Second Canadian Edition

Business in Action

To my beautiful wife Nitsa. Over the years, we've seen
our share of good times and bad times; we've shared
success and dealt with pain. Thanks for the great
advice and encouragement. Your positive attitude
and outlook toward life is truly special.

I would also like to thank my family, friends,
and colleagues for their support.

Second Canadian Edition

Business in Action

Courtland L. Bovée Grossmont College

John V. Thill Communication Specialists of America

George Dracopoulos Vanier College

ICE

CANADIAN IN-CLASS EDITION

PEARSON

Prentice
Hall

Toronto

Library and Archives Canada Cataloguing in Publication

Bovée, Courtland L.
     Business in action / Courtland L. Bovée, John V. Thill, George
Dracopoulos.—2nd Canadian ed.

Includes index.
In-class edition.
Previous ed. issued under title: Business in action.
ISBN 978-0-13-206691-4

     1. Business—Textbooks.   2. Commerce—Textbooks.   3. Industrial management—
Textbooks.   I. Thill, John V   II. Dracopoulos, George, 1970–   III. Title.

HF1008.B89 2008   650   C2007-905468-4

ISBN-13: 978-0-13-206691-4
ISBN-10: 0-13-206691-2

Vice-President, Editorial Director: Gary Bennett
Executive Marketing Manager: Cas Shields
Acquisitions Editor: Karen Elliott
Developmental Editors: Mary Wong, Pam Voves, and Lisa Cicinelli
Production Editor: Leanne Rancourt
Copy Editor: Leanne Rancourt
Proofreader: Anne Borden
Senior Production Coordinator: Patricia Ciardullo
Indexer: Audrey Dorsch
Page Layout: Macmillan Publishing Solutions
Photo and Permissions Research: Dawn du Quesnay
Art Director: Julia Hall
Interior Design: Brett Miller
Cover Design: Anthony Leung
Cover Image: Veer Incorporated

Statistics Canada information is used with the permission of Statistics Canada. Users are
forbidden to copy the data and redisseminate them, in an original or modified form, for
commercial purposes, without the expressed permission of Statistics Canada. Information on
the availability of the wide range of data from Statistics Canada can be obtained from
Statistics Canada's Regional Offices, its World Wide Web site at http://www.statcan.ca, and its
toll-free access number 1-800-263-1136.

5 6 7   14 13 12
Printed and bound in Canada.

Brief Contents

Preface   xiii

Part 1   Conducting Business in the Global Economy   1

Chapter 1   Understanding the Fundamentals of Business and Economics   1
Chapter 2   Competing in the Global Economy   35
Chapter 3   Practising Ethical Behaviour and Social Responsibility   68

Part 2   Starting and Organizing a Small Business   105

Chapter 4   Starting and Financing a Small Business   105
Chapter 5   Selecting the Proper Form of Business Ownership and Exploring Business Combinations   133

Part 3   Managing a Business   165

Chapter 6   Understanding the Functions and Roles of Management   165
Chapter 7   Organizing and Working in Teams   195
Chapter 8   Producing Quality Goods and Services   227

Part 4   Managing Employees   265

Chapter 9   Managing Human Resources   265
Chapter 10   Motivating Today's Workforce and Handling Employee-Management Relations   293

Part 5   Developing Marketing Strategies to Satisfy Customers   331

Chapter 11   Developing Product and Pricing Strategies   331
Chapter 12   Developing Distribution and Promotional Strategies   369

Part 6   Managing Financial Information and Resources   405

Chapter 13   Analyzing and Using Financial Information   405
Chapter 14   Understanding Banking and Securities   439

Appendixes

Appendix A   The Canadian Legal System   477
Appendix B   Your Business Plan   484

Answers to Study Guide Questions   486
References   488
Company/Brand/Organization Index   508
Subject Index   512
Photo Credits   523

Contents

Preface   xiii

Part 1
Conducting Business in the Global Economy   1

Chapter 1   Understanding the Fundamentals of Business and Economics   1

■ BEHIND THE SCENES BlackBerry: The High-Tech Maple Leaf?   2

Why Study Business?   3
■ Learning from Business Blunders   3

What Is a Business?   4
Goods-Producing Businesses versus Service Businesses   5
■ Technologies That Are Revolutionizing Business   6
Growth of the Service Sector   6
■ Redefining Reality in the Electronic Economy   8

What Is an Economic System?   8
Types of Economic Systems   10
The Trend toward Privatization   12

How Does a Free-Market Economic System Work? (A Microeconomic View)   13
The Theory of Supply and Demand in a Free-Market System   13

Free-Market System (A Macroeconomic View)   15
Competition   15
■ LivePerson Puts a Pulse on the Web   16
Government's Role in a Free-Market System   17
How a Free-Market System Monitors Its Economic Performance   24
■ Economic Indicators and the New World Order: Windsor and the Shifting Front Lines   25

Challenges of a Global Economy   26
Moving Forward   28
BEHIND THE SCENES BlackBerry: Communicating, Defending, and Expanding Its Global Reach   28

TEST YOUR KNOWLEDGE   29
PRACTISE YOUR KNOWLEDGE   30
EXPAND YOUR KNOWLEDGE   30
STUDY GUIDE   31
Summary of Learning Objectives   31

Key Terms   32
Questions   32
SEE IT ON THE WEB   34

Chapter 2   Competing in the Global Economy   35

■ BEHIND THE SCENES Molson Canadian, eh?   36

Fundamentals of International Trade   37
Why Nations Trade   37
How International Trade Is Measured   38
Trade Restrictions   40
Agreements and Organizations Promoting International Trade   42
Trading Blocs   43
The Undeniable Force of Emerging Markets: BRIC and Beyond   47
Foreign Exchange Rates and Currency Valuations   48

The Global Business Environment   49
■ Technologies That Are Revolutionizing Business   50
Cultural Differences in the Global Business Environment   50
■ Learning from Business Blunders   52
Legal Differences in the Global Business Environment   52
■ China's Counterfeit Economy   54
Forms of International Business Activity   55
Product Strategies for International Markets   58
■ How to Avoid Business Blunders Abroad   59

Dealing with Economic Shocks in a Global Business Environment   60
BEHIND THE SCENES Molson Coors: A Global Partnership   61

TEST YOUR KNOWLEDGE   62
PRACTISE YOUR KNOWLEDGE   62
EXPAND YOUR KNOWLEDGE   63
STUDY GUIDE   64
Summary of Learning Objectives   64
Key Terms   65
Questions   65
SEE IT ON THE WEB   67

Chapter 3   Practising Ethical Behaviour and Social Responsibility   68

■ BEHIND THE SCENES Telus: Setting Clear Profit and Sustainability Targets   69

Ethics and Social Responsibility in the Workplace   70
What Is Ethical Behaviour?   72
■ Learning from Business Blunders   73
Factors Influencing Ethical Behaviour   74
■ Actions Speak Louder than Codes   77
How Do You Make Ethical Decisions?   79
Perspectives on Corporate Social Responsibility   80
The Traditional Perspective: The Business of Business Is Making Money   80
The Contemporary Perspective: Ethics Pays   81
An Emerging Perspective: Dynamically Balancing Ethics and Profits   82
Business's Efforts to Increase Social Responsibility   84
Responsibility toward Society and the Environment   84
■ Banning Light Bulbs: Greener Days Ahead   88
■ Ben & Jerry's: A Double Scoop of Irony?   89
Responsibility toward Consumers   90
■ Technologies That Are Revolutionizing Business   91
■ Voisey's Bay: Native Canadians Exercise Right to Be Heard   92
Responsibility toward Investors   92
Responsibility toward Employees   93
Ethics and Social Responsibility Around the World   95
BEHIND THE SCENES Telus: Green Leadership   95

TEST YOUR KNOWLEDGE   96
PRACTISE YOUR KNOWLEDGE   96
EXPAND YOUR KNOWLEDGE   97
STUDY GUIDE   98
Summary of Learning Objectives   98
Key Terms   99
Questions   99
SEE IT ON THE WEB   101
CBC VIDEO CASE Hollywood North: The Big Chill   101
ON LOCATION VIDEO CASE Entering the Global Marketplace: Lands' End and Yahoo!   102
E-BUSINESS IN ACTION The Biggest Audience in the Whole Wide World Wide Web   103
BUSINESS PLANPRO EXERCISES   104

**Part 2
Starting and Organizing a Small Business   105**

Chapter 4   Starting and Financing a Small Business   105

■ BEHIND THE SCENES Itech: An Entrepreneur's Clear Vision   106

Understanding the World of Small Business   107
Economic Roles of Small Businesses   107
Characteristics of Small Businesses   108

Factors Contributing to the Increase in the Number of Small Businesses   110
■ Technologies That Are Revolutionizing Business   110
■ Create a Winning Website   111
Starting a Small Business   113
Characteristics of Entrepreneurs   113
Importance of Preparing a Business Plan   114
■ Learning from Business Blunders   115
■ Blueprint for a Comprehensive Business Plan   116
Small Business Ownership Options   117
The Franchise Alternative   118
Why New Businesses Fail   121
Sources of Small Business Assistance   122
Financing a New Business   123
Length of Term   123
Cost of Capital   123
Debt versus Equity Financing   124
Private Financing Sources   125
BEHIND THE SCENES Mission-Itech: Growing, Diversifying, and Competing   127
TEST YOUR KNOWLEDGE   128
PRACTISE YOUR KNOWLEDGE   128
EXPAND YOUR KNOWLEDGE   129
STUDY GUIDE   130
Summary of Learning Objectives   130
Key Terms   130
Questions   131
SEE IT ON THE WEB   132

Chapter 5   Selecting the Proper Form of Business Ownership and Exploring Business Combinations   133

■ BEHIND THE SCENES Canadian Home Renovation Centres: Strategic Battleground   134

Choosing a Form of Business Ownership   135
Sole Proprietorships   135
Partnerships   137
Corporations   139
■ Technologies That Are Revolutionizing Business   140
■ Pattison: The Potential of the Private Corporation   142
Cooperatives   146
Income Trusts   146
Understanding Business Combinations   148
Mergers and Acquisitions   148
■ Learning from Business Blunders   149
■ Hey, Wanna Lose a Few Billion? We Have a Sure Deal for You   151
Strategic Alliances and Joint Ventures   152
BEHIND THE SCENES Recruiting the Independent Retailer   153
TEST YOUR KNOWLEDGE   154
PRACTISE YOUR KNOWLEDGE   154

EXPAND YOUR KNOWLEDGE   155

STUDY GUIDE   156

Summary of Learning Objectives   156

Key Terms   157

Questions   157

SEE IT ON THE WEB   159

CBC VIDEO CASE Funny Business: Creating a Comedy Club   160

ON LOCATION VIDEO CASE Doing Business Privately: Amy's Ice Creams   161

E-BUSINESS IN ACTION Why Did the Dot.Coms Fall to Earth?   162

BUSINESS PLANPRO EXERCISES   164

Part 3
Managing a Business   165

Chapter 6   Understanding the Functions and Roles of Management   165

■ BEHIND THE SCENES Apple iTunes and Steve Jobs: A Strong Leader with a Clear iVision   166

The Four Basic Functions of Management   167

The Planning Function   167

The Organizing Function   172

The Leading Function   174

■ Learning Simple Lessons Can Define a Leader's Legacy   174

■ How Much Do You Know about the Company's Culture?   179

The Controlling Function   180

■ Learning from Business Blunders   181

Key Management Skills for Success   185

Interpersonal Skills   185

Technical Skills   185

Conceptual Skills   185

Why Managers Fail   186

■ Technologies That Are Revolutionizing Business   187

BEHIND THE SCENES Moving Music at Apple iTunes and Taking Advantage of New Opportunities   188

TEST YOUR KNOWLEDGE   189

PRACTISE YOUR KNOWLEDGE   190

EXPAND YOUR KNOWLEDGE   190

STUDY GUIDE   191

Summary of Learning Objectives   191

Key Terms   192

Questions   192

SEE IT ON THE WEB   194

Chapter 7   Organizing and Working in Teams   195

■ BEHIND THE SCENES The Teamwork Behind the Events at Altitude Concepts   196

Designing an Effective Organization Structure   197

Identifying Job Responsibilities   198

■ Technologies That Are Revolutionizing Business   199

Defining the Chain of Command   199

■ Learning from Business Blunders   202

Organizing the Workforce   203

Working in Teams   207

What Is a Team?   207

■ Team-Building Activities   208

Types of Teams   209

■ Don't Leave Home to Go to Work: American Express Company's Virtual Environment   211

Advantages and Disadvantages of Working in Teams   212

Characteristics of Effective Teams   213

Five Stages of Team Development   216

Team Conflict   216

Conducting Productive Team Meetings   218

BEHIND THE SCENES Once in a Lifetime, Twice in a Month: The Rogers Cup   220

TEST YOUR KNOWLEDGE   221

PRACTISE YOUR KNOWLEDGE   222

EXPAND YOUR KNOWLEDGE   222

STUDY GUIDE   223

Summary of Learning Objectives   223

Key Terms   224

Questions   224

SEE IT ON THE WEB   226

Chapter 8   Producing Quality Goods and Services   227

■ BEHIND THE SCENES Magna International: Assembling, Designing, Engineering, and Planning in the Dynamic Auto Sector   228

Understanding Production and Operations Management   229

What Is Production?   229

The Value Chain and the Conversion Process   230

The Unique Challenges of Service Delivery   230

Mass Production, Customized Production, and Mass Customization   232

Outsourcing   233

■ Smart Car, Interesting Process   234

■ Offshoring: Profits—Yes, but at What Cost?   235

Designing the Production Process   235

Establishing the Supply Chain   235

Forecasting Demand   237

Planning for Capacity   237

Choosing a Facility Location   238

Designing a Facility Layout   239

■ A Bike That Really Travels   239

Scheduling Work   241

Improving Production Through Technology   244

Computer-Aided Design and Computer-Aided Engineering   244

Computer-Aided Manufacturing and Computer-Integrated Manufacturing   244

Flexible Manufacturing Systems 245
■ Technologies That Are Revolutionizing Business 245

Electronic Data Interchange 247
Managing and Controlling the Production Process 247
Coordinating the Supply Chain 247
■ Learning from Business Blunders 251

Assuring Product Quality 251
BEHIND THE SCENES Planning Capacity and Exploring New Opportunities 254

TEST YOUR KNOWLEDGE 255
PRACTISE YOUR KNOWLEDGE 255
EXPAND YOUR KNOWLEDGE 256
STUDY GUIDE 257
Summary of Learning Objectives 257
Key Terms 258
Questions 258
SEE IT ON THE WEB 260
CBC VIDEO CASE The Big Switcheroo: Vancity 261
ON LOCATION VIDEO CASE Feeling like Part of the Family: Kingston Technology 262
E-BUSINESS IN ACTION Whatever Happened to B2B Exchanges? 263
BUSINESS PLANPRO EXERCISES 264

Part 4
Managing Employees 265

Chapter 9   Managing Human Resources 265

■ BEHIND THE SCENES Human Resources at WestJet: Smiles and Jokes Take Front Stage 266

Understanding What Human Resources Managers Do 267
Planning for a Company's Staffing Needs 267
Forecasting Supply and Demand 267
■ Technologies That Are Revolutionizing Business 269

Evaluating Job Requirements 270
Recruiting, Hiring, and Training New Employees 270
The Hiring Process 271
■ New-Age Job Interviews: Are you Camera Friendly? 272

Training and Development 275
■ Click and Learn: E-Training Today's Employees 276

Appraising Employee Performance 278
Administering Compensation and Employee Benefits 279
Wages and Salaries 279
■ Show Me the Money: A Tale of Two Compensation Scales 280

Incentive Programs 280
Employee Benefits and Services 281
■ Learning from Business Blunders 282
Overseeing Changes in Employment Status 285
Promoting and Reassigning Employees 285
Terminating Employees 286
Retiring Employees 286
■ You're e-Fired! 287

BEHIND THE SCENES HR Policies Designed to Avoid Turbulent Labour Issues 287

TEST YOUR KNOWLEDGE 288
PRACTISE YOUR KNOWLEDGE 289
EXPAND YOUR KNOWLEDGE 289
STUDY GUIDE 290
Summary of Learning Objectives 290
Key Terms 290
Questions 291
SEE IT ON THE WEB 292

Chapter 10   Motivating Today's Workforce and Handling Employee-Management Relations 293

■ BEHIND THE SCENES Bombardier: Employee Relations in Good Times and Bad Times 294

Understanding Human Relations 295
Motivating Employees 295
What Is Motivation? 295
Theories of Motivation 297
■ Learning from Business Blunders 301

Motivational Strategies 302
Keeping Pace with Today's Workforce 304
Staffing Challenges 304
■ Too Many Workers? Not For Long 305

Demographic Challenges 308
■ Chuckle While You Work 308

Alternative Work Arrangements 312
■ Technologies That Are Revolutionizing Business 314

Working with Labour Unions 315
The Collective Bargaining Process 315
■ Wal-Mart and the U-Word 316

The Labour Movement Today 319
BEHIND THE SCENES Bombardier's Adjusted Flight Plans 320

TEST YOUR KNOWLEDGE 321
PRACTISE YOUR KNOWLEDGE 322
EXPAND YOUR KNOWLEDGE 322
STUDY GUIDE 323
Summary of Learning Objectives 323
Key Terms 324

Questions   324

SEE IT ON THE WEB   326

CBC VIDEO CASE Work–Life Special:
Voices of Canadians   327

ON LOCATION VIDEO CASE Recruitment and
Placement   328

E-BUSINESS IN ACTION Job Recruiting Moves
Online   329

BUSINESS PLANPRO EXERCISES   330

Part 5
Developing Marketing Strategies to Satisfy Customers   331

Chapter 11   Developing Product and Pricing Strategies   331

■ BEHIND THE SCENES Shoppers Drug Mart Gets a
Facelift: Updating a Marketing Strategy   332

What Is Marketing?   333
The Role of Marketing in Society   334
The Marketing Concept   336
■ Learning from Business Blunders   339

■ Your Right to Privacy versus the Marketing
Databases   341

■ Technologies That Are Revolutionizing
Business   342

Planning Your Marketing Strategies   343
Step 1: Examining Your Current Marketing Situation   344
*Step 2: Assessing Your Opportunities and Setting Your
Objectives*   346
Step 3: Developing Your Marketing Strategy   346
■ Questionable Marketing Tactics on Campus   347

Developing Product Strategies   352
Types of Products   353
The Product Life Cycle   355
Product Identities   356
Product-Line and Product-Mix Strategies   358
Developing Pricing Strategies   360
Cost-Based and Price-Based Pricing   360
Price Skimming   361
Penetration Pricing   361
Price Discounts   361
BEHIND THE SCENES Shoppers Cosmetics: Makeup
Beautifies the Bottom Line   362

TEST YOUR KNOWLEDGE   363
PRACTISE YOUR KNOWLEDGE   364
EXPAND YOUR KNOWLEDGE   364
STUDY GUIDE   365
Summary of Learning Objectives   365
Key Terms   366
Questions   367
SEE IT ON THE WEB   368

Chapter 12   Developing Distribution and Promotional Strategies   369

■ BEHIND THE SCENES MEC: Climbing Toward the
3 Million Member Mark   370

Developing Distribution Strategies   371
*Understanding the Role of Marketing
Intermediaries*   371
Selecting Your Marketing Channels   372
Managing Physical Distribution   377
*Incorporating the Internet into Your Distribution
Strategies*   380
Promotional Strategies   381
Setting Your Promotional Goals   381
Analyzing Product Variables   381
■ Learning from Business Blunders   382

■ Where Did the Audience Go?   384

Selecting Your Promotional Mix   385
■ Technologies That Are Revolutionizing
Business   387

■ Zoom Media: A Good Place for an Ad   390

Integrating Your Marketing Communications   392
BEHIND THE SCENES MEC's Effective Blend of Retail and
E-tail Channels   394

TEST YOUR KNOWLEDGE   395
PRACTISE YOUR KNOWLEDGE   395
EXPAND YOUR KNOWLEDGE   396
STUDY GUIDE   397
Summary of Learning Objectives   397
Key Terms   398
Questions   398
SEE IT ON THE WEB   399
CBC VIDEO CASE The Bay's Wishlist: Redefining a Retail
Giant   400
ON LOCATION VIDEO CASE In Consumers' Shoes:
Skechers   401
E-BUSINESS IN ACTION Clicks and Bricks: Bridging the
Physical and Virtual Worlds   402
BUSINESS PLANPRO EXERCISES   403

Part 6
Managing Financial Information and Resources   405

Chapter 13   Analyzing and Using Financial Information   405

■ BEHIND THE SCENES Corporate Reputation:
Once a Tremendous Asset, Now a Clear Liability for
Nortel   406

What Is Accounting?   407
What Accountants Do   407

The Rules of Accounting   410
■ Putting Accountability Back into Public Accounting   412
■ Technologies That Are Revolutionizing Business   413

Fundamental Accounting Concepts   414
The Accounting Equation   414
Double-Entry Bookkeeping and the Matching Principle   415
■ Software Simplifies Accounting Tasks   415

Using Financial Statements   417
Understanding Financial Statements   417
Analyzing Financial Statements   423

What Does Financial Management Involve?   427
Developing and Implementing a Financial Plan   428
Monitoring Cash Flow   428
Developing a Budget   429
■ How to Read an Annual Report   429
■ Learning from Business Blunders   430

BEHIND THE SCENES How Long Will It Take? Nortel's Troubles Resurface   431

TEST YOUR KNOWLEDGE   432
PRACTISE YOUR KNOWLEDGE   433
EXPAND YOUR KNOWLEDGE   434
STUDY GUIDE   435
Summary of Learning Objectives   435
Key Terms   436
Questions   436
SEE IT ON THE WEB   438

Chapter 14   Understanding Banking and Securities   439

■ BEHIND THE SCENES Retooling Canada's Banks: Despite Merger Restrictions, Some Positive Results   440

Money and Financial Institutions   441
Characteristics and Types of Money   441
■ Technologies That Are Revolutionizing Business   443
Financial Institutions and Services   443
■ Surprise! You've Been Swiped   444
Bank Safety   447
The Evolving Canadian Banking Environment   447

Types of Securities Investments   448
Shares   448
Bonds   449
■ Income Trusts: Playing the Blame Game   453

Securities Markets   454
Securities Exchanges   454
How to Buy and Sell Securities   454
How to Analyze Financial News   457
■ Put Your Money Where Your Mouse Is!   458
Industry Challenges   460
■ Put the Experts to the Test: Stocks That Can Stand Up to the Storm   462
Regulation of Securities Markets   463
■ Learning from Business Blunders   464
BEHIND THE SCENES Separating Facts from Fiction: Canadian Bank Mergers   466

TEST YOUR KNOWLEDGE   467
PRACTISE YOUR KNOWLEDGE   467
EXPAND YOUR KNOWLEDGE   468
STUDY GUIDE   469
Summary of Learning Objectives   469
Key Terms   470
Questions   470
SEE IT ON THE WEB   472
CBC VIDEO CASE Card Tricks: The Credit Card Web of Rules   473
ON LOCATION VIDEO CASE Accounting for Billions of Burgers: McDonald's   474
E-BUSINESS IN ACTION Cyberbanks Hit a Brick Wall   475
BUSINESS PLANPRO EXERCISES   476

Appendix A   The Canadian Legal System   477
Appendix B   Your Business Plan   484

Answers to Study Guide Questions   486
References   488
Company/Brand/Organization Index   508
Subject Index   512
Photo Credits   523

Preface

A GUIDED TOUR of the text that lets students experience *Business in Action!*

As part of Pearson Education Canada's commitment to providing students with value, choice, and tools for educational success, *Business in Action*, Second Canadian Edition, has been designed as an In-Class Edition. This approach enables students to experience business first-hand through a variety of highly engaging activities and real-world examples that no other textbook can match. Students will appreciate the broad selection of featured companies along with the text's user-friendly layout, manageable length, eye-catching graphics, conversational tone, and tie-in with Business PlanPro software. From the global economy to the world of small business, *Business in Action* takes students on an engaging exploration of the fundamentals, strategies, and dynamics that make the business world work.

Business in Action is a compelling model of today's most effective instructional techniques. The text uses an extraordinary number of devices that simplify teaching, promote active learning, stimulate critical thinking, and develop career skills. This text is the most effective teaching and learning tool you'll find for an introductory business course. As you'll see on the pages that follow, *Business in Action* will make your classes livelier, more relevant, and more enjoyable.

WHAT'S NEW TO THIS EDITION

It's an "In-Class Edition"

More than just a text, *Business in Action* is a study partner that gives students the extra help they need. It includes the following features:

- **Test Yourself:** Questions at the beginning of each chapter that cover the main objectives of the chapter. They can be used to review for tests and exams.
- **In-Class Notes:** Brief summaries of key points that appear in the text with space for students to take notes during class.
- **Study Guide:** A complete guide to the chapter, including a summary of learning objectives, a list of key terms, and a series of questions will test students' understanding of key concepts. The answers to the Study Guide questions are provided at the back of the book.
- **Study Card:** This handy tear-out card is perfect for preparing for exams and reviewing key concepts.

Two New Boxed Features

- **Learning from Business Blunders:** Small developing companies make mistakes that hinder their ability to grow. Large companies often make major mistakes. In each chapter, we examine a business blunder that hurt the growth of a particular brand or led to a specific product failure. The examples are based on the key chapter concepts and are both entertaining and relevant. What happens when a major corporation realizes that their ads are actually helping the competition? (A major rebranding campaign in the frozen pizza wars was based on this real blunder.) Is there such a thing as a bad customer? (YES! A major automobile manufacturer learned that lesson the hard way.) This feature is a great conversation piece in the classroom that provides vivid examples students will remember.
- **Technologies That Are Revolutionizing Business:** Each chapter highlights a particular form of new technology and identifies how the technology is impacting the business environment. Cutting-edge developments such as

nanotechnology, virtual meetings, RFID, and wireless networking applications are explored throughout the text. The mini-boxes explain the basics of the technology, describe the potential impact and future applications, and encourage students to find out more by directing them to appropriate websites.

In addition, more than 95 percent of the opening cases, boxed inserts, and end-of chapter cases are either new or updated. There is increased coverage of globalization's impact on Canadian business, including emerging markets, and increased coverage on change management.

HALLMARK FEATURES—ALL UPDATED FOR THIS EDITION

Behind the Scenes

Chapter-Opening Vignette

Each chapter begins with a slice-of-life vignette that attracts student interest by vividly portraying a challenge faced by a company or businessperson. These opening cases help students understand the origins of the company's growth and success. Each vignette ends with thought-provoking self-test questions that draw students into the chapter.

Chapter-Ending Case

Each chapter ends with a case that expands on the chapter-opening vignette. The case includes critical-thinking questions that require students to apply the concepts covered in the text. Plus, students can find out more about the company featured in the case by completing the "Learn More Online" exercise that follows the case.

Learning Objectives

In each chapter, clearly stated learning objectives signal important concepts to be mastered. The Summary of Learning Objectives, contained in the end-of-chapter Study Guide, reinforces basic concepts by reviewing chapter highlights for students.

Special Feature Boxes

There are 38 special feature boxes in the text. Each chapter contains between two and four boxes that make the world of business come alive with current examples to further enhance student learning. Each box includes critical-thinking questions that are ideal for developing team or individual problem-solving skills.

BEHIND THE SCENES

Shoppers Drug Mart Gets a Facelift: Updating a Marketing Strategy

www.shoppersdrugmart.ca

Shoppers Drug Mart (Pharmaprix in Quebec) faces many new challenges. Wal-Mart and Loblaw have increased their pharmacy businesses and are offering clients the ability to fill prescriptions while shopping. Shoppers is feeling the heat from traditional competitors like the Edmonton-based Katz Group, which has 1800 stores under such banners as Rexall, IDA, and Pharma Plus. Jean Coutu has a dominant share in Quebec and has stores in Ontario and New Brunswick as well. In addition, Jean Coutu will soon own a 32 percent stake in Rite Aid, the third-largest pharmacy chain in the United States. The competitors each have their own strategies that will likely result in more intense competition ahead.

Shoppers Drug Mart was founded in 1962 by Murray Koffler. At the time, he wanted to build a national chain that could provide the personalized service available at independent local pharmacies. Today there are more than 1000 Shoppers Drug Mart outlets and 58 Shoppers HomeHealthCare centres across the country. Mission accomplished. However, to continue its success the firm will need to make some changes.

Faced with new competitive threats and a consumer

Shoppers Drug Mart is updating its image to improve service and bolster the bottom line. Key initiatives in this phase include bigger stores in more central locations; more private-label brand sales; and the expansion of the cosmetics lines to include upscale brands.

These house brands provide obvious cost advantages for customers (they are about 25 percent cheaper than national brands) and profit advantages for retailers (there is an approximately 15 percent better profit margin). In addition, retailers like Shoppers hope to achieve brand loyalty similar to what Loblaw has achieved with its President's Choice label. If consumers identify with a brand that is only available in their stores, the retail chain will benefit.

BEHIND THE SCENES

Shoppers Cosmetics: Makeup Beautifies the Bottom Line

Can you remember the last time that you walked into a new or newly renovated Shoppers Drug Mart big-box pharmacy? Close your eyes for a second. What is the first thing that you see as you enter the store? Cosmetics! A few years ago Shoppers decided to increase their cosmetics lines and try to capture the upscale cosmetics market, which was traditionally controlled by department stores. They had tried, for some time, to convince companies like Estée Lauder to bring high-end brands like Clinique into their stores without success. Why the big emphasis in this area? Profits! High-end cosmetics can carry margins of 40 percent or more. That is significant in the competitive retail industry. Compare that to the 3 to 4 percent margins typically earned by grocery stores and the strategic leap of faith is easy to understand.

Why would a manufacturer resist the opportunity to be sold in 1000 additional outlets in Canada? As you have read in this chapter, the answer is quite simple: Companies, especially high-end cosmetics firms like Estée Lauder, protect their brands and try to ensure that they are sold in outlets that reflect their image and respect the expectations of their core customers. High-end brands need to ensure that their target market consumer does not get alienated. Clearly, the traditional drugstore model was ideal for lower-end brands

like Revlon and Maybelline—consumers flocked to purchase reasonably priced makeup in drugstores—but they were traditionally no place for the likes of Chanel, Clinique, and other higher-end names.

Despite being denied in the past, Shoppers Drug Mart was unwilling to accept this rejection. Rather, they decided to take appropriate measures to make Shoppers a destination worthy of the lucrative business from high-end cosmetics. But how could they do it? Remember the old saying: You have to spend money to make money. As you saw in the opening case, Shoppers was investing heavily in building new locations and improving or moving older locations. These updated stores have dedicated primary space that directs traffic flow to the cosmetics section. Appealing layouts and improved service is changing the image of pharmacy shopping, and Shoppers is at the front of the pack—and has the cosmetics sales to prove it.

All of the work paid off. A recent announcement sent shivers up the spines of department store executives in 2007 when Shoppers became the first North American drugstore chain to carry Clinique. Initially only a handful of locations earned the right to carry the line, but within a year about 150 updated or well-designed locations were expected to carry the brand. This deal helped turn Shoppers into a destination

---

New-Age Job Interviews: Are you Camera Friendly?

Smile for the camera and make sure to practise your delivery! Many initial interviews today are being conducted via videoconferencing.

Have you taken a drama course? How are your acting skills? Do you come across well on screen? Are you afraid of the lights of a camera? You may be wondering where we're going with this line of questioning. Let's begin with some new-age human resource trends. According to Gordon Orlikow, a senior partner in the Toronto office of the executive recruiting company Korn/Ferry International, "approximately 30 percent of initial job interviews are conducted using a video link between candidates and human resources managers. This figure is up dramatically from about 2 percent just two years earlier."

A few years ago, Donald Trump packaged his extended interview into a TV program meant to entertain and provide some indication of a bizarre version of

the hiring process—*The Apprentice*. The show faded but the use of the camera lens is not far-fetched or unrealistic; real practitioners are seeing the merits of using video equipment to manage their increasing time demands and to decrease costs. This video approach appears to be especially important for high-end executive positions, which tend to extend candidate searches over long distances to other parts of Canada and the world.

Many firms have used unconventional techniques for years, such as asking employees to perform improvisational skits to demonstrate their reactions to a fabricated situation. These approaches force candidates out of their comfort zone and put them under the spotlight. Now human resources managers are truly placing the spotlight on interviewees. So what can a candidate do to prepare for a video interview? A personal face-to-face interview allows the HR manager to focus on what the interviewee is saying, however, in a video interview on-screen appearance and presentation style tend to be more memorable. You can't approach this type of interview with the same mindset.

Will this method continue to grow in popularity? We'll find out. In the meantime, remember that you must tailor your interview preparation to the type of company, organizational culture, industry expectations and now the medium of delivery to be truly effective in any given situation.[17]

Questions for Critical Thinking

1. What are the advantages and disadvantages of the video interview? Debate the issue with a classmate.
2. How would you prepare for a video interview? What additional steps should you take beyond what you would do to prepare for a regular face-to-face interview?

Test Your Knowledge

Questions for Review

End-of-chapter questions that reinforce learning and help students review the chapter material.

Questions for Analysis

End-of-chapter questions that help students analyze chapter material. Selected questions are ethics based and labelled "Ethical Considerations."

Questions for Application

End-of-chapter questions that give students the opportunity to apply principles presented in the chapter material. Selected questions labelled "Integrated" ask students to tie material learned in previous chapters to the topics in the chapter they're currently studying.

TEST YOUR KNOWLEDGE

Questions for Review

1. Explain what is meant by the marketing concept.
2. Describe the product development process.
3. How can legal and regulatory factors affect a company's short-term marketing objectives?
4. Describe the four stages of the product life cycle.
5. Explain what is meant by niche marketing and provide an example of a company that is using this approach effectively.

Questions for Analysis

6. How have new techniques in database marketing revolutionized the way companies communicate with their core customers? What tools have enabled them to improve their data collection processes?
7. How do consumer purchases differ from organizational purchases? Describe the difference between the processes of a consumer buying an automobile for personal use versus an organization purchasing a fleet of delivery cars.
8. What is meant by brand equity? What can companies do to maintain or improve brand equity?
9. Why is it important to review the objectives of a strategic marketing plan before setting a product's price?
10. **Ethical Considerations.** Why might an employee with high personal ethical standards act less ethically when developing packaging, labelling, or pricing strategies?

Questions for Application

11. How does a hotel chain like Holiday Inn deal with the specific challenges of the service industry (intangibility and perishability)? What impact do these factors play in pricing?
12. Think of a product you recently purchased and review your decision process. Why did you need or want that product? How did the product's marketing influence your purchase decision? How did you investigate the product before making your purchase decision? Did you experience cognitive dissonance after your purchase?
13. A technology firm has just developed a new Internet browsing device that is designed for practical home use and can free up the problem parents have with children fighting over the computer—not to mention the parents' lack of access. The product can be produced at a very low manufacturing cost. What pricing approach should they use—skimming or price penetration? Explain.
14. **Integrated.** Why is it important to analyze a firm's marketing plan before designing the production process for a service or a good? (Production processes were discussed in Chapter 8.) What kinds of information are generally included in a marketing plan that might affect the design of the production process?
15. **Integrated.** Discuss how the following economic indicators discussed in Chapter 1 might affect a company's marketing decisions: consumer price index, inflation, unemployment.

Practise Your Knowledge

Sharpening Your Communication Skills

These exercises call on students to practise a wide range of communication activities, including one-on-one and group discussions, personal interviews, panel sessions, oral and written papers, and letter- and memo-writing assignments.

Building Your Team Skills

These exercises teach students important team skills, such as brainstorming, collaborative decision making, developing a consensus, debating, role playing, and resolving conflict.

PRACTISE YOUR KNOWLEDGE

SHARPENING YOUR COMMUNICATION SKILLS

Collect some examples of mail communications you have received from companies trying to sell you something. How do these communications try to get your attention? Highlight all instances in which these communications use the word *you* or even your personal name. How is using the word *you* an effective way to communicate with customers? Does the communication appeal to your emotions or to your logic? How does the company highlight the benefits of its products or services? How does the company approach price? Finally, how does the company motivate you to act? Bring samples to class and be prepared to present your analysis to your classmates.

BUILDING YOUR TEAM SKILLS

In the course of planning a marketing strategy, marketers need to analyze the external environment to consider how forces outside the firm may create new opportunities and challenges. One important environmental factor for merchandise buyers at Canadian Tire is weather conditions. For example, when merchandise buyers for lawn and garden products think about the assortment and number of products to purchase for the chain's stores, they don't place any orders without first poring over long-range weather forecasts for each market.

In particular, temperature and precipitation predictions are critical to the company's marketing plan, because they offer clues to consumer demand for barbecues, lawn furniture, gardening tools, and other merchandise. What other products would benefit from examining weather forecasts? With your team, brainstorm to identify at least three types of products (in addition to lawn and garden items) for which Canadian Tire should examine the weather as part of its analysis of the external environment. Share your recommendations with the entire class. How many teams identified the same products your team did?

Expand Your Knowledge

Exploring Career Opportunities

Students are given the opportunity to explore career resources on campus, observe businesspeople in their jobs, interview businesspeople, and perform self-evaluations to assess their own career skills and interests.

Developing Your Research Skills

These exercises familiarize students with the wide variety of business reference material that's available, and they give students practice in developing research skills.

EXPAND YOUR KNOWLEDGE

DISCOVERING CAREER OPPORTUNITIES

Jobs in the four P's of marketing cover a wide range of activities, including personal selling, advertising, marketing research, product management, and public relations. You can get more information about various marketing positions by consulting your local job bank, as well as online job search websites like Monster.ca.

1. Select a specific marketing job that interests you. Using one or more of the preceding resources, find out more about this chosen job. What specific duties and responsibilities do people in this position typically handle?
2. Search through help-wanted ads in newspapers, specialized magazines, or websites to find two openings in the field you are researching. What educational background and work experience are employers seeking in candidates for this position? What kind of work assignments are mentioned in these ads?
3. Now think about your talents, interests, and goals. How do your strengths fit with the requirements, duties, and responsibilities of this job? Do you think you would find this field enjoyable and rewarding? Why?

DEVELOPING YOUR RESEARCH SKILLS

From recent issues of business journals and newspapers (print or online editions), select an article that describes in some detail a particular company's attempt to build relationships with its customers (either in general or for a particular product or product line).

1. Describe the company's market. What geographic, demographic, behavioural, or psychographic segments of the market is the company targeting?
2. How does the company hold a dialogue with its customers? Does the company maintain a customer database? If so, what kinds of information does it gather?
3. According to the article, how successful has the company been in understanding its customers?

See It on the WEB

End-of-chapter "See It on the WEB" exercises acquaint students with the wealth of information on the web that relates to the content of each chapter. These exercises direct students to the Companion Website where they can explore websites and answer questions that reinforce and extend chapter learning.

Video Cases

There are two video cases at the end of each of the six sections of the text. These cases help students see how real-life businesses and the people who run them apply fundamental business principles on a daily basis.

E-Business in Action

From the smallest dot.coms to lumbering global giants, e-business is influencing the way all companies do business. While the Internet bubble has burst, Internet technology and e-commerce remain very much a part of the business environment. "E-Business in Action" is a dedicated section that appears at the end of each text part and will expand student learning by explaining in depth the important challenges companies face in the world of e-business.

Business PlanPro Exercises

The end-of-part "Business PlanPro Exercises" enable students to apply the knowledge they've gained from reading the chapters to the Business PlanPro software. Each exercise has two tasks. "Think Like a Pro" tasks require students to navigate the software, find and review information in sample business plans, and evaluate and critique some of the thinking that went into these plans. "Create Your Own Business Plan" tasks provide students with an opportunity to apply their skills to create their own winning business plan.

Business Plan (Appendix B)

Instructors who want a more complete business-planning experience for their students will want to take advantage of this appendix. Using Business PlanPro software as a foundation, this appendix carefully takes students through each step of creating a winning business plan. By completing the chapters in the text, and after studying numerous business plan examples, students will be able to build their own complete business plan by the end of the term.

Four-Way Approach to Vocabulary Development

This text's four-way method of vocabulary reinforcement helps students learn basic business vocabulary with ease. First, each term is printed in boldface within the text. Second, a definition appears in the margin adjacent to the term. Third, an alphabetical list of key terms appears at the end of each chapter, with convenient cross-references to the pages in the chapter where the terms are defined. Fourth, all marginal definitions are assembled in an alphabetical glossary on the Companion Website.

TEACH WITH AN UNPARALLELED SUPPLEMENTS PACKAGE

The instructional resource package accompanying this text is specially designed to simplify the tasks of teaching and learning.

Instructor's Resource CD-ROM

The Instructor's Resource CD-ROM includes the Instructor's Resource Manual, TestGen, PowerPoint Presentations, PRS Questions, and Image Library.

Instructor's Resource Manual

The Instructor's Resource Manual contains a set of completely integrated support materials. The manual is designed to assist instructors in quickly finding and assembling the resources available for each chapter of the text and includes the following material:

- Learning objectives
- Learning objectives summarized
- Brief chapter outline
- Detailed lecture outlines and notes with suggested classroom activities integrated throughout
- A list of the difficulties (for each chapter) that students often face with material presented and suggestions for overcoming each challenge
- Real-world cases with discussion questions
- Answers to all end-of-chapter questions, problems, and assignments
- A detailed video guide with answers to video exercise questions
- One 10- to 15-question pop quiz for each chapter
- Sample syllabus

TestGen

The TestGen contains 14 chapters of 100–125 questions per chapter, all of which have been carefully checked for accuracy and quality. It consists of multiple-choice, true/false, fill-in-the-blank, and essay questions. Each test question is ranked based on Bloom's Taxonomy and by level of difficulty (easy, moderate, or difficult) and contains page references to give the instructor a quick and easy way to balance the level of exams or quizzes.

The user-friendly TestGen software allows you to generate random tests with our extensive bank of questions. You can also edit our questions and answers and even add your own. You can create an exam, administer it traditionally or online, and analyze your success with a simple click of the mouse.

PowerPoint® Presentations

Enhance your classroom presentations with this well-developed PowerPoint presentation set, which contains more than 250 text-specific slides that highlight fundamental concepts by integrating key graphs, figures, and illustrations from the text. Free to adopters, these PowerPoint slides are available on the Instructor's Resource CD-ROM or can be downloaded from Pearson's online catalogue at vig.pearsoned.ca.

PRS Questions

Gauge your students' course progress with this Personal Response System that enables you to pose questions, record results, and display those results instantly in your classroom. Questions are provided in PowerPoint format.

Image Library

Selected full-colour figures and graphs from the text are available for viewing in the Image Library of the IRCD.

Videos

Twelve videos are linked to end-of-part cases and exercises to help students see how real-life businesses operate and how the people who run them apply fundamental business principles on a daily basis. The videos are available in DVD and VHS format, and are also available on our Video Central website.

VangoNotes Audio Study Guide

Study on the go with VangoNotes. Just download chapter reviews from your text and listen to them on any mp3 player. Now wherever you are—whatever you're doing—you can study by listening to the following for each chapter of your textbook:

- **Big Ideas:** Your "need to know" for each chapter
- **Practice Test:** A gut check for the Big Ideas—tells you if you need to keep studying
- **Key Terms:** Audio "flashcards" to help you review key concepts and terms
- **Rapid Review:** A quick drill session—use it right before your test

VangoNotes are **flexible**; download all the material directly to your player, or only the chapters you need. And they're **efficient**. Use them in your car, at the gym, walking to class, wherever. So get yours today. And get studying.

VangoNotes.com

Career Portfolio Supplement

This unique saleable booklet, written by James O'Rourke, University of Notre Dame, takes students through the process of building their individualized career portfolio. Students walk through the process of self-assessment, matching career opportunities, initiating the job search using the latest Internet-based search vehicles, preparing all job-search–related documents, and following up. Upon completion of the supplement, students will have a career portfolio they can use and build on as their career progresses. To order, please contact your local Pearson Education sales representative (ISBN: 978-0-13-172798-4).

Business Ethics in Uncertain Times: A Special Supplement

This special booklet by Marian Woods covers key issues in contemporary business ethics, including the following:

- Management's responsibility for accountability; conflicts of interest, protection of employees, protection of shareholders, and compliance with legal and regulatory standards
- Corporate governance, including how and why it's supposed to work but doesn't always; outside directors versus insiders with conflicts of interest; and audit committees
- Accounting practices, including why and how public corporations hide debt and misrepresent expenses, how previously accepted accounting practices are now being questioned, the role of CPA firms in auditing statements, and ways to manage conflicts of interest with consulting clients
- Stakeholder relations, including the importance of honest and complete financial statements to inform current and potential shareholders, ways to maintain employee trust, and relations with unions
- Ethical decisions and behaviour, including what can be done to encourage and support ethical actions, such as codes of conduct, ethical training, whistle-blower and ombudsman structures, legal and regulatory oversight of auditors and managers, separation of consulting and auditing, and director accountability

Chapter-ending pedagogy includes "Questions for Review," "Questions for Discussion and Analysis," "For Further Research," and "Ethics Resources Online." This supplement can be packaged with the text for no additional cost. To order, contact your local Pearson Education Canada sales representative (ISBN: 978-0-13-141422-4).

Business PlanPro Software

Business PlanPro Business PlanPro software provides students with a step-by-step approach to creating a comprehensive business plan. Preformatted report templates, charts, and tables do the mechanics so students can focus on the thinking. Business PlanPro software can be packaged with the textbook for a nominal fee of $15 (ISBN: 978-0-13-195519-6).

PREVIEW THE COMPANION WEBSITE FOR *BUSINESS IN ACTION*, SECOND CANADIAN EDITION

The Companion Website is your personal tool to the free online resources for this book. Access the Companion Website at **www.pearsoned.ca/bovee**.

The website features one-click access to all of the resources created by an award-winning team of educators. Here is a preview of its exciting features.

For the Student

- **Self-tests:** Test your knowledge with this interactive quiz that offers a wide variety of self-assessment questions for each chapter. Results from the automatically graded questions for every chapter provide immediate feedback that can serve as practice or can be emailed to the instructor for extra credit.
- **Internet Exercises:** These exercises are drawn directly from the book's end-of-chapter material. Students can link to a variety of websites and answer questions based on both website and text content.
- **Student Resources:** Access the websites featured in the text by using the hotlinks, review chapter content by viewing the student version of the PowerPoint slides, or use the additional study materials developed for this course.

For the Instructor

Online Faculty Support: In this password-protected area, get the most current and advanced support materials available, including downloadable supplements, such as the Instructor's Resource Manual, PowerPoints, and TestGen.

OFFER *BUSINESS IN ACTION* AS AN ONLINE COURSE

Online Learning Solutions: Pearson Education Canada supports instructors interested in using online course management systems. We provide text-related content in WebCT, Blackboard, and Course Compass. To find out more about creating an online course using Pearson content in one of these platforms, contact your Pearson Education Canada sales representative.

PERSONAL ACKNOWLEDGMENTS

Many individuals assisted in the development of this text; their comments, ideas, and recommendations were vital elements in shaping the second Canadian edition of *Business in Action*.

Joel Bernard, BCIT
Hugh Drolle, Mohawk College
Cathie M. Hurley, University of New Brunswick

Suzanne Iskander, Humber College
Paul Myers, St. Clair College
Jeffrey Rudolph, Marianopolis College

I would like to acknowledge all the staff at Pearson Canada for their contributions to this project. In particular, I would like to recognize Karen Elliott, Acquisitions Editor, for her leadership and clear vision for the project; Lisa Cicinelli, Assistant Editor, Pam Voves, Senior Developmental Editor, and Mary Wong, Assistant Editor, for their guidance and creative ideas; and Leanne Rancourt, Production Editor, for her attention to detail and great feedback.

I would also like to thank Gary Bennett, Vice-President, Editorial Director, for providing strong support for this project, as well as Allen Dykler, Senior Sales and Editorial Representative, and Cas Shields, Executive Marketing Manager.

I would also like to recognize my colleagues at Vanier College and Concordia University for providing valuable feedback and support.

George Dracopoulos

A Great Way to Learn and Instruct Online

Companion
Website

The Pearson Education Canada Companion Website is easy to navigate and is organized to correspond to the chapters in this textbook. Whether you are a student in the classroom or a distance learner you will discover helpful resources for in-depth study and research that empower you in your quest for greater knowledge and maximize your potential for success in the course.

[**www.pearsoned.ca/bovee**]

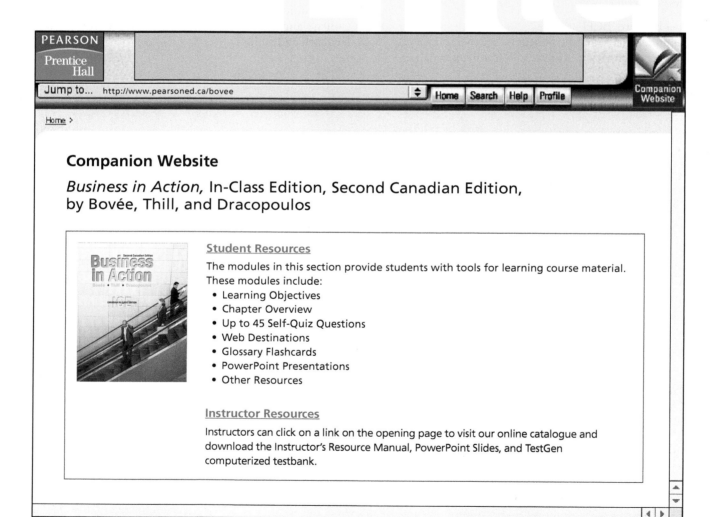

PEARSON
Prentice
Hall

Companion
Website

Jump to...   http://www.pearsoned.ca/bovee | Home | Search | Help | Profile |

Home >

Companion Website

Business in Action, In-Class Edition, Second Canadian Edition, by Bovée, Thill, and Dracopoulos

Student Resources

The modules in this section provide students with tools for learning course material. These modules include:

- Learning Objectives
- Chapter Overview
- Up to 45 Self-Quiz Questions
- Web Destinations
- Glossary Flashcards
- PowerPoint Presentations
- Other Resources

Instructor Resources

Instructors can click on a link on the opening page to visit our online catalogue and download the Instructor's Resource Manual, PowerPoint Slides, and TestGen computerized testbank.

PART I

CONDUCTING
BUSINESS IN THE
GLOBAL ECONOMY

CHAPTER 1
Understanding the Fundamentals of
Business and Economics

CHAPTER 2
Competing in the Global Economy

CHAPTER 3
Practising Ethical Behaviour and Social
Responsibility

CHAPTER I

UNDERSTANDING THE FUNDAMENTALS OF BUSINESS AND ECONOMICS

LEARNING OBJECTIVES
After studying this chapter, you will be able to

1 Define what a business is and identify four key social and economic roles that businesses serve

2 Differentiate between goods-producing and service businesses. List five factors that explain the rise in the number of service businesses

3 Differentiate between a free-market system and a planned system

4 Explain how supply and demand affect price

5 Explain the four major economic roles of the Canadian government

6 Explain how a free-market system monitors its economic performance

7 Identify five challenges that businesses are facing in the global economy as well as how companies are using the Internet to improve efficiency

BEHIND THE SCENES

BlackBerry: The High-Tech Maple Leaf?

www.rim.net

Research in Motion (RIM) began operations in Waterloo, Ontario, back in 1984. At the time, the company founders could not have imagined that they would create a product and brand that would be so well-recognized and embraced around the world. But through the tremendous success of the BlackBerry, the company has surpassed its initial dreams. Tremendous success has continued despite important setbacks and competitors trying to take a piece of their BlackBerry pie.

By all accounts, RIM is an extremely successful Canadian company. Over the years, the workforce has expanded from 200 in 1998 to 6200 in 2007. If a high-tech flag were created for Canada, it would most likely have a BlackBerry at the centre. In the first quarter of fiscal 2008, RIM's revenue amounted to over $1 billion, up 76.5 percent from $613.1 million in the same quarter the previous year; RIM shipped approximately 2.4 million devices; and the total number of BlackBerry subscriber accounts increased by approximately 1.2 million, to over 9 million total accounts. The company earned about 76 percent of its revenue from devices, 16 percent from services (carriers like Bell and Rogers pay RIM $7 to $9 per customer every month), 5 percent from software, and 3 percent from other revenue. Recent financial statistics continue to help make the case: Research in Motion's BlackBerry is high-tech royalty.

Most aspiring business owners can only hope of conducting business discussions that use product and dollar figures in the millions and billions. RIM achieved that status long ago. The entrepreneurial push behind RIM's success began with company co-founders Mike Lazaridis, co-CEO, and Douglas Fregin, vice-president of operations. The addition of co-CEO Jim Balsillie back in 1992 was a vital piece of the puzzle. RIM went public a little over a decade ago, and since that time Jim Balsillie and Mike Lazaridis have become "golden boys" of the wireless communications world. According to Barry Richards, analyst at Paradigm Capital, "the co-CEOs are like the guys who invented the cell phone." RIM's entrepreneurs are respected role models because of their great market vision.

As wise businessmen, Balsillie and Lazaridis understand that accomplishments require proper inputs: from natural resources to labour to capital to knowledge. In

The co-CEOs of Research in Motion, Jim Balsillie and Mike Lazaridis, proudly hold their BlackBerry devices.

particular, developing human resources and contributing to the knowledge field are of key strategic importance for this company. RIM pushes the learning philosophy internally and is also willing to give back to the community to foster even more innovation. For example, the company donated $100 million to create the Institute for Theoretical Physics and another $50 million for the Institute for Quantum Computing at the University of Waterloo.

In today's connected world, financial figures are examined very closely—yearly, quarterly, monthly, even hourly—and things can change in a digital moment. Building a dream—even one as grand as this one—is an accomplishment, but maintaining and continuing the growth is quite another achievement altogether. The competition is fierce and everyone is looking to undercut or bury the opposition. The BlackBerry is no different; it has low-cost, knock-off competitors like the boldly named RedBerry from China as well as legitimate global competitors such as Motorola's Q, Palm's Treo, and Nokia's E62. The launch of the Apple iPhone has also proven to be a significant threat. Margins are being threatened on the service and software side of the business as well. Despite it all, RIM's officials do not seem overly concerned; the company has taken on all challengers and continued to innovate. Rumours recently surfaced of a potential buyout attempt from Microsoft, but this news was quickly dismissed by both sides. RIM is soaring high, but even with this confidence the CEOs are painfully aware that things change quickly in the world of high tech.[1]

TEST YOURSELF

Answers to these questions can be found on the website: www.pearsoned.ca/bovee.

1. Does Research in Motion function in the goods-producing or service sector?

2. How does Research in Motion's history demonstrate the power and motivation behind the capitalist system, as advocated by Adam Smith?

3. Explain the role that the *factors of production* play in the economy by providing examples from Research in Motion's business activities.

4. Explain the basic theory of supply and demand using the BlackBerry as an example.

WHY STUDY BUSINESS?

L.O. 1

No matter where your career plans take you, the dynamics of business will affect your work and life in many ways. If you want to be a manager or an entrepreneur, knowing how to run a business is very important. If you plan a career in a professional specialty such as law, engineering, or finance, knowing how businesses operate will help you interact with clients and colleagues more effectively and contribute to your career success. Even if you plan to work in government, education, or another non-commercial setting, business awareness can help you as well; many organizations look to business for new ideas and leadership techniques. In your role as a consumer and taxpayer, knowing more about business will help you make better financial decisions.

In fact, your experiences as a consumer have already taught you a great deal about the business world. Whether you're logged on to a website, flying in an airplane, watching a movie, buying music over the Internet, enjoying your favourite coffee drink, or withdrawing money from an ATM, you're involved in someone else's business. But like many students, for most of your life you've been observing and enjoying the efforts of others. As you progress through this course, though, you'll begin to look at things from the eyes of an employee, a manager or an entrepreneur instead of a consumer. You'll develop a fundamental business vocabulary that will help you keep up with the latest

Learning from Business Blunders

OOPS

Filling out a loan application can be an unpleasant task; it's hard to avoid the feeling that you're being forced to reveal your most private, personal secrets. Imagine how it must feel to see all those secrets on display on the World Wide Web. Dealerskins, a company that hosts websites for car dealers, failed to take even the most basic steps to protect the private financial information of a thousand car-loan applicants. Anyone could view the applications simply by clicking on "View Source" in Internet Explorer.

WHAT YOU CAN LEARN

In today's electronic economy, all businesses have an obligation to protect any confidential data they collect from customers. No system is absolutely foolproof, but readily available e-commerce systems provide secure, reliable ways to protect data.[2]

IN-CLASS NOTES

Why Study Business?

- Learn what it takes to run a business
- Build business vocabulary
- Develop workplace skills
- Learn about a variety of jobs
- Appreciate today's business career opportunities

_____

_____

_____

_____

_____

_____

business
An activity and enterprise that provide goods and services a society needs

profit
Money that remains after expenses and taxes have been deducted from revenue generated by selling goods and services

news and make more-informed decisions. By participating in classroom discussions and completing the chapter exercises, you'll gain some valuable critical-thinking, problem-solving, team-building, and communication skills that you can use on the job and throughout your life.

This course will also introduce you to a variety of jobs in business fields such as accounting, economics, human resources, management, finance, marketing, and so on. You'll see how people who work in these fields contribute to the success of a company as a whole. You'll gain insight into the types of skills and knowledge these jobs require—and you'll discover that a career in business today is fascinating, challenging, and often quite rewarding.

In addition, a study of business management will help you appreciate the larger context in which businesses operate and the many legal and ethical questions managers must consider as they make business decisions. Both government regulators and society as a whole have numerous expectations regarding the ways businesses treat employees, shareholders, the environment, other businesses, and the communities in which they operate.

WHAT IS A BUSINESS?

Like Jim Balsillie and Mike Lazaridis, many people create and build a **business**—a profit-seeking activity that provides goods and services that satisfy consumers' needs. For example, Research in Motion provides products that satisfy consumer and business communications needs. In addition to providing a society with necessities such as housing, clothing, food, transportation, communication, health care, and so on, businesses provide people with jobs and a means to prosper; they pay taxes that are used to build highways, fund education, and provide grants for scientific research (as the University of Waterloo can attest to); and they reinvest their profits in the economy, thereby creating a higher standard of living and quality of life for society as a whole.

The driving force behind most businesses is the prospect of earning a **profit**—what remains after all expenses have been

If Irving Oil follows through on its plans to build a new refinery in Saint John, New Brunswick, it will be the first major refinery to be built in North America in 25 years. The company has already purchased 3000 acres of land for the project, even though it would only need about 400 or 500 for the project.

deducted from business revenue. Such a prospect is commonly referred to as a *profit motive*. For example, Irving Oil is thinking of building a new refinery in Saint John, New Brunswick, at a cost of $5 to $7 billion. This project would lead to the creation of 5000 jobs during construction and employ 100 people on a permanent basis once it is completed in 2012 or 2013. Of course, beyond the environmental studies under way, the company is conducting major feasibility studies aimed at understanding oil-capacity needs, especially on the north-east coast of the United States where most of the new supply would be heading. There are many economic benefits of the project, but in the end the decision will be based on long-term profit.[3]

Businesses may keep and use their profits as they wish, within legal limits. Still, not every organization exists to earn a profit. **Non-profit organizations** such as museums, public schools and universities, symphonies, libraries, government agencies, and charities exist to provide society with a social or educational service. The Canadian Red Cross, for example, provides relief to victims of disasters and helps people prevent, prepare for, and respond to emergencies. The organization takes in approximately $270 million annually and spends almost all of that money on its programs and supporting services.[4] From domestic relief efforts like those for people affected by forest fires in British Columbia, to international crises such as the 2006 tsunami relief effort or providing mosquito nets to people in Sierra Leone, the Canadian Red Cross is there. In addition, the Red Cross runs programs that help the elderly, teach people to swim, and provide first aid and CPR training, just to name a few of their community-based initiatives. Although non-profit organizations like the Red Cross do not have a profit motive, they must operate efficiently and effectively to achieve their goals. Thus, the business opportunities, challenges, and activities discussed throughout this textbook apply to both profit-seeking and non-profit organizations. Moreover, to be successful, both profit-seeking and non-profit organizations must be socially responsible and ethical when dealing with investors, employees, customers, the community, and society (as Chapter 3 discusses).

The Canadian Red Cross promises to be ready "Anytime, Anyplace." Non-profit organizations need to be professionally run and well-organized to reach their goals.

non-profit organizations
Firms whose primary objective is something other than returning a profit to their owners

L.O. 2

Goods-Producing Businesses versus Service Businesses

Most organizations can be classified into two broad categories (or industry sectors): goods producing and service businesses. **Goods-producing businesses** produce tangible goods by engaging in activities such as manufacturing, construction, mining, or agriculture. Boeing, the world's largest manufacturer of commercial jetliners, military aircraft, and satellites, is a perfect example. The company has the largest building, by volume, in the world. Spanning 98 acres under one roof, the facility is big enough to handle construction of 20 wide-body jets at once.[5] Of course, most manufacturing operations do not require a facility as big as Boeing's. Nonetheless, it's difficult to start a goods-producing business without substantial investments in buildings, machinery, and equipment. For this reason, most goods-producing organizations are **capital-intensive**; they generally require large amounts of money or equipment to get started and to operate. Overall, goods-producing employment in Canada has been in decline for the past two decades. Between 2002 and 2007, approximately 149 000 jobs were lost in the manufacturing sector alone.[6]

Service businesses produce intangible products (ones that cannot be held in your hand) and are created in fields such as finance, insurance, transportation, utilities, wholesale and retail trade, banking, entertainment, health care, repairs, and information. AOL Canada, Fairmont Hotels & Resorts, CIBC, and eBay are all examples of service businesses. Most service businesses are **labour-intensive**. They rely

goods-producing businesses
Businesses that produce tangible products

capital-intensive businesses
Businesses that require large investments in capital assets

service businesses
Businesses that provide intangible products or perform useful labour on behalf of another business

labour-intensive businesses
Businesses in which labour costs are more significant than capital costs

Technologies That Are Revolutionizing Business

INSTANT MESSAGING

If you're a serious user of instant messaging (IM), do you remember what it was like those first few times you communicated? Chances are it changed the way you interacted with friends and family.

HOW IT'S CHANGING BUSINESS

IM may have started as a way for individual computer users to stay in touch, but it is now a major communication tool for businesses worldwide. Businesses use IM to replace in-person meetings and phone calls, to supplement online meetings, and to interact with customers. Key benefits include rapid response to urgent messages and lower costs than both phone calls and email. Business-class IM systems offer a range of advanced capabilities in addition to basic chat, including *presence awareness* (the ability to quickly see if someone is at his or her desk and available to IM), remote display of documents, remote control of other computers, video capabilities, and even automated *bot* capabilities that mimic simple conversations with human beings.[7]

WHERE YOU CAN LEARN MORE

To learn more about how IM works, check out http://communication.howstuffworks.com/instant-messaging.htm. For the latest on the business applications of IM, log on to www.instantmessagingplanet.com.

---

more on human resources than on buildings, machinery, and equipment to prosper. A consulting firm is an example of a labour-intensive service business because its existence depends heavily on the knowledge and skills of its consultants. A group of consultants can go into business simply by purchasing some computers and telephones.

Goods and services are useful categories, but the line between the two is often blurry. As discussed in the opening case, RIM sells BlackBerry devices, but it also earns monthly fees from services it provides to carriers for each of its subscriber accounts. IBM is primarily a manufacturer of computers and other business machines, but at least one-third of the company's sales come from computer-related services such as systems design, consulting, and product support.[8] Bombardier provides flight training, maintenance technician training, fleet and logistics support, and a number of aviation services to support sales of its commercial aircraft.[9] As more and more manufacturers such as RIM, Bombardier, and IBM focus on servicing and supporting their products, it becomes increasingly difficult to classify a company as either a goods-producing business or a service business.

Growth of the Service Sector

Over the past two decades, service businesses have grown from providing about half of the nations output to providing roughly three quarters of the output today (see Exhibit 1.1).[10] In fact, most of the increase in Canadian employment in the last two decades has been generated by the service sector. About half of the 1000 largest North American companies today are service based.[11] Economists project that the number of service-related jobs will continue to increase. In contrast, employment growth in the goods-producing sector is under increasing pressure. Wal-Mart's (a service company) rise to the top spot as the world's largest company underscores the changing face of the global economic system.[12] An increasing number of individuals are employed in the service sector and this growth is based on five key factors:

- *Consumers have more disposable income.* The dominant baby-boomer population (people born between 1947 and 1966) have been an extremely financially successful

Exhibit 1.1   **Goods and Services: Employment Breakdown**

The service sector (finance, professional services, trade, transportation, education, etc.) accounts for 75.8 percent of Canadian employment while the goods-producing sector (manufacturing, construction, agriculture, etc.) accounts for the remaining 24.2 percent.

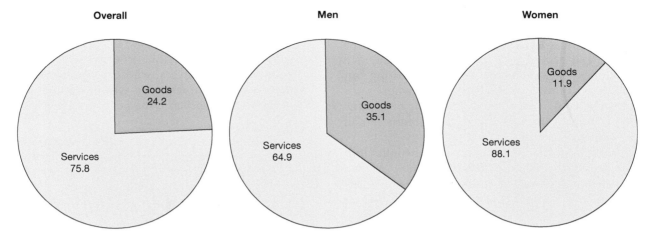

Source: "Employment by Industry and Sex (in percent) 2006," adapted from Statistics Canada website, http://www40.statcan.ca/l01/cst01/labor10b.htm.

generation, and many are still in their peak earning years. These consumers find themselves with more disposable income and look for services to help them invest, travel, relax, and stay fit.[13]

■ *Services target changing demographic patterns and lifestyle trends.* Canada has more elderly people, more single people living alone, more two-career households, and more single parents than ever before. These trends create opportunities for service companies that can help people with all the tasks they no longer have time for, including home maintenance, food service, and child care.[14]

■ *Services are needed to support complex goods and new technology.* Computers, home entertainment centres, recreational vehicles, security systems, and automated production equipment are examples of products that require specialized installation, repair, user training, or extensive support services. As new technology is incorporated into more and more products, companies will need to provide more of these types of product-support services to remain competitive.

■ *Companies are increasingly seeking professional advice.* To compete in the global economy, many firms turn to consultants and professional advisers for help as they seek ways to cut costs, refine their business processes, expand overseas, and engage in **electronic commerce (e-commerce)**—buying and selling over the Internet.

■ *Barriers to entry are low for service businesses.* Capital-intensive manufacturing businesses generally have high **barriers to entry**, which are the requirements a company must meet before it can start competing in a given market. Conditions vary widely by industry, but manufacturers sometimes need to invest millions of dollars in facilities and equipment before they can produce a single product. Other barriers to entry can include government testing and approval, high learning curves, tightly controlled markets, strict licensing procedures, supplies of raw materials, and the need for highly skilled employees. Of course, many of these barriers apply to various service businesses as well, but in general, service businesses are easier to start than manufacturing businesses of comparable size.

Whether you're running a service or a goods-producing business, the global economy is having an impact on all businesses to some extent. The service sector is

electronic commerce (e-commerce)
The general term for the buying and selling of goods and services on the Internet

barriers to entry
Factors that make it difficult to launch a business in a particular industry

Redefining Reality in the Electronic Economy

Jumping on the Internet to check your test scores, reserve a plane ticket, or find an apartment might feel like business as usual to you these days, but the business and technology revolution that enabled these online conveniences has been anything but usual and it's not over yet. No matter where your career takes you, inside the business arena or not, the electronic economy will affect you personally and professionally.

Throughout this course, you'll get insights into the interplay of technology and business. As you explore the ins and outs of business management, pay attention to the Internet's impact in areas such as these:

- *Competitive opportunities and threats.* The Internet creates new business opportunities for some companies and creates new competitive threats for others. Small companies can now reach customers halfway around the world—but the customers they used to have across the street can now shop just about anywhere as well.

- *The speed of business.* The good news is that technology can accelerate virtually every aspect of business. That's also the bad news. The faster things go, the faster everybody expects them to go. The pace can lead to rushed decision making and wear out both employees and managers.

- *Consumer power.* Researching and shopping for many products used to be a time-consuming

chore in many cases, leaving buyers wondering if they had really explored all their options and gathered enough information to make smart decisions. Not anymore. The Internet shifts power from sellers to buyers, who can usually gather mountains of information within minutes and jump from one seller to the next with the click of a mouse.

- *Security and privacy.* Online security issues are significant and cause many individuals to shy away from fully using the potential of the Internet. Dealing with issues like credit card scams, security breaches, and even spam is an unfortunate side of the medium.

- With the dot.com boom and collapse far behind in the rear-view mirror, technology is getting down to business with an emphasis on sensible solutions to real-world problems. As you move into your career, you'll no doubt encounter all these issues—and perhaps make your mark somewhere in the ever-changing world of electronic business.[15]

Questions for Critical Thinking
1. Select a business that you purchase from regularly; how could the Internet help or threaten this company?
2. How has the Internet helped (or perhaps hurt) your college experience?

not immune to the challenges facing the manufacturing sector. According to former Bank of Canada governor David Dodge, the relentless pressure of globalization will soon spread to the service sector. On a positive note, though, Dodge is confident that firms are flexible enough to handle it.[16] Thus, running a successful business today requires a firm understanding of basic economic principles, of the different economic systems operating in the world, and of how businesses compete in the global and electronic economy (see the box entitled "Redefining Reality in the Electronic Economy").

WHAT IS AN ECONOMIC SYSTEM?

economics
The study of how society uses scarce resources to produce and distribute goods and services

Economics is the study of how a society uses its resources to produce and distribute goods and services. All societies must deal with the same basic questions: How should limited economic resources be used to satisfy society's needs? What goods and services should be produced? Who should produce them? How should these goods and services be divided among the population? In some countries these

IN-CLASS NOTES

Goods-Producing vs. Service Businesses

- *Goods-producing industries* create tangible goods and are more *capital-intensive* (i.e., manufacturing, construction, etc.)
- *Service industries* provide intangible products and are more *labour-intensive* (i.e., banking, health care, repairs)
- About 76% of the Canadian workforce is employed within the service sector
- Reasons for service sector growth include low barriers to entry, changing demographics and lifestyles, complex goods and technologies, need for professional advice, more disposable income

_____

_____

_____

_____

_____

_____

_____

_____

_____

decisions are made by individuals (or households) when they decide how to spend or invest their income and by businesses when they decide what kinds of goods and services to produce; in other countries these decisions are primarily made by governments.

Economists call the resources that societies use to produce goods and services *factors of production*. To maximize a company's profit, businesses use five **factors of production** in the most efficient way possible:

- **Natural resources**—things that are useful in their natural state, such as land, forests, minerals, and water

- **Human resources**—anyone (from company presidents to grocery clerks) who works to produce goods and services

- **Capital**—resources (such as money, computers, machines, tools, and buildings) that a business needs to produce goods and services

- **Entrepreneurs**—people like RIM's co-CEOs Jim Balsillie and Mike Lazaridis who are innovative and willing to take risks to create and operate new businesses (see Exhibit 1.2)

- **Knowledge**—the collective intelligence of an organization

Traditionally, a business was considered to have an advantage if it was located in a country with a large supply of natural resources, human resources, capital, and entrepreneurs. But in the global marketplace, intellectual assets are the key. Today companies can obtain capital from one part of the world, purchase supplies from another, and

factors of production
Basic inputs that a society uses to produce goods and services, including natural resources, labour, capital, entrepreneurial skills, and knowledge

natural resources
Land, forests, minerals, water, and other tangible assets usable in their natural state

human resources
All of the people who work for an organization

capital
The physical, human-made elements used to produce goods and services, such as factories and computers; can also refer to the funds that finance the operations of a business

entrepreneurs
People who accept the risk of failure in the private enterprise system

knowledge
Expertise gained through experience or association

Exhibit 1.2   **Success Stories**

Few start-up companies are resource rich. Still, they become successful because an entrepreneur substitutes ingenuity for capital resources.

THE COMPANY	ITS START
McCain Foods Ltd.	Began producing frozen french fries in 1957 out of a small factory based in Florenceville, New Brunswick, with 30 employees. Today the company has over 20 000 employees worldwide and net sales in the $6 billion range.
Coca-Cola	Pharmacist John Pemberton invented a soft drink in his backyard in 1886. Asa Chandler bought the company for US$2300 in 1891.
Nike	In the early 1960s, Phil Knight and his college track coach sold imported Japanese sneakers from the trunk of a station wagon. Start-up costs totalled US$1000.
United Parcel Service	In 1907, two teenagers pooled their cash, came up with US$100, and began a message and parcel delivery service for local merchants.
Cirque du Soleil	In the early 1980s, a group of young street performers began entertaining people in the Old Port of Montreal. Two decades later, these dreamers and unconventional entrepreneurs have turned Cirque du Soleil into an international success story. The company has unique shows playing across the world, including five main shows in Las Vegas and touring shows in Asia, Europe, and North America.[17]
Amazon.com	In 1994, Jeff Bezos came across a report projecting annual Web growth at 2300 percent. He left his Wall Street job, headed to Seattle in an aging Chevy Blazer, and drafted his business plan en route. His e-business, Amazon.com, initially focused on selling books over the Internet, but Bezos later expanded his product offerings to include toys, consumer electronics, software, home improvement products, and more. Today, Amazon.com is a role model for aspiring online retailers.
WestJet	Four Calgary entrepreneurs who saw an opportunity to provide low-rate air travel to western Canadians founded WestJet in 1996. They began operations with three Boeing 737 planes. Today WestJet has expanded to 65 planess with plans to add another 20 planes in the next two years.

locate production facilities in still another. They can relocate their operations to wherever they find a steady supply of affordable workers. Thus, countries with the greatest supply of knowledge workers and ones with economic systems that give workers the freedom to pursue their own economic interests will have an advantage in the new economy (see Exhibit 1.3).

Types of Economic Systems

economic system
Means by which a society distributes its resources to satisfy its people's needs

The role that individuals and governments play in allocating a society's resources depends on the society's **economic system**, the basic set of rules for allocating a society's resources to satisfy its citizens' needs. Two main economic systems exist in the world today: *free-market systems* and *planned systems*.

L.O. 3

Free-Market System

free-market system
An economic system in which decisions about what to produce and in what quantities are made by the market's buyers and sellers

capitalism
An economic system based on economic freedom and competition

In a **free-market system**, individuals are free to decide what products to produce, how to produce them, whom to sell them to, and at what price to sell them. Thus, they have the chance to succeed—or to fail—based on their own efforts. **Capitalism** is the term most often used to describe the free-market system—one in which individuals own and operate the majority of businesses and where competition, supply, and demand determine which goods and services are produced. Capitalism owes its philosophical origins to eighteenth-century philosophers like Adam Smith. According to Smith, in the ideal capitalist economy (pure capitalism) the *market* (an arrangement between buyer and

Exhibit 1.3	**What's New about the New Economy?**

The new economy is different from the old economy in a number of key ways. Besides being faster and more volatile, it's highly dependent on the use of information technology to gain a competitive advantage.

	OLD ECONOMY	NEW ECONOMY
General Characteristics	■ Competitive advantage based on physical assets	■ Competitive advantage based on intellectual assets
	■ Profits maximized by controlling costs	■ Profits maximized by adding value to products and services
Technology	■ Mechanical technology is main influence on economic growth	■ Information technology is main influence on economic growth
Workforce	■ Job-specific skills	■ Transferable skills and lifelong learning
Geography	■ Firms locate near resource to reduce costs	■ Firms locate near collaborators and competitors to boost innovation
Capital	■ Debt financing	■ Venture capital

Source: Adapted from Monica Kearns, "Whatever Happened to the New Economy?" *State Legislatures,* February 2002, 24–27.

seller to trade goods and services) serves as a self-correcting mechanism—an "invisible hand" to ensure the production of the goods that society wants in the quantities that society wants, without regulation of any kind.[18]

Because the market is its own regulator, Smith was opposed to government intervention. He believed that if anyone's prices or wages strayed from acceptable levels that the forces of competition would drive them back. In modern practice, however, governments sometimes interfere in free-market systems to accomplish goals that leaders think are economically or socially desirable. This practice of limited intervention is characteristic of a *mixed economy* or *mixed capitalism,* which is the economic system in Canada. For example, federal, provincial, and local governments intervene in the economy in a variety of ways, such as influencing particular allocations of resources through tax incentives, prohibiting or restricting the sale of certain goods and services, or setting *price controls.* Price controls can involve both maximum allowable prices (such as limiting rent increases or capping the price on gasoline or other products during emergencies and shortages) and minimum allowable prices (such as supplementing the prices of agricultural goods to ensure producers a minimum level of income or establishing minimum-wage levels).[19] Other countries with variations of this economic system include (but are not limited to) the United States, Germany, and Japan.

Mixed economies, particularly those with a strong capitalist emphasis, offer opportunities for wealth creation, but usually attach an element of risk to the potential reward. For instance, it is relatively easy to start a company in a mixed economy, but you could lose all of your start-up money if the company isn't successful. Entrepreneurs and investors willing to face these risks are an important force in capitalist economies, and they can be rewarded handsomely when they are successful.

Planned System

In a **planned system**, governments control all or part of the allocation of resources and limit the freedom of choice in order to accomplish government goals. Because social equality is a major goal of planned systems, private enterprise and the pursuit of private gain are generally regarded as wasteful and exploitive.

The planned system that allows individuals the least degree of economic freedom is **communism**, which still exists in such countries as North Korea and Cuba. (Keep in mind that even though communism and socialism are discussed here as economic

planned system
An economic system in which the government controls most of the factors of production and regulates their allocation

communism
An economic system in which all productive resources are owned and operated by the government and private property essentially doesn't exist

systems, they can be political and social systems as well.) The degree to which communism is actually practised varies. In its purest form, almost all resources are under government control. Private ownership is restricted to personal and household items. Resource allocation is handled through centralized planning by a handful of government officials who decide what goods to produce, how to produce them, and to whom they should be distributed.[20] Although pure communism still has its supporters, the future of communism is not bright. As economists Lester Thurow and Robert Heilbroner put it, "It's a great deal easier to design and assemble the skeleton of a mighty economy than to run it."[21]

socialism
An economic system characterized by public ownership and operation of key industries combined with private ownership and operation of less vital industries

Socialism lies somewhere in between capitalism and communism in the degree of economic freedom that it permits. Like communism, socialism involves a relatively high degree of government planning and some government ownership of land and capital resources (such as buildings and equipment). However, government involvement is limited to industries considered vital to the common welfare, such as transportation, utilities, medicine, steel, and communications. In these industries, the government owns or controls all of the facilities and determines what will be produced and how the output will be distributed. Private ownership is permitted in industries that are not considered vital, and in these areas both businesses and individuals are allowed to benefit from their own efforts. Taxes are high in socialist states because the government must cover public-care costs. Canada falls under the category of a mixed capitalist economy because many programs such as universal health care, subsidized education, and housing are borrowed from the socialist model. As such, Canada is more closely linked to this model than the United States, which provides fewer public services.

The Trend toward Privatization

Although varying degrees of socialism and communism are practised around the world today, several socialist and communist economies are moving toward free-market systems. Even some mixed capitalist economies are unloading unprofitable businesses for badly needed cash. Countries such as Great Britain, Mexico, Argentina, Israel, France, Sweden, and China are **privatizing** some of their government-owned enterprises by selling them to privately held firms. Great Britain, for example, has sold the national phone company, the national steel company, the national sugar company, Heathrow Airport, water suppliers, and the company that makes Rover automobiles. Like Great Britain, China is also privatizing its major industries and plans to convert

privatizing
The conversion of public ownership to private ownership

  IN-CLASS NOTES

Economic Systems
- To maximize profits, businesses use five **factors of production** as efficiently as possible: *natural resources, human resources, capital, knowledge,* and *entrepreneurs*
- Types of economic systems that exist today:
  - **Free-market systems** include *capitalism* and *mixed capitalism*
  - **Planned systems** include *communism* and *socialism*

_____

_____

_____

_____

_____

_____

_____

the majority of its state-owned industries.[22] The Canadian government went through a similar divestment process during the last two decades. Recently, the federal government sold its remaining shares in Petro-Canada.[23]

How Does a Free-Market Economic System Work? (A Microeconomic View)

Earlier in this chapter we noted that in a free-market system, the marketplace determines what goods and services get produced. In this section we will discuss three underlying elements that differentiate a free-market system from other economic systems: supply and demand, competition, and limited government intervention.

The Theory of Supply and Demand in a Free-Market System

The theory of supply and demand is the driving force of the free-market system. It is the basic tool that economists use to describe how the market works in determining prices and the quantity of goods produced. **Demand** refers to the amount of a good or service that consumers will buy at a given time at various prices. **Supply** refers to the quantities of a good or service that producers will provide on a particular date at various prices. Simply put, *demand* refers to the behaviour of buyers, whereas *supply* refers to the behaviour of sellers. Both forces work together to create order in the free-market system.

On the surface, the theory of supply and demand seems little more than common sense. Consumers should buy more when the price is low and buy less when the price is high. Producers would offer more when the price is high and offer less when the price is low. The quantity supplied and the quantity demanded continuously interact, and the balance between them at any given moment should be reflected by the current price on the open market. However, a quick look at any real-life market situation shows you that balancing supply with demand by adjusting price isn't quite that simple.

Consider the airline industry. Airline travel is a cyclical business; its revenues rise and fall with the economy. When the economy is strong, consumers and businesses are willing to spend more on discretionary travel. When the economy is weak, they cut back on such discretionary spending (see Exhibit 1.4[24]). Airlines can respond by

Over the years the Canadian government has followed the trend toward privatization; it sold its remaining 19% stake in Petro-Canada a few years ago.

L.O. 4

demand
Buyers' willingness and ability to purchase products

supply
The specific quantity of a product that the seller is able and willing to provide

---

Exhibit 1.4 **Effect of Faltering Economy on Demand for Business Travel**

During poor economic times, demand for business travel softens as companies take steps such as these to reduce their travel costs.

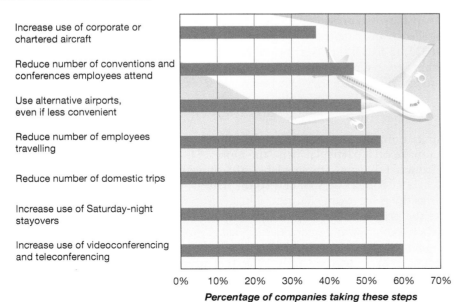

Percentage of companies taking these steps

Increase use of corporate or chartered aircraft

Reduce number of conventions and conferences employees attend

Use alternative airports, even if less convenient

Reduce number of employees travelling

Reduce number of domestic trips

Increase use of Saturday-night stayovers

Increase use of videoconferencing and teleconferencing

0% 10% 20% 30% 40% 50% 60% 70%

By adjusting prices, airlines can influence demand for their services to a degree, but factors such as security threats and the health of the economy have a tremendous influence on consumer airline behaviour.

reducing ticket prices, offering promotions, or scaling back the number of flights. But airlines must plan their businesses years in advance, which means they must always be able to provide a base level of service regardless of how many people want to use it. Maintaining a fixed network of scheduled flights as traveller demand fluctuates is expensive. A new commercial jet costs from several million dollars (e.g., Bombardier's regional narrow-body jet) to several *hundred* million dollars (e.g., wide-body jets such as Boeing's 767s and 747s and Airbus's A340s and A330s). Further complicating the matter, new planes must be ordered years before they are needed. Air Canada has major fixed costs; it operated 329 airplanes in 2007.[25] Add the costs of airport leases, landing fees, jet fuel, and employees such as pilots, flight attendants, and maintenance crews, and you can begin to see why airlines simply can't shrink their way back to profitability when demand falls. In recent years, Air Canada has served as a prominent case study of the industry's challenges.

Nevertheless, in broad terms, the interaction of supply and demand regulates a free-market system by determining what is produced and in what amounts. For example, a movie studio might produce more comedies if ticket sales for similar films are strong. On the other hand, it might decide to produce fewer comedies and more action-adventure movies if attendance at comedies lags. The result of such decisions—in theory, at least—is that consumers will get what they want and producers will earn a profit by keeping up with public demand.

Buyer's Perspective (Simple Example)

The forces of supply and demand determine the market price for products and services. Say you're shopping for a hat, and the one you want is priced at $35. This is more than you can afford, so you don't make the purchase. When the store puts the hats on sale the following week for $18, you run right in and buy one.

But what if the store had to buy the hats from the manufacturer for $20? It would have made a profit selling them to you for $35, but it loses money selling them for $18. What if the store tries to buy more from the manufacturer at $10 or $15 but the manufacturer refuses? Is there a price that will make both the supplier and the customer happy? The answer is yes—the price at which the quantity of hats demanded equals the quantity supplied.

This relationship is shown in Exhibit 1.5. A range of possible prices is listed vertically at the left of the graph, with the lowest at the bottom and the highest at the top. Quantity of hats is represented along the horizontal axis. The points plotted on the curve labelled *D* indicate that on a given day the store would sell 10 hats if they were priced at $35, 15 hats if they were priced at $27, and so on. The curve that describes this relationship between price and quantity demanded is a *demand curve*. (Demand curves are not necessarily curved; they may be straight lines.)

Seller's Perspective

Now think about the situation from the seller's point of view. The more profit the store can make on a particular item, the more of that item it will want to sell. Take a look at Exhibit 1.5 again. The line labelled *S* shows that the store would be willing to offer 30 hats at $35, 25 at $30, and so on. The store's willingness to carry the item increases as the price it can charge and its profit potential per item increase. In other words, as the price goes up, the quantity supplied goes up. The line tracing the relationship between price and quantity supplied is called a *supply curve*.

As much as the store would like to sell 30 hats at $35, you and your fellow consumers are likely to want only 10 at that price. If the store offered 30 hats at that price, it would probably be stuck with some that it would have to mark down.

Exhibit 1.5   **The Relationship between Supply and Demand**

In a free-market system, prices aren't set by the government; nor do producers alone have the final say. Instead, prices reflect the interaction of supply (S) and demand (D). The equilibrium price (E) is established when the amount of a product that producers are willing to sell at a given price equals the amount that consumers are willing to buy at that price.

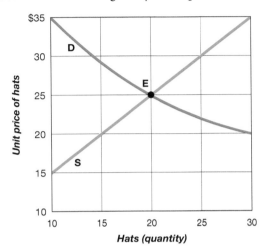

How does the store avoid this problem? It looks for the point at which the demand curve and the supply curve intersect—the point at which the intentions of buyers and sellers coincide. The point marked *E* in Exhibit 1.5 shows that when hats are priced at $25, consumers are willing to buy 20 and the store is willing to sell 20. In other words, at $25 the quantity supplied and the quantity demanded are in balance. The price at this point is known as the **equilibrium price**. Note that this intersection represents both a specific price—$25 in our example—and a specific quantity of goods—20 hats. It is also tied to a specific point in time. Note also that it is the mutual interaction between quantity demanded and quantity supplied that determines the equilibrium price.

FREE-MARKET SYSTEM (A MACROECONOMIC VIEW)

Competition

In a free-market system, customers are free to buy whatever and wherever they please. Therefore, companies must compete with rivals for potential customers. For example, Reitmans competes with other fashion apparel outlets across the country. In addition, the company serves specific needs and competes in the marketplace under various additional retail brands such as Smart Set, RW&CO., Penningtons, MXM, Thyme Maternity, Addition Elle, and Cassis. **Competition** is the situation in which two or more suppliers of a product are rivals in the pursuit of the same customers.

The nature of competition varies widely by industry. In theory, the ideal type of competition is **pure competition**, which is characterized by three conditions: a marketplace of multiple buyers and sellers, a product or service with nearly identical features such as wheat or cotton, and low barriers of entry (that is, the ability to easily enter and exit the marketplace). When these three conditions exist, no single firm or group of firms in an industry becomes large enough to influence prices and thereby

equilibrium price
The point at which quantity supplied equals quantity demanded

competition
Rivalry among businesses for the same customer

pure competition
The situation in which so many buyers and sellers exist that no single buyer or seller can individually influence market prices

Reitman's has been in business for over 70 years. There are 343 Reitman's stores across Canada, offering a full line of ready-to-wear clothing and accessories that cater to the active woman— everything from career wear to casual wear, all available in petite to full sizes.

monopoly
A market in which there are no direct competitors and only one company dominates

oligopoly
A market dominated by a few producers

monopolistic competition
The situation in which many sellers differentiate their products from those of competitors in at least some small way

competitive advantage
The ability to perform in one or more ways that competitors cannot match

distort the workings of the free-market system. At the other extreme, in a **monopoly** there is only one producer of a product in a given market, and thus the producer is able to determine the price. A situation in which an industry (such as commercial aircraft manufacturing) is dominated by only a few producers (wide-body jets: Boeing and Airbus; narrow-body regional jets: Bombardier and Embraer) is called an **oligopoly**.

Between pure competition and monopoly lay a number of forms with varying degrees of competitive power. Most of the competition in advanced free-market economic systems is **monopolistic competition**, where a large number of sellers (none of which dominates the market) offer products that can be distinguished from competing products in at least some small way. Toothpaste, cosmetics, soft drinks, Internet search engines, and restaurants are examples of products that can vary in the features each offers.

When markets become filled with competitors and products start to look alike, companies use price, speed, quality, service, or innovation to gain a **competitive advantage**—something that sets one company apart from its rivals and makes its products more appealing to consumers (see the box entitled "LivePerson Puts a Pulse on the Web"). For example, WestJet built its reputation by offering low fares and good value. Fast-food outlets compete on speed and convenience. Harvey's locations further distinguish themselves by allowing customers to customize their hamburgers and view final preparation. Second Cup competes on quality by delivering a premium product to the mass of caffeine-craving individuals. And Mountain Equipment Co-op (MEC) competes based on its customer service. Not only are MEC's customers allowed to return their online purchases to any physical MEC store, but those who live near one of MEC's retail outlets can arrange to pick up online sales at the store or receive them at home.

LivePerson Puts a Pulse on the Web

You're shopping online, but you want some more information. Does that sweater come in red? Will you get free shipping? Before you click and buy, sometimes you need the help of a real live person. That's why Robert LoCascio developed LivePerson.com, a software company that puts the human touch into online shopping. Bell Canada is one of the many large corporations that uses the company's services.

LoCascio knows that many retail websites are ineffective. They confuse and frustrate shoppers and force them to look through page after page of details to find the information they need. As a result, many consumers give up and abandon their electronic shopping carts. But LoCascio's LivePerson helps companies doing business on the Internet maximize their customers' online shopping experience. Websites with LivePerson services invite online shoppers to chat with a real live person. Shoppers simply click on the LivePerson icon and a pop-up window appears on the screen. Type in your name and you're instantly greeted by a customer service rep who asks, "What can I do for you?"

Bell Canada uses LivePerson's online sales solution to engage customers as they browse its business solutions website. This initiative targets small and medium enterprises (SME) and focuses on high-speed Internet and Web-hosting services.

The LivePerson reps can also help customers with unique product questions and selections. For instance, reps can suggest alternatives to customers by clicking on different web pages to show similar products. They can also supply customers with valuable information about their past purchases and previous visits to the website. As LoCascio explains, the reps "embrace the customer and help them through the process of shopping."

All in all, LoCascio's company helps e-commerce firms compete by providing a high level of customer service. "If you walk into a store and there's no person there to help you, the experience is pretty bad," says LoCascio. "The same thing is true online."[26]

Questions for Critical Thinking
1. How can a service like LivePerson help Internet retailers gain a competitive advantage?
2. A business is a profit-seeking activity that provides goods and services that satisfy consumer needs. What consumer need does LivePerson try to satisfy?

IN-CLASS NOTES

Free-Market System Fundamentals

- In a free-market system, the interaction of **supply** and **demand** determines what is produced and in what amounts
- **Competition** varies widely by industry
  - *Pure competition*: multiple buyers and sellers, products with nearly identical features, low barriers of entry
  - *Monopoly*: one producer in a given market
  - *Oligopoly*: industry is dominated by a few producers
  - *Monopolistic competition*: large number of sellers offering products that can be distinguished in at least some small way

_____

_____

_____

_____

_____

_____

_____

_____

_____

_____

Product innovation is another way that companies compete in the free-market economy. For nearly a century, 3M's management has promoted innovation by giving employees the freedom to take risks and try new ideas. Beginning with the invention of sandpaper in 1904, 3M has produced such staples as masking tape, cellophane tape, magnetic tape, videotape, and Post-it Notes. Sometimes product innovation can revolutionize an entire industry, just as Rollerblades and Burton and Sims snowboards did by creating new market opportunities for the sporting goods industry.[27]

Government's Role in a Free-Market System

L.O. 5

Although the free-market system generally works well, it's far from perfect. If left unchecked, the economic forces that make capitalism succeed may also create severe problems for some groups or individuals. To correct these types of problems, the government serves four major economic roles:

1. It enacts laws and creates regulations to foster competition;
2. It regulates and deregulates certain industries;
3. It protects stakeholders' rights; and
4. It intervenes to contribute to economic stability.

Fostering Competition

In Canada, the *Competition Act* is a key piece of legislation that regulates business practices. The purpose of this act is to maintain and encourage competition and the efficiency of the Canadian economy. The *Competition Act* also protects the rights of small- and medium-sized businesses while ensuring that consumers have access to competitive prices and product choices. It clearly sets out the laws and consequences of unhealthy economic practices such as illegal trading, double-ticketing, bid-rigging, disseminating deceptive notices of winning a prize, giving false or misleading representations, deceptive telemarketing, and conspiracy.[28]

Because competition generally benefits the Canadian economy, the federal government as well as the provincial governments create laws and regulations every year to preserve competition and ensure that no single enterprise becomes too powerful. For instance, if a company has a monopoly, it can harm consumers by raising prices, cutting output, or stifling innovation. Furthermore, because most monopolies have total control over certain products and prices and the market share for those products, it is extremely difficult for competitors to enter markets where monopolies exist. For these reasons, over the last century or so, a number of laws and regulations have been established to help prevent individual companies or groups of companies from gaining control of markets in ways that restrain competition or harm consumers.

Mergers and Acquisitions   To preserve competition, the government may also create requirements that companies must gain approval of a proposed merger or acquisition. This has been a hot area of debate in recent years since the Canadian government has repeatedly blocked or delayed the domestic chartered banks from merging. If left unchecked, the Canadian banking system would probably be dominated by three huge banks instead of the "Big Six" that reign today. The Canadian government rejected proposed mergers between the Royal Bank and the Bank of Montreal, as well as a merger between the Canadian Imperial Bank of Commerce and the Toronto-Dominion Bank. According to the Competition Bureau, the proposed bank mergers would lessen competition and result in many branches closing their doors. Thus Canadians would pay more for less.[29] Nearly a decade later the debate still rages on and the government is once again hinting that there could be some movement, but it stops short of committing. A Bank of Canada study indicated that bank mergers would not necessarily lessen competition.[30] Adding fuel to the fire, a recent analysis from the C.D. Howe Institute, a Toronto think tank, suggested that there is a misconception that bank mergers would result in fewer branches and would be harmful to consumers. Canadian bank mergers would allow them to move more aggressively.[31]

Regulating and Deregulating Industries

Sometimes the government imposes regulations on specific industries to ensure fair competition, ethical business practices, safe working conditions, or general public safety. The banking industry exemplifies the serious role of government in creating rules of conduct and outlining a framework for the system. In a *highly regulated industry,* close government control is substituted for free competition, and competition is either limited or eliminated. In extreme cases, regulators may even decide who can enter an industry, what customers they must serve, and how much they can charge. For years, the electric utility industries were under strict government control.

Hydro-Québec is a closely run government-controlled entity. Other utilities such as Ontario Hydro and BC Hydro have begun to experiment with free-market approaches, with mixed results.[32] The trend in most industries over the past few decades has been to open up competition in regulated industries by removing or relaxing existing regulations. Hopes are that such *deregulation* will allow new industry competitors to enter the market, create more choices for consumers, and keep prices in check. But the debate is ongoing about whether deregulation actually achieves these goals.

Protecting Stakeholders

stakeholders
Individuals or groups to whom a business has a responsibility

In addition to fostering competition, another important role the government plays is to protect the stakeholders of a business. Businesses have many **stakeholders**—groups that are affected by (or that affect) a business's operations, including employees, investors, customers, suppliers, governments, and society at large. In the course of serving one or more of these stakeholders, a business may sometimes neglect the interests of other stakeholders. For example, managers who are too narrowly focused on generating wealth for shareholders might not spend the funds necessary to create a safe work environment for employees or to reduce waste. Similarly, a public company that withholds information about its true financial performance may hurt the ability of investors to make sound decisions and may even harm the wealth of stakeholders. Nortel, once the pride of Canadian investors, has fallen on hard times. Originally it was hurt by a free-falling stock price as the stock market high-tech bubble burst. Further damaging its reputation was the firm's forced admission that the financial results for previous years required restatement to reflect more accurately the financial position of the company.[33] More recently, Research in Motion's shiny image was hurt when it was forced to reveal that the company had illegally backdated stock options. The actions were addressed, and in the end stakeholders were protected.[34]

To protect consumers, employees, shareholders, and the environment from the potentially harmful actions of business, the government has established several regulatory agencies (see Exhibit 1.6). Many of these agencies have the power to pass and enforce rules and regulations within their specific area of authority. Such regulations are intended to encourage businesses to behave ethically and in a socially responsible manner. Chapter 3 takes a closer look at society's concerns for ethical and socially responsible behaviour.

Contributing to Economic Stability

A nation's economy never stays exactly the same size. Instead it grows and contracts in response to the combined effects of such factors as technological breakthroughs, changes in investment patterns, shifts in consumer attitudes, world events, and basic economic forces. *Economic expansion* occurs when the economy is growing and people are spending more money. Consumer purchases stimulate businesses to produce more goods and services, which in turn stimulates employment. *Economic contraction* occurs when such spending declines. Businesses cut back on production, employees are laid off, and the economy as a whole slows down. If the period of downward swing is severe, the nation may enter into a **recession**, traditionally defined as two consecutive quarters of decline in real gross domestic product.

recession
A period during which national income, employment, and production all fall

When a downward swing or recession is over, the economy enters into a period of *recovery*: Companies buy more, factories produce more, employment is high, and workers spend their earnings. These recurrent up-and-down swings are known as the **business cycle** (see Exhibit 1.7). Despite the fact that economic swings are natural, and to some degree predictable, they cause hardship nonetheless. In an attempt to avoid such hardship and to foster economic stability, the government can create new taxes or adjust the current tax rates, raise or lower interest rates, and regulate the total amount of money circulating in our economy. These government actions have two facets: monetary policy and fiscal policy.

business cycle
Fluctuations in the rate of growth that an economy experiences over a period of several years

Monetary Policy **Monetary policy** involves adjusting the nation's money supply by increasing or decreasing interest rates to help control inflation. In Canada, monetary policy is controlled primarily by the Bank of Canada (BOC). It directly influences the money supply with policy decisions and indirectly with its implied vision for future decisions. The BOC must be certain that enough money and credit are available to fuel a healthy economy. However, it must act carefully—altering the money supply affects interest rates, inflation, and the economy (see Exhibit 1.8). When the money supply is increased, more money is available for loans so banks can charge lower interest rates to borrowers. On the other hand, an increased money supply can lead to greater consumer spending and can result in the demand for goods exceeding supply. When demand exceeds supply, sellers may raise their prices, leading to inflation. In turn, inflation can

monetary policy
Government policy and actions taken by the Bank of Canada to regulate the nation's money supply

Exhibit 1.6   **Major Canadian Government Agencies and What They Do**

Government agencies protect stakeholders by developing and promoting standards, regulating and overseeing industries, and enforcing laws and regulations.

GOVERNMENT AGENCY OR COMMISSION	MAJOR AREAS OF RESPONSIBILITY
Competition Bureau	Promotes fair competition so that Canadians can benefit from lower prices, product choice, and quality services. Administration and enforcement of the *Competition Act*, the *Consumer Packaging and Labelling Act*, the *Textile Labelling Act*, and the *Precious Metals Marking Act*.
Environment Canada	Preserves and enhances the quality of the natural environment, including water, air, and soil quality; conserve Canada's renewable resources; protect Canada's water resources; carry out meteorology.
Industry Canada	Helps make Canadians more productive and competitive in the knowledge-based economy. Give consumers, investors, and businesses the confidence that the marketplace is fair, efficient, and competitive.
The Business Development Bank of Canada (BDC)	Provides small and medium-sized businesses with flexible financing, affordable consulting services, and venture capital.
Export Development Canada (EDC)	Devoted to providing trade finance services to support Canadian exporters and investors in some 200 markets, 130 of which are in developing markets.
Canadian Radio-television and Telecommunications Commission (CRTC)	Regulates and supervises all aspects of the Canadian broadcasting system, as well as telecommunications common carriers and service providers that fall under federal jurisdiction.
Transport Canada	Ensures that Canadians have the best transportation system by developing and administering policies, regulations, and programs for a safe, efficient, and environmentally friendly transportation system.
National Energy Board	Promotes safety, environmental protection, and economic efficiency in the *Canadian public interest* within the mandate set by Parliament in the regulation of pipelines, energy development, and trade.
Fisheries and Oceans Canada	Responsible for developing and implementing policies in support of Canada's economic, ecological, and scientific interests in oceans and inland waters.
Health Canada	In partnership with provincial and territorial governments, Health Canada provides national leadership to develop health policy, enforce health regulations, promote disease prevention, and enhance healthy living for all Canadians.
Canadian Food Inspection Agency (CFIA)	Protects consumers by contributing to food safety, the protection of plants, and the health of animals in Canada. CFIA is responsible for the administration and enforcement of the numerous acts, including the *Fish Inspection Act*, the *Meat Inspection Act*, the *Plant Protection Act*, the *Consumer Packaging and Labelling Act* as it relates to food, and the enforcement of the *Food and Drugs Act* as it relates to food.
Canadian Wheat Board (CWB)	Farmer-controlled organization that markets wheat and barley grown by western Canadian producers. The CWB is the largest single seller of wheat and barley in the world, holding more than 20 percent of the international market.
Department of Human Resources & Skills Development (HRSD)	Responsible for providing Canadians with the tools they need to thrive and prosper in the workplace by supporting human capital development and labour market development and establishing a culture of lifelong learning for Canadians.
Canadian Centre for Occupational Health and Safety (CCOHS)	The CCOHS promotes a safe and healthy working environment and assists in the maintenance and development of policies and programs. The CCOHS reports to the Minister of Labour.

Source: Government of Canada website, www.gc.ca/depts/major//depind_e.html

Exhibit 1.7   **The Business Cycle**

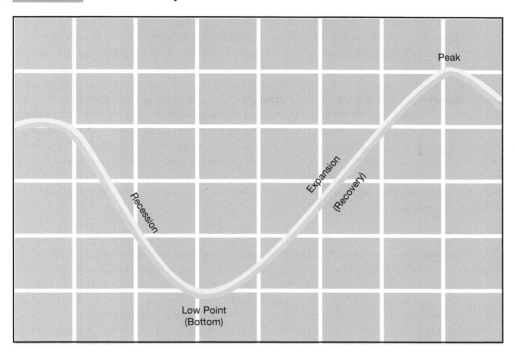

slow economic growth—a situation the BOC wants to avoid. Since so many companies now buy and sell across national borders, the BOC's changes may also affect the interlinked economies of many countries and vice versa.[35]

The BOC can change the **target for the overnight rate**, which represents the midpoint of the bank's operating band for overnight financing. This is the average rate the BOC wants to see in the marketplace for such short-term loans. The official rate was formerly the *bank rate*, which is at the upper level of the operating band and is set one-quarter percent above the target rate.[36] When the Bank of Canada raises the target for the overnight rate, banks generally raise the **prime interest rate**, the lowest interest rate on short-term loans offered to preferred borrowers. This discourages loans and tightens the money supply, which can slow down economic growth. In contrast, lowering the target for the overnight rate results in lower lending rates, which can encourage borrowing and stimulate economic growth.

target for the overnight rate
The midpoint rate the Bank of Canada wants to see in the marketplace for short-term loans

prime interest rate
The lowest interest rate banks offer on short-term loans to preferred borrowers

Exhibit 1.8   **Influencing the Money Supply**

The Bank of Canada cautiously adjusts the money supply as it attempts to stimulate economic growth while keeping inflation and interest rates at acceptable levels.

The Bank of Canada can also conduct open-market operations. It can influence the money supply by selling and buying government bonds. If the BOC is concerned about inflation, it can reduce the money supply by selling Canadian government bonds, which takes cash out of circulation. When the BOC wants to boost the economy, it can buy back government bonds, putting cash into circulation and increasing the money supply.

Keep in mind that money injected into the economy has a *multiplier effect* as it makes its way through the system. For example, if a company spends money to build a large office complex, hundreds of construction workers will earn wages. If some of these workers decide to spend their extra income to buy new cars, car dealers will have more income. The car dealers might spend their income on new clothes, and the sales clerks (who earn commissions) might buy electronic products, and so on. This *circular flow* of money through the economic system links all elements of the Canadian economy by exchanging goods and services for money, which is then used to buy more goods and services, and so on.

fiscal policy
The use of government revenue collection and spending to influence the business cycle

Fiscal Policy **Fiscal policy** involves changes in the government's revenues and expenditures to stimulate or dampen the economy. Government spending is indeed an important factor in Canadian economic stability. For one thing, the Canadian federal, provincial, and municipal governments are responsible for supplying and maintaining such *public goods and services* as: highways, military, public water works, fire and police protection, health care, and so on. The Canadian government gets money to provide such public goods by collecting a variety of taxes, such as those listed in Exhibit 1.9.

When the Canadian government spends more money than it takes in, it creates annual budget deficits. Over the past 10 years the government has reversed the negative ritual of annual government deficits. In fact, since it achieved a surplus in 1997–98, thus ending a nearly three-decade-old habit of deficits, the federal government has avoided the "D" word. Reducing the accumulated amount of annual budget deficits (the national debt) is a target on which the government has recently focused. The gross domestic product (GDP) represents the value of all final goods and services produced by businesses in the country. The Canadian government is determined to lower the debt-to-GDP ratio to 25 percent by 2012–13 by paying down the debt with a portion of the budget surpluses (see Exhibit 1.10). The debt-to-GDP ratio stood at 68.4 percent in 1995–96 and had fallen to 35.1 percent by 2005–06.[37]

Exhibit 1.9   **Types of Taxes**

From road repair to regulation, running a government is an expensive affair. To fund government operations and projects, national governments, provinces, towns, and cities apply and collect a variety of revenue-raising taxes.

TYPE OF TAX	LEVIED ON
Income taxes	Income earned by individuals and businesses. Income taxes are the government's largest single source of revenue.
Property taxes	Assessed value of the land and structures owned by businesses and individuals.
Sales taxes (GST, PST, HST)	Retail purchases made by customers. Sales taxes are collected by retail businesses at the time of the sale and then forwarded to the government.
Excise taxes	Selected items such as gasoline, tobacco, and alcohol. Often referred to as "sin" taxes, excise taxes are implemented to help control potentially harmful practices.
Payroll taxes	Earnings of individuals to help fund programs such as education, health care, and employment insurance.

Exhibit 1.10 **Federal Debt-to-GDP Projections (Accumulated Deficit)**

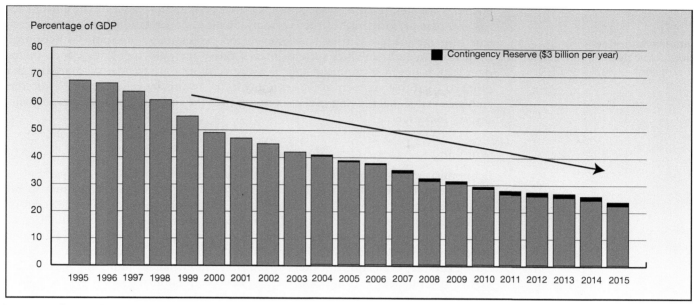

Source: Reproduced with permission of the Minister of Public Works and Government of Canada.

 IN-CLASS NOTES

Government Role in the Economy
- Free-market systems work well, but capitalist practices can also create problems for individuals
- The government serves four major economic roles:
  - **Enacts laws** and creates regulations to foster competition (i.e., *Competition Act*)
  - **Regulates and deregulates** industries (i.e., banking)
  - **Protects** stakeholders' rights (i.e., Health Canada)
  - **Intervenes** for economic stability (fiscal and monetary policy)

How a Free-Market System Monitors Its Economic Performance

Each day we are presented with complex statistical data that describe the current status and past performance of the economy. Sorting, understanding, and interpreting this information are difficult tasks even for professional economists. **Economic indicators** include statistics such as interest rates, unemployment rates, and housing data that are used to monitor and measure economic performance. Statistics that point to what may happen to the economy in the future are called *leading indicators;* statistics that signal a swing in the economy after the movement has begun are called *lagging indicators.*

economic indicators
Statistics that measure variables in the economy

Watching Economic Indicators

Economists monitor the performance of the economy by watching a variety of indicators. Unemployment statistics, for example, signal future changes in consumer spending. When unemployment rises, people have less money to spend and the economy suffers. Housing starts, another leading indicator, show where several industries are headed. Housing is very sensitive to interest rate changes. If mortgage rates are high, fewer people can afford to build new homes. When housing starts drop, builders stop hiring and may even lay off workers. Meanwhile, orders fall for plumbing fixtures, carpets, and appliances, so manufacturers decrease production and workers' hours. These cutbacks ripple through the economy and lead to slower income and job growth and weaker consumer spending. Another leading indicator is durable-goods orders, or orders for goods that typically last more than three years (which can mean everything from desk chairs to airplanes). A rise in durable-goods orders is a positive indicator that business spending is turning around. Besides unemployment data, housing starts, and durable-goods orders, economists closely monitor a nation's price changes and output.

Measuring Price Changes

Price changes, especially price increases, are another important economic indicator. **Inflation** refers to a steady rise in the prices of goods and services throughout the economy. In a period of rising prices, the purchasing power of a dollar declines, which means that you can purchase fewer items with today's dollar than you could in a prior period. Over time, price increases tend to lead to wage increases, which in turn add pressure for higher prices, setting a vicious cycle in motion. On the other hand, a sustained fall in the general price level for goods and services is known as **deflation**. In this case, purchasing power increases because a dollar held today will buy more tomorrow. In a deflationary period, investors postpone major purchases in anticipation of lower prices.

Keep in mind that although prices in the overall economy tend to increase year after year, not all industries and product categories necessarily follow this trend. In the electronics industry, for instance, prices tend to drop as technology advances and production becomes more efficient.

inflation
An economic condition in which prices rise steadily throughout the economy

deflation
An economic condition in which prices fall steadily throughout the economy

Consumer Price Index   The **consumer price index (CPI)** measures the rate of inflation by comparing the change in prices of a representative basket of goods and services, such as clothing, food, housing, and utilities, over time. A numerical weight is assigned to each item in the representative basket to adjust for each item's relative importance in the marketplace. The CPI has always been a hot topic because it is used by the government to index programs, and it is widely used by businesses in private contracts to calculate cost-of-living increases. But, like most economic indicators, the CPI is far from perfect. For one thing, the representative basket of goods may not accurately represent the prices and consumption patterns of the area in which you live. For another, the mix in this basket may not include new innovations or capture the shift of consumer purchases to products with falling prices.

consumer price index (CPI)
A monthly statistic that measures changes in the prices of about 400 goods and services that consumers buy

Economic Indicators and the New World Order: Windsor and the Shifting Front Lines

The government of Canada carefully measures unemployment statistics, housing starts, durable-goods orders and many other key bits of information to make decisions about lowering interest rates, adjusting taxes, or taking other actions that will influence the economy and ensure that the system runs smoothly. Governments have a complicated task in trying to satisfy opposing needs in a vast economy like Canada. Despite errors and cynical opinions about bureaucrats, officials usually have the best intentions in mind and they try to balance the diverse needs as best they can.

But what happens when old models meet abnormal economic forces? Chrysler just signed an assembly deal with Chinese automaker Chery Automobile Company. Workers on the assembly line in the province of Anhui earn 83 cents per hour as opposed to $73 per hour (when you add in all the benefits) for a US employee. Canadian workers are slightly more of a bargain compared to their American counterparts, but how do you compete with figures as low as those offered by the Chery Automobile Company? You don't need to put those figures into a supply and demand graph to get the picture. Major job cuts in North American plants are largely based on such figures. There is only so much that efficiency and cost reduction can accomplish.

With an average wage rate of 83 cents per hour for assembly workers in China's Chery Automobile Company, it's no wonder that North American manufacturing employees are concerned.

How does this news affect Canadian autoworkers? Windsor, Ontario, has a long history as a manufacturing hub, especially in the auto sector. With Detroit just across the bridge, it is ideally located for traditional economic ties. Its status as a vital Canadian–US gateway city has led to a special connection and probably a greater awareness of economic forces. Since they are at the front lines of the traditional manufacturing sector "the people of Windsor are fond of saying that when it comes to economic slowdowns, their city is first in and first out. Windsor serves as a barometer for the country." In the past, you could have even described the City of Windsor itself as a leading indicator. But something is changing and the old patterns are not quite the same anymore. A recent *Globe and Mail* article entitled "Welcome to a New Economic Cycle" was published on the same day that Statistics Canada announced that the economy had created 88 900 jobs in the previous month. Good News! However, it all seemed like a terrible joke to Windsor residents. With manufacturing plants shutting their doors and an unemployment rate nearly in double digits, the community that was accustomed to seeing the good news before it read about it in government reports wasn't seeing it this time around.

But Windsor is still sending signals to the rest of the country. The message, in case you have not heard the first 20 warning bells, is that the economy has shifted and employees and communities had better adapt and focus on new opportunities. But also beware that the 83-cents-per-hour worker is interested in the service sector, too. Adapt, but don't get too comfortable. Most people no longer get a gold watch after 30 years of service because employees shift from job to job and career to career so often. Stay current and don't be afraid to change because nobody is quite sure what the economy will look like in another 10 or 15 years.[38]

Questions for Critical Thinking

1. Why does the government examine key economic indicators such as unemployment and durable-goods orders?

2. What can companies and workers in the manufacturing sector do to help maintain a manufacturing base in Canada?

IN-CLASS NOTES

How a Free-Market System Monitors Performance

- Economists watch *economic indicators* closely: unemployment rates, housing starts, etc.
- *Consumer price index (CPI)* measures the rate of *inflation* or *deflation* by comparing the change in prices of a representative basket of goods
- The *GDP* and *GNP* measure a country's output; GNP considers who is responsible for the production; GDP considers where the production occurs

_____

_____

_____

_____

_____

_____

_____

_____

_____

Measuring a Nation's Output

gross domestic product (GDP)
The dollar value of all the final goods and services produced by businesses located within a nation's borders; it excludes receipts from overseas operations of domestic companies

The broadest measure of an economy's health is the **gross domestic product (GDP)**. The GDP measures a country's output—its production, distribution, and use of goods and services—by calculating the sum of all goods and services produced for *final* use in a market during a specified period (usually a year). Either domestic or foreign companies may produce the goods—as long as these companies are located within a nation's boundaries. Sales from a Honda assembly plant in Ontario would be included in the GDP.

gross national product (GNP)
The dollar value of all the final goods and services produced by domestic businesses that includes receipts from overseas operations and excludes receipts from foreign-owned businesses within a nation's borders

A less popular measure of a country's output is the **gross national product (GNP)**. This measure excludes the value of production from foreign-owned businesses within a nation's boundaries (such as Honda Canada), but it includes receipts from the overseas operations of domestic companies—such as Canadian companies like Aldo Shoes in the United States. Put another way, GNP considers *who* is responsible for the production, and GDP considers *where* the production occurs. Although far from perfect, the GDP enables a nation to evaluate its economic policies and to compare its current performance with prior periods or with the performance of other nations.

L.O. 7

CHALLENGES OF A GLOBAL ECONOMY

globalization
Tendency of the world's economies to act as a single interdependent economy

Whether economic indicators suggest that the economy is in a period of contraction or expansion, businesses must be prepared to meet the many challenges of a global economy. One of the reasons countries measure economic activity is to gauge their relative success in the global marketplace. Overall, Canada seems to be doing quite well; despite worrisome headlines and difficult announcements, Canada ranked in the top spot according to one G7 report card (See Exhibit 1.11). **Globalization** refers to the increasing integration of the world's economies. This evolution can be credited to technological and human innovation that has forced independent markets to slowly evolve and embrace the new world market. With this transformation we have seen a

Exhibit 1.11   **G7's Economic Report Card**

Canada ranked first overall in this 2006 economic evaluation of G7 countries.[39]

	INFLATION (%)	JOBLESS RATE (%)	BUDGET DEFICIT (% OF GDP)	CURRENT ACCOUNT DEFICIT (% OF GDP)	GROWTH FACTOR*	OVERALL GRADE (EPI†)
Canada	2.0%	6.3%	Surplus	Surplus	0.1%	91.8%
United States	3.2	4.6	2.3	6.5	0.5	83.9
Japan	0.3	4.2	4.6	Surplus	0.1	91.6
Britain	2.2	5.5	3.0	2.4	0.4	87.3
Germany	1.7	8.0	2.3	Surplus	0.8	88.8
France	2.0	9.1	2.7	1.7	−0.1	86.1
Italy	2.2	7.1	4.8	2.2	−0.1	83.6
Euro zone	2.2	7.9	2.1	0.3	0.5	88.0
OECD	2.2	6.0	2.0	2.0	0.4	88.2

*Growth in real GDP per capita less long-term trend.
†Economic Performance Indicator (100 minus first four columns, plus the fifth): All variables are full-year estimates.

Source: BMO Nesbitt Burns

move toward labour mobility and the freer flow of technology and knowledge across international borders. This has created new opportunities for a company's goods and services, but at the same time it has created tougher competition and new challenges for businesses.

- *Producing quality products and services that satisfy customers' changing needs.* Today's customer is well informed and has many product choices. For businesses like Research In Motion, competing in the global economy means competing on the basis of *speed* (getting products to market sooner), *quality* (doing a better job of meeting customer expectations), and *customer satisfaction* (making sure buyers are happy with every aspect of the purchase, from the shopping experience to using the finished product).

- *Starting and managing a small business in today's competitive environment.* Starting a new business or successfully managing a small company in today's global economy requires creativity and a willingness to exploit new opportunities. Small companies often lack the resources to fight the competition. Furthermore, once a new product or process is brought to the market, competitors need only a short time to get up and running with something similar. Thus, the biggest challenge for small businesses today is to make a product or provide a service that is hard to imitate.

- *Thinking globally and committing to a culturally diverse workforce.* Globalization opens new markets for a company's goods, increases competition, and changes the composition of the workforce into one that is more diverse in race, gender, age, language, physical and mental abilities, lifestyle, culture, education, ideas, and background. Thus, to be competitive in the global economy, companies must commit to a culturally diverse workforce, think globally, and adopt global standards of excellence.

- *Behaving in an ethically and socially responsible manner.* As businesses become more complex through global expansion and technological change, they must deal with an increasing number of ethical and social issues. These include the marketing of unhealthy products, the use of questionable accounting practices to calculate financial results, and the pollution of the environment (as Chapter 3 discusses). In the future, businesses can expect continued pressure from environmental groups, consumers, employees, and government regulators to act ethically and responsibly.

■ *Keeping pace with technology and electronic commerce.* Everywhere we look, technology is reshaping the world. The Internet and innovations in computerization, miniaturization, and telecommunication have made it possible for people anywhere in the world to exchange information and goods. Such technologies are collapsing boundaries and changing the way customers, suppliers, and companies interact.

Moving Forward

As these challenges suggest, doing business in the twenty-first century means working in a world of increasing uncertainty where change is the norm, not the exception. In the coming chapters, we explore specific challenges that businesses are facing in the global economy and provide real-world examples of how companies are tackling and meeting these challenges. As you read through the text be sure to pay attention to the "E-Business in Action" cases, which appear at the end of each Part and show the relationship between the chapter material and e-business practices that companies are using to gain a competitive advantage. Also make sure to go to the Companion Website at www.pearsoned.ca/bovee and read the detailed information in the **Web Appendix** on Internet and e-commerce fundamentals.

BEHIND THE SCENES

BlackBerry: Communicating, Defending, and Expanding Its Global Reach

Research in Motion is a dynamic company that evolved from a small operation, full of ideas, into a large, diverse international enterprise. Despite the change, the company retains much of its entrepreneurial spirit: Jim Balsillie and Mike Lazaridis have kept the essence of the company intact. Innovation is vital for the long-term future of RIM, and the organization is not sitting back and resting on its past success. New products are being developed and new markets are aggressively being pursued.

A BlackBerry in Every Corner of the World

A major challenge for all companies is to effectively access a new market; this task is especially difficult in the high-tech communications industry. For example, in France the BlackBerry was banned from the government because of fears that messages sent and routed through US and British servers could be read by the US National Security Agency. But that was only a minor public relations problem when compared to the years and effort that RIM put forward to gain the right to sell BlackBerrys in China. In 2007, eight years after making its first application, RIM finally received

permission from the Ministry of Information Industry. With almost 500 million cell phone users in China, Balsillie and Lazaridis surely feel it was well worth the effort. Analysts are predicting that this move could lead to a 25 percent growth in worldwide customers within a couple of years. In Japan (although not for the same reasons) it also took time for RIM to penetrate the market. Just a few months before the China announcement, RIM struck a deal with DoCoMo, Japan's largest mobile phone carrier, to sell its BlackBerry devices to corporate customers. It remains to be seen how the BlackBerry will be received in a country that is so technologically advanced (cell phones had already been using 3G technology for five years in Japan before this launch).

RIM has averaged two-year growth of 38 and 34 percent in the US and Canadian markets, whereas the growth in the rest of the world has averaged 84.23 percent. With access to China and Japan and new projects on the way, the overseas opportunities should justify all that buzz about RIM in the financial markets. Regardless of short-term results, these moves are defining moments in the relatively young history of Research in Motion.

Competitive Threats

But while RIM was busy planning to conquer the world (or more of it), the competition had its own plans. The usual suspects (Motorola, Palm, Nokia, etc.) were continuing to launch new smart phones with features to compete with the BlackBerry and carve out a bigger share of the market. However, as RIM entered their second quarter of fiscal 2008 everyone was talking about the newly launched Apple iPhone; part iPod, part phone, part . . . you name it. Speaking at a technology conference, Mike Lazaridis said that "he sees no real competition between the BlackBerry and the iPhone and even thanked Apple CEO Steve Jobs for increasing interest in smart phones." After all, the iPhone is more of a consumer product with limited business potential, the initial price tag was significantly higher, and the iPhone launch was only taking place in the United States. Despite the comments, it is clear that unless the iPhone flops in a short period of time, prices will fall, the market will expand, and RIM will have yet another suitor for its crown.

Future Messages

What comes next for Research in Motion? It is difficult to say. Over the past few years it has taken on all competitors, fought off and settled a patent lawsuit, and survived an options scandal. Despite merger and acquisition talk, RIM was still intact and moving along. Through it all, RIM remains a solid profit-oriented company run by innovative thinkers. With Jim Balsillie and Mike Lazaridis at the helm, RIM should continue to be an interesting piece of the Canadian and global economy.[40]

Critical Thinking Questions

1. Describe how RIM meets the four key social and economic roles that businesses serve, as described in the chapter.
2. What challenges and opportunities does RIM encounter in today's global economy?
3. Describe the role of governments as it relates to RIM. Refer to the foreign examples, but also examine the Canadian government. How does RIM's experience help exemplify the difference between a planned and a free-market economy?

Learn More Online

Find out the latest news about this company. Has RIM increased its subscription accounts in the last year or quarter? Has it secured any new markets with foreign governments? Go to Chapter 1 of the Companion Website at www.pearsoned.ca/bovee, and click on the RIM hotlink to read the latest news releases about the company and its plans for expansion.

TEST YOUR KNOWLEDGE

Questions for Review

1. How do non-profit organizations apply the concepts that we associate with profit-seeking businesses?
2. Employment trends have shown a definite shift toward services and away from manufacturing. What are some of the key reasons for this shift?
3. How is capitalism different from communism and socialism in the way that it achieves key economic goals?
4. Describe Adam Smith's beliefs about the power of the capitalist system. What did Smith warn against?
5. What is the difference between an oligopoly market and a monopoly market?

Questions for Analysis

6. What role do entrepreneurs play in the economy? Relate your answer to the factors of production.
7. Why is it often easier to start a service business than a goods-producing business?

8. How do governments intervene in a free-market system? Describe the difference between fiscal and monetary policy.
9. How do countries know whether their economic system is working?
10. **Ethical Considerations.** Because knowledge workers are in such high demand, John decides to enrol in an evening MBA program. His company has agreed to reimburse him for 80 percent of his tuition. He hasn't revealed, however, that once he earns his degree, he plans to apply for a management position at a different company. Is it ethical for John to accept his company's tuition reimbursement, given his intentions?

Questions for Application

11. Company sales are skyrocketing and projections show that your computer consulting business will outgrow its current location by next year. What factors should you consider when selecting a new site for your business?
12. How would a decrease in government old age security (OAS) benefits affect the economy?

13. Think about the many ways in which technology has changed your life as a consumer. Record your thoughts on a sheet of paper. On that same sheet of paper, make a second list of how you envision technology will change your life in the near future. Compare your thoughts to those of your classmates.

PRACTISE YOUR KNOWLEDGE

SHARPENING YOUR COMMUNICATION SKILLS

Select a local service business you are familiar with. How does that business try to gain a competitive advantage in the marketplace? Write a brief summary, as directed by your instructor, describing whether the company competes on speed, quality, price, innovation, service, or a combination of these attributes. Be prepared to present your analysis to your classmates.

BUILDING YOUR TEAM SKILLS

Economic indicators help businesses and governments determine where the economy is headed. You may have noticed news headlines such as the following, each of which offers clues to the direction of the Canadian economy:

1. Housing Starts Lowest in Months
2. The Bank of Canada Lowers the Target for the Overnight Rate and Interest Rates Tumble
3. Retail Sales Up 4 Percent over Last Month
4. Business Debt Down from Last Year
5. Businesses Are Buying More Electronic Equipment
6. Industry Jobs Go Unfilled as Area Unemployment Rate Sinks to 6 Percent
7. Telephone Reports 30-Day Backlog in Installing Business Systems

Working in teams, discuss each of these headlines. Is each item good news or bad news for the economy? Why? What does each item mean for large and small businesses? Report your team's findings to the class as a whole. Did all of the teams come to the same conclusions about each headline? Why or why not? Within your team, discuss how these different perspectives might influence the way you interpret economic news in the future.

EXPAND YOUR KNOWLEDGE

DISCOVERING CAREER OPPORTUNITIES

Thinking about a career in economics? Find out what economists do by reviewing the *Occupational Outlook Handbook* in your library or online at www.bls.gov/oco. This is an authoritative resource for information about all kinds of occupations. Click on Search and enter "economists."

1. Briefly describe what economists do and their typical working conditions.
2. What is the job outlook for economists? What is the average salary for starting economists?
3. What training and qualifications are required for a career as an economist? Are the qualifications different for jobs in the private sector as opposed to those in government?

DEVELOPING YOUR RESEARCH SKILLS

Gaining a competitive advantage in today's marketplace is critical to a company's success. Look through recent copies of business journals and newspapers (online or in print) to find an article about a company whose practices have set it apart from its competitors. Use your favourite search engine to find more information about that company online.

1. What products or services does the company manufacture or sell?
2. How does the company set its goods or services apart from its competitors? Does the company compete on price, quality, service, or innovation?
3. Does the company have a website? If so, how does the company use it? What kinds of information does the company include on its website?

STUDY GUIDE

SUMMARY OF LEARNING OBJECTIVES

1. Define what a business is and identify four key social and economic roles that businesses serve

A business is a profit-seeking activity that provides goods and services to satisfy consumer needs. The driving force behind most businesses is the chance to earn a profit; however, non-profit organizations exist to provide society with a social or educational service. Businesses serve four key functions: they provide society with necessities; they provide people with jobs and a means to prosper; they pay taxes that are used by the government to provide services for its citizens; and they reinvest their profits in the economy, thereby increasing a nation's wealth.

2. Differentiate between goods-producing and service businesses. List five factors that explain the rise in the number of service businesses

Goods-producing businesses produce tangible goods and tend to be capital-intensive, whereas service businesses produce intangible goods and tend to be labour-intensive. The number of service businesses is increasing because (1) consumers have more disposable income to spend on taking care of themselves; (2) many services target consumer needs brought about by changing demographic patterns and lifestyle trends; (3) consumers need assistance with using and integrating new technology into their business operations and lifestyles; (4) companies are turning to consultants and other professionals for advice to remain competitive; and (5) in general, barriers to entry are lower for service companies than they are for goods-producing businesses.

3. Differentiate between a free-market system and a planned system

In a free-market system, individuals have a high degree of freedom to decide what is produced by whom and for whom. Moreover, the pursuit of private gain is regarded as a worthwhile goal. In a planned system, governments limit the individual's freedom of choice to accomplish government goals, control the allocation of resources, and restrict private ownership to personal and household items. The pursuit of private gain is non-existent under a planned system.

4. Explain how supply and demand affect price

In the simplest sense, supply and demand affect price in the following manner: When the price goes up, the quantity demanded goes down but the supplier's incentive to produce more goes up. When the price goes down, the quantity demanded increases but the quantity supplied may (or may not) go down. When the interests of buyers and sellers are in balance, an equilibrium price is established. However, adjusting price or supply to meet or spur demand does not guarantee profitability, as the airline example on page 13 illustrates. The important thing to remember is that in a free-market system the interaction of supply and demand determines what is produced and in what amounts.

5. Explain the four major economic roles of the Canadian government

The Canadian government fosters competition by enacting laws and regulations and by approving mergers and acquisitions, retaining the power to block those that might restrain competition. It regulates certain industries where competition would be wasteful or excessive. It protects stakeholders from potentially harmful actions of businesses. Finally, the government contributes to economic stability by regulating the money supply and by spending for the public good.

6. Explain how a free-market system monitors its economic performance

Economists evaluate economic performance by monitoring a variety of indicators, such as unemployment statistics, housing starts, durable-goods orders, and inflation. They calculate the consumer price index (CPI) to keep an eye on price changes—especially inflation. In addition, economists measure the productivity of a nation by calculating the country's gross domestic product (GDP)—the sum of all goods and services produced by both domestic and foreign companies as long as they are located within a nation's borders.

7. Identify five challenges that businesses are facing in the global economy as well as how companies are using the Internet to improve their efficiency

The five challenges identified in the chapter are (1) producing quality products and services that satisfy customer's changing needs; (2) starting and managing a small business in today's competitive environment; (3) thinking globally and committing to a culturally diverse workforce;

(4) behaving in an ethically and socially responsible manner; and (5) keeping pace with technology and electronic commerce. Nearly all aspects of business can be improved with the help of Internet technology. From improved communication in the supply chain to efficient 24-hour sales information to improved customer service and delivery, the Internet is a tool that, when used properly, can be a weapon for competitive advantage.

KEY TERMS

barriers to entry   (7)
business   (4)
business cycle   (19)
capital   (9)
capital-intensive businesses   (5)
capitalism   (10)
communism   (11)
competition   (15)
competitive advantage   (16)
consumer price index (CPI)   (24)
deflation   (24)
demand   (13)
economic indicators   (24)
economic system   (10)
economics   (8)
electronic commerce
   (e-commerce)   (7)

entrepreneurs   (9)
equilibrium price   (15)
factors of production   (9)
fiscal policy   (22)
free-market system   (10)
globalization   (26)
goods-producing businesses   (5)
gross domestic product (GDP)   (26)
gross national product (GNP)   (26)
human resources   (9)
inflation   (24)
knowledge   (9)
labour-intensive businesses   (5)
monetary policy   (19)
monopolistic competition   (16)
monopoly   (16)
natural resources   (9)

non-profit organizations   (5)
oligopoly   (16)
planned system   (11)
prime interest rate   (21)
privatizing   (12)
profit   (4)
pure competition   (15)
recession   (19)
service businesses   (5)
socialism   (12)
stakeholders   (18)
supply   (13)
target for the overnight rate   (21)

QUESTIONS

Multiple Choice   Circle the correct answer and then check the answers in the back of the book to chart your progress.

1. Why is the Canadian economy becoming more and more service based?

   a. Heavy industry, such as steel, cars, and chemicals, are hiring more workers.
   b. Services are actually less important in the new Internet-based economy.
   c. Major industries like the steel sector are creating jobs.
   d. Services are increasingly important as products become more complex.

2. Which of the following is the BEST definition of a business?

   a. Any activity that provides goods to satisfy consumer needs.
   b. Any activity that provides services to meet society's needs.
   c. Any activity that provides goods or services to satisfy society's needs and wants.
   d. Profit-seeking organizations that provide goods and services to supply society's needs and wants.

3. Which of the following is a feature of the Canadian economic system?

   a. There is no government interference with business activities.
   b. Government planners decide what and how much is to be produced.
   c. Markets are generally left to the participants, but governments have a limited role.
   d. The government owns all the important enterprises, such as railroads, television, and telephone lines.

4. What happens when the price of a popular blue jean brand falls from $85 to $28?

   a. Consumers are likely to buy more jeans.
   b. The manufacturer will make more jeans.
   c. Consumers are likely to buy fewer jeans.
   d. The jeans will become less expensive to manufacture.

5. Which of the following describes an oligopoly market?

   a. The market is served by many small sellers, such as farmers.
   b. The market is served by only one seller, such as an electric utility.
   c. A few major competitors dominate the industry.
   d. There are a large number of sellers, providing differentiated products, such as fast-food restaurants.

6. _____ involves government adjustments in revenue and spending to stimulate or dampen the economy.

   a. Monetary policy
   b. Ethical policy
   c. Target policy
   d. Fiscal policy

7. The federal government tries to guide the national economy and carefully monitors the stages of the business cycle. Based on this information, which of the following statements is accurate?

   a. During a recession jobs are available and the economy prospers.
   b. Recessions encourage consumers to buy more.
   c. The economy produces more jobs and more products during times of expansion.
   d. The government never interferes with the national economy.

8. Which of the following is a tool used to measure inflation?

   a. CPI
   b. GDP
   c. GNP
   d. Unemployment rate

9. Which of the following statements is correct?

   a. More than half of the workforce is employed in the manufacturing sector.
   b. Approximately three out of every four workers are in the service industry.
   c. There are more women than men in the manufacturing sector.
   d. Both men and women are employed in equal proportions in both the service and manufacturing sectors.

10. Which of the following does NOT represent one of the five *factors of production*?

    a. Clean, fresh water
    b. A loaf of bread
    c. An aircraft factory
    d. Aircraft factory workers

True/False

1. True or false? In a free-market economy, profit-seeking businesses have no role in supplying necessities such as food, clothing, and shelter.

2. True or false? The electric utility industry is usually a regulated industry in a mixed economy.

3. True or false? The seller is likely to produce more goods if the price falls.

4. True or false? Competition is fierce in free-market economies because government regulations require businesses to compete.

5. True or false? Service industries are an increasingly important part of the Canadian economy.

Fill-in-the-Blank

1. _____ such as universities, symphonies, libraries, government agencies, and charities exist to provide society with a social or educational service.

2. Goods-producing organizations tend to be _____; they generally require large amounts of money or equipment to get started and to operate.

3. _____ rely more on human resources than on buildings, machinery, and equipment to prosper.

4. Capital-intensive businesses generally have high _____, which are the requirements a company must meet before it can start competing in a given market.

5. The basic inputs that a society uses to produce goods and services, including natural resources, labour, capital, entrepreneurship, and knowledge, are collectively known as _____.

6. _____ is an economic system that is characterized by public ownership and operation of key industries combined with private ownership and operation of less vital industries.

7. The specific quantity of a product that the seller is able and willing to provide at a given price is known as _____ .

8. _____ is a situation where a large number of sellers offer products that can be distinguished from each other in at least some small way.

9. _____ policy is the term that refers to the actions taken by the Bank of Canada to regulate the nation's money supply.

10. _____ measures the dollar value of all the final goods and services produced by businesses located within a nation's borders; it excludes receipts from overseas operations of domestic companies.

Companion Website

See It on the WEB

Visit the Companion Website at **www.pearsoned.ca/bovee**, review the exercises, and complete the following assignments for Chapter 1:

1. Find the Right Stuff
2. Step Inside the Economic Statistics Briefing Room
3. Discover What's in the CPI

CHAPTER 2

COMPETING IN THE GLOBAL ECONOMY

LEARNING OBJECTIVES

After studying this chapter, you will be able to

1 Explain why nations trade

2 Explain why nations restrict international trade and list four forms of trade restrictions

3 Highlight three protectionist tactics nations use to give their domestic industries a competitive edge

4 Explain how trading blocs affect trade

5 Identify the role of emerging markets and the importance of the countries referred to as BRIC

6 Understand the fundamental elements of currency exchange

7 Highlight the opportunities and challenges of conducting business in other countries

8 List five ways to improve communication in an international business relationship

9 Identify five forms of international business activity

10 Discuss the economic and social impact of global events such as avian flu, SARS, mad cow disease, and terrorism as they relate to globalization

Behind the Scenes

Molson Canadian, eh?

From brand names to logos to bottle caps, the Maple Leaf is proudly displayed as a symbol of Molson's heritage.

www.molson.com

For over 220 years, Molson has stood firmly behind the Canadian border as master of its home territory, with its competitor Labatt by its side for most of that time period. Proudly Canadian, it displays its heritage in brand names, logos, and of course, in the very famous former slogan: "I Am Canadian." A large portion of the company's brewing heritage took place in a much simpler time, though. Borders were considered an obstacle and companies enjoyed a clear home-market advantage. Governments routinely helped local companies fight foreign competition (through restrictions, tariffs, etc.) in the name of the local economy.

Of course, governments still intervene to support national interests, but it's not quite the same. Protectionism has become a dirty word in international business; these practices now come with consequences. Countries are constantly accusing each other of providing unfair support to companies; many disputes end up at the World Trade Organization. Free trade is now the official policy of most industrialized nations. In the past few decades countries have joined forces like never before by creating powerful trading blocs (NAFTA, the European Union, etc.) to slowly open borders and eliminate trade restrictions. Companies that were once protected are now actively competing in the "global economy." Large multinational companies don't see borders—they see opportunities. There is nowhere to hide. Governments are still a factor but, in comparison to the norm decades ago, companies are on their own to compete, consolidate, excel, or disappear.

Despite its tremendous success on this side of the border, Molson has never really managed to create a truly powerful, elite global brand (like Heineken, for example). Despite reasonable attempts, Molson's brand recognition and sales are fairly modest outside of Canada. At the turn of the millennium, with brewers from around the world increasingly knocking at the door and consolidating into large corporations, Molson was feeling the heat of the competition. Its market share in Canada was under threat by cheap US brands and premium beers from all over the world. At the time, Molson's international brewing strategies consisted of exporting, importing, and holding licensing agreements for international brands like Corona and Heineken. To compete effectively, though, Molson felt the need to take further steps to build its brand mix and distribution capacity.

BRIC is a term used to describe four very important emerging markets: Brazil, Russia, India, and China. In 2002, Molson made a major move and set its sights on one of these markets: Brazil. It purchased a majority stake in Cervejarias Kaiser for US$765 million. This purchase was accompanied by a belief that Molson could improve its operations and marketing in Brazil and also launch the Kaiser and A Marca Bavaria brands in Canada. However, the realization came quickly that this was not going to be a successful proposition. Tuning into tastes of the Brazilian market and creating efficiencies in its Brazilian operations was a greater challenge than expected. Establishing and selling the Brazilian brands in Canada was no easy task either. The Brazilian operations bled money from the beginning, and Molson was not able to get the benefits it had so enthusiastically expected. BRIC turned out to stand for **B**ad **R**esults **I**n that **C**ountry for Molson as the losses piled up.

After looking at all options and considering various partners, Molson decided to merge its operations with Adolph Coors Company to form Molson Coors in 2005. The merger made Molson Coors the fifth-largest brewer in the world. In 2006, as it was deciding on its global strategy, the new firm sold off 68 percent of its shares in Cervejarias Kaiser for only US$68 million. As Molson entered into this new global partnership many questions remained: Would this partnership be the answer? Would Molson Coors become an acquisition target for the four biggest breweries? How should the company expand its global reach?[1]

TEST YOURSELF

Answers to these questions can be found on the website: www.pearsoned.ca/bovee.

1. Why are established companies under increased pressure to compete with foreign-based companies? What factors are influencing this pattern? Explain.

2. Why did Molson's Brazilian acquisition pose such a challenge for the company?

3. Did Molson really need a partner? Do you think that Coors was a good choice?

FUNDAMENTALS OF INTERNATIONAL TRADE

L.O. 1

The success of businesses such as Molson Coors, McCain Foods, Bombardier, RIM, Whirlpool, Scotiabank, UPS, and others that operate in the global marketplace depends, in part, on the international economic relationships forged between nations. From a Canadian perspective it is important that the government create policies that balance the interests of local firms, Canadian workers, foreign firms operating in Canada, and Canadian consumers. Other countries are trying to do the same thing. As you might expect, the many players in world trade sometimes have conflicting goals.

Why Nations Trade

No single country has the resources to produce everything its citizens want or need. Businesses and countries specialize in the production of certain goods and engage in international trade to obtain raw materials and goods that are unavailable to them or too costly for them to produce. International trade has many benefits: it increases a country's total output, it offers lower prices and greater variety to consumers, it subjects domestic oligopolies and monopolies to competition, and it allows companies to expand their markets and achieve cost, production, and distribution efficiencies, known as **economies of scale**.[2]

How does a country know what to produce and what to trade for? In some cases, the answer is easy: A nation may have an **absolute advantage**, which means it can produce a particular item more efficiently than all other nations, or it is virtually the only country producing that product. Absolute advantages rarely last, however, unless they are based on the availability of natural resources. Saudi Arabia, for example, has an absolute advantage in crude oil production because of its huge developed reserves. Thus, it makes sense for Saudi Arabia to specialize in providing the world with oil and to trade for other items it needs.

In most cases, a country can produce many of the same items that other countries do. The **comparative advantage theory** explains how a country chooses which items to produce and which items to trade for. The theory states that a country should produce and sell to other countries those items it produces more efficiently or at a lower cost, and it should trade for those it can't produce as economically. Canada has an abundance of natural resources. Canada's strongest markets include lumber, aluminium, and wheat exports, but Canada does not compete in the world marketplace for bananas. With enough money and technology, Canadians could make an attempt to mass-produce bananas (government programs have sponsored questionable projects in the past). However, in this case the cost cannot possibly match the pennies per kilogram that

economies of scale
Savings from manufacturing, marketing, or buying in large quantities

absolute advantage
A nation's ability to produce a particular product with fewer resources per unit of output than any other nation

comparative advantage theory
A theory that states that a country should produce and sell to other countries those items it produces most efficiently

IN-CLASS NOTES

Why Do Nations Trade?
- Greater total output
- Wider variety of goods
- Expanded markets
- Lower prices
- Increased local competition
- Economies of scale

_____

_____

_____

_____

_____

_____

Canadian wholesalers pay Caribbean, South American, and Central American nations to keep supermarkets well-stocked with bananas. This example is extreme and provides an obvious course to follow, but in other industries—despite a less efficient cost and resource structure—Canadian firms continue to produce less efficient products.

The basic argument behind the comparative advantage theory is that specialization and exchange will increase a country's total output and allow both trading partners to enjoy a higher standard of living. Like many theories, it is based on a solid foundation of logic, but it is not always put into practice. Traditionally, some industries have been protected in Canada and elsewhere, a situation which has corrupted such comparisons. With trade barriers being removed it would seem as though comparative advantage theory should be increasingly respected, but the global nature of business today makes these bilateral (two-country) comparisons seem a bit simplistic in practice.

How International Trade Is Measured

In Chapter 1 we discussed how economists monitor certain key economic indicators to evaluate how well a country's economic system is performing. One trend that economists watch carefully is the level of a nation's imports and exports. For instance, at any given time a country may be importing more than it is exporting. Two key measurements of a nation's level of international trade are the *balance of trade* and the *balance of payments*.

The total value of a country's exports *minus* the total value of its imports, over some period of time, determines its **balance of trade**. When the value of goods and services exported by Canada exceeds the value of goods and services it imports, Canada's balance of trade is said to be positive: People in other countries buy more goods and services from Canada than Canadians buy from them, creating a **trade surplus** (see Exhibit 2.1). The trade surplus in 2006 amounted to more than $43 billion.[3] Conversely, if Canadians purchase more from foreign countries than the foreign countries buy from Canada, the balance of trade would be negative. That is, imports exceed exports, creating a **trade deficit**.

The **balance of payments** is the broadest indicator of international trade. It is the total flow of money into the country *minus* the total flow of money out of the country, over some period of time. The balance of payments includes the balance of trade plus the net dollars received and spent on foreign investment, military spending, tourism, foreign aid, and other international transactions. For example, when Canadian media giant Thomson bought England-based Reuters, that investment was counted in the balance of payments, but not in the balance of trade.[4] Similarly, when India-based Essar purchased Algoma Steel (headquartered in Sault Ste. Marie, Ontario) for $1.85 billion, or when foreign firms purchase Canadian stocks, bonds, or real estate, those transactions are

balance of trade
Total value of the products a nation exports minus the total value of the products it imports, over some period of time

trade surplus
A favourable trade balance created when a country exports more than it imports

trade deficit
An unfavourable trade balance created when a country imports more than it exports

balance of payments
The sum of all payments one nation receives from other nations minus the sum of all payments it makes to other nations, over some period of time

Exhibit 2.1   **Canada's Trade Balance**

The Canadian trade balance is consistently in a surplus position mainly because of tremendous exports to the United States ($141 billion trade surplus with the US in 2006).

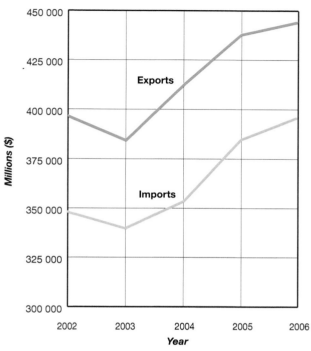

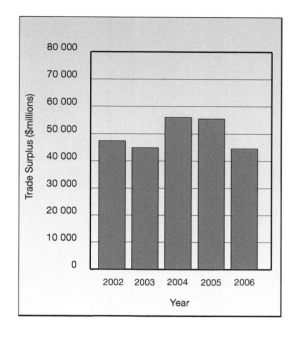

Source: *Canada's Trade Balance*, based on Statistics Canada data (Extracted from Strategis website, http://strategis.gc.ca, December 3, 2007).

part of the balance of payments. The Canadian government, like all governments, desires a favourable balance of payments, which means that more money is coming into the country than is flowing out of it.

In theory, the balance of payments is always zero. "If Canada buys more goods and services than it sells (i.e., if it has a current account deficit), it has to sell its assets to finance the spending (i.e., run a capital account surplus) or go into debt."[5]

IN-CLASS NOTES

Measuring Trade
- **Balance of trade:** exports–imports
  - *Trade surplus*: exports are greater than imports
  - *Trade deficit*: imports are greater than exports
- **Balance of payments:** total flow of money into the country minus flow of money out

It is not just developed countries who are playing the high-stakes game of corporate takeovers anymore. Emerging economies are now major players.

Bidder	Home Country	Target
Svenskt Stal AB	Sweden	IPSCO
Essar Global	India	Algoma Steel
Bowater	United States	Abitibi-Consolidated
Dubai Aerospace Enterprise	United Arab Emirates	Standard Aero
Norilsk Nickel Group	Russia	LionOre Mining International
Statoil ASA	Norway	North American Oil Sands Corporation
Xstrata PLC	Switzerland	LionOre Mining

Source: Modified from Jacquie McNish and Lori Mcleod, "All the Rules Have Changed," *Globe and Mail*, 4 May 2007, B6.

protectionism
Government policies aimed at shielding a country's industries from foreign competition

Trade Restrictions

Even though international trade has many economic advantages, sometimes countries practise **protectionism**; that is, they restrict international trade for one reason or another. Sometimes they restrict trade to shield specific industries from foreign competition and the possible loss of jobs in these industries. Sometimes they try to protect certain industries that are key to their national defence and the health and safety of their citizens. At other times they engage in protectionist measures to give new or weak industries an opportunity to grow and strengthen.[6] With the recent wave of foreign-based acquisitions in the resource sector, Canadian companies are being snatched up by companies based in Sweden, Russia, Switzerland, Norway and the United Arab Emirates. Emerging markets are now in the game and people are getting worried (see Exhibit 2.2). There have been calls for the government to do something . . . anything! However, the truth is that banks, life insurance companies, media companies, telecom firms, and airlines are already protected from foreign takeovers and they make up 35 percent of the S&P/TSX Composite Index. If the government guards additional industries in a protectionist move it would be going in the opposite direction of its official policy. True believers in free trade cannot act in this manner to protect national interests. Although it is tempting to deal with short-term public relations problems, the government must think of the long term.[7] Firms must become more competitive to truly function in the global economy. Molson Coors is an example of a confident company that feels it can face the competition more effectively after merging operations.

Despite its leadership position in the fight to reduce trade barriers, the United States uses protectionist tools with some regularity. From Canadian lumber to Chinese bras, the United States is often out of step with its official stance on free trade. In fact, the United States has been involved in more than 50 percent of the trade disputes brought to the World Trade Organization (WTO) since 1995.[8] Of course, the United States is also the economic leader in international trade and therefore is involved in a tremendous amount of transactions open to dispute. American officials argue that their tactics are appropriate, but many in the world see a double standard and the official rulings have often supported these claims. Is the United States acting like a child who goes home and takes her ball with her when things don't go her way on the playground?

Are trade restrictions a good idea or a bad idea? Study after study has shown that in the long run, they hurt a country because they remove competition, stifle innovation, and allow domestic producers to charge more for their goods. The most commonly used forms of trade restrictions include:

■ **Tariffs** are taxes, surcharges, or duties levied against imported goods. Sometimes tariffs are levied to generate revenue for the government, but more often they are imposed to restrict trade or to punish other countries for disobeying international trade laws.

■ **Quotas** limit the amount of a particular good that countries can import during a year. Limits may be set in quantities, such as kilograms of salt, or in values, such as total dollars' worth of peanuts.

■ In its most extreme form, a quota becomes an **embargo**, a complete ban on the import or export of certain products. The Canadian beef industry suffered an embargo after a single case of mad cow disease was discovered in 2003. Strict embargoes on Canadian beef set by the United States and other countries have translated into lost revenues. More than four years after the embargo, the Canadian Beef Industry was still trying to re-establish trade with some countries. South Korea is the latest to indicate that it will reopen its borders.[9]

■ Sanctions are politically motivated embargoes that revoke a country's normal trade relations status; they are often used as forceful alternatives short of war. Sanctions can include arms embargoes, foreign-assistance reductions and cut-offs, trade limitations, tariff increases, import-quota decreases, visa denials, air-link cancellations, and more. Most governments use sanctions sparingly, because studies show that they are ineffective at getting countries to change.[10]

In addition to restricting foreign trade, governments sometimes provide their domestic producers a competitive edge by using these protectionist tactics:

■ Countries can assist their domestic producers by establishing *restrictive import standards*, such as requiring special licences for doing certain kinds of business and then making it difficult for foreign companies to obtain such a licence. For example, Saudi Arabia restricts import licences for a variety of products, including chemicals, pasteurized milk, and information technology products.[11] Here in Canada, Quebec's Regulation respecting dairy product substitutes restricts the sale of yellow margarine in the province. This issue was recently taken to the Supreme Court of Canada, but the law was not overturned. Quebec remains the only jurisdiction in North America where yellow margarine is illegal.[12] Trading blocs also impose standards that ensure local content. Toyota recently complained of unfair restrictions in the North American Free Trade Agreement (NAFTA), which requires vehicle manufacturers to have 62.5 percent NAFTA content for products sold within the trading bloc. Canada, the United States, and Mexico are each re-evaluating the agreement more than a decade after the deal. Toyota would like to see this particular rate reduced to 50 percent.[13]

■ Rather than restrict imports, some countries give **subsidies** to domestic producers so that their prices can compete favourably in the global marketplace. Bombardier and Embraer have continuously accused each other of receiving unfair subsidies from their respective home governments, Canada and Brazil. The disputes have routinely ended up at the WTO. Recently, the Canadian government lodged a complaint against the United States for corn and other agricultural subsidies.[14]

■ *Dumping*: The practice of selling large quantities of a product at a price lower than the cost of production or below what the company would charge in its home market is called **dumping**. Back in 2002, the US government accused the Canadian lumber industry of dumping and imposed a 27.2 percent duty. Canada launched separate actions at the WTO and with the NAFTA panel, which

tariffs
Taxes levied on imports

quotas
Fixed limits on the quantity of imports a nation will allow for a specific product

embargo
A total ban on trade with a particular nation (a sanction) or of a particular product

subsidies
Government support provided to businesses in the form of money, tax breaks, or low-rate/interest-free loans

dumping
Charging less than the actual cost or less than the home country's price for goods sold in other countries

Automobiles are just one of the many products that have been subject to trade restrictions by governments over the years.

The dispute between Canada and the US over softwood lumber has been resolved, for now. The fight went to the WTO and NAFTA panels before a resolution was reached to address the 27.2 percent duty imposed by the US on Canadian softwood lumber.

free trade
International trade without restrictive measures

ruled that the duties were not warranted. The dispute dragged on for years with accusations and threats coming from both sides. The dispute was resolved with a somewhat controversial deal in late 2006. Under the deal, the United States agreed to return $5 billion worth of duties collected from Canadian timber firms but kept $1 billion for American-based initiatives. The deal is expected to be in place for at least seven years, but there are clauses that could see it renewed beyond that date or even revoked much sooner.[15]

Agreements and Organizations Promoting International Trade

To prevent trade disputes from escalating into full-blown trade wars, and to ensure that international business is conducted in a fair and orderly fashion, countries worldwide have created trade agreements and organizations. Philosophically, most of these agreements and organizations support the basic principles of **free trade**. The assumption is that each nation will ultimately benefit by freely exchanging the goods and services it produces most efficiently for the goods and services it produces less efficiently. The major trade agreements and organizations include GATT, the WTO, the IMF, the World Bank, and APEC.

The General Agreement on Tariffs and Trade (GATT)

The General Agreement on Tariffs and Trade (GATT) is a worldwide pact that was first established in the aftermath of World War II. The pact's guiding principle—most favoured nation (MFN)—is one of non-discrimination. Any trade advantage a GATT member gives to one country must be given to all GATT members, and no GATT nation can be singled out for punishment. In 1995, GATT established the World Trade Organization, which has replaced GATT as the world forum for trade negotiations.

The World Trade Organization (WTO)

The World Trade Organization (WTO) is a permanent forum for negotiating, implementing, and monitoring international trade procedures and for mediating trade disputes among its 150 member countries. The organization's goals include facilitating

IN-CLASS NOTES

Free Trade vs. Protectionism
- *Protectionism*: government policies to protect country's industries from foreign competition
  - tariffs, quotas, embargoes, subsidies, restrictive import standards
- *Free trade*: international trade without government restrictions

_____

_____

_____

_____

_____

_____

free trade, lowering the costs of doing business, enhancing the international investment environment, simplifying customs, and promoting technical and economic cooperation. The WTO builds upon the principles of GATT and in addition provides a formal legal structure for settling disputes.

Admission to the WTO is by application process and requires approval by two-thirds of the members. All WTO members enjoy "favoured" access to foreign markets in exchange for respecting a long list of fair-trading rules and laws governing patents, copyrights, and trademarks. After 15 years of negotiations, China was finally admitted to the WTO in 2001. As a condition of its membership, China made concessions to eliminate many tariffs and quotas and open its market of 1.4 billion people to foreign goods. Other fairly new members include Armenia, Cambodia, Croatia, Jordan, and Oman.[16]

The International Monetary Fund (IMF)

The International Monetary Fund (IMF) is an international organization of 185 member countries. Founded in 1945, its primary function is to promote international monetary cooperation and foster economic growth. The IMF provides short-term loans to countries that are unable to meet their budgetary expenses. As such, the IMF is often looked upon as a lender of last resort. The IMF also helps countries with loans after an emergency or conflict. In the past two years, Haiti and the Central Republic of Africa have benefited from this program.[17]

The World Bank

The World Bank was initially founded to finance reconstruction after World War II. It now provides low-interest loans to developing nations for improvement of transportation, telecommunications, health, and education. Currently, the World Bank is focused on bringing the Internet to the less-developed regions of the world, like Africa. World Bank officials and telecommunication executives hope that Internet connections will attract more companies to the region and lead to more rapid economic development.[18] Both the IMF and the World Bank are funded by deposits from its 185 member nations.

The Asia-Pacific Economic Cooperation (APEC)

The Asia-Pacific Economic Cooperation (APEC) is an organization of 21 countries making efforts to liberalize trade in the Pacific Rim (the land areas that surround the Pacific Ocean). Some member nations include Canada, Japan, China, Thailand, Mexico, Australia, South Korea, and the United States. "APEC members account for more than a third of the world's population (2.6 billion people), over 50 percent of world GDP (US$19 254 billion) and in excess of 41 percent of world trade. APEC also proudly represents the most economically dynamic region in the world having generated nearly 70 percent of global economic growth in the past decade." In 1994, the members established the "Bogor Goals." They agreed to work toward the elimination of all tariffs and trade barriers among industrialized countries of the Pacific Rim by 2010 and among developing countries by 2020.[19] The objectives are lofty; only time will tell if this agreement will live up to its enormous promise.

Trading Blocs

L.O. 4

Trading blocs are another type of organization that promotes international trade. Generally composed of neighbouring countries, trading blocs promote free trade among regional members. Although specific rules vary from group to group, their primary objective is to ensure the economic growth and benefit of members. As such, trading blocs generally promote trade inside the region while creating uniform barriers against goods and services entering the region from non-member countries. Trading blocs are becoming a significant force in the global marketplace.[20]

trading blocs
Organizations of nations that remove barriers to trade among their members and that establish uniform barriers to trade with non-member nations

Trading blocs can be advantageous or disadvantageous in promoting world trade, depending on one's perspective. Some economists are apprehensive about the growing importance of regional trading blocs. They fear that the world is splitting into three camps, revolving around the Americas, Europe, and Asia. Any nation that does not fall into one of these economic regions could suffer, they say, because members of the trading blocs could place severe restrictions on trade with non-member countries. The critics fear that overall world trade could decline as members become more protective of their own regions. As a result, consumers could find themselves with fewer choices, and many producers could lose sales in lucrative foreign markets.

Others claim that trading blocs could improve world trade. The growth of commerce and the availability of customers and suppliers within a trading bloc can be a big advantage for smaller or younger nations that are trying to build strong economies. The lack of trade barriers within the bloc could help member industries compete with producers in more-developed nations, and in some cases, member countries could reach a wider market than before.[21] Furthermore, close ties to more stable economies could help shield emerging nations from fluctuations in the global economy and could promote a greater sharing of knowledge and technology.

The four most powerful trading blocs today are the Association of Southeast Asian Nations (ASEAN), South America's Mercosur, the North American Free Trade Agreement (NAFTA), and the European Union (EU), with the latter two being the largest and most powerful (see Exhibit 2.3). Because many trading nations see Latin America as having great potential for large-scale economic growth in the future, they are eager to establish ties with Mercosur, which links Argentina, Brazil, Paraguay, Uruguay, and Venezuela (Bolivia, Chile, Colombia, Ecuador, and Peru are associate members) and encompasses a population of 250 million that produces more than US$1 trillion in goods and services.[22] Like other trading blocs, Mercosur's objectives include the free movement of goods and services across the borders of its member nations. Furthermore, the group seeks an economic integration that it hopes will make the four countries more competitive in the global marketplace.[23] Some NAFTA officials hope that Mercosur will eventually join NAFTA to form a Free Trade Area of the Americas (FTAA).[24]

The European Union (EU)

One of the largest trading blocs is the European Union (EU). It combines 27 countries, with two countries—Romania and Bulgaria—gaining membership in 2007, increasing the EU's population to nearly half a billion people. Other candidate countries awaiting membership include Croatia, Albania, and Turkey, but entering the EU may be getting more difficult as many Western Europeans feeling that the bloc is already overstretched.[25] EU nations are working to eliminate hundreds of local regulations, variations in product standards, and protectionist measures that limit trade among member countries. Eliminating barriers enables the nations of the EU to function as a single market, with trade flowing among member countries as it does among regions within a country. This is no small feat considering the nationalistic feelings and a long history of war and conflict among many member nations. The challenge of forming the EU and other such trading blocs is to deal with cultural resistance, respect fragile national identities, deal with inflation and conversion costs, integrate national institutions (like central banks), and in effect give up some autonomy for a cooperative arrangement that will hopefully bring greater peace and economic prosperity to the region.

The EU's Impact on the Rules of Global Trade   Increasingly, the rules governing the food we eat, the software we use, and the cars we drive are set in Brussels, the unofficial capital of the European Union. The EU sets regulations frequently and rigorously when it comes to consumer protection, and it has significantly affected global product standards. Twenty years ago if manufacturers designed something to North American standards, they could pretty much sell it around the world. Now items must conform to EU standards. When it comes to consumer or environmental protections, EU regulators

Exhibit 2.3   **Members of Major Trade Blocs**

As the economies of the world become increasingly linked, many countries have formed powerful regional trade blocs that trade freely with one another and limit foreign competition.

European Union (EU)*	North American Free Trade Agreement (NAFTA)	Association of Southeast Asian Nations (ASEAN)	Mercosur
Austria	Canada	Brunei	Argentina
Belgium	Mexico	Cambodia	Bolivia[†]
Bulgaria	United States	Indonesia	Brazil
Cyprus*		Laos	Chile[†]
Czech Republic		Malaysia	Colombia[†]
Denmark		Myanmar	Ecuador[†]
Estonia		Philippines	Paraguay
Germany		Singapore	Peru[†]
Greece		Thailand	Uruguay
Finland		Vietnam	Venezuela
France			
Hungary			
Ireland			
Italy			
Latvia			
Lithuania			
Luxembourg			
Malta			
The Netherlands			
Poland			
Portugal			
Romania			
Slovakia			
Slovenia			
Spain			
Sweden			
United Kingdom			

* Only the Southern part of Cyprus is a member; [†] Bolivia, Chile, Colombia, Ecuador, and Peru are associate members

believe it's better to be safe than sorry. That approach evolved partly from a series of food scares, including mad cow disease, in Europe over the past two decades. It also reflects the fact that Europeans are more inclined to expect governments to protect their citizens. The EU is also a powerful voice in the area of fair competition, as Intel is finding out. An important case between Intel and rival AMD is being investigated by the EU Antitrust Commissioner.[26]

The Euro   In 1999, 11 EU countries formed the economic and monetary union (EMU) and turned over control of their individual monetary policies to the newly created European Central Bank. Greece joined in January 2002 and Slovenia in January of 2007. With a combined population of more than 315 million, these 13 countries account for about 20 percent of the world's gross domestic product (GDP), making them the world's second-largest economy.[27] One of the driving forces behind the decision to join the EMU was the anticipated advantages these countries would enjoy by creating a unified currency called the **euro**.

The decision to move to the euro was a complicated issue for all member nations. Some did not want to change for nationalistic or sentimental reasons. Other countries,

euro
The currency used by 13 European nations

The euro eases price comparisons for products sold in the member countries of the European Union.

such as the United Kingdom and Denmark, decided to maintain their currencies (the British pound and the Danish crown) in order to preserve more direct control over their economic policies.[28]

Before being integrated into the euro family, applicant nations must meet certain standards: they must attempt to curb inflation, cut interest rates, reduce budget deficits to a maximum of 3 percent of GDP, and limit public borrowing to a maximum of 60 percent of GDP thus stabilizing the currency's exchange rate. Cyprus and Malta are expected to be the next two nations that will try to meet the standards and join the ranks of the official euro nations.[29]

Officially launched in 1999 (with notes and coins available in 2002), the euro got off to a rocky start. But European leaders believed it would build a bond among Europe's cities and improve trade. Moreover, the euro could wipe out some US$65 billion annually in currency exchange costs among participants and cut the intermediary out of trillions of dollars' worth of foreign exchange transactions. The initial difficulties were resolved and the currency has flourished. With prices in member nations now visible in one currency, consumers can compare prices on similar items whether they are sold in Lisbon, Paris, Athens, Milan, Vienna, or Berlin.[30]

Despite this strength in numbers, the euro, like older established currencies such as the US dollar, is subject to price variations. Joining forces can lead to more economic power and stability; however, balancing opinions can also lead to political and economic instability, which tends to put downward pressure on currency values (see Exhibit 2.4).[31]

NAFTA

In 1994, Canada, the United States, and Mexico formed a powerful trading bloc called the North American Free Trade Agreement (NAFTA). The agreement paves the way for the free flow of goods, services, and capital within the bloc by eliminating all tariffs and quotas on trades among the three nations.[32] So far the scorecard for NAFTA seems positive. It has been a huge success in promoting trade between Canada and its Mexican and American partners. Canada and Mexico send more than 80 percent of their exports to the United States and get a similar percentage of their imports from the United States.[33] Fears that NAFTA would move Canadian jobs to Mexico have, for the most part, proved unfounded. The majority of Canadian manufacturing job losses have gone to places like China without the benefits of a trading bloc. Many

Exhibit 2.4   Exchange Rates: Recent History of the Canadian Dollar

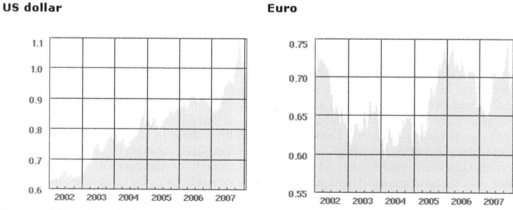

Source: Available at the Bank of Canada website at http://bankofcanada.ca/en/graphs/currencies.html#us

IN-CLASS NOTES

Important Role of Trading Blocs
- **Arguments for:**
  - wider markets
  - fosters economic growth
  - helps smaller countries
  - promotes competition
- **Arguments against:**
  - trade restrictions for non-members
  - economic isolation
  - decline in overall world trade
  - fewer choices

needle-trade jobs have already been lost to locations around the world. For example, Gildan Activewear, which primarily makes t-shirts and sweatshirts, has moved its production to Central America and the Caribbean.[34] Ultimately, NAFTA's supporters would like to see the agreement expanded to include all of Central and South America—making it the largest free-trade zone on the planet.[35]

The Undeniable Force of Emerging Markets: BRIC and Beyond

L.O. 5

BRIC is not another name for a regional trading bloc; these initials stand for four important emerging markets that are constantly in the business press: Brazil, Russia, India, and China. These four emerging markets have had a tremendous impact on all the world's economies, whether they belong to a trading bloc or not. Trading blocs are designed to strengthen their members' economies, but BRIC and other emerging markets are changing the dynamics of global trade. For example, Mexico surely expected to benefit more from the NAFTA agreement than it has, but many of the jobs that Mexico expected to acquire from Canada and the United States have instead shifted to places like China.

The BRIC nations have been a magnet for investment from developed countries and they are growing in power. Brazil is strong in commodities and agriculture, and their fundamental economic structure is improving. Russia is a powerful energy supplier with an increasingly powerful domestic demand. India is a fast-growing provider of services ranging from engineering to customer-service call centres. China has grown into the major centre for manufacturing as money has poured into the country from firms around the world who have built factories there to increase capacity.[36] Each of these countries has seen tremendous growth and presents many opportunities ahead. The BRIC nations have also proven to be a popular choice for diversified investment portfolios offered by financial companies. Emerging markets provide tremendous opportunities, but they are still volatile and risky. For example, the Chinese stock market increased by 700 percent from 2001 to 2006, but the market was full of corruption and was being influenced by a still somewhat unpredictable government.[37]

BRIC
An acronym representing four important emerging markets: Brazil, Russia, India, and China

Emerging markets are not limited to these four countries. There are many important nations such as Eastern European countries like Ukraine, which has fertile plains, vast fossil-fuel riches, and a developed industrial base. South Africa is also poised to move forward years after shedding their oppressive Apartheid system. Asian markets like South Korea, Thailand, and Taiwan also have a great deal of additional potential.[38] But for now, the diversity of strengths the BRIC countries offer makes them extremely important players in the global economy.

L.O. 6

Foreign Exchange Rates and Currency Valuations

When companies buy and sell goods and services in the global marketplace, they complete the transaction by exchanging currencies. For instance, if a Japanese company borrows money from a Canadian bank to build a manufacturing plant in Japan, it must repay the loan in Canadian dollars. Or if a South Korean car manufacturer imports engine parts from Japan, it must pay for them in yen (Japan's currency). To do so, companies exchange their currency at any international bank that handles *foreign exchange*, the conversion of one currency into an equivalent amount of another currency. The number of yen, zloty, or pounds that must be exchanged for every dollar, koruna, or won is known as the **exchange rate** between currencies.

exchange rate
The rate at which the money of one country is traded for the money of another

Most international currencies operate under a *floating exchange rate system*; thus, a currency's value or price fluctuates in response to the forces of global supply and demand. The supply and demand of a country's currency is determined in part by what is happening in the country's own economy. Moreover, because supply and demand for a currency are always changing, the rate at which it is exchanged for other currencies may change a little each day. Japanese currency might be trading at 115.94 yen to the Canadian dollar on one day and 117.05 on the next.

Even though most governments allow the value of their currency to respond to the forces of supply and demand, sometimes a government will intervene and adjust the exchange rate of its country's currency. Why would a government do this? One reason is to keep the price of a nation's goods and services more affordable in the global marketplace and to protect the nation's economy against trade imbalances. Another is to either boost or slow down the country's economy.

Devaluation, or the drop in the value of a nation's currency relative to the value of other currencies, can at times boost a country's economy because it makes the country's products and services more affordable in foreign markets while it increases the price of imports. Because fewer units of foreign currency are required to purchase the devalued currency, such situations tend to raise a country's exports and lower its imports. Conversely, a strong currency boosts imports and dampens exports. The drop in the US dollar over the past few years in comparison to the euro, the Canadian dollar, and other world currencies has made American products more competitive or less costly to buy for other countries. When the Canadian dollar reached parity (US$1 = CDN$1) for the first time in three decades in late 2007, it meant that Canadians could look for bargains in the United States, but it also meant that Canadian products were less attractive for Americans.

Some countries fix, or peg, the value of their currencies to the value of more stable currencies such as the euro, the US dollar, or the yen instead of letting it float freely. Hong Kong, for example, pegs its currency to the US dollar. If a currency is pegged, its value fluctuates proportionately with the value of the foreign currency to which it is linked. So if the US dollar declines, so will the other currencies that are pegged to it. This system works well as long as the

In recent years, the Canadian dollar has traded as low as US$0.62 and as high as US$1.10. Currency valuation changes affect the economy in many ways, creating winners and losers each time a currency rises or falls.

IN-CLASS NOTES

Foreign Exchange Rates and Currency Valuations

- *Floating exchange rate*: a currency's value/price changes with global supply and demand
- *Fixed value system*: when a currency fluctuates with the value of the foreign currency it is linked to
- *Currency devaluation*: a drop in value of a nation's currency relative to other currencies
- *Government intervention*

proportionate relationship between the two currencies remains valid. This has been a major issue between China and the United States in recent years. If one partner suffers economic hardship, demand for its currency will decline significantly and the exchange rate at which the two are pegged will become unrealistic. Such was the case a few years ago with Thailand's currency (the baht), Indonesia's currency (the rupiah), and Argentina's currency (the peso). When these countries un-pegged their currencies from the US dollar to let them gradually seek their true value, the currencies went into a free fall.

THE GLOBAL BUSINESS ENVIRONMENT

L.O. 7

Like Molson, more and more enterprises are experiencing the excitement of conducting business in the global marketplace. Even firms that once thought they were too tiny to expand into a neighbouring city have discovered that they can tap the sales potential of overseas markets with the help of fax machines, overnight delivery services, email, and the Internet (see the box entitled "Technologies that Are Revolutionizing Business"). Because of the advances in communication technologies, small companies can also tap into resources overseas to meet client needs. For example, The Portables, based in Richmond, British Columbia, is a maker of trade show displays and exhibits, and about 20 percent of their business is outsourced to two manufacturing plants in the southern Chinese city of Shenzhen. Regardless of the scope of business interactions abroad, companies must learn how to effectively conduct business overseas.[39]

Entire industries have been transformed by global accessibility. It was not long ago that Hollywood had a virtual monopoly over the North American filmmaking industry. Today, North American films are produced around the world in places like Ireland, the Czech Republic, Australia, and New Zealand. Of course, Canada has been a major winner in the globalization of the film industry. In particular, Vancouver is the leading location with Toronto in second and Montreal in third. In 2006, $1.7 billion was spent by filmmakers in Canada, leading directly to 16 700 jobs and to an additional 26 700

Technologies That Are Revolutionizing Business

TELEPRESENCE

Telepresence systems start with the basic idea of video-conferencing but go far beyond with imagery so real that colleagues thousands of miles apart appear to be in the same room together. Business executives dissatisfied with the delays and image quality of conventional videoconferencing are turning to telepresence systems to stay connected with colleagues and customers—while avoiding the disruptions, costs, or perceived risks of international travel.

HOW IT'S CHANGING BUSINESS

Telepresence enhances communication for teams spread around the country or around the world. Participants sit down at a table in one city, and virtual participants from the other city appear to be sitting on the other side of the table. The effect is so real that some people think it's downright eerie. Participants can make eye contact from across the Atlantic or across the province. Developers are even working on robotic telepresence, in which you'll be able to control a robot surrogate hundreds or thousands of miles away. Before long, you'll be able to run your global empire from the conference room down the hall.[40]

WHERE YOU CAN LEARN MORE

Teliris is one of the early innovators in telepresence technology; check out the company's website at www.teliris.com. You can also visit the Cisco Systems website at www.cisco.com.

Russell Crowe starred in Cinderella Man, *which was based on the true story of a boxer from the 1930s named Jim Braddock; the movie was filmed in Toronto.*

indirect jobs from foreign film production. These figures represented a rebound after a couple of bad years that were a result of the rise in the Canadian dollar and competition from locations around the world.[41]

Companies know that selling goods and services in foreign markets can generate increased sales, produce operational efficiencies, expose companies to new technologies, and provide greater consumer choices. But venturing abroad also exposes companies to many new challenges, as Molson discovered with their move into Brazil. For instance, each country has unique ways of doing business that must be learned: laws, customs, consumer preferences, ethical standards, labour skills, and political and economic stability. All of these factors can affect a firm's international prospects. Furthermore, volatile currencies and international trade relationships can make global expansion a risky proposition.

Still, in most cases the opportunities of the global marketplace greatly outweigh the risks. Consider UPS. When this company began its rapid global expansion program in the 1980s, it had to attain air rights into each country, unravel a patchwork of customs laws, learn how to deal with varying work ethics and employment policies, and so on. But the company's efforts paid off. Today UPS has revenue of US$47.5 billion, and delivers more than 15.6 million packages and documents daily in more than 200 countries. The company has more than 427 000 employees, including approximately 67 000 international employees.[42]

L.O. 8   Cultural Differences in the Global Business Environment

Cultural differences present a number of challenges in the global marketplace. For one thing, companies must recognize and respect differences in language, social values, ideas of status, decision-making habits, attitudes toward time, use of space, body language, manners, and ethical standards. Otherwise, such differences can lead to misunderstandings in international business relationships, particularly if differences in business practices also

IN-CLASS NOTES

Global Business Environment
- **Opportunities**
  - Growth potential
  - Increased sales
  - Operating efficiencies
  - New technologies
  - More consumer choice
- **Challenges**
  - Laws and customs
  - Consumer preferences
  - Ethical standards
  - Labour skills
  - Politics and economics

exist (see Exhibit 2.5). Furthermore, companies that sell their products overseas must often adapt these products to meet the unique needs of international customers.

The best way to prepare for doing business with people from another culture is to study that culture in advance. Learn everything you can about the culture's history, religion, politics, and customs—especially its business customs. Who makes decisions? How are negotiations usually conducted? Is gift giving expected? What is the proper attire for a business meeting? In addition to the suggestion that you learn about the

Exhibit 2.5 **Going Global Has Its Barriers**

Learning a country's business customs and cultural differences is the first step in going global.

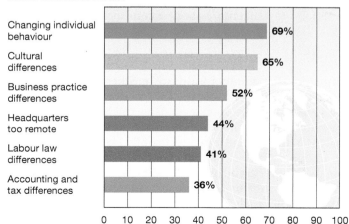

Challenges senior executives say they face when managing across different countries:

Challenge	Percentage
Changing individual behaviour	69%
Cultural differences	65%
Business practice differences	52%
Headquarters too remote	44%
Labour law differences	41%
Accounting and tax differences	36%

Source: Adapted from "Going Global Has Its Barriers," *USA Today*, 3 May 2000, B1.

Learning from Business Blunders

OOPS

Toyota thought it had a clever ad slogan that played off the Chinese proverb, "When you get to the foot of the mountain, a road will appear." The Japanese automaker launched an advertising campaign with the slogan, "Wherever there is a road, there is a Toyota." Not precisely true, to be sure, but it's the sort of advertising-speak that consumers are used to just about everywhere in the world. Not in China; government authorities accused Toyota of false advertising.

WHAT YOU CAN LEARN

Most advertisers wouldn't think twice about saying things like "Wherever there is a road, there is a Toyota," but the Chinese government has strict rules about truth in advertising and, after all, there really isn't a Toyota on every road—in China or anywhere else. The message: Don't assume anything when you're doing business in another country—research is vital.[43]

culture, seasoned international businesspeople offer the following tips for improving intercultural communication:

- *Be aware of the other person's customs.* Expect the other person to have values, beliefs, expectations, and mannerisms different from yours. For instance, don't be surprised when business people in Pakistan excuse themselves in the middle of a meeting to conduct prayers.
- *Deal with the individual.* Don't stereotype the other person or react with preconceived ideas. Regard the person as an individual first, not as a representative of another culture.
- *Clarify your intent and meaning.* The other person's body language may not mean what you think, and the person may read unintentional meanings into the messages you're sending—both verbal and nonverbal. Clarify your true intent by repetition and examples. Ask questions and listen carefully. The Japanese are generally appreciative when foreigners ask them about proper behaviour, because it shows respect for the Japanese way of doing things.[44]
- *Adapt your style to suit the other person's.* If the other person appears to be direct and straightforward, follow suit. If not, adjust your behaviour to match. In many African countries, people are suspicious of others who seem to be in a hurry. Therefore, you should allow plenty of time to get to know the people you are dealing with.
- *Show respect.* Learn how respect is communicated in various cultures—through gestures, eye contact, and so on. For example, in Spain, let a handshake last five to seven strokes; pulling away too soon may be interpreted as a rejection. In France, however, the preferred handshake is a single stroke.

These are just a few tips for doing business in the global marketplace. Exhibit 2.6 can guide you in your efforts to learn more about a country's culture before doing business abroad.

Legal Differences in the Global Business Environment

All Canadian companies that conduct business in other countries must be familiar with Canadian law, international law, and the laws of the specific countries where they plan to trade or do business. Corporate legal departments work hard to ensure that firms can take every advantage within the boundaries of the law. However, quite often laws and norms across nations come into direct conflict with each other. Practices that are frowned upon in one nation are tolerated and even encouraged in others (see the box entitled "China's Counterfeit Economy"). What is a firm to do if it is trying to earn a deal with a foreign company or a foreign nation that sees bribery as a routine part of doing business? How far should a company go in dealing with local problems? Chiquita Brands International recently pled guilty to paying terrorists in Colombia in return for protection of its profitable banana-growing operation. In a deal made with prosecutors, the company agreed to pay a fine of US$25 million.[45]

Exhibit 2.6   **Checklist for Doing Business Abroad**

Use this checklist as a starting point when investigating a foreign culture.

UNDERSTAND SOCIAL CUSTOMS

✓ How do people react to strangers? Are they friendly? Hostile? Reserved?

✓ How do people greet each other? Should you bow? Nod? Shake hands?

✓ How are names used for introductions?

✓ What are the attitudes toward touching people?

✓ How do you express appreciation for an invitation to lunch or dinner, or to someone's home? Should you bring a gift? Send flowers? Write a thank-you note?

✓ How, when, or where are people expected to sit in social or business situations?

✓ Are any phrases, facial expressions, or hand gestures considered rude?

✓ How close do people stand when talking?

✓ How do you attract the attention of a waiter? Do you tip the waiter?

✓ When is it rude to refuse an invitation? How do you refuse politely?

✓ What are the acceptable patterns of eye contact?

✓ What gestures indicate agreement? Disagreement? Respect?

✓ What topics may or may not be discussed in a social setting? In a business setting?

✓ How is time perceived?

✓ What are the generally accepted working hours?

✓ How do people view scheduled appointments?

LEARN ABOUT CLOTHING AND FOOD PREFERENCES

✓ What occasions require special clothing? What colours are associated with mourning? Love? Joy?

✓ Are some types of clothing considered taboo for one sex or the other?

✓ What are the attitudes toward human body odours? Are deodorants or perfumes used?

✓ How many times a day do people eat?

✓ How are hands or utensils used when eating?

✓ What types of places, food, and drink are appropriate for business entertainment?

✓ Where is the seat of honour at a table?

ASSESS POLITICAL PATTERNS

✓ How stable is the political situation? Does it affect businesses in and out of the country?

✓ How is political power manifested? Military power? Economic strength?

✓ What are the traditional government institutions?

LEARN ABOUT ECONOMIC AND BUSINESS INSTITUTIONS

✓ Is the society homogeneous?

✓ What minority groups are represented?

✓ What languages are spoken?

✓ Do immigration patterns influence workforce composition?

✓ What are the primary resources and principal products?

✓ What vocational/technological training is offered?

✓ What are the attitudes toward education?

✓ Are businesses generally large? Family controlled? Government controlled?

✓ Is it appropriate to do business by telephone? By fax? By email?

✓ Do managers make business decisions unilaterally, or do they involve employees?

✓ How are status and seniority shown in an organization? In a business meeting?

✓ Must people socialize before conducting business?

APPRAISE THE NATURE OF ETHICS, VALUES, AND LAWS

✓ Is money or a gift expected in exchange for arranging business transactions?

✓ What ethical or legal issues might affect business transactions?

✓ Do people value competitiveness or cooperation?

✓ What are the attitudes toward work? Toward money?

✓ Is politeness more important than factual honesty?

✓ What qualities are admired in a business associate?

Source: John V. Thill and Courtland L. Bovée, *Excellence in Business Communication* (Upper Saddle River, NJ: Prentice Hall, 2002), 33.

China's Counterfeit Economy

The vast economy in the People's Republic of China has come alive in recent years now that the communist government is embracing many principles of free-market economics. Despite the recent headlines and product recalls, the quality of most Chinese products has risen dramatically, and many of the world's best-known companies now rely on Chinese manufacturers to build some of their products for them.

Unfortunately, the Chinese manufacturing phenomenon is not limited to legitimate products. China also produces more counterfeit products than any other nation—everything from cars to aircraft parts, beer to razor blades, soap to shampoo, and TVs to toilets. Nearly half of the world's 14 billion batteries are produced in China, but most of them are fake versions of Panasonic, Duracell, and other big brands. Bikes with names like Yamaha zip along the roads from Beijing to Tibet, but Yamaha didn't make most of them. Procter & Gamble (P&G) claims counterfeiters sell $150 million of fake P&G products annually. More than 90 percent of all music CDs sold in China are pirated copies, and according to the Motion Picture Association of America, Chinese pirating of DVDs costs the industry more than $2 billion in lost revenue each year. Microsoft has invested several billion dollars in China, but has yet to generate a nickel of profit, since more than 90 percent of the application software sold in the country is counterfeit.

Most counterfeiters work at small to mid-sized factories, but many stay at home, doing things like filling Head & Shoulders bottles with concoctions from large vats in their living rooms, or translating subtitles for

According to estimates, 90 percent of DVDs and CDs sold in China are pirated copies.

pirated movies. Overall, the amount of China's manufacturing base that is dependent on illegal knockoffs is estimated to be 10 to 30 percent . . . and growing.

Raids do occur daily, but even the government's efforts aren't reducing the number of counterfeiters. Local officials are hesitant to stop the pirates because they create millions of jobs. "Entire villages live off counterfeiting. If you suddenly throw these people out of work, you'll have riots," says one spokesperson for a leading private anti-counterfeiting agency. Shutting down the fakes at Yiwu—China's largest wholesale distribution centre, where it is estimated that 80 percent of the consumer goods sold are counterfeits—would cripple the city's economy because many hotels, restaurants, and businesses cater to the trade.

The sale of fake or pirated products is not limited to the Chinese market either; these items are exported around the globe—to Europe, Russia, and the Middle East. Unilever says that fake Dove soap is making its way from China into Europe. Bose, a maker of high-end audio systems, is also finding Chinese fakes in overseas markets. These exports are made possible by the growing sophistication of Chinese manufacturing. Ten years ago, China's knockoffs were below Western standards. Now, many fake Duracell batteries look so genuine that Gillette (the maker of Duracell batteries) has to send them to a forensics lab to analyze them.

So what are pirated brand owners to do? For the most part, companies hope to encourage greater government enforcement, but it's a tough task. Although US-based Oakley has convinced Chinese authorities to close counterfeit sunglasses factories, new ones just pop up in their place.

Some multinationals are shutting down or shrinking some product lines in China because these products are overrun by counterfeits. But China's market is so vast and promising that few companies are willing to pull out. General Motors recently announced a US$3 billion additional investment based on the expectation that China will become the world's largest car market by 2025. Given the magnitude of the problem and the number of people who are dependent on this shadow economy, the situation won't be solved anytime soon, if ever.[46]

Questions for Critical Thinking

1. Honda recently set up a joint venture to make and sell motorcycles with a Chinese company that used to produce Honda knockoffs. Why would Honda do this?

2. How might product counterfeiting in China affect consumers in Canada?

Laws and policies have been put in place to deal with problems of international conduct. According to the *Corruption of Foreign Public Officials Act*, "every person commits an offence who, in order to obtain or retain an advantage in the course of business, directly or indirectly gives, offers or agrees to offer a loan, reward, advantage or benefit to a foreign public official."[47] These offences are punishable by imprisonment. Export Development Canada does not provide support to firms convicted of corruption unless the firm has instituted severe anti-corruption policies and implemented reforms.[48] Despite the policies and laws to deter business corruption, many firms will still make attempts to subvert the law.

Do honest companies lose out to foreign competitors and domestic firms willing to operate in grey areas? The answer is yes. In order to even the playing field, the Organisation for Economic Co-operation and Development (OECD) along with national governments and regulators are attempting to create an accepted international order.

Forms of International Business Activity

L.O. 9

Once a company decides to operate in the global marketplace, it must decide on the level of involvement it is willing to undertake and develop strategies for marketing its products internationally. Five common forms of international business activities are importing and exporting, licensing, franchising, strategic alliances and joint ventures, and foreign direct investment. Each has varying degrees of ownership, financial commitment, and risk.

Importing and Exporting

Importing, the buying of goods or services from a supplier in another country, and **exporting**, the selling of products outside the country in which they are produced, have existed for centuries. In the last few decades, however, the increased level of these activities has caused the economies of the world to become tightly linked.

importing
Purchasing goods or services from another country and bringing them into one's own country

Exporting, one of the least risky forms of international business activity, permits a firm to enter a foreign market gradually, assess local conditions, and then fine-tune its product to meet the needs of foreign consumers. In most cases, the firm's financial exposure is limited to market research costs, advertising costs, and the costs of either establishing a direct sales and distribution system or hiring intermediaries.

exporting
Selling and shipping goods or services to another country

Such intermediaries include *export management companies*, which are domestic firms that specialize in performing international marketing services on a commission basis, and *export trading companies*, which are general trading firms that will buy a company's products for resale overseas as well as perform a variety of importing, exporting, and manufacturing functions. Still another alternative is to use foreign distributors. Working through a foreign distributor with connections in the target country is often helpful to both large and small companies because such intermediaries can provide the connections, expertise, and market knowledge needed to conduct business in a foreign country.[49] In addition, many countries now have foreign trade offices to help importers and exporters interested in doing business within their borders. Other helpful resources include professional agents, local businesspeople, and agencies like Export Development Canada. This government organization offers a variety of services, including credit insurance, political risk insurance, direct loans, and lines of credit to encourage buyers to choose Canadian products.[50]

International Licensing

Licensing is another popular approach to international business. Licensing agreements entitle one company to use some or all of another firm's intellectual property (patents, trademarks, brand names, copyrights, or trade secrets) in return for a royalty payment. Underwear manufacturer Jockey licenses the rights to use the Jockey name to certain foreign manufacturers of women's activewear, sleepwear, and slippers. Jockey licenses its products in more than 120 countries, but is careful that all such arrangements add value to the Jockey name.[51] Likewise, Molson has licensing agreements to sell Corona and Heineken in Canada.

licensing
An agreement to produce and market another company's product in exchange for a royalty or fee

In the past few years, China's major cities have sprouted Western franchises like McDonald's.

Many firms choose licensing as an approach to international markets because it involves little out-of-pocket money; the other firm has already incurred the costs of developing the intellectual property to be licensed. Pharmaceutical firms, for instance, routinely use licensing to enter foreign markets. Once a pharmaceutical firm has developed and patented a new drug, it is often more efficient to grant existing local firms the right to manufacture and distribute the patented drug in return for royalty payments. Israel's Teva Pharmaceutical Industries, for example, has a licence to manufacture and market Merck's pharmaceutical products in Israel. This arrangement saves Merck the expense of establishing its own Israeli sales force.[52] Of course, licensing agreements are not restricted to international business. A company can also license its products or technology to other companies in its domestic market.

International Franchising

Some companies choose to expand into foreign markets by *franchising* their operation. International franchising is among the fastest-growing forms of international business activity today. Under this arrangement, a franchisor enters into an agreement whereby the franchisee obtains the rights to duplicate a specific product or service—perhaps a restaurant, photocopy shop, or video rental store—and the franchisor obtains a royalty fee in exchange. In recent years, Tim Hortons has slowly expanded its franchise base into the United States by focusing mainly on border states, with a significant entry into New England and Michigan. There are now 336 stores in the United States (82 percent of them are franchised).[53] Other firms look far beyond their initial borders. Holiday Inn has used this approach to reach customers globally and now consists of nearly 1500 hotels. KFC, McDonald's, and scores of other companies have also used this approach. Even some smaller companies have found that franchising is a good way for them to enter the global marketplace.[54] By franchising its operations, a firm can minimize the costs and risks of global expansion and bypass certain trade restrictions. (The advantages and disadvantages of franchising will be discussed in detail in Chapter 4.)

International Strategic Alliances and Joint Ventures

strategic alliance
A long-term relationship in which two or more companies share ideas, resources, and technologies to establish competitive advantages

A **strategic alliance** is a long-term partnership between two or more companies to jointly develop, produce, or sell products in the global marketplace. To reach their individual but complementary goals, the companies typically share ideas, expertise, resources, technologies, investment costs, risks, management, and profits.

Strategic alliances are a popular way to expand one's business globally. Starbucks uses this approach in venturing overseas by partnering with local businesses.[55] In Canada, Starbucks formed a strategic alliance with Indigo and Chapters bookstores to increase its presence. The benefits of this form of international growth include ease of market entry, shared risk, shared knowledge and expertise, and synergy. Companies that form a strategic alliance with a foreign partner can often compete more effectively than if they entered the foreign market alone. Consider the 17-member Star Alliance, which includes notable airlines such as Air Canada, Air New Zealand, Lufthansa, United Airlines, and Singapore Airlines. The network provides various advantages. For example, Star Alliance travellers have access to more than 855 lounges in airports worldwide and the ability to earn and redeem frequent flyer miles on any member airline.[56]

joint venture
A cooperative partnership in which organizations share investment costs, risks, management, and profits in the development, production, or selling of products

A **joint venture** is a special type of strategic alliance in which two or more firms join together to create a new business entity that is legally separate and distinct from its parents. The CAMI automotive plant, located in Ingersoll, Ontario, is an example of a joint venture between General Motors and Suzuki. The vehicles produced in this plant include the Chevrolet Equinox and the Suzuki XL7.[57] Magna International recently signed a deal to jointly build a new economy-car and assembly plant in Russia with AvtoVaz. The project will require an investment of about $2 billion and will give Magna a relationship with the rapidly expanding Russian auto market, which is expected to double its annual vehicle sales by 2021 from 1.589 million cars to 3.3 million.[58]

In some countries, foreign companies are prohibited from owning facilities outright or from investing in local business. Thus, establishing a joint venture with a local partner may be the only way to do business in that country. In other cases, foreign companies may be required to move some of their production facilities to the country to earn the right to sell their products there. For instance, the Chinese government would not allow Boeing to sell airplanes in China until the company agreed to move half of the tail-section production for its 737s to Xian.[59] Despite similar pressure, Bombardier has held off on making a substantial investment for its aerospace division. However, Bombardier has shown a tremendous commitment to China by creating three railway industry joint ventures: one for signalling equipment, one for subway cars, and one for mainline cars. It also recently signed a 20-year deal to supply the country with high-speed trains.[60]

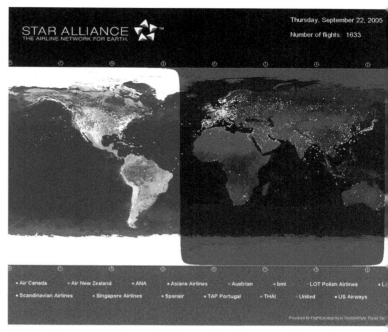

Air Canada passengers, along with clients of the other 17 member airlines of the Star Alliance, enjoy the benefits of shared resources and operational cooperation.

Foreign Direct Investment

Exporting, licensing, franchising, and strategic alliances allow a firm to enter the global marketplace without investing in foreign factories or facilities. However, many firms prefer to enter international markets through ownership and control of assets in foreign countries.

The most comprehensive form of international business is a wholly owned operation run in another country, without the financial participation of a local partner. Many Canadian firms conduct business this way, as do companies based in other countries. These operations vary in form, size, and purpose. Some are started from scratch; others are acquired from local owners. The Bank of Nova Scotia is probably the most internationally oriented of the Canadian banks with a strong presence in places like Mexico, the Caribbean, and a commitment to China and India where they have had a presence for over two decades. It is a slow process getting through government regulations, with each location in China going through a very tough approval process (there are only six branches in China). Things are moving at a snail's pace, but the company is willing to be patient in markets with such tremendous potential.[61] On the other hand, Couche-Tard, a leader in the Canadian convenience store industry, provides a countering example. A few years ago, the firm purchased Circle K, a southern-US convenience chain with 2290 stores, for $1.1 billion. The expansion from strong national player to international giant happened quickly. There are now over 2000 stores in Canada and more than 3000 stores in the United States. Couche-Tard is further expanding the Circle K brand internationally; there are approximately 3500 Circle K licensed locations in seven other regions worldwide (Japan, Hong Kong, China, Indonesia, Guam, Macao, and Mexico).[62]

Some international operations are small sales offices; others are full-scale manufacturing facilities. Some are set

The Chevrolet Equinox is built in the Suzuki/GM joint-venture plant located in Ingersoll, Ontario.

International Business Activity

- Importing and exporting
- Licensing
- Franchising
- Strategic alliances and joint ventures
- Direct foreign investment

_____

_____

_____

_____

_____

up to exploit the availability of raw materials; others take advantage of low wage rates; still others minimize transportation costs by choosing locations that give them direct access to markets in other countries. In almost all cases, at least part of the workforce is drawn from the local population.

multinational corporations (MNCs)
Companies with operations in more than one country

foreign direct investment (FDI)
Investment of money by foreign companies in domestic business enterprises

Companies with a physical presence in numerous countries are called **multinational corporations (MNCs)**. Some multinational corporations increase their involvement in foreign countries by establishing **foreign direct investment (FDI)**. That is, they either establish production and marketing facilities in the countries where they operate or purchase existing foreign firms. Such foreign direct investment constitutes the highest level of international involvement. Moreover, it carries much greater economic and political risk and is more complex than any other form of entry into the global marketplace.[63]

The ability to attract foreign direct investment is an important element of national economic competitiveness. Among developed countries, Canada, Italy, France, and Australia are no longer among the world's top 10 spots for foreign direct investment. As discussed earlier in this chapter, emerging markets such as the BRIC countries (Brazil, Russia, India, and China), as well as Mexico, Poland, and others have grown significantly in this area. In fact, China has overtaken the United States as the world's preferred location for FDI.[64]

Product Strategies for International Markets

Whether exporting, licensing, or franchising its products in a foreign country, a company must decide on an appropriate product strategy. For instance, it must decide whether to *standardize* the product, selling the same product everywhere in the world, or to *customize* the product to accommodate the lifestyles and habits of local target markets. Keep in mind that the degree of customization can vary. A company may change only the product's name or packaging, or it can modify the product's components, size, and functions. Of course, understanding a country's culture and regulations helps a company make these important decisions. But even the most successful companies have blundered (see the box entitled "How to Avoid Business Blunders Abroad").

After being slammed for its ignorance of European ways and losing US$1 billion in Euro Disney's first year of operation, Disney realized that Paris was not Orlando or Anaheim. Disney had insulted French employees with its required dress code and angered its European customers, who were not accustomed to standing in line for rides or eating fast food standing up. "When we first launched Euro Disney there was the belief that it was enough to be Disney," says Euro Disney CEO Jay Rasulo. "Now we

How to Avoid Business Blunders Abroad

Doing business in another country can be extremely tricky. Here are some issues to consider when you conduct business abroad.

THE IMPORTANCE OF PACKAGING

Numerous problems result from the failure to adapt packaging for other cultures. Sometimes only the colour of the package needs to be altered to enhance a product's sales. For instance, white symbolizes death in Japan and much of Asia; green represents danger or disease in Malaysia. Using the wrong colour in these countries might produce negative reactions.

THE LANGUAGE BARRIER

Some product names travel poorly. For instance, Esso found out that its name means "stalled car" in Japan. However, some company names have travelled well. Kodak may be the most famous example. A research team deliberately developed this name after searching for a word that was pronounceable everywhere but had no specific meaning anywhere. Canadian firms have an advantage over companies that operate in a unilingual country with a more homogeneous population; domestic companies are trained in cultural diversity just from dealing with the idiosyncrasies of cultural and linguistic adaptation here at home. For example, before expanding into the Quebec market, Medicine Hat, Alberta–based Spitz Sunflower Seeds sent personnel to the market to assess the competition, design packaging, and adapt its approach for the francophone market.

PROBLEMS WITH PROMOTIONS

In its promotions, one company had effectively used this sentence: "You can use no finer napkin at your dinner table." The company decided to use the same commercials in England because, after all, the British do speak English. To the British, however, the word *napkin* or *nappy* actually means "diaper." The ad could hardly be expected to boost sales of dinner napkins in England.

LOCAL CUSTOMS

Social norms vary greatly from country to country and it is difficult for any outsider to be knowledgeable about all of them, so local input is vital. For example, one firm promoted eyeglasses in Thailand with commercials featuring animals wearing glasses. However, in Thailand animals are considered a lower life form; humans would never wear anything worn by an animal.

RIM's famous BlackBerry has finally entered into the Japanese market with the help of NTT DoCoMo, Japan's largest mobile phone operator. It remains to be seen if the BlackBerry will gain equivalent acceptance in a country where most important business communication is still conducted face to face and email plays a smaller role, with employees routinely lingering in their offices after hours.

TRANSLATION PROBLEMS

The best translation of an advertising message conveys the concept of the original but does not precisely duplicate it. PepsiCo learned this lesson when it discovered that its slogan "Come alive with Pepsi" was translated into German as "Come alive out of the grave with Pepsi." In Asia, the slogan was once translated as "Bring your ancestors back from the dead." This did not go over well in a region that reveres their elders and ancestors.

THE NEED FOR RESEARCH

Proper market research may reduce or eliminate most international business blunders. Market researchers can uncover needs for product adaptations, potential name problems, promotional requirements, and useful market strategies. Good research may even uncover potential translation problems.

As you can see, doing business in other cultures can be risky if a company is unprepared. However, awareness of differences, consultations with local people, and concern for host-country feelings can reduce problems and save money.[65]

Questions for Critical Thinking

1. If you were thinking of selling a breakfast cereal in Japan, what issues might you want to consider?
2. What steps can companies take to avoid business blunders abroad?

After learning valuable lessons in Europe about cultural differences, Disney continues to expand its powerful brand worldwide.

realize that our guests need to be welcomed on the basis of their own culture and travel habits."[66] To cease alienating the Europeans, Disney switched from a standardized to a customized product strategy by modifying its theme park for the European culture. The company ditched its controversial dress code, authorized wine with meals, lowered admission prices, hired a French investor relations firm, and changed the name of the complex from Euro Disney to Disneyland Paris to lure French tourists. Today, Disneyland Paris is a strong tourist attraction and the company has learned a few things about operating in foreign markets. In another global leap, Disney has recently signed a deal to set up 150 stores in India to sell their branded products with a local company called RJ Corp.[67]

Like Disney, many manufacturers have customized their products after learning that international customers are not all alike. For instance, KFC believes that business, like politics, is local. So it doesn't just open restaurants based on the North American model and expect success—it adapts KFC's product offerings to local tastes. In Japan KFC sells tempura crispy strips; in northern England KFC stresses gravy and potatoes; in Thailand it offers fresh rice with soy or sweet chili sauce; in Holland the company makes a potato-and-onion croquette; in France it sells pastries alongside chicken; and in China the chicken gets spicier the farther inland you travel.[68]

On the other hand, Kellogg sells the same Corn Flakes in Europe that it sells in Canada. Only recently has Kellogg made significant inroads in European markets, however, thanks to television advertising and lifestyle changes that favour bigger breakfasts.[69] The latest twist is for companies to adapt products or brands from their foreign operations to their local markets, as Molson unsuccessfully attempted with A Marca Bavaria.

L.O. 10

DEALING WITH ECONOMIC SHOCKS IN A GLOBAL BUSINESS ENVIRONMENT

The global market is intertwined more than at any other time in history. In recent years, the avian influenza ("bird flu"), SARS, mad cow disease, and other health-related fears have had a major impact on global trade and travel. Mad cow disease discoveries have led to old protectionist measures. Natural disasters—hurricanes, tornadoes, tsunamis—in one part of the world can have a large impact on industries on the other side of the world. The war in Iraq has had an impact on the gas pumps across the globe. A few years earlier, the world experienced the Asian economic flu, which did not create potential medical fears like SARS or the avian flu, but still managed to cause pain and hardship as markets, firms, and investors suffered worldwide.

In the global marketplace, the problems of one country can greatly affect world economics. There is an old joke that says when the United States sneezes, Canada catches a cold. In today's global environment the Canadian economy is susceptible to ailments from all around the world, not just our neighbours to the south. What does this new global reality translate into? One example can be found in the airline industry, where the fear of terrorist attacks have led to major changes in security and safety protocols that cause to some annoying yet worthwhile time delays. Rules have been adjusted; however, organizations will not shy away from their global pursuits. For example, despite the avian flu, which has led to many concerns over poultry products, Yum! Brands, owner of KFC, Taco Bell, Pizza Hut, and other restaurant chains, is one firm that has not hit the brakes. There are 11 000 KFC restaurants in 80 countries, and KFC is increasing its presence in strategic markets. It already has stores in 402 cities in China, with 1822 restaurants in total. Yum! Brands has no plans to slow down—avian flu or not.[70]

Behind the SCENES

Molson Coors: A Global Partnership

After more than two centuries of successful business operations, Molson formed a bonding relationship with Coors. Strangely enough, there is nothing odd about this move—there are many similar examples from around the world in recent years. Within weeks of the merger, the famous slogan for Molson Canadian was symbolically switched from "I Am Canadian" to "It Starts Here." The change was appropriate because despite the clear statements that both companies would continue and traditions would be respected (Molson had been in business for 219 years and Coors for 178 years at the time of the merger), it was a new start. Molson Coors has two powerful identities slowly integrating into a new system. By becoming the world's fifth largest brewery—behind companies like Anheuser-Busch and SABMiller PLC—Molson Coors had effectively consolidated each individual company's respective strengths. After the initial shakeout, the company has been reporting the benefits of the move. In the first quarter of 2007 alone, Molson Coors reported savings of $14 million from synergies directly linked to the merger. The company has also exceeded expectations of reaching $175 million in savings by the end of its first three years—it is expected to reach that goal by the end of 2007.

The new company has set a clear direction for the future to build on their impressive portfolio of brands. The global approach now has three centres of operation. The 2006 annual report makes this clear from page one with a picture of three bottles of beer: Molson Canadian, Coors Light, and Carling. All three of these images are important to their regional markets.

Canada
In the new company, Molson is responsible for Canadian operations, which accounted for 19 percent of sales in 2006. The major priorities include the expansion of the Coors Light brand and a concerted effort to rebuild momentum with the Molson Canadian brand.
Key Brands: Molson Canadian, Coors Light, Rickard's, Carling, and Pilsner
Key Licensed Brands: Amstel Light, Heineken, Corona, Tiger

United States
The Coors Brewing Company looks after the US operations, which accounted for 56 percent of sales in 2006. According to a recent press release, the primary goal is to re-establish Coors Light's growth trends. Building Molson brands are not listed as a top priority.
Key Brands: Coors, Coors Light, George Killian's, Keystone, and Molson brands

United Kingdom, Europe, and Asia
Coors Brewers Limited looks after the United Kingdom, Europe, and Asia, which accounted for 25 percent of 2006 sales. The key focus in this market is on increasing sales of Carling, Grolsch, and Coors Fine Light. No clear focus has been set on building Molson brands here, either.
Key Brands: Carling, Coors Fine Light, Caffrey's, Screamers
Key Joint Venture Brand: Grolsch

The New Road Ahead
For old-fashioned, protectionist-minded Canadians the following stats are alarming. In the new Molson Coors statistics chart, Coors Light accounted for 45 percent of total sales volume, Carling was second at 19 percent, and Keystone was third with approximately 8 percent. Is there any wonder why Molson brands are not a huge priority for short-term growth? But don't panic. Molson brands will not be disappearing from Canadian shelves. Molson Coors may have great plans down the road for the beloved local brands, but at the moment this global player is more concerned with building known brands. Who can blame them? It's a business decision. Why invest millions to promote a lesser-known brand to global interests when you can take advantage of better known commodities?

The merger gave Molson additional financial support and stability, but the true global Molson beer brand may take another 200 years to develop. Molson's shareholders are in a better position, but the brands will need to fight with their new siblings if they are to take advantage of the benefits of the Molson Coors arrangement.[71]

Critical Thinking Questions
1. How does Molson's partnership with Coors enhance the company's market position?
2. How does the three region strategy help Molson Coors capitalize on market opportunities?
3. What role do licensed brands play in the success of Molson Coors's Canadian operations?

Learn More Online
Find out how Molson Coors is faring with its global strategy. Go to Chapter 2 of this text's website at www.pearsoned.ca/bovee, and click on the Molson Coors hotlink to read the latest news releases about their financial performance, international operations, and plans for expansion. How do their international sales figures look? Where is the company strongest? Where is it struggling? In late 2007, Molson Coors and SABMiller announced a joint venture to combine their US operations. How is this partnership progressing? What changes, if any, is the company making to its global strategy?

TEST YOUR KNOWLEDGE

Questions for Review

1. What is meant by the term absolute advantage? What is meant by comparative advantage? Explain both and provide examples.

2. What is the balance of trade and how is it related to the balance of payments?

3. What are the advantages and disadvantages of trading blocs like NAFTA and the European Union?

4. What is meant by currency devaluation?

5. What two fundamental product strategies do companies choose between when selling their products in the global marketplace?

Questions for Analysis

6. What is the difference between an embargo and a tariff? Which one is more restrictive from a manufacturer's point of view?

7. The trend away from protectionism and toward free trade has been undeniable in recent years and has been pushed by the big developed countries like Canada and the United States. However, governments sometimes fall back on their old protectionist ways while dealing with trading partners. Under what circumstances might a country do this?

8. Why would a company choose to work through intermediaries when selling products in a foreign country?

9. Which of the following international expansion strategies is more risky: foreign direct investment or joint ventures (with foreign companies)? Why?

10. **Ethical Considerations.** Should the Canadian government more closely regulate the practice of giving trips and other incentives to foreign managers to win their business? Is this bribery?

Questions for Application

11. Suppose you own a small company that manufactures hockey equipment. You are aware that Russia is a large market, and you are considering exporting your products there. What steps should you take? Who might be able to provide assistance?

12. Because your Brazilian restaurant caters to western businesspeople and tourists, much of the food you buy is imported from North American sources. Lately, the value of the real (Brazil's currency) has been falling relative to the US dollar. This change makes your food imports much more costly, and it negatively affects your profitability. You have three options; which one will you choose? (a) Raise menu prices across the board. (b) Accept only US dollars from customers. (c) Try to purchase more of your food items locally. Please explain your selection.

13. **Integrated.** Review the theory of supply and demand discussed in Chapter 1. Using this theory, explain how a country's currency is valued and why governments sometimes adjust the values of their currency.

14. **Ethical Considerations.** You just received notice that a large shipment of manufacturing supplies you have been waiting for has been held up in customs for two weeks. A local business associate tells you that you are expected to give customs agents some "incentive money" to see that everything clears easily. How will you handle this situation?

PRACTISE YOUR KNOWLEDGE

SHARPENING YOUR COMMUNICATION SKILLS

Languages never translate on a word-for-word basis. When doing business in the global marketplace, choose words that convey only their most specific denotative meaning. Avoid using slang or idioms (words that can have meanings far different from their individual components when translated literally). For example, if a Canadian executive tells an Egyptian executive that a certain product "doesn't cut the mustard," chances are that communication will fail.

Team up with two other students and list 10 examples of slang (in your own language) that would probably be misinterpreted or misunderstood during a business conversation with someone from another culture. Next to each example, suggest other words you might use to convey the same message. Make sure the alternatives mean exactly the same as the original slang or idiom. Compare your list with those of your classmates.

BUILDING YOUR TEAM SKILLS

After nearly three decades in the shadows of the US dollar the Canadian loonie is making a stand and is now outperforming the US greenback. In recent years, the dollar climbed from a low of 61.79 on January 21, 2002, to a 31-year high of

1.09 on November 7, 2007.[72] Of course, these rates vary daily. By the time you read this, the dollar may have slipped or may be in new, uncharted territory.

a. With your team, brainstorm a list of at least three Canadian companies and describe some of the ways that a rising/falling Canadian dollar influences their financial performance.

b. Consider the probable short-term effect of the rising dollar on each of the following companies:

- A Canadian film production studio that caters to US movie production companies.

- A Canadian steel manufacturer that sells 70 percent of its production to US companies.

- A US food producer that sells its products in Sobeys and Loblaw stores across Canada.

Select a spokesperson to provide and explain your answers and your team's reasoning to the rest of the class. Compare your recommendation with those of your classmates.

EXPAND YOUR KNOWLEDGE

DISCOVERING CAREER OPPORTUNITIES

If global business interests you, consider working for a Canadian government agency that supports or regulates international trade. For example, Export Development Canada (EDC) offers a student summer employment program. The EDC provides trade finance services to support Canadian exporters and investors in more than 200 markets. Visit its website at www.edc.ca, go to the Student Summer Employment Program section, and then answer these questions: Who can apply for these positions? Where are the work terms located? What positions are available for this upcoming summer?

DEVELOPING YOUR RESEARCH SKILLS

Companies involved in international trade have to watch the foreign exchange rates of the countries in which they do business. Use your research skills to locate and analyze information about the value of the Canadian dollar relative to the US dollar. As you complete this exercise, make a note of the sources and search strategies you used.

1. How many Canadian dollars do you need to purchase one US dollar? Find yesterday's foreign exchange rate for the US dollar in the *Globe and Mail* or on the Internet.

2. Investigate this foreign exchange rate over the past month. Is the Canadian dollar growing stronger (buying more US dollars) or growing weaker (buying fewer US dollars)?

STUDY GUIDE

SUMMARY OF LEARNING OBJECTIVES

1. Explain why nations trade

Nations trade to obtain raw materials and goods that are unavailable to them or that are too costly to produce domestically. International trade benefits nations by increasing a country's total output, offering lower prices and greater variety to its consumers, subjecting domestic oligopolies and monopolies to competition, and allowing companies to expand their markets and achieve production and distribution efficiencies.

2. Explain why nations restrict international trade and list four forms of trade restrictions

Nations restrict international trade to boost local economies, shield domestic industries from head-to-head competition with overseas rivals, save specific jobs, give weak or new industries a chance to grow strong, or protect a nation's security. The four most commonly used forms of trade restrictions are tariffs (taxes, surcharges, or duties levied against imported goods), quotas (limitations on the amount of a particular good that can be imported), embargoes (the banning of imports and exports of certain goods), and sanctions (politically motivated embargoes).

3. Highlight three protectionist tactics nations use to give their domestic industries a competitive edge

From time to time countries give their domestic producers a competitive edge by imposing restrictive import standards, such as requiring special licences or unusually high product standards; by subsidizing certain domestic producers so they can compete more favourably in the global marketplace; or by dumping or selling large quantities of a product at a lower price than it costs to produce the good or at a lower price than the good is sold for in its home market.

4. Explain how trading blocs affect trade

Trading blocs are regional groupings of countries in which trade barriers have been removed. These alliances ease trade among bloc members and strengthen barriers for non-members. Critics of trading blocs fear that as members become more protective of their regions, those not in the bloc could suffer. Proponents see them as a way to help smaller or younger nations compete with producers in more-developed nations. The four most

powerful trading blocs today are the Association of Southeast Asian Nations (ASEAN), Mercosur, the North American Free Trade Agreement (NAFTA), and the European Union (EU).

5. Identify the role of emerging markets and the importance of the countries referred to as BRIC

Emerging markets provide access to natural resources, inexpensive labour, and are important potential markets that all major companies want to access. Brazil, Russia, India, and China are four particularly interesting nations that have a huge population base and have been targeted by firms in recent years for their tremendous potential.

6. Understand the fundamental elements of currency exchange

Foreign exchange refers to the conversion of one currency into an equivalent amount of another currency. Most international currencies operate under a floating exchange rate system, which means that its price fluctuates in response to the forces of global supply and demand. Other countries fix their currencies to another foreign currency like the euro. As the euro rises, their currency rises proportionately. Devaluation, or the decline of a country's currency, is not necessarily bad. It makes that country's products cheaper to buy for foreigners and can actually boost the local economy by creating additional foreign demand for products. In general, an increase in the dollar is good for importers but bad for exporters and vice versa.

7. Highlight the opportunities and challenges of conducting business in other countries

Conducting business in other countries can provide such opportunities as increased sales, better operational efficiencies, and exposure to new technologies and consumer markets. At the same time, it poses challenges such as the need to learn local laws, customs, and ethical standards. Furthermore, it exposes companies to the risks of political and economic instabilities, volatile currencies, international trade relationships, and the threat of global terrorism.

8. List five ways to improve communication in an international business relationship

To improve international communication, learn as much as you can about the culture and customs of the people you are working with, keep an open mind and avoid stereotyping, anticipate misunderstandings and guard against them by clarifying your intent, adapt your style to match the style of others, and learn how to show respect in other cultures.

9. **Identify five forms of international business activity**

Importing and exporting, licensing, franchising, strategic alliances and joint ventures, and foreign direct investment are five of the most common forms of international business activity. Each provides a company with varying degrees of control and entails different levels of risk and financial commitment.

10. **Discuss the economic and social impact of global events such as avian flu, SARS, mad cow disease, and terrorism as they relate to globalization**

The growing mutual dependence and interrelation between countries in the global business environment is inevitable. This fact leaves multinational firms vulnerable to events across the globe, but at the same time protects them from facing financial ruin when a devastating event occurs in any one region. Whether it is avian flu, mad cow disease, SARS, or terrorism, companies and governments will handle each event and then legislate and create protection measures to deal with these new threats.

KEY TERMS

absolute advantage (37)	exchange rate (48)	protectionism (40)
BRIC (47)	exporting (55)	quotas (41)
balance of payments (38)	foreign direct investment (FDI) (58)	strategic alliance (56)
balance of trade (38)	free trade (42)	subsidies (41)
comparative advantage theory (37)	importing (55)	trade deficit (38)
dumping (41)	joint venture (56)	trade surplus (38)
economies of scale (37)	licensing (55)	tariffs (41)
embargo (41)	multinational corporations	trading blocs (43)
euro (45)	(MNCs) (58)	

QUESTIONS

Multiple Choice   Circle the correct answer and then check the answers in the back of the book to chart your progress.

1. Which of the following does not represent a major trading bloc?

   a. NAFTA
   b. Mercosur
   c. EU
   d. WTO

2. Which of the following is the most comprehensive form of international business?

   a. Importing and exporting
   b. Licensing
   c. Strategic alliances
   d. Foreign direct investment

3. Assume that Canada is more efficient at producing aluminium and Brazil is more efficient at producing coffee. What should both countries produce?

   a. Both countries should produce both coffee and steel, at the levels preferred by each country's customers.
   b. Canada should produce coffee and Brazil should produce aluminium so they can improve their efficiency.
   c. Canada should produce aluminium and Brazil should produce coffee. The countries should trade with each other so that both of the country's consumers get more.
   d. Both Canada and Brazil should grow more vegetables.

4. Which of the following contributes to a favourable balance of payments?

   a. Imports are greater than exports.
   b. Best Buy purchased Future Shop.
   c. Canada spends more on military policing activities in Afghanistan.
   d. Canadian investors buy stocks in Asian high-technology companies.

5. Which of the following is the best justification for tariffs or other trade restrictions?

   a. They remove competition from domestic businesses.
   b. They save domestic jobs.
   c. They allow domestic producers to charge higher prices.
   d. They reduce the incentives for innovation.

6. Which of the following is *not* a trade restriction?

   a. Tariffs
   b. Quotas
   c. Restrictive import standards
   d. NAFTA

7. Which of the following needs to be considered when a company expands internationally?

   a. Products
   b. Promotion
   c. Pricing
   d. All of the above

8. _____ are taxes, surcharges, or duties applied to imported goods.

   a. Quotas
   b. Subsidies
   c. Tariffs
   d. Boycotts

9. Four very important developing nations that are impacting global commerce are collectively referred to as BRIC. What does BRIC stand for?

   a. Brazil, Russia, India, and China
   b. Bolivia, Rwanda, India, and China
   c. Brazil, Romania, Indonesia, and China
   d. Brazil, Russia, Ireland, and Czech Republic

10. What is it called when a nation has the ability to produce a particular product with fewer resources per unit of output than any other nation?

   a. Comparative advantage
   b. Trading bloc
   c. Absolute advantage
   d. Subsidized dumping

True/False

1. True or false? The Canadian trade deficit has been steadily growing in the past decade.

2. True or false? Licensing is an excellent way to enter a market if the company is not willing to establish facilities in the foreign nation.

3. True or false? Under the theory of comparative advantage, if each country specializes in those products they can produce best, then all countries will enjoy a higher standard of living.

4. True or false? Governments subsidize certain industries to help companies compete in the global market.

5. True or false? The World Bank is used by central banks such as the Bank of England and the Bank of Canada to settle transactions between countries.

Fill-in-the-Blank

1. The total value of products a nation exports minus the total value of products it imports, over some period of time, is known as the _____.

2. _____ is the term used to describe government policies aimed at shielding a country's industries from foreign competition.

3. When companies sell their products in foreign markets at a price lower than their cost of production, the exporting country can be charged with _____.

4. A total ban on trade with a particular nation or of a particular product is known as a(n) _____.

5. _____ is an international organization with 185 member countries; its primary function is to promote international monetary cooperation and foster economic growth.

6. The four most powerful trading blocs today are the Association of Southeast Asian Nations (ASEAN), South America's Mercosur, the North American Free Trade Agreement (NAFTA), and the _____.

7. Most international currencies operate under a _____ rate system.

8. Purchasing goods or services from another country and bringing them into one's own country is known as _____.

9. A _____ is a cooperative partnership in which organizations share investment costs, risks, management expertise, and profits in the development, production, or selling of goods.

10. Companies that have a physical presence in many countries are called _____.

Companion Website

See It on the WEB

Visit the Companion Website at **www.pearsoned.ca/bovee**, review the exercises, and complete the following assignments for Chapter 2:

1. Navigating Global Business Differences
2. Banking on the World Bank

CHAPTER 3

PRACTISING ETHICAL BEHAVIOUR AND SOCIAL RESPONSIBILITY

LEARNING OBJECTIVES

After studying this chapter, you will be able to

1   Discuss what it means to practise good business ethics and highlight three factors that influence ethical behaviour

2   Identify three steps that businesses are taking to encourage ethical behaviour and explain the advantages and disadvantages of whistle-blowing

3   List four questions you might ask yourself when trying to make an ethical decision

4   Explain the difference between an ethical dilemma and an ethical lapse

5   Discuss the relationship between corporate social responsibility and profits

6   Explain how businesses can become more socially responsible

7   Outline activities that the government and businesses are undertaking to improve the environment

leading the way

corporate social responsibility report

Telus has earned a reputation as a firm that embraces socially responsible practices.

www.telusmobility.com

You are no doubt aware of the Telus brand name. Many of you have a Telus-served phone in your bag, purse, or pocket as you sit through your lectures. So it should be no surprise that Telus is the largest telecommunications company in western Canada and the second-largest in the country with a 23 percent market share and $8.7 billion in annual revenue. Telus sets very clear objectives that are divided into five sustainability categories: economic growth, environmental sustainability, community welfare, workplace well-being, and governance and integrity.

Beyond its continued expansion and market success, Telus has a strong commitment to social responsibility and ethical conduct. In fact, the company has become a standard example cited by *Corporate Knights*, the magazine for Canadian corporate social responsibility. According to Patricia Mackenzie, Telus's assistant vice-president of environmental health and safety, "Telus envisions a day when telecommunications will allow them to move ideas and information instead of goods, services, and people." Telus has been delivering on their goal by creating various pilot projects. For example, the "teleworking" project saved Telus employees almost 14 000 hours of commute time, created and increased job satisfaction, and helped reduce greenhouse gas emissions by 114 tonnes. Additionally, the green agenda pushed forward a recovery and recycling program that allowed Telus to recycle 7183 metric tonnes of material that would otherwise have ended up in landfills. For these and other achievements, Telus has been listed on the Dow Jones Sustainability Index for the past six years. Telus was also listed by Canadian Business Online as being in the top 10 percent of companies worldwide that make their business practices sustainable for long-term growth. How do they deliver consistently? When *Corporate Knights* magazine conducted an assessment they identified three key factors:

1. *The environmental agenda is not isolated in a corner collecting dust.* Telus does not simply leave it to the public relations department to look after its environmental image. Instead it has empowered the finance department and created a system in which environmental performance reports are provided to the audit committee on a quarterly basis. Telus also pushes the agenda forward by continuously training its workforce. In each of the past three years, more than 6000 courses were completed by Telus employees.

2. *Telus sets hard targets.* If a company wants to reach a goal, it must be specific in setting a target. Telus has established targets for many environmental goals, including water use, paper use, air emissions, reclamation activity, energy use, fuel consumption, and training.

3. *Telus is willing to take the lead.* The firm was a key player in the development of the Communications Environmental Excellence Initiative, a North American telecommunications commitment to improve environmental accountability.

Were you aware of Telus's environmentally friendly track record? Does it influence your purchase decisions in any way?[1]

TEST YOURSELF

Answers to these questions can be found on the website: www.pearsoned.ca/bovee.

1. How does Telus balance their profit-seeking motive with their environmental agenda?

2. What concrete measures can a company like Telus take to ensure that it is acting in a responsible and sustainable manner?

3. Does a good corporate conscience translate into customer loyalty benefits?

L.O. 1

ETHICS AND SOCIAL RESPONSIBILITY IN THE WORKPLACE

Telus works hard to make sure that the company behaves in an ethical and socially responsible manner; businesses can't control each action or individual decision, but they can set expectations and enforce policies and codes. From the CEO to the newest entry-level clerk, every individual in an organization makes choices and decisions that have moral implications. These choices and decisions affect the company and its stakeholders. Moreover, they ultimately determine whether the company is recognized as a responsible corporate citizen.

This chapter explains what it means to conduct business in an ethically and socially responsible manner and discusses the importance of doing so. Many people use the terms *social responsibility* and *ethics* interchangeably, but the two are not the same. **Social responsibility** is the idea that business has certain obligations to society beyond the pursuit of profits. **Ethics** is defined as the principles and standards of moral behaviour that are accepted by society as right versus wrong. To make the "right choice" individuals must think through the consequences of their actions. *Business ethics* is the application of moral standards to business situations.

Thanks to a number of high-profile scandals involving finances or product safety, corporate social responsibility and managerial ethics have been a hot topic in the media in recent years. Several of these cases clearly and often painfully demonstrate that corporate responsibility and ethics are not just philosophical questions but real-life issues, where mistakes by just a handful of people can erase billions of dollars (including the life savings of many employees), put thousands of people out of work, and affect families and communities for years. Throughout your business studies and into your career, you'll continue to hear references to many of the following cases (lawsuits are still active in several of these cases):

social responsibility
The concern of businesses for the welfare of society as a whole

ethics
The rules or standards governing the conduct of a person or group

- *Enron.* Once the seventh-largest company in the United States and a poster child for the "new economy," Enron collapsed in 2001 thanks to a complex structure of hidden partnerships (designed to inflate profits and hide losses from investors), managerial mistakes, and insider trading. Thousands of employees lost their jobs, and many lost their life savings when Enron stock became almost worthless. More than 20 executives have been investigated and many have been sentenced to prison terms. Most notably, founder and former chairman Kenneth Lay and former CEO Jeffrey Skilling were both convicted for their actions. Lay died two months later, before he could serve his prison term, while Skilling was sentenced to 24 years in prison.[2] Charges were also brought against several of Enron's banks for their role in hiding financial information from investors.[3] The

CIBC agreed to pay $80 million in penalties because of their involvement with Enron. The bank also agreed to abandon large portions of its structured finance business for three years.[4]

■ *Arthur Andersen.* One of the world's oldest and most distinguished accounting firms, Arthur Andersen served as both Enron's independent financial auditor and management adviser. The company shred Enron accounting documents and was convicted of obstruction of justice for hiding information about Enron's finances. It was the first major accounting firm ever convicted of a felony. As a consequence, Arthur Andersen was required to stop performing public audits—the core of its business—and let go two-thirds of its employees.[5]

■ *Nortel.* Years after the decline of one of Canada's greatest symbols of the stock boom, which characterized the late nineties and early days of the new millennium, Nortel is still trying to get its house in order. Nortel has had to restate its financial statements for 2003, 2004, and 2005, and in 2007 the company announced a delay in filing its 2006 statements in order to continue to address its accounting issues. Nortel also recently settled two lawsuits for US$2.5 billion.[6]

■ *Tyco.* Former Tyco CEO Dennis Kozlowski is currently serving a 25-year prison sentence. Kozlowski and several other top executives were convicted of taking $600 million from Tyco, a diversified manufacturing company. In 2007, the company agreed to pay nearly $3 billion to settle 32 class-action lawsuits and announced plans to split the company into three separate entities.[7]

■ *WorldCom.* Telecommunications giant WorldCom (which now goes by the name MCI) filed for bankruptcy and cut more than 22 000 jobs after revealing accounting frauds totalling $11 billion.[8] In 2006, former CEO Bernie Ebbers began serving a 25-year prison sentence for his involvement in the fraudulent actions.[9]

■ *Conrad Black (Hollinger International).* Lord Conrad Black, who once sat on top of a global media empire, Hollinger International, faced eight fraud-related charges that he and three associates diverted $84 million from investor's pockets. The court case revealed all sorts of questionable acts. For example, a $62 000 birthday party for Barbara Amiel, Black's wife, was billed to the company. In his defence, Black said that he discussed a building project with Donald Trump at the party. There is also the issue of the 12 boxes that were taken out of the back door of Hollinger's Toronto offices even though there was a court order to seek approval before removing any items. It was all caught on surveillance cameras. Black was convicted of fraud and obstruction of justice in July 2007 and was sentenced to a six-and-a-half-year jail term in December 2007.[10]

■ *Ford and Firestone.* Faulty Firestone tires on Ford Explorers have been blamed for 271 deaths and more than 800 injuries worldwide—numbers that could have been much lower if both companies had reacted sooner to evidence of product failure, which was brought to their attention back in 2000. Firestone blamed the problem on Ford (and on Explorer drivers); Ford blamed the problem on Firestone. Firestone refused to recall the tires, so Ford stepped in and replaced the tires on nearly 50 000 vehicles in 16 countries. A new $2 billion class-action lawsuit was launched in 2007; clearly, consumers have not forgotten.[11]

Conrad Black removing 12 boxes through the back door of Hollinger's Toronto offices, and in the process violating a court order.

Although these cases involve only a few companies, the fallout from their actions continues to affect managers in thousands of companies. For instance, publicly traded companies (those that sell stock to investors) in the United States must now comply with the *Sarbanes-Oxley Act*, which requires much more careful financial reporting. Stricter laws are also being adopted in Canada under Bill C-198. This new level of information

IN-CLASS NOTES

Ethics and Social Responsibility in the Workplace

- *Social responsibility*: acting in a manner that shows concern for society's welfare
- *Ethical conduct*: conforming to standards governing the actions of a person or group
- *Consumer expectations in the 21st century*: be a responsible corporate citizen; provide a positive contribution

_____

_____

_____

_____

_____

_____

disclosure may be a good thing for investors, but it comes at a cost. Estimates vary, but businesses will probably spend several billion dollars and countless hours of employee and executive time in complying with new regulations—time and money that could have been invested in creating better products, improving customer service, or other productive activities.[12] Consumers ultimately pay the price when these added costs are passed along. Even though these new costs are a small fraction of the amount investors lost in the scandals outlined above, it is unfortunate that the unethical behaviour of a small group of executives have raised costs for everyone else.

The news is not all bad, of course. As you read about illegal (or legal but unethical) behaviour on the part of a few managers, bear in mind that the vast majority of businesses are run by ethical managers and staffed by ethical employees whose positive contributions to their communities are sometimes overshadowed by headline-generating scandals. But to be an ethical manager or employee, you need to know about ethics and corporate social responsibility. In this chapter, we will first explain what it means to behave ethically. Next we highlight factors that influence ethical behaviour and provide examples of what some companies are doing to improve their ethical behaviour. We continue by showing how a business's behaviour affects its many stakeholders. In the second part of the chapter, we discuss what it means to be a socially responsible business and explore business's efforts to become more socially responsible.

What Is Ethical Behaviour?

Wanting to be an ethical corporate citizen isn't enough; people in business must actively practise ethical behaviour. In business, besides obeying all laws and regulations, practising good ethics means competing fairly and honestly, communicating truthfully, and not causing harm to others.

Competing Fairly and Honestly

Businesses are expected to compete fairly and honestly and not knowingly deceive, intimidate, or misrepresent customers, competitors, suppliers, clients, or employees. While most companies compete within the boundaries of the law, some knowingly break laws or take questionable steps in their rush to maximize profits and gain a competitive advantage. For example, to get ahead of the competition, some companies have engaged in corporate spying, stealing patents, hiring employees from competitors to gain trade secrets, and eavesdropping electronically. Although businesses need to gather as much strategic information as they can, ethical companies steer clear of such practices.

An example is Air Canada and WestJet, who have been fighting to control air travel in Canada for quite some time. More recently the fight moved into the courtroom with a $220 million lawsuit when Air Canada accused WestJet of using corporate spying to illegally access company information. A former Air Canada employee allowed his employee code to be used thousands of times by WestJet executives to gain valuable information about routes, seats sold, and load factor (percentage of available seats filled). The case was settled out of court. Apparently, Clive Beddoe, chairman of WestJet, and Robert Milton, chairman and CEO of Air Canada, met over dinner and agreed on the terms. WestJet agreed to pay $5.5 million in legal fees to Air Canada and to donate $10 million to a children's charity for their actions.[13]

The headline catching 'Airline Espionage' dispute between WestJet and Air Canada was settled out of court.

In some cases, the line between legal and ethical behaviour is blurred. For instance, breaking into an office to gather sensitive information or crucial documents from the trash is illegal, but once the trash makes its way to a dumpster on public property, it's fair game. Still, rifling through a competitor's trash bins—a practice commonly referred to as *dumpster diving*—is unethical. Companies that practise good ethical behaviour frown on dumpster diving and even take corrective steps to make sure their employees compete fairly and honestly in the workplace.

Communicating Truthfully

Companies that practise good ethical behaviour refrain from issuing false or misleading communications. Publishers Clearing House learned this ethical lesson the hard way. The company paid more than US$34 million to settle lawsuits that claimed it deceived consumers by mailing "you are a winner" notices that looked like cheques for large amounts. The company was also charged with accompanying such notices with deceptive communications that led consumers to believe they could increase their chances of winning a grand prize by purchasing magazine subscriptions. As part of the settlement agreement, Publishers Clearing House promised it would stop mailing simulated cheques and sending consumers misleading information. It also promised

Learning from Business Blunders

OOPS

When KFC launched a new ad campaign that presented fried chicken as an acceptable part of a "healthy, balanced diet" (or at least healthier than other fast-food alternatives), consumer advocates were quick to point out that the bucket of chicken being advertised contained more than 3000 calories. *Advertising Age* magazine attacked the campaign, calling it "laughable." KFC quickly pulled the ads.

WHAT YOU CAN LEARN

Whether people can occasionally enjoy fried chicken as part of a generally healthy diet is probably an issue for dieticians to resolve, but one thing is clear: Showing a 3000-calorie, deep-fried product while talking about healthy diets is only asking for criticism. Many businesses now operate under constant scrutiny, so any suspect product claims are likely to come under close, critical examination from any number of regulators and advocacy groups.[14]

that future mailings would disclose the odds of winning and inform the public that buying subscriptions would not increase their chances of winning.[15]

Not Causing Harm to Others

According to a recent *BusinessWeek* poll, 79 percent of the general population believe that corporate executives put their own personal interests ahead of workers' and shareholders' interests.[16] Placing one's personal welfare above the welfare of the organization can cause harm to others. For instance, every year tens of thousands of people are the victims of investment scams. Lured by promises of high returns, people sink more than a billion dollars annually into non-existent oil wells, gold mines, and other fraudulent operations sold by complete strangers over the telephone and the Internet.[17] Does anyone remember Bre-X? In the late 1990s, many Canadian and international investors bought this stock based on false information about a remarkable gold discovery in Busang, Indonesia. The reports were fabricated and investors lost fortunes. The head geologist mysteriously fell off of a helicopter right at the time that the scandal was being revealed. Nearly a decade after his death, his wife reported that she mysteriously received $25 000 dollars and is certain that he is not dead. Unfortunately, the money that investors lost will not be resurrected in such a miraculous fashion.[18]

Shady companies use other types of scams to take people's money. For example, con artists can fool investors by offering shares in start-up companies that don't exist. They can also misrepresent the potential of an investment while staying within the boundaries of the law. For example, with a little "creative accounting," a business that is in financial trouble can be made to look reasonably good to all but the most educated investors, as the Nortel example illustrated earlier shows.

One major source of fraud is the often-criticized world of telemarketing (see Exhibit 3.1). According to the National Fraud Information Center, the most popular scams include credit card offers, fake cheque scams, advance fee loans, lotteries (false claims that require an upfront tax fee), and telephone slamming (switching consumers' phone service without consent). In terms of regional breakdown, Ontario and Quebec both made the North American top-10 list with 7 percent and 3 percent, respectively, of North American cases.[19]

Some business executives take advantage of the investor by using the company's earnings or resources for personal gain. Perhaps the most common approach is to cheat on expense accounts. Padding invoices and then splitting the overcharge with the supplier is another common ploy. As we saw from the Tyco and Hollinger examples, big executives—with matching large egos—can do a lot more than pad an expense account. Other tactics include selling company secrets to competitors and using confidential, non-public information gained from one's position in a company to benefit from the purchase and sale of stocks. Such **insider trading** is illegal and is closely checked by the appropriate governing body (Ontario Securities Commission, British Columbia Securities Commission, etc.).

insider trading
The use of unpublicized information that an individual gains from the course of his or her job to benefit from fluctuations in the stock market

Another way that businesspeople can harm others is by getting involved in a **conflict of interest** situation. A conflict of interest exists when choosing a course of action will benefit one person's interests at the expense of another, or when an individual chooses a course of action that advances his or her personal interests over those of the employer. For example, a lawyer would find himself in a conflict of interest situation if he represented both the plaintiff and the defendant in a lawsuit. Similarly, independent auditors could be in a conflict of interest situation if their firm also served as the client's consultants, as Chapter 13 discusses in detail.

conflict of interest
A situation in which a business decision may be influenced by the potential for personal gain

L.O. 2

Factors Influencing Ethical Behaviour

Although a number of factors influence the ethical behaviour of businesspeople, three in particular appear to have the greatest impact: cultural differences, knowledge, and organizational behaviour.

| Exhibit 3.1 | The National Consumers League Top-10 Telemarketing Scams |

Beware of the following common telemarketing scams aimed at taking your hard-earned money illegally.

CATEGORY	PERCENTAGE OF ALL COMPLAINTS	AVERAGE LOSS*
1. **Fake Cheque Scams** Consumers paid with phony cheques for work or items sold, instructed to wire money back	31%	$3278
2. **Prizes/Sweepstakes** Requests for payment to claim prizes that never materialize	26%	$2749
3. **Magazine Sales** Misrepresent the cost of subscriptions or pretend to be publisher offering renewals	8%	$77
4. **Scholarships/Grants** Falsely promise to help get scholarships or grants for a fee	6%	$236
5. **Advance Fee Loans** False promises of business or personal loans, even if credit is bad, for a fee upfront	6%	$1164
6. **Lotteries/Lottery Clubs** Requests for payment to claim lottery winnings or to get help to win	5%	$3189
7. **Credit Card Offers** False promises of credit cards, for a fee, even if credit is bad	4%	$237
8. **Phishing** Calls pretending to be from a well-known source, asking to confirm personal information	3%	$387
9. **Work-at-Home Plans** Materials sold on false promises of big profits working at home	1%	$104
10. **Travel/Vacation** Offers of free or discount travel that never materialize	1%	$812

*Loss values given in US dollars.

Source: National Consumers League: http://fraud.org/stats/2006/telemarketing.pdf

IN-CLASS NOTES

What Is Ethical Behaviour?

- *Competing fairly and honestly*: do not knowingly deceive, intimidate, or misrepresent customers, competitors, suppliers, clients, or employees
- *Communicating truthfully*: avoid false or misleading communications
- *Not causing harm to others*: ensure stakeholder interests are protected

_____

_____

_____

_____

_____

_____

_____

Cultural Differences

Globalization exposes businesspeople to a variety of different cultures and business practices. What does it mean for a business to do the right thing in Thailand? In Africa? In Norway? What may be considered unethical in Canada may be an accepted practice in another culture. Consider bribes, for example. In Canada, bribing officials is illegal, but to get something done in Mexico it's common to pay officials *una mordida* ("a small bite"). In China businesses pay *huilu*, and in Russia they pay *vzyatka*.

To crack down on illegal payoffs, industrialized nations have now signed a treaty that makes bribes to foreign officials a criminal offence. Still, bribery won't end just because a treaty has been signed or because it is illegal.

Knowledge

In most cases, a well-informed person is in a position to make better decisions and avoid ethical problems. Making decisions without all of the facts or a clear understanding of the consequences could harm employees, customers, the company, and other stakeholders. As an employee or manager, you are held accountable for your decisions and actions. So be sure to ask questions and gather enough information before making a decision or choosing a course of action. For instance, if a business superior tells you to shred a drawer full of documents, you might want to ask why and inquire whether doing so would be in violation of the law.

Organizational Behaviour

The foundation of an ethical business climate is ethical awareness. Organizations that strongly enforce company codes of conduct and provide ethics training help employees recognize and reason through ethical problems. Similarly, companies with strong ethical practices set a good example for employees to follow. On the other hand, companies that commit unethical acts in the course of doing business open the door for employees to follow suit.

code of ethics
A written statement setting forth the principles that guide an organization's decisions

To avoid such situations, many companies proactively develop programs designed to improve their ethical conduct. Additionally, more than 80 percent of large companies have adopted a written **code of ethics**, which defines the values and principles that should be used to guide decisions (see Exhibit 3.2 for an example). By itself, however, a code of ethics cannot accomplish much. "You can have big goals, but if your employees don't see them, they aren't going to mean anything," says one ethics manager.[20] To be effective, a code must be supported by employee communications efforts, a formal

---

Exhibit 3.2   **Bell Canada Code of Business Conduct**

Bell Canada has set nine key principles of business conduct for its employees, officers, and directors. It is interesting to note the addition of codes #4 and #9 in the past three years.

1. To comply with applicable laws, regulations, and company policies and procedures;
2. to carry out work duties and conduct business relationships with integrity, honesty and fairness;
3. to avoid all conflicts of interest;
4. to avoid acts or omissions that give the appearance of misconduct;
5. to foster a work environment based on trust and respect for all stakeholders of the Bell Canada Enterprises community;
6. to foster a work environment which encourages open communication;
7. to maintain a safe and secure workplace and protect the environment;
8. to sustain a culture in which ethical conduct is recognized, valued and exemplified by us all;
9. to promptly report violations of the Code or non-compliance with applicable laws, regulations, or company policies or procedures.

Source: Code of Business Conduct, Bell Canada website, www.bce.ca

training program, employee commitment to follow it, and a system through which employees can get help with ethically difficult situations.[21]

Like most firms, Petro-Canada has created a code of business conduct for all employees. In addition, Petro-Canada has created a specific code of ethics for senior financial officers to promote honest and ethical conduct, proper disclosure of financial information, and compliance with appropriate laws and rules. After the Enron scandal, energy firms are being watched closely and have responded with increased attention to the ethical questions facing their firms. To guide employees in their day-to-day activities, Petro-Canada has even set up an anonymous ethics telephone hotline available to employees through the company intranet.[22] This practice has swept across the business landscape (see Exhibit 3.2).

Codes of ethics are an important starting point that can be used as a reference. As one ethics expert explains, "If you have an active ethics program in place ahead of time, then bad things shouldn't happen; but if they do happen, it won't hurt you as badly."[23] Perhaps inspired by these guidelines, some companies have created an official position—the ethics officer—to guard morality. Originally hired to oversee corporate conduct—from stealing company pens to endangering the environment to selling company secrets—many ethics officers today function as corporate coaches for ethical decision making. Keep in mind, however, that ethical behaviour starts at the top. The CEO and other senior managers must set the tone for people throughout the company (see the box entitled "Actions Speak Louder than Codes").

As the Petro-Canada example demonstrates, companies that support ethical behaviour can establish a system for reporting unethical or illegal actions at work with an ethics hotline. Companies that value ethics will try to correct reported problems. If a serious problem persists, or in cases where management is involved, an employee can

Actions Speak Louder than Codes

Once you write a code of ethics and establish an ethics hotline, what more does your business need to do? A lot more, according to experts. Some companies develop detailed codes of behaviour and establish ethics hotlines only to pay them lip service. Perhaps that's why 81 percent of top managers believe they use ethics in day-to-day decision making, whereas 43 percent of employees believe managers routinely overlook ethics. When leaders make decisions that clearly show profits winning out over ethics, employees become skeptical and mistrustful—attitudes that lead to unethical behaviour.

To avoid the lip-service trap, support your ethics programs with a dose of reality:

■ *Inspire concretely.* Tell employees how they will personally benefit from participating in ethics initiatives. People respond better to personal benefits than to company benefits.

■ *Acknowledge reality.* Admit errors. Discuss what went right and what went wrong. Solicit employee opinion: What do you think? What's your view? Act on those opinions.

■ *Incorporate reality into your solutions.* Use practical strategies that can be accomplished in the time

available. Obtain real feedback by asking employees to name three realities the company isn't facing, three reasons the company won't meet its goals, and three competitive weaknesses the company exhibits in the marketplace.

■ *Be honest.* Tell employees what you know as well as what you don't know. Talk openly about real results, not about what you'd like them to be. Accept criticism—and listen to it.

Make personal benefits, company errors, and tactical solutions more concrete by being straightforward and specific. By acknowledging the realities in every situation, you turn your words into action and build trust with your employees.[24]

Questions for Critical Thinking

1. How does building trust encourage employees to be more ethical?

2. Some companies ask job candidates to take pre-employment tests such as drug tests or lie-detector tests. Does such testing build trust with potential employees? Explain.

Exhibit 3.3	**Doing the Right Thing**

According to a recent survey of 1002 randomly selected adults, when it comes to ethics in the workplace, most employees try to do the right thing.

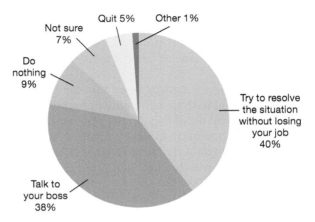

If you found out your employer was doing something contrary to your ethical standards, you would:

Quit 5%
Other 1%
Not sure 7%
Do nothing 9%
Try to resolve the situation without losing your job 40%
Talk to your boss 38%

speak up in an ethically conscious company. *Whistle-blowing* is an employee's disclosure to the media or authorities of illegal, unethical, or harmful practices by the company. But whistle-blowing can bring with it high costs: a public accusation of wrongdoing hurts the business's reputation, requires attention from managers who must investigate the accusations, and damages employee morale. Moreover, whistle-blowers risk being fired or demoted, and they often suffer career setbacks, financial strain, and emotional stress. The fear of such negative repercussions may allow unethical or illegal practices to go unreported. Still, all things considered, many employees do the right thing, as Exhibit 3.3[25] suggests.

According to a recent poll conducted by the Environics Research Group, an overwhelming majority—89 percent—want the government to create new laws to improve protection for whistle-blowers.[26] Many firms today have incorporated a whistle-blowing clause in their code of conduct. At the Bank of Montreal, employees are instructed that they can file reports at the FirstPrinciples website and are protected under the Whistle-Blower Protection and Prohibition against Retaliation clause.[27] Despite such policies, individual behaviour is usually guided by the individual's perception of the firm's true commitment to upholding rules of conduct.

IN-CLASS NOTES

Keys to Building an Ethical Organization
- Top-management commitment
- Code of ethics
- Ethics officer
- Reporting system
  - Hotlines

How Do You Make Ethical Decisions?

L.O. 3

Determining what's ethically acceptable in any given situation can be difficult. One approach is to measure each act against certain absolute standards. In Canada, these standards are often grounded in teachings such as "Do not lie" and "Do not steal." Another place to look for ethical guidance is the law. If saying, writing, or doing something is clearly illegal, you have no decision to make—you must obey the law.

Even though legal considerations will resolve some ethical questions, you'll often need to rely on your own judgment and principles. When trying to decide the most ethical course of action, you might apply the golden rule: Do unto others as you would have them do unto you. Or you might examine your motives: If your intent is honest, the decision is ethical; however, if your intent is to mislead or manipulate, the decision is unethical. You might also consider asking yourself a series of questions, such as the following:

L.O. 4

1. Is the decision legal? (Does it break any laws?)
2. Is it balanced? (Is it fair to all concerned?)
3. Can you live with it? (Does it make you feel good about yourself?)
4. Is it feasible? (Will it actually work in the real world?)

When you need to determine the ethics of any situation, these questions will get you started. You may also want to consider the needs of stakeholders, and you may want to investigate one or more philosophical approaches, such as those mentioned in the third column of Exhibit 3.4. These approaches are not mutually exclusive alternatives. On the contrary, most businesspeople combine them to reach decisions that will

Exhibit 3.4   **Itemized Lists for Making Ethical Decisions**

Companies with the most success in establishing an ethical structure are those that balance their approach to making decisions.[28]

IS THE DECISION ETHICAL?	DOES IT RESPECT STAKEHOLDERS?	DOES IT FOLLOW A PHILOSOPHICAL APPROACH?
IS IT LEGAL?	**WILL OUTSIDERS APPROVE?**	**IS IT A UTILITARIAN DECISION?**
Does it violate civil law?	Does it benefit customers, suppliers, investors, public officials, media representatives, and community members?	Does it produce the greatest good for the greatest number of people?
Does it violate company policy?		**DOES IT UPHOLD INDIVIDUAL, LEGAL, AND HUMAN RIGHTS?**
IS IT BALANCED?	**WILL SUPERVISORS APPROVE?**	
Is it fair to all concerned, in both the short and the long term?	Did you provide management with information that is honest and accurate?	Does it protect people's own interests?
CAN YOU LIVE WITH IT?	**WILL EMPLOYEES APPROVE?**	Does it respect the privacy of others and their right to express their opinion?
Does it make you feel good about yourself?	Will it affect employees in a positive way?	Does it allow people to act in a way that conforms to their religious or moral beliefs?
Would you feel good reading about it in a newspaper?	Does it handle personal information about employees discreetly?	**DOES IT UPHOLD THE PRINCIPLES OF JUSTICE?**
IS IT FEASIBLE?	Did you give proper credit for work performed by others?	
Does it work in the real world?		Does it treat people fairly and impartially?
Will it improve your competitive position?		Does it apply rules consistently?
Is it affordable?		Does it ensure that people who harm others are held responsible and make restitution?
Can it be accomplished in the time available?		

satisfy as many stakeholders as possible without violating anyone's rights or treating anyone unjustly.

When making ethical decisions, keep in mind that most ethical situations can be classified into two general types: ethical dilemmas and ethical lapses. An **ethical dilemma** is a situation in which one must choose between two conflicting but arguably valid sides. All ethical dilemmas have a common theme: the conflict between the rights of two or more important groups of people. The second type of situation is an **ethical lapse**, in which an individual makes a decision that is clearly wrong, such as divulging trade secrets to a competitor. A company faces an ethical dilemma when it must decide whether to continue operating a production facility that is suspected, but not proven, to be unsafe. A company makes an ethical lapse when it continues to operate the facility even after the site has been proven unsafe. Other examples of ethical lapses include inflating prices for certain customers, hiring employees from competitors to gain trade secrets, selling trade secrets to unfriendly foreign governments, switching someone's long-distance service without their consent (*slamming*), slipping unauthorized charges into phone bills (*cramming*), and using insider information to profit on the sale of company securities.

ethical dilemma
A situation in which both sides of an issue can be supported with valid arguments

ethical lapse
A situation in which an individual makes a decision that is morally wrong, illegal, or unethical

PERSPECTIVES ON CORPORATE SOCIAL RESPONSIBILITY

Conflicts over ethics and social responsibility are often fuelled by differing perspectives on the issues at hand. People with equally good intentions can arrive at different conclusions based on their perspective about the role of business in society. These perspectives can be grouped into three general categories:

1. The only responsibility of business is to make money
2. Businesses have a larger responsibility to society, and ethical behaviour will lead to financial success
3. Businesses must balance social responsibility and financial objectives

The Traditional Perspective: The Business of Business Is Making Money

The classic perspective on this issue states that the sole responsibility of business is to make money for the investors who put their money at risk to fund companies. In the nineteenth and early twentieth centuries, the main view among industrialists was that business had only one responsibility: to make a profit. "The public be damned," said railroad tycoon William Vanderbilt, "I'm working for the shareholders."[29] *Caveat emptor*—"Let the buyer beware"—was the rule of the day. If you bought a product, you paid the price and took the consequences.

In 1970, influential economist Milton Friedman updated this perspective, saying "There is only one social responsibility of business: to use its resources and engage in activities designed to increase its profits so long as it stays within the rules of the game, which is to say, engages in open and free competition without deception or fraud." Friedman argued that only real people, not corporations, could have responsibilities and that dividends and profit maximization would allow the shareholders to contribute to the charities and causes of their choice.[30] As he saw it, the social responsibility of business was to provide jobs and pay taxes.

The issue that is sometimes overlooked by critics of this perspective of business is that companies cannot offer decent wages; provide health care, child care, and community assistance; and fund philanthropic endeavours if they don't make enough money. The benefits of a healthy economy are numerous, from lower crime rates to better education, but socially healthy economies cannot exist without financially healthy companies, because business is the primary generator of wealth in the economy.

The Contemporary Perspective: Ethics Pays

L.O. 5

Most people (as much as 95 percent of the population, according to one survey) now reject the notion that a corporation's only role is to make money.[31] A new view of corporate social responsibility has replaced the classic view in the minds of many people both inside and outside business. This perspective states that businesses not only have a responsibility to society, but that doing good deeds for society helps companies do well for themselves. In other words, ethics pays. This line of thinking was best captured by a *New York Times* headline: "Do Good? Do Business? No, Do Both!" In recent years, GE has embraced this motto as CEO Jeffrey Immelt has launched an ambitious environmental strategy called "Ecomagination." The early returns are quite positive; the company earned $12 billion from its eco-products in 2006, and this figure is expected to grow to $20 billion annually by 2010.[32]

Companies that support this line of thinking link the pursuit of socially responsible goals with their overall strategic planning. Such socially responsible companies are just as dedicated to building a viable, profitable business as they are to adhering to a mission—and they think strategically to make both happen. Increasingly, companies and employees are caring about their communities and want to be a part of the greater cause (see Exhibit 3.5[33]). They want to be good corporate citizens while also satisfying shareholders' needs for a return on their investment. Still, finding the right balance can be challenging.

The Ethical Funds Company is an example of a firm that has successfully merged these two goals. The company was launched in 1986 as the first socially responsible mutual fund company in Canada. The goal was quite clear: help investors earn a good return on investment without sacrificing ethical or socially responsible duties. In addition to examining financial criteria in their investment decision making, The Ethical Funds Company assesses a company's social and environmental performance using the criteria set out in their core values (see Exhibit 3.6). The firm continues to exclude companies who are primarily involved in

GE is investing heavily in its "Ecomagination" program, which is aimed at capitalizing on the green technologies of the future. California Governor, Arnold Schwarzenegger, attended GE's "Ecomagination" news conference.

Exhibit 3.5   **Civic Responsibilities**

Executives generally support the notion that companies should serve their communities and be socially responsible citizens in a number of ways.

PERCENTAGE OF EXECUTIVES WHO "STRONGLY AGREE" OR "AGREE" THAT COMPANIES SHOULD:	PERCENTAGE
Be environmentally responsible	100
Be ethical in operations	100
Earn profits	96
Employ local residents	94
Pay taxes	94
Encourage and support employee volunteering	89
Contribute money and leadership to charities	85
Be involved in economic development	75
Be involved in public education	73
Involve community representatives in business decisions that affect the community	62
Target a proportion of purchasing toward local vendors	61
Help improve quality of life for low-income populations	54

Exhibit 3.6   **The Ethical Funds Company Core Values**

The Ethical Funds Company bases its entire Sustainable Investing Program efforts on three core values.

■ **Respect for the environment**
We believe that ecosystems have intrinsic value to all of us, and are essential to human well-being and growth. We encourage all companies to reduce adverse impacts, adopt a precautionary approach to the environment, and help restore ecological health.

■ **Respect for stakeholders**
Shareholders, employees, customers, suppliers, and communities all share in the successes and failures of an organization's business endeavours. It's important that companies offer solid financial performance while also contributing positively to the local economy, demonstrating good ethics, governance, and accountability. We also encourage companies to develop progressive approaches to incorporate stakeholder priorities into their strategies and operations.

■ **Respect for human rights**
We want companies to acknowledge their responsibility to protect and promote human and labour rights within their spheres of influence. This includes avoiding complicity in human rights abuses, helping to reduce poverty, improving health and safety for workers, contributing to civil society, and encouraging the peaceful resolution of conflict.

Source: The Ethical Funds Company website, https://www.ethicalfunds.com/en/Investor/ChangingTheWorld/HowWeWork/Pages/CoreValus.aspx

weapons manufacturing, tobacco farming, and nuclear power generation. The good corporate image helps distinguish The Ethical Funds Company and has had a positive impact on marketing and public relations. It is hard to make a name in this competitive industry, but their clear ethical positioning helps to attract a significant, growing number of environmentally friendly, socially responsible clients. Acting responsibly can really pay off.

Exactly how much can businesses contribute to social concerns? This is a difficult decision for most companies because they have limited resources. They must allocate their resources to a number of goals, such as upgrading facilities and equipment, developing new products, marketing existing products, and rewarding employee efforts, in addition to contributing to social causes. This juggling act is a challenge that every business faces. If a company consistently ignores its stakeholders, it will suffer and eventually fold. For example, if the company disregards society's needs, voters will demand laws to limit the offensive business activities, consumers who feel their needs and values are being ignored will spend their money on a competitor's products, investors who are unhappy with the company's performance will invest elsewhere, and employees whose needs are not met will become unproductive or will quit and find other jobs. As Exhibit 3.7 demonstrates, stakeholders' needs sometimes conflict. In such cases, businesses must decide which stakeholders should be served first—society, consumers, suppliers, government, investors, or employees?

An Emerging Perspective: Dynamically Balancing Ethics and Profits

Some business theorists now promote a third view: Ethics needs to be one of the cornerstones of business, but in the real world profits and ethics are often at odds. Managers need to evaluate every situation within the context of the organization's "moral personality." In some cases, the ethical approach will pay off financially, but in others it won't.[34] The decision by 3M to discontinue Scotchgard Fabric Protector is a

Exhibit 3.7 **Balancing Business and Stakeholders' Rights**

Balancing the individual needs and interests of a company's stakeholders is one of management's most difficult tasks.

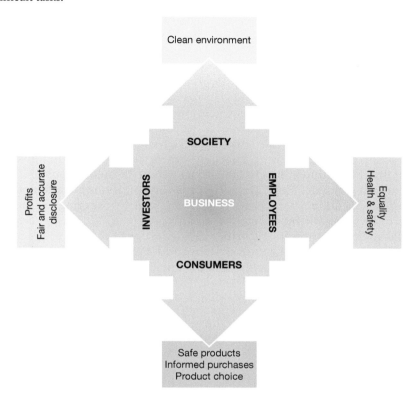

noteworthy example of this perspective. The government did not order 3M to stop manufacturing products with perfluorooctane sulfonate (PFOs), and there was no solid evidence that PFOs harmed humans. But when traces of the chemical showed up in humans, 3M decided to pull the plug on the product and not wait until scientific

---

IN-CLASS NOTES

Perspectives on Corporate Social Responsibility

There are three common perspectives on the role of business in society:

1. The only responsibility of business is to make money

2. Businesses have a larger responsibility to society, and ethical behaviour will lead to financial success

3. Businesses must balance social responsibility and financial objectives

_____

_____

_____

_____

_____

_____

_____

_____

_____

evidence linked PFOs to a disease. This decision cost 3M $500 million in annual sales because the company did not have a substitute product to fill Scotchgard's void.[35] Even though the decision had painful financial implications, it fit the moral personality that 3M's leaders want to maintain for the organization. After addressing the problem, 3M released a new generation of PFO-free Scotchguard.

L.O. 6

BUSINESS'S EFFORTS TO INCREASE SOCIAL RESPONSIBILITY

As The Ethical Funds Company, 3M and Telus demonstrate, socially responsible businesses can make a difference in the world. Some work to curb child abuse or domestic violence; others provide generous benefits packages for employees; still others have strong recycling programs to keep the environment clean. Those that give back to society are finding that their efforts can lead to a more favourable public image and stronger employee morale. Thus, more and more organizations are attempting to be socially responsible citizens by conducting a *social audit*, by engaging in *cause-related marketing*, or by being *philanthropic*.

social audit
An assessment of a company's performance in the area of social responsibility

philanthropic
A descriptive term for altruistic actions such as donating money, time, goods, or services to charitable, humanitarian, or educational institutions

pollution
Damage or destruction of the natural environment caused by the discharge of harmful substances

A **social audit** is a systematic evaluation and reporting of the company's social performance. The report typically includes objective information about how the company's activities affect its various stakeholders. Companies can also engage in *cause-related marketing*, in which a portion of product sales helps support worthy causes. For example, Johnson & Johnson gives the World Wildlife Fund a cut from sales of a special line of children's toiletries. Similarly, PeaceWorks is a snack-food company that encourages joint business ventures among people of different backgrounds who live in volatile regions of the world. One of the company's product lines is Spraté, which are uniquely flavoured spreads produced in Israel by a Jewish-owned company that buys all of its ingredients from Israeli Arabs and Palestinians. When consumers buy a jar of Spraté, they not only get a tasty spread but also support the peace process in the Middle East.[36]

Some companies choose to be socially responsible by being **philanthropic**; that is, they donate money, time, goods, or services to charitable, humanitarian, or educational institutions. Telus has donated $76 million to various charities in the past six years.[37]

Responsibility toward Society and the Environment

Mountain Equipment Co-op (MEC) sends a portion of sales to environmental concerns. The company serves outdoor enthusiasts who appreciate nature and have a vested interest in the environment. But for many firms, environmental issues exemplify the difficulty that businesses encounter when they try to reconcile conflicting interests. Society needs as little pollution as possible from businesses, but producing quality products to satisfy customers' needs can cause pollution to some degree. Business executives try to strike a balance by making environmental management a formal part of their business strategy—along with quality, profit, safety, and other daily business operations.

Merging industrialism with environmentalism is not an easy task, but some companies have stepped up to the plate. For example, Canadian Tire launched an annual Community Environmental Award program to support projects that improve the environment in local communities served by the retailer. In recent years, these programs have included tree planting in Cochrane, Alberta; a beach cleanup initiative in Saint John, New Brunswick; a lake cleanup in Rouyn-Noranda, Quebec; a schoolyard naturalization program in Corner Brook, Newfoundland; and a river shore cleanup and naturalization in Windsor, Ontario.

The Pervasiveness of Pollution

For decades, environmentalists have warned businesses and the general public about the dangers of **pollution** (the contamination of the natural environment by the discharge of harmful substances). Our air, water, and land can easily be tainted by industrial

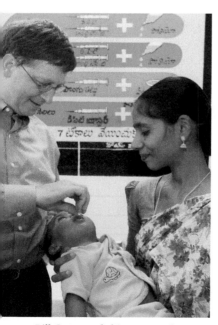

Bill Gates made his name as the co-founder and guiding force behind Microsoft, but in recent years he and his wife Melinda (not pictured) have become well-known for their generous contributions to worldwide health care and education.

waste, aircraft and motor vehicle emissions, and a number of chemicals that spill into the environment. Moreover, the pollution in any one element can easily taint the others. For instance, when emissions from coal-burning factories and electric utility plants react with air, they can cause acid rain, which damages lakes and forests. No business is immune from pollution issues, either. Internet-based companies such as Yahoo! or Google strike some people as "clean" because there seems to be no visible pollution, but the Internet has a big appetite for electricity, and the generation of electricity nearly always affects the environment. For example, two-thirds of the electricity used in the United States is generated by burning coal, oil, or natural gas.[39]

Government Efforts to Reduce Pollution

Widespread concern for the environment has been growing since the 1960s with the popularization of **ecology**, the study of the balance of nature. The new *Canadian Environmental Protection Act* entitles companies, individuals, and government agencies to request independent reviews of Environmental Protection Compliance Orders (EPCOs). According to Environmental Protection Review Canada, "since 1999, EPCOs allow enforcement officers to act immediately to stop suspected illegal activities, as well as to prevent or remedy an action."[40] International treaties have recognized the importance of environmental concerns, too. For example, the North American Agreement on Environmental Cooperation (NAAEC) was signed when the North American Free Trade Agreement came into effect: "The key objectives of the NAAEC are to promote sustainable development, encourage pollution prevention and enhance compliance with environmental laws."[41] Agreements and laws such as these should help eliminate the risk of environmental disasters like the Sydney Tar Ponds—700 000 tonnes of toxic sludge as a result of 100 years of runoff from a local steel mill.[42]

But our love affair with the automobile has slowed progress toward cleaner air. Three of the most popular types of vehicles—pickup trucks, minivans, and sport-utility vehicles—are considered light trucks by government regulators and aren't required to meet the more stringent pollution standards set for passenger cars. The situation is not helped by the runaway success of gas guzzlers such as the Hummer H2 and the Cadillac Escalade, or moves like the one Subaru recently made to get

Through its Foundation for Families, Canadian Tire has donated over $27 million to charitable organizations that help ensure that life's basic needs are met for families in local communities.[38]

L.O. 7

ecology
Study of the relationships among living things in the water, air, and soil, their environments, and the nutrients that support them

IN-CLASS NOTES

Business Efforts to Improve Social Responsibility

- *Social audit*: transparent reviews force companies to find and correct problem areas
- *Philanthropy*: donating money, time, goods, or services
- *Cause-related marketing*: donating a portion of sales to a worthy cause

_____

_____

_____

_____

_____

_____

_____

A modern economy needs metals, minerals, and fuels, but the effort to extract these materials can create unsafe conditions for nearby populations.

its popular Outback sedan reclassified as a small truck to avoid passenger-car fuel-efficiency requirements.[43]

Progress has been made in reducing water pollution, though. Both government and private businesses have made major expenditures to treat and reuse waste water, as well as to upgrade sewage systems. Unfortunately, the war on toxic waste has not been quite as successful. Government attempts to force businesses to clean up certain sites have yielded more disappointing results. At some sites, the groundwater may never be restored to drinking-water purity again.

The Kyoto Protocol and Clean Air Initiatives

In recent years, greenhouse gas emissions have been a hot topic in the political arena. You would think this would mean that there has been significant progress in this area, but the results seem to indicate something different.

In December 1997, 160 countries met in Kyoto, Japan, to discuss the reduction of greenhouse gas (GHG) emissions and agree on specific reduction targets. This was a landmark event with firm commitments to follow. In December 2002, Canada's ratification of the Kyoto Protocol marked another step in a very long road toward a cleaner environment. Under the Kyoto Protocol, Canada agreed to reduce GHG emissions to 6 percent below 1990 levels by 2012. The Protocol took effect on February 16, 2005, after it met key conditions and was ratified by a minimum of 55 countries, covering at least 55 percent of the emissions addressed by the protocol. Making a commitment is one thing, but taking concrete action is quite another. So far, the results are not very positive; in fact they are a bit embarrassing for a country symbolized by the maple leaf (see Exhibit 3.8). In addition, some countries backed away from Kyoto, most notably the United States and Australia.

So at the very least an undeniable direction has been set, right? Certainly the past few years have been filled with discussions and proposals, but politicians have yet

---

Exhibit 3.8   **Climate Scores in Black and White: Failing Grades for Canada**

The United States is the highest emitter of greenhouses gases with the highest per capita rate. Canada has nothing to be proud of with an equally dismal per capita rate. Numbers represent tonnes of CO_2 per capita, with G8 countries in bold. The numbers on the right represent changes in emissions between 1990 and 2004 (* denotes 1990 and 2005).

Country	Tonnes CO_2 per capita	Change
Canada	24	▲ +27%
United States*	24	▲ +16.3%
Russia*	15	▼ −28.7%
Germany*	12	▼ −18.4%
Britain*	11	▲ +12.1%
Japan	11	▼ −14.8%
South Africa	11	▲ +29.7%
Italy*	10	▲ +12.1%
France*	9	▼ −1.8%
Brazil	5	▲ +40.7%
China	5	▲ +72.7%
Mexico	5	▲ +38.6%
India	2	▲ +57.5%

Source: Martin Mittelstaedt, "Canada's Green Record Beyond Pale," *Globe and Mail*, 4 June 2007, A4.

to come to an agreement on how to proceed. With the election of the Conservative government in 2006, Canada's position on the Kyoto Protocol officially changed. Government officials now say that there is no chance that Canada will meet their Kyoto commitments. Instead, the Conservatives tabled Bill C-30, the *Clean Air Act*, in November 2006. The proposed legislation sets intensity-based targets, meaning that environmental emissions would be relative to the economic output of various industries (that is, as production increases in an industry, so do the allowable emissions).[44] If companies exceed the targets set out in the Bill, they would be forced to pay between $20 to $30 for each additional tonne of GHGs. This Bill has been criticized by the opposition, who want major alterations more in line with the Kyoto Protocol. Many critics say that this Bill is, in fact, already dead.[45]

Beyond Kyoto, the international community is searching for consensus, but the EU is pushing in one direction and the United States in another. At a recent G8 summit meeting a tentative deal was struck between these eight powerful nations to cut emissions in half by 2050. Of course, critics were not impressed by the fact that there were no firm targets set.[46] What does this all mean? Governments have come to a conclusion that the issue matters and that their citizens care, but now they have to figure out how to deal with the problem without causing economic hardship or losing votes.

Not all the news is bad, though—some real initial efforts have been made. Progress has been reported in many industries, including the oil and gas sector. Ottawa managed to avoid a messy fight with the auto sector, reaching a voluntary deal where auto makers agreed to cut GHG emissions from vehicles by 5.3 million tonnes by the year 2010. This goal will be achieved through more fuel-efficient technologies, more hybrid vehicles, improved technology in areas like vehicle air conditioning, and joint advertising deals with Ottawa to encourage people to switch to more fuel-efficient cars.[47] Real action like this is more important than ever, and the government is trying to take steps toward a greener environment (see the box entitled "Banning Light Bulbs: Greener Days Ahead").

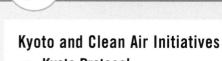

IN-CLASS NOTES

Kyoto and Clean Air Initiatives
- **Kyoto Protocol**
  - Canada agreed to reduce GHG emissions to 6 percent below 1990 levels by 2012
  - In 2007, Canada was above 1990 levels by 27 percent
  - Government officials now say there is no chance Canada will meet their Kyoto commitments
- Additional agreements are being negotiated to deal with GHGs

Banning Light Bulbs: Greener Days Ahead

No, we are not heading into the Dark Ages. According to a recent announcement, traditional light bulbs will be banned by 2012. In their place will be more energy-efficient products such as compact fluorescents and halogen light bulbs. Traditional 60-watt light bulbs are replaced with 15-watt compact fluorescent bulbs that provide an equivalent light source with reduced energy consumption and a longer life. Many people have already begun to make the environmentally friendly change.

LIGHT BULB MATH

Light bulbs are often used as a symbol to display the emergence of a great idea. So is this new legislation a good idea? Let's examine a few important questions:

Q: How many households are there in Canada?

A: Approximately 12 million households.

Q: How many light bulbs does that represent?

A: If each household replaces 16 light bulbs it would amount to 192 million light bulbs.

Q: What impact, if any, would that have on greenhouse gas emissions?

A: It would reduce GHG emissions by 6.3 million tonnes per year—the same as removing 1 million cars from the road.

Who knew? The lowly light bulb is taking its place in the fight for a greener environment. Now you can change your light bulbs and go fire up your SUV with a guilt-free grin. You get the picture—even small changes can make a big difference.

Of course, every piece of legislation that restricts access or forces a change is greeted by resistance or concern, especially from those in the industry being affected. That is not the case for the Montreal-based Globe Electric Company, though. CEO Edward Weinstein says that the company got a head start in the North American market a few years ago when it observed the trends in Europe and Asia and invested heavily to establish its presence as a leader in energy-efficient lighting. The company created its Globe Enersaver brand and was confident that the North American market would catch up with more energy-efficient parts of the world. This consciousness is being accelerated as the environmental debate moves more and more to the forefront and governments begin to legislate on the issue. Consumers see new products, some companies see problems, but the smart companies see opportunities just ahead of the curve and take advantage.[48]

Questions for Critical Thinking

1. Do you believe that governments should force people and companies to take environmentally friendly actions? Do you think incentive programs or energy-saving rebates are more appropriate?

2. How can companies like Globe Electric take advantage of such legislation in their marketing efforts for the mutual benefits of the firm and the environment?

The Business Effort to Reduce Pollution

While some companies must be pressured by the federal government or private citizens to stop polluting the environment, others do a good job of regulating themselves (see the box entitled "Ben & Jerry's: A Double Scoop of Irony?"). For example, Cascades, a pulp and paper company, is showing some leadership. It has the lowest water consumption of any Canadian company in the industry, and it has also gradually abandoned coal and heavy oil in favour of less polluting energy sources. Furthermore, Cascades recently worked with Greenpeace in changing several aspects of its manufacturing process for bathroom tissue. In so doing, Greenpeace has included the tissue in its "green products" category.[49] Zellers was recognized with a Natural Resources Canada award for its energy reduction in existing buildings. In 2006, Zellers reported savings of 61 488 gigajoules, which is the equivalent of taking 1300 cars off the road or planting 154 200 trees and growing them for 10 years.[50] Like Cascades and Zellers, many companies are addressing environmental concerns by taking the following actions:[51]

- Considering environmental issues a part of everyday business and operating decisions
- Accepting environmental staff members as full-fledged partners in improving the company's competitiveness
- Measuring environmental performance
- Linking compensation to environmental performance
- Determining the long-term environmental costs *before* such costs occur
- Considering environmental impact in the product development process
- Challenging suppliers to improve environmental performance
- Conducting environmental training and awareness programs

In addition to these actions, companies are reducing the amount of solid waste they send to landfills by implementing companywide recycling programs. Companies and individuals alike generate enormous amounts of solid waste, much of which is electronic waste (computer monitors, circuit boards, and so on), which emit toxic

Ben & Jerry's: A Double Scoop of Irony?

Few companies have a better reputation for environmental and social responsibility than Ben & Jerry's, the folksy ice cream company. Since its origins in 1978, the company has donated 7.5 percent of pre-tax profits to various causes, including saving the family farm, promoting world peace, saving the world's rainforests, and keeping French nuclear testing out of the South Pacific. Even as the company grew, it managed to stay focused on Ben Cohen and Jerry Greenfield's mission and their intent to be a different kind of company. Cohen and Greenfield brought in professional management to balance the desire to do good with the need to maintain financial viability. To the surprise of many, the vision even survived a corporate buyout in 1999, when the company was purchased by Unilever, a $45 billion global food giant. Today, Ben & Jerry's continues to put its money where its mouth is, promoting a variety of admirable causes.

Here's the catch. Well, three of them, actually. First, even with the company's high standards of environmental responsibility—and you'd have to look far and wide to find a company with higher standards—it can be hard to make a case that the production of ice cream is an environmentally friendly process. For instance, ice cream requires refrigeration at every step of the manufacturing and distribution process, and refrigeration requires large amounts of electricity. And while the company has done a great job of removing chlorine and other nasty elements from the production of its ice cream cartons, those cartons are delivered to your local grocery store by fume-spewing diesel trucks. Second, obesity is now considered a huge health problem, and most of Ben & Jerry's products are high in fat and high in calories. Third, all of this discussion concerns products that no one really needs. After all, this is ice cream, not medical supplies or drinking water.

Ben & Jerry's may well be the most environmentally and socially responsible ice cream company in history, but that still leaves the question: Should *anybody* be in the ice cream business?[52]

Questions for Critical Thinking
1. Could Ben & Jerry's environmental stance be considered hypocritical, given the electricity demands of the ice cream industry? Why or why not?
2. How might Ben & Jerry's respond to the three issues discussed above while still remaining true to its philosophical roots?

Electronics recycling centres like this one near the Lianjiang River in China are releasing toxic pollutants, environmental groups say.

consumerism
A movement that pressures businesses to consider consumer needs and interests

pollutants.[53] Some companies are using high-temperature incineration to destroy hazardous wastes or are giving their wastes to other companies that can use them in their manufacturing processes.

Businesses that recognize the link between environmental performance and financial well-being are discovering that spending now to prevent pollution can end up saving more money down the road (by reducing cleanup costs, litigation expense, and production costs). From building eco-industrial parks to improving production efficiency, these activities are a part of the *green marketing* movement in which companies distinguish themselves by using fewer packaging materials, recycling more waste, and developing new products that are easier on the environment. In addition to ethical and financial concerns, green marketing efforts can also help companies build goodwill with customers, communities, and other stakeholders.

Responsibility toward Consumers

The 1960s activism that awakened business to its environmental responsibilities also gave rise to **consumerism**, a movement that put pressure on businesses to consider consumer needs and interests. Consumerism prompted many businesses to create consumer affairs departments to handle customer complaints. It also prompted federal and provincial agencies to set up bureaus to offer consumer information, assistance, and protection and an outlet to file complaints. In Canada, the Competition Bureau is an agency that gives consumers an avenue of complaint when a company policy or action violates the *Competition Act, Consumer Packaging and Labelling Act, Textile Labelling Act,* or *Precious Metals Marking Act.* South of the border, a key moment for the consumerism movement can be traced to President John F. Kennedy, who announced a "bill of rights" for consumers, laying the foundation for a wave of consumer-oriented legislation. These rights include the right to safe products, the right to be informed, the right to choose, and the right to be heard. This movement also led to the creation of non-profit organizations like the Automobile Protection Association (APA), which offers an annual Canadian used car guide to its members along with the very popular *Lemon-Aid* review of the industry's worst cars.

The Right to Safe Products

The Canadian Standards Association (CSA) is a membership-based, non-profit organization that serves government, industry, and consumers. The CSA develops standards and codes that help ensure reasonable safety requirements, and its seal is recognized as a comforting symbol.[54] The federal government along with the various provincial governments impose safety standards that range from food inspection to drug approval to emission controls. Theoretically, companies that do not comply with these rules are forced to take corrective action. The threat of liability suits and declining sales motivates many companies to meet safety standards. However, many consumer advocates complain that some unsafe products still slip through the cracks.

The Right to Be Informed

Consumers have a right to know what is in a product and how to use it. They also have a right to know the sales price of goods or services and the details of any purchase contracts. For example, the *Consumer Packaging and Labelling Act* regulates everything from units of measurement to the representation of the number of servings to pictures on food labels.[55] If a product is sufficiently dangerous, a warning label is required by law, as in the case of cigarettes. However, warning labels can be a mixed blessing for consumers. To some extent, it protects the manufacturer from product liability suits, but the label may not stop people from using the product or from using it incorrectly. The billions of dollars per year still spent on cigarettes illustrate this point.

The Canadian government, through the Competition Bureau, also works to ensure that consumers are accurately informed through transparent information. For example, the Forzani Group agreed to pay a record $1.7 million to settle a federal Competition Bureau investigation of their Sport Chek and Sport Mart stores. The bureau accused Forzani of significantly inflating regular prices to make sales appear larger. Forzani is

Technologies That Are Revolutionizing Business

LOCATION AND TRACKING TECHNOLOGIES

Science fiction movies sometimes feature amazing technologies that can track people anywhere in the universe. They might still be amazing, but they're no longer science fiction; a variety of tracking devices can now keep tabs on both people and products.

HOW THEY'RE CHANGING BUSINESS

Location and tracking technologies cover a wide range of capabilities, some already in use and some just now hitting the market. Here are some of the more common uses and a few examples:

- *Personal security.* Parents and caregivers can use tracking technologies to check on children, elderly relatives, and medical patients.

- *Inventory management.* Radio frequency identification (RFID) tags combine tiny computer chips with small antennas. Retail giant Wal-Mart is moving to require all its suppliers to attach RFID tags to incoming merchandise to improve inventory management.

- *Location-based services and marketing campaigns.* Customers who are on the move can benefit from instant information that reflects their immediate shopping needs—and marketers would love to offer the right information at the right time, including notifications of nearby sales.

These new capabilities present considerable technological, social, and ethical issues; expect to hear plenty of discussion about them in the coming years. For instance, privacy advocates launched a boycott campaign (www.boycottbenetton.org) when a supplier to the Italian apparel retailer Benetton announced that the company planned to embed RFID tags in its clothing items. (The premature announcement was denied by the company.)[56]

WHERE YOU CAN LEARN MORE

This is a broad and dynamic field, with new information available nearly every day. Here are two of the many sources online: MIT's Auto-ID Lab, autoidlabs .mit.edu, and *RFID Journal*, www.rfidjournal.com.

---

threatening to sue the bureau for its handling of the case; the company has agreed to pay the fine but admits no wrongdoing in the process. The previous record for such a case in Canada was imposed on Suzy Shier for $1 million.[57] The bureau also pursued Sears Canada for pitching exaggerated savings on automobile tires in its advertisements. Sears is examining its options after the tribunal ruled against it. While the penalty has not yet been decided, it is expected to be in the area of $500 000.[58]

The Right to Choose Which Products to Buy

The number of products available to consumers is truly amazing. But how far should the right to choose extend? Are we entitled to choose products that are potentially harmful, such as cigarettes, liquor, or guns? To what extent are we entitled to learn about these products? Consumer groups and businesses are concerned about these questions, but no clear answers have emerged. Some consumer groups say that government does not do enough. For example, when a product has been proven to be dangerous, does the fact that it is legal justify its sale? Should the government take measures to make the product illegal, or should consumers be allowed to decide for themselves?

Scientists determined long ago that the tar and nicotine in tobacco are both harmful and addictive. Cigarette legislation has become increasingly aggressive over the years. Anti-tobacco legislation restricts tobacco advertising and has now removed the traditional domain of event sponsorship from the hands of tobacco manufacturers. Furthermore, the graphic warning labels that became law in June 2000 ushered in a new age, as Canada became the first nation to implement such strong labelling and reporting measures. You are no doubt familiar with the warning labels that Health Canada forces tobacco manufacturers to include on their packages, such as: "Cigarettes hurt babies," "Idle but deadly," "Cigarettes cause strokes," and "Tobacco use makes you impotent."[59] Even so, consumers can still purchase cigarettes in the marketplace.

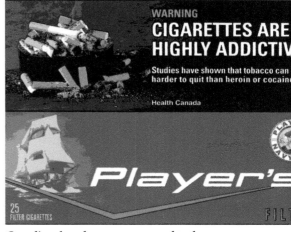

Canadians have become accustomed to the strong warning labels on cigarette packages.

Voisey's Bay: Native Canadians Exercise Right to Be Heard

When Inco (CVRD Inco as of 2007) purchased the rights to the Voisey's Bay property back in 1996 for $4.3 billion, they could not have imagined that obstacles would delay this potential site from reaching operational status for nearly a decade. Inco spent the next few years negotiating the terms of the project with the Newfoundland-Labrador government and stakeholders such as the local Innu and Inuit. The early years of the project were characterized by a drop in the price of nickel and costly, time-consuming environmental reviews.

The right to be heard is a concept that extends beyond consumer rights. Various stakeholders can play key roles in project approval and development stages, in influencing opinions of corporate image, and in pressuring governments to respond to local needs. In the Voisey's Bay case, the Innu and Inuit population had a tremendous stake in the potential development of this project. Inco was spending its time considering estimated reserves, annual production capacity, and expected daily activity and workforce requirements. Meanwhile, locals were considering how the increased ship traffic would affect hunting season, which is dictated largely by ice in Labrador. What did these miners know about the way in which local communities use the waterways and land? Did they care? According to some locals, the company saw ice as something that needed to be broken whereas the native population sees it as a way to get around. Needless to say, the education process was lengthy.

In 2002, after years of negotiating and many lessons, Inco, through its subsidiary Voisey's Bay Nickel Company, struck a deal with the Innu nation and the Labrador Inuit Association. The agreement addresses issues ranging from employment targets to supplying traditional food on-site to plans that nurture aboriginal joint ventures. Furthermore, Inco managed to agree that shipping would be suspended twice a year—when ice is forming and when it is melting—to minimize impact on wildlife and hunting patterns.

Since this agreement was reached, Inco has made attempts to solidify the relationship. For example, it sponsored the Nunatsiavut Drum Dancers and brought the group to Toronto to participate in the First Night Festival. Inco finally began production in 2005 and has bridged the stakeholder gap. It has also given back by donating $20 million to Memorial University for the development and operation of the Inco Innovation Centre located at the St. John's campus. It appears that the company has learned from the experience and is making every effort to engage its stakeholders.[60]

Questions for Critical Thinking

1. What were three key factors behind the Voisey's Bay project delays?
2. What lesson(s) can other companies learn from Inco's experience at Voisey's Bay? What is the significance of Inco's donation to Memorial University?

The Right to Be Heard

Many companies have established toll-free numbers for consumer information and feedback, and print these numbers on product packages. In addition, more and more companies are establishing websites to provide product information and as a vehicle for customer feedback. Companies use such feedback to improve their products and services and to make informed decisions about offering new ones. However, the right to be heard extends beyond simple customer product feedback; smart firms are aware of the importance of their various stakeholders (see the box entitled "Voisey's Bay: Native Canadians Exercise Right to Be Heard").

Responsibility toward Investors

A growing number of investors today are concerned about the ethics and social responsibility of the companies in which they invest. Allegations range from executives dumping stock ahead of bad news to companies using dirty accounting tricks to misrepresenting the investment.

The job of looking out for a company's investors falls to its board of directors. Lately, more investors are turning up the heat on the individuals who sit on those boards. Concerned investors are targeting board members who fail to attend meetings, who sit on the boards of too many companies, who are underinvested (own very little stock in the companies they direct), or who sit on boards of companies with which their

IN-CLASS NOTES

Consumer Rights
- The right to safe products
- The right to be informed
- The right to choose
- The right to be heard

own firms do business. Recently, Cinar shareholders went to court to get details about an $8.1 million trust fund that was transferred in the name of Joseph Groia, a lawyer who represented Ronald Weinberg and Micheline Charest, the company's co-founders.[61]

Angry investors are filing lawsuits not just against the management of companies that admit to "accounting irregularities," but also against their boards of directors and audit committees (the audit committee signs off on all financial statements and is supposed to protect shareholders). Looking out for investors is no easy task, but investors are finding that holding individual directors more accountable improves overall performance.[62] Of course, any action that cheats the investors out of their rightful profits is also unethical. An Ontario Superior Court judge recently awarded damages worth as much as $10 million to unhappy investors of Danier Leather because of claims that management withheld critical information.[63]

Responsibility toward Employees

For some companies, the past 30 years have brought dramatic changes in the attitudes and composition of the workforce. These changes have forced businesses to modify their recruiting, training, and promotion practices, as well as their overall corporate values and behaviours. Respecting employees and addressing their needs is sometimes difficult. (Consult Chapter 10 for an in-depth discussion of the staffing and demographic challenges employers face in today's workplace.)

The Push for Equality in Employment

Canadians have always supported economic freedom and the individual's right to pursue opportunity. Unfortunately, until the past few decades many people were targets of economic **discrimination**, relegated to low-paying, menial jobs and prevented from taking advantage of many opportunities solely on the basis of their gender, disability, ethnic background, or religion.

discrimination
In a social and economic sense, denial of opportunities to individuals on the basis of some characteristic that has no bearing on their ability to perform in a job

Employment Equity Act   The *Employment Equity Act* has been featured often in newspaper headlines over the past few years. Since it was first introduced in 1995, the Act has been the catalyst in the fight to eliminate perceived injustices, especially as they apply to professions deemed to be female dominated where workers have traditionally earned lower wages. The other three key groups addressed are Aboriginals, visible minorities, and the disabled. The Canadian government along with other branches of government have faced challenges as they moved to eliminate their own systematic injustices.

The stated goal of the *Employment Equity Act* is as follows:

To achieve equality in the workplace so that no person shall be denied employment opportunities or benefits for reasons unrelated to ability and, in fulfillment of that goal, to correct the conditions of disadvantage in employment experienced by women, aboriginal peoples, persons with disabilities and members of visible minorities, by giving effect to the principle that employment equity means more than treating persons in the same way but also requires special measures and the accommodation of differences.[64]

The *Employment Equity Act* directly applies to federally regulated companies and those doing business with the government under the federal contractor's program, which accounts for about 1425 organizations. With Canadian baby boomers set to vacate the workforce in the coming years and the birth rate at low levels, this legislation grows in importance. If the Canadian economy is to reach its full potential and continue to grow, it must not shut out key groups. Each year 220 000 newcomers arrive, and 70 to 80 percent are visible minorities. The aboriginal population is quite small in western Canada; however, Aboriginals will play a major role in the next 10 to 20 years. For example, by 2015 Aboriginals are expected to account for 20 percent of the population of Saskatchewan. Based on such trends, it is not surprising that many firms are creating their own workforce **diversity initiatives**.[65] These initiatives include increasing minority employment and promotion, contracting with more minority vendors, adding more minorities to boards of directors, and targeting a more diverse customer base. Many companies also offer employees diversity training to promote understanding of the unique cultures, customs, and talents of all employees.

diversity initiatives
Company policies designed to enhance opportunities for minorities and to promote understanding of diverse cultures, customs, and talents

Occupational Safety and Health

In Canada, there were 340 502 workplace injuries and 928 workplace fatalities in one recent year (see Exhibit 3.9).[66] The problem exists in varying degrees around the world. The Canadian Centre for Occupational Health and Safety was established in 1978 as a federal departmental corporation that reports to Parliament through the minister of labour. The centre's mandate is to promote health and safety in the workplace; facilitate cooperation among federal, provincial, and territorial jurisdictions; assist in the development of policies and programs; and serve as a national information centre.

Enbridge Inc., a leading energy transportation and distribution company, earned top marks in health and safety in the *Corporate Knights* ranking.[67] Most firms have implemented strict policies and procedures to reduce risks. However, concerns for employee safety have been raised by the international expansion of businesses. Many Canadian companies subcontract production to companies in foreign countries, making it even more difficult to maintain proper standards of safety and compensation for workers.

Exhibit 3.9	**Workplace Killers**

Transportation accidents are the leading workplace killer.

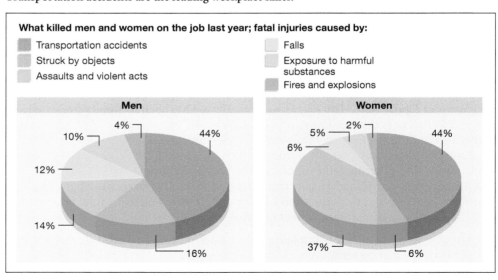

What killed men and women on the job last year; fatal injuries caused by:

- Transportation accidents
- Struck by objects
- Assaults and violent acts
- Falls
- Exposure to harmful substances
- Fires and explosions

Men
4% 44% 10% 12% 14% 16%

Women
2% 44% 5% 6% 37% 6%

ETHICS AND SOCIAL RESPONSIBILITY AROUND THE WORLD

As complicated as ethics and social responsibility can be for Canadian businesses, these issues grow even more complex when cultural influences are applied in the global business environment. As discussed in Chapter 2, ethical codes of conduct, laws, and cultural differences vary greatly from country to country. Corporate executives may face simple questions regarding the appropriate amount of money to spend on a business gift or the legitimacy of a payment to "expedite" business. Or they may encounter out-and-out bribery, environmental abuse, and other unscrupulous business practices.

BEHIND THE SCENES

Telus: Green Leadership

Many firms are willing to make a token verbal commitment to socially responsible and ethical behaviour; however, few take a leadership position in this particular area. Telus is not afraid to declare, implement, and influence other firms in this pursuit. It begins with the company's commitment to triple bottom-line reporting, which addresses economic, environmental, and social aspects of the firm's performance. It continues with lobbying efforts; Telus has urged the government to make triple bottom-line reporting a requirement for corporate accounting in Canada, to create a website that evaluates corporate social responsibility performance, and to educate investors on the merits of investing in such socially responsible firms.

Leadership is characterized by an ability to initiate change in others. Telus has used its large purchasing power through its environmentally responsible procurement policy to force its suppliers to be more environmentally friendly. The company prefers to purchase products that contain the maximum level of post-consumer waste or recycled content. The company has also managed to save 9792 kilograms of paper per year by employing paperless invoices for its top 100 clients.

Although Telus operates in an industry that is fairly environmentally friendly, the company has made additional efforts to increase its positive impact on the Earth. They have adopted an environmental management system (EMS) that includes the elements of the ISO 14000 model. Working with stakeholders is a key part of this tool. Telus gathers and analyzes both internal and external information and collaborates with various groups, including the Canadian Chamber of Commerce and the Conference Board of Canada.

A true test of a company's dedication is its reaction to a system failure. Despite all good intentions and attention to environmental detail, Telus was guilty of releasing waste (diesel) into the environment as a result of a fuel system failure at Strathcona Mountain, British Columbia. The firm paid $50 000 to the Habitat Conservation Trust Fund to compensate for the failure. It also spent considerable time and effort to clean up the site and improve its fuel systems to avoid possible future recurrence. The company has also vastly improved its prevention program with 558 site assessments in 2006 alone. Telus is also involved in various green projects. When Vancouver's Stanley Park was devastated by a severe windstorm, Telus stepped up and contributed $125 000. This generosity is not limited to the aftermath of natural disasters, either. Telus pledged $1 million over three years to the Montreal Green Fund, which is aimed at increasing green spaces in the city.

Telus employees are faced with obstacles and decisions in performing their day-to-day duties. However, extensive systems are in place to guide them. From the EMS, to the ethics hotline, to ethics e.learning courses, to training programs, to triple bottom-line reporting and external lobbying, Telus demonstrates leadership in the area of socially responsible ethical management.[68]

Critical Thinking Questions

1. Which of Telus's stakeholders are most affected by the company's environmentalism?
2. What is meant by triple bottom-line reporting? Should this practice be implemented as a standard accounting practice in Canada?
3. Telus's system failure at Strathcona Mountain, BC, was a test of the company's green image. If you were the public relations officer at that time, what elements would you include in a press release to deal with the problem? Would you deny the allegations?

Learn More Online

Go to Chapter 3 of this text's website at www.pearsoned.ca/bovee, and click on the Telus hotlink to read more about the company.

TEST YOUR KNOWLEDGE

Questions for Review

1. What factors influence ethical behaviour in a company?

2. What is insider trading? How does this practice hurt investors and damage the reputation of a company?

3. Why do companies spend considerable time creating and implementing practices that are written in a code of ethics?

4. What is a social audit?

5. What rights do consumers have?

Questions for Analysis

6. Why can't legal considerations resolve every ethical question?

7. Why is it increasingly important that the government and the private sector continue to pay attention to diversity initiatives?

8. Whether it is Kyoto or some other clean-air legislation, do you think the government is doing enough to reduce greenhouse gas emissions? Explain.

9. Why is it important for a company to balance its social responsibility efforts with its need to generate profits?

10. **Ethical Considerations.** How do business scandals such as Enron, Nortel, and WorldCom impact all businesses?

Questions for Application

11. You sell musical gifts on the web and in quarterly catalogues. Your two-person partnership has quickly grown into a 27-person company, and you spend all of your time on quality matters. You're losing control of important environmental choices about materials suppliers, product packaging, and even the paper used in your catalogues. What steps can you take to be sure your employees continue making choices that protect the environment?

12. At quitting time, you see your new colleague filling a briefcase with expensive software programs that aren't supposed to leave the premises. What do you do? Explain.

13. **Integrated.** In Chapter 1 we identified knowledge workers as the key economic resource of the twenty-first century. If an employee leaves a company to work for a competitor, what types of knowledge would it be ethical for the employee to share with the new employer and what types of knowledge would it be unethical to share?

14. **Ethical Considerations.** Is it ethical for provincial and municipal governments to entice businesses to relocate their operations to that province or city by offering them special tax breaks that are not extended to other businesses operating in that area?

PRACTISE YOUR KNOWLEDGE

SHARPENING YOUR COMMUNICATION SKILLS

All organizations, not just corporations, can benefit from having a code of ethics to guide decision making. But whom should a code of ethics protect, and what should it cover? In this exercise, you and your team are going to draft a code of ethics for your school.

Start by thinking about who will be protected by this code of ethics. What stakeholders should the school consider when making decisions? What negative effects might decisions have on these stakeholders? Then think about the kinds of situations you want your school's code of ethics to cover. One example might be employment decisions; another might be disclosure of confidential student information.

Next, using Exhibit 3.2 as a model, draft your school's code of ethics. Write a general introduction explaining the purpose of the code and who is being protected. Then write a positive statement to guide ethical decisions you identified earlier in this exercise. Your statement about promotion decisions, for example, might read: "School officials will encourage equal access to job promotions for all qualified candidates, with every applicant receiving fair consideration."

Compare your code of ethics with the codes drafted by your classmates. Did all of the codes seek to protect the same stakeholders? What differences and similarities do you see in the statements guiding ethical decisions?

BUILDING YOUR TEAM SKILLS

Choosing to blow the whistle on your employees or co-workers can create all kinds of legal, ethical, and career complications. Here are five common workplace scenarios that might cause you to search your soul about whether to go public with damaging charges. Read them carefully and discuss them with your teammates. Then decide what your team would do in each situation.

1. You believe your company is overcharging or otherwise defrauding a customer or client.

2. With all of the headlines generated by sexual harassment cases lately, you'd think employees wouldn't dare break the law, but it's happening right under your company's nose.

3. You discover that your company, or one of its divisions, products, or processes, presents a physical danger to workers or to the public.

4. An employee is padding overtime statements, taking home some of the company's inventory, or stealing equipment.

5. You smell alcohol on a co-worker's breath and notice that his or her work hasn't been up to standard lately.

 EXPAND YOUR KNOWLEDGE

DISCOVERING CAREER OPPORTUNITIES

Businesses, government agencies, and non-profit organizations offer numerous career opportunities related to ethics and social responsibility. How can you learn more about these careers?

1. Search through Appendix C on the website to identify jobs related to ethics and social responsibility. One example is an occupational health and safety manager, a job concerned with a company's responsibility toward its employees. What are the duties and qualifications of the jobs you have identified? Are the salaries and future outlooks attractive for all of these jobs?

2. Select one job for further consideration. Following the suggestions in Appendix C, what sources of employment information might provide more details about this job? Which of these sources are available in your school or public library? What additional sources can you consult for more information about the daily activities of this job and for ideas about locating potential employers?

3. What skills, educational background, and work experience do you think employers are seeking in applicants for the specific job you are researching? What key words do you think employers would search for when scanning electronic resumés submitted for this position?

DEVELOPING YOUR RESEARCH SKILLS

Articles on corporate ethics and social responsibility regularly appear in business journals and newspapers. Look in recent issues (print or online editions) to find one or more articles discussing one of the following ethics or social responsibility challenges faced by a business:

- Environmental issues, such as pollution, acid rain, and hazardous waste disposal
- Employee or consumer safety measures
- Consumer information or education
- Employment discrimination or diversity initiatives
- Investment ethics
- Industrial spying and theft of trade secrets
- Fraud, bribery, and overcharging
- Company codes of ethics

1. What was the nature of the ethical challenge or social responsibility issue presented in the article? Does the article report any wrongdoing by a company or agency official? Was the action illegal, unethical, or questionable? What course of action would you recommend the company or agency take to correct or improve matters now?

2. What stakeholder groups are affected? What lasting effects will be felt by (a) the company; (b) the stakeholder groups?

3. Writing a letter to the editor is one way consumers can speak their mind. Review some of the letters to the editor in newspapers or journals. Why are letters to the editor an important feature for that publication?

STUDY GUIDE

SUMMARY OF LEARNING OBJECTIVES

1. Discuss what it means to practise good business ethics and highlight three factors that influence ethical behaviour

Businesspeople who practise good business ethics obey all laws and regulations, compete fairly and honestly, communicate truthfully, and do not cause harm to others by putting themselves ahead of others or by placing themselves in a conflict of interest situation. Of the many factors that influence ethical behaviour, the three most common are cultural differences, knowledge of the facts and consequences involving a decision or action, and the ethical practices and commitment to ethical behaviour at a place of work.

2. Identify three steps that businesses are taking to encourage ethical behaviour and explain the advantages and disadvantages of whistle-blowing

Businesses are adopting codes of ethics, appointing ethics officers, and establishing ethics hotlines. In spite of these efforts, if illegal, unethical, or harmful practices persist, an employee may need to blow the whistle or disclose such problems to outsiders. Doing so may force the company to stop the problematic practices. But bringing these issues into the public eye has consequences. It can hurt the company's reputation, take up managers' time, damage employee morale, and affect the informant's job with the company.

3. List four questions you might ask yourself when trying to make an ethical decision

When making ethical decisions, ask yourself: (1) Is the decision legal? (Does it break any law?); (2) Is it balanced? (Is it fair to all concerned?); (3) Can you live with it? (Does it make you feel good about yourself?); (4) Is it feasible? (Will it work in the real world?).

4. Explain the difference between an ethical dilemma and an ethical lapse

An ethical dilemma is an issue with two conflicting but arguably valid sides, whereas an ethical lapse occurs when an individual makes a decision that is illegal, immoral, or unethical.

5. Discuss the relationship between corporate social responsibility and profits

For years many companies believed that the only role of a company was to make money and that social problems were the concern of the government. It was believed that socially responsible companies could not be profitable. But supporters of social responsibility now argue that a company has an obligation to society beyond the pursuit of profits and that companies can be both socially responsible and profitable. In fact, being a socially responsible company can help improve profits and being profitable can help companies stick to their social mission.

6. Explain how businesses can become more socially responsible

Companies can conduct social audits to assess whether their performance is socially responsible, they can engage in cause-related marketing by using a portion of product sales to help support worthy causes, or they can become philanthropic by donating their money, time, goods, or services to charitable, humanitarian, or educational institutions. Companies can also protect and improve the environment by taking a variety of actions to reduce pollution. They can become good citizens by considering consumers' needs and respecting their four basic rights: the right to safe products; the right to be informed—which includes the right to know a product's contents, use, price, and dangers; the right to choose which products to buy; and the right to be heard (that is, the right to voice a complaint or concern). Businesses can look out for a company's investors and protect the value of their interests and they can foster good employee relationships by treating employees fairly and equally and by providing a safe working environment.

7. Outline activities that the government and businesses are undertaking to improve the environment

The federal government improved upon the *Canadian Environmental Protection Act* in 1999, making changes that went much further than the previous Act. The Canadian government is actively working with the international community and ratified the Kyoto Protocol in 2002. Even though it doesn't appear that Canada will be able to honour its Kyoto commitments by 2012, the government is still working with industries to reduce pollution as much as possible. The federal government also signed the North American Agreement on Environmental Cooperation as part of the North American Free Trade Agreement.

Companies are taking the following steps to improve the environment: (1) considering it a part of everyday business and operating decisions; (2) making environmental staff members full-fledged partners in improving competitiveness; (3) measuring environmental performance; (4) tying compensation to environmental performance; (5) determining environmental costs before they occur; (6) considering the environmental impact of the product development process; (7) helping suppliers improve their environmental performance; and (8) conducting training and awareness programs.

KEY TERMS

code of ethics   (76)
conflict of interest   (74)
consumerism   (90)
discrimination   (93)
diversity initiatives   (94)

ecology   (85)
ethical dilemma   (80)
ethical lapse   (80)
ethics   (70)
insider trading   (74)

philanthropic   (84)
pollution   (84)
social audit   (84)
social responsibility   (70)

QUESTIONS

Multiple Choice   Circle the correct answer and then check the answers in the back of the book to chart your progress.

1. According to Milton Friedman, what is the most important responsibility of business?

   a. Care for the environment
   b. Increase profits
   c. Take care of employees
   d. Contribute to the community

2. _____ is switching someone's long distance service without their prior consent.

   a. Cramming
   b. Breaking
   c. Slamming
   d. Enhancing

3. Which of the following is *not* a method companies use to address environmental concerns?

   a. Measuring environmental performance
   b. Conducting environmental training programs
   c. Considering environmental impact in product development
   d. Delegating environmental responsibility to the appropriate government agencies

4. What happens if a company makes unsafe products?

   a. The unsafe products can improve the company's reputation.
   b. The company can improve its profits.

   c. Customers will accept the unsafe products because they have no choice.
   d. The company may have to recall the product and replace it at great expense.

5. Which is of the following is *not* a responsibility that businesses owe to their shareholders?

   a. Managers have a responsibility to inform shareholders and the public as soon as they learn of any potentially bad news.
   b. Managers have a responsibility to prepare annual and quarterly financial reports that accurately reflect the results of the company's activities.
   c. Managers have a responsibility to provide steady dividends for those shareholders who need it for retirement.
   d. Managers have a responsibility to use their best judgment in developing, manufacturing, and marketing their products.

6. The *Employment Equity Act* focuses primarily on women and the perceived discrimination against female-dominated professions. The Act also focuses on which of the following groups?

   a. Aboriginals
   b. Disabled people
   c. Visible minorities
   d. All of the above are addressed in the *Employment Equity Act*.

7. Which of the following approaches to ethical decision making will certainly result in an unethical decision?

    a. Apply existing laws to the situation.
    b. Apply the golden rule to the situation.
    c. Strive to treat people impartially and consistently.
    d. Remain within the letter of the law while intending to mislead people.

8. The 1960s activism that awakened business to its environmental responsibilities also gave rise to _____, a movement that put pressure on businesses to consider consumer needs and interests.

    a. consumerism
    b. breaking
    c. enhancing
    d. responsiveness

9. *Caveat emptor* is a Latin term that refers to a traditional view of business. Which of the following statements reflect this view?

    a. Take care of each stakeholder as if he or she was a member of your family.
    b. Let the buyer beware.
    c. Pollution must be reduced at all costs.
    d. Social causes over profits.

10. A key moment for the consumerism movement can be traced to President John F. Kennedy, who announced a "bill of rights" for consumers, laying the foundation for a wave of consumer-oriented legislation. These rights include the right to safe products, the right to be informed, the right to choose, and what?

    a. The right to be heard
    b. The right to make profits
    c. The right of first refusal
    d. The right to a clear rebate

True/False

1. True or false? Only the CEO takes ethical actions and makes ethical decisions in a business.

2. True or false? Companies can pursue ethical behaviour by establishing training programs.

3. True or false? The Kyoto Protocol will eliminate 90 percent of greenhouse gas emissions by 2012.

4. True or false? The threat of product liability suits often motivates companies to produce safe products.

5. True or false? Proper warning labels protect the manufacturer completely from lawsuits.

Fill-in-the-Blank

1. _____ is defined as the use of unpublicized information uncovered in a job function to capitalize on fluctuations in the stock market.

2. Governments around the world are slowly waking up to the realities of global warming. The _____ is an important deal that aims to reduce greenhouse gas emissions.

3. Organizations that are truly serious about ethical conduct have created a _____ mechanism to asses the company's performance in this area.

4. A _____ situation occurs when a business decision may be influenced by the potential for personal gain.

5. The new _____ entitles companies, individuals, and governments to request environmental protection reviews.

6. A written statement that establishes the principles that guide an organization's decisions are known as _____.

7. An _____ occurs when an individual makes a decision that is morally wrong, illegal, or unethical.

8. The _____ is a membership-based, non-profit organization that serves government, industry, and consumers in Canada and develops standards and codes that help ensure reasonable safety requirements.

9. Company policies designed to enhance opportunities for minorities and to promote understanding of diverse cultures, customs, and talents are known as _____.

10. _____ organizations and individuals donate money, time, goods, or services to charitable, humanitarian, or educational institutions.

See It on the **WEB**

Visit the Companion Website at **www.pearsoned.ca/bovee**, review the exercises, and complete the following assignments for Chapter 3:

1. Build a Better Business
2. Protect the Environment

CBC ✦ VIDEO CASE

Hollywood North: The Big Chill

LEARNING OBJECTIVES

The purpose of this video is to help you

1. Identify the methods that governments use to stimulate growth and protect industries.

2. Recognize uncontrollable macroeconomic threats and implement appropriate protection measures.

3. Understand the obstacles and opportunities that companies face in the global economy.

SYNOPSIS

Select the word that does not fit: *stars, movies, glamour, Hollywood, Canada.* A couple of decades ago the choice would have been obvious. At that time, Canadian film production was primarily limited to creating content for the CBC and CTV. But with the Canadian dollar declining and local costs rising, Hollywood looked north. The weak Canadian dollar enabled US film producers to create films and TV programs at bargain prices. Production in Vancouver and across the nation spread quickly and a prosperous domestic industry, worth more than $5 billion, soon developed.

Today, Canadians have become accustomed to film production trailers, movie stars, and blocked streets in their cities. The cheap Canadian currency fuelled the industry's growth, but currency rates vary and can take a turn with little notice. When the Canadian dollar climbed more than 20 percent in one recent year, it posed a direct threat to film production in the nation. At the time, Arnold Schwarzenegger, the "Terminator" governor, began a campaign to bring film production back to California. The

subsequent move of the Canadian dollar to parity with the US dollar did not help either. In addition, "reality TV" reduced the need for conventional television productions. Finally, because of global competition, dollars continued to flow out of Hollywood, but much of them began to flow past Canada to other low-cost locations such as Romania and Timbuktu. What does the future hold? Will film-production remain in Canada if the Canadian dollar remains strong? It is difficult to predict, as doing business in the global economy is a dynamic challenge. The playing field can change in the blink of an eye, or in this case, in a single movie frame.

Discussion Questions

1. *For analysis*: Why did Hollywood film producers set up shop in Canada?

2. *For analysis*: How does pressure from politicians like Arnold Schwarzenegger affect company decisions?

3. *For application*: How can Canadian film production companies protect their investment and help ensure that facilities are running despite the new economic pressures?

4. *For application*: Look up the current exchange rate between the US and Canadian dollars. A film production company is considering two production locations for a new movie: one in the United States and one in Canada. Assume that the film will cost US$60 million to produce south of the border. How much money would they have saved back in 2002 when the Canadian dollar was worth US62.5 cents? How much money would it cost today (assuming equal costs, paid in Canadian dollars)? Is there still a savings? Does it still seem worthwhile?

5. *For debate*: Should governments provide subsidies and tax breaks to lure film production to their country, province, or city?

ON LOCATION VIDEO CASE

Entering the Global Marketplace: Lands' End and Yahoo!

LEARNING OBJECTIVES

The purpose of this video is to help you

1. Understand the different reasons that businesses undertake international expansion.

2. Identify the financial and marketing issues of selling goods and services internationally.

3. Recognize the influence of culture on business decisions in an international firm.

SYNOPSIS

Yahoo! is a US-based Internet company with offices around the world. The company's service offerings have expanded from a search engine and web directory to a wide array of content and e-commerce offerings. Lands' End began in 1963 by selling sailing equipment by catalogue. Today the publicly owned firm is one of the largest apparel brands with a variety of catalogues and a high-volume e-commerce site. This video segment shows how these two very different companies approached the same goal: Expansion into international business. You will see how each copes with cultural, financial, monetary, and marketing differences as well as differences in language and method of payment. See whether you can identify those areas in which each firm chose to adapt to the needs and expectations of the international marketplace and where it maintained its original product or policy.

Discussion Questions

1. *For analysis*: Compare the different reasons why Lands' End and Yahoo! decided to expand internationally.

2. *For analysis*: How did Lands' End succeed in establishing itself in the United Kingdom and Japan?

3. *For application*: In addition to hiring local employees in countries such as France and China, how could Yahoo! help educate US employees about the nuances of doing business in these countries?

4. *For application*: How should Lands' End alter its online marketing efforts in countries that have different expectations of personal modesty?

5. *For debate*: Both Yahoo! and Lands' End expect their employees to behave in an ethical manner in all business dealings. However, experienced managers recognize that definitions of ethical behaviour can vary from country to country. Should both companies demand a consistent ethical code in all cases across all regions of the world? Why or why not?

ONLINE EXPLORATION

Visit Yahoo!'s Canadian website (www.yahoo.ca) and explore some of the features and functions that appeal to you. Then select one of the international sites listed at the bottom of the Yahoo! homepage and compare it to the Canadian site. Identify the differences made to suit the particular country's language and customs, and observe what elements of the site are identical. What do you think is the motivation behind the design and content choices Yahoo! made in the overseas sites? Do you think these choices would make it is successful in its market?

Anywhere between 150 to 200 million Chinese residents were estimated to be online in 2007, and that number is expected to grow substantially in the next few years. The game company Kingsoft provides a good example of how rapidly Chinese consumers are embracing new online offerings. After attempting to sell software to consumers for years, the company gave up and shifted to the Internet, starting with an action game called Sword Online. Within six months Kingsoft had signed up 1.7 million customers. Forecasters expect the online game market in China to surpass $2.1 billion by 2010, so the possibilities for companies like Kingsoft are virtually endless.

Internet + Mobile Phones = Profits

The marriage of the Internet and wireless technology promises to be another hot business across China. Portals now deliver a variety of information and entertainment services to phone users—news, games, dating services, even voice greeting cards featuring NBA star Yao Ming. Kingsoft is among the companies developing phone games that combine movies, voice, and data.

Multimedia phone services proved to be an enormous blessing for China's leading web portals, which include Sina, Sohu and NetEase. (A web portal is a multifaceted website such as www.yahoo.ca that provides a variety of information and entertainment offerings along with site directories, search engines, and other services.) Because advertising opportunities in China were so minuscule in the beginning, Sina and the other Chinese portals avoided a misstep that hobbled many e-commerce companies during the early days of the Internet boom—trying to support themselves by selling online advertising. In contrast, the Chinese portals are already profitable, thanks to wireless content services.

Rapid Evolution

This sizzling growth is a far cry from just a few years ago, when the Chinese government generally viewed e-commerce as a threat to its tight control over the economy and consumer behaviour. Now the country's leadership is intent on making China a global technology leader, showing strengths in both networking and wireless technologies. In rapid succession, the country is evolving from a low-cost manufacturer to a high-quality manufacturer and is on its way to being a technical innovator as well. As Robert Mao, CEO of greater China operations for Nortel, put it China is now "part of the leading edge."

This isn't to say that growth is easy, by any means. Dangdang.com, which roughly models itself after Amazon.com,

faced the challenge of selling products online without a financial feature that marketers in many countries take for granted—credit cards (most Chinese citizens don't have them yet). To get around this hurdle, the company accepts money orders and lets customers pay in cash when products are delivered.

Internet entrepreneurs are becoming role models for a new generation who see that they can get ahead on their own initiative. In an economy under tight government control, "people used to think you could only get rich with stocks or smuggling," says one Chinese CEO. "Now, with the Internet, they know they can get rich using their intelligence."

Freedom to Profit, Not Freedom of the Press

Does all this free-market fervour mean that China's communist government is relaxing its control over its citizens? Hardly. Site operators are forbidden to publish information about Falun Gong, an outlawed religious group, or to raise the call for political reform. Moreover, the government has been known to demand free advertising space on portal sites.

Blogs also come under close scrutiny in China. The government shut down blogs for carrying content it deemed objectionable—one was rumoured to be discussing issues related to the 1989 crackdown on a student protest in Beijing's Tiananmen Square.

In addition, Internet cafés, popular with students and travellers all over the world, can also prompt government crackdowns. At one point, officials banned the establishment of new Internet cafés close to primary or middle schools or within residential buildings for fear that illegal online content might corrupt young minds.

Building a Bubble?

In spite of the technical and political challenges, the World Wide Web is in China to stay. The Internet economy may have taken a while to catch a spark in China, but it's been on fire ever since. In fact, market watchers liken the frantic growth to the dot.com boom in the late 1990s. Stock prices for China's leading Internet companies are growing as fast as their markets, leading some to worry that the bubble will soon burst, much as the dot.coms did in North America a few years ago. However, executives insist things are different in China. Not only are the companies already making money, but they tend not to be saddled by much debt and they run their operations in a much more frugal manner.

Where do giants like Yahoo! and AOL show up in the list of China's most popular online sites? Not much more than a blip on the radar screen, actually. Yahoo! China ranks way down the list in popularity behind Sina, Sohu, and NetEase. As one investor put it, "Everybody thought AOL was going to take over the world. They didn't." Experts and users both say that foreign-owned sites don't seem to have a good feel for the Chinese market yet. With the world's largest Internet population in their sights, though, you can bet that the world's leading Internet companies aren't about to ignore China's vast online market.[69]

Questions for Critical Thinking

1. What advantages do North American e-commerce companies have over their Chinese counterparts? What disadvantages?

2. Why is a country's infrastructure an important factor in e-commerce development and success?

3. How might government control of information affect the growth of e-commerce in China?

BUSINESS PLANPRO EXERCISES EXERCISES

Conducting Business in the Global Economy

Review Appendix B, "Your Business Plan," to learn how to use Business PlanPro Software so you can complete these exercises.

Think Like a Pro

Objective: By completing these exercises you will become acquainted with the sections of a business plan that address forms of competition, company and product/service descriptions, and the economic outlook for the related industry. You will use the sample business plan for Adventure Excursions Unlimited (listed as Travel Agency–Adventure Sports in the Sample Plan Browser) in this exercise. Use the table of contents to move from section to section as you explore the plan and answer the following questions:

1. What products and services does Adventure Excursions provide? Will the company compete on the basis of price, speed, quality, service, or innovation to gain a competitive advantage?

2. What is the economic outlook for the travel industry? What competition does Adventure Excursions face?

3. How does Adventure Excursions plan to use the Internet?

Create Your Own Business Plan

Now start a new plan for your own business. Answering the following questions will help you think about different aspects of your business plan. Enter your answers in the appropriate sections of the new business plan.

1. What information should you include about your product or service when creating a business plan? Describe in detail the product or service your company will provide. Indicate whether you will compete on price, speed, quality, service, or innovation.

2. What are some of the things you should discuss about your competition in a business plan? What kinds of competition do you expect to face?

3. In what industry will you compete? What is the economic outlook for that industry?

PART 2

STARTING AND ORGANIZING A SMALL BUSINESS

CHAPTER 4
Starting and Financing a Small Business

CHAPTER 5
Selecting the Proper Form of Business Ownership and Exploring Business Combinations

CHAPTER 4

STARTING AND FINANCING A SMALL BUSINESS

LEARNING OBJECTIVES
After studying this chapter, you will be able to

1 Highlight the major contributions small businesses make to the Canadian economy

2 Identify the key characteristics that differentiate small businesses from larger ones

3 Discuss three factors contributing to the increase in the number of small businesses

4 Cite the key characteristics common to most entrepreneurs

5 List three ways of going into business for yourself

6 Identify three sources of small business assistance

7 Highlight several factors you should consider when evaluating financing options, and discuss the principal sources of small business private financing

BEHIND THE SCENES

Itech: An Entrepreneur's Clear Vision

www.itech.com

Like many Canadians, Robin Burns grew up on an outdoor rink playing hockey with passion and pride. Frozen purple toes along with bumps and bruises were accepted and expected. Unlike most, in 1967 his dream led him to the NHL and an opportunity to play with the Montreal Canadiens. His career also took him to the Pittsburgh Penguins, the Colorado Rockies, and the Kansas City Scouts. As a child of that time, it never occurred to him to wear a helmet, mask, or mouth guard. According to Burns, "losing your four front teeth was a badge of honour." Yet the business of protective hockey gear was to hold the key to his post-NHL future.

After a decade in the NHL, Burns returned to Montreal and joined the start-up Micron, a company that produced a unique skate in the early 1980s. Throughout his playing years, Burns had been involved with the development, marketing, and sales of hockey equipment. However, this entrepreneur's moment of clarity would soon take him on a new venture. Like many players before and after him, Burns was hit in the eye by an errant stick during an old-timers' match. This moment triggered the idea for Itech's clear hockey visor. Burns quit his job at Micron and began developing the prototype for the initial product in his basement. The risky move did not come without its trials and tribulations. As with most innovations, the bar for successful commercialization was set high. According to Randy Burns, vice-president of marketing, "one of the biggest obstacles was achieving official certification with the CSA [Canadian Standards Association] in Canada and the HECC [Hockey Equipment Certification Council] in the US." But, of course, jumping through hoops comes with the territory when creating a new segment in the market. People naturally doubt the unknown.

Itech is the pioneer of clear full-face hockey visors. The company was founded on this product but soon expanded its product line.

From these humble origins, Itech emerged as a pioneer that changed the face of hockey by developing the first clear full-face shield. The company grew to a stage where it had more than 200 employees and an extensive product line including (but not limited to) shoulder pads, elbow pads, sticks, shin protectors, neck protectors, gloves, jocks, and goalie pads. Itech has also paid attention to the key industry players and has formed alliances with organizations like Hockey Canada, USA Hockey, USA Hockey InLine, and the Central Hockey League (CHL).

The Itech story is a classic Canadian tale that most of us can identify with. This business's success is an inspiring example of innovation fuelled by market knowledge and an entrepreneur's clear vision. Growth and evolution inevitably lead to change. Like most industries, the hockey equipment segment is consolidating. As Itech entered its twentieth year of operations back in 2004, it needed to examine all possible avenues to continue its growth and maintain its industry standing.[1]

TEST YOURSELF

Answers to these questions can be found on the website: www.pearsoned.ca/bovee.

1. What are the challenges of starting a business from scratch? Provide examples from Robin Burns's experience in creating Itech.

2. What entrepreneurial characteristics did Robin Burns demonstrate in creating his company?

3. How do companies like Itech help to fulfill the economic roles of society?

4. How can Itech diversify its product line? Should it consider a merger with another industry player?

UNDERSTANDING THE WORLD OF SMALL BUSINESS

Many small businesses start out like Itech: with an entrepreneur, an idea, and a drive to succeed. In fact, Canada was originally built by people involved in small businesses—the family farmer, the shopkeeper, the craftsperson. Successive waves of immigrants carried on this tradition, launching restaurants and laundries, providing repair and delivery services, and opening newsstands and bakeries. This trend continued for decades, until improvements in transportation and communication enabled large producers to manufacture goods at low costs and pass the savings on to consumers. Many smaller businesses could not compete with larger retailers on price, so many of them closed their doors and big business emerged as the primary economic force. The trend toward bigness continued for several decades—and then it reversed.

The 1990s was a golden decade for entrepreneurship in Canada. Entrepreneurs launched small companies in great numbers to fill new consumer needs. Many took advantage of Internet technologies to gain a competitive edge. Some succeeded; others failed. However, the resurgence of small businesses helped propel the Canadian economy forward.

There are more than 2.3 million business establishments in Canada.[2] But defining what constitutes a small business is surprisingly tricky, because *small* is a relative term. For example, a manufacturing firm with 500 employees might be considered small if it competes against much larger companies, but a retail establishment with 500 employees might be classified as big when compared with its competitors.

One reliable source of information for small businesses is Industry Canada. This government agency serves as a resource and advocate for small firms by promoting investment, trade, and scientific research, and through other supportive initiatives.[3] A **small business** can be defined as a firm that is independently owned and operated; is not dominant in its field; is relatively small in terms of annual sales; and has fewer than 500 employees.[4]

small business
A company that is independently owned and operated, is not dominant in its field, and meets certain criteria for the number of employees and annual sales revenue

Economic Roles of Small Businesses

L.O. 1

Small businesses are the cornerstone of the Canadian economy. They bring new ideas, processes, and energy to the marketplace and fill a niche market that generally is not served by large businesses. Here are just some of the important roles small businesses play in the economy:

■ *They provide jobs.* In Canada, small businesses and the self-employed are an engine for economic growth. Small and medium-sized businesses (SMEs) account for about 64 percent of private sector employment and around 45 percent of private sector output.[5]

■ *They introduce new products.* According to a recent study, Canadian SMEs accounted for 41 percent of world or Canadian firsts.[6] Small firms tend to develop a high percentage of "radical" new products.

■ *They supply the needs of large corporations.* Many small businesses act as distributors, servicing agents, and suppliers to large corporations. Consider Terpac Plastics Inc., a niche player that identified and filled a need in the market; this Montreal-based clothes hanger manufacturer seized an opportunity in the early 1980s to service the retail market in a city with an established needle trade. At the time, no local company was churning out this basic but vital product in

While recuperating from a broken ankle, Perry Klebahn decided to try out a pair of snowshoes he found in his friend's closet. Today, his company, Atlas Showshoes, sells products across North America in more than 1000 stores, including retailers like Mountain Equipment Co-op, Sport Mart, Hikers Haven, Bernard Trottier, and Baron Sport.

the clothing business cluster. Today, Terpac serves the needle trade with this product and has an impressive client list that includes Wal-Mart, The Bay, Zellers, Federated Department Stores, Reitmans, Costco, and numerous high-end boutiques across North America.[7]

■ *They provide specialized goods and services.* When Mike Woods tried to teach his son how to read, he couldn't find any toys that helped teach phonics. So he left his job as a partner in a big law firm and started LeapFrog. The company's initial product was the Phonics Disk, a US$50 toy that teaches children shapes, sounds, and pronunciation of letters and words. LeapFrog, now a division of Knowledge Universe Education, has created more than 50 interactive learning products and 40 interactive books.[8]

Today, people are experiencing more pressure to balance personal demands with work responsibilities. Many small businesses have been created to deal with this problem.

Characteristics of Small Businesses

Small businesses are of two distinct types: lifestyle businesses and high-growth ventures. Roughly 80 to 90 percent are modest operations with little growth potential (although some have attractive income potential for the solo businessperson). The self-employed consultant working part-time from a home office, the corner florist, and the neighbourhood pizza parlour fall into the category of *lifestyle businesses*—firms built around the personal and financial needs of an individual or a family.[9] Lifestyle businesses aren't designed to grow into large enterprises. For example, Richard Mund Pottery out of Neustadt, Ontario, was featured in a *Globe and Mail* article entitled "Staying Small—and Loving It." Richard Mund's approach was simple: carry no debt. He decided to stay away from the hustle and bustle of city life and created a popular shop en route to cottage country. Not everyone is looking for the big corporate buyout.[10]

In contrast to lifestyle businesses, some firms are small simply because they are new. Many companies—such as Magna International, Microsoft, and Bombardier—started out as small entrepreneurial firms but quickly outgrew their small business status. Magna International started off as a one-man Toronto-based tool and die shop in 1957, with sales of $13 000. Today Frank Stronach's company employs more than 83 000 people in 235 manufacturing divisions in 23 countries. Annual sales have increased from $13 000 to $24.2 billion.[11] *High-growth ventures* are usually run by a team rather than by one individual, and they expand rapidly by obtaining sizable investment capital and introducing new products or services to a large market. But expanding from a small firm into a large enterprise is no easy task; there's a world of difference between the two.

The typical small business has few products or services, focuses on a narrow group of customers, and remains in close contact with its markets. In addition, most small business owners work with limited resources and tend to be more innovative.

Limited Resources

Small companies tend to have limited resources, so owners and employees must perform a variety of job functions to get the work done. Being a jack-of-all-trades is not for everyone, however (see Exhibit 4.1[12]); many executives who leave the corporate world to start a small business have trouble adjusting to the daily grind of entrepreneurship. They miss the support services, conveniences, and fringe benefits they enjoyed in large corporations.[13]

Innovation

Small businesses also tend to be more open-minded and willing to try new things more often than big businesses. Case studies show that being small can stimulate innovation: (1) small businesses can make decisions faster; (2) the owners are more

Exhibit 4.1 **How Entrepreneurs Spend Their Time**

The men and women who start their own companies are jacks-of-all-trades, but they spend most of their time selling and producing the product.

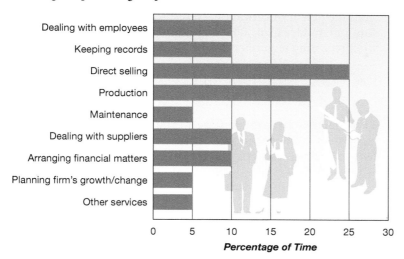

Percentage of Time

accessible; and (3) employees have a greater opportunity for individual expression. Small companies continue to energize the technology sector with leading-edge ideas. According to a recent survey, more than half of Deloitte's "Technology Fast 50" were self-funded ventures, and small companies are blazing the trail.[14]

Putting an idea into action in big companies often means filing formal proposals, preparing research reports, and attending many meetings. This process could kill an idea before it has a chance to take off. Consider Microsoft, for example. One manager quit out of frustration at the company's snail's pace for decision making. It took 10 meetings and three months to act on his suggestion to add a feature to Hotmail (the company's free Internet email service) that would quickly take 40 million users to Microsoft's MSN website. In contrast, it took only 30 minutes to write the code for this feature.[15]

To compete with small companies, many big companies now divide their organizations into smaller work units. Xerox, Motorola, and others have launched their

IN-CLASS NOTES

Small Business Defined
Characteristics:
- Independently owned and operated
- Not dominant in its field
- Relatively small annual sales
- Fewer than 500 employees
- Limited resources, but tend to be innovative

_____

_____

_____

_____

_____

_____

Retired Worker addresses a particular niche for older workers who are not adequately serviced by the main job websites like Monster.ca. Linda Welstead is its founder and spokesperson.

own small enterprises to keep new ideas from falling through the cracks. Run by *intrapreneurs*—people who create innovation of any kind from *within* an organization (not to be confused with *entrepreneurs*, risk takers in the private enterprise system)—these ventures get funding and support from the parent organization. Nevertheless, some intrapreneurial ventures continue to face giant obstacles because the parent corporation imposes strict reporting requirements and formal procedures.[16]

Factors Contributing to the Increase in the Number of Small Businesses

Three factors are contributing to the increase in the number of small businesses today: technological advances, an increase in the number of female business owners, and corporate downsizing and outsourcing.

Technology and the Internet

L.O. 3

The Internet, together with e-commerce, has produced thousands of new business ventures. Retired Worker is one such firm. Linda Welstead, a former teacher, along with her daughter, Sarah Welstead, founded this small online business to serve the needs of retired workers looking for part-time or occasional work. Welstead saw an opportunity when she noticed that the main job sites like Monster.ca and Workopolis.com were mainly serving the needs of workers at the beginning of their careers. She then set out to create a site geared toward the specific needs of older workers; larger fonts and easy-to-read pages forego flashy options, and the site presents information in a clear, concise manner. With the baby boomers aging and increasingly fighting the stereotypical Florida retirement, Retired Worker is on to something. It now serves customers from coast to coast.[17]

Technologies That Are Revolutionizing Business

SOCIAL NETWORK APPLICATIONS (CYBERNETWORKING)

Social networking sounds like the time you spend wandering around a party trying to meet people, but it's actually a new category of technology that is changing the way many professionals communicate. Many of you are probably quite familiar with the basic concept and spend a great deal of time on Facebook. Social network applications, which can be stand-alone software products or websites, help to identify potential business connections by indexing email and instant messaging address books, calendars, and message archives. For instance, you might find that the sales lead you've been struggling to contact at a large customer is a golf buddy of one of your suppliers or a relative of your child's soccer coach.

HOW THEY'RE CHANGING BUSINESS

One of the biggest challenges small business owners face is finding the right people and making those connections, whether you're looking for a new employee, an investor, a potential customer, or anyone else who might be important to the future of your business. With social network applications, businesspeople can reach more people than they could ever hope to reach via traditional, in-person networking. For example, Elmer Sotto, director of marketplace development for eBay Canada, received six solid recommendations within four hours of putting the word out that he needed a consultant for a short-term project. One person was recommended by four people that he knew and trusted.[18]

WHERE YOU CAN LEARN MORE

Visit the websites of LinkedIn (www.linkedin.com), Ryze Business Networking (www.ryze.com), Spoke (www.spoke.com), and BNI (www.bni.com) to learn more about their services. To find other information about social network applications, enter "business networking" or "social networking" into your favourite search engine.

The Internet makes it possible for small companies to compete on a level playing field with larger ones. Small businesses can use the Internet to communicate with customers and suppliers all over the world—any time of the day—and to access the types of resources and information that were previously available only to larger firms. The Internet also makes it easier to start a small home-based business (see the box entitled "Create a Winning Website"). With the Internet and online resources, accountants, writers, lawyers, and consultants can set up shop at home—or on the Web. Other firms like Whittier Canada Enterprise Inc., a company that sells snow-making equipment to ski resorts, even have virtual secretaries who process invoices, send emails and deal with company accountants from a distance.[19] Experts predict that as much as half the workforce may soon be involved in full- or part-time home-based businesses.[20]

Rise in Number of Female Small Business Owners

An increase in the number of women entrepreneurs is also fuelling small business growth. According to Statistics Canada there are approximately 877 000 self-employed

Create a Winning Website

These days, anyone can learn to design and construct web pages. All you need is the right web-authoring software and a reasonably good computer to create pages with text, photos, and animated graphics. An estimated 75 percent of small Canadian businesses are on the Web. But if you want to create a winning website, here are a few tips to consider:

- *Present a professional corporate image.* Be sure to provide a corporate profile that tells people a little bit about your company. Include news releases or articles about your business so that customers can see how well-known or dynamic you are in the industry. Make sure your material is accurate, interesting, and related to your products. Identify the key benefits of your product (include product details on a second page). Check out other websites for inspiration—especially your competitors' sites—and decide what you like or dislike about their appearance. Think of ways to distinguish your site.

- *Don't forget the basics.* Always give visitors a person to call and a place to send a request for more information to. Be sure to list your postal and email addresses and phone and fax numbers. Remember that the Internet is international, so list the nation where your company or its dealers are located.

- *Make your website easy to use.* Web surfers have a short attention span, so keep large graphics (which take forever to load) to a minimum. If you must include any large, embedded graphics or photos, provide an option for users to select a text-only interface, or provide small images of photos (called

thumbnails) for users to click on if they want to view larger, more detailed versions. Always provide hyperlinks at the bottom of each page to allow users to move backwards and forward through a multi-page site.

- *Anticipate your customers' needs.* Plan ahead. By including answers to frequently asked questions, chances are you'll cover about 90 percent of your customers' concerns. Remember, users tend to provide both frank and useful input, but only if you ask them for it. So be sure to include an active customer feedback mechanism such as email, open feedback forms, or structured survey forms. Don't require users to register before they can see your site. You may drive them away.

- *Promote your website.* Be sure to list with numerous search engines—giant indexes that allow web users to find information by entering key words. Most of these listings are free. Maximize the number of times your site will be listed by jamming in as many words as you can that best describe your site. Take out an ad in the newspaper and list your company in the Internet yellow pages. Finally, don't just sit back and expect your website to perform magic. Use it to find out as much as possible about your customers. Ask yourself: How can I benefit from all this customer information?[21]

Questions for Critical Thinking

1. Why do web surfers have a short attention span?
2. List some of the ways companies can benefit from having a website on the Internet.

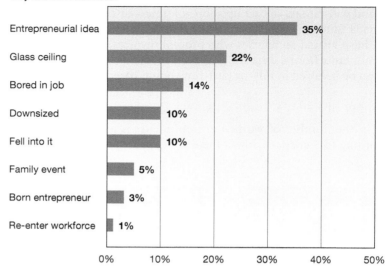

Exhibit 4.2   **Women Starting Businesses**

More than half of all women business owners started their own businesses because they had an entrepreneurial idea or wished to further advance their careers.

What women with companies less than a decade old say is the main reason they started a business:

Entrepreneurial idea	35%
Glass ceiling	22%
Bored in job	14%
Downsized	10%
Fell into it	10%
Family event	5%
Born entrepreneur	3%
Re-enter workforce	1%

women in the country. In fact, over the last ten years, the number of self-employed women has increased by 18 percent, compared to 14 percent for men. By 2010, the number of self-employed women in Canada is expected to reach 1 million.[22] Some of these women would not classify themselves as entrepreneurs; however, they are an important growing element in the economy. It is also estimated that 47 percent of SMEs have at least some degree of female ownership.[23] Although men still account for about 60 percent of new start-ups, the statistics indicate that women tend to stick to a business over the long haul; in other words, the survival rate for female-run start-ups is higher.[24]

As Exhibit 4.2[25] shows, women are starting small businesses for a number of reasons. Some choose to run their own companies so they can enjoy a more flexible work arrangement; others start their own business because of barriers to corporate advancement, known as the *glass ceiling*. Christine Nicholls from Victoria, British Columbia, chose to leave a successful career in a high-tech company where she worked as a consultant in the health care field. After earning her MBA and starting a family, she decided to look into operating a home-based business that she could run while raising her children. She came up with the idea to sell children's mail-order crafts and now sells them primarily online at www.creativekidsathome.com.[26]

Downsizing and Outsourcing

Contrary to popular wisdom, business start-ups soar when the economy sours. During hard times, many companies downsize or lay off talented employees who then have little to lose by pursuing self-employment. In fact, several well-known companies were started during recessions. For example, Bill Gates started Microsoft during the 1975 recession.

outsource
Subcontracting work to outside companies (often in other countries)

To make up for layoffs of permanent staff, some companies **outsource** or subcontract special projects and secondary business functions to experts outside the organization. Others turn to outsourcing as a way to permanently eliminate entire company

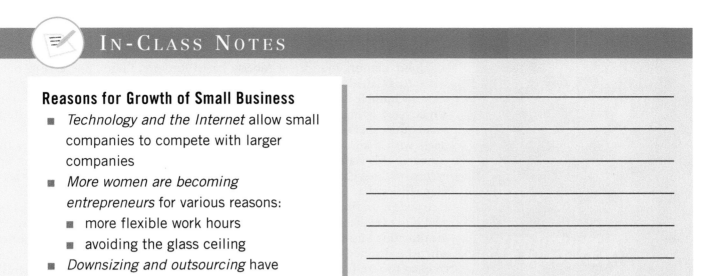

departments. Regardless of the reason, the increased use of outsourcing provides opportunities for smaller businesses to service the needs of larger enterprises.

STARTING A SMALL BUSINESS

According to a recent CIBC survey, as many as 100 000 new small businesses will be started over the next five years.[27] Could you or should you join the thousands of entrepreneurs who start new businesses every year? What qualities would you need? What tasks would you have to perform to get started?

Characteristics of Entrepreneurs

L.O. 4

Contrary to what you might expect, most entrepreneurs are not glamorous adventurers; instead, they are often ordinary people who have a good idea. But it takes more than a good idea to launch a successful business. Most entrepreneurs have these qualities in common:

- They are highly disciplined.
- They like to control their destiny.
- They listen to their intuitive sense.
- They relate well to others.
- They are eager to learn whatever skills are necessary to reach their goal.
- They learn from their mistakes.
- They stay abreast of market changes.
- They are willing to exploit new opportunities.
- They are driven by ambition.
- They think positively.
- They prefer the excitement and potential rewards of risk taking over security.[28]

John Stanton literally ran into a business opportunity. After changing his lifestyle—from overweight smoker to avid jogger—he noticed that the service in many of the footwear retail shops was subpar and came up with the Running Room lifestyle concept.

While most entrepreneurs are anxious to become their own boss, surprisingly they cite making money as the secondary reason for starting their own business.[29]

John Stanton, founder of Alberta-based Running Room, operates 89 outlets across Canada and the United States. The company has made great strides since its humble beginnings two decades ago. The original store was located in a renovated living room of an old Edmonton home. The goal was to create a retail outlet that serviced the needs of its client base. The retailer distinguishes itself with a simple philosophy: Running Room is a store for runners by runners. This statement must be qualified, because Running Room is not an exclusive, elitist club; the firm has a tradition of creating runners and holds regular clinics that cost about $69 for 10 to 18 lessons. These lessons include instruction on fitness, walking, running, sports medicine, and nutrition. The goal is to ease the individual into the world of running. Stanton initially got the idea for this business based on the poor service he received in a retail outlet when he decided to transform himself from an overweight executive who smoked two-and-a-half packs a day into a healthy, avid runner. On the twentieth anniversary of the firm's inception, Stanton celebrated, along with 20 000 runners across Canada, with a special 20-minute run. The firm is involved in many events and promotes the sport by example. Healthy living has meshed effectively with entrepreneurial pursuits in this case.[30]

Entrepreneurs like Itech's Robin Burns start with relatively small sums of money and operate informally from their homes, at least for a while. Most have diverse backgrounds in terms of education and business experience. Some come from companies unlike the ones they start; others use their prior knowledge and skills—such as editing, telemarketing, public relations, or selling—to start their own businesses. Still others have less experience but an innovative idea or a better way of doing something. Like John Stanton and Robin Burns, they find an overlooked corner of the market, exploit a demographic trend unnoticed by others, or meet an unsatisfied consumer need through better service or a higher-quality product. Moreover, they often plan and develop their product quickly, while the rest of the business world ponders whether a market for the product exists.

Importance of Preparing a Business Plan

Getting started in a new business requires a lot of work (see Exhibit 4.3), not the least of which is planning. Although many successful entrepreneurs claim to have done little formal planning, even the most intuitive of them have *some* idea of what they're trying to accomplish and how they hope to do it. Jeff Bezos, founder of Amazon.com, planned the world's first online bookstore in the backseat of his car as his wife drove them from New York to Seattle. As Bezos and other entrepreneurs know, planning is essential for success. No amount of hard work can turn a bad idea into a profitable one.

Planning forces you to think ahead. Before you rush in to supply a product, you need to be sure that a market exists. You must also try to predict some of the problems that might arise and figure out how you will deal with them. For instance, what will you do if one of your suppliers suddenly goes out of business? Can you locate another supplier quickly? What if the neighbourhood starts to change—even for the better? An influx of wealthier neighbours may cause such a large increase in rent that your business must move. Tough competition may also move into the neighbourhood along with the fatter wallets. Do you have an alternative location staked out? What if styles suddenly change? Can you switch quickly from, say, hand-painted crafts to some other kind of artwork?

One of the first steps you should take toward starting a new business is to develop a **business plan**, a written document that summarizes an entrepreneur's proposed

business plan
A written document that provides an orderly statement of a company's goals and how it intends to achieve those goals

Exhibit 4.3 Business Start-up Checklist

You have many tasks to perform before you start your own business. Here are just a few.

- ✓ Choose a business name, verify the right to use it, and register it.
- ✓ Reserve a corporate name if you will be incorporating.
- ✓ Register or reserve trademarks.
- ✓ Apply for a patent if you will be marketing an invention.
- ✓ Write a business plan.
- ✓ Choose a location for the business.
- ✓ File partnership or corporate papers.
- ✓ Get any required business licences or permits.
- ✓ Have business phone lines installed.
- ✓ Check into business insurance needs.
- ✓ Apply for a sales tax number.

- ✓ Apply for an employee identification number if you will have employees.
- ✓ Open business bank account(s).
- ✓ Have business cards and stationery printed.
- ✓ Purchase equipment and supplies.
- ✓ Order inventory.
- ✓ Order signage.
- ✓ Order fixtures.
- ✓ Print brochures and other sales literature.
- ✓ Send out publicity releases.
- ✓ Call everyone you know and tell them you are in business.

Source: Business Know How website, www.businessknowhow.com.

business venture, communicates the company's goals, highlights how management intends to achieve those goals, and shows how consumers will benefit from the company's products or services.

Preparing a business plan serves two important functions: First, it guides the company's operations and outlines a strategy for turning an idea into reality; second, it helps persuade lenders and investors to finance your business. In fact, without a business plan, many investors won't even grant you an interview. According to Jacques Lemoine, senior

Learning from Business Blunders

OOPS

Carol Skonberg's company, Swasko Jewels, made sterling silver charms that dinner guests could wrap around the stems of their wineglasses to prevent confusion over which glass belongs to whom. Not a life-and-death problem, to be sure, but one of the things people would readily pay a few dollars to avoid, she figured. Her hunch proved correct, and she convinced 90 retailers in her home state of Texas to carry the product. Sales looked promising—then quickly plummeted as competitors with similar products but more aggressive marketing appeared out of nowhere. Skonberg and her business partner disbanded the company soon after.

WHAT YOU CAN LEARN

According to small business experts, Skonberg made several common rookie mistakes. The first was that she

believed that she had a unique product. It's not unusual for more than one company to come up with the same solution to a given problem. The second mistake was failing to investigate legal protection earlier. Although she couldn't patent her designs (jewellery usually can't be patented), she could have come up with a catchy brand name and eye-catching logo and trademarked those. The third—and probably biggest—mistake was not being prepared to go nationwide quickly. Two competitors did expand rapidly, signing up sales reps around the country and getting into catalogues with wide distribution.

The story does have a happy ending, though. Skonberg learned from her experience and tried again, this time with a jewellery company called HipIce that makes chains that drape off beltlines. So far, so good.[31]

vice-president of Ontario operations for the Business Development Bank of Canada, writing an effective plan is often the difference between getting financing and walking out empty handed.[32] Keep in mind that sometimes the greatest service a business plan can provide an entrepreneur is the realization that "the concept just won't work." Discovering this on paper can save you considerable time and money (see the box entitled "Blueprint for a Comprehensive Business Plan").

Blueprint for a Comprehensive Business Plan

Although the business plan has a simple, straightforward purpose, it still requires a great deal of thought. For example, before you open your doors, you have to make important decisions about personnel, marketing, facilities, suppliers, and distribution. A written business plan forces you to think about those issues and develop programs that will help you succeed. If you are starting out on a small scale and using your own money, your business plan may be relatively informal. But at a minimum, you should describe the basic concept of the business and outline its specific goals, objectives, and resource requirements. A formal plan, suitable for use with banks or investors, should cover the following points:

- *Summary.* In one or two pages, summarize your business concept. Describe your product or service and its market potential. Highlight some things about your company and its owners that will distinguish your firm from the competition. Summarize your financial projections and the amount of money investors can expect to make on their investment. Be sure to indicate how much money you will need and for what purposes.

- *Mission and objectives.* Explain the purpose of your business and what you hope to accomplish.

- *Company and industry.* Give full background information on the origins and structure of your venture and the characteristics of its industry.

- *Products or services.* Give a complete but concise description of your product or service, focusing on its unique attributes. Explain how customers will benefit from using your product or service instead of those of your competitors.

- *Market and competition.* Provide data that will persuade the investor that you understand your target market and can achieve your sales goals. Be sure to identify the strengths and weaknesses of your competitors.

- *Management.* Summarize the background and qualifications of the principals, directors, and key management personnel in your company. Include resumés in the appendix.

- *Marketing strategy.* Provide projections of sales and market share, and outline a strategy for identifying and contacting customers, setting prices, providing customer services, advertising, and so forth. Whenever possible, include evidence of customer acceptance, such as advance product orders.

- *Design and development plans.* If your product requires design or development, describe the nature and extent of what needs to be done, including costs and possible problems.

- *Operations plan.* Provide information on the facilities, equipment, and labour needed.

- *Overall schedule.* Forecast development of the company in terms of completion dates for major aspects of the business plan.

- *Critical risks and problems.* Identify all negative factors and discuss them honestly.

- *Financial projections and requirements.* Include a detailed budget of start-up and operating costs, as well as projections for income, expenses, and cash flow for the first three years of business. Identify the company's financing needs and potential sources.

- *Exit strategy.* Explain how investors will be able to cash out or sell their investment, such as through a public stock offering, sale of the company, or a buyback. When covering these points, keep in mind that your audience wants short, concise information—not lengthy volumes—and realistic projections for growth.[33]

Questions for Critical Thinking

1. What details should you know about your business before writing a business plan?
2. Why is it important to identify critical risks and problems in a business plan?

IN CLASS NOTES

Starting a New Business from Scratch

ADVANTAGES
- Control your destiny
- Reach your potential
- Unlimited profits
- Recognition
- Doing what you enjoy

DISADVANTAGES
- Uncertain income
- Risk of loss
- Long hours and hard work
- Total responsibility
- High stress levels

_____

_____

_____

_____

_____

_____

_____

_____

Small Business Ownership Options

L.O. 5

Once you've done your research and planning, if you decide to take the risk you can get into business for yourself in three ways: start from scratch, buy an existing business, or obtain a franchise. Roughly two-thirds of business founders begin **start-up companies**; that is, they start from scratch rather than buy an existing operation or inherit a family business. Starting a business from scratch has many advantages and disadvantages. A new business enables the owner to maintain control over all aspects of the business and benefit from all of the profits if the business succeeds. It allows the entrepreneur to achieve recognition for their efforts, hopefully while working in a line of work they enjoy. However, there are many potential disadvantages. For example, income is no longer secure and there is a risk of losing the initial investment. Recognition is great, but it does not come for free. In this case it is attached to long, hard work hours, total responsibility for all decisions, and a great deal of stress. Of the three options for going into business for yourself, starting a new business is the most common route and, in many cases, the most difficult.

Another way to go into business for yourself is to buy an existing business. This approach tends to reduce the risks—provided, of course, that you check out the company carefully. When you buy a business, you generally purchase an established customer base, functioning business systems, a proven product or service, and a known location. You don't have to go through the painful period of building a reputation, establishing a clientele, finding suppliers, and hiring and training employees. In addition, financing an existing business is often much easier than financing a new one; lenders are reassured by the company's history and existing assets and customer base. With these major details already settled, you can concentrate on making improvements.

start-up companies
New ventures that start from scratch

Danvin, a recent start-up company, obtains the distribution rights to sell branded food products in the Canadian market. The company sells to supermarkets, such as Sobeys, Metro, and Loblaw, as well as to restaurants and hotels. Danvin owns the rights to Sweet Baby Ray's Barbecue Sauce, Simply Potatoes, My Grandma's of New England Coffee Cakes, and Arriba! Salsa.

Still, buying an existing business is not without disadvantages. For one thing, the business may be overpriced. For another, inventories and equipment may be obsolete. Furthermore, the location may no longer be satisfactory, the previous owner may have created ill will, your personality may clash with those of existing managers and employees, and outstanding bills owed by customers may be difficult to collect. Keep in mind that no matter how fast you learn and how much investigating you do, you're likely to find that the challenges of running an existing business are far greater than you anticipated.[34]

The Franchise Alternative

franchise
A business arrangement in which a small business obtains the rights to sell the goods or services of the supplier (franchisor)

franchisee
A small business owner who contracts for the right to sell goods or services of the supplier (franchisor) in exchange for some payment

franchisor
A supplier that grants a franchise to an individual or group (franchisee) in exchange for payments

An alternative to buying an existing business is to buy a **franchise** in somebody else's business. This approach enables the buyer to use a larger company's trade name and sell its products or services in a specific territory. In exchange for this right, the **franchisee** (the small business owner who contracts to sell the goods or services) pays the **franchisor** (the supplier) an initial fee (and often monthly royalties as well). Franchises are a factor of rising importance in the Canadian economy. According to BeTheBoss.ca there are 75 809 franchisees in Canada with annual sales in excess of $100 billion.[35] The Canadian Franchise Association (CFA) is a trade association that represents firms in a wide variety of industries that use the franchise format. Information can be obtained from their website, www.cfa.ca, by phone, or in person at their annual franchising show in Toronto. The show offers a variety of seminars, discussion panels, and workshops on important aspects of the process, such as financing, marketing, buying contracts, and obligations. The CFA also publishes *Franchise Canada Magazine*, a bimonthly magazine geared toward entrepreneurs interested in buying a franchise.[36]

Types of Franchises

Franchises are of three basic types. A *product franchise* gives you the right to sell trade-marked goods, which are purchased from the franchisor and resold. Car dealers and gasoline stations fall into this category. A *manufacturing franchise*, such as a soft-drink bottling plant, gives you the right to produce and distribute the manufacturer's products, using supplies purchased from the franchisor. A *business-format franchise* gives you the right to open a business using a franchisor's name and format for doing business. Chains such as Harvey's, Second Cup, Tim Hortons, Pizza Hut, Chez Cora, and White Spot typify this form of franchising.

How to Evaluate a Franchise

How do you protect yourself from a poor franchise investment? The best way is to study the opportunity carefully before you commit. Speak to knowledgeable and experienced individuals, attend the CFA trade show, and do your homework before signing an agreement. By studying this information, you can determine the financial condition of the franchisor and discover whether the company has been involved in lawsuits with franchisees. Before signing a franchise agreement, it's also wise to consult an attorney. Exhibit 4.4 suggests some points to consider as you study the package of information on the franchise.

Nevertheless, some people find out too late that franchising isn't the best choice for them. They make a mistake common among prospective franchisees—buying without really understanding the day-to-day business. Often, prospects simply don't get beyond the allure of the successful name or concept—or the mistaken notion that a franchise brings instant success. "People go into a sub shop at the noon hour and see the cash register opening and closing," says the president of Franchise Solutions, "what they don't see is having to get there at 4 a.m. to bake the bread." Buying a franchise is much like buying any other business: It requires analyzing the market, finding capital, choosing a site, hiring employees, and buying equipment. The process also includes an element not found in other businesses—evaluating the franchisor.[37]

Exhibit 4.4 **Ten Questions to Ask Before Signing a Franchise Agreement**

A franchise agreement is a legally binding contract that defines the relationship between the franchisee and the franchisor. Because the agreement is drawn up by the franchisor, the terms and conditions generally favour the franchisor. Before signing the franchise agreement, be sure to consult an attorney and make sure you know the answers to these questions.

1. What does the initial franchise fee cover? Does it include a starting inventory of supplies and products?
2. How are the periodic royalties calculated and when are they paid?
3. Are all trademarks and names legally protected?
4. Who provides and pays for advertising and promotional items?
5. Who selects the location of the business?
6. Is the franchise assigned an exclusive territory?
7. If the territory is not exclusive, does the franchisee have the right of first refusal on additional franchises established in nearby locations?
8. Is the franchisee required to purchase equipment and supplies from the franchisor or other suppliers?
9. Under what conditions can the franchisor and/or the franchisee terminate the franchise agreement?
10. Can the franchise be assigned to heirs?

Before entering into a franchise agreement with Vancouver-based 1-800-GOT-JUNK? Cameron Neufeld and Ben Hopper asked a simple question: Tell us about the franchises that have failed. They were impressed by the fact that company representatives were open to discussing failures and the reasons behind them. Knowing they were signing on with a brand that had tried-and-true systems gave them the confidence to sign a franchise agreement and open 1-800-GOT-JUNK? in Winnipeg. Neufeld and Hopper earned $320 000 in revenue in their first year, far surpassing their goal of $240 000. They added two trucks in the same year and continued growth is projected; they expect to reach $1 million in revenue within two years.[38]

One of the best ways to evaluate a prospective franchisor is by talking to other franchisees. At a minimum, you should find out what other franchisees think of the opportunity. If they had it to do over again, would they still invest? You might even want to spend a few months working for someone who already owns a franchise you're interested in. Finally, evaluating a franchise means more than assessing the current operation. What the market will be like tomorrow is just as important an issue to consider. New competition is always searching for opportunities to step in and take advantage of the traffic flow generated by a known franchise.

Advantages of Franchising

Why is franchising so popular? For one thing, when you invest in a franchise you know you are getting a viable business, one that has "worked" many times before. If the franchise is well established, you get the added benefit of instant name recognition, national advertising programs, standardized quality of goods and services, and a proven formula for success. Buying a franchise also gives you instant access to a support network, and in many cases a ready-made blueprint for building a business. For an initial investment (from a few thousand dollars to upward of a million, depending on the franchise), you get services such as site-location studies, market research, training, and technical assistance, as well as help with building or leasing your premises, decorating the building, purchasing supplies, and operating the business for 6 to 12 months. Since few franchisees are able to write a cheque for the amount of the total investment, some franchisors also provide financial assistance (see Exhibit 4.5).

1-800-GOT-JUNK? is a company that enables franchisees to build equity by literally gathering and hauling away junk.

Exhibit 4.5   **The Franchise Solution: How Much Does it Cost?**

Selecting a franchise depends on a lot of factors, but potential franchisees need to complete some calculations before entering into an agreement. Below you will find some figures from companies in different industries that offer franchise opportunities in Canada.

COMPANY NAME	TYPE OF BUSINESS	NUMBER OF FRANCHISES	INITIAL INVESTMENT	FRANCHISE FEE	ROYALTIES	CASH NEEDED
Second Cup	Café	375	$140 000–$280 000	$25 000	9%	Varies
Mad Science	Educational services	156	$36 000–$78 500	$23 500	8%	$15 000–$30 000
1-800-GOT-JUNK?	Junk removal	317	$70 000–$100 000	$20 000	8%	$70 000
Burger King	Fast food	12 642	$294 000–$2 800 000	$50 000	4.5%	$500 000
UPS Store	Postal and business service centres	4601	$131 000–$239 700	$29 950	5%	$50 000
RE/MAX International	Real estate	4611	$20 000–$200 000	$10 000–$25 000	Varies	N/A
Play It Again Sports	Sporting goods retailer	433	$285 000–$400 000	$28 000	5%	$80 000–$115 000
Kumon	Educational services	1568	$9000–$40 000	$1000	$30/student/month	$0

Sources: Canadian Franchise Association website, www.cfa.ca/CFA_HTM/Home.html; Franchise Opportunities website, www.mysitespace.com/franchise_opportunities/top_franchises_canada.asp?offset=30

Disadvantages of Franchising

Although franchising offers many advantages, it is not the ideal choice for everyone. First, owning a franchise is no guarantee of wealth. Even though it may be a relatively easy way to get into business, not all franchises are hugely profitable. Some franchisees barely survive. One of the biggest disadvantages of franchising is the monthly payment, or royalty, that must be turned over to the franchisor. For example, Second Cup franchisees are charged 9 percent royalty fees plus 3 percent for advertising fees.[39] Royalties are not necessarily bad as long as the franchisee receives ongoing assistance in return. Royalty fees vary from nothing at all to 20 percent of sales. Harvey's charges a monthly royalty fee of 5 percent.[40] The Harvey's restaurant concept is owned by Cara Operations along with Swiss Chalet, Kelsey's, Montana's, and Milestone's.[41]

Another drawback of franchises is that many allow individual operators little independence. Franchisors can prescribe virtually every aspect of the business, down to the details of employee uniforms and the colour of the walls. Furthermore, when a chain loses its cutting edge in the marketplace, being stuck with a franchise can be painful. By contrast, if independent retailers run into trouble with their product lines, they can change suppliers or switch to a whole new line of business. Franchisees can't. They're usually bound by contracts to sell only authorized goods, often supplied by the franchisor itself at whatever price the franchisor wants to charge.

Although franchisors can make important decisions without consulting franchisees, the days of franchisors exercising such control are ending. In many cases the relationship between franchisor and franchisee is

Prospective Subway franchisees must attend company training classes and pass a final exam before they can own a Subway sandwich shop.

becoming more of a joint venture. Some franchisors are rewriting contracts to become less dictatorial. Newer contracts offer stock options, automatic contract renewals, and empowerment through franchise advisory boards.[42] Some franchisors are even giving franchisees a voice in how advertising funds are used.

Why New Businesses Fail

Even if you carefully evaluate a prospective franchisor or write a winning business plan, you have no guarantee of success. In fact, you may have heard some depressing statistics about the number of new businesses that fail. Some reports say your chances of succeeding are only one in three; others claim that the odds are even worse, stating that 85 percent of all new business ventures fail within 10 years. Actual statistics, however, show otherwise. Among all companies that close their doors, only about one in seven actually fails—that is, goes out of business leaving behind unpaid debts. Moreover, the true failure rate is much lower if you remove those operations that Dun & Bradstreet (D&B) business analysts say aren't "genuine businesses." For instance, a freelancer who writes one article for a magazine and then stops writing would be counted as a failed business under the traditional measurement (which is based on tax returns).[43]

Most new businesses fail for a number of reasons. Lack of management skills, experience, and proper financing are among the top 10 reasons for failure. So is uncontrolled growth. Growth forces changes throughout the organization that affect every aspect of the business operation. In general, growing companies need to install more sophisticated systems and processes. They must staff positions that never existed and learn how to delegate responsibilities and control. They must hire experienced managers and stay focused. They must also measure success and failure like a fitness fanatic measures their workout results. According to a recent PricewaterhouseCoopers study, only 43 percent of small companies in Canada set financial targets to measure progress.[44]

When growth is too rapid, it can force so much change that things spin out of control; and nothing can kill a successful business faster than chaos. Once the firm starts to expand, it takes the entrepreneur a while to realize he or she is not running a mom-and-pop operation anymore. The tendency to avoid delegating work and attempting to do it all are common. However, at a certain stage the firm must put key people in place to serve

IN-CLASS NOTES

Top 10 Reasons Why New Businesses Fail

1. Management incompetence
2. Lack of industry experience
3. Inadequate financing
4. Poor business planning
5. Unrealistic goals
6. Failure to attract and keep target clients
7. Uncontrollable growth
8. Poor location
9. Poor inventory and financial control
10. Lack of entrepreneurial skills

the needs of the operation. Besides growing too rapidly, another common mistake entrepreneurs make is to stray too far from the original product or market.

Even when signs of failure begin to surface, some entrepreneurs don't pull the plug fast enough. Jeff Schwarz worked three years without drawing a salary and used up $100 000 of his personal savings before closing his photography business, Remarkable Moments.[45] Keep in mind that failure isn't always the end of the world. Many presidents of big successful companies, including Fred Smith of FedEx, can tell stories about how failure got them where they are today or how failure was a valuable learning experience.[46] Moreover, many sources of small business assistance exist to help you plan your new business and overcome these obstacles.

L.O. 6

Sources of Small Business Assistance

Many local business professionals are willing to serve as mentors and can help you avoid the pitfalls of running your own business. As a small business owner, you may turn to small business resources such as the Business Development Bank of Canada, the Canadian Youth Business Foundation (CYBF), incubators, and the Internet. These resources can help you evaluate your business idea, develop a business plan, locate start-up funding sources, and show you how to package your business image professionally.

Business Development Bank of Canada

The Business Development Bank of Canada (BDC) is a financial institution wholly owned by the Government of Canada. BDC has been servicing Canadian business needs for over 60 years and offers a variety of financial products designed to help Canadian businesses grow, such as term loans, subordinate financing, and venture capital. BDC is also a major player in helping businesses improve their management techniques by providing tailored consulting services through a national network of consultants. BDC's financing and consulting solutions are readily accessible from 85 locations nationwide or by calling 1-877-BDC-BANK.

Incubators

incubators
Facilities that house small businesses during their early growth phase

Incubators are centres that provide "newborn" businesses with just about everything a company needs to get started—office space, expert advice, legal and accounting services, clerical services, marketing support, contacts, and more.[47] Some incubators are open to businesses of all types; others specialize in a specific industry or product. For example, Nova Scotia's AgriTECH Park caters to developing technology companies; the Toronto Fashion Incubator nurtures young fashion designers; and the Centre d'Entreprises et d'Innovation de Montréal (CEIM) offers support to various sectors from e-commerce to manufacturing.[48] Regardless, the goal is to convert "tenant" firms into "graduates," so most incubators set limits—from 18 months to 5 years—on how long a company can stay in the nest.[49]

Studies show that firms that start out in incubators typically increase sales by more than 400 percent from the time they enter until the time they leave.[50] Furthermore, 8 out of 10 businesses nurtured in incubators succeed beyond five years. Incubators, of course, are not a new idea. Thousands of them hatch successful businesses each year. Visit the Canadian Association of Business Incubation for more information (www.cabi.ca).

The Internet

The Internet is another source of small business assistance. It provides entrepreneurs the opportunity to test ideas on prospective customers and access to instant market research on topics ranging from favourite brands to useful product features to pricing expectations. Of course there are also countless traditional "how-to" websites available for more basic business questions. For information on Canadian business fundamentals visit www.businessgateway.ca. This federal government site provides a variety of sources and information on taxes and regulations, start-ups, importing and exporting, research and development tax credits, human resources, and so on. The site also has convenient links to information divided by province.

FINANCING A NEW BUSINESS

Once you've decided to go into business for yourself, you will probably need some money to get started. Start-up companies must pay employees, purchase inventory, and acquire assets such as land, production facilities, and equipment before they can generate revenue.

Where can firms obtain the money they need to launch and operate a new business? Most new businesses turn to private financing sources, such as family, friends, and loans from banks, finance companies, or other commercial lenders. As the start-up grows, owners can raise additional funds by selling shares of stock to the public. For instance, The Brick was founded in 1971 as a prototypical small business with only four employees. William Comrie, founder and CEO, preferred to retain tight control of the firm for years. More than 30 years after founding the company—and after the former small business had been transformed into the top Canadian furniture, appliance, and electronics chain—the company raised $272 million by tendering an initial public offering (IPO) in the income trust market.[49] Other firms embrace major external financing in their infant years as a means to grow or survive.

As you can imagine, financing an enterprise is a complex undertaking. The process begins by assessing the firm's financing needs and determining whether funds are needed for the short or the long term. You must also evaluate the cost of obtaining financing, and you must weigh the advantages and disadvantages of financing through debt or equity, taking into consideration the firm's special needs and circumstances. In short, choosing the right sources of financing can be just as important as choosing the right location. Your decision will affect your company's *capital structure*—the mix of debt and equity—forever.

Length of Term

Short-term financing is any financing that will be repaid within one year, whereas *long-term financing* is any financing that will be repaid over a period of more than one year. The primary purpose of short-term debt financing is to ensure that a company maintains its liquidity, or its ability to meet financial obligations (such as inventory payments) as they become due. By contrast, long-term financing is used to acquire long-term assets such as buildings and equipment or to fund a start-up or expansion via any number of growth options.

Cost of Capital

In general, a company wants to obtain money at the lowest cost and least amount of risk. However, lenders and investors want to receive the highest possible return on investment at the lowest risk. A company's *cost of capital*, the average rate of interest it must pay on its financing, depends on three main factors: the risk associated with the company, the current interest rates, and management's selection of funding vehicles. Obviously, the more financially solid a company is, the less risk investors face. However, time also plays a vital role. Because a dollar will be worth less tomorrow than it is today (since you could presumably invest that dollar today and earn a return on it by tomorrow), lenders need to be compensated for waiting to be repaid. As a result, long-term financing generally costs a company more than short-term financing.

Regardless of how financially solid a company is, the cost of money will vary over time because interest rates fluctuate. Companies must take such interest rate fluctuations into account when making financing decisions. For instance, a company planning to finance a short-term project when interest rates are 8.5 percent would want to re-evaluate the project if interest rates rose to, say, 10 percent a few months later. Even though companies try to time their borrowing to take advantage of drops in interest rates, this option is not always possible. A firm's need for money doesn't always coincide with a period of favourable rates. At times, a company may be forced to borrow when rates are high and then renegotiate the loan when rates drop. Sometimes projects must be put on hold until interest rates become more affordable.

Debt versus Equity Financing

secured loans
Loans backed up with something of value that the lender can claim in case of default, such as a piece of property

unsecured loans
Loans requiring no collateral but a good credit rating

stock
Shares of ownership in a corporation

initial public offering (IPO)
A corporation's first offering of stock to the public

Debt financing refers to what we normally think of as a loan. A creditor agrees to lend money to a debtor in exchange for repayment, with accumulated interest, at some future date. Loans can be secured or unsecured. **Secured loans** are those backed by something of value, known as *collateral,* which may be seized by the lender in the event that the borrower fails to repay the loan. The most common types of collateral are accounts receivable; inventories; and property such as marketable securities, buildings, and other assets. **Unsecured loans** are ones that require no collateral. Instead, the lender relies on the general credit record and the earning power of the borrower.

Equity financing is achieved by selling shares of a company's stock. Whenever a corporation offers its shares of ownership, or **stock**, to the public for the first time, the company is said to be *going public.* The initial shares offered for sale are the company's **initial public offering (IPO)**. Going public is an effective method of raising needed capital, but it can be an expensive and time-consuming process. Public companies must file a variety of statements, pay costly fees, and prepare audited financial statements.

When choosing between debt and equity financing, you should weigh the advantages and disadvantages of each (see Exhibit 4.6). In addition to considering whether the financing is for the short or the long term and assessing the cost of the financing, such as interest, fees, and other charges, you must also evaluate your desire for ownership control. Two of the biggest benefits of debt financing are (1) the lender does not gain an

Exhibit 4.6   Debt versus Equity

When choosing between debt and equity financing, companies evaluate the characteristics of both types of funding.

CHARACTERISTIC	DEBT	EQUITY
Maturity	**Specific:** Specifies a date by which it must be repaid.	**Non-specific:** Specifies no maturity date.
Claim on income	**Fixed cost:** Company must pay interest on debt held by bondholders and lenders before paying any dividends to shareholders. Interest payments must be met regardless of operating results.	**Discretionary cost:** Shareholders may receive dividends after creditors have received interest payments; however, the company is not required to pay dividends.
Claim on assets	**Priority:** Lenders have prior claims on assets.	**Residual:** Shareholders have claims only after the firm satisfies claims of lenders.
Influence over management	**Little:** Lenders are creditors, not owners. They can impose certain restrictions (e.g., ratio limits) on management when interest payments are not received.	**Varies:** As owners of the company, shareholders can vote on some aspects of corporate operations. Shareholder influence varies, depending on whether stock is widely distributed or closely held.

ownership interest in the business, and (2) a firm's obligations are limited to repaying the loan even if the company earns tremendous profits. The obligation can be difficult to meet when the business is suffering, but it is a clear advantage when the business thrives. By contrast, equity financing involves an exchange of money for a share of business ownership. It allows firms to obtain funds without pledging to repay a specific amount of money at a particular time, but in exchange for this benefit the firm must give up some ownership control.

Private Financing Sources

Most new companies obtain start-up capital from personal assets, family and friends, or strategic partners or customers. Another source of private financing is big business. Companies such as Coca-Cola and Procter & Gamble fund young companies in exchange for stock or exclusive rights to future products. By working with start-ups, larger companies hope to hasten product development and infuse their own operations with more of the entrepreneurial spirit.[52]

Bank loans are another source of private financing, but obtaining such financing can be difficult for most start-ups. For one thing, banks consider start-ups risky so they tend to shy away from lending money to new businesses. For another, the risk associated with some start-ups justifies higher interest rates than banks are allowed to charge by law. Thus, most banks will finance a start-up only if they can obtain payment guarantees from other financially sound parties or to the extent that the business has marketable collateral, such as buildings and equipment, to back the loan.[53] The Canada Small Business Financing (CSFB) Program helps some businesses access bank loans by having the federal government guarantee up to 85 percent of the lender's losses in case of default. Of course, each business must meet certain criteria to be considered for the program.

In addition to friends, corporate financing, and bank loans, other sources of private financing assistance include venture capitalists, angel investors, credit cards, and government programs.

Venture Capitalists

Venture capitalists are investment specialists who raise pools of capital from large private and institutional sources (such as pension funds) to fund ventures that have a high rapid-growth potential and a need for large amounts of capital. Venture capitalists, or VCs as they're called in entrepreneurial circles, do not simply lend money to a small business as a bank would. Instead, they provide money and management expertise in return for a sizable ownership interest in the business. Once the business becomes profitable, venture capitalists reap the reward by selling their interest to other long-term investors for a sizable profit.

Burned by the dot.com fallout at the end of the millennium, many VCs have become more selective in whom they lend money to. In the last four years VC investment has been fairly steady from $1.67 to 1.84 billion (see Exhibit 4.7), but fewer firms received funding in each of the last four years. Furthermore, dollars invested have not approached the enthusiastic levels found at the turn of the millennium.[54] In addition to being more selective, venture capitalists are also becoming more aggressive in their oversight and management of firms they've already funded. For instance, they are shutting down firms that show little promise and pumping extra cash into those they think can survive. VCs are also examining business plans of capital seekers more skeptically. Applicants must now show real revenue, real customers, and a clear path to profits.[55] Still, most Canadian venture capitalist firms will finance only companies that need $1 million or more.[56] Thus, if you're looking for a more modest amount of financing, you might want to find an angel instead.

venture capitalists
Investment specialists who provide money to finance new businesses or turnarounds in exchange for a portion of the ownership, with the objective of making a considerable profit on the investment; also called VCs

Angel Investors

Comfortable with risks that scare off many banks, *angel investors* put their own money into start-ups with the goal of eventually selling their interest for a large profit. These

Exhibit 4.7 **Venture Capital in Canada**

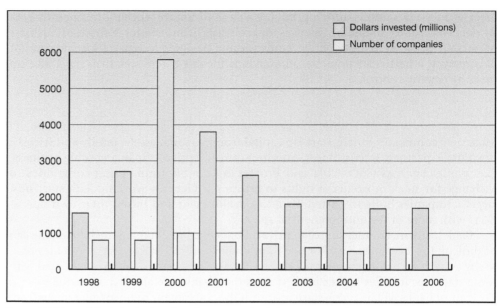

Source: 2006 Annual Statistics Review, Canadian Venture Capital Association website www.cvca.ca/files/Downloads/Final_English_Q4_2006_VC_Data_Deck.pdf, page8.

wealthy individuals are willing to loan smaller amounts of money than VCs, and they are willing to stay involved with the company for a longer period of time.

Start-ups that seek out angels typically have spent their first $50 000 to $100 000 and are now looking for the next $250 000 to grow their business. In addition to providing financing, angels can be a great source of business expertise and credibility. High-profile angels include individuals like Bill Gates and Dave Chilton. For example, when Greta and Janet Podleski decided to write their own corny and creative cookbook called *Looneyspoons*, they had a great idea but lacked financing. Many of their early initiatives were financed by credit cards and their limited personal funds. But when push came to shove, the sisters recruited Dave Chilton, author of the Canadian bestseller *The Wealthy Barber*. He ended up taking a much more active role in the company than he had initially planned, since the book quickly entered the bestseller's list and a production cash crunch followed. The relationship has been successful and the follow-up cookbook, *Crazy Plates*, also earned bestseller status.[57] The two also have a successful show, *Eat, Shrink, and Be Merry*, on Food Network Canada.

Burdened with debt and struggling to cope with their project, Greta and Janet Podleski turned to an angel investor for help. In Dave Chilton, they found the financing and the experience they needed.

Credit Cards

According to one study, one-third of businesses with 19 or fewer employees use credit cards to finance their new business ventures.[58] Many people turn to credit cards because credit card companies don't care how borrowers spend the money just as long as they pay the bill. Others use credit cards because they are the only source of funding available to them. But with high interest rates, credit cards are a risky way to finance a business, as Jorge de la Riva discovered. He used personal credit cards to start his industrial wholesale business—an experience he calls "playing with the tiger." As de la Riva put it, "You can make it work only if you have a definite plan to pay back the debt."[59] Unfortunately, many do not. As we have examined, there are much more intelligent ways to build your dream.

IN-CLASS NOTES

Key Decisions in Financing a Business

- *Length of term* makes a difference to the interest rate you will pay
- *Cost of capital* is determined by factors such as risk level and current interest rates
- *Debt vs. equity* financing is a major decision
- *Financing sources* range from family to venture capitalists to angel investors

BEHIND THE SCENES

Mission-Itech: Growing, Diversifying, and Competing

As Itech celebrated its twentieth year of operation, the company was thriving under a diversified product umbrella. Competition for its core visor product was coming from conventional sources like Bauer, Nike, and Easton, as well as from new industry players like Oakley. Despite these challengers, Itech could still proudly lay claim to about two-thirds of the full-face guard visor market. However, the hockey gear industry was transforming itself from a collection of independent firms into a select group of powerful, consolidated companies. Bauer had been acquired by Nike a decade earlier, and more recently, The Hockey Company, which markets the CCM, Koho, Jofa, and Heaton brands, was acquired by Reebok. Itech had previously gone its own way and resisted the merger temptation. However, in May 2004, Itech, the market leader in hockey facial protection, announced that it was merging with Mission Hockey, the California-based market leader in roller hockey equipment and a strong marketer of sticks, skates, and gloves. Each company possessed a diversified but largely complementary product mix with growing brands.

The new consolidated entity was named Mission-Itech. The combined power of these organizations makes the new company one of the top four players in the market along with The Hockey Company, Bauer/Nike, and Easton. According to

Itech's founder, "The merger is a dream come true. It's rare when you find individuals that share your personal faith, love of product, and passion for hockey. With the strengths of the brands, and the commitment of this ownership team to winning, the future of Mission-Itech is limitless."

The two brands have maintained their grassroots and build on each other's strengths. Mission-Itech continues to be a generous contributor to Canadian minor hockey associations, providing $150 000 worth of equipment annually. It also continues to build on and secure agreements with various leagues. It recently signed a deal with the British Columbia Hockey League (BCHL) to become the league's exclusive helmet and facial-protection provider. A similar deal was struck with the Saskatchewan Junior Hockey League (SJHL).

Mission-Itech's future is exciting. The company has established itself as a full-service hockey organization with a proven track record of success. It will be interesting to see how this marriage evolves.[60]

Critical Thinking Questions

1. Do you believe that the merger with Mission was a good fit for Itech? Why or why not?
2. How will this agreement allow the new firm to compete more effectively in the industry?

Learn More Online
Go to Chapter 4 of this text's website at www.pearsoned.ca/bovee and click on the Mission-Itech hotlink to read more about the company. Has the company secured any additional

contracts with any other hockey leagues? Is there any news about the integration of the Mission and Itech operations? Are any new products being launched?

TEST YOUR KNOWLEDGE

Questions for Review

1. What are the primary economic roles of small businesses?
2. Explain the terms "downsizing" and "outsourcing."
3. What role does the Business Development Bank of Canada play in the economy?
4. What are the elements of an effective business plan?
5. What are the advantages and disadvantages of buying a franchise?
6. List five potential sources of financing for a new business and briefly describe each.
7. What occurs when a company goes public? What is meant by an initial public offering?

Questions for Analysis

8. Why is writing a business plan an important step in starting a new business?
9. What's the difference between a secured and an unsecured loan?
10. Why is it important to establish a time limit for a new business to generate a profit?
11. Take a look at Exhibit 4.7. How do you explain the recent trend in venture capital financing in Canada?
12. Is it easier to start a business form scratch or to purchase a franchise? In answering this question evaluate each option both in the short term and in the long term.
13. If you were opening up a new business would you try to get the support of a local business incubator? In what practical ways do incubators help businesses survive? What psychological advantage is gained by the support provided by these organizations?

14. **Ethical Considerations.** You're thinking about starting your own hot dog and burger stand. You have the perfect site in mind, and you've analyzed the industry and all of the important statistics. It looks as if all systems are go. Uncle Daniel is even going to back you on this one. You really understand the fast-food market. In fact, you've become a regular at a competitor's operation (down the road) for over a month. The owner thinks you're his best customer—he even wants to name a sandwich creation after you! But you're not there because you love the fancy fries. No, you're actually spying. You're learning everything you can about the competition so you can outsmart it. Is this behaviour ethical? Explain your answer.

Questions for Application

15. Briefly describe an incident in your life pertaining to a particular failure. What was it and what did you learn from this experience?
16. Take the entrepreneur test at www.wd.gc.ca/tools/xindex_e.asp to assess your entrepreneurial skills. What did you learn about yourself from this test? How can tests like these help you fine-tune your business skills?
17. **Integrated.** Entrepreneurs are one of the five factors of production, as discussed in Chapter 1. Review that material plus Exhibit 1.2 and explain why entrepreneurs are an important factor for economic success.
18. **Integrated.** Pick a local small business or franchise that you visit frequently and discuss whether that business competes on price, speed, innovation, convenience, quality, or any combination of those factors. Be sure to provide some examples.

PRACTISE YOUR KNOWLEDGE

SHARPENING YOUR COMMUNICATION SKILLS

Effective communication begins with identifying your primary audience and adapting your message to your audience's needs. This is true even for business plans. One of the primary reasons for writing a business plan is to obtain financing. With that in mind, what do you think are the most important things investors will want to know? How

can you convince them that the information you are providing is accurate? What should you assume investors know about your specific business or industry?

BUILDING YOUR TEAM SKILLS

The 10 questions shown in Exhibit 4.4 on page 119 cover major legal issues you should explore before putting down money for a franchise. In addition, however, there are many more questions you should ask when deciding whether to buy a particular franchise.

With your team, think about how to investigate the possibility of buying a Harvey's franchise. First, brainstorm with your team to draw up a list of sources (such as printed sources, Internet sources, and any other suitable sources) where you can locate basic background information about the franchisor. Also list at least two sources you might consult for detailed information about buying and operating a

Harvey's franchise. Next, generate a list of at least 10 questions any interested buyer should ask about this potential business opportunity.

Select a spokesperson to present your team's ideas to the class. After all the teams have reported, hold a class discussion to analyze the lists of questions generated by all teams. Which questions were on most teams' lists? Why do you think those questions are so important? Can your class think of any additional questions that were not on any lists but seem important?

EXPAND YOUR KNOWLEDGE

DISCOVERING CAREER OPPORTUNITIES

Would you like to own and operate your own business? Whether you plan to start a new business from scratch or buy an existing business or a franchise, you will need certain qualities to be successful. Start your journey to entrepreneurship by reviewing this chapter's section on entrepreneurs. Now you are ready to look deeper into the career opportunities of owning and running a small business.

1. Which of the entrepreneurial characteristics mentioned in the chapter describe you? Which of those characteristics can you develop more fully in advance of running your own business?

2. Using library sources, find a self-test on entrepreneurial qualities. Analyze the test's questions. Which of the characteristics discussed in this chapter are mentioned or suggested by the questions included in the test?

3. Answer all of the questions in the self-test you have selected. Which questions seem most critical for entrepreneurial success? How did you score on this self-test

and on the questions you think are most critical? Before you go into business for yourself, which characteristics will you need to work on?

DEVELOPING YOUR RESEARCH SKILLS

Scan issues of print or online editions of business journals and newspapers for articles describing problems or successes faced by small businesses in Canada. Clip or copy three or more articles that interest you and then answer the following questions.

1. What problem or opportunity does each article present? Is it an issue faced by many businesses, or is it specific to one industry or region?

2. What could a potential small business owner learn about the risks and rewards of business ownership from reading these articles?

3. How might these articles affect someone who is thinking about starting a small business?

STUDY GUIDE

SUMMARY OF LEARNING OBJECTIVES

1. Highlight the major contributions small businesses make to the Canadian economy

Small businesses bring new ideas, processes, and vigour to the marketplace. According to Statistics Canada's Survey of Employment Payroll and Hours (SEPH), 48 percent of the private labour force was employed by small enterprises with fewer than 100 employees.[61] Small businesses introduce new goods and services, provide specialized products, and supply the needs of large corporations. Additionally, they spend almost as much as big businesses in the economy each year.

2. Identify the key characteristics that differentiate small businesses from larger ones

In general, small businesses tend to sell fewer products and services to a more targeted group of customers. They have closer contact with their customers and tend to be more open-minded and innovative because they have less to lose than established companies. Small business owners generally make decisions faster and give employees more opportunities for individual expression and authority. Because they have limited resources, however, small business owners must work harder and perform a variety of job functions.

3. Discuss three factors contributing to the increase in the number of small businesses

One factor is the advancement of technology and the Internet, which makes it easier to start a small business, compete with larger firms, or work from home. A second factor is the increase in the number of women and minority entrepreneurs entering the workforce. Finally, corporate downsizing and outsourcing have made self-employment or small business ownership an attractive and viable option.

4. Cite the key characteristics common to most entrepreneurs

Entrepreneurs are highly disciplined, intuitive, innovative, ambitious individuals who are eager to learn and like to set trends. They prefer excitement and are willing to take risks to reap the rewards. Few start businesses for the sole purpose of making money.

5. List three ways of going into business for yourself

You can start a new company from scratch, you can buy a going concern, or you can invest in a franchise. Each option has advantages and disadvantages when it comes to cost, control, certainty, support, and independence.

6. Identify three sources of small business assistance

One source for small business assistance is the Business Development Bank of Canada (BDC), a federally owned organization that provides financial and consulting services to a select group of firms. Incubators are another source. They provide facilities, business resources, and all types of start-up support. Finally, the Internet is an excellent resource for product and market research, business leads, advice, and contacts.

7. Highlight several factors you should consider when evaluating financing options, and discuss the principal sources of small business private financing

When assessing financing options, you should consider the cost and risk of capital and the firm's special needs and circumstances. You should also weigh the term for which financing is needed and the advantages and disadvantages of debt versus equity financing, including impact on ownership control. Bank loans are a principal source of private financing. Family and friends are another. Other alternatives include big businesses, venture capitalists, angel investors, and credit cards. Finally, the Canadian Small Business Financing (CSBF) Program can assist entrepreneurs by guaranteeing small bank loans for up to 85 percent of the amount borrowed.

KEY TERMS

business plan   (114)
franchise   (118)
franchisee   (118)
franchisor   (118)
incubators   (122)

initial public offering (IPO)   (124)
outsource   (112)
secured loans   (124)
small business   (107)
start-up companies   (117)

stock   (124)
unsecured loans   (124)
venture capitalists   (125)

QUESTIONS

Multiple Choice   Circle the correct answer and then check the answers in the back of the book to chart your progress.

1. Which of the following does *not* represent one of the economic roles of small businesses?

   a. Small businesses tend to be bureaucratic.
   b. Small businesses provide specialized goods and services.
   c. Small businesses provide jobs.
   d. Small businesses are innovative.

2. Which of the following best describes female small business owners?

   a. Female entrepreneurs are declining in numbers.
   b. Female-owned businesses have a much lower success rate.
   c. Women are discouraged from owning their own businesses.
   d. Women tend to stick to a business longer; the survival rate for female start-ups is higher.

3. Small businesses are usually more innovative. Which of the following statements describes a reason for this?

   a. Unlike employees in large corporations, small business employees are able to specialize in one specific function.
   b. Small businesses have a much longer decision-making process.
   c. Small business owners are more difficult to reach.
   d. Small business employees have a greater opportunity for individual expression.

4. Which of the following is the best reason for workers to leave big companies to start small businesses?

   a. The worker may make less money.
   b. The worker will not have the support services of the large company.
   c. The individual has the satisfaction of running their own business.
   d. The worker spends more time at work.

5. Which of the following is *not* an advantage of small businesses?

   a. Small businesses can make decisions faster.
   b. Small businesses have more resources than large businesses.
   c. The owners are more accessible.
   d. Employees have greater opportunities for self-expression.

6. Which of the following is true about venture capital (VC) investing?

   a. VC investing has been non-existent in the past decade.
   b. There was a significant decline in VC investing after the dot.com bubble burst.
   c. VC investing has been stable in the past decade.
   d. VC investing has been consistently increasing in the past decade.

7. Which of the following is *not* a common attribute of successful entrepreneurs?

   a. They are glamorous adventurers.
   b. They are highly self-disciplined.
   c. They are eager to learn whatever skills are necessary to reach their goal.
   d. They learn from their mistakes.

8. Which of the following is the most popular reason entrepreneurs tend to provide as to why they started their own business?

   a. They want to be their own boss.
   b. They want to make money.
   c. They want security and are not willing to take risks.
   d. They care about the environment and are willing to sacrifice profits.

9. Which of the following is the best reason for developing a business plan?

   a. All business textbooks tell you to prepare a business plan.
   b. It guides the company's operations and outlines a strategy for turning your vision into reality.
   c. Business plans ensure success.
   d. Preparing the business plan gives you something to do while searching for customers.

10. Which of the following is most likely to fail?

    a. Starting your business from scratch.
    b. Buying an existing local business.
    c. Buying a franchise.
    d. All small businesses are equally likely to fail.

True/False

1. True or false? Lifestyle businesses are usually run by a team rather than an individual, and they expand rapidly by obtaining a sizeable supply of investment capital and by introducing products to a large market.

2. True or false? Most small businesses are high-tech start-ups that are in the process of becoming large.

3. True or false? An advantage of small business is closer contact with customers.

4. True or false? Most small business owners cite making money as a secondary reason for starting their own business.

5. True or false? Working at a franchise operation is a good way to learn if you should invest in your own franchise.

Fill-in-the-Blank

1. _____ are people who create innovation of any kind from *within* an organization (not to be confused with *entrepreneurs,* risk takers in the private enterprise system).

2. A _____ is a written document that provides an orderly statement of a company's goals and how it intends to achieve those goals.

3. A _____ is a small business owner who contracts for the right to sell goods or services of the supplier (franchisor) in exchange for some payment.

4. Secured loans are backed by something of value, known as _____, which may be seized by the lender in the event that the borrower fails to repay the loan.

5. An _____ occurs when a corporation offers its shares of ownership, or stock, to the public for the first time.

6. _____ are investment specialists who raise pools of capital from large private and institutional sources (such as pension funds) to fund companies that have a high rapid-growth potential and a need for large amounts of capital.

7. _____ put their own money into start-ups with the goal of eventually selling their interest for a large profit

8. To make up for layoffs of permanent staff, some companies _____ or subcontract special projects and secondary business functions to experts outside the organization.

9. The _____ offers a wide range of services aimed at helping businesses grow (term loans, venture capital, consulting, etc.)

10. _____ are centres that provide "newborn" businesses with just about everything a company needs to get started, including office space, legal advice, marketing support, contacts, and so on.

See It on the WEB

Visit the Companion Website at **www.pearsoned.ca/bovee**, review the exercises, and complete the following assignments for Chapter 4:

1. The ABCs of IPOs
2. Starting a Business in Canada
3. Financing a New Business

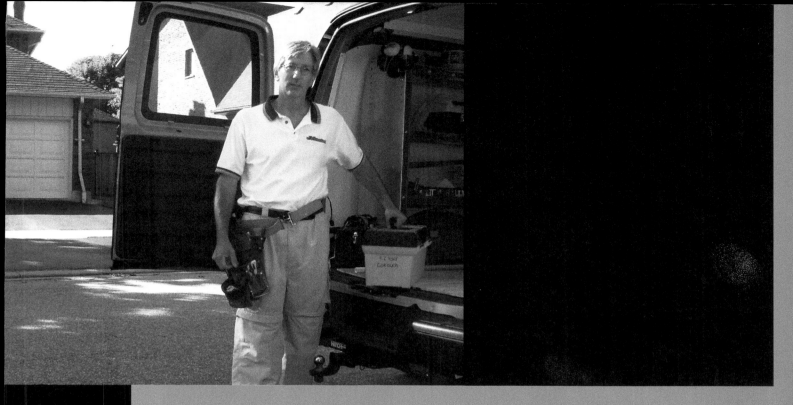

Chapter 5

Selecting the Proper Form of Business Ownership and Exploring Business Combinations

LEARNING OBJECTIVES
After studying this chapter, you will be able to

1 List five advantages and four disadvantages of sole proprietorships

2 List five advantages and five disadvantages of partnerships

3 Explain the differences between common and preferred shares from a shareholder's perspective

4 Highlight the advantages and disadvantages of public share ownership

5 Cite four advantages and three disadvantages of corporations

6 Describe the three groups that govern a corporation and the role of each

7 List advantages and disadvantages offered by the cooperative business format

8 Explain the important role of income trusts to the economy in recent years

9 Identify some of the synergies companies hope to achieve by combining their operations

10 Identify methods a public company can use to fight a hostile takeover

BEHIND THE SCENES

Canadian Home Renovation Centres: Strategic Battleground

www.rona.ca
www.homehardware.ca

In recent years, the most notable change in the home renovation retail industry has been the expansion of The Home Depot into the Canadian marketplace. However, two Canadian companies have chartered their own plans for growth and an increased share in this growing industry. Both offer an interesting look at changing business models in the face of an evolving market.

Rona and Home Hardware possess a shared history; they were both created to protect small independent hardware retailers from the threat of large industry discounters. Rona was founded in 1939 as a loose coalition of Quebec hardware merchants; by the 1960s the group had emerged as a dealer-owned cooperative. Around this time, Walter Hachborn founded Home Hardware in Ontario as a privately held, dealer-owned cooperative. The company has not changed much in the past four decades. According to Hachborn, Home Hardware's philosophy has remained the same: "Maybe I'm stubborn, and I hope that the rest of our dealers are stubborn as well, but I feel that we have to protect the independent from the invasion of large corporations." While Home Hardware hasn't varied from its original strategy, even two decades after Hachborn's retirement in 1988, Rona has definitely changed its course. It now represents one of those large publicly traded, growth-oriented corporations that Hachborn warned against. But Home Hardware is not a helpless victim; it is now a powerful cooperative with more than 1000 retail outlets and is more than capable of fighting the competition.

The links between Home Hardware and Rona do not end with their initial founding missions. Home Hardware and Rona actually joined forces to create a national wholesaler called United Hardware Wholesalers in 1964. Along with this mutually beneficial partnership came a gentleman's agreement that neither firm would invade the other's territory. Neither firm actively tried to recruit across provincial boundaries and the relationship remained intact for decades.

External pressure from indirect competitors like Canadian Tire, the market entry of retailers like The

Home Hardware and Rona represent two different business models in the increasingly competitive home renovation industry.

Home Depot Canada, and the threat of other potential entrants like US-based Lowe's led to a new era of relations that would redefine the game. In recent years, Rona has acquired Cashway Building Centres, Totem Building Supplies, Revy, Lansing, Chester Dawe, Mountain Building Supplies, and Réno-Dépôt (Building Box), to name just a few. For its part, Home Hardware doubled its sales with the acquisition of Beaver Lumber. The gentleman's agreement is history and former allies have become bitter rivals across the nation.

Rona boldly set a goal to achieve $7 billion in revenue by 2007 and 25 percent market share. By mid-2007 it was approaching $6 billion in revenue and a 16.4 percent market share—up from $1.8 billion and 11.1 market share in 2001. These figures represent tremendous growth, but still fall short of the company's lofty goals at this point. However, Rona is still pushing the expansion pedal. Home Hardware is not backing down either; it is out to defend its territory. The true battleground in the next few years is the fight for independent proprietors who still own nearly half this retail market.[1]

CHOOSING A FORM OF BUSINESS OWNERSHIP

One of the most fundamental decisions you must make when starting a business is selecting a form of business ownership. This decision can be complex and have far-reaching consequences for your business. Picking the right ownership structure involves knowing your long-term goals and how you plan to achieve them. Your choice also depends on your desire for ownership and your tolerance for risk. Furthermore, as your business grows, chances are you may change the original form you selected.

The four common forms of business ownership are sole proprietorships, partnerships, corporations, and cooperatives. Each form has its own characteristic internal structure, legal status, size, and fields to which it is best suited (see Exhibit 5.1). Each has key advantages and disadvantages for the owners, as we will discuss in this section.

Sole Proprietorships

L.O. 1

sole proprietorship
A business owned by a single individual

A **sole proprietorship** is a business owned by one person (although it may have many employees), and it is the easiest and least expensive form of business to start. Many farms, retail establishments, and small service businesses are sole proprietorships, as are many home-based businesses (such as caterers, consultants, and computer programmers).

Advantages of Sole Proprietorships

A sole proprietorship has many advantages. One is ease of establishment—all you have to do to launch a sole proprietorship is obtain necessary licences, open a chequing account for the business, register a name with the provincial government, and open your doors. Another advantage is the satisfaction of working for yourself. As a sole proprietor, you can make your own decisions about when to work, whom to hire, what prices to charge, whether to expand, and whether to shut down. Best of all, you can keep all after-tax profits and the company is taxed at individual levels, which can be advantageous in the early stages when the company has modest returns.

As a sole proprietor, you also have the advantage of privacy; you do not have to reveal your performance or plans to anyone. Although you may need to provide financial information to a banker if you need a loan, and you must provide certain financial information when you file tax returns, you do not have to prepare any reports for outsiders as you would if the company were a public corporation.

Disadvantages of Sole Proprietorships

unlimited liability
The legal condition under which any damages or debts attributable to the business can also be attached to the owner because the two have no separate legal existence

One major drawback of a sole proprietorship is the proprietor's **unlimited liability**. From a legal standpoint, the owner and the business are one and the same. Any legal damages or debts of the business are the owner's responsibility. As a sole proprietor,

Exhibit 5.1   **Characteristics of the Forms of Business Ownership**

The "best" form of ownership depends on the objectives of the people involved in the business.

STRUCTURE	OWNERSHIP RULES AND CONTROL	TAX CONSIDERATIONS	LIABILITY EXPOSURE	EASE OF ESTABLISHMENT AND TERMINATION
Sole Proprietorship	One owner has complete control.	Profits and losses flow directly to the owner and are taxed at individual rates.	Owner has unlimited personal liability for business debts.	Easy to set up. Owner must generally sell the business to get his or her investment out.
Partnership	Two or more owners; each partner is entitled to equal control unless the agreement specifies otherwise. In a limited partnership the general partner controls the business; limited partners don't participate in the day-to-day management.	Profits and losses flow directly to the partners and are taxed at individual rates. Partners share income and losses equally unless the partnership agreement specifies otherwise.	Personal assets of operating partners are at risk from business creditors. In a limited partnership the limited partners are only liable for the amount of their investment.	Easy to set up. Partnership agreement is recommended but not required. Partners must generally sell their share in the business to recoup their investment.
Corporation	Unlimited number of shareholders for public corporations; no limits on stock classes or voting arrangements. Ownership and management of the business are separate. Shareholders in public corporations are not involved in daily management decisions; in private or closely held corporations, owners are more likely to participate in managing the business.	Profits and losses are taxed at corporate rates. Profits are taxed again at individual rates when they are distributed to investors as dividends. The dividend tax credit was created to offset the effects of this double taxation.	Investor's liability is limited to the amount of his or her investment.	Expense and complexity of incorporation varies depending on the jurisdiction; it can be costly. In a public corporation, shareholders may trade their shares on the open market; in a private corporation, shareholders must find a buyer for their shares to recoup their investment.

you might have to sell personal assets like your home to satisfy a business debt. If someone sues you over a business matter, you might lose many of your personal possessions if you do not have the proper types and amount of business insurance.

In some cases, the sole proprietor's independence can also be a drawback because it means that the business depends on the talents and managerial skills of one person. If problems crop up, the sole proprietor may not recognize them or may be too proud to seek help, especially given the high cost of hiring experienced managers and consultants. Other disadvantages include the difficulty of a single-person operation obtaining large sums of capital and the limited life of a sole proprietorship. Although some sole proprietors pass their business on to their heirs, the owner's death may mean the demise of the business. Even if the business does transfer to an heir, the founder's unique skills may have been crucial to the successful operation of the business.

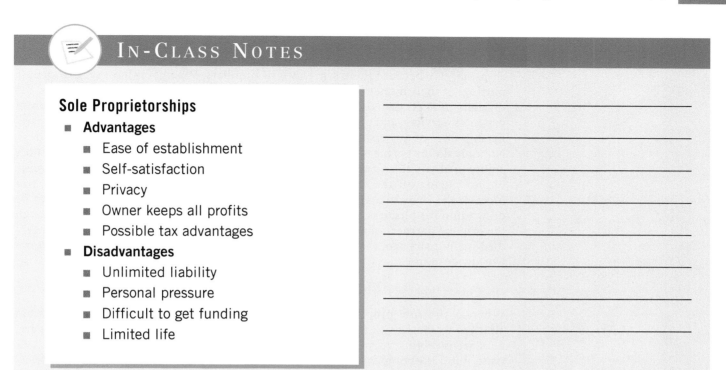

IN-CLASS NOTES

Sole Proprietorships
- **Advantages**
  - Ease of establishment
  - Self-satisfaction
  - Privacy
  - Owner keeps all profits
  - Possible tax advantages
- **Disadvantages**
  - Unlimited liability
  - Personal pressure
  - Difficult to get funding
  - Limited life

Partnerships

L.O. 2

If starting a business on your own seems intimidating, you might decide to share the risks and rewards with a partner. In that case, you would form a **partnership**—a legal association of two or more people as co-owners of a business for profit. You and your partners would share the profits and losses of the business and perhaps the management responsibilities. Your partnership might remain a small, two-person operation or it might have multiple partners.

Partnerships are of two basic types. In a **general partnership** all partners are considered equal by law, and all are liable for the business's debts. To guard against personal liability exposure, some organizations choose to form a **limited partnership**. Under this type of partnership one or more persons act as *general partners* who run the business, while the remaining partners are passive investors (that is, they are not involved in managing the business). These partners are called *limited partners* because their liability (the amount of money they can lose) is limited to the amount of their capital contribution.

Some North American jurisdictions now recognize **limited liability partnerships** (LLPs). Under this form, all partners in the business are limited partners and have limited liability for the debts and obligations of the partnership. The LLP was created to protect partners from legal claims pursued against another partner who acts negligently. Under this format the limited partners are only liable if they are personally negligent. However, the partnership's assets are at risk from all partners' actions. Most jurisdictions restrict LLPs to professionals such as attorneys, physicians, dentists, and accountants.[2] This form originated in the United States in 1991 and is slowly gaining popularity in Canada, with Alberta, Ontario, Quebec, Saskatchewan, Manitoba, and Nova Scotia enacting various forms of LLPs in recent years.[3]

Advantages of Partnerships

Proprietorships and partnerships have some of the same advantages. Like proprietorships, partnerships are easy to form. Partnerships also provide the same tax advantages as proprietorships, because profits are taxed at individual rates rather than at

partnership
An unincorporated business owned and operated by two or more people under a voluntary legal association

general partnership
A partnership in which all partners have the right to participate as co-owners and all are liable for the business's debts

limited partnership
A partnership composed of one or more general partners and one or more partners whose liability is limited to the amount of their capital investment

limited liability partnership
A partnership where all of the partners are limited partners and have limited liability

corporate rates. This can lead to savings while the company is in its infancy and profits are fairly modest.

However, in a couple of respects, partnerships are superior to sole proprietorships, largely because there's strength in numbers. When you have several people putting up their money, you can start a more ambitious enterprise. In addition, the diversity of skills that good partners bring to an organization leads to innovation in products, services, and processes, which improves your chances of success.[4] The partnership form of ownership also broadens the pool of capital available to the business. Not only do the partners' personal assets support a larger borrowing capacity, but the ability to obtain financing also increases because general partners are legally responsible for paying off the debts of the group. Finally, by forming a partnership you increase the chances that the organization will survive, because new partners can be drawn into the business to replace those who die or retire. For example, even though the original partners of the accounting firm KPMG Peat Marwick (founded in 1897) died many years ago, the company has maintained operations and expanded into a worldwide entity.

Disadvantages of Partnerships

Whereas the sole proprietor reaps all the profits of success, shared profits are attached to shared risk in a partnership. If the organization is thriving and all partners are receiving adequate rewards for their investments it may not be a major issue, but if the company is barely making any profit the partners may begin to wonder if all the additional opinions are worth it. Since all general partners have unlimited liability, if one of the firm's partners makes a serious business or professional mistake and is sued by an unhappy client, all general partners are accountable. At the same time, general partners are also responsible for any debts incurred by the partnership.

Another disadvantage of partnerships is the potential for interpersonal problems. Difficulties often arise because each partner wants to be responsible for managing

---

In-Class Notes

Partnerships
- **Advantages**
  - Easy to establish
  - Strength in numbers
  - Increased capital
  - Potential tax advantages
  - Diversity of skills
  - Extended life
- **Disadvantages**
  - Unlimited liability
  - Interpersonal problems
  - Sharing profits
  - Dealing with an unproductive partner
  - Decision-making complications

_____

_____

_____

_____

_____

_____

_____

_____

_____

the organization. Making major decisions can lead to serious arguments. Electing a managing partner to lead the organization may diminish the conflicts, but disagreements are still likely to occur. Moreover, the partnership may have to face the question of what to do with unproductive partners. Additionally, if a partner wants to leave the firm, conflicts can arise over claims on the firm's profits and on capital the partner invested. Provisions for handling the departure and addition of partners are usually covered in the partnership agreement.

Partnership Agreement

A *partnership agreement* is a written document that states the terms of operating the partnership by spelling out the partners' rights and responsibilities. Although the law does not require a written partnership agreement, it is wise to work with a lawyer to develop one. One of the most important features of such an agreement is to address potential sources of conflict that could result in battles between partners. The agreement spells out such details as the division of profits, decision-making authority, expected contributions, and dispute resolution. Moreover, a key element of this document is the buy/sell agreement, which defines the steps a partner must take to sell his or her partnership interest or what will happen if one of the partners dies.

Corporations

A **corporation** is a legal entity with the power to own property and conduct business. The modern corporation evolved in the nineteenth century when large sums of capital were needed to build railroads, steel mills, and manufacturing plants. Such endeavours required so much money that no single individual or group of partners could hope to raise enough. The solution was to sell shares in the business to numerous investors who would get a cut of the profits in exchange for their money. These investors got a chance to vote on certain issues that might affect the value of their investment, but they were not involved in managing the day-to-day operations. The investors were protected from the risks associated with such large undertakings by having their liability limited to the amount of their investment.

It was a good solution, and the corporation quickly became a vital force in the economy. As rules and regulations developed to define what corporations could and could not do, corporations acquired the legal attributes of people. Like you, a corporation can receive, own, and transfer property; make contracts; and sue and be sued. Unlike sole proprietorships and partnerships, a corporation's legal status and obligations exist independently of its owners.

corporation
A legally chartered enterprise having most of the legal rights of a person, including the right to conduct business, to own and sell property, to borrow money, and to sue or be sued; owners of the corporation enjoy limited liability

shareholders
Proportionate owners of a corporation; based on the number of shares held

stock certificate
A document that proves stock ownership

common shares
Shares whose owners have voting rights and have the last claim on distributed profits and assets

L.O. 3

Ownership

The corporation is owned by its **shareholders**, who are issued shares in return for their investments. These shares are represented by a **stock certificate**, and they may be passed down (inherited) or sold to someone else. As a result, the company's ownership may change drastically over time while the company and its management remain intact (as long as the company is economically sound). The corporation's unlimited lifespan combined with its ability to raise capital gives it the potential for significant growth.

Common Shares   Most shares issued by corporations are **common shares**. Owners of common shares have voting rights and get one vote for each share they own. They can elect the company's board of directors in addition to voting on major policies that will affect ownership—such as mergers, acquisitions, and takeovers. For example, when Google purchased YouTube for US$1.65 billion, investors in YouTube earned a great reward for their early investment. In the deal, company co-founders

YouTube is a site that many of you visit on a daily basis. Co-founders Chad Hurley and Steven Chen earned these big grins when the company was acquired by Google, leading to big paydays for YouTube's early shareholders.

Avis has never paid cash dividends to shareholders. The company believes that shareholders are best served by reinvesting profits into the company to foster long-term growth.

dividends
Distributions of corporate assets to shareholders in the form of cash or other assets

preferred shares
Shares that give their owners first claim on a company's dividends (before common shareholders) and assets if the company goes out of business (after all debts have been paid)

Chad Hurley and Steven Chen acquired shares of Google worth US$346 million and US$326 million, respectively. The riches were shared by many employees and investors. Julie Supan, a spokeswoman for YouTube, had shares evaluated at nearly US$5 million on the day the deal was announced.[5]

Besides conferring voting privileges, common shares frequently pay **dividends**, which are payments to shareholders from the company's profits. Dividends can be paid in cash or shares (called *stock dividends*). They are declared by the board of directors, but their payment is not mandatory. Some companies, especially young or rapidly growing ones, pay no dividends. Instead, they reinvest their profits in new product research and development, equipment, buildings, or other assets so they can grow and earn future profits. Research in Motion (RIM), the Waterloo, Ontario–based designer, manufacturer, and marketer of wireless communications tools like the BlackBerry, does not pay cash dividends. RIM chooses to focus on a long-term growth strategy.[6]

In addition to dividends, common shareholders can earn a return on their investment. If shareholders sell their shares in good times for more than they paid for them, they stand to pocket a handsome gain. Since the value or price of a company's common shares is subject to many economic variables besides the company's own performance, investing in common shares is risky and shareholders may not get any profit at all.

Preferred Shares   In contrast to common shares, **preferred shares** do not usually carry voting rights. They do, however, give preferred shareholders the right of first claim on the corporation's assets (in the form of dividends) after all of the company's debts have been paid if the company ever goes out of business. Moreover, preferred shareholders get their dividends before common shareholders do. The amount of preferred dividend is usually set (or fixed) at the time the preferred shares are issued and can provide investors with a source of steady income. Like common shares, however, dividends on preferred shares are not mandatory and may be omitted in hard times. Still, most preferred shares are *cumulative preferred shares*, which means that any unpaid dividends owed to preferred shareholders must be paid before dividends are paid to common shareholders.

Technologies That Are Revolutionizing Business

GROUPWARE

Groupware is an umbrella term for systems that let people communicate, share files, present materials, and work on documents simultaneously.

HOW IT'S CHANGING BUSINESS

Groupware is changing the way employees interact with one another—and even the way businesses work together. In fact, groupware is changing the way many companies are structured. *Shared workspaces* are "virtual offices" that give everyone on a team access to the same set of resources and information: databases, calendars, project plans, archived instant messages and emails, reference materials, and team documents. These workspaces (which are typically accessible through a web browser) let you and your team organize your work files

into a collection of electronic folders, making it easy for geographically dispersed team members to access shared files anytime, anywhere. Employees no longer need to be in the same office or even in the same time zone. They don't even need to be employees. Groupware makes it easy for companies to pull together partners and temporary contractors on a project-by-project basis.

Groupware is often integrated with web-based meeting systems that combine instant messaging, shared workspaces, videoconferencing, and other tools like *virtual whiteboards* that let teams collaborate in real time.[7]

WHERE YOU CAN LEARN MORE

Log on to www.zdnet.com and use the search button to find descriptions, cases, blogs, and news items about the topic.

Public versus Private Ownership   The shares of a **private corporation** like Cirque du Soleil are held by only a few individuals or companies and is *not publicly traded*. By withholding their shares from public sale, the owners retain complete control over their operations and ownership. Other companies like McCain Foods, The Jim Pattison Group, Kruger, and Hyatt Hotels have opted to remain private corporations (also referred to as *closed corporations* or *closely held companies*). These companies finance their operating costs and growth from company earnings or other sources like bank loans. In contrast, the shares of a **public corporation** are held by and available for sale to the general public; thus the company is said to be *publicly traded*.

In an interview conducted by *60 Minutes*, Guy Laliberté, founder of Cirque du Soleil, was asked why he had not taken his company public. He began to laugh and assured the interviewer that the Cirque was comfortable as a private corporation. He pointed to his organization's need for creativity that investors, shareholders, and accountants should not be a part of. As a private corporation, Cirque du Soleil does not have to jump through hoops to please investors. Cirque Du Soleil is another shining example of the potential of a private corporation (see the box entitled "Pattison: The Potential of the Private Corporation"). Cirque du Soleil has shows around the world and a virtual domination of the Las Vegas strip with shows at the Bellagio, MGM Grand, Mirage, New York New York, and Treasure Island hotel casinos. Laliberté was named Ernst and Young's World Entrepreneur of the Year in 2007. His philosophy seems to be paying off.[8]

In Chapter 4 we discussed the concept of going public in the context of financing the enterprise. Bear in mind that in addition to providing a ready supply of capital, public ownership has other advantages and disadvantages. Among the advantages are increased liquidity, enhanced visibility, and the establishment of an independent market value for the company. Moreover, having publicly traded shares gives companies flexibility to acquire other firms. Rona first issued shares back in 2002, an important step in its plan to expand and become a true national retailer. Nevertheless, selling shares to the public has distinct disadvantages: (1) the cost of going public is high; (2) filing requirements are burdensome; (3) some ownership control is lost; (4) management must be ready to handle the administrative and legal demands of heightened public exposure; and (5) the value of the company's shares becomes subject to external forces beyond the company's control.

Advantages of Corporations

No other form of business ownership can match the success of the corporation in bringing together money, resources, and talent; in accumulating assets; and in creating wealth. (Exhibit 5.2 lists the top 10 Canadian companies as ranked by market capitalization). As a corporation grows it capitalizes on a diverse labour pool, greater financing options, and expanded research and development capabilities. The corporation has certain qualities that make it the best vehicle for reaching those objectives. One such quality is limited liability. Although a corporate entity can assume tremendous liabilities, it is the corporation that is liable and not the private shareholders. For example, Johannes Schwartlander ran his marble and granite business as a sole proprietorship for seven years. When the company began to grow, Schwartlander decided to incorporate to protect himself. According to a close source, "When they added so many employees and started installing marble panels ten stories high, he realized that if something fell down, he would be responsible." Incorporation also protects people like Schwartlander from personal liability should his business go bankrupt.[9]

In addition to limited liability, corporations that sell shares to the general public have the advantage of **liquidity**, which means that investors can easily convert their shares into cash by selling it on the open market. This option makes buying shares in a corporation attractive to many investors. In contrast, liquidating the assets of a sole proprietorship or a partnership can be difficult. Moreover, shareholders of public corporations can easily transfer their ownership by selling their

According to founder Guy Laliberté, Cirque du Soleil's business model is not really suited to investor constraints. Creativity is its key to success, and the systems involved in running a public company could dampen this vital force. How could you justify a new risky acrobatic act to an accountant?

Pattison: The Potential of the Private Corporation

You may be thinking that for a corporation to truly reach its potential it must go public and reap the rewards of being a listed company on the stock exchange. However, there are many successful companies in a range of businesses from production to entertainment to retailing to advertising that show how the private corporation has a great deal of potential for growth and long-term success.

The Jim Pattison Group is one such company. Jim Pattison may be known in some circles as the invisible billionaire, but his influence is clear. If you live in British Columbia you are all too familiar with the Pattison

Pattison Outdoor Advertising's reach is evident on sidewalks, metros, bus stops, and highways across the nation.

empire. From car dealerships to media outlets, the company is front and centre. However, the reach of this company extends well beyond BC. In fact, it reaches more than 400 worldwide locations. The employee roster totals over 29 000 people, and its revenues surpass $6.3 billion. The Jim Pattison Group, Canada's third-largest private corporation, has diverse businesses that include automotive, media, packaging, food sales and distribution, magazine distribution, entertainment, exports, and financial industries. Jim Pattison also has substantial investments in companies like Canfor, a major lumber producer with 30 production plants in the United States and Canada and $3.6 billion in annual sales.

Without the pressure of the public eye watching their every step, private corporations can thrive and focus on long-term goals. Far too often, public corporations are caught looking at the scoreboard (share prices) rather than focusing on the game (the company's goals). Next time you are driving down the highway or strolling down a street, pay attention to the billboards or bus stop posters—you will more than likely find a Pattison logo attached to it.[10]

Questions for Critical Thinking

1. Why do you think The Jim Pattison Group has resisted the temptation to become a public corporation?
2. Go to The Jim Pattison Group website at www.jimpattison.com and list all the various businesses that fall under the umbrella of this diverse company.

| Exhibit 5.2 | **Top 10 Canadian Corporations Ranked by Market Cap** |

Insurers, banks, and resource companies dominate the top 10—Canadian investors still have very traditional tastes.

RANK	COMPANY	MARKET CAP ($MILLION)	INDUSTRY
1	Manulife Financial	54 070	Financial
2	Royal Bank of Canada	53 600	Financial
3	EnCana Corporation	44 934	Energy
4	Bank of Nova Scotia	42 568	Financial
5	Toronto-Dominion Bank	39 647	Financial
6	Imperial Oil Ltd.	38 388	Energy
7	Shell Canada	34 696	Energy
8	Suncor Energy	33 556	Energy
9	Canadian Natural Resources	30 910	Energy
10	Bank of Montreal	28 918	Financial

Source: Courtesy of *Report on Business*, "The Top 1000," 2006 Edition, www.theglobeandmail.com/v5/content/tp1000/index.php?view=top_100_market_cap

IN-CLASS NOTES

Corporations
- **Characteristics**
  - Owners enjoy limited liability
  - Can enter into contracts
  - Can own and sell property
  - Can sue or be sued
- **Public Corporation**
  - Many shareholders
  - Publicly traded
- **Private Corporation**
  - Few shareholders
  - Not publicly traded

shares to someone else. Thus, corporations tend to be in a better position than proprietorships and partnerships to make long-term plans because of their unlimited lifespan and easy access to funding through the sale of shares. As they grow, corporations can benefit from the diverse talents and experience of a large pool of employees and managers. Moreover, large corporations are often able to finance projects internally.

Keep in mind that a company need not be large to incorporate. Most corporations, like most businesses, are relatively small, and most small corporations are privately held. The big ones, however, are *really* big. Wal-Mart employs more than 1.8 million people worldwide. To put that figure in perspective, only three Canadian cities (metropolitan areas) have a population that surpasses Wal-Mart's employee roster: Vancouver, Toronto, and Montreal.[11]

Disadvantages of Corporations

Corporations are not without some disadvantages. The paperwork and costs associated with incorporation can be burdensome, particularly if you plan to sell shares. The complexity varies by jurisdiction, but regardless of where you live it is wise to consult an attorney and an accountant before incorporating. In addition, corporations are taxed twice. They must pay corporate income tax on the company's profits, and individual shareholders must pay income taxes on their share of the company's profits received as dividends.

Another drawback relates to publicly owned corporations. As mentioned earlier, such corporations are required by the government to publish information about their finances and operations. Disclosing financial information increases the company's vulnerability to competitors and to those who might want to take control of the company against the wishes of the existing management. It also increases the pressure on corporate managers to achieve short-term growth and earnings targets to satisfy shareholders and to attract potential investors. Some cite such earnings pressure as the driving force behind the aggressive accounting practices recently adopted by some corporations, as we will discuss in Chapter 13.

IN-CLASS NOTES

Evaluating the Corporate Option
- **Advantages**
  - Access to capital
  - Limited liability
  - Increased liquidity
  - Unlimited lifespan
- **Disadvantages**
  - Excessive paperwork
  - Double taxation
  - Disclosure requirements

_____

_____

_____

_____

_____

_____

_____

subsidiary corporations
Corporations whose shares are owned entirely or almost entirely by another corporation

parent company
A company that owns most, if not all, of another company's shares and takes an active part in managing that company

Some corporations are not independent but actually owned by a single entity. For example, **subsidiary corporations** are partially or wholly owned by another corporation, known as the **parent company**, which supervises the operations of the subsidiary. For example, Mac's Convenience Stores LLC is a subsidiary of Quebec-based Alimentation Couche-Tard. Many of Canada's largest corporations are subsidiaries of foreign companies. For example, The Home Depot Canada and General Motors Canada are subsidiaries of their American parent companies.

L.O. 6

Corporate Governance

Although a corporation's common shareholders own the business, they are rarely involved in managing it, particularly if the corporation is publicly traded. Instead, the common shareholders elect a board of directors to represent them, and the directors select the corporation's top officers, who actually run the company (see Exhibit 5.3).

chief executive officer (CEO)
The person appointed by a corporation's board of directors to carry out the board's policies and supervise the activities of the corporation

The centre of power in a corporation usually lies with the **chief executive officer**, or **CEO**. Together with the chief financial officer (CFO) and the chief operating officer (COO), the CEO is responsible for establishing company policies, managing corporate direction, and making big decisions that will affect the company's growth and competitive position, as Chapter 6 discusses in detail. Keep in mind that the CEO may also be the chairman of the board, the president of the corporation, or both. Moreover, because corporate ownership and management are separate, the owners may get rid of the managers (in theory, at least) if the owners vote to do so.

Shareholders   Shareholders of a corporation can be individuals, other companies, non-profit organizations, pension funds, or mutual funds. All shareholders who own

Exhibit 5.3   **Corporate Governance**

In theory, the shareholders of a corporation own the business, but in practice they elect others to run it.

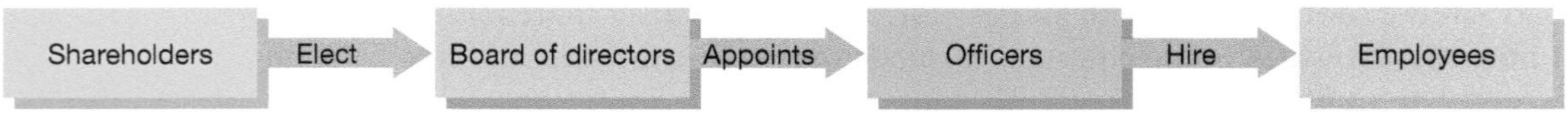

Shareholders → Elect → Board of directors → Appoints → Officers → Hire → Employees

voting shares are invited to an annual meeting to choose directors, select an independent accountant to audit the company's financial statements, and attend to other business. Those who cannot attend the annual meeting in person vote by **proxy**, signing and returning a slip of paper that authorizes management to vote on their behalf. Since shareholders elect the directors, in theory they are the ultimate governing body of the corporation. In practice, however, most individual shareholders in large corporations—where the shareholders may number in the millions—accept the recommendations of management. For example, the Bank of Nova Scotia has 990 000 000 shares outstanding.[12] An individual investor with a few hundred shares will not make an impact on the major policy decisions of this corporation.

Typically, the more shareholders a company has, the smaller the influence each shareholder has on the corporation. However, some shareholders have more influence than others. In recent years, *institutional investors* such as pension funds (e.g., Ontario Teachers' Pension Plan, Caisse de dépôt), insurance companies, and mutual funds have accumulated an increasing number of shares in Canadian corporations. As a result, these large investors are playing a powerful role in governing the corporations in which they own substantial shares, especially with regard to the election of a company's board of directors.[13] Furthermore, at companies such as Avis and Bombardier, employees are major shareholders so they have a voice in how the company is run.

Volkswagen executives address shareholders at the company's annual meeting.

proxy
A document authorizing another person to vote on behalf of a shareholder in a corporation

Board of Directors Representing the shareholders, the **board of directors** is responsible for declaring dividends, guiding corporate affairs, reviewing long-term strategic plans, selecting corporate officers, and overseeing financial performance. Depending on the size of the company, the board might have anywhere from 3 to 35 directors, although 15 to 25 is the typical range for traditional corporations, with a smaller number for e-businesses. The board has the power to vote on major management decisions, such as building a new factory, hiring a new president, or buying a new subsidiary. The board's actual involvement in running a corporation varies from one company to another. Some boards are strong and independent and serve as a check on the company's management. Others act as a "rubber stamp," simply approving management's recommendations. The level of board independence has been steadily improving. According to a recent *Report on Business* review, only 7 percent of companies in Canada's benchmark S&P/TSX index do not have a majority of independent directors on their boards.[14]

board of directors
A group of people, elected by the shareholders, who have the ultimate authority in guiding the affairs of a corporation

Retired CEOs and politicians are popular choices to serve on boards. Peter Godsoe, former chairman and CEO of the Bank of Nova Scotia, serves on several boards. Former CEOs are popular choices because they possess a wide range of knowledge and invaluable business experience.[15] Former politicians are attractive candidates because they possess connections at the highest levels of political and business circles. Former prime minister Brian Mulroney sits on the following boards: The Blackstone Group, Avis Budget Group, Wyndham Worldwide, Barrick Gold, Archer Daniels Midland, and Quebecor.[16] Women are slowly catching up in the boardroom, but still make up only 13.5 percent of directors at the top 100 companies. Former deputy prime minister Anne McLellan has moved back to her law practice in Edmonton and has recently joined three boards: Nexen, Agrium, and Cameco.[17]

Former prime minister Brian Mulroney serves on the board of directors of various companies, including Archer Daniels Midland, Quebecor, and Blackstone. Recent allegations of misconduct will need to be cleared up if Mulroney is to remain a sought-after individual for this function.

At most large corporations, boards are composed exclusively of directors from outside the company, with only the CEO and a senior executive or two from inside the organization. This arrangement helps ensure that the board provides diligent and independent oversight.[18] But the debate over the optimal number of inside versus outside directors continues. Too many insiders can give management too much power over a group whose function is to protect shareholders' rights and investments. However, outside directors are at a serious information disadvantage. Thus, they must rely largely on the CEO's portrayal of the firm's condition and prospects.

Every director at The Home Depot must make formal visits to at least 20 stores each year to gain hands-on knowledge of the company's operation.

L.O. 7

To compensate directors for their time and contributions, most large companies pay their directors a sizable fee and issue them stock options—the right to purchase a set number of shares at a specific price (see Chapter 10). Some think compensation in the form of company shares aligns the directors' interests with those of other shareholders, while critics of this practice claim that directors with excessive shareholdings could compromise their independent decision making by placing too much focus on a company's short-term share performance.

Cooperatives

Cooperatives are organized and controlled by their members, who pool their resources to create benefits for themselves and their clients. The cooperative form is characterized by open voluntary membership and a democratic control mechanism that provides each member with one decision-making vote. Unlike public corporations, which can be controlled by individuals who possess the majority of shares, cooperatives are designed to give each member an equal say.[19] As we saw in the opening feature, Home Hardware operates as a retail cooperative. Membership in this group permits retailers to enjoy the benefits of bulk buying power and centralized advertising, which allows them to compete more effectively. There are various forms of cooperatives ranging from financial to housing to retail and beyond. Among the top financial cooperatives are recognizable names such as Desjardins Group, Vancity Savings Credit Union, Coast Capital Savings Credit Union, The Co-operators, and the Credit Union Central of Saskatchewan.[20]

Advantages of Cooperatives

The primary advantage of the cooperative form is the strength provided by being affiliated with a group. When a cooperative negotiates with a manufacturer on behalf of its members, it possesses the buying power that each individual member would not possess if it negotiated alone. The cooperative form champions the little guy because each member possesses one equal vote—all voices are heard. Furthermore, at the end of the year surplus earnings are distributed to members based on their level of service usage. Finally, members of a cooperative enjoy the protection of limited liability.[21]

Disadvantages of Cooperatives

Of course the cooperative form has its share of drawbacks. The cooperative structure tends to lead to a longer decision-making process and it also demands extensive record keeping. There is also less incentive to invest in additional capital as members may choose short-term surplus dividends over long-term investments. Finally, as with all collections of opinions, cooperatives can lead to disagreements and or conflicts among members.[22]

L.O. 8

Income Trusts

In recent years, income trusts have been a major topic of discussion in Canadian business circles. Income trusts have been around for decades; they are especially popular in the real estate and energy sectors of the economy. The bright spotlight was truly placed on trusts between 2002 and 2006 when a growing trend emerged. By mid-2006 it seemed like most companies were either converting into trusts or having discussions to that effect (see Exhibit 5.4). Major announcements by Telus and BCE seemed to indicate the continued wave of the future. However, this trend abruptly changed when the federal government announced a new Tax Fairness Plan in late 2006 that took direct aim at the income trust sector.

IN-CLASS NOTES

Cooperatives
- Organized and controlled by members
- **Advantages**
  - Bargaining power
  - Democratic structure
  - Surplus earnings distribution
  - Limited liability
- **Disadvantages**
  - Longer decision-making processes
  - Extensive record keeping
  - Less incentive to invest in additional capital
  - Potential conflict among members

So what was the big attraction? Trusts have many features that are similar to corporations (shares or "trust units" are traded on exchanges), but the profits generated by a trust flow straight to investors and can lead to significant cash flow and tax advantages. In addition, income trusts tend to pay significant distributions. To level the playing field, the federal government slapped a 34 percent levy on trusts in October 2006.

Exhibit 5.4   **Market Capitalization of Publicly Traded Trusts (1995–2006)**

The trend clearly demonstrated in this graph placed great pressure on the federal government to act and address the growing (and tax draining) numbers of income trusts.

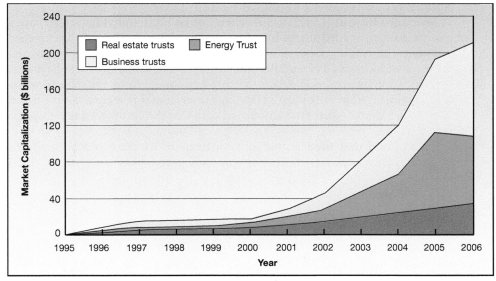

Source: Department of Finance Canada. "Canada's New Government Announces Tax Fairness Plan." Ottawa, October 31, 2006. Retrieved September 24, 2007, from http://www.fin.gc.ca/news06/06-061e.html. Reproduced with the permission of the Minister of Public Works and Government Services, 2008.

This measure was taken to reverse the income-trust trend and recapture some of the tax revenue losses the government was experiencing. But it was not just a money grab, as the cynics claimed. Under the income trust format executives are under pressure to distribute all profits to unitholders, when in fact the long-term growth of the company may depend on capital investments. Long-term productivity was often being sacrificed at the expense of short-term payout expectations.[23] The move worked, and the growing trend of converting to income trusts was halted.

UNDERSTANDING BUSINESS COMBINATIONS

L.O. 9

Companies have been combining in various configurations since the early days of business. Joining two companies is a complex process because it involves every aspect of both companies. For instance, executives have to agree on how the combination will be financed and how the power will be transferred and shared. Marketing departments need to figure out how to blend advertising campaigns and sales forces. Data processing and information systems, which seldom mesh, must be joined together seamlessly.

Mergers and Acquisitions

merger
A form of business combination in which two companies combine forces to create a new single entity

acquisition
A form of business combination in which one company buys another company's voting shares

leveraged buyout (LBO)
A situation in which individuals or a group of investors purchase a company primarily with debt secured by the company's assets

Two of the most popular forms of business combinations are mergers and acquisitions. In a **merger**, two companies combine forces to create a new entity. The closing case in Chapter 4 discussed how two famous hockey equipment companies, Itech and Mission, merged a few years ago; the two companies ceased to exist as independent companies and a new entity called Mission-Itech was created.[24] Sometimes a merger is referred to as a consolidation; there is a minor technical difference between the two, but the terms are used interchangeably.

A company can acquire another firm by purchasing that firm's voting shares. This transaction is generally referred to as an **acquisition** and is completed when the shareholders of the acquired firm tender their shares for either cash or shares in the acquiring company. For example, Reebok paid CDN$21.25 per outstanding share of The Hockey Company—the total transaction was worth US$204 million.[25] Another recent acquisition took place when Imvescor (owner of Pizza Delight) acquired the Bâton Rouge restaurant chain through its Imvescor Restaurants Inc. division for $43 million.[26]

A **leveraged buyout (LBO)** occurs when one or more individuals purchase a company's publicly traded shares by using borrowed funds. The debt is expected to be repaid with funds generated by the company's operations and, often, by the sale of some of its assets. For an LBO to be successful, a company must have reasonably priced shares and easy access to borrowed funds. Unfortunately, in many cases the acquiring company must make huge interest and principal payments on the debt, which then depletes the amount of cash that the company has for operations and growth.

Keep in mind that the purpose and outcome of mergers and acquisitions are basically the same, which is why you will often hear these terms used interchangeably.

Advantages of Mergers and Acquisitions

Business combinations provide several financial and operational advantages. Combined companies hope to eliminate expenses for redundant resources, increase their buying power, increase revenue by cross-selling products to each other's customers, increase market share, eliminate manufacturing overcapacity, and gain access to new expertise and systems. Often these advantages are grouped under umbrella terms such as *economies of scale*, *efficiencies*, or *synergies*, which

Imvescor inc., which operates out of Moncton, New Brunswick, owns over 250 restaurants in the Maritimes, Quebec, Ontario, and Alberta under the following banners: Pizza Delight®, Mikes® Baton Rouge®, and Scores®.

generally mean that the benefits of working together will be greater than if each company continued to operate independently.

Disadvantages of Mergers and Acquisitions

Despite the promise of economies of scale, studies of merged companies show that 65 to 85 percent of these deals fail to actually achieve promised efficiencies.[27] One such study even found that the profitability of acquired companies on average declined.[28] "Bigger" does not always mean "better."

Part of the problem with mergers is that companies often borrow large amounts of money to acquire a firm, and the loan payments on this corporate debt gobble up cash needed to run the business. Managers must help combine the operations of the two entities, pulling them away from their normal day-to-day responsibilities. Another obstacle that companies face when combining forces is that they tend to underestimate the difficulties of merging two distinct corporate cultures (we will discuss organizational culture in detail in Chapter 6). Culture includes not only management style and practices, but also the way people dress, how they communicate, and whether they punch a time clock. *Culture clash* occurs when two joining companies have different beliefs about what is really important, how to make decisions, how to supervise people, how to communicate, and so on. In too many deals, the acquiring company imposes its values and management systems on the acquired company without any regard to what worked well there.

Current Trends in Mergers and Acquisitions

Mergers and acquisitions are nothing new. Companies have been dancing to this beat for quite some time. Smart companies are constantly looking for companies in the same business or in complementary businesses to buy out or form a new partnership with. The major difference in recent years has been the origins of the suitors. As global competition increases companies are no longer able to hide behind government-imposed barriers, and many firms are looking for acquisitions or partners to remain competitive. Businesses of various sizes, including some of the biggest players in the world, are being targeted. From telecommunications to banking to oil to automobiles, mass consolidation

Learning from Business Blunders

OOPS

When new-school Internet upstart America Online (AOL) acquired old-school publishing and cable TV titan Time Warner, a company with five times AOL's revenues, it was a sure sign that the digital revolution was reshaping the world economy. Sadly, the deal of the century didn't take long to turn into one of the biggest business blunders of all time, destroying $200 billion in shareholder wealth and throwing tens of thousands of people out of work. Lawsuits followed and settlements were reached, but the promised success was elusive.

WHAT YOU CAN LEARN

Perhaps more than anything else, the AOL–Time Warner deal is a painful reminder that mergers and acquisitions are extremely complicated, difficult, and prone to failure, even under the best of circumstances. In the perfect storm of the AOL–Time Warner deal, failure was virtually guaranteed. Corporate egos clashed as the buttoned-down Time Warner crew and the free-spirited AOL crew failed to harmonize. The purchase was made with hyper-inflated dot.com shares that were ready for a collapse (as most new economy shares were at the time). Finally, the success of the deal was based on the unproven assumption that advertisers would flock en masse to online media outlets, which didn't happen.[29]

IN-CLASS NOTES

Mergers and Acquisitions
- **Pros**
  - Economies of scale
  - Efficiencies
  - Synergies
- **Cons**
  - High risk from debt
  - Management distractions
  - Corporate culture clashes

_____

_____

_____

_____

_____

_____

_____

L.O. 10

hostile takeovers
Situations in which an outside party buys enough shares in a corporation to take control against the wishes of the board of directors and corporate officers

Alcan has 68 000 employees in 61 countries with revenues of $23 billion annually. It has successfully acquired some competitors and has also been able to stave off others in the global takeover game.

among industry competitors is one strategy for competing in the global marketplace. Although some people think the answer is for governments to protect domestic companies from foreign takeovers, protectionist measures are frowned upon in economic circles. As one economist put it, "If you don't play the game as a global company, you're going to wind up a niche player."[30]

Still, after over a decade of unprecedented mega-mergers, some of the largest companies are shedding some unprofitable acquisitions and focusing on generating internal growth from their core businesses. Well before the Molson Coors merger (discussed in the opening case to Chapter 2), Molson sold off various assets, including the Montreal Canadiens hockey club, to focus on its core business of selling beer. Factors contributing to this trend reversal include economic slowdowns, increased political uncertainty, global market saturation, and pressure from shareholders to generate profits. (See the box entitled "Hey, Wanna Lose a Few Billion? We Have a Sure Deal for You!")

Merger and Acquisition Defences

Although 95 percent of all business combinations are friendly deals, some 5 percent are **hostile takeovers**, in which one party fights to gain control of a company against the wishes of the existing management.[31] A few years ago, Alcan Inc., the Canadian aluminium giant, launched a successful $5 billion hostile bid to acquire French competitor Pechiney SA.[32] Since that time Alcan has been the target of an unsuccessful hostile bid from Alcoa, and other companies are lining up to take a run at Alcan. Only time will tell if the company will eventually be bought out or continue to acquire.

As mentioned earlier, every corporation that sells shares to the general public is vulnerable to a takeover by any individual or company that buys enough shares to gain a controlling interest. Basically, a hostile takeover can be launched in one of two ways: by tender offer or by proxy fight. In a *tender offer* the raider offers to buy a certain number of shares in the corporation at a specific price. The price offered is generally more than the current share price so that shareholders are motivated to sell. The raider hopes to get enough shares to take control of the corporation and to replace the existing board of directors and management. In a *proxy fight*, the raider launches a public relations battle for shareholder votes,

Hey, Wanna Lose a Few Billion? We Have a Sure Deal for You

If you were about to make a multibillion-dollar deal but statistics suggested you had an 80 percent chance of failure, would you go for it? Sure you would, if you work in the slightly wacky world of corporate mergers and acquisitions.

Studies consistently show that the vast majority of mergers and acquisitions fail to meet their primary goal of increasing shareholder value. In many cases, the only people who win in these deals are the shareholders in acquired companies, when eager buyers shell out more for their shares than they are really worth.

How can so many otherwise talented people keep making so many mistakes? Although no one answer applies to every situation, experts cite these common mistakes:

■ Companies often rush into deals in search of synergies, but then fail to develop them. Once the merger is done, management doesn't follow through to make sure that the computer programmers, sales representatives, engineers, and others responsible for carrying out the details are able to cut costs and boost revenues according to plan.

■ Companies pay excessively high premiums for the companies they acquire. According to one expert, any time an acquiring company pays a premium of 25 percent or more over the trading price of the acquired company's shares, the acquiring company is exposing itself and its shareholders to substantial risk.

■ Companies are unable to deal with differences in corporate cultures. A successful merger requires more than simply respecting each partner's differences. Procedures must be established to settle disputes and to integrate workforces and product lines strategically.

Without question, some mergers and acquisitions are beneficial to companies and shareholders in both the short term and the long term. However, managers need to approach mergers and acquisitions with caution by answering these questions: Will the regulatory environment change? How will competitors respond? Do the expected gains justify the up-front costs and disruption to business operations? Will the cultures, systems, processes, and product lines of the two companies blend well? Executives will continue to believe they can beat the odds and craft successful deals, but without seeking honest answers to these questions first they're likely to only find themselves adding to the depressing statistics about mergers and acquisitions.[33]

Questions for Critical Thinking

1. If you were on the board of directors at a company and the CEO announced plans to merge with a competitor, what types of questions would you want answered before you gave your approval?

2. If a CEO has the opportunity to merge with or acquire another company and is reasonably certain that the transaction will benefit shareholders, is the CEO obligated to pursue the deal? Why or why not?

hoping to enlist enough votes to remove the board and management. Proxy fights sound easy enough, but they are tough to win. The insiders have certain advantages: They can get in touch with shareholders, and they can use money from the corporate treasury in their campaign.

Corporate boards and executives have devised a number of schemes to defend themselves against unwanted takeovers:

■ *The poison pill.* This plan makes the company less valuable to the potential raider; the idea is to discourage the takeover from actually happening. The company could create a special sale of newly issued shares to current shareholders at prices below the market value of the company's existing shares. Such action increases the number of shares the raider has to buy, making the takeover more expensive. Many shareholders believe that poison pills are bad for a company because they can protect weak management and discourage takeover attempts that would improve company value.[34]

- *The golden parachute.* This method is designed to benefit a company's top executives by guaranteeing them generous compensation packages if they ever leave or are forced out after a takeover. These packages often total millions of dollars for each executive and therefore make the takeover much more expensive for the acquiring company. Thus, a golden parachute has an effect similar to that of a poison pill.

- *The shark repellent.* This tactic is more direct; it is simply a requirement that shareholders representing a large majority of shares approve of any takeover attempt. Such a plan is possible only if management has the support of the majority of shareholders.

- *The white knight.* This tactic uses a friendly buyer to take over the company before a raider can. White knights usually agree to leave the current management team in place and to let the company continue to operate in an independent fashion.

Sometimes a group of investors is able to take a publicly traded company off the open market by purchasing all of the company's shares. This tactic is known as "taking the company private." Descendants of Levi Strauss, for example, borrowed US$3 billion to buy back all of Levi's shares so that the family could maintain control of the company.[35]

Although companies like Levi Strauss may go private to avoid unwanted takeovers, this is a radical action. First, shareholders must be willing to sell, and second, buyers must have enough cash on hand to repurchase all of the company's shares. Furthermore, going private eliminates the firm's ability to raise future capital by selling authorized shares to the public.

Strategic Alliances and Joint Ventures

In Chapter 2 we discussed strategic alliances and joint ventures from the perspective of international expansion. We defined a *strategic alliance* as a long-term partnership between companies to jointly develop, produce, or sell products, and we defined a *joint venture* as a special type of strategic alliance in which two or more firms jointly create a new business entity that is legally separate and distinct from its parents. In this chapter we look at these forms of business combinations as an alternative to a merger or acquisition.

Many strategic alliances are driven by the realization that no single company can offer customers everything they need. Strategic alliances can accomplish many of the same goals as a merger or acquisition without a long process of integration.[36] They can help a company gain credibility in a new field, expand its market presence, gain access to technology, diversify offerings, and share best practices without forcing the partners to become fast friends for life. If the arrangement does not work out or its usefulness expires, the partners can simply go their separate ways.

Companies can also form joint ventures to get the same benefits enjoyed by strategic alliances. Joint ventures are similar to partnerships except that they are formed for a specific, limited purpose. They allow companies to use each other's complementary strengths that might otherwise take too long to develop on their own, and they allow companies to share what may be the substantial costs and risks of starting a new operation.[37] This was the motivation behind the creation of Virgin Mobile Canada, a joint venture between Bell Mobility and Richard Branson's Virgin Group. Neither company needed the other to launch a new cell phone service, but the venture made sense to both parties because the deal enabled them to share expertise, knowledge, and networks. Virgin provides specific expertise and brand equity in the youth market whereas Bell provides the best cell phone infrastructure network in Canada.[38]

BEHIND THE SCENES

Recruiting the Independent Retailer

An estimated 5000 independent retailers still control approximately 50 percent of the home renovation industry. The race to recruit them is intensifying between Home Hardware and Rona. Meanwhile, The Home Depot continues to build more big-box stores and has also created a new smaller neighbourhood format (small by The Home Depot standards, that is). Lowe's has finally made its long-awaited entry into Canada by opening a few locations in Ontario. This is a small first step, but industry experts are watching this company for its next big move. The small independents will continue to feel pressure to pick sides or continue to fight on their own. The following outlines the options Home Hardware and Rona offer to existing retailers.

Comparing Business Models

Home Hardware's cooperative network consists of more than 1000 owner-operated retail outlets. The system is served by regional warehouses that are stocked by a single companywide buying arm. Home Hardware also provides a nationwide marketing campaign that emphasizes the diversity of these outlets. Home Hardware is positioned as anti–big box, service-first outlets. This non-imposing approach is a key selling point, especially in rural areas.

Rona has a unique approach: it is a publicly traded company with various business models. It consists of a combination of big-box, medium-sized, and neighbourhood outlets with both corporate and dealer-owned franchise stores as well as affiliated independent dealers. This allows it to absorb independent retailers of all sizes. According to CEO Robert Dutton, "With three types of ownership options and three types of stores the firm now offers nine possible combinations to suit retailers and ensure Rona's growth." The hybrid system offers something for everyone.

Costs and Commitment

Rona expects an initial investment of $96 000 in Rona shares over a four-year period. It also expects its retailers to sign a 10-year contract. Home Hardware does not require a time commitment and the initial investment amounts to just $1500 in member fees.

Final Thoughts

Paul Strauss, Home Hardware's CEO, is very secretive about the company's plans and he points to this as one of the advantages of running a privately held organization. According to Strauss, his dealers and not some analyst on Bay Street are his first priority. In addition to keeping members informed and placing reasonable investment demands, this model champions the little guy. On the other hand, Rona's CEO, Robert Dutton, can point out that although there is a substantial initial investment, Rona's original dealers each now own $3 to $4 million worth of Rona shares because of the appreciation of their corporate shares. Rona also offers the flexibility of a hybrid system that includes corporate, franchise, and affiliated stores. Critics argue that there is a danger that the small independent affiliated store is so low on the pecking order that it doesn't have much say despite its commitment.

Rona's growth ambitions are being displayed in all its actions. By mid-2007 it was digesting recent purchases like Newfoundland-based Chester Dawe and Burnaby, BC–based Curtis Lumber. Rona is also set to move into the United States with stated ambitions to become the third-largest US home improvement retailer. The initial steps are planned for the Northeast. As Rona moves forward, each additional share of the Canadian market will be tougher to earn than the previous one. Home Hardware has its own plans, and so do the other competitors. It is the independent retailers who are standing in the centre of this intensifying market share battlefield.[39]

Critical Thinking Questions

1. Rona's decision to become a publicly traded company was an important element of their expansion plan. How has this decision helped Rona in realizing additional growth?
2. Home Hardware has maintained its strategy as a privately held cooperative. What is the primary goal of such a cooperative?
3. Evaluate the business decision being faced by independent Canadian retailers. Make a list of pros and cons for each option: joining Rona, joining Home Hardware, or staying independent.
4. If you owned an independent home renovation retail outlet, which model would you opt for? Explain your answer.

Learn More Online

Go to Chapter 5 of this text's website at www.pearsoned.ca/bovee and click on the Rona hotlink to learn about the company's latest financial results. What were Rona's revenues in the most recent fiscal year? How many stores do they possess? Have they made any major acquisitions in the past 12 months?

TEST YOUR KNOWLEDGE

Questions for Review

1. What are the main advantages of a cooperative?

2. What is the difference between preferred and common shares?

3. What is meant by liquidity? Why is this an advantage for corporations over the sole proprietorship and partnership business formats?

4. What is a leveraged buyout?

5. What is the difference between a merger and an acquisition?

Questions for Analysis

6. Why is it advisable for partners to enter into a formal partnership agreement?

7. The small landscaping company that you started two years ago is growing quickly. You have hired three new workers in the past year and have added a second truck. New contracts are being negotiated with some large industrial clients. Is it wise to incorporate at this point in time? Explain.

8. Should the board of directors be composed almost exclusively of members from outside the organization? What are the benefits of such an arrangement? What are the potential drawbacks?

9. If you were an executive for a company that was the target of a takeover attempt, which type of defence would you recommend? Explain.

10. **Ethical Considerations.** Your father sits on the board of directors of a large, well-admired public company. Yesterday, while looking for an envelope in his home office, you stumbled upon a confidential memorandum. Unable to resist the temptation to read the memo, you discovered that your father's company is talking with another publicly traded company about the possibility of a merger, with your father's company being the survivor. Dollar signs flash before your eyes. Should the merger occur, the value of the other company's shares is likely to soar. You're tempted to log on to your E*TRADE Canada account in the morning and place an order for 1000 of that company's shares. Better still, maybe you'll give a hot tip to your best friend in exchange for the four Nickelback tickets that your friend has been flashing in your face all week. Would either of those actions be unethical? Explain your answer.

Questions for Application

11. Suppose you and some friends want to start a business to take tourists on wilderness backpacking expeditions. None of you has much extra money, so your plan is to start small. However, if you are successful, you would like to expand into other types of outdoor tours and perhaps even open up branches in other locations. What form of ownership should your new enterprise take and why?

12. Selling antiques on the Internet has become more successful than you originally imagined. Overnight your website has grown into a full-fledged business— now generating some $200 000 in annual revenue. It's time to think about the future. Several competing online antique dealers have approached you with a proposal to merge their websites with yours to create the premier online antique store. The money sounds good, but you have some concerns about joining forces. What might they be? What other growth options should you consider before joining forces with another business?

13. **Integrated.** In Chapter 2 we discussed international strategic alliances and joint ventures. Why might a Canadian company want to enter into those types of arrangements instead of merging with a foreign concern?

14. **Integrated.** Look back at Chapter 4. How might each of the following small business scenarios affect your selection of a form of business ownership?

    a. You have decided to purchase a franchise operation instead of starting a business from scratch.

    b. You can't tap into your personal financial resources or rely on friends or family for financial assistance.

    c. You are a hard worker, visionary, a risk-taker, highly disciplined, and very bright. But you lack managerial experience.

PRACTISE YOUR KNOWLEDGE

SHARPENING YOUR COMMUNICATION SKILLS

You have just been informed that your employer is going to merge with a firm in Germany. Because you know very little about German culture or business practices, you think it might be a good idea to do some preliminary research—just in case you have to make a quick trip overseas. Using the Internet or library sources, find information on the German culture and customs and prepare a short report discussing such cultural differences as German social values, decision-making customs, concepts of time, use of body language, social behaviour and manners, and legal and ethical behaviour.

BUILDING YOUR TEAM SKILLS

Directors often have to ask tough questions and make difficult decisions, as you will see in this exercise. Imagine that the director general of your college or university has just announced plans to retire. Your team, playing the role of the school's board of directors, must decide how to choose a new director general to fill this vacancy next semester.

First, generate a list of the qualities and qualifications you think the school should seek in a new director general. What background and experience would prepare someone for this key position? What personal characteristics should this individual possess? What questions would you ask to find out how each candidate measures up against the list of credentials you have prepared? Now list all the stakeholders that your team, as directors, must consider before deciding on a replacement for the retiring director general. Of these stakeholders, whose opinions do you think are most important? Whose are least important? Who will be directly and indirectly affected by the choice? Of these stakeholders, which should be represented as participants in the decision-making process?

Select a spokesperson to deliver a brief presentation to the class summarizing your team's ideas and the reasoning behind your suggestions. After all the teams have completed their presentations, discuss the differences and similarities among credentials proposed by all the teams for evaluating candidates. Then compare the teams' conclusions about stakeholders. Do all teams agree on the stakeholders who should participate in the decision-making process? Have a class discussion on a board's responsibility to its stakeholders.

EXPAND YOUR KNOWLEDGE

DISCOVERING CAREER OPPORTUNITIES

Are you best suited to working as a sole proprietor, as a partner in a business, or in a different role within a corporation? For this exercise, select three businesses with which you are familiar: one run by a single person, such as a dentist's practice or a local landscaping firm; one run by two or three partners, such as a small accounting or law firm; and one that operates as a corporation, such as Petro-Canada or Telus.

1. Write down what you think you would like about being the sole proprietor, one of the partners, or the corporate manager or an employee in the businesses you have selected. For example, would you like having full responsibility for the sole proprietorship? Would you like being able to consult with other partners in the partnership before making decisions? Would you like having limited responsibility when you work for other people in the corporation?

2. Now write down what you might dislike about each form of business. For example, would you dislike the risk of bearing all legal responsibility in a sole proprietorship? Would you dislike having to talk with your partners before spending the partnership's money? Would you dislike having to write reports for top managers and shareholders of the corporation?

3. Weigh the pluses and minuses you have identified in this exercise. Based on your comparison, which form of business most appeals to you?

DEVELOPING YOUR RESEARCH SKILLS

Review recent issues of business newspapers or periodicals (print or online editions) to find an article or series of articles illustrating one of the following business developments: merger, acquisition, hostile takeover, or leveraged buyout.

1. Explain in your own words what steps or events led to this development.

2. What results do you expect this development to have on (a) the company itself; (b) consumers; and (c) the industry the company is part of? Write down and date your answers.

3. Follow your story in the business news over the next month (or longer, as your instructor requests). What problems, opportunities, or other results are reported? Were these developments anticipated at the time of the initial story, or did they seem to catch industry analysts by surprise? How well did your answers to question 2 predict the results?

STUDY GUIDE

SUMMARY OF LEARNING OBJECTIVES

1. List five advantages and four disadvantages of sole proprietorships

Sole proprietorships have five advantages: (1) They are easy to establish; (2) they provide the owner with control and independence; (3) the owner reaps all the profits; (4) profits are taxed at individual rates; and (5) the company's plans and financial performance remain private. The four main disadvantages of a sole proprietorship are (1) the company's financial resources are usually limited; (2) management talent may be thin; (3) the owner is liable for the debts and damages incurred by the business; and (4) the business may cease when the owner dies.

2. List five advantages and five disadvantages of partnerships

In addition to being easy to establish and having profits taxed at individual rates, partnerships offer a greater ability to obtain financing, longevity, and a broader base of skills. The main disadvantages of partnerships are unlimited liability for general partners, the potential for personality and authority conflicts, having to share profits (regardless of how abundant or meagre they may be), the potential of having to deal with an unproductive partner, and the added complexity to decision making.

3. Explain the differences between common and preferred shares from a shareholder's perspective

Common shareholders can vote and can share in the company's profits through discretionary dividends and adjustments in the market value of their shares. In other words, they can profit from their investment if the value of the shares rise above the price they paid for them, or they can lose money if the value of the shares fall below the price they paid for them. In contrast, preferred shareholders cannot vote, but they can get a fixed return (dividend) on their investment, and they have a priority claim on assets after creditors if the business ceases operations.

4. Highlight the advantages and disadvantages of public shares ownership

Public shares ownership offers a company increased liquidity, enhanced visibility, financial flexibility, and an independently established market value for the shares. The disadvantages of public ownership are high costs, burdensome filing requirements, loss of ownership control, heightened public exposure, and loss of direct control over the market value of the company's shares.

5. Cite four advantages and three disadvantages of corporations

Because corporations are a separate legal entity, they have the power to raise large sums of capital, they offer shareholders protection from liability, they provide liquidity for investors, and they have an unlimited lifespan. In exchange for these advantages, businesses pay large fees and have to file excessive paperwork to incorporate, and they are subject to double taxation. Finally, if publicly owned, corporations must adhere to strict government reporting requirements.

6. Describe the three groups that govern a corporation and the role of each

Shareholders are the basis of the corporate structure. They elect the board of directors, who in turn elect the officers of the corporation. The corporate officers carry out the policies and decisions of the board. In practice, the shareholders and board members usually follow the lead of the chief executive officer. However, some board members are more active than others. This is especially true of young dot.com corporations that appoint directors for their management expertise and industry connections.

7. List advantages and disadvantages offered by the cooperative business format

Cooperatives provide the following advantages: strength in numbers, buying power, a democratic system, and year-end surplus earnings. Cooperatives have the following disadvantages: a long decision-making process, extensive record keeping, less incentive to invest in additional capital, and potential conflicts among members.

8. Explain the important role of income trusts in the economy in recent years

The growing popularity of income trusts from 2002 to 2006 became a political issue when many major corporations began to convert. This format has the advantage of allowing profits to flow directly to unitholders to be taxed at individual rates (as opposed to the double taxation profits from corporations are subject to). This was beginning to become a drain on government revenues, causing the federal government to eventually step in and announce a 34 percent levy on income trusts to level the playing field with corporations.

9. Identify some of the synergies companies hope to achieve by combining their operations

By combining their operations, companies hope to eliminate redundant costs, increase their buying power,

increase their revenue, improve their market share, eliminate manufacturing overcapacity, and gain access to new expertise and personnel.

10. Identify methods a public company can use to fight a hostile takeover

Corporate boards and executives have come up with a number of techniques (poison pill, golden parachute, shark repellent, white knight) to defend public companies against unwanted takeovers. These approaches can devalue a company in the eyes of potential investors and transform an attractive opportunity into something far less desirable.

KEY TERMS

acquisition   (148)
board of directors   (145)
chief executive officer (CEO)   (144)
common shares   (139)
corporation   (139)
dividends   (140)
general partnership   (137)
hostile takeovers   (150)

leveraged buyout (LBO)   (148)
limited liability partnership   (137)
limited partnership   (137)
liquidity   (141)
merger   (148)
parent company   (144)
partnership   (137)
preferred shares   (140)

private corporation   (141)
proxy   (145)
public corporation   (141)
shareholders   (139)
sole proprietorship   (135)
stock certificate   (139)
subsidiary corporations   (144)
unlimited liability   (135)

QUESTIONS

Multiple Choice   Circle the correct answer and then check the answers in the back of the book to chart your progress.

1. How many owners can participate in a partnership?

    a. One
    b. Only two
    c. Only three
    d. Two or more

2. Which of the following is an advantage of the sole proprietorship form of business organization?

    a. Unlimited liability
    b. Limited liability
    c. Easy and inexpensive to set up
    d. Access to capital

3. What is the major advantage of forming a corporation?

    a. Limited liability
    b. Only one owner is permitted
    c. Most major businesses are corporations
    d. The corporation pays corporate income tax, and the owners pay personal income tax on dividends

4. What is a document authorizing another person to vote on behalf of a shareholder known as?

    a. Dividend
    b. Proxy
    c. Preferred share
    d. Shark repellent

5. Which of the following is a major disadvantage of becoming a public company owned by shareholders throughout the world?

    a. The company gains access to funds.
    b. The company must pay as much as $500 000 to have its shares listed on the stock market.
    c. The company gains a worldwide reputation for excellence.
    d. The company continues to have unlimited liability.

6. Which of the following statements accurately reflects an advantage of the cooperative form of business?

   a. The cooperative structure leads to a longer decision-making process.
   b. The cooperative structure requires extensive record keeping.
   c. Members of a cooperative have limited liability.
   d. Cooperatives often lead to disagreements and conflicts among members.

7. Which of the following is an important reason for companies to merge?

   a. Combined companies can eliminate overlapping expenses.
   b. Mergers are required by law to encourage bigger companies.
   c. Mergers promote diversity in the workforce of the combined entity.
   d. Mergers sharpen the marketing focus of the combined entity.

8. Which group of shareholders is having an increasing influence on corporations?

   a. Small-time investors
   b. Bondholders
   c. Entrepreneurs
   d. Institutional investors

9. In a hostile takeover attempt, the raider can make a proposal to buy a certain number of shares for a specified amount of money per share. What is this called?

   a. Proxy fight
   b. Vertical offer
   c. Tender offer
   d. Leveraged proxy bid

10. Which of the following is *not* a defence against unwanted takeovers?

   a. Poison pill
   b. Golden handcuffs
   c. Shark repellent
   d. White knights

True/False

1. True or false? Being a sole proprietor guarantees a shorter work week.

2. True or false? Regardless of how many owners a corporation has, the law generally treats the corporation the same way it treats an individual person.

3. True or false? Mergers often fail because companies have a difficult time merging corporate cultures.

4. True or false? The board of directors guarantees the owners of common shares dividend payments every quarter.

5. True or false? All companies, regardless of the form of organization, must submit their financial statements to the appropriate securities commission, which makes them available to the public.

Fill-in-the-Blank

1. Sole proprietors are subject to great financial risk because they do not have the protection of _____ enjoyed by shareholders in a corporation.

2. _____ shareholders have voting rights and have the last claim on the distribution of profits and assets.

3. Doctors, lawyers, and some other professionals often join forces in a special type of company called a _____ .

4. Mac's Convenience Stores LLC is a _____ company of parent company Alimentation Couche-Tard.

5. In a _____ scenario, one or more individuals buy all the shares of a publicly traded company using borrowed funds.

6. In a _____ , all partners are considered equal by law, and all are liable for the business's debts.

7. Distributions of corporate assets to shareholders in the form of cash or other assets are known as _____ .

8. _____ does not usually carry voting rights, but it provides the holder the right of first claim on the corporation's assets (in the form of dividends) after all of the company's debts have been paid.

9. Corporations that sell shares to the general public have the advantage of _____, which means that investors can easily convert their shares into cash by selling it on the open market.

10. The _____ defence to a hostile takeover requires shareholders representing a large majority of shares to approve of any takeover attempt. Such a plan is possible only if management has the support of the majority of shareholders.

See It on the WEB

Visit the Companion Website at **www.pearsoned.ca/bovee**, review the exercises, and complete the following assignments for Chapter 5:

1. Choose a Form of Ownership
2. Follow the Fortunes of the Fortune 500
3. *Globe and Mail* Top 1000 Canadian Businesses
4. Building a Great Board

CBC 🔴 VIDEO CASE

Funny Business: Creating a Comedy Club

LEARNING OBJECTIVES

The purpose of this video is to help you

1. Understand the various challenges entrepreneurs face when starting a business from scratch.

2. Identify the advantages and disadvantages of dealing with partners.

3. Examine the importance of leadership vision and energy in small business endeavours.

SYNOPSIS

After years of living out of a suitcase and running from city to city, playing gigs in sites across North America, Rick Bronson seized an opportunity to build his own business. He found this opportunity when Yuk Yuk's moved out of the West Edmonton Mall. But how could someone who makes people laugh for a living handle the stress involved in starting a business from scratch? Like all aspiring entrepreneurs, Bronson soon realized that plans can be drawn up but they must constantly be adapted to deal with complications. Some of his problems were standard issues that young entrepreneurs face. His construction deadlines were threatened because of delays, and he spent much of his time dealing with contractors. He had trouble getting food and beverage licences, which is a typical problem when dealing with government bureaucracy. Bronson also began to feel the competitive squeeze when Yuk Yuk's cancelled one of

his shows in Ottawa citing conflict of interest. However, all of these problems were minor. Like most start-ups, there were plenty of additional issues that Bronson had not counted on. He soon discovered that turning a good idea into reality required total commitment and tireless energy on his part.

Discussion Questions

1. *For analysis*: Based on the definition in the text, does Rick Bronson possess the traits of an entrepreneur?
2. *For analysis*: Did he possess a clear vision of his ultimate goal?
3. *For analysis*: What impact (positive or negative) did Bronson's partners have on the process of transforming his vision into reality?
4. *For application*: Launching a new business is very difficult, but sustaining one and growing it is where entrepreneurs earn their stripes. What should Bronson do to attract more customers and ensure the long-term success of the business?
5. *For debate*: For an entrepreneur to be successful, he or she must have an intimate knowledge of the industry with direct applicable experience.

ONLINE EXPLORATION

Visit The Comic Strip website at www.thecomicstrip.ca and follow the links to find out more about Rick Bronson and his comedy club. Has he opened any new locations?

On Location VIDEO CASE

Doing Business Privately: Amy's Ice Creams

LEARNING OBJECTIVES

The purpose of this video is to help you

1. Consider the advantages and disadvantages of incorporation.

2. Understand the role that shareholders play in a privately held corporation.

3. Examine the various challenges of entrepreneurship.

SYNOPSIS

Amy's Ice Creams, based in Texas, is a privately held corporation formed in 1984 by Amy Miller and is owned by Miller and a group of family members and friends. At the outset, one of the most important decisions Miller faced was choosing an appropriate legal ownership structure for the new business. Fuelled by the founder's dedication to creating happy ice cream memories for customers, Amy's has continued to evolve and grow. The company now operates 11 stores and rings up close to US$4 million in annual sales. Applying for a job is an adventure in creativity, and Miller welcomes employees' suggestions for new flavours and new promotions to keep sales growing.

Discussion Questions

1. *For analysis*: How does Amy's Ice Creams differ from a publicly held company?

2. *For analysis*: What are some of the particular advantages for a firm such as Amy's Ice Creams?

3. *For application*: How well do you think Amy Miller is working to ensure her company continued survival and success? Looking ahead to future growth, what marketing, financial, or other suggestions would you make?

4. *For application*: What are some of the issues that Miller may have to confront because her 22 investors are family members?

5. *For debate*: Should Amy's Ice Creams become a publicly held corporation? Support your chosen position.

ONLINE EXPLORATION

Find out what is required to incorporate a business in your province. Begin by searching this Industry Canada web page: http://strategis.ic.gc.ca/epic/internet/incd-dgc.nsf/en/cs01134e.html for "provincial registrars." The site provides links on incorporating in the various provinces as well as incorporating federally. If you were going to start a small business would you choose to incorporate, or would you choose a different form of legal organization? List the pros and cons of incorporation for the type of business you have selected.

On April 8, 1999, Craig Winn, founder of Value America, became a dot.com billionaire. Investors flocked to his idea of a "Wal-Mart" on the Internet, where shoppers could order jars of caviar along with gas barbecues or desktop computers. The company served as a go-between: It transmitted customer orders immediately to manufacturers, who would ship the merchandise directly to buyers. The company's IPO was a success; its stock closed the first day at US$55 a share, valuing the three-year-old profitless company at US$2.4 billion.

Running on Empty

Twelve months later, Value America filed for bankruptcy protection, and the price of the company's shares fell to 72 cents. The cyberstore was supposed to take advantage of every efficiency promised by the Internet: no inventory, no shipping costs, no warehouse, no physical store. But like many Internet entrepreneurs, Winn tried to do too much too soon. Company computers crashed, customers waited to get their orders filled, returned merchandise piled up in the halls of the company's offices, and discounting and advertising drained the company's cash, wiping out any chance of profitability.

Instant Paper Millions

The mid to late 1990s was an era of great optimism; investors displayed an appetite for risk that would have been considered reckless a few years earlier. A raging bull market, free-flowing capital, and technological advances created so many opportunities at the turn of the millennium that it was difficult to separate a calculated risk from foolish speculation. Just about any dot.com company that wanted to sell over the Internet found plenty of eager investors hoping to earn huge profits. The Web was like a vast, underdeveloped prairie. The new economy boom led many entrepreneurs to believe that the rules of business had changed. Young entrepreneurs with a good idea and a half-baked business plan could make a couple of phone calls to venture capitalists (VCs) and raise millions. Enthusiastic investors raced to claim a stake in the new frontier at Internet speed. Most went in with their eyes wide shut.

The Lights Go Out

Like a thrill ride at an amusement park, however, the whole affair soon screeched to a halt. Entrepreneurs learned the hard way that successfully launching a public company is much different than successfully running one. Cyberspace got crowded. New dot.coms went unnoticed. Desperate to get consumers'

attention and business, e-tailers spent large amounts on advertising. Some pumped out discount offers and free-shipping promises—hemorrhaging cash and piling up losses. This turn of events led investors to take a second look and change their minds—overnight. Profits, it seemed, mattered after all. Many investors watched in shock as dot.com share prices fell through the floor.

Some, of course, had predicted the dot.com fallout. History, they said, would repeat itself. After all, from 1855 to 1861 the number of start-up telegraph companies in the United States alone shrank by 87 percent—from 50 to 6. The Internet, they predicted, would not escape a shakedown of its own. Why did the dot.coms run out of steam? Experts now cite these reasons:

- *Poor management.* Many dot.coms were founded by people with cool ideas but no business sense. Some entrepreneurs were in such a rush to go public they forgot one small detail: a sound business plan. They were more attracted by the potential to get rich than by the need to create a company "built to last." Craig Winn's business background, for instance, consisted mainly of leading another public company into bankruptcy. His technology experience? None. Only during such an aggressive period of shallow optimism could someone with Winn's background amass the funds to launch such a risky venture.

- *Unrealistic goals.* Many dot.com start-ups were dedicated to achieving the impossible—launching companies in weeks and attracting millions of customers in months. But the evolution of consumers was far slower than most people predicted. Companies like Kanetix (a Canadian online insurance broker) have now emerged and appear to be gaining acceptance in today's market. But at the time people were not ready to buy mortgages and new cars in volume over the Internet. In fact, most Internet firms found that hoped-for volume simply wasn't there. Take online grocers, for example. Buying groceries online requires consumers to make a big change in the way they shop for basic household goods. Online grocers soon discovered that going to the grocery store wasn't as terrible as e-companies had hoped. Moreover, to build a base of customers from scratch, the newcomers had to spend heavily on advertising and other types of marketing. The online grocer Webvan, for instance, spent 25 to 35 percent of its revenue on advertising, compared with an average of about 1 percent spent by traditional grocers.

- *Going public too soon.* Venture capitalists (VCs), eager to back the next AOL or Amazon, tossed huge sums of money at companies that had barely a prayer of prospering.

In many cases, the VCs took the dot.coms public way too soon. Instead of waiting the customary four to five years, dot.coms were taken public in two years or less—long before the company or its management could prove consistent performance to the public. Meanwhile, investors overlooked business fundamentals and threw money at these businesses—driving their share prices ridiculously high.

■ *Fighting the laws of supply and demand.* Demand-driven start-ups such as Cisco are born to fulfill existing needs of consumers or businesses. By contrast, supply-driven start-ups are born in the mind of the entrepreneur with little more than a gut feeling that someone will eventually need or want the company's product or service. Thus, supply-driven start-ups leave the company with the enormous task of establishing a market rather than participating in one. Moreover, with relatively low barriers to entry, other dot.coms could easily copy a good idea. At the turn of the twenty-first century, the supply of start-ups greatly exceeded their demand.

■ *Extravagant spending.* Companies spent recklessly to lure customers with special promotions and silly marketing campaigns—no matter the cost. For instance, drkoop.com, an online health site, burned through three-quarters of the US$84 million it raised in an IPO in less than one year. Losses, of course, were excused as a necessary evil in the pursuit of new customers. Some dot.coms even began to act like conventional retailers—building costly warehouses and adding staff—to compete. Webvan officials argued in the company's early stages that the centres, which could handle up to 8000 orders a day (many times more than a traditional warehouse) would give it a big cost advantage over its traditional competitors. But it never gained the sales volume to take full advantage of the efficiencies, and so its gross margins trailed behind those of large traditional grocers. After spending US$830 million in start-up and IPO funds, Webvan sought bankruptcy protection and began liquidating its assets.

■ *Locked out of cash.* Most dot.coms were started with venture capital. When they burned through that money, they had to find new funding or go public. For many, neither happened. Once more and more dot.coms began to fail, investors forced companies to cut costs vigorously, postpone or scrap their plans to go public, find a buyer at any price, or close up shop.

As quickly as they'd jumped on the bandwagon, investors, the press, and the general public turned on the whole idea of dot.coms. VCs and individual investors licked their wounds and looked for safer places to invest whatever money they had left. Workers who had been lured away from big companies with the dream of IPO riches tried to return. Most people seemed to write it off as some big, crazy experiment that went wildly wrong.

Internet entrepreneurs learned a lot during the dot.com boom, everything from fundamentals of supply and demand (when there's no demand, there's not much point in having supply) to the truth about those traditional business models they once scoffed at as outmoded (there's a reason those models have been in use for years . . . they work!). Online companies learned how hard it was to compete in businesses that often had razor-thin profit margins, such as retailing, and how hard it was to change consumer habits.

A Funny Thing Happened on the Way to the Trash Heap

A year or two after the bleakest point of the dot.com story, an amazing thing began to happen: Some of the dot.coms started to succeed. Amazon.com became a multibillion-dollar retailer that started to turn a profit on its massive investment in e-commerce. eBay reinvented the world of flea markets and auctions on its way to becoming the most popular shopping site in the world and continues to show strong profits. Yahoo! attracts more than 4 billion visits annually to its global network of web portals. Google has become a household name and has become synonymous with searching online. Old-school retailers like Wal-Mart and manufacturers like Dell learned from dot.com mania and now harness the Internet successfully themselves. Finally, sites like YouTube and Facebook are now an integral part of everyday life for most young people. So while the dot.com party certainly got out of control in the late 1990s, it seems there were some ideas worth celebrating after all.

The companies listed above are the who's who of the Internet world, but there are many other smaller examples. Quebec-based Mediagrif Interactive Technologies is a publicly traded company with 370 employees and offices in China, the United States, India, and the United Arab Emirates. The company links buyers and sellers in diverse industries such as automotive parts, medical supplies, and heavy equipment. Even more shocking, in comparison to the early pioneers of e-commerce exchanges, the company announced net earnings of nearly $10 million in 2006.[40]

Critical Thinking Questions

1. Why did so many dot.com businesses fail at the beginning of the twenty-first century?

2. How did the attitude of dot.com investors change? Why did it change?

3. If you had the opportunity to invest in a dot.com business today, what questions would you ask before investing your money?

BUSINESS PLANPRO EXERCISES

Starting and Organizing a Small Business

 Review Appendix B, "Your Business Plan" to learn how to use Business PlanPro Software so you can complete these exercises.

Think Like a Pro

Objective: By completing these exercises you will become acquainted with the sections of a business plan that address forms of ownership, financing the enterprise, and the franchising alternative. You will use the sample business plan for Pegasus Sports (listed as Inline Skating Products in the Sample Plan Browser) in this exercise.

1. What form of ownership does Pegasus currently use? What are the advantages of selecting that form of ownership? What change in ownership form is Pegasus planning to make?

2. How is Pegasus financing its start-up operations? Has the company gone public (or does the plan indicate it wants to go public)?

3. Would you recommend that Pegasus use franchising to grow its business? Explain your answer.

Create Your Own Business Plan

Think about your own business. What form of ownership will you choose? Why? How much start-up money will you need? How will you finance your start-up costs? Where will you obtain the money you will need to grow your business? Enter your answers in the appropriate sections of your business plan.

PART 3

MANAGING A BUSINESS

CHAPTER 6
Understanding the Functions and Roles of Management

CHAPTER 7
Organizing and Working in Teams

CHAPTER 8
Producing Quality Goods and Services

CHAPTER 6

UNDERSTANDING THE FUNCTIONS AND ROLES OF MANAGEMENT

LEARNING OBJECTIVES
After studying this chapter, you will be able to

1 Define the four basic management functions

2 Outline the tasks involved in the strategic planning process

3 Explain the purpose of a mission statement

4 List the benefits of setting long-term goals and objectives

5 Cite three leadership styles and describe when each style is most appropriate to use

6 Identify the importance of contingency leadership and distinguish between transactional and transformational leadership

7 List the challenges involved in managing organizational change and identify strategies to overcome them

8 Explain how total quality management (TQM) is changing the way organizations are managed

9 Identify and explain the three types of managerial skills

10 Understand some of the reasons why managers fail and identify key strategies for success

Behind the Scenes

Apple iTunes and Steve Jobs: A Strong Leader with a Clear iVision

Apple CEO Steve Jobs spotted an opportunity in linking online music with his company's popular iPod digital music players.

www.apple.com/itunes

A little over a decade ago Steve Jobs returned to Apple, the company that he co-founded, to provide a boost to an organization looking to reinforce its brand image, reputation for innovation, and sales results. Success in business is often a matter of connecting the dots—looking at your own strengths and weaknesses, exploring customer needs, and analyzing the various legal, technical, and social forces at work in the marketplace. You consider what you're capable of doing, what your competitors might do, what customers would like you to do, and what forces are changing the business landscape. Then you look for opportunities. How can you capitalize on changing markets? What can you do to meet customer needs better than anyone else?

Apple Computer CEO Steve Jobs has spent his career connecting those dots and using his charismatic leadership style to push his company in the development of innovative products that have changed the way people work and play—including the way people listen to music. Although Apple didn't start out in the music business, by 2003 the company was a significant force in the industry, at least indirectly. Many musicians and creative professionals favoured Apple computers, and the company's sleek new iPod portable music players were a must-have item for trendsetting music fans everywhere.

Outside the company, though, the music industry was in a state of turmoil. Music fans, tired of buying entire CDs for just one or two favourite songs, were downloading millions of songs for free from the Internet despite legal and ethical issues. Performers, songwriters, and music companies were all looking for better ways to address customer complaints about the industry while protecting their legal rights and financial assets. As is often the case, technology seemed to be one step ahead of business strategy. Everybody agreed that online distribution was central to the future of the music business, but nobody had quite figured out how to make it work.

Jobs wasn't the only person pondering this situation, of course. A diverse group of companies, from Wal-Mart and Sony to RealNetworks and a reborn Napster, wanted a piece of the new online music market. Amazon.com, eBay, and other companies had proven the potential for selling over the Internet, but was it possible to make money selling something as inexpensive as an individual song? If you were Steve Jobs, how would you approach the challenges and opportunities of online music? How would you connect the dots between Apple's strengths and the complex dynamics of the marketplace?[1]

TEST YOURSELF

Answers to these questions can be found on the website: www.pearson.ca/bovee.

1. How does this case demonstrate the important concept of managerial vision?

2. How has Apple used its strengths to take advantage of the online music business?

3. What external threats and opportunities are looming over the music industry in the next few years?

4. How does this case relate to the four functions of management?

THE FOUR BASIC FUNCTIONS OF MANAGEMENT

L.O. 1

Steve Jobs knows that when managers possess the right combination of vision, skill, experience, and determination they can lead an organization to success. Jobs also knows that not everyone is equipped to be an effective manager. So he focuses on finding the right managers to help him turn his vision into reality. In this chapter we explore the four basic functions of **management**: planning, organizing, leading, and controlling resources (land, labour, capital, and information) to efficiently reach a company's goals (see Exhibit 6.1).[2] We also highlight and examine the skills required for effective management.

In the course of performing the four management functions, managers play a number of **roles** that fall into three main categories:

management
Process of coordinating resources to meet organizational goals

- *Interpersonal roles.* Managers perform ceremonial obligations; provide leadership to employees; build a network of relationships with bosses, peers, and employees; and act as a liaison to groups and individuals both inside and outside the company (suppliers, competitors, government agencies, consumers, special-interest groups, and interrelated workgroups).

roles
Behavioural patterns associated with or expected of certain positions

- *Informational roles.* Managers spend a fair amount of time gathering information by questioning people both inside and outside the organization. They also distribute information to employees, their managers, and outsiders.

- *Decisional roles.* Managers use the information they gather to encourage innovation, to resolve unexpected problems that threaten organizational goals (like reacting to an economic crisis), and to decide how organizational resources will be used to meet planned objectives. They also negotiate with many individuals and groups, including suppliers, employees, and unions.[3]

Being able to move among these roles while performing the four basic management functions is just one of the many skills that managers must possess. But these functions are not discrete; they overlap and influence one another. Let's examine them in detail.

The Planning Function

Planning is the primary management function—the one on which all others depend. Managers engaged in **planning** to develop strategies for success, establish goals and objectives for the organization, and turn strategies and goals into action plans. To develop long-term strategies and goals, managers must be well informed on a number of key issues and topics that could influence their decisions. A closer look at the strategic planning process will give you a better idea of the types of information managers need to help them plan for the company's future.

planning
Establishing objectives and goals for an organization and determining the best ways to accomplish them

Understanding the Strategic Planning Process

L.O. 2

Strategic plans outline the firm's long-range (two to five years) goals and set a course of action for the firm to pursue. These long-term goals encompass eight major areas of concern: market standing, innovation, human resources, financial resources, physical resources, productivity, social responsibility, and financial performance.[4] A good strategic plan answers the questions, Where are we going? What is the environment? How do we get there?

strategic plans
Plans that establish the actions and the resource allocation required to accomplish goals; usually defined for periods of two to five years and developed by top managers

---

Exhibit 6.1 **The Four Basic Functions of Management**

Although these functions tend to occur in a somewhat progressive order, sometimes they occur simultaneously, and often the process is ongoing.

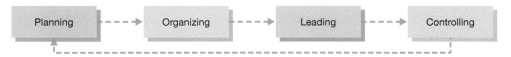

When Wendelin Wiedeking took over as CEO of Porsche back in 1992, the company was racing toward record losses of $150 million. Few people believed that Wiedeking could get Porsche back on track. But Wiedeking had a clear vision for the company—one that adopted lean and efficient Japanese production systems at Porsche. Thanks to Wiedeking's vision and leadership, Porsche is back in the fast lane. It is racking up some of the highest profit margins of any manufacturer in the automobile industry even as it expands production.

vision
A viable view of the future that is rooted in but improves on the present

L.O. 3

mission statement
A statement of the organization's purpose, basic goals, and philosophies

To answer these questions and establish effective long-term goals, managers require extensive amounts of information. For instance, managers must study budgets, production schedules, industry and economic data, customer preferences, internal and external data, the competition, and so on. Managers use this information to set a firm's long-term course of direction during a process called *strategic planning*, which consists of six steps: developing a clear vision, creating a mission statement, developing forecasts, analyzing the competition, establishing goals and objectives, and developing action plans.

Develop a Clear Vision   Most organizations are formed to realize a **vision**—a realistic, credible, and attainable view of the future that grows out of and improves on the present.[5] Fred Smith (founder of FedEx) envisioned making FedEx an information company (besides being a transportation company). Bill Gates (chair of Microsoft) envisioned empowering people through great software, anytime, anyplace, and on any device. Henry Ford envisioned making affordable transportation available to every person. If Ballard Power Systems, the Burnaby, BC–based fuel cell maker, successfully commercializes a truly effective alternative to the combustion engine it will represent an equally important achievement. Steve Jobs envisioned the potential to revolutionize and enable people's relationship with music through the iPod, iTunes, and now the iPhone. Without such visionaries, who knows how the world would be different? Thus, developing a clear vision is a critical task in the strategic planning process. But having a vision alone is no guarantee of success; it must be communicated to others, executed, and modified as conditions change.

Translate the Vision into a Meaningful Mission Statement   To transform vision into reality, managers must define specific organizational goals, objectives, and philosophies. A starting point is to write a company **mission statement**, a brief document that defines why the organization exists, what it seeks to accomplish, and the principles that the company will follow as it tries to reach its goals (see Exhibit 6.2). A mission statement communicates what the company is, what it does, and where it's headed. Typical components of a mission statement include the company's product or service; primary market; fundamental concern for survival, growth, and profitability; managerial philosophy; and commitment to quality and social responsibility.

Another important function of a mission statement is to bring clarity of focus to members of the organization. A mission statement helps employees understand how their role is tied to the organization's greater purpose. Thus, it should inspire and guide employees and managers in such a way that they can understand the firm's vision and identify with it. Furthermore, the statement must fit with the organization's core values. Managers should use it to see whether new project proposals are within the scope of the company's mission.[6]

Develop Forecasts   To develop forecasts, managers must make a number of educated assumptions about future trends and events and modify those assumptions once new information becomes available. Some managers rely on expert forecasts such as those found in *IndustryWeek*'s "Trends and Forecasts," *BusinessWeek*'s "Survey of Corporate Performance," and Standard & Poor's *Earnings Forecast* as a foundation for their projections. However, these sources may not always include key variables specific to an individual company or industry. Therefore, managers must also develop their own forecasts.

Managerial forecasts fall under two broad categories: *quantitative forecasts,* which are typically based on historical data or tests and which involve complex statistical calculations, and *qualitative forecasts,* which are based on intuitive judgments or consumer research. Statistically analyzing the cycles of economic growth and recession over several decades to predict when the economy will take a downward turn is an

Exhibit 6.2   **Mission Statement**

The mission statement for Dell Computer embodies the firm's high standards for quality and customer service.

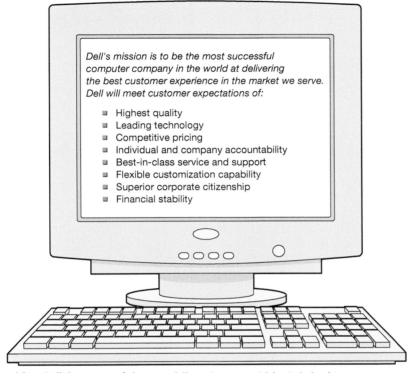

Dell's mission is to be the most successful computer company in the world at delivering the best customer experience in the market we serve. Dell will meet customer expectations of:

- Highest quality
- Leading technology
- Competitive pricing
- Individual and company accountability
- Best-in-class service and support
- Flexible customization capability
- Superior corporate citizenship
- Financial stability

Source: Adapted from Dell Computer website, www.dell.com/corporate/vision/mission.htm.

example of quantitative forecasting. Making predictions about sales of a new product on the basis of experience and consumer responses to a survey is an example of qualitative forecasting. Neither method is foolproof, but both are valuable tools to help managers deal with unknown variables that come up in the planning process.

Analyze the Competition   All business decisions take place within a competitive context, so understanding who your competitors are and how you stack up against them is a critical part of planning. "Business is like any battlefield. If you want to win the war, you have to know who you're up against," says one management consultant.[7] Managers can assess their competition by asking five questions:[8]

- Who are our competitors, both our current competitors and any who might join the market in the future?
- What are their strengths and weaknesses?
- What strategies and tactics have they employed in the past?
- What strategies and tactics are they likely to employ in the future, particularly in response to moves we might make?
- How will their future moves affect both the industry in general and our company in particular?

Analyzing your own company is just as important as analyzing competitors. Many managers use a technique known as a **SWOT analysis**, which identifies strengths, weaknesses, opportunities, and threats. Strengths and weaknesses are your internal capabilities and represent things that you have direct control over. For example, Volvo is known for producing high-quality, safe automobiles. The reputation is based on a real commitment by the company to being a leader in the production of safe automobiles. On the other

SWOT analysis
Analyzing a company by identifying the strengths, weaknesses, opportunities, and threats

Exhibit 6.3   SWOT Analysis

A SWOT analysis is a tool that allows companies to examine internal strengths and weaknesses while identifying possible external threats and opportunities.

Internal Factors	External Factors
Strengths	Opportunities
Weaknesses	Threats

hand, opportunities and threats are based on assessment of external factors that the company does not control. Companies must take advantage of opportunities and deal with threats. For example, a company may have developed a great new product, but if it is released in the middle of a major economic recession sales will suffer. Companies cannot control the economy, the weather, or the political climate, but they must make plans to deal with these external situations (see Exhibit 6.3).

Conducting a SWOT analysis of competitors is a helpful exercise as well. In addition to analyzing their strengths and weaknesses, as you would normally do in competitive analysis, a SWOT analysis lets you put yourself in their shoes and try to identify the opportunities and threats they're likely to perceive in the marketplace. If you can see the world as they see it, you have a better chance of predicting their future behaviour.

With insight into its own capabilities and those of its competitors, a company can then work to gain a competitive edge through at least one of three strategies:

- *Differentiation.* A company using differentiation develops a level of service, a product image, unique product features (including quality), or new technologies that distinguish its products from the competition. Volvo stresses the safety of its cars; Caterpillar (maker of construction equipment) emphasizes product durability.

- *Cost leadership.* Businesses that pursue this strategy aim to become the low-cost leader in an industry by producing or selling products more efficiently and economically than competitors. Cost leaders have a competitive advantage by reaching buyers whose primary purchase criterion is price. Wal-Mart is a typical industry cost leader; its suppliers must justify all aspects of price to earn Wal-Mart's business.

- *Focus.* When using a focus strategy, companies concentrate on a specific regional market or consumer group, such as the Maritime provinces or drivers of economy cars. This type of strategy enables organizations to develop a better understanding of their customers and to tailor their products specifically to customer needs.[9] For example, Holt Renfrew retail outlets tailor their offerings to meet the needs of an upscale, sophisticated, brand-conscious clientele.

Many firms gain a competitive advantage by excelling in two of these areas at once, such as Toyota's efforts to excel at both quality (a differentiation strategy) and lower cost. However, pursuing more than one strategic focus at a time can be risky if it leads to mediocre efforts across the board.[10]

Establish Company Goals and Objectives   As mentioned earlier, establishing goals and objectives is the key task in the planning process. Although these terms are often used interchangeably, a **goal** is a broad, long-range accomplishment that the organization wishes to attain in typically five or more years, whereas an **objective** is a specific, short-range target designed to help reach that goal. For Nokia Canada, a goal might be to increase market share of mobile phone sales in Canada by 25 percent over the next five years, and an objective might be to sell 100 000 mobile phones to Canadian customers by year end. To be effective, organizational goals and objectives should be specific, measurable, relevant, challenging, attainable, and time bound. For example, it is better to state "increase our sales by 25 percent over the next five years" than "substantially increase our sales."

L.O. 4

goal
A broad, long-range target or aim

objective
A specific, short-range target or aim

Apple has set clear sales objectives and goals for its revolutionary new iPhone. In the first year Apple has set a target sales figure of 10 million iPhones, and the company plans to sell 45 million iPhones by 2009.

IN-CLASS NOTES

The Planning Function

1. *Set a clear vision*: Realistic, credible, attainable view of the future
2. *Create a solid mission statement*: Communicate what the company is, what it does, and where it's heading
3. *Forecast*: Make educated assumptions about future trends and events
4. *Competitive analysis*: Identify current and potential competition. Do a SWOT analysis
5. *Goals and objectives*: Goals are broad long-range targets; objectives are short-term targets
6. *Develop action plans*: Tactical plans are typically 1–3 years; operational plans are less than 1 year

_____
_____
_____
_____
_____
_____
_____
_____
_____

Setting appropriate goals has many benefits: It increases employee motivation, establishes standards for measuring individual and group performance, guides employee activity, and clarifies management's expectations. By establishing organizational goals, managers set the stage for the actions needed to achieve those goals. If actions aren't planned, the chances of reaching company goals are slim.

Develop Action Plans   Once managers have established a firm's long-term strategic goals and objectives, they must then develop a plan of execution. **Tactical plans** lay out the actions and the allocation of resources necessary to achieve specific, short-term objectives that support the company's broader strategic plan. Tactical plans typically focus on departmental goals and cover a period of one to three years. Their limited scope permits them to be changed more easily than strategic plans. **Operational plans** designate the actions and resources required to achieve the objectives of tactical plans. Operational plans usually define actions for less than one year and focus on accomplishing a firm's specific objectives, like developing a strategic partnership with another company.

Many highly admired CEOs have stumbled not because they didn't have strategies for success, but because they didn't execute their strategies or deliver on their commitments. That's because developing a strategy or vision is less than half the battle. In today's information age, strategies quickly become public property. Everyone knows Dell's direct business model, for example, yet few companies, if any, have successfully copied its execution.

Planning for a Crisis

No matter how well a company plans for its future, any number of problems can arise to threaten its existence. An ugly fight for control of a company, a product failure, a

tactical plans
Plans that define the actions and the resource allocation necessary to achieve tactical objectives and to support strategic plans; usually defined for a period of one to three years and developed by middle managers

operational plans
Plans that lay out the actions and the resource allocation needed to achieve operational objectives and to support tactical plans; usually defined for less than one year and developed by first-line managers

crisis management
A system for minimizing the harm that might result from some unusually threatening situations

organizing
The process of arranging resources to carry out an organization's plans

management pyramid
An organizational structure comprising top, middle, and lower management

top managers
Those at the highest level of the organization's management hierarchy; they are responsible for setting strategic goals, and they have the most power and responsibility in the organization

breakdown in routine operations (as a result of fire, for example), or an environmental accident could develop into a serious and crippling crisis. Managers can help a company survive these setbacks through **crisis management**, a plan for handling such unusual and serious problems.

The goal of crisis management is to keep the company functioning smoothly both during and after a crisis. Successful crisis management requires comprehensive contingency plans in addition to speedy, open communication with all who are affected by the crisis. Experts suggest setting up a crisis communications team with a knowledgeable spokesperson to handle the many requests for information that arise during a crisis. The individuals selected should be able to remain honest and calm when a crisis hits. Moreover, top managers should be visible in the hours immediately following the crisis to demonstrate that the company will do whatever is necessary to control the situation as best it can, find the cause, and prevent a future occurrence.[11]

Even the most efficient systems can go down and create chaos. When the Royal Bank (RBC) experienced a major computer glitch, company executives and public relations people scrambled to calm their clients and fix the problem. The computer glitch occurred during a routine software upgrade; the end result was that millions of transactions were not processed over a two-day period. In the hours and days following the incident, RBC addressed all aspects of the problem: It fixed the technical malfunction, extended its business hours, opened more locations on Saturdays to temporarily service concerned customers, and finally addressed its stakeholders with statements like the following from Rod Pennycook, an executive vice-president at the bank: "We recognize this has caused not only our own clients but also clients of some other institutions considerable inconvenience and for this we sincerely apologize." Many firms spent countless hours and dollars preparing for the Y2K crisis at the end of the twentieth century, but the problem never materialized. However, all of that preparation and crisis planning helped RBC deal with this unexpected event.[12]

The Organizing Function

Organizing, the process of arranging resources to carry out the organization's plans, is the second major function of managers. During the organizing stage, managers think through all activities that employees carry out (from programming the organization's computers to mailing its letters), as well as all facilities and equipment employees need to complete those activities. They also give people the ability to work toward organizational goals by determining who will have the authority to make decisions, to perform or supervise activities, and to distribute resources.

The organizing function is particularly challenging because most organizations undergo constant change. Long-time employees leave and new employees arrive. Equipment breaks down or becomes obsolete and replacements are needed. The public's tastes and interests change and the organization has to re-evaluate its plans and activities. Shifting political and economic trends can lead to employee cutbacks—or perhaps expansion. Long-time competitors take unexpected actions and new competitors enter the market. Every week the organization faces new situations, so management's organizing tasks are never finished. Consider Microsoft. The company continually challenges itself by asking: "Are we making what customers want and working on products and technologies they'll want in the future? Are we staying ahead of all our competitors? What don't our customers like about what we do? What are we doing about it? Are we organized most effectively to achieve our goals?"[13]

The organizing function will be discussed in detail in Chapter 7. In this chapter, however, we will discuss the three levels of a corporate hierarchy—top, middle, bottom—commonly known as the **management pyramid** (see Exhibit 6.4). In general, **top managers** are the upper-level managers who

Quick action and contingency planning enabled RBC to recover quickly after a routine computer upgrade triggered a processing disruption that led to millions of unprocessed transactions. The bank addressed all stakeholders, temporarily adjusted operational procedures, and reassured the general public.

Exhibit 6.4 **The Management Pyramid**

Separate job titles are used to designate the three basic levels in the management pyramid.

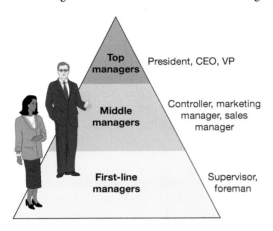

- Top managers — President, CEO, VP
- Middle managers — Controller, marketing manager, sales manager
- First-line managers — Supervisor, foreman

have the most power and who take overall responsibility for the organization, like the chief executive officer (CEO). Top managers establish the structure for the organization as a whole, and they select the people who fill the upper-level positions. Top managers also make long-range plans, establish major policies, and represent the company to the outside world at official functions and fundraisers.

Middle managers have similar responsibilities, but usually for just one division or unit. They develop plans for implementing the broad goals set by top managers, and they coordinate the work of first-line managers. In traditional organizations, managers at the middle level are plant managers, division managers, branch managers, and other similar positions, all reporting to top-level managers. But in more innovative management

middle managers
Those in the middle of the management hierarchy; they develop plans to implement the goals of top managers and coordinate the work of first-line managers

IN-CLASS NOTES

The Organizing Function
- Managers decide on the following areas:
  - Employee activities
  - Facilities and equipment
  - Decision making
  - Supervision
  - Resource distribution
- *Top managers* make long-range plans (e.g., president, CEO, VP)
- *Middle managers* implement goals, make decisions (e.g., controller, marketing manager)
- *First-line managers* implement plans, oversee workers (e.g., supervisor, foreman)

structures, middle managers often function as team leaders who are expected to supervise and lead small groups of employees in a variety of job functions. Similar to consultants, they must understand every department's function, not just their own area of expertise. Furthermore, they are granted decision-making authority previously reserved for only high-ranking executives.[14]

first-line managers
Those at the lowest level of the management hierarchy; they supervise the operating employees and implement the plans set at the higher management levels; also called supervisory managers

leading
The process of guiding and motivating people to work toward organizational goals

At the bottom of the management pyramid are **first-line managers** (or *supervisory managers*). They oversee the work of operating employees, and they put into action the plans developed at higher levels. Positions at this level include supervisor, department head, and office manager.[15] Even though more managers are at the bottom level than at the top (see Exhibit 6.4), today's leaner companies tend to have fewer levels, flattening the organizational structure, as Chapter 7 will discuss.

The Leading Function

Leading, the process of influencing and motivating people to work effectively and willingly toward company goals, is the third basic function of management. Leading becomes

Learning Simple Lessons Can Define a Leader's Legacy

Business texts, journals, and newspapers are full of fancy terms that try to capture the essence of effective leadership. Important studies have yielded valid terms describing leader types under headings like Architect, Coach, Mobilizer, Taskmaster, and Expert, to name just a few. All of these terms try to highlight a different angle of leadership. One thing is certain, leaders come in many forms. Steve Jobs is a strong business leader but so is Jack Welch who has taught and influenced many additional leaders from his days as chairman and CEO at GE. A recent article in the *Globe and Mail* had the following headline: "Looking for a Leader? Just Look for a GE Graduate." Of course, leadership is not reserved for the business field. Wayne Gretzky is a great leader and so are Oprah Winfrey, Ghandi, and Nelson Mandela. It takes quite a list to pinpoint what makes each of these unique people effective. Instead of defining the ultimate characteristics of a leader, we will just examine some keys lessons for success:

- *Don't Limit Yourself.* If you believe it, it is possible. If you stop yourself, your organization will not grow. You will not succeed. If you make the effort and work hard, you have a chance. Most people are capable of much more than they ever accomplish but their fear limits them. A leader must be willing to push the boundaries.

- *Good Leaders Listen.* There is a time to talk and a time to listen. It is not a sign of weakness to step back for a moment and hear what others have to say. No leader can accomplish anything without the hard work and support of a team. Motivation can come from great speeches but it also develops when an employee feels that their opinions are being acknowledged (observe, show interest, and learn) and they feel connected to the process.

- *Be Open and Honest.* Don't be afraid to address issues up front and be responsive to the feedback and expectations of others.

- *Confidence not Arrogance.* There is nothing more frustrating than an indecisive leader. A leader should get the facts straight, analyze a situation, and make clear decisions, but a leader must not get too full of himself or herself. Confidence crosses over to arrogance when leaders dismiss other views and expect their subordinates to conform.

SIMPLE ADVICE

According to Jack Welch, the best advice he ever received came during his first or second board meeting at GE. It was from Paul Austin, a former chairman of Coke, who looked at a slightly nervous Welch and said, "Be yourself!" There are so many terms used to describe leaders because there are so many types of individual leaders. Effective leaders don't try to conform to a simple definition. They use their own talents and strengths to become successful and lead organizations and causes to success in their own way. So whether you are leading your football team, work team, non-profit organization, business team, or political party—BE YOURSELF— just don't be scared to IMPROVE YOURSELF.[16]

Questions for Critical Thinking

1. Be yourself! This simple advice is a powerful message when it is actually applied. Take a few moments and list your strengths and weaknesses.

2. From your experience as a student, work partner, employee, or manager, which lesson from this mini-case do you consider to be the most important? Provide examples to support your answer.

even more challenging in today's business environment, where individuals who have different backgrounds and unique interests, ambitions, and personal goals are placed into a productive work team. Managers with good leadership skills have a greater success rate in influencing the attitudes and actions of others, both through the demonstration of specific tasks and through the manager's own behaviour and spirit. Furthermore, effective leaders are good at *motivating*, or giving employees a reason to do the job and to put forth their best performance (see Chapter 10). See the box entitled "Learning Simple Lessons Can Define a Leader's Legacy" for some key lessons for success as a leader.

What makes a good leader? When early researchers studied leadership they looked for specific characteristics, or *traits*, common to all good leaders. At the time, they were unable to prove any link between particular traits and leadership ability. However, researchers found that leaders who have specific traits, such as decisiveness and self-confidence, are likely to be more effective.[17] Additional studies have shown that managers with strong interpersonal skills and high emotional quotients (EQs) tend to be more effective leaders. The characteristics of a high EQ include:[18]

- *Self-awareness.* Self-aware managers have the ability to recognize their own feelings and how they, their job performance, and other people are affected by those feelings. Managers who are highly self-aware know where they are headed and why.

- *Self-regulation.* Self-regulated managers have the ability to control or reduce disruptive impulses and moods. They can suspend judgment and think before acting. Moreover, they know how to use the appropriate emotion at the right time and in the right amount.

- *Motivation.* Motivated managers are driven to achieve beyond expectations—their own and everyone else's. They can capture people's attention and guide them to reach goals. (Chapter 10 takes a comprehensive look at motivating employees.)

- *Empathy.* Empathetic managers thoughtfully consider employees' feelings along with other factors in the process of making intelligent decisions.

- *Social skill.* Socially skilled managers tend to have a wide circle of acquaintances, and they have a knack for finding common ground with people of all kinds. They assume that nothing important gets done by one person alone and have a network in place when the time for action comes.

Keep in mind that these traits alone do not define a leader. Different leadership traits are appropriate under different leadership situations.[19]

Adopting an Effective Leadership Style

L.O. 5

Leadership style is the way a manager uses authority to lead others. Every manager, from the baseball coach to the university chancellor, has a definite style. The three broad categories of leadership style are *autocratic, democratic,* and *laissez-faire.*

Autocratic leaders make decisions without consulting others. "My way or the highway" summarizes this style, which tends to go well with traditional, hierarchical organizational structures. Although autocratic leadership can be highly effective when quick decisions are necessary, it does little to empower employees or encourage innovation. Al Dunlap, former CEO of Sunbeam, used an autocratic leadership style to try to turn the failing household appliance maker around. True to his word, Dunlap turned Sunbeam inside out and upside down—and nearly destroyed the company with his "chainsaw" management style—crushing employee morale and creating unbearable stress by exerting excruciating pressure on his staff. As Dunlap liked to brag, "I don't get heart attacks, I give them."[20]

autocratic leaders
Leaders who do not involve others in decision making

In contrast, **democratic leaders** delegate authority and involve employees in decision making. Even though their approach can lead to slower decisions, getting input from people familiar with particular situations or issues may result in better decisions. An effective democratic leader also builds a work environment in which employees are not afraid to make a mistake and are encouraged to step out and make suggestions. This breeds organizational growth and creativity.[21] As more companies adopt the principles of teamwork, democratic leadership continues to gain in popularity.

democratic leaders
Leaders who delegate authority and involve employees in decision making

Meg Whitman, CEO of eBay, is a perfect example of a democratic leader. She attributes much of eBay's success to involvement of employees and managers in decision making. "I'm really proud of what we've created at eBay, but I haven't done it alone," says Whitman. "It really has been our management team and the people that come to eBay and build our community. It's a partnership." Fortune recently named Meg Whitman the most powerful businesswoman.[22]

L.O. 6

laissez-faire leaders
Leaders who leave the actual decision making up to employees

contingency leadership
Adapting the leadership style to what is most appropriate given current business conditions

situational leadership
A variation on contingency leadership in which the manager adapts his or her style based on the readiness of employees to accept changes or task responsibilities

transactional leaders
Leaders who focus on meeting established goals and making sure current business operations run smoothly

transformational leaders
Leaders who can reshape the destinies of their organizations by inspiring employees to rise above self-interest and create new levels of success for the company as a whole

coaching
Helping employees reach their highest potential by meeting with them, discussing problems, and offering suggestions and encouragement

The third leadership style, laissez faire, is sometimes referred to as free-rein leadership. The French term *laissez faire* can be translated as "leave it alone," or more roughly as "hands off." **Laissez-faire leaders** take the role of consultant, encouraging employees' ideas and offering insights or opinions when asked. The laissez-faire style may fail if workers pursue goals that do not match the organization's goals. However, the style has proven effective in some situations. Managers at Hewlett-Packard's North American distribution organization adopted a laissez-faire style when they were given nine months to reorganize their order-fulfillment process. The managers eliminated all titles, supervision, job descriptions, and plans, and they made employees entirely responsible for the project. At first there was chaos. However, employees soon began to try new things, make mistakes, and learn as they went. In the end, the team finished the reorganization ahead of schedule, reduced product delivery times from 26 days to 8 days, and cut inventory by 20 percent. Moreover, the employees experienced a renewed sense of challenge, commitment, and enjoyment in their work.[23]

More and more businesses are adopting democratic and laissez-faire leadership as they reduce the number of management layers in their corporate hierarchies and increase the use of teams. However, experienced managers know that no one leadership style works every time. In fact, new research shows that leaders with the best results do not rely on only one leadership style; instead they adapt their approach to match the requirements of the particular situation.[24] Adapting leadership style to current business circumstances is called **contingency leadership**. One of the more important contingency styles is **situational leadership**, in which leaders adapt their style based on the readiness of employees to accept the changes or responsibilities the manager wants them to accept.[25] You can think of leadership styles as existing along a continuum of possible leadership behaviours, as suggested by Exhibit 6.5.

Aside from these styles, leaders also differ in the degree to which they try (or need) to reshape their organizations. **Transactional leaders** tend to focus on meeting established goals, making sure employees understand their roles in the organization, making sure the correct resources are in place, and so on. In contrast, some leaders can "take it up a notch," inspiring their employees to perform above and beyond the everyday responsibilities of their jobs. These **transformational leaders** can reshape the destinies of their organizations by inspiring employees to see the world in new ways, to find creative solutions to business challenges, to rise above self-interest, and to create new levels of success for the company as a whole.[26] Well-known transformational leaders include Jeff Bezos of Amazon.com and Bill Gates of Microsoft, both of whom have inspired thousands of employees to feats that have changed entire industries. But many other leaders have transformational qualities in less spectacular ways.

Coaching and Mentoring

Managers can provide effective leadership by coaching and mentoring their employees. On a winning sports team, the coach focuses on helping all team members perform at their highest potential. In a similar way, *coaching* managers strive to bring out the best in their employees.

Coaching involves taking the time to meet with employees, discussing any problems that may hinder their ability to work effectively, and offering suggestions and encouragement to help them find their own solutions to work-related challenges.

Exhibit 6.5   **Continuum of Leadership Behaviour**

Leadership style occurs along a continuum, ranging from boss-centred to employee-centred. Situations that require managers to exercise greater authority fall toward the boss-centred end of the continuum. Other situations call for a manager to give workers leeway to function more independently.

Boss-centred leadership						Employee-centred leadership
Use of authority by manager						**Area of freedom for workers**
Manager makes decision, announces it	Manager "sells" decision	Manager presents ideas, invites questions	Manager presents tentative decision subject to change	Manager presents problems, gets suggestions, makes decisions	Manager defines limits, asks group to make decision	Manager permits workers to function within defined limits

Source: Adapted from and reprinted by permission of *Harvard Business Review*, an exhibit from "How to Choose a Leadership Pattern" by Robert Tannenbaum and Warren H. Schmidt, May–June 1973. Copyright © 1973 by the President and Fellows of Harvard College, all rights reserved.

This process requires keen powers of observation, sensible judgment, and both a willingness and an ability to take appropriate action. However, just as a sports coach cannot play the game for team members, a coaching manager must step back and let employees perform when it's "game time." Coaching managers develop a solid game plan and empower their team to carry it out. If the team gets behind, the manager offers encouragement to boost morale. When team members are victorious, the manager recognizes and praises their outstanding achievement.[27]

Acting as a mentor is similar to coaching, but mentoring also emphasizes helping employees understand how the organization works. A **mentor** is usually an experienced manager or employee who can help guide other employees through the corporate maze. Mentors have a deep knowledge of the business and a useful network of industry colleagues. In addition, they can explain office politics, serve as a role model for appropriate business behaviour, and provide valuable advice about how to succeed within the organization.

Your mentor won't necessarily be your boss. Relationships with mentors often develop informally. However, some companies have established formal mentoring programs. In the program at Xerox, women employees can spend a few hours every month discussing work or career issues with any of the participating female executives.[28] Mentoring offers benefits for both parties: the less-experienced employee gains from the mentor's advice and ideas, and the mentor gains new networking contacts in addition to personal satisfaction.

mentor
An experienced manager or employee with a wide network of industry colleagues who can explain office politics, serve as a role model for appropriate business behaviour, and help other employees negotiate the corporate structure

Managing Change

L.O. 7

Another important leadership function is managing the process of change. The stimulus for change can come from any direction, both inside and outside the organization. Internally, a shift in strategy might require changes to the structure of the organization and to the jobs of many people within the company. In others cases, managers might identify a need to improve performance or fix organizational weaknesses. For instance, when Rick Wagoner took over as CEO of General Motors he inherited problems that had been growing for decades, including factory productivity that lagged far behind Japanese competitors, a pension program for GM retirees that was underfunded by as much as $23 billion, a bureaucratic corporate hierarchy, and bland products. To begin to solve these problems, Wagoner had to institute many changes, including bringing in executives from other companies to create strict financial controls.[29]

Outside the organization, changes can come from many directions, in many flavours. Some develop over time and are relatively easy to prepare for, like shifts in demographics. If your company markets exclusively to teenagers and you observe that birthrates have been declining, you know it won't be too many years before your market will start to shrink. At other times, you know that change is heading your way but you can't reliably predict the effects it will have on your organization. This is often the case with new competitors, new technologies, new regulations, and shifts in political influence. Still other changes come without warning, such as natural disasters. Leaders in these situations need to take decisive and dramatic changes.

Managing change is a difficult process; even previous experience does not guarantee success. For example, Paul Tellier is a highly respected CEO who has received many awards for his leadership. He was largely credited with turning Canadian National Railway "from a bloated turkey into one of the continent's biggest and most profitable transportation players." More recently the change initiatives at his former post, as CEO of Bombardier, did not achieve the same level of success. His leadership was questioned and he was rather abruptly removed from his position just a few months after the company sold off its recreational division (which sells the company's founding product, the Ski-Doo, as well as the popular Sea-Doo vehicles).[30]

Change presents a major leadership challenge for one simple reason: Most people don't like it. They may fear the unknown, they may be unwilling to give up current habits or benefits, and they may believe that the change is bad for the organization, or they may not trust the motives of the people pushing the change.[31] As a result, many— perhaps most—change initiatives fail.[32] To improve the chances of success when the organization needs to change, managers can follow the following steps:[33]

1. *Identify what needs to change.* Changes can involve the structure of the organization, technologies and systems, or people's attitudes, beliefs, skills, or behaviours.

2. *Identify the forces acting for and against the change.* By understanding these forces, managers can work to amplify the forces that will facilitate the change and remove or diminish the forces that will resist the change. For instance, if uncertainty is one of the forces working against the change, education and communication may help reduce these forces and thereby reduce resistance to the change.

3. *Choose the approach or combination of approaches best suited to the situation.* Managers can institute change through a variety of techniques, including communication, education, participation in the decision-making process, negotiation with groups opposed to the change, visible support from top managers or other opinion leaders, or coercive use of authority (usually recommended only for crisis situations). Helping people understand the need for change is often called *unfreezing* existing behaviours.

4. *Reinforce changed behaviour and monitor continued progress.* Once the change has been made, managers need to reinforce new behaviours and make sure old behaviours don't creep back in. This effort is commonly called *refreezing* new behaviours.

5. *Cultivating constant change on a small scale.* This can prepare employees for even larger changes; it's the difference between asking someone to run a race who has never even practised versus asking someone to run a race that jogs every day.[34]

In many industries and markets, change now appears to be a constant aspect of business, making change management a vital skill for leaders at all levels of the organization.

Building a Strong Organizational Culture

Strong leadership is a key element in establishing a productive *organizational culture*—the set of underlying values, norms, and practices shared by members of an organization. When you visit an organization, observe how the employees work, dress, communicate, address each other, and conduct business. Each organization has a special way of doing things. In corporations, this force is often referred to as **corporate culture**.

A company's culture influences the way people treat and react to each other and to customer and suppliers. It shapes the way employees feel about the company and the work they do; the way they interpret and perceive the actions taken by others; the

corporate culture
A set of shared values and norms that support the management system and that guide management and employee behaviour

How Much Do You Know about the Company's Culture?

Before you accept a job at a new company, it's a good idea to learn as much as possible about the company's culture. Use this list of questions to guide you in your investigation.

COMPANY VALUES

- Is there a compelling vision for the company?
- Is there a mission statement supporting the vision that employees understand and can implement?
- Do employees know how their work relates to this vision?
- Is there a common set of values that binds the organization together?
- Do officers/owners follow these values, or is there a gap between what they say and what they do?

PEOPLE

- How are people treated?
- Is there an atmosphere of civility and respect?
- Is teamwork valued and encouraged, with all ideas welcomed?
- Are employee ideas acknowledged, encouraged, and acted upon?
- Are employees given credit for their ideas?
- Is there a positive commitment to a balance between work and life?
- Is there a commitment from top management to support working parents?

COMMUNITY INVOLVEMENT

- Is the company involved in the community?
- Is there a corporate culture of service?

- Is there a stated policy of community involvement by the company and its employees?

COMMUNICATION

- Is there open communication?
- Do officers/owners regularly communicate with employees at all levels?
- Are the customer service and financial results widely distributed?
- Is there meaningful two-way communication throughout the organization?
- Are employee surveys on workplace issues conducted and published? Are employees asked for input on solutions?
- Is there an open-door policy for access to management?

EMPLOYEE PERFORMANCE

- How are personnel issues handled?
- Is employee feedback given regularly?
- Are employee evaluations based on agreed-upon objectives that have been clearly communicated?
- Are employees asked to provide a summary of their accomplishments for placement into their evaluations?[35]

Questions for Critical Thinking

1. How might a job candidate find the answers to these questions?
2. Why is it important to learn about the company's culture before accepting a job?

---

expectations they have regarding changes in their work or in the business; and their ability to lead, be productive, and choose the best course of action (see the box entitled "How Much Do You Know about the Company's Culture?").

Enron, once the world's leading market maker in electricity and natural gas, didn't fail just because of improper accounting or corruption at the top. It also failed because of its culture—one that emphasized earnings growth and rewarded aggressive behaviour to such an extent that it fostered unethical corner cutting. Top performers were rewarded with huge cash bonuses and stock options—a system that encouraged "every man for himself" instead of teamwork. Monetary and stock rewards were granted by a performance review committee. This system bred a culture in which people were afraid to go against anyone who could influence their reviews, and the whole culture at the vice-president level and above turned into a "yes-man" culture. Things weren't much better in the lower ranks.

In-Class Notes

The Leading Function
- Effectively influencing and motivating people
- *Emotional quotient (EQ)*: Self-awareness, self-regulation, motivation, empathy, social skills
- *Leadership styles*: Autocratic ("my way or the highway"); democratic (delegate and involve employees); laissez-faire (consultant role); employees take the lead
- *Transactional vs. transformational leadership*: Task oriented vs. inspirational
- Managing change
- Building a strong organizational culture

Young people—many just out of undergraduate or MBA programs with little experience and perspective—were handed extraordinary authority and decision-making power. Some were even swiftly advanced to senior-level positions. It was like a bunch of kids running loose without adult supervision. So if senior managers were fudging earnings, the inexperienced managers assumed that this was the way it was done at most businesses.[36]

Of course, Enron is not the first or the last example of corruption and corporate culture gone bad. Even seasoned veterans have been known to push the limits into the domain of the illegal. For example, allegations surrounding the Woodbridge, Ontario–based Royal Group Technologies emerged and seemed eerily familiar. The company's senior executives were accused of "systematically deceiving and defrauding shareholders in a scheme to transfer money to a luxury Caribbean resort development owned by Chairman Victor De Zen."[37]

The Controlling Function

Controlling is the fourth basic managerial function. In management, **controlling** means monitoring a firm's progress toward meeting its organizational goals and objectives, resetting the course if goals or objectives change in response to shifting conditions, and correcting deviations if goals or objectives are not being attained.

The Control Cycle

Managers strive to maintain a high level of **quality**—a measure of how closely goods or services conform to predetermined standards and customer expectations. Many firms control for quality through a four-step cycle that involves all levels of management and all employees (see Exhibit 6.6). In the first step, top managers set **standards**, or criteria for measuring the performance of the organization as a whole. At the same time, middle and first-line managers set departmental quality standards so they can

controlling
The process of measuring progress against goals and objectives and correcting deviations if results are not as expected

quality
A measure of how closely a product conforms to predetermined standards and customer expectations

standards
Criteria against which performance is measured

Exhibit 6.6   **The Control Cycle**

The control cycle has four basic steps: (1) On the basis of strategic goals, top managers set the standards by which the organization's overall performance will be measured. (2) Managers at all levels measure performance. (3) Actual performance is compared with the standards. (4) Appropriate corrective action is taken (if performance meets standards, nothing other than encouragement is needed; if performance falls below standards, corrective action may include improving performance, establishing new standards, changing plans, reorganizing, or redirecting efforts).

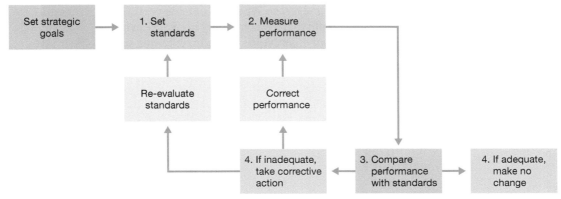

Source: Adapted from Courtland Bovée et al., *Management* (New York: McGraw-Hill, 1993), 678.

meet or exceed company standards. Establishing control standards is closely tied to the planning function and depends on information supplied by employees, customers, and other external sources. Examples of specific standards might be "produce 1500 circuit boards monthly with less than 1 percent failures."

Learning from Business Blunders

OOPS

When the worst blackout in North American history shut off electrical power to 50 million people in Canada and the eastern United States and drained up to $10 billion from the Canadian and US economies in the summer of 2003, both countries discovered just what a complicated managerial challenge the power industry faces. Electrical suppliers and customers are connected via a complex grid of transmission lines that ensure continued power even as supply and demand ebb and flow in various parts of the grid. Every power station has automatic controls that prevent the grid from drawing too much power, which can happen when demand rises across the grid or when other stations reduce the power they make available to the grid. The system can usually respond to localized power shortages by managing availability, but power station operators need to know what's going on to make these decisions.

Believe it or not, a few trees triggered this economic disaster. Three high-voltage lines in Ohio, owned by power company FirstEnergy Capital Corporation, shorted out when they came into contact with trees that should have been trimmed but weren't. Then FirstEnergy's monitoring facility didn't detect the problem because its computer system wasn't operating properly and employees weren't trained adequately. Because the company didn't respond to its own problems or alert other power generators, a surge of unmet demand for electricity began to roll through the grid—which triggered automatic protection systems at other stations and continued to amplify the problem until it rolled all the way to the east coast.

WHAT YOU CAN LEARN

The blackout led to several key business lessons: (1) Monitoring and control, based on reliable data, are essential to the operation of every business; (2) unless they are detected and dealt with quickly, relatively small mistakes can mushroom into huge problems—moreover, complex systems need vigorous, constant scrutiny; (3) employee training and system maintenance are crucial—managers can't just assume that people or systems will work properly; (4) when various independent business entities are connected (either literally connected, as in the power industry, or financially connected, as in banking), problems can spread quickly. The bottom line: Know yourself—and your business partners.[38]

In the second step of the control cycle, managers assess performance using both quantitative (specific, numerical) and qualitative (subjective) performance measures. In the third step, managers compare performance with the established standards and search for the cause of any discrepancies. If the performance falls short of standards, the fourth step is to take corrective action, which may be done by either adjusting performance or re-evaluating the standards. If performance meets or exceeds standards, no corrective action is taken. As Exhibit 6.6 shows, if everything is operating smoothly, controls permit managers to repeat acceptable performance. If results are below expectations, controls help managers take any necessary action.

Take a company like Nokia Canada, who has set an objective of selling 100 000 mobile phones to Canadian customers by their year end. What happens if they don't reach that target? With proper control systems in place, managers will evaluate why this objective was not reached. Perhaps they will find that a shortage of parts created manufacturing delays. Or perhaps the market where sales were targeted became saturated with cell phones made by competitors like the exciting new entry of the Apple iPhone. Regardless, management will search for the cause of the discrepancies before modifying the company's objectives or trying a different approach to achieve the company's long-term goals. Control methods are examined in greater detail in Chapter 8.

| L.O. 8 |

Total Quality Management

The controlling function is an important part of total quality management, which is sometimes referred to as *total quality control*. In the past, *control* often meant those little sticky tags attached to new items that say "inspected by #47." Companies would inspect finished products and rework or discard items that didn't meet quality standards. Today, this inspection step is only one small part of the total control process.

total quality management (TQM)
A comprehensive strategic management approach that builds quality into every organizational process as a way of improving customer satisfaction

Total quality management (TQM) is both a management philosophy and a strategic management process that focuses on delivering the optimum level of quality to customers by building quality into every organizational activity (see Exhibit 6.7). Total quality management draws its ideas, principles, and tools from psychology, sociology, statistics, management, and marketing. The goal of TQM is to create an environment that encourages people to grow as individuals and to learn to bring about continuous and breakthrough improvements. Companies that adopt TQM create a value for all stakeholders—customers, employees, owners, suppliers, and the community.[39] Additionally, many companies seek out and attain ISO 9000 certification, which is a global standard set by the International Organization for Standardization that establishes a minimum level of quality management. This will be discussed in greater detail in Chapter 8.

The four key elements of TQM are employee involvement, customer focus, benchmarking, and continuous improvement.

participative management
Sharing information with employees and involving them in decision making

- *Employee involvement.* Total quality management involves every employee in quality assurance. Workers are trained in quality methods and are empowered to stop a work process if they feel that products or services are not meeting quality standards. Managers also encourage employees to speak up when they think of better ways of doing things. This approach exemplifies a **participative management** style—the sharing of information at all levels of the organization (also known as *open-book management*). By directly involving employees in decision making, companies increase employees' power in an organization and improve the flow of information between employees and managers. BorgWarner Automotive (BWA) is a global player in the auto industry with facilities in 14 countries, including a plant in Simcoe, Ontario. BWA is a manufacturer of highly engineered components and systems for vehicle engines and transmissions, and participatory management is ingrained in the company's culture. The product emphasis at BWA is high tech and the workforce emphasis is high involvement. Management understands that people are the true drivers of improvement.[40]

| Exhibit 6.7 | **Total Quality Management** |

These 14 points, based on the work of W. Edwards Deming, can help managers improve their goods and services through total quality management.

1. **Create constancy of purpose for the improvement of goods and services.** The organization should constantly strive to improve quality, productivity, and consumer satisfaction to improve performance today and tomorrow.

2. **Adopt a new philosophy to reject mistakes and negativism.** Customers, managers, and employees all need to change their attitudes toward unacceptable work quality and sullen service.

3. **Cease dependence on mass inspection.** Instead of inspecting products after production to weed out bad quality, improve the process to build in good quality.

4. **End the practice of awarding business on price alone.** Create long-term relationships with suppliers who can deliver the best quality.

5. **Improve constantly and forever the system of production and service.** Improvement is not a one-time effort; managers must lead the way to continuous improvement of quality, productivity, and customer satisfaction.

6. **Institute training.** Train all organization members to do their jobs consistently well.

7. **Institute leadership.** Managers must provide the leadership to help employees do a better job.

8. **Drive out fear.** Create an atmosphere in which employees are not afraid to ask questions or to point out problems.

9. **Break down barriers between units.** Ensure that people in organizational departments or units do not have conflicting goals and are able to work as a team to achieve overall goals.

10. **Eliminate slogans, exhortations, and targets for the workforce.** These alone cannot help anyone do a better job, and they imply that employees could do better if they tried harder; rather, management should provide methods for improvement.

11. **Eliminate numerical quotas.** Quotas count only finished units, not quality or methods, and they generally lead to defective goods, wasted resources, and demoralized employees.

12. **Remove barriers to pride in work.** Most people want to do a good job but are prevented from doing so by misguided management, poor communication, faulty equipment, defective materials, and other barriers that managers must remove to improve quality.

13. **Institute a vigorous program of education and retraining.** Both managers and employees have to be educated in the new quality methods.

14. **Take action to accomplish the transformation.** With top-management commitment, have the courage to make the changes throughout the organization that will improve quality.

- *Customer focus.* Focusing on the customer simply means finding out what customers really want and then providing it. This approach requires casting aside assumptions about customers and relying on accurate research. It also requires developing long-term relationships with customers. Harry Rosen retail outlets have earned a reputation for excellent customer service with their core clients. The company's approach goes far beyond the sales experience. Harry Rosen spends a lot of time getting in tune with clients, conducting research, organizing special parties for its clients, and using its database to meet the needs of the consumer.

- *Benchmarking.* This element of TQM involves comparing your company's processes and products against the standards of the world's best companies and then working to match or exceed those standards. This process involves rating the manufacturing process, product development, distribution, and other key functions against those of acknowledged leaders; analyzing how those role models achieve their outstanding results; and then applying that knowledge to make quality improvements. World-class organizations frequently cited as benchmarks include Toyota for production, FedEx for distribution, and American Express for customer service.[41]

Harry Rosen retail outlets have been serving Canadians for more than 50 years. The company has been recognized as one of the top 50 managed companies three years in a row.

■ *Continuous improvement.* This key feature of TQM requires an ongoing effort to reduce defects, cut costs, slash production and delivery times, and offer customers innovative products. Improvements are often small incremental changes that add up to greater competitiveness over the long run. Because responsibility for such improvement often falls on employees, it becomes management's job to provide employee incentives that will motivate them to want to improve.

Although many companies are enjoying greater success as a result of total quality initiatives, a recent study of the largest companies indicates that such initiatives have fallen short of expectations in a large number of organizations. However, the fact that total quality principles played a significant role in propelling Japanese businesses from postwar ruins to pillars of innovation and productivity suggests that much can be gained from the process. What may be lacking in North America is a firm commitment to TQM. Many companies have jumped on the TQM bandwagon hoping for a quick boost in performance without really thinking about how to make total quality a part of their long-term strategy. Such companies often fail to provide the necessary managerial and financial support for the programs. In about half of the firms studied, less than 40 percent of workers and less than 80 percent of management teams were sufficiently knowledgeable about TQM philosophy, concepts, and tools.[42] Experts agree that the entire organization—from the bottom all the way up to the CEO—must be actively and visibly involved for TQM to work. Companies that make a half-hearted commitment should not expect dramatic improvements.[43]

At the same time, pursuing TQM is not necessarily a prerequisite for success. Many successful companies do not have TQM programs.[44] However, no business that operates in a competitive environment can expect long-term success unless managers strive to meet customers' needs, improve processes, lower costs, and empower employees in one way or another.

IN-CLASS NOTES

The Controlling Function
■ **The control cycle**
1. Set standards
2. Measure performance
3. Compare to standard
4. Take action (correct performance if needed, re-evaluate standards)

■ **Total quality management**
 ■ Employee involvement
 ■ Customer focus
 ■ Benchmarking
 ■ Continuous improvement

KEY MANAGEMENT SKILLS FOR SUCCESS

Interpersonal Skills

The skills required to communicate with other people, work effectively with them, motivate them, and lead them are called **interpersonal skills**. Because managers mainly get things done through people at all levels of the organization, they use good interpersonal skills in countless situations. Encouraging employees to work together toward common goals, interacting with employees and other managers, negotiating with partners and suppliers, developing employee trust and loyalty, and fostering innovation—all these activities require interpersonal skills.

Communication, or exchanging information, is the most important interpersonal skill that managers use. Effective communication not only increases the manager's and the organization's productivity, but also shapes the impressions made on colleagues, employees, supervisors, investors, and customers. Communication allows you to perceive the needs of these stakeholders and it helps you respond to those needs.[45] In addition, as the workforce becomes more diverse, managers will need to adjust their interactions with others, communicating in a way that considers the different needs, backgrounds, and experiences of people.

Technical Skills

A person who knows how to operate a machine, prepare a financial statement, program a computer, or pass a football has **technical skills**; that is, the individual has the knowledge and ability to perform the mechanics of a particular job. Technical skills are most important at lower organizational levels because managers at these levels work directly with employees who are using the tools and techniques of a particular specialty, such as automotive assembly or computer programming. Still, twenty-first–century managers must have a strong technology background. They must find new computer applications that can complete daily work routines faster or provide more accurate information sooner.

Managers at all levels use **administrative skills**, which are the technical skills necessary to manage an organization. Administrative skills include the abilities to make schedules, gather information, analyze data, plan, and organize. Managers often develop such skills through education and then improve them by working in one or more functional areas of an organization, such as accounting or marketing.[46] Project management skills are becoming an increasingly important administrative skill. Managers must know how to start a project or work assignment from scratch, map out each step in the process to its successful completion, develop project costs and timelines, and establish checkpoints at key project intervals.

Conceptual Skills

Managers need **conceptual skills** to see the organization as a whole, in the context of its environment, and to understand how its various parts relate. Conceptual skills are especially important to top managers. These managers are the strategists who develop the plans that guide the organization toward its goals. Managers like Steve Jobs use their conceptual skills to acquire and analyze information, identify both problems and opportunities, understand the competitive environment in which their companies operate, develop strategies, and make decisions.

A key managerial activity requiring conceptual skills is **decision making**, a process that has five distinct steps: (1) recognizing the need for a decision; (2) identifying, analyzing, and defining the problem

interpersonal skills
Skills required to understand other people and to interact effectively with them

technical skills
The ability and knowledge to perform the mechanics of a particular job

administrative skills
Technical skills in information gathering, data analysis, planning, organizing, and other aspects of managerial work

conceptual skills
The ability to understand the relationship of parts to the whole

decision making
The process of identifying a decision situation, analyzing the problem, weighing the alternatives, choosing an alternative and implementing it, and evaluating the results

Dominic D'Alessandro was recently named the Canadian Business Leader of 2007 by the University of Alberta School of Business. He has previously earned the Most Respected CEO of 2004 and Most Outstanding CEO for 2002 awards from his peers. This respect comes from his skilful efforts in leading Manulife Financial to a world leader position in the financial services business. He took the company public in 1999 and led the company to its acquisition of John Hancock Financial in 2004 and continues to push Manulife to new heights.[47]

Exhibit 6.8   **Monumental Management Decisions**

Great decisions change things. Here are a few of the management decisions that made the greatest impact in the twentieth century.

Coca-Cola	During World War II Robert Woodruff, president of Coca-Cola, committed to selling bottles of Coke to members of the armed services for a nickel per bottle. Customer loyalty never came cheaper.
Holiday Inn	When the Wilson family went on a motoring vacation, they discovered it was not much fun staying in motels that were either too expensive or too slovenly. Kemmons Wilson decided to build his own hotels; the first Holiday Inn opened in 1952.
Honda	When Honda arrived in North America in 1959 to launch its big motorbikes, customers weren't keen on their problematic performance. However, they did admire the little Super Cub bikes that Honda's managers used. So Honda bravely changed direction and transformed the motorbike business overnight.
CNN	Ignoring market research, Ted Turner launched the Cable News Network in 1980. No one thought a 24-hour news network would work.
Dell	In 1984 Michael Dell decided to sell personal computers direct and built to order. Now everybody in the industry is trying to imitate Dell's strategy.

Source: Stuart Crainer, "The 75 Greatest Management Decisions Ever Made," *Management Review*, November 1998, 17–23.

or opportunity; (3) generating alternatives; (4) selecting an alternative and implementing it; and (5) evaluating the results. Managers monitor the results of decisions over time to see whether the chosen alternative works, whether any new problem or opportunity arises because of the decision, and whether a new decision must be made (see Exhibit 6.8).[48]

Keep in mind that a company's managerial structure defines the way decisions are made. Today's flatter organizations, for example, allow information to flow more freely among all levels of the organization, and they push decision making down to lower organizational levels. As Chapter 7 discusses in detail, more and more organizations are empowering their employees and teams by giving them increasing discretion over work-related issues.[49]

L.O. 10

Why Managers Fail

A wide variety of reasons can be listed to explain why some managers thrive and others fail miserably. Many companies make a very common and simplistic error in judgment. They promote their best employee to the position of manager without really examining their strengths and weaknesses to see if they would be a good fit in the new position. Companies compound this error by providing poor training and assuming that the star employee will thrive in the new job without proper guidance. Of course, internal promotion is a great tool for motivation, but you can't just assume people will fit the job. The most skilled employee in a workshop may lack the interpersonal skills to effectively lead. The best salesperson may lack the ability to communicate with groups of employees. The most knowledgeable accountant or engineer may have tremendous process or product development skills but lack the ability to see the big picture or may lack market knowledge. Far too often, the department will lose their most valuable employee and gain a poor manager all in one move (see Exhibit 6.9).[50]

Managers rely on a number of skills to perform their functions and maintain a high level of quality in their organizations. These skills can be classified into three basic categories: *interpersonal, technical,* and *conceptual.* As managers rise through the organization's hierarchy, they may need to strengthen their abilities in one or more of these skills; fortunately, managerial skills can usually be learned.[51]

Exhibit 6.9   Why Managers Fail

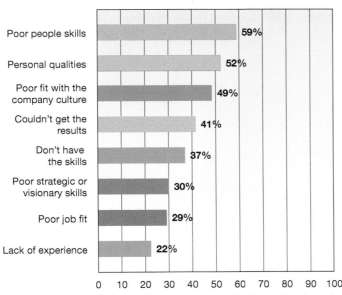

Source: Roma Luciw, "No.1 Employee Not Always Your No.1 Manager," *Globe and Mail,* 17 February 2007, B10.

Technologies That Are Revolutionizing Business

BUSINESS INTELLIGENCE SYSTEMS

One of the maddening ironies of contemporary business is that many decision makers are bombarded by data but starved for true information and insights. *Business intelligence* (BI) systems aim to harness all that data and turn it into the insights that managers need.

The good news is that a number of companies are now offering BI solutions. The bad news is there's a dizzying array of terminology in use today. The wide range of technologies that fall under the BI umbrella include *executive information systems* (a general term for systems that present top managers with vital operational information), *decision support systems* (which collect and analyze data then model various scenarios to let managers study the likely outcomes of the decisions they face), and a variety of other systems and tools. You'll also encounter such terms as *online analytical processing (OLAP)* and *business analytics* (data analysis tools that help managers discover trends and relationships in operating data), *performance metrics* (systems that measure and report on progress toward organizational goals), and *executive dashboards* (specialized web pages that present performance metrics in easy-to-read formats).

HOW THEY'RE CHANGING BUSINESS

Business intelligence systems are helping managers and professionals in many industries deal with both strategic and tactical problems. For instance, Boeing tracks the complex process of custom-building each of its aircraft, and DaimlerChrysler analyzes millions of owner contact records to learn more about customer needs and expectations.[52]

WHERE YOU CAN LEARN MORE

Because business intelligence is a broad term that describes a variety of approaches, technologies, and specific products, you can expect to find a wide range of information. Start with www.businessintelligence.com, then try several of the leading vendors, including Cognos, www.cognos.com; Business Objects, www.businessobjects.com; and Hyperion, www.hyperion.com.

IN-CLASS NOTES

Management Skills

- *Interpersonal skills*: required to communicate with other people
- *Technical skills*: most important at lower levels because managers at these levels work directly with employees
- *Administrative skills*: abilities to make schedules, gather information, analyze data, plan, and organize
- *Conceptual skills*: top managers need to be able to see the organization as a whole

_____

_____

_____

_____

_____

_____

_____

BEHIND THE SCENES

Moving Music at Apple iTunes and Taking Advantage of New Opportunities

When Steve Jobs evaluated the marketplace for online music, he no doubt liked some of the things he saw more than others. On the plus side, Apple was well known and highly regarded in both the computer and music industries, so almost anything the company chose to do would have the support and respect of many consumers and potential business partners. At the time, 2 million people were already walking around with the enormously popular iPod. Moreover, Apple's design team had a proven knack for making technology easier to use, a critical issue in the technically complicated arena of digital music.

On the minus side, Jobs knew there would be serious challenges in any effort to turn online music into a success-ful business venture. The technology would be complex, starting from the need to collect and store hundreds of thousands of songs and to make them easily available to thousands or even millions of online customers at once. But the technology might have been the easiest part of the whole problem. The music business is a complex stew of personalities, traditions, and legal contracts, with lots of people who want a piece of the financial action. Some artists refuse to sell songs individually out of fear it will hurt album sales (and some refuse to sell their music online at all). As a result, Apple and other companies often need to negotiate deals one song at a time—all of which takes time and costs

money. To complicate matters even further, contractual terms differ from country to country, requiring a new round of negotiations each time. Then there are the millions of music listeners who were already in the habit of simply making copies of pirated songs. How could they be con-vinced to pay for something they were getting for free?

Steve Jobs has never been one to back down from a chal-lenge. He added up those pluses and minuses and decided to lead Apple into the arena. In 2003, the company launched iTunes.com, a web-based music store that offers legal music downloads—all for just 99 cents each. iTunes enjoyed wide-spread media coverage when it was launched and even more when it was expanded to support Windows-based personal computers. Industry experts applaud its simplicity and vol-ume of musical offerings. Apple's efforts were no doubt also helped by some high-profile lawsuits that the recording industry launched against hundreds of people who had been downloading pirated tunes. However, by early 2004 iTunes had sold only 75 million or so of the 100 million songs it had hoped to sell by then. Jobs claimed to be thrilled with the new business's performance nonetheless, despite a difficult profit equation. When Apple collects those 99 cents for each song it sells, it first hands over 70 cents to whichever company controls the rights to the song (typically a record company). This company then has to divide those 70 cents among music publishers, performers, and songwriters. From the 29 cents Apple keeps, it needs to cover its costs for advertising, staffing, computer systems, and other business expenses. A single nationwide advertising campaign can cost millions of dollars, so you can get an idea of how hard it is to stretch those 29 cents to cover costs and turn a profit.

Despite serious questions and evaluations, Jobs and his leadership team did not retreat. They reinforced their actions and found additional ways to improve the service and revenues. They added movies and TV shows to the iTunes mix; they created a premium service called iTunes Plus enabling clients to pay $1.29 for improved downloads that provided sound quality comparable to the original recordings. The commitment and vision seems to be slowly paying off, and Apple's confidence seems to be justified. By mid-2007 iTunes had sold more than 2.5 billion songs, 50 million TV shows, and 2 million movies. At the time, online music sales only made up 10 percent of all music sales. This number was expected to grow to 25 percent by 2010 with Apple as a major beneficiary. In addition, iTunes was just one element of a linked family that helped reinforce sales of all Apple's products. For example, iTunes helps fuel the king of the Apple court, the iPod, which has sold over 100 million units—not to mention the sales of its over 4000 accessory products.

New Horizons

Where do Steve Jobs and Apple go from here? The job of planning, leading, organizing and controlling an organization like Apple is not simple. Effective leaders are constantly juggling their duties to stay ahead of the competition. The opportunities are vast. Apple has already launched the Video iPod and iTV, to name just two products. However, the product that has received the most press and created fear among cell phone manufactures is the iPhone—part phone, part iPod, and part wireless computer. This device has no buttons and no keyboards, and executives at competitive firms are scrambling. This is nothing new for Jobs and his team—innovation sparks fear in the unimaginative. Will the iPhone become the holy grail of gadgets? Only time will tell, but it will surely fit nicely into the portfolio of Apple products and push sales, while also helping to fuel the innovative image of Apple and its various iProducts with current and future generations of consumers.[53]

Critical Thinking Questions

1. Based on this case, would you describe Steve Jobs as a transactional or a transformational leader?
2. In the context of this case, explain the importance of setting clear goals and objectives.
3. Perform a SWOT analysis for the Apple iTunes business unit. What do you think the future of this division will be? Will it continue to grow? What challenges does it face?

Learn More Online

Go to Chapter 6 of this text's website at www.pearsoned/bovee and click on the Apple iTunes hotlink. Why does the website appeal to customers? What other services are offered? In what ways does the website encourage visitors to make purchases?

TEST YOUR KNOWLEDGE

Questions for Review

1. Explain the important role of management vision. How does management vision relate to the mission statement?
2. What is the purpose of a SWOT analysis?
3. What is the difference between transactional and transformational leadership?
4. What are the four key elements of total quality management (TQM)?
5. Strong conceptual skills are most important for managers at which level of the organization?

Questions for Analysis

6. How do effective managers balance the demands of the four functions of management as described in this chapter?
7. What is meant by the term *emotional quotient*? How does this term relate to effective management?
8. Describe the three main leadership styles discussed in this chapter. Is there an ideal leadership style? Explain.
9. Mentoring and coaching techniques have been adopted by many high-profile companies. What is the value of such programs from the perspective of the participants? What is the value from the organization's perspective?

10. **Ethical Considerations.** When an organization learns about a threat that could place the safety of its workers or its customers at risk, is management obligated to immediately inform these parties of the threat? Explain your answer.

Questions for Application

11. What are your long-term goals? Develop a set of long-term career goals for yourself and several short-term objectives that will help you reach those goals. Make sure your goals are specific, measurable, and time bound.
12. Do you have the skills it takes to be an effective manager? Find out by taking the Keirsey Temperament Sorter II personality test at www.keirsey.com.
13. **Integrated.** Using Dell Computer's mission statement in Exhibit 6.2 as a model and the material you learned in Chapter 3 on social responsibility, develop a mission statement for a socially responsible company such as Telus or Ben & Jerry's.
14. **Integrated.** What is the principal difference between a business plan (as discussed in Chapter 4) and a strategic plan?

PRACTISE YOUR KNOWLEDGE

SHARPENING YOUR COMMUNICATION SKILLS

As the manager of Martin's Restaurant Supply, you see a huge potential for selling company products on the Internet to customers around the world. Your company already has a website but it's geared to Canadian sales only. Before you propose your idea to senior management, however, you're going to do your homework. Studies have shown that companies selling products in the global marketplace benefit by modifying their websites to accommodate cultural differences. For instance, a mailbox with a raised flag has no meaning in many foreign countries.

Your task is to review the websites of several leading global companies and take notes on how they adapt their websites for global audiences. Once you've gathered your notes, write a short memo to management highlighting (via bullet points) some of the ways these leaders make their websites effective for a global audience.

BUILDING YOUR TEAM SKILLS

A good mission statement should define the organization's purpose and ultimate goals and outline the principles that are to guide managers and employees in working toward those goals. Using library sources like annual reports or Internet sources like organizational websites locate mission statements from one non-profit organization, such as a school or a charity, and one company with which you are familiar.

Bring these statements to class and, with your team, select four mission statements to evaluate. How many of the mission statements contain all five of the typical components (product or service; primary market; concern for survival, growth, and profitability; managerial philosophy; and commitment to quality and social responsibility)? Which components are most often absent from the mission statements you are evaluating? Which components are most often included? Of the mission statements your team is analyzing, which is the most inspiring? Why?

Now assume that you and your teammates are the top management team at each organization or company. How would you improve these mission statements? Rewrite the four mission statements so that they cover the five typical components, show all organization members how their roles are related to the vision, and inspire commitment among employees and managers.

Summarize your team's work in a written report or oral presentation to the class. Compare the mission statement that your team found most inspiring with the statements that other teams found most inspiring. What do these mission statements have in common? How do they differ? Of all the inspiring mission statements reported to the class, which do you think is the best? Why? Does this mission statement inspire you to consider working for or doing business with this organization?

EXPAND YOUR KNOWLEDGE

DISCOVERING CAREER OPPORTUNITIES

If you become a manager, how much of your day will be spent performing each of the four basic functions of management? This is your opportunity to find out. Arrange to shadow a manager (such as a department head, a store manager, or a shift supervisor) for a few hours. As you observe, categorize the manager's activities in terms of the four management functions and note how much time each activity takes. If observation is not possible, interview a manager to complete this exercise.

1. How much of the manager's time is spent on each of the four management functions? Is this the allocation you expected?

2. Ask whether this is a typical workday for this manager. If it isn't, what does the manager usually do differently? During a typical day, does this manager tend to spend most of the time on one particular function?

3. Of the four management functions, which does the manager believe is most important for good organizational performance? Do you agree?

DEVELOPING YOUR RESEARCH SKILLS

Find two articles in business journals or newspapers (print or online editions) that profile senior managers who lead a business or a non-profit organization.

1. What experience, skills, and business background does each leader have? Do you see any striking similarities or differences in their backgrounds?

2. What kinds of business challenges have these leaders faced? What actions did they take to deal with those challenges? Did they establish any long-term goals or objectives for their company? Did the articles mention a new change initiative?

3. Describe the leadership strengths of each person as they are presented in the articles you selected. Is either leader known as a team builder? Long-term strategist? Shrewd negotiator? What are each leader's greatest strengths?

STUDY GUIDE

SUMMARY OF LEARNING OBJECTIVES

1. Define the four basic management functions

The four basic management functions are: (1) planning—establishing objectives and goals for the organization and translating them into action plans; (2) organizing—arranging resources to carry out the organization's plans; (3) leading—influencing and motivating people to work effectively and willingly toward company goals; and (4) controlling—monitoring progress toward organizational goals, resetting the course if goals or objectives change in response to shifting conditions, and correcting deviations if goals or objectives are not being attained.

2. Outline the tasks involved in the strategic planning process

The strategic planning process begins with a clear vision for the company's future. This vision is then translated into a mission statement so it can be shared with all members of the organization. Next, managers develop forecasts about future trends that affect their industry and products. Then they analyze the competition, paying close attention to their strengths and weaknesses so this information can be used to gain a competitive edge. With an eye on the company's vision and mission as well as on competition, managers establish company goals and objectives. Finally, they translate these goals and objectives into action plans.

3. Explain the purpose of a mission statement

A mission statement defines why the organization exists, what it does, what it hopes to achieve, and the principles it will follow to meet its goals. It is used to bring clarity of focus to members of the organization and to provide guidelines for the adoption of future projects.

4. List the benefits of setting long-term goals and objectives

Goals and objectives establish long- and short-range targets that help managers fulfill the company's mission. Setting appropriate goals increases employee motivation, establishes standards by which individual and group performance can be measured, guides employee activity, and clarifies management's expectations.

5. Cite three leadership styles and describe when each style is most appropriate to use

Three leadership styles are autocratic, democratic, and laissez faire (also called free-rein). Each may work best in different situations—autocratic when quick decisions are needed, democratic when employee participation in decision making is desirable, and laissez faire when fostering creativity is a priority.

6. Identify the importance of contingency leadership and distinguish between transactional and transformational leadership

Contingency leadership emphasizes the need to adapt—good leaders are flexible enough to respond with the best approach for the situation. The difference between a transactional and a transformational leader is important. The transactional leader focuses on the task at hand and emphasizes getting the specific job done, while the transformational leader has the ability to inspire and lead beyond the tedious day-to-day tasks.

7. List the challenges involved in managing organizational change and identify the strategies to overcome them

People don't like change because they tend to fear the unknown and are comfortable in their routines. They may distrust the motives of the change or just feel that the change is bad for the company. To facilitate change in an organization, managers can take the following steps: (1) identify what needs to change; (2) identify the forces acting for and against the change; (3) choose the approach or combination of approaches best suited to the situation; (4) reinforce changed behaviour and monitor continued progress; (5) cultivate constant change on a small scale.

8. Explain how total quality management (TQM) is changing the way organizations are managed

Total quality management is both a management philosophy and a management process that focuses on delivering quality to customers. TQM redirects management to focus on four key elements: (1) employee involvement, including team building and soliciting employee input on decisions; (2) customer focus, which involves gathering customer feedback and then acting on that feedback to better serve customers; (3) benchmarking, which involves measuring the company's standards against the standards of industry leaders; (4) continuous improvement, which requires an ongoing commitment to reducing defects, cutting costs, slashing production and delivery times, and offering customers innovative products.

9. Identify and explain the three types of managerial skills

Managers use (1) interpersonal skills to communicate with other people, work effectively with them, and lead them; (2) technical skills to perform the mechanics of a particular job; and (3) conceptual skills (including decision making) to see the organization as a whole, to see it in the context of its environment, and to understand how the various parts relate.

10. Understand some of the reasons why managers fail and identify key strategies for success

Managers fail for many reasons, including poor people skills, personal qualities, poor fit with the organization, lack of skills, or lack of experience. Companies must carefully pick management personnel to match the needs of the job. Simply promoting a star employee without evaluating the needs of the position can often lead to both the loss of a star employee and the hiring of an ineffective manager all in one action.

KEY TERMS

administrative skills   (185)
autocratic leaders   (175)
coaching   (176)
conceptual skills   (185)
contingency leadership   (176)
controlling   (180)
corporate culture   (178)
crisis management   (172)
decision making   (185)
democratic leaders   (175)
first-line managers   (174)
goal   (170)
interpersonal skills   (185)

laissez-faire leaders   (176)
leading   (174)
management   (167)
management pyramid   (172)
mentor   (177)
middle managers   (173)
mission statement   (168)
objective   (170)
operational plans   (171)
organizing   (172)
participative management   (182)
planning   (167)
quality   (180)

roles   (167)
situational leadership   (176)
standards   (180)
strategic plans   (167)
SWOT analysis   (169)
tactical plans   (171)
technical skills   (185)
top managers   (172)
total quality management (TQM)
   (182)
transactional leaders   (176)
transformational leaders   (176)
vision   (168)

QUESTIONS

Multiple Choice   Circle the correct answer and then check the answers in the back of the book to chart your progress.

1. Which of the following is the primary management function on which all the others depend?

   a. Planning
   b. Organizing
   c. Leading
   d. Controlling

2. Which of the following is *not* one of the three main roles that managers serve?

   a. Interpersonal
   b. Philosophical
   c. Informational
   d. Decisional

3. Which of the following best describes the environment that positive organizational cultures create?

   a. Cutthroat and very competitive
   b. Concentrates solely on the "bottom line"

   c. Ever changing, even if it doesn't have a direction to change in
   d. Encourages employees to make ethical decisions for the good of the company and its customers

4. Which of the following typically comes first in the planning process?

   a. Vision
   b. Mission statement
   c. Strategic plan
   d. Tactical plan

5. Which of the following does *not* appear in a mission statement?

   a. A statement of why the organization exists
   b. An employment contract for key employees
   c. A general description of the company's primary market(s)
   d. A summary of managerial philosophy

6. Studies indicate that leaders who possess a high emotional quotient (EQ) are more effective. According to the definition, which of the following is *not* a quality exhibited by managers with a high emotional quotient?

   a. Self-regulation
   b. Autocratic skills
   c. Empathy
   d. Self-awareness

7. What is the main advantage of the autocratic style of management?

   a. The autocratic manager can "get the job done," especially in a crisis.
   b. The autocratic leader makes sure each worker is involved in the decision-making process.
   c. The autocratic leader makes sure each worker is involved in the planning process.
   d. The autocratic manager can hurt employee morale.

8. Which of the following is the managerial function that involves arranging resources to carry out a firm's plans?

   a. Controlling
   b. Evaluating
   c. Leading
   d. Organizing

9. Which of the following is *not* an advantage of mentoring?

   a. The less-experienced worker gains ideas and advice.
   b. The less-experienced worker could gain automatic raises and quicker promotions.
   c. The more-experienced worker gets contacts in other areas of the company.
   d. The more-experienced worker gets personal satisfaction from helping others.

10. Which of the following is a successful strategy for business leaders to manage change?

    a. Refusing to change
    b. Understanding that change is inevitable, so workers will eventually figure out how to do it
    c. Building trust with employees before the change is necessary
    d. Avoiding small changes over long periods of time and then radically changing operations all at once

True/False

1. True or False? A controller, a marketing manager, and a sales manager are all considered first-line managers.

2. True or False? Companies can be successful only by developing and selling unique, popular items.

3. True or False? The best leaders adapt their leadership styles to match the requirements of the situation.

4. True or False? Managers who use "coaching" behaviour encourage their workers to find their own solutions.

5. True or False? A company using a differentiation strategy distinguishes its products from the competitors based on the level of service, product image, unique product features, or new technologies provided by its company.

Fill-in-the-Blank

1. _____ plans outline a firm's long-range (two to five years) goals and set a course of action for the firm to pursue.

2. Managers perform ceremonial obligations; provide leadership to employees; build a network of relationships with bosses, peers, and employees; and act as a liaison to groups and individuals both inside and outside the company. In performing these functions managers execute their _____ roles.

3. _____ forecasts are typically based on historical data or tests and involve complex statistical calculations.

4. Managers who can reshape the destinies of their organizations by inspiring employees to rise above self-interest and create new levels of success for the company as a whole are referred to as _____ leaders.

5. _____ refers to the set of shared values and norms that support the management system and that guide management and employee behaviour.

6. _____ is a comprehensive strategic management approach that builds quality into every organizational process as a way of improving customer satisfaction.

7. _____ leadership involves adaptation; it is based on the readiness of employees and the situation.

8. _____ involves comparing key functions against the same functions in businesses recognized to be world class.

9. The _____ includes setting standards, measuring performance, comparing results, and adjusting if necessary.

10. A manager that has the ability to understand the relationship of the parts to the whole possesses good _____ skills.

Companion
Website

See It on the WEB

Visit the Companion Website at **www.pearsoned.ca/bovee**, review the exercises, and complete the following assignments for Chapter 6:

1. Become a Better Manager
2. Learn from the Best—and the Worst
3. Looking to Organizational Change

CHAPTER 7

ORGANIZING AND WORKING IN TEAMS

LEARNING OBJECTIVES

After studying this chapter, you will be able to

1   Discuss the function of a company's organizational structure

2   Explain the concepts of accountability, authority, and delegation

3   Define five major types of organizational structure

4   Describe the five most common forms of teams

5   Highlight the advantages and disadvantages of working in teams

6   List the characteristics of effective teams

7   Review the five stages of team development

8   Highlight six causes of team conflict and three styles of conflict resolution

9   Identify key factors that lead to effective team meetings

Behind the Scenes

www.altitude-concepts.com

Welcome to the exciting and stressful world of event planning! You may not be familiar with Altitude Concepts's name, but you will be familiar with some of the events and organizations that they have been associated with: the Rogers Cup, the Telus World Skins Game, BDC's Small Business Week, and Bombardier's events at the Salt Lake City Winter Olympics, to name just a few. How do you turn a shabby old warehouse into a top-notch event space designed to entertain members of the business community? How do you create just the right ambiance in a VIP lounge at a tennis tournament? How do you design an event space to create an exciting setting for a new business product launch? Answer: With a lot of creativity and imagination, a bit of elbow grease, and a solid team pulling together to make sure that the events run seamlessly. After all, event planning, like many businesses, is based on reputation and referrals; ensuring that the client paying the bill is totally satisfied is a matter of survival.

Many of you may have some experience planning events like an office party, a company picnic, a school dance, or a fashion show. If you have had the opportunity, you know just how stressful it can be. You want to ensure that everything goes well but there are always challenges. Imagine what it is like to plan multiple events on a large scale, in locations across the continent, with 500 to 3000 people typically attending and organizations expecting a unique exciting experience each time. At Altitude Concepts, that is exactly what they do.

The company's seeds were planted when founder Jean-François Grenier was still a student and became involved in organizing comedy shows. His knack for theatrics and his love of entertainment evolved into the idea for Altitude Concepts. Today the company consists of 14 full-time staff members with a wide range of skills and 25 regularly subcontracted specialists including

It takes a lot of creativity, great vision, clear organization skills and a hard-working team of talented individuals to turn an old warehouse into a dynamic business event site, or a cavernous empty space into an intimate show experience. But that is exactly what Altitude Concepts prides itself on.

sound engineers, lighting specialists, and so on. Many of these subcontractors earn as much as 80 percent of their revenue from Altitude Concepts so they are, in essence, part of the extended business family.

The various event preparations are led by individual project managers that are in charge of executing the details negotiated between Altitude Concepts and the client. But the project managers couldn't do it alone. Each event is worked on by a core team consisting of a production manager, creative director, as well as individuals with diverse skills and experience. According to Grenier, the secret to effectively managing teams is to train team members, put good people in place, and create a supportive environment with good communication that allows teams to thrive and function as independent units.[1]

Test Yourself

Answers to these questions can be found on the website: www.pearson.ca/bovee.

1. As organizations like Altitude Concepts grow, formal organizational structures replace informal planning approaches. Why is a company's organizational structure so important? Can two companies in the same industry take different approaches?

2. What are the challenges of working in teams and how do these challenges apply to an event-planning organization like Altitude Concepts?

3. What are the benefits of using a cross-functional team approach to plan an event?

Designing an Effective Organization Structure

L.O. 1

A company's **organizational structure** has a dramatic influence on the way employees and managers make decisions, communicate, and accomplish important tasks. As entrepreneurial organizations like Altitude Concepts grow they transform from being simply intuitive and free-flowing into more structured companies. Large multinational companies like McCain Foods or Irving Oil have clear lines of authority. An organizational structure helps the company achieve its goals by providing a framework for managers to divide responsibilities, effectively distribute the authority to make decisions, coordinate and control the organization's work, and hold employees accountable for their work. In some organizations this structure is a relatively rigid vertical hierarchy like the management pyramid described in Chapter 6 (see Exhibit 6.4). In other organizations, teams of employees and managers from various levels and functions work together to make decisions and achieve the organization's goals.[2]

When managers design the organization's structure they use an **organization chart** to provide a visual representation of how employees and tasks are grouped and how the lines of communication and authority flow. Exhibit 7.1 shows the organization chart for a grocery store chain. An organization chart depicts the official design for accomplishing tasks that lead to achieving the organization's goals, a framework known as the **formal organization**. Every company also has an **informal organization**—the network of interactions that develop on a personal level among workers. Sometimes the interactions among people in the informal organization parallel their relationships in the formal organization, but often interactions don't follow formal boundaries. An employee who is lower on the organizational chart may actually have more power to influence opinion than an individual higher up on the chart because of his or her informal influence. Crossing formal boundaries can help establish a more pleasant work

organizational structure
A framework enabling managers to divide responsibilities, ensure employee accountability, and distribute decision-making authority

organization chart
A diagram showing how employees and tasks are grouped and where the lines of communication and authority flow

formal organization
A framework officially established by managers for accomplishing tasks that lead to achieving the organization's goals

informal organization
A network of informal employee interactions that are not defined by the formal structure

Exhibit 7.1   **Organization Chart for a Grocery Store Chain**

Many organization charts look like this one. The traditional model of an organization is a pyramid in which numerous boxes form the base and lead up to fewer and fewer boxes at higher levels, ultimately arriving at one box at the top. A glance at this grocery store chain's organization chart reveals who has authority over whom, who is responsible for whose work, and who is accountable to whom.

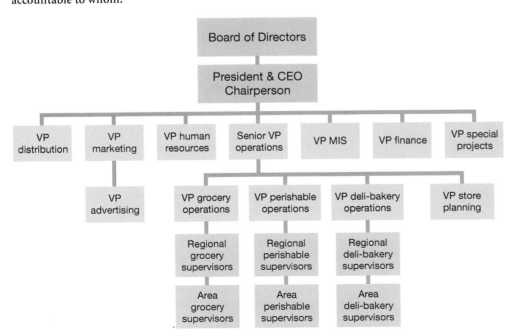

environment, but it can also undermine formal work processes and hurt a company's ability to get things done.[3]

How do companies design an organizational structure, and which organizational structure is the most effective? In the past, organizations were designed around management's desire to control workers and were set up as a hierarchy. Today, however, more and more companies are designing organizational structures around the customers' needs for fast decisions. As this chapter will discuss later, companies are eliminating layers of management, or flattening their organizational structures, to give more decision-making authority to employees who deal directly with customers. In fact, as management guru Peter Drucker saw it, "There is no such thing as one right organization. Each has distinct strengths, distinct limitations, and specific applications." In other words, today's managers require a toolbox full of organizational structures so they can select the right tool for each specific task.[4] To identify the best structure for their organizations, managers need to identify job responsibilities, define the chain of command, and organize the workforce in a way that maximizes effectiveness and efficiency.

Identifying Job Responsibilities

The nature of the work employees are expected to do is a critical aspect when choosing an organizational structure. Before designing a structure, management must first decide on the optimal level of **work specialization**—the degree to which organizational tasks are broken down into separate jobs.[5] Few employees have the skills to perform every task a company needs. Therefore, work specialization can improve organizational efficiency by enabling each worker to perform tasks that are well defined and that require specific skills. For example, in 1776 Scottish economist Adam Smith found that if each of 10 workers went through every step needed to make a pin, the entire group could make 200 pins a day. However, if each worker performed only a few steps and no one made a pin from start to finish, the same 10 workers could make 48 000 pins a day. When employees concentrate on specialized tasks they can perfect their skills and perform their tasks more quickly. A classic example of work specialization is the automobile assembly line.

Work specialization continues to be an important feature in business organizations, from the various responsibilities along an automobile assembly line, to an accounting firm in which various staff members specialize in different aspects of taxation.

work specialization
Specialization in or responsibility for some portion of an organization's overall work tasks; also called division of labour

In addition to matching skills with job tasks, specialization prevents overlapping responsibilities and communication breakdowns. For instance, in business-to-business markets, the ongoing relationship between a supplier and a customer can sometimes involve dozens or even hundreds of employees. To ensure efficient communication, *relationship managers* (frequently senior salespeople) are often put in charge of the relationship on both sides. Other employees will communicate back and forth, but significant issues such as contract negotiations and scheduling updates are left to these two people.

However, organizations can overdo specialization. If a task is defined too narrowly employees may become bored with performing the same repetitive job over and over again. They may also feel unchallenged and alienated. Managers must think carefully about how specialized or how broad each task should be. In fact, a growing number of companies are balancing specialization and employee motivation with teamwork. This approach allows group members to decide how to break down a complex task, and it allows employees to rotate among the jobs that the team is collectively responsible for. The team then shares credit for the results, and workers feel

This photo shows a Bombardier factory assembly shop where employees perform specialized work tasks to create a unified product. Each employee is an expert in one area of the process.

Technologies That Are Revolutionizing Business

WIRELESS NETWORKING

You already spend part of your days or evenings in the midst of a wireless network—around your campus, at your favourite coffeehouse, or in one of the many other locations that now provide wireless access points. Instead of working on class assignments or writing a great novel, businesspeople use wireless networking to conduct business more efficiently and effectively.

HOW IT'S CHANGING BUSINESS

Wireless networking gives businesses two major benefits. The first is making information available where and when it can be most useful. For example, Tesco, a large retail firm based in the United Kingdom, uses handheld wireless devices in its stores to let sales staff check prices, inventory levels, and other information on the spot. Similarly, many warehouses now use wireless networks to help workers find and organize products. Some hospitals now provide medical staff with wireless devices to access patient records on the spot.

By giving employees the information they need to perform tasks, wireless networks are improving inventory management, customer service, sales productivity, and other vital business functions.

The second major benefit is simplifying the connection between people and computers. This can help in a variety of ways, from making it easier to add networking to an older building that doesn't have wires running through the walls to making it easier for business teams to move around large corporate campuses (to attend team meetings, for example) without losing their connections to the company network.[6]

WHERE YOU CAN LEARN MORE

The Web is full of information about wireless networking, although much of this information is rather technical. For some basic information, visit www.about .com and search for "wireless networking." For more technical information, visit Network World Fusion, www.networkworld.com/topics/wireless.html.

---

that they have created something of value. The team approach to organization is discussed in more depth later in this chapter.

Defining the Chain of Command

L.O. 2

Once the various jobs and their individual responsibilities have been identified, the next step is defining the **chain of command**, the lines of authority that connect the various groups and levels within an organization. The chain of command helps organizations function smoothly by making two things clear: who is responsible for each task, and who has the authority to make official decisions.

All employees have a certain amount of **responsibility**—the obligation to perform the duties and achieve the goals and objectives associated with their jobs. As they work toward the organization's goals, employees must also maintain their **accountability**, their obligation to report the results of their work to supervisors or team members and to justify any outcomes that fall below expectations. Managers ensure that tasks are accomplished by exercising **authority**, the power to make decisions, issue orders, carry out actions, and allocate resources to achieve the organization's goals. Authority is vested in the positions that managers hold, and it flows down through the management pyramid. **Delegation** is the assignment of work and the transfer of authority and responsibility to complete that work.[7]

Look again at Exhibit 7.1. The senior vice-president of operations delegates responsibilities to the vice-presidents of grocery operations, perishable operations, deli-bakery operations, and store planning. These department heads have the authority to make certain decisions necessary to fulfill their roles, and they are accountable to the senior vice-president for the performance of their respective divisions. In turn, the senior vice-president is accountable to the company CEO.

The simplest and most common chain-of-command system is known as **line organization** because it establishes a clear line of authority flowing from the top down, as Exhibit 7.1 depicts. Everyone knows who is accountable to whom, as well as which tasks

chain of command
Pathway for the flow of authority from one management level to the next

responsibility
Obligation to perform the duties and achieve the goals and objectives associated with a particular position

accountability
Obligation to report results to supervisors or team members and to justify outcomes that fall below expectations

authority
Power granted by the organization to make decisions, take actions, and allocate resources to accomplish goals

delegation
Assignment of work and the authority and responsibility required to complete it

line organization
A chain-of-command system that establishes a clear line of authority flowing from the top down

Exhibit 7.2   **Simplified Line-and-Staff Structure**

A line-and-staff organization divides employees into those who are in the direct line of command (from the top level of the hierarchy to the bottom) and those who provide staff (or support) services to line managers at various levels. Staff report directly to top management.

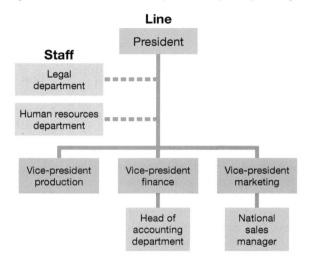

line-and-staff organization
An organization system that has a clear chain of command but also includes functional groups of people who provide advice and specialized services

span of management
The number of people under one manager's control; also known as span of control

flat organizations
Organizations with a wide span of management and few hierarchical levels

and decisions each is responsible for. However, line organization sometimes falls short because the technical complexity of a firm's activities may require specialized knowledge that individual managers don't have and can't easily acquire. A more elaborate system called **line-and-staff organization** was developed out of the need to combine specialization with management control. In such an organization, managers in the chain of command are supplemented by functional groupings of people known as *staff*, who provide advice and specialized services but who are not in the line organization's chain of command (see Exhibit 7.2).

Span of Management

The number of people a manager directly supervises is called the **span of management** or *span of control*. When a large number of people report directly to one person, that person has a wide span of management. This situation is common in **flat organizations**, which are characterized by relatively few levels in the management hierarchy. Sun Microsystems, Visa, and Oticon (a hearing-aid manufacturer in Denmark) are all companies that have flat organizations. British Petroleum (BP) is also amazingly flat and lean for an organization with $266 billion in revenues and 97 000 employees.

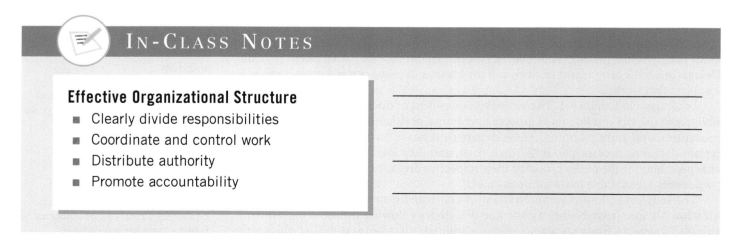

IN-CLASS NOTES

Effective Organizational Structure
- Clearly divide responsibilities
- Coordinate and control work
- Distribute authority
- Promote accountability

Exhibit 7.3   **Tall versus Flat Organizations**

A tall organization, like a national army, has many levels with a narrow span of management at each level so that relatively few people report to each manager on the level above them. In contrast, a flat organization, like the Catholic Church, has relatively few levels with a wide span of management so that more people report to each hierarchical level.

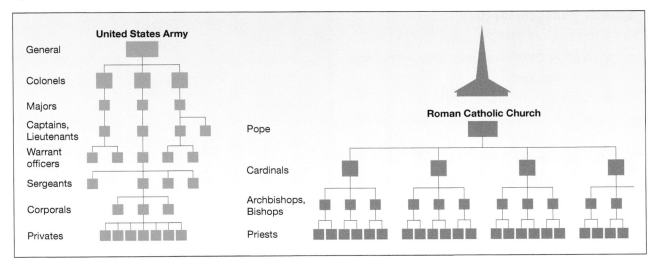

At BP there is no level between the general managers of the business units and the group of nine operating executives who oversee the businesses.[8] The shift toward a larger span of control has been the trend in recent years as downsizing, restructuring, and empowerment have swept through organizations and altered the employment landscape.

In contrast, **tall organizations** have many hierarchical levels, usually with only a few people reporting to each manager. In such cases, the span of management is narrow (see Exhibit 7.3). General Motors traditionally had a tall organization structure with as many as 22 layers of management. Under tall organization structures, employees who want to institute a change must ask a supervisor, who in turn must ask a manager, who in turn must ask another manager at the next level up, and so on. To reduce the time it takes to make decisions, many companies are flattening their organizational structures by removing layers of management and by delegating increased responsibilities and authority to middle managers, work teams, and individual employees.[9]

No formula exists for determining the ideal span of management. How well people work together is more important than the number of people reporting to one person. Still, several factors affect the number of people a manager can effectively supervise, including the manager's personal skill and leadership ability, the skill of the workers, the motivation of the workers, and the nature or complexity of the job. In general, employees who are highly skilled or who are trained in many work tasks don't require as much supervision as employees who are less skilled.

tall organizations
Organizations with a narrow span of management and many hierarchical levels

Centralization versus Decentralization

Organizations that focus decision-making authority near the top of the chain of command are said to be centralized. **Centralization** benefits a company by using top management's rich experience and broad view of organizational goals. Both line organizations and line-and-staff organizations tend to be centralized.

The trend in business today, though, is moving in a different direction. **Decentralization** pushes decision-making authority down to lower organizational levels like department heads while control over essential companywide matters remains with top management. Implemented properly, decentralization can stimulate responsiveness because decisions don't have to be passed up the hierarchy.[10] To accelerate the

centralization
Concentration of decision-making authority at the top of the organization

decentralization
Delegation of decision-making authority to employees in lower-level positions

IN-CLASS NOTES

Span of Management (Control)

- Wide span of control
  - A large number of employees report to one manager
  - Common in "flat organizations" where there are fewer management layers
- Narrow span of control
  - Small number of employees report to each manager
  - Common in "tall organizations" with many bureaucratic layers

_____

_____

_____

_____

_____

_____

_____

_____

_____

development of new drugs, the pharmaceutical giant GlaxoSmithKline recently divided the 15 000 scientists in its research and development lab into six smaller labs, each with independent responsibility to pursue products in a specific area, such as heart disease or cancer.[11] Magna's automotive manufacturing divisions operate as independent profit centres. The decentralized approach discourages bureaucratic mentality and makes the divisions more customer-oriented.[12]

However, decentralization does not work in every situation or in every company. At times, strong authority from the top of the chain of command may be needed to keep the organization focused on immediate goals. Managers should select the level of

Learning from Business Blunders

OOPS

In an attempt to accelerate innovation by decentralizing decision making, telecommunication equipment maker Lucent Technologies (now known as Alcatel-Lucent) split its three operating divisions into 11 largely independent business units. Unfortunately, the move toward decentralization apparently made matters worse. Decision making slowed down, new communication and control issues were created, and another layer of cost and complexity was added to the organizational structure. Experts say the reorganization played a significant role in a decline that saw the company lose money every quarter for more than three years and shed more than

100 000 jobs. (To be fair, at the time just about everybody in the telecommunications business was hit, but Lucent's losses were extraordinarily painful.)

WHAT YOU CAN LEARN

Decentralization works only if the various units of a company can truly work independently. Lucent makes extremely complex systems that require close coordination across many groups within the company to be successful. After the failed experiment in decentralization, the company has become more efficient by becoming even more centralized than it was before.[13]

decision making that will most effectively serve the organization's needs given its circumstances.[14]

Organizing the Workforce

The decisions regarding job responsibilities, span of management, and centralization versus decentralization provide the insights managers need to choose the best organizational structure. The arrangement of activities into logical groups that are then clustered into larger departments and units that form the total organization is known as **departmentalization**.[15] The choice must involve both the *vertical structure*—how many layers the chain of command is divided into from the top of the company to the bottom—and the *horizontal structure*—how the various business functions and work specialties are divided across the company. For instance, looking back at Exhibit 7.1 you can see the grocery store company divides the chain of command into six vertical layers from the board of directors down to the area supervisors, and the operations group is departmentalized into four horizontal subgroups.

departmentalization
Grouping people within an organization according to function, division, matrix, network, or a hybrid that combines features of two or more types

Variations in the vertical and horizontal designs of the organization can produce many structures—some flat, some wide, some simple and clear, others confusing and complex. For instance, a retailer like Wal-Mart is likely to duplicate a single organizational structure across all of its stores, whereas a large high-technology firm might use one structure in its hardware division, a different structure in its software division, and a third structure in its sales and support division, since the nature of these activities differs widely. Two similar companies in the same industry may decide to organize in different ways, based on their unique competitive strengths and weaknesses, company history, and the preferences of the owners or top executives.

Within this endless variety of structure possibilities, most designs fall into one of five types: functional, divisional, matrix, network, or hybrids that combine features of two or more types. Keep in mind that large companies often combine structure choices at different levels in the organization. For example, a company might first divide into divisions, then use a functional structure within each of those divisions.

Functional Structures

The **functional structure** groups employees according to their skills, resource use, and job requirements. Common functional departments include marketing and sales, human resources, operations, finance and accounting, and research and development, with each department working independently from the others.[16] As shown in Exhibit 7.1, functional departmentalization is highly centralized.

functional structure
Grouping workers according to their similar skills, resource use, and expertise

Splitting the organization into separate functional departments offers several advantages: (1) Grouping employees by specialization allows for the efficient use of resources and encourages the development of in-depth skills; (2) centralized decision making enables unified direction by top management; and (3) centralized operations improve communication and the coordination of activities within departments. Despite these advantages, functional departmentalization can create communication barriers between departments, thereby slowing response to change and effective planning for products and markets, and overemphasizing work specialization (which alienates employees).[17] Moreover, employees may become too narrowly focused on departmental goals and lose sight of larger company goals. For instance, the research and development departments in some companies have been criticized for designing new products then "throwing them over the wall" to manufacturing and marketing, leaving those other departments to figure out what to do with the new products. Firms that use functional structures often try to counter these weaknesses by using *cross-functional teams* to coordinate efforts across functional boundaries, as you'll see later in this chapter.

Divisional Structures

The **divisional structure** establishes self-contained departments that encompass all the major functional resources required to achieve their goals, such as research and design, manufacturing, finance, and marketing.[18] These departments are typically formed according to similarities in product, process, customer, or geography. In some

divisional structure
Grouping departments according to similarities in product, process, customer, or geography

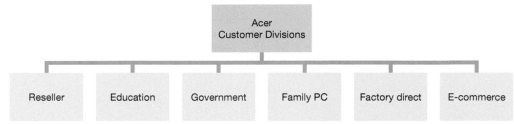

Exhibit 7.4   **Departmentalization by Customer Divisions**

Acer's organizational structure supports the company's mission to be more customer focused.

Source: Adapted from Steven Burke, "Acer Restructures into Six Divisions," *Computer Reseller News*, 13 July 1998, 10.

companies, these divisions operate with great autonomy, almost as multiple small companies within a larger company.

product divisions
A divisional structure based on the various products produced by the firm

- *Product divisions.* Many organizations use a structure based on **product divisions**—grouping departments around each of the company's products or family of products. The logic behind this organizational structure is that each department can manage all the activities needed to develop, manufacture, and sell a particular product or product line. For example, Rogers is divided into three entities: Rogers Wireless, Rogers Cable, and Rogers Media. Rogers Media is further divided to reflect the various aspects of the business: publishing, television, radio, and its shopping channel.[19]

process divisions
A divisional structure based on the major steps of a production process

- *Process divisions.* **Process divisions**, also called *process-complete* departments, are based on the major steps of a production process. For example, a table-manufacturing company might have three divisions, one for each phase of manufacturing a table. A pharmaceutical company that markets anti-ulcer and anti-hypertension drugs can be organized around process divisions, including drug development and distribution.

customer divisions
A divisional structure that focuses on types of clients

- *Customer divisions.* The third approach, **customer divisions**, concentrates activities on satisfying specific groups of customers. For example, Acer, a manufacturer of computer equipment, restructured into six customer-centric divisions to facilitate the fulfillment of the company's mission—to provide customers with the highest level of quality, reliability, and support (see Exhibit 7.4).[20]

geographic divisions
A divisional structure based on location of operations

- *Geographic divisions.* **Geographic divisions** enable companies spread over a national or an international area to respond more easily to local customs, styles, and product preferences. For example, Nova Scotia–based Sobeys operates 1300 locations, with stores in all 10 provinces, and employs more than 75 000 people. Its stores operate under various retail names: Sobeys, IGA, IGA Extra, and Price Chopper. The company structure is divided into four geographic divisions: Atlantic, Quebec, Ontario, and West.[21]

Divisional structures offer both advantages and disadvantages. First, because divisions are self-contained, they can react quickly to change, making the organization more flexible. In addition, because each division focuses on a limited number of products, processes, customers, or locations, divisions can offer better service to customers. Top managers can focus on problem areas more easily, and managers can gain valuable experience by dealing with the various functions in their divisions. However, divisional departmentalization can also increase costs by duplicating the use of resources such as facilities and personnel. Furthermore, poor coordination between divisions may cause them to focus too narrowly on divisional goals and neglect the organization's overall goals. Finally, divisions may compete with one another for resources and customers, causing rivalries that hurt the organization as a whole.[22]

matrix structure
A structure in which employees are assigned to both a functional group and a project team (thus using functional and divisional patterns simultaneously)

Matrix Structures

A **matrix structure** is an organizational design in which employees from functional departments form teams to combine their specialized skills (see Exhibit 7.5). This structure allows the company to pool and share resources across divisions and functional

| Exhibit 7.5 | **Departmentalization by Matrix** |

In a matrix structure, each employee is assigned to both a functional group (with a defined set of basic functions) and a project team (which consists of members of various functional groups working together on a project, such as launching new consumer product).

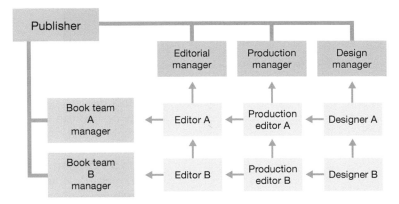

groups. The matrix may be a permanent feature of the organization's design, or it may be established to complete a specific project. For instance, the tool and appliance manufacturer Black & Decker shifted to a matrix organization in the early 1990s. Departments such as mechanical design, electrical engineering, and model shop assigned employees with specific technical skills to work on product-development projects in such categories as saws, cordless appliances, and woodworking.[23]

The matrix structure can help big companies function like smaller ones by allowing teams to devote their attention to specific projects or customers without permanently reorganizing the company's structure. But matrix structures are not without drawbacks. One problem of a matrix structure is that team members usually continue to report to their functional department heads as well as to a project team leader. Another drawback is that authority tends to be more ambiguous and up for grabs, creating power struggles and other interpersonal conflicts. Black & Decker realized this problem soon after implementing its matrix organization. The manager with the most authority was always the functional department head, and the project team did not really hold any control. The company has since redesigned its organizational structure, which is now based on product divisions that employ teams of people from many functional areas.[24]

In a matrix organization, excellent communication and coordination are necessary to avoid conflicts. In addition, companies may find it difficult to coordinate the tasks of diverse functional specialists so that projects are completed efficiently.[25] However, because it facilitates the pooling of resources across departments, a matrix organization can also enable a company to respond better to changes in the business environment.

Network Structures

A **network structure** stretches beyond the boundaries of the company to connect a variety of partners and suppliers that perform selected tasks for a headquarter organization. Also called a *virtual organization*, the network organization can *outsource* engineering, marketing, research, accounting, production, distribution, or other functions. That is, the organization hires other organizations under contracts to handle one or more of those functions. In fact, companies such as Nike, Liz Claiborne, and Dell sell hundreds of millions of dollars worth of products even though they outsource most of their manufacturing. As these companies have learned, the network approach is especially appropriate for international operations, allowing every part of the business to draw on resources no matter where in the world they may be.[26]

The biggest advantage of the network structure is its flexibility. Companies hire whatever services are needed and then change them once they are no longer needed. The limited hierarchy required to manage a network organization also permits the company to make decisions and react to change quickly. Additional advantages are that the organization can continually redefine itself, and a lean structure usually means employees have

network structure
A structure in which individual companies are connected electronically to perform selected tasks for a headquarter organization

greater job variety and satisfaction. However, the network approach lacks hands-on control because the functions are not in one location or company. Also, if one company in the network fails to deliver, the headquarter organization could suffer or even go out of business. Finally, strong employee loyalty and team spirit are less likely to develop because the emotional connection between the employee and the organization is weak.[27]

Hybrid Structures

hybrid structure
A structure design that combines elements of functional, divisional, matrix, and network organizational structures

Some companies find it most effective to adopt a **hybrid structure**, which combines various elements from the four standard types of organizational structures. For example, employees from various departments or functions can be grouped around a few companywide, cross-functional core processes, and they are responsible for an entire core process from beginning to end. Employees who create new product designs, for instance, work with engineers and marketing personnel to make sure the designs can be manufactured and marketed successfully. A typical core process group might include staff from finance, research and development, manufacturing, and customer service. All core processes lead to one objective: creating and delivering something of value to the customer.

Xerox uses a hybrid structure by organizing its operations around five core processes based on five types of products. The core processes are supported by two companywide operations: technology management and customer service. This way, researchers are not constrained by specific markets, and customers have to deal with only one customer service representative, even if they buy different product types.[28]

By now you can see that whether it uses a traditional tall structure or an innovative horizontal or hybrid structure, every organization must coordinate activities and communication among its employees. Without such coordination, functional departments would be isolated from one another, and they would be unable to align their objectives.[29] Another important facet of organizational effectiveness is the use of teams, because no matter what the structure, teamwork is crucial to every organization's success.

IN-CLASS NOTES

Organizing the Workforce
- *Functional structure*: Grouping employees based on their skills, resource use, and expertise (marketing, accounting, etc.)
- *Divisional structure*: Self-contained departments that possess all the functions needed to achieve their goals (product, process, customer, geography)
- *Matrix structure*: Employees are assigned to both a functional group and a project team
- *Network structure*: Individual companies are connected electronically to perform selected tasks for a headquarter organization
- *Hybrid structure*: Combining parts of the other four approaches

WORKING IN TEAMS

While the vertical chain of command is a tried-and-true method of organizing for business, it is limited by the fact that decision-making authority is often located high up the management hierarchy. Companies that organize vertically may become slow to react to change, and high-level managers may overlook many great ideas for improvement that originate in the lower levels of the organization. As this section will show, the value of involving employees from all levels and functions of the organization in the decision-making process cannot be overstated. As a result, most companies now use a variety of team formats in day-to-day operations.

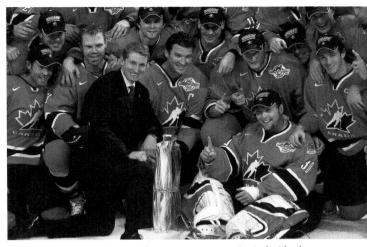

Great sports teams, like great business teams, require individuals to take their roles seriously and move forward as a unit to achieve their ultimate goals.

Even though the team approach has many advantages, shifting to a team structure often requires a fundamental shift in the organization's culture. Management must show strong support for team concepts by empowering teams to make important decisions about the work they do. Teams must also have clear goals that are tied to the company's strategic goals, and their outcomes need to be measured and compared with benchmarks. Moreover, employees must be motivated to work together in teams. Such motivation requires extensive training and a compensation system that is based, at least in part, on team performance. This last objective is sometimes accomplished by using stock options, profit sharing, performance bonuses, and other employee incentives.

What Is a Team?

A **team** is a unit of two or more people working together to achieve a goal. Teams differ from workgroups in that workgroups interact primarily to share information and to make decisions to help one another perform within each member's area of responsibility. In other words, the performance of a workgroup is merely the summation of all group members' individual contributions.[30] By contrast, the members of a team have a shared mission and are collectively accountable for their work. By coordinating their efforts, team members generate a positive synergy and achieve a level of performance that exceeds what would have been accomplished if members had worked individually.[31]

team
A unit of two or more people who share a mission and collective responsibility as they work together to achieve a goal

The concept of the business work team has gained popularity in recent years. However, many companies still pay lip service to the idea of teamwork but fail to properly implement a team environment. A recent survey released by Ipsos Reid and Microsoft Canada revealed that 86 percent of Canadian executives believe that teamwork is a critical element of business success. However, only 31 percent believed that their firms were meeting the standards of "effective teamwork." According to David Saffran, senior vice-president of Ipsos Reid, "Business expectations have evolved faster than organizations have been able to keep pace. There appears to be a big gap between what a CEO expects and what an information worker is able to fulfill based on the tool set their employer provides." Not surprisingly, the findings pointed to the need for companies to use solutions like Microsoft-based Office Systems to improve communications and help companies in their quest.[32]

As for Microsoft, the company practises what it preaches. At corporate headquarters and beyond, almost all work is completed by teams. Two factors that have made Microsoft teams so successful are clear goals and strong leadership. This atmosphere has created a positive reputation for the firm that draws many new recruits to apply and to rate Microsoft at the top of their job wish list.[33]

Although the team's goals may be set by either the team or upper management, it is the job of the team leader to make sure the team stays on track to achieve those goals.

Team leaders are often appointed by senior managers, but sometimes they emerge naturally as the team develops. To foster teamwork and to train employees to understand the techniques and the value of teamwork, many managers and executives are turning to experiential exercises like the ones offered by Outward Bound Canada (see the box entitled "Team-Building Activities").

Team-Building Activities

Creating an effective work team is not an easy task. For the most part, we were all taught at a young age that individuals excel. From elementary school we learned that good boys and girls earn stars for their performance. As adults we often find the same reward systems in place. Based on these simple individualistic socialization factors it should not be surprising that companies often struggle to transform workgroups into highly functioning work teams. To improve the transition process, many firms are using experiential group activities. These activities are designed to force groups to work together effectively and transform into teams. Companies can spend between $5000 and $15 000 for a session. Some major firms are spending as much as $50 000 per session to have employees learn valuable teamwork skills through diverse activities like mountain climbing, cooking, rowing, and improv theatre. Here are just a few companies that offer team-building exercises for employees:

- Outward Bound Canada is an organization that offers a wide variety of outdoor experiences such as canoeing and mountaineering. They organize activities across the country, including expeditions to the Yukon, the Rockies, and the east coast. Outward Bound's client list includes companies like Sobeys, HSBC Bank Canada, and Purolator Courier. www.outwardbound.ca

- At Niagara-based Good Earth Cooking, teamwork essentials are taught in the kitchen. The chefs assign groups the task of cooking a four- or five-course meal that forces team members to work together. The setting is less threatening than an obstacle course and yet the same group dynamics need to be employed to achieve success. www.goodearthcooking.com

- Fort Angrignon in Montreal offers obstacle courses and brain-teasing activities that pit groups of individuals against each other in team competitions. The groups are awarded points for each activity. The competition concludes with a ceremony identifying the most effective teams and leads naturally to a discussion on effective strategies for success. www.fortangrignon.com

Outward Bound Canada offers a wide variety of activities and experiences that many high-profile companies use for leadership training and team building.

- Alberta-based Mountain Quest offers a hands-on program that costs companies about $150 per person and forces individuals to work together to accomplish tasks like conquering the "Electric Fence." www.mountainquest.ca

Regardless of the approach, these activities share certain common results: They force employees to break down imaginary walls and move away from the routine. They help nurture bonds among employees and open lines of communication in a team setting. Each of these programs offers a different approach, but the goals are essentially the same.[34]

Questions for Critical Thinking

1. What are the advantages and disadvantages of holding team-building activity days?
2. If you were in charge of organizing a corporate group activity, which option would you choose? Explain your answer.

IN-CLASS NOTES

Teams versus Groups
- A group ≠ a team
- What sets a team apart is that members
    - have a shared goal or task
    - are mutually accountable
    - have a high level of interdependence
    - have a commitment to mutual growth

Types of Teams

L.O. 4

The type, structure, and composition of individual teams within an organization all depend on the organization's strategic goals and the objective for forming the team. The five most common forms of teams are *problem-solving teams, self-managed teams, functional teams, cross-functional teams*, and *virtual teams*. Such classifications are not exclusive. For example, a problem-solving team may also be self-managed and cross-functional. Similarly, some teams are established on an informal basis. That is, they are designed to encourage employee participation but do not become part of the formal organizational structure.

Problem-Solving Teams

The most common type of informal team is the **problem-solving team**. Also referred to as *quality circles*, problem-solving teams usually consist of 5 to 12 employees from the same department who meet voluntarily to find ways of improving quality, efficiency, and the work environment. Any recommendations they come up with are then submitted to management for approval.[35] Land Rover, a manufacturer of luxury sport-utility vehicles, was able to save millions of dollars, improve productivity, and sell more vehicles by using problem-solving teams.[36] If such teams are able to successfully contribute to the organization, they may evolve into formal teams, a change that represents a fundamental shift in the way the organization is structured.

problem-solving team
An informal team of 5 to 12 employees from the same department who meet voluntarily to find ways of improving quality, efficiency, and the work environment

Self-Managed Teams

Self-managed teams take problem-solving teams to the next level. As the name implies, **self-managed teams** manage their own activities and require minimum supervision. Typically, they control the pace of work and determination of work assignments. Fully self-managed teams select their own members. As you might imagine, many managers are reluctant to embrace self-managed teams because it requires them to give up significant control.

self-managed teams
Teams in which members are responsible for an entire process or operation

SEI Investments administers more than $344.9 billion in mutual funds and pooled assets, and manages more than $168.9 billion in assets. SEI operates 20 offices in 12 countries including Canada, and its defining unit of operation is the self-managed team. Finding itself indistinguishable from the competition, SEI took a wrecking ball to the traditional corporate pyramid. It formed 140 self-managed teams at its head office to speed up reaction time, innovate more quickly, and get closer to the customer. Some SEI teams are permanent, designed to serve big customers or important markets; others are temporary—they come together to solve a problem and disband when their work is done. This flexible team structure is supported by having all office furniture on wheels so that teams can easily create their own work areas. In fact, employees move their desks so often that SEI has created software to map every employee's location.[37]

Functional Teams

functional teams
Teams whose members come from a single functional department and that are based on the organization's vertical structure

Functional teams, or *command teams,* are organized along the lines of the organization's vertical structure and thus may be referred to as *vertical teams.* They are composed of managers and employees within a single functional department. For example, look again at Exhibit 7.1. Functional teams could be formed in the grocery chain's marketing, human resources, and finance departments. The structure of a vertical team typically follows the formal chain of command. In some cases, the team may include several levels of the organizational hierarchy within the same functional department.[38]

Cross-Functional Teams

cross-functional teams
Teams that draw together employees from different functional areas

In contrast to functional teams, **cross-functional teams**, or *horizontal teams,* draw together employees from various functional areas and expertise. In many cross-functional teams, employees are cross-trained to perform a variety of tasks. Cross-functional teams have many benefits: (1) They facilitate the exchange of information between employees; (2) they generate ideas for how to best coordinate the organizational units that are represented; (3) they encourage new solutions for organizational problems; and (4) they aid in the development of new organizational policies and procedures.[39]

To develop its 777 airplane, Boeing used hundreds of "design-build" teams that integrated design engineers and production workers.[40] Cross-functional teams have also become a way of life at Harley-Davidson. At the heart of Harley's organizational structure are three cross-functional teams or circles—the Create Demand Circle, the Produce Product Circle, and the Provide Support Circle. Each circle includes design engineers, purchasing professionals, manufacturing personnel, marketing personnel, and others. The cross-functional circles are responsible for every motorcycle produced by Harley—from product conception to final design. Within each circle, the leadership role moves from person to person, depending on the issue being addressed.[41]

Besides permanent circles such as the ones used at Harley-Davidson, cross-functional teams can take on a number of formats:

task force
A team of people from several departments who are temporarily brought together to address a specific issue

- *Task forces.* A **task force** is a type of cross-functional team formed to work on a specific activity with a completion point. Several departments are usually involved so that all parties who have a stake in the outcome of the task are able to provide input. However, once the goal has been accomplished, the task force is disbanded.[42] Organizations may establish a task force to find ways to reduce the cost of supplies, reduce operational inefficiencies, or solve a systematic problem. For example, the largest blackout in North American history knocked out service in Ontario as well as eight US states and affected 50 million households. Months later, a joint Canadian–US task force, formed by Natural Resources Canada and the US Secretary of Energy, rendered its analysis of the problem. They looked at the sequence of events, the responses, and the system failures and concluded by recommending necessary preventive actions to their respective government agencies.[43]

special-purpose teams
Temporary teams that exist outside the formal organizational hierarchy and are created to achieve a specific goal

- *Special-purpose teams.* Like task forces, **special-purpose teams** are created as temporary entities to achieve specific goals. However, special-purpose teams are different because they exist outside the formal organizational hierarchy. Such teams remain a part of the organization but have their own reporting structures, and members view themselves as separate from the normal functions of the organization. A special-purpose team might be used to develop a new product when complete creative freedom is needed. By operating outside the formal organizational structure, the team would be able to test new ideas and new ways of accomplishing tasks.[44]

committee
A team that may become a permanent part of the organization and is designed to deal with regularly recurring tasks

- *Committees.* In contrast to a task force, a **committee** usually has a long lifespan and may become a permanent part of the organizational structure. Committees typically deal with regularly recurring tasks. For example, a grievance committee may be formed as a permanent resource for handling employee complaints and concerns. Because many committees require official representation to achieve their goals, committee members are usually selected on the basis of their titles or positions rather than their personal expertise.

Virtual Teams

Virtual teams are groups of physically dispersed members who work together to achieve a common goal. Virtual team members communicate using a variety of technological formats and devices such as company intranets, email, electronic meeting software, and telephones. Occasionally, they may meet face to face. The biggest advantage of virtual teams is that members are able to work together even if they are thousands of miles and several time zones apart. At Texas Instruments, for instance, microchip engineers in India, Texas, and Japan are able to pool ideas, design new chips, and collaboratively debug them—even though they're separated by more than 12 000 kilometres and 12 time zones.[45]

The three primary factors that differentiate virtual teams from face-to-face teams are the absence of nonverbal cues, a limited social context, and the ability to overcome time and space constraints. Since virtual teams must function with less direct interaction, team members require certain competencies: project-management skills, time management skills, the ability to use electronic communication and collaboration technologies, the ability to work across cultures, as well as a heightened interpersonal awareness.[46] (See the box entitled "Don't Leave Home to Go to Work: American Express Company's Virtual Environment.")

In many cases, virtual teams are as effective as teams that function under a single roof. At the Bank of Montreal a manager was able to retain her position even though she left Toronto to join her husband, who was retiring in Dorset, England. Since the bank wanted to keep a key employee it arranged for her to manage the group using

virtual team
A team that uses communication technology to bring geographically distant employees together to achieve goals

---

Don't Leave Home to Go to Work: American Express Company's Virtual Environment

"Don't leave home without it!" sends a powerful message about the dangers of travelling without an American Express card tucked into your pocket. Millions of customers listen to that advice each day, making American Express (Amex) the world's largest travel agency and a leading provider of financial services. But providing a seamless network of services for customers around the globe requires effective teamwork from all employees, whether they're working from the New York headquarters or from locations in Edmonton, Halifax, or Ottawa or telecommuting from home in Los Angeles. Employees have everything they need to work together and contribute to the company's success—even if they don't leave home to go to work.

The president of American Express Global Establishment Services (GES), the division that recruits new American Express merchants, encourages his staff members to work together to achieve their goals. But uniting employees in sales offices across long distances demands more than a few rousing pep talks. To build a successful team, Amex uses technology to promote communication within the division. They provide every employee with access to the company's highly efficient computer network. Amex offers employees the opportunity to work from home, eliminating the time, expense, and stress of daily commutes to the

office. They even provide employees with computer training, software and hardware setup, and selection and delivery of office furniture to complete their virtual office environment.

Nevertheless, American Express has learned that effective teams need more than equipment to produce quality work. They need to communicate. Telecommuters conduct virtual meetings with colleagues around the world, taking advantage of email and videoconferencing to brainstorm and collaborate on projects. Several units in the division use a buddy system that requires remote workers to chat with on-site colleagues by phone every morning, covering topics from new customers to office politics. Other telecommuters report to a local or regional office several times each week, meeting with co-workers for specific purposes.

Not only do virtual teams save the company time and travel costs, but they have increased employee productivity and improved customer satisfaction rates. Moreover, by using virtual teams, the company initially reduced the number of field offices from 85 to 7, resulting in large cost savings.[47]

Questions for Critical Thinking

1. How does American Express support virtual teams?
2. How do American Express telecommuters stay in touch with the company and with each other?

IN-CLASS NOTES

Common Types of Teams

- *Problem-solving teams*: Five to twelve employees who find ways to improve quality, efficiency, and the work environment
- *Self-managed teams*: Members are responsible for the entire process or operation
- *Functional teams*: Members come from a single department
- *Cross-functional teams*: Draw together employees from various departments
- *Virtual teams*: Draw together geographically distant employees using communication technology

_____

_____

_____

_____

_____

_____

_____

_____

_____

teleconferencing, email, and voice mail. Most of her team was in a glass building in downtown Toronto while she was in an old-fashioned British cottage. Worlds apart, the manager and employees were able to function in this new virtual reality.[48] At British Petroleum, virtual teams link workers in the Gulf of Mexico with those working in the eastern Atlantic and around the globe. By using a virtual team network, the company has decreased the number of helicopter trips to offshore oil platforms, avoided refinery shutdowns because technical experts at other locations were able to handle problems remotely, and experienced a significant reduction in construction rework, among other benefits.[49]

L.O. 5

Advantages and Disadvantages of Working in Teams

Even though teams can play a vital role in helping an organization reach its goals, they are not appropriate for every situation. Managers must weigh both the advantages and the disadvantages of teams when deciding whether to use them.[50]

One of the biggest advantages of teams is that the interaction of the participants leads to higher-quality decisions based on the combined intelligence of the group. Moreover, teams lead to increased acceptance of a solution. Team members who participate in making a decision are more likely to enthusiastically support the decision and encourage others to accept it.[51] Another big advantage is that teams have the potential to uncover large amounts of creativity and energy in workers. Techniques such as **brainstorming** can be used to access the thoughts of various employees in a non-threatening environment. Motivation and performance are often increased as workers share a sense of purpose and mutual accountability. Teams can also fill the individual worker's need to belong to a group. They can reduce boredom, increase feelings of dignity and self-worth, reduce stress and tension between workers. Teams empower employees to bring more knowledge and skill to the tasks they perform and thereby often lead to greater efficiency and cost reduction. Organizational flexibility is another key benefit of using teams in the workplace. Such flexibility means employees are able to exchange jobs,

brainstorming
A preliminary technique often used in group situations to generate and develop ideas in a non-threatening environment

workers can be reallocated as needed, managers can delegate more authority and responsibility to lower-level employees, and the company can meet changing customer needs more effectively.

In short, using teams can add up to more satisfied employees performing higher-quality work that helps the organization achieve its goals. Studies of individual industries show that companies using teamwork to organize, plan, and control activities enjoy greater productivity, increased profits, fewer defects, lower employee turnover, less waste, and even increased market value.[52] Consider the results these companies achieved by using employee teams: Kodak has halved the amount of time it takes to move a new product from the drawing board to store shelves; Texas Instruments increased revenue per employee by more than 50 percent; and Ritz-Carlton Hotels jumped to the top of the J.D. Power and Associates consumer survey of luxury hotels.[53]

Although teamwork has many advantages, it also has a number of potential disadvantages. For one thing, power within the organization sometimes becomes realigned with teams. Successful teams mean that fewer supervisors are needed, and usually fewer middle and front-line managers. Adjusting to changing job roles, or even to the loss of their jobs, is understandably difficult for many people. Another potential disadvantage is the emergence of **free riders**—team members who don't contribute their fair share to the group's activities because they aren't being held individually accountable for their work. The free-ride attitude can lead to the non-fulfillment of certain tasks. Still another drawback to teamwork is the high cost of coordinating group activities. Aligning schedules, arranging meetings, and coordinating individual parts of a project can eat up a lot of time and money. A team may also develop **groupthink**, a situation in which pressure to conform to the norms of the group causes members to withhold contrary or unpopular opinions. Groupthink can hinder effective decision making because some possibilities will be overlooked.[54]

Another variation of groupthink that team leaders should be aware of was examined in a recently published book called *The Innovation Killer* by Cynthia Barton Rabe, a former Intel innovation strategist. In her book, she highlights the problem of **expert-think**, which she describes as "the tendency to make decisions that experts in the field would agree with—groupthink on steroids." After all how could you disagree with the great experts in the field? If you are constantly trying to fit into the accepted norm you are limiting your long-term possibilities. The problem with such patterns is that they crush innovation and stop new ideas from developing. She proposes inserting "zero-gravity" thinkers into teams—people whose role is to ask the naïve questions and help teams, at the very least, explore new horizons.[55]

Most people look at groups from the perspective that two heads are better than one and believe that teamwork works as follows: one plus one equals two. Some would argue that the equation is more closely related to multiplication. In a team full of halfwits the following calculations would apply: halfwit × halfwit = a quarter-wit. This of course represents a cynical look at teams, but at the very least it sarcastically emphasizes the importance of building effective teams rather than just loosely throwing individuals together.[56]

A creative director at the TBWA/Chiat/Day ad agency attempts to stimulate this team of advertising people to think creatively by walking on the conference room table.

free riders
Team members who do not contribute sufficiently to the group's activities because members are not being held individually accountable for their work

groupthink
Pressure to conform to the norms of the group can cause members to withhold contrary or unpopular opinions, which can lead to poor or even dangerous decisions

expert-think
The tendency of groups to censor new ideas and follow the consensus of the experts in the field without even exploring new possibilities, which can destroy innovation

Characteristics of Effective Teams

L.O. 6

Size is one factor that contributes to a team's overall effectiveness. The optimal size for teams is generally thought to be between 5 and 12 members. Teams that contain fewer than five members may be lacking in skill diversity and may be less effective at solving

IN-CLASS NOTES

Advantages and Disadvantages of Teams
- **Advantages**
    - Higher-quality decisions
    - Improved commitment
    - Creativity and motivation
    - Flexibility
- **Disadvantages**
    - Power realignment
    - Free riders
    - Increased costs
    - Groupthink
    - Expert-think

_____

_____

_____

_____

_____

_____

_____

problems. Teams of more than 12 people may be too large for group members to bond properly and may discourage some individuals from sharing their ideas. Larger groups are also prone to disagreements and factionalism because so many opinions must be considered, thus making the team leader's job more difficult. Moreover, studies have shown that turnover and absenteeism are higher in larger teams because members tend to feel that their presence makes less of a difference.

For a team to be successful over time, it must also be structured to accomplish its task and to satisfy its members' needs for social well-being. Effective teams usually fulfill both requirements with a combination of members who assume one of four roles: task specialist, socioemotional role, dual role, or non-participator. People who assume the *task-specialist role* focus on helping the team reach its goals. In contrast, members who take on the *socioemotional role* focus on supporting the team's emotional needs and strengthening the team's social unity. Some team members are able to assume *dual roles*, contributing to the task and still meeting members' emotional needs. These members often make effective team leaders. At the other end of the spectrum are members who are *non-participators*, contributing little to reaching the team's goals or to meeting members' emotional needs. Exhibit 7.6 outlines the behaviour patterns associated with each of these roles.

Other characteristics of effective teams include the following:[57]

- *Clear sense of purpose.* Team members clearly understand the task at hand, what is expected of them, and their role on the team.

- *Open and honest communication.* The team culture encourages discussion and debate. Team members speak openly and honestly without the threat of anger, resentment, or retribution. They listen to and value feedback from others. As a result, all team members participate.

- *Creative thinking.* Effective teams encourage original thinking, considering options beyond the usual.

- *Focus.* Team members get to the core issues of the problem and stay focused on key issues.

- *Decision by consensus.* All decisions are arrived at by consensus. No easy, quick votes are taken.

Exhibit 7.6 **Team Member Roles**

Team members assume one of these four roles. Members who assume a dual role often make effective team leaders.

High	**Task specialist role** Focuses on task accomplishment over human needs Important role, but if adopted by everyone, team's social needs won't be met	**Dual role** Focuses on task and people May be a team leader Important role, but not essential if members adopt task specialist and socioemotional roles
Member task behaviour	**Non-participator role** Contributes little to either task or people needs of team Not an important role—if adopted by too many members, team will disband	**Socioemotional role** Focuses on people needs of team over task Important role, but if adopted by everyone, team's tasks won't be accomplished
Low		

Low   Member social behaviour   High

Of course, learning effective team skills takes time and practice, so many companies now offer employees training in building their team skills. At Saturn, for example, every team member goes through a minimum of 92 hours of training in problem solving and people skills. Saturn teaches team members how to reach a consensus point they call "70 percent comfortable but 100 percent supportive." At that level of consensus, everybody supports the solution.[58] For a brief review of characteristics of effective teams, see Exhibit 7.7.

Exhibit 7.7 **Characteristics of Effective Teams**

Effective teams practise these good habits.

Build a sense of fairness in decision making
- ✓ Encourage debate and disagreement without fear of reprisal
- ✓ Allow members to communicate openly and honestly
- ✓ Consider all proposals
- ✓ Build consensus by allowing team members to examine, compare, and reconcile differences
- ✓ Avoid quick votes
- ✓ Keep everyone informed
- ✓ Present all the facts

Select team members wisely
- ✓ Involve stakeholders
- ✓ Limit size to no more than 12 members
- ✓ Select members with a diversity of views
- ✓ Select creative thinkers

Make working in teams a top management priority
- ✓ Recognize and reward individual and group performance

- ✓ Provide ample training opportunities for employees to develop interpersonal, decision-making, and problem-solving skills
- ✓ Allow enough time for the team to develop and learn how to work together

Manage conflict constructively
- ✓ Share leadership
- ✓ Encourage equal participation
- ✓ Discuss disagreements
- ✓ Focus on the issues, not the people
- ✓ Keep things under control

Stay on track
- ✓ Make sure everyone understands the team's purpose
- ✓ Communicate what is expected of team members
- ✓ Stay focused on the core assignment
- ✓ Develop and adhere to a schedule
- ✓ Develop rules and obey norms

Five Stages of Team Development

Developing an effective team is an ongoing process. Like the members who form them, teams grow and change as time goes by. You may think that each team evolves in its own way. However, research shows that teams typically go through five definitive stages of development: forming, storming, norming, performing, and adjourning.[59]

- *Forming.* The forming stage is a period of orientation and breaking the ice. Members get to know each other, determine what types of behaviours are appropriate within the group, identify what is expected of them, and become acquainted with each other's task orientation.
- *Storming.* In the storming stage, members show more of their personalities and become more assertive in establishing their roles. Conflict and disagreement often arise during the storming stage as members jockey for position or form coalitions to promote their own perceptions of the group's mission.
- *Norming.* During the norming stage these conflicts are resolved and team harmony develops. Members come to understand and accept one another, reach a consensus on who the leader is, and reach an agreement on each member's role.
- *Performing.* In the performing stage, members are really committed to the team's goals. Problems are solved and disagreements are handled with maturity in the interest of task accomplishment.
- *Adjourning.* Finally, if the team has a limited task to perform, it goes through the adjourning stage after the task has been completed. In this stage, issues are wrapped up and the team is dissolved.

As the team moves through the various stages of development two things happen. First, the team develops a certain level of **cohesiveness**, a measure of how committed the members are to the team's goals. The team's cohesiveness is reflected in meeting attendance, team interaction, work quality, and goal achievement. This element is vital if the team is to work together to achieve their common goals.[60] Strong team cohesiveness generally results in high morale. Cohesiveness is influenced by many factors. Two primary factors are competition and evaluation. If a team is in competition with other teams, cohesiveness increases as the team strives to win. Furthermore, if a team's efforts and accomplishments are recognized by the organization, members tend to be more committed to the team's goals. When cohesiveness is coupled with strong management support for team objectives, teams tend to be more productive.

The second thing that happens as teams develop is the emergence of **norms**—informal standards of conduct that members share and that guide their behaviour. Norms define acceptable behaviour, set limits, identify values, clarify what is expected of members, and facilitate team survival. Norms can be established in many ways: early behaviours that set precedents for future actions, significant events in the team's history, behaviours that come to the team through outside influences, and a leader's or member's explicit statements that have an impact on other members.[61]

Team Conflict

By now you can see that being an effective team member requires many skills. However, none is more important than the ability to handle **conflict**—the antagonistic interactions resulting from differences in ideas, opinions, goals, or ways of doing things. Conflict can be both constructive and destructive to a team's effectiveness. Conflict is constructive if it increases the involvement of team members and results in a solution to a problem. Conflict is destructive if it diverts energy from more important issues, destroys the morale of the team or individual team members, or polarizes or divides the team.[62]

Causes of Team Conflict

Team conflicts can arise for a number of reasons. First, teams and individuals may feel they are in competition for scarce or declining resources, such as money, information,

cohesiveness
A measure of how committed the team members are to their team's goals

norms
Informal standards of conduct that guide team behaviour

conflict
Antagonistic interactions resulting from differences in ideas, opinions, goals, or ways of doing things

IN-CLASS NOTES

Stages of Team Development

- *Five stages*: forming, storming, norming, performing, and adjourning
- As the team transforms from a group into a team the following occurs:
  - Teams become more *cohesive*, which is reflected in meeting attendance, team interaction, work quality, and goal achievement
  - Teams develop *norms*, informal standards of conduct that guide member behaviour

_____

_____

_____

_____

_____

_____

_____

and supplies. Second, team members may disagree about who is responsible for a specific task; this type of disagreement is usually the result of poorly defined responsibilities and job boundaries. Third, poor communication can lead to misunderstandings and misperceptions about other team members or other teams. In addition, intentionally withholding information can undermine trust among members. Fourth, basic differences in values, attitudes, and personalities may lead to clashes. Fifth, power struggles may result when one party questions the authority of another or when people or teams with limited authority attempt to increase their power or exert more influence. Finally, conflicts can arise because individuals or teams are pursuing different goals.[63]

A British cardboard manufacturer switched from a hierarchical, functionally oriented organization to a team-based structure with the hope of empowering employees and reducing scrap. However, once they got started the teams realized that the company had many problems to solve. Conflicts resulted when team members couldn't agree on which problems to tackle first.[64] Some team conflicts intensify and transform into issues that can lead to workplace bullying and intimidation. This issue has become more visible in recent years and has led to the creation of websites like Vancouver-based No Bully for Me, www.nobullyforme.ca, which is trying to draw attention to the problem of workplace intimidation.[65]

How to Resolve Team Conflict

Each team member has a unique style of dealing with conflict, but the members' styles are primarily based on how competitive or cooperative team members are when a conflict arises. Depending on the particular situation, the same individual may use one of several styles, which include avoidance, defusion, and confrontation.[66] *Avoidance* may involve ignoring the conflict in the hope that it will disappear on its own, or it may even involve physically separating the conflicting parties. *Defusion* may involve several actions, including downplaying differences and focusing on similarities between team members or teams, compromising on the disputed issue, taking a

The important thing to remember about resolving conflict is that people can usually get what they want if they are willing to work together. In many cases, the resolution process is an exchange of opinions and information that gradually leads to a mutually acceptable solution.

vote, appealing to a neutral party or higher authority, or redesigning the team. *Confrontation* is an attempt to work through the conflict by getting it out in the open, which may be accomplished by organizing a meeting between the conflicting parties.

These three styles of conflict resolution come into play after a conflict has developed, but team members and team leaders can take several steps to prevent conflicts. First, by establishing clear goals that require the efforts of every member the team reduces the chance that members will battle over their objectives or roles. Second, by developing well-defined tasks for each member the team leader ensures that all parties are aware of their responsibilities and the limits of their authority. Finally, by facilitating open communication the team leader can ensure that all members understand their own tasks and objectives as well as those of their teammates. Keep in mind that communication builds respect and tolerance and provides a forum for bringing misunderstandings into the open before they turn into full-blown conflicts. But remember, "it takes two to tango." So look at your own behaviour as well: be self-aware, check your reactions, be supportive, and keep everything in perspective.[67]

L.O. 9

Conducting Productive Team Meetings

Meetings are the primary communication venue for business teams, whether they take place in formal conference rooms or over the Internet in *virtual meetings*. Well-run meetings can help you solve problems, develop ideas, and identify opportunities. Much of your workplace communication will take place in small-group meetings; therefore, your ability to contribute to the company and to be recognized for those contributions will depend on your meeting participation skills. If you're ever in the position of leading a meeting, remember that "the most productive meetings are those where the leader is in tune with the group dynamics and major concerns of the group."[68]

Unfortunately, many meetings are unproductive. In a recent study, senior and middle managers reported that only 56 percent of their meetings were actually productive and that 25 percent of them could have been replaced by a phone call or a memo.[69] The

IN-CLASS NOTES

Dealing with Conflict
- Keys to prevention:
  - Open communication
  - Clear goals
  - Well-defined tasks
- Common resolution approaches:
  - Confrontation
  - Defusion
  - Avoidance

_____

_____

_____

_____

_____

_____

three most frequently reported problems with meetings are getting off topic, not having an agenda, and running too long.[70] Given such demoralizing statistics and the high cost of meetings—which can run hundreds or thousands of dollars per hour in lost work time and travel expenses—it's no wonder that companies are focusing on making their team meetings more productive. Companies can make better use of valuable meeting time by following these steps:

- *Clarify the purpose of the meeting.* Although many meetings combine purposes, most focus on one of two types. *Informational meetings* involve sharing information and perhaps coordinating action. *Decision-making meetings* involve persuasion, analysis, and problem solving and often include a brainstorming session followed by a debate on the alternatives. Effective decision-making meetings require that each participant be aware of the nature of the problem and the criteria for its solution. Whatever your purpose, make sure it is clear and clearly communicated to all participants.

- *Select participants carefully.* With a clear purpose in mind it's easier to identify the right participants. If the session is purely informational and one person will do most of the talking, you can invite a large group. For problem-solving and decision-making meetings, invite only those people who are in a direct position to help the meeting reach its objective. The more participants, the more comments you're likely to get and the longer the meeting will take. However, make sure you invite all the key decision makers, or your meeting will fail to satisfy its purpose.

- *Establish a clear agenda.* The success of any meeting depends on the preparation of the participants. Distribute a carefully written agenda to participants, giving them enough time to prepare as needed. A productive agenda answers three key questions: (1) What do we need to do in this meeting to accomplish our goals? (2) What issues will be of greatest importance to all participants? (3) What information must be available to discuss these issues?[71] In addition to improving productivity, this level of agenda detail shows respect for participants and the other demands on their time.

- *Keep the meeting on track.* A good meeting draws out the best ideas and information the group has to offer. Good leaders occasionally guide, mediate, probe, stimulate, and summarize, but mostly they encourage participants to share. Experience will help you recognize when to be dominant and press the group forward and when to step back and let people talk. If the meeting lags, you'll need to ask questions to encourage participation. Conversely, there will be times when you have no choice but to cut off a discussion to stay on schedule.

- *Follow agreed-upon rules.* Business meetings run from informal to extremely formal, complete with detailed rules for speaking, proposing new items to discuss, voting on proposals, and so on. The larger the meeting, the more formal it will need to be to maintain order. Whatever system of rules you employ, make sure everyone is clear about the expectations.

- *Encourage participation.* As the meeting gets under way you'll discover that some participants are too quiet and others are too talkative. The quiet participants might be shy, they might be expressing disagreement or resistance, or they might be answering email or instant messages on their laptop computers. Draw them out by asking for their input on issues that pertain to them. For the overly talkative, simply say that time is limited and others need to be heard.

- *Close effectively.* At the conclusion of the meeting, verify that the objectives have been met; if not, arrange for follow-up work as needed. Either summarize the general conclusion of the discussion or list the actions to be taken. Make sure all participants agree on the outcome and give people a chance to clear up any misunderstandings.

Effective teams know how to keep meetings on track while ensuring full participation from everyone involved.

BEHIND THE SCENES

Once in a Lifetime, Twice in a Month: The Rogers Cup

Creating unique and appealing events is quite challenging, especially since each client must be treated as if they are unique despite the fact that Altitude Concepts is busy planning equally important events in various locations simultaneously. For example, the Rogers Cup is one of the most high-profile events that Altitude Concepts works on, and yet this account actually represents two separate events, usually spanning two weeks, in two different cities: Montreal and Toronto. Altitude Concepts is in charge of creating an appealing players and VIP lounge experience at the Rogers Cup and also creating the "Once in a Lifetime" tennis experience for a few lucky fans.

So what happens behind the scenes? How does an idea become reality for an event-planning company like Altitude Concepts? The company holds daily "cardio" meetings either in person, over the phone, or through any medium available, depending on the time of year and the amount of "live" projects. At these meetings, project managers are asked questions like "What is the next 'priority action' and how is it progressing?" This is where the project manager may describe a major upcoming challenge or an expected milestone. This is also where they would reveal any critical delays that require additional resources. If there are serious issues, then there is a "call to action" to support a team in need and ensure that the problems

don't become critical. The project managers are also asked to report on the team's most recent success. This aspect is all about recognizing the small victories that lead to the ultimate success of any project. With so many small moving parts to create a unified project, it is important to recognize the small steps and share the victories. This process leads to important lessons, well-deserved recognition, shared knowledge, and a more motivated work team. In addition to these short "cardio" meetings, the general manager meets with the project manager, the creative director, and the production manager of each project once a week to get a hands-on feel for how the work is progressing. When the workload is at its peak and multiple setups are occurring at the same time the company creates support staff specialists, such as a logistics specialist who helps the process flow and a research specialist who focuses on scheduling and booking issues. These individuals can help to reduce the project manager's load by as much as 20 percent, improving their ability to focus on the big picture.

The project mangers are the information gatekeepers. They ensure proper relations and open communication with the client; they pass the appropriate messages on to the team; they ensure that the team members are motivated and on task; and they communicate with the organizational hierarchy. The project manager is the person on the ground, so it's up to them to ensure client satisfaction by discussing strategies to accommodate VIPs, ensuring promotional material is well exhibited, and consulting and advising the client on the pros and cons of various ideas. A big part of the job is troubleshooting, and the project manager is given plenty of latitude to get the job done. For example, at the Rogers Cup, what seemed to be going as planned took a slight detour when the "hot seats" were being installed. Even though approval had been granted from Tennis Canada and the Association of Tennis Professionals (ATP), there was a last-minute hurdle when TV broadcasters made demands. Since the "guests" were within site lines of the camera, they had to ensure that no brands were visible other than the ones from official sponsors—everything from water bottles to sunglasses were in question. Brand labels were hidden and the platform was lowered by two inches to meet approval. All in a day's work for a quick-acting team.

Clearly you don't need to be a large multinational corporation to deal with the issues of organizational structure

Providing a "Once in a Lifetime" experience is what Altitude Concepts aims to achieve with each event. A couple of lucky tennis fans at the Rogers Cup were treated to these "hot seats" that give a new meaning to front row.

discussed in this chapter. All professionally run organizations must come up with a structure that makes sense for their needs and enables them to efficiently get the job done. Altitude Concepts uses a system that is heavily centred on the team concept. To remain flexible and lean and meet the diverse needs of the client, the company has adopted a hybrid approach that touches on various models examined in the chapter.

Regardless of labels, the organization known as Altitude Concepts has come a long way from the time when it landed its first project. Company growth has brought a system that makes sense for the company, which continues to adjust to find the right formula for their business model. Judging from their client list and their repeat business it appears as though they have found a good mix. As the company continues to evolve they will necessarily need to make more structural adjustments, but any company that can transform a warehouse into an elite business event should be capable of creating the necessary changes and creatively meeting the challenges for continued growth.[72]

Critical Thinking Questions

1. Describe the role of meetings at Altitude Concepts. How do communications flow in this organization and why are the "cardio" meetings essential?
2. A quickly evolving business like Altitude Concepts is not always easy to define. Using terminology from the chapter, describe the structure of this organization.
3. Teams have many advantages and disadvantages. In your opinion, what is the likelihood that a work team at Altitude Concepts may experience (a) free riders and (b) groupthink?

Learn More Online

Effective teamwork and communication have helped Altitude Concepts and many other companies become successful. Go to Chapter 7 of this text's website at www.pearsoned.ca/bovee and click on the Altitude Concepts hotlink to learn more about the company.

TEST YOUR KNOWLEDGE

Questions for Review

1. What is the difference between the formal and informal organization?
2. What are the characteristics of tall organizations and flat organizations?
3. What factors are considered when determining the span of management?
4. What are the advantages and disadvantages of decentralization?
5. What steps can a manager take to help ensure that a meeting is as effective as possible?

Questions for Analysis

6. Why would you expect a manager of a group of nuclear physicists to have a wide span of management?
7. Why is it important as a team leader to understand the five stages of team development?
8. Under what circumstances would a task force be more appropriate than a committee to address an issue?
9. How can companies benefit from using virtual teams?
10. **Ethical Considerations.** You were honoured that you were selected to serve on the salary committee of the employee-negotiations task force. As a member of that committee you reviewed confidential company documents listing the salaries of all department managers. You discovered that managers at your level are earning $5000 more than you, even though you've been at the company the same amount of time. You feel that a raise is justified on the basis of this confidential information. How will you handle this situation?

Questions for Application

11. You are the leader of a cross-functional work team whose goal is to find ways of lowering production costs. Your team of eight employees has become stuck in the storming stage. They disagree on how to approach the task, and they are starting to splinter into factions. What can you do to help the team move forward?
12. Your warehouse operation is currently functioning at capacity. To accommodate anticipated new business your company must either build a major addition to your current warehouse operation or build a new warehouse that would be located at a distant site. As director of warehouse operations, you would like several people to participate in this decision. Should you form a task force, a committee, or a special-purpose team? Explain your choice.
13. **Integrated.** One of your competitors has approached you with an intriguing proposition. The company would like to merge with your company. The economies

of scale are terrific. So are the growth possibilities. There's just one issue to be resolved. Your competitor is organized under a horizontal structure and uses a lot of cross-functional teams. Your company is organized under a traditional vertical structure that is departmentalized by function. Using your knowledge about culture clash, what are the likely issues you will encounter if these two organizations merge?

14. **Integrated.** In Chapter 6 we discussed three styles of leadership: autocratic, democratic, and laissez faire. Using your knowledge about the differences in these leadership styles, which style would you expect to find under the following organizational structures: (a) a vertical organization departmentalized by function; (b) a vertical organization departmentalized by matrix; (c) a horizontal organization; or (d) self-directed teams?

PRACTISE YOUR KNOWLEDGE

SHARPENING YOUR COMMUNICATION SKILLS

Write a brief memo to your instructor describing a recent conflict you had with a peer at work or at school. Be sure to highlight the cause of the conflict and steps you took to resolve it. Which of the three conflict-resolution styles discussed in this chapter did you use? Did you find a solution that both of you could accept?

BUILDING YOUR TEAM SKILLS

What's the most effective organizational structure for your college or university? With your team, obtain a copy of your school's organization chart. If this chart is not readily available, gather information by talking with people in administration and then draw your own chart of the organizational structure.

Analyze the chart in terms of span of management. Is your school a flat or a tall organization? Is this organizational structure appropriate for your school? Does decision making tend to be centralized or decentralized? Do you agree that this approach to decision making is the most effective for your school?

Finally, investigate the use of formal and informal teams in your school. Are there any problem-solving teams, task forces, or committees at work in your school? Are any teams self-directed or virtual? How much authority do these teams have to make decisions? What is the purpose of teamwork in your school? What kinds of goals do these teams have?

Share your team's findings during a brief classroom presentation and then compare the findings of all teams. Is there agreement on the appropriate organizational structure for your school?

EXPAND YOUR KNOWLEDGE

DISCOVERING CAREER OPPORTUNITIES

Whether you're a top manager, middle manager, or first-line manager (supervisor), your efforts will affect the success of your organization. To get a closer look at what the responsibilities of a manager are, log on to the Prentice Hall Student Success Supersite at www.prenhall.com/success. Click on "Majors Exploration" and select "Business" then "Management" in the drop-down menu. Then scroll down and read about careers in management.

1. What can you do with a degree in management?

2. What is the future outlook for careers in management?

DEVELOPING YOUR RESEARCH SKILLS

Although teamwork can benefit many organizations, introducing and managing team structures can be a real challenge.

Search past issues of business journals or newspapers (print or online editions) to locate articles about how an organization has overcome problems with teams.

1. Why did the organization originally introduce teams? What types of teams are being used?

2. What problems did each organization encounter in trying to implement teams? How did the organization deal with these problems?

3. Have the teams been successful from management's perspective? From the employees' perspective? What effect has teamwork had on the company, its customers, and its products?

STUDY GUIDE

SUMMARY OF LEARNING OBJECTIVES

1. Discuss the function of a company's organizational structure

An organizational structure provides a framework through which a company can coordinate and control the work, divide responsibilities, distribute authority, and hold employees accountable. An organization chart provides a visual representation of this framework.

2. Explain the concepts of accountability, authority, and delegation

Accountability is the obligation to report work results to supervisors or team members and to justify any outcomes that fall below expectations. Authority is the power to make decisions, issue orders, carry out actions, and allocate resources to achieve the organization's goals. Delegation refers to the assignment of work and the transfer of authority and responsibility to complete that work.

3. Define five major types of organizational structure

Companies can organize in four primary ways: by function, which groups employees according to their skills, resource use, and expertise; by division, which establishes self-contained departments formed according to similarities in product, process, customer, or geography; by matrix, which assigns employees from functional departments to interdisciplinary project teams and requires them to report to both a department head and a team leader; and by network, which connects separate companies that perform selected tasks for a headquarter organization. In addition, many companies now combine elements of two or more of these organizational designs into hybrid structures.

4. Describe the five most common forms of teams

The five most common forms of teams are (1) problem-solving teams, which seek ways to improve a situation and then submit their recommendation to management; (2) self-managed teams, which manage their own activities and seldom require supervision; (3) functional teams, which are composed of employees within a single functional department; (4) cross-functional teams, which draw together employees from various departments and expertise and which can be set up in a number of formats, such as task forces, special-purpose teams, or committees;

and (5) virtual teams, which bring together employees from distant locations.

5. Highlight the advantages and disadvantages of working in teams

Teamwork has the potential to increase creativity, motivation, performance, and satisfaction of workers and thereby can lead to greater company efficiency, flexibility, and cost savings. The potential disadvantages of working in teams include the difficulties of managing employees' changing roles; the possibilities of free riders, groupthink, and expert-think; and the costs and time needed to coordinate members' schedules and project parts.

6. List the characteristics of effective teams

Effective teams have a clear sense of purpose, communicate openly and honestly, build a sense of fairness in decision making, think creatively, stay focused on key issues, manage conflict constructively, and select team members wisely by involving stakeholders, creative thinkers, and members with diverse views. Effective teams have an optimal size of between 5 and 12 members.

7. Review the five stages of team development

Teams typically go through five stages of development. In the *forming* stage, team members become acquainted with each other and with the group's purpose. In the *storming* stage, conflict often arises as coalitions and power struggles develop. In the *norming* stage, conflicts are resolved and harmony develops. In the *performing* stage, members focus on achieving the team's goals. In the *adjourning* stage, the team dissolves upon completion of its task.

8. Highlight six causes of team conflict and three styles of conflict resolution

Conflict can arise from competition for scarce resources; confusion over task responsibility; poor communication and misinformation; differences in values, attitudes, and personalities; power struggles; and goal incongruity. Conflict can be resolved by *avoiding* it and hoping that it will go away, by *defusing* it through downplaying team member differences or focusing on member similarities, or by *confronting* it and working hard to resolve the issues at hand.

9. **Identify key factors that lead to effective team meetings**

A meeting can lead to a productive session or a waste of valuable time. The tone of the meeting is set by the team leader. Here are some important tips to remember:

(1) Clarify the purpose of the meeting; (2) Select participants carefully; (3) Establish a clear agenda; (4) Keep the meeting on track; (5) Follow agreed-upon rules; (6) Encourage participation; (7) Close effectively.

KEY TERMS

accountability   (199)
authority   (199)
brainstorming   (212)
centralization   (201)
chain of command   (199)
cohesiveness   (216)
committee   (210)
conflict   (216)
cross-functional teams   (210)
customer divisions   (204)
decentralization   (201)
delegation   (199)
departmentalization   (203)
divisional structure   (203)
expert-think   (213)

flat organizations   (200)
formal organization   (197)
free riders   (213)
functional structure   (203)
functional teams   (210)
geographic divisions   (204)
groupthink   (213)
hybrid structure   (206)
informal organization   (197)
line organization   (199)
line-and-staff organization   (200)
matrix structure   (204)
network structure   (205)
norms   (216)
organization chart   (197)

organizational structure   (197)
problem-solving team   (209)
process divisions   (204)
product divisions   (204)
responsibility   (199)
self-managed teams   (209)
span of management   (200)
special-purpose teams   (210)
tall organizations   (201)
task force   (210)
team   (207)
virtual team   (211)
work specialization   (198)

QUESTIONS

Multiple Choice   Circle the correct answer and then check the answers in the back of the book to chart your progress.

1. Which of the following is a good reason to use an organization chart?

    a. It lists the employees in alphabetical order.
    b. It lists the employees in order of seniority.
    c. It represents the lines of authority.
    d. It represents the informal, personal interactions.

2. Which of the following is *not* a factor used to identify the best structure for an organization?

    a. Identify job responsibilities
    b. Define the chain of command
    c. Organize the workforce for effectiveness and efficiency
    d. Adopt a preconceived model from another organization

3. Which of the following is a major advantage of work specialization?

    a. Specialization can lead to greatly increased efficiency.
    b. Specialization can make work boring and repetitive.
    c. Specialized workers may not understand the purpose of their work.
    d. Specialized workers may have no room for advancement.

4. What is a disadvantage of the line organization?

    a. Employees know who is accountable to whom.
    b. Employees know who is responsible for which tasks.
    c. Employees may not have the specialized knowledge or skills that are needed.
    d. Line organizations are easy to understand.

5. Which of the following is an advantage of a flat organization?

    a. Only a few people report to each manager.
    b. A flat organization requires a large span of management.
    c. Decisions can be made and implemented quickly in a flat organization.
    d. Top managers can be sure that lower employees are following policies.

6. Which of the following is an advantage of decentralization?

    a. Decisions do not have to be authorized at each level of the hierarchy.
    b. The most experienced managers make important decisions.
    c. Top managers can see how decisions will affect all parts of the company.
    d. Top managers want workers to follow orders, not make decisions.

7. Which team member role is described by the following statement: They focus on the "people needs" of the team over the task of the project.

    a. Dual role
    b. Socioemotional role
    c. Task specialist role
    d. People-person role

8. Which of the following is *not* a requirement of successful work teams?

    a. Top management must empower teams to make decisions about their work.
    b. Teams must have clear goals that are tied to the company's goals.
    c. Employees must be motivated to work together in teams.
    d. The company must have centralized management and a tall organization.

9. Which of the following is a possible disadvantage of working in teams?

    a. Teams can make high-quality decisions with the participation of all the members.
    b. Team members are more likely to support the decisions.
    c. Some team members may be free riders.
    d. Individuals benefit from feeling like they're part of a group.

10. Which of the following is *not* one of the five stages of team development?

    a. Adjourning
    b. Building
    c. Storming
    d. Performing

True/False

1. True or false? Firms that use functional structures often try to counter problems by using cross-functional teams.

2. True or false? There is no difference between a group and a team.

3. True or false? Many mid-size companies are structured by function so that specialists in each business field can work with other experts in their field.

4. True or false? A team composed exclusively of individuals with a socioemotional approach will likely fail to reach its goal.

5. True or false? Effective teams require a minimum of 12 members.

Fill-in-the-Blank

1. _____ refers to an employee's obligation to report results to supervisors or team members and justify outcomes that fall below expectations.

2. _____ is the obligation to perform specified duties.

3. When Todd was hired, he was assigned to both a functional group and a project team simultaneously. The company that Todd works for appears to be set up in a departmentalization by _____ format.

4. The _____ refers to the network of interactions that develop on a personal level among workers.

5. The _____ refers to the lines of authority that connect the various groups and levels within the organization.

6. A _____ organization has a wide span of management and few hierarchical levels.

7. Organizations that focus decision-making authority near the top of the chain of command are said to be _____.

8. A _____ is a team of people from several departments who are temporarily brought together to address a specific issue.

9. _____ is a preliminary technique often used in group situations to generate and develop ideas in a non-threatening environment.

10. A team may develop _____, a situation in which pressure to conform to the norms of the group causes members to withhold contrary or unpopular opinions.

Companion Website

See It on the **WEB**

Visit the Companion Website at **www.pearsoned.ca/bovee**, review the exercises, and complete the following assignments for Chapter 7:
1. Build Teams in the Cyber Age
2. Be Direct
3. Resolve Conflict like a Pro

CHAPTER 8

PRODUCING QUALITY GOODS AND SERVICES

LEARNING OBJECTIVES
After studying this chapter, you will be able to

1 Explain what production and operations managers do

2 Highlight the unique challenges of providing efficient and effective service-delivery systems

3 Explain the role of the supply chain and identify key tasks in designing a production process

4 Discuss the role of computers and automation technology in production

5 Explain the strategic importance of coordinating the supply chain and managing inventory

6 Distinguish among JIT, MRP, and MRP II inventory management systems

7 Highlight the differences between quality control and quality assurance

BEHIND THE SCENES

www.magna.com

Here's a quick quiz for you. What do all of the following cars have in common: Chrysler 300 and 300C, BMW X3, Mini Cooper, Mercedes A, B, C, and E class vehicles, Dodge Magnum, Pontiac Pursuit, Volkswagen Golf, and Saab 9-3? Answer: They are connected in some commercial way with Magna International, the world's most diversified automotive supplier. These associations range from simple component assembly to developing and manufacturing complete modules to engineering and assembling complete vehicles for sale to original equipment manufacturers (OEMs).

Magna International started off as a one-man tool-and-die shop in 1957 with sales of $13 000. Today, Frank Stronach's company employs more than 83 000 people in 23 countries, with 235 production divisions and 62 engineering and research and development divisions. Annual sales have increased from $13 000 to $24.2 billion.

As you read through this chapter you will learn more about outsourcing, which is loosely defined as removing an internal task and paying another company to provide the service. For Magna, outsourcing is not a dirty word—it is the lifeline of the company. Magna's strength lies in finding opportunities in an ever-changing automotive sector and getting contracts to complete work for OEMs. The company has benefited in recent years since companies are farming out more assembly, design, and engineering functions. By the end of 2006, Magna's average content per vehicle had risen to $775, up from $172 a decade earlier.

Assembling, Designing, and Engineering

Magna supplies the complete cockpit and door modules, door panels, sun visors, fuel filler systems, exterior trim, and more for the Mini Cooper. Magna actually produces entire vehicles that have been outsourced from major brands like Mercedes, Jeep, and Volkswagen. Magna Steyr, a subsidiary of Magna International, performs complete vehicle assembly of the BMW X3 while also serving as a supplier for various parts. BMW also outsourced the engineering of the X3, and with the help

Magna Corporation is involved in practically all aspects of the volatile automotive business. The company is successful because it effectively deals with the dynamic market expectations and has built strong links with the major players in the industry by continually supplying their assembly, design, or engineering needs.

of some 500 engineers, Magna Steyr was able to bring the project from concept to production in a record-breaking 28 months. This process is actually better than the average figure BMW produces in-house and represents a vast improvement from the standard seven to eight years that was the industry norm for many years. As you can see, the Aurora, Ontario–based company and its subsidiaries are involved in practically all aspects of the automotive business.

In 2007, despite five decades of accomplishments, it was no time to rest on old victories. Magna was feeling pressure on all fronts. To effectively plan for the future—adjust supply chains, forecast demand, plan for capacity, choose new facility locations, consolidate existing operations, design layouts, and schedule work—the company would need to stay in tune with an evolving market. Key trends were identified that were creating new opportunities and threats: (1) Shifts in market share away from the traditional big three Detroit automakers, especially in North America; (2) Growth in low-cost regions such as Russia and China; (3) Continued consolidation among auto-parts suppliers; (4) More niche vehicles being built. In addition, there was word that BMW might be moving the production of the next generation X3 in-house. In this business, contracts expire and competition is fierce; to survive and thrive for another 50 years Magna will need to continue to embrace change.[1]

TEST YOURSELF

Answers to these questions can be found on the website: www.pearson.ca/bovee.

1. Why do companies like GM, BMW, and Mercedes outsource their production to companies like Magna?

2. Describe the challenges of managing the supply chain for a company like Magna International.

3. What are some of the industry tools used to reduce design and engineering development times?

4. What elements need to be considered in developing the production process?

UNDERSTANDING PRODUCTION AND OPERATIONS MANAGEMENT

L.O. 1

As managers at Magna know, the extremely competitive nature of the global business environment requires companies to produce high-quality goods and services in the most efficient way possible. Few defects, fast production, low costs, excellent customer service, broad market reach, innovative products and processes, less waste, and high flexibility are all objectives that improve quality by adding value to the good or service being produced. Companies pursue these objectives to maintain a competitive advantage.[2] Moreover, managers understand that the level of quality a company aspires to in the production of goods and services affects its long-term ability to address the needs of its customers.

Like most aspects of business, production tends to get more complex and technologically advanced with each passing year. To get a sense of what production means today and how it might affect your career, it's important to first clarify what production really is, explain how it fits in the value chain, identify the unique challenges of service production, understand the difference between mass production and customization, and explore the impact that outsourcing is having on businesses and employers all over the world.

What Is Production?

To most people, the term "production" suggests images of factories, machines, and assembly lines staffed with employees making automobiles, computers, furniture, motorcycles, or other tangible goods. That's because in the past people used the terms *production* and *manufacturing* interchangeably. With the growth in the number of service-based businesses and their increasing importance to the economy, however, the term **production** is now used to describe the transformation of resources into goods and services that people need or want. The broader term **production and operations management (POM)**, or simply *operations management*, refers to all of the activities involved in producing a firm's goods and services.

Like other types of management, POM involves the basic functions of planning, organizing, leading, and controlling. It also requires careful consideration of a company's goals, the strategies for attaining those goals, and the standards against which results will be measured. In both manufacturing and service organizations, the production and operations manager is the person responsible for performing these functions. One of the principal responsibilities of the production and operations manager is to

production
The transformation of resources into goods or services that people need or want

production and operations management (POM)
Coordination of an organization's resources in manufacturing goods or delivering services

Exhibit 8.1   **The Conversion Process**

Production of goods or services is basically a process of conversion. Inputs (the basic ingredients) are transformed (by the application of labour, equipment, and capital) into outputs (the desired product or service).

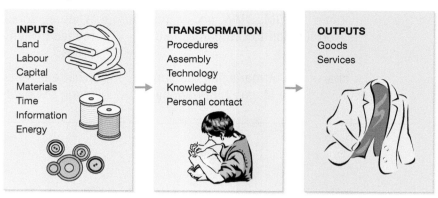

INPUTS
Land
Labour
Capital
Materials
Time
Information
Energy

TRANSFORMATION
Procedures
Assembly
Technology
Knowledge
Personal contact

OUTPUTS
Goods
Services

value chain
All of the functions required to transform inputs into outputs (goods and services) along with the business functions that support the transformation process

analytic system
A production process that breaks incoming materials into various component products and divisional patterns simultaneously

synthetic system
A production process that combines two or more materials or components to create finished products; the reverse of an analytic system

L.O. 2

design and oversee an efficient conversion process—one that lowers costs by optimizing output from each resource used in the process. These resources include money, materials, inventories, people, buildings, and time.

The Value Chain and the Conversion Process

Every business, from neighbourhood coffeehouses to car manufacturers, tries to create value by transforming inputs (such as labour, information, and raw materials) into outputs (goods and services that customers want to purchase). This transformation, often called the *conversion process*, is at the core of a company's **value chain**, which includes all the business functions necessary to support the transformation process— marketing, accounting, human resources, and so on.

This transformation concept applies to tangible goods and intangible services. An airline like WestJet uses such processes as booking flights, flying airplanes, maintaining equipment, and training crew to transform tangible and intangible inputs (such as the plane, pilot's skill, fuel, time, and passengers) into the delivery of customers to their destinations. For a clothing manufacturer to produce a jacket, inputs such as cloth, thread, and buttons are transformed by the seamstress into the finished product (see Exhibit 8.1).

Conversion is of two basic types. An **analytic system** breaks raw materials into one or more distinct products, which may or may not resemble the original material in form and function. In meatpacking, for example, a steer is divided into hide, bone, steaks, and so on. A **synthetic system** combines two or more materials to form a single product. For example, in steel manufacturing, iron is combined with small quantities of other minerals at high temperatures to make steel.

The Unique Challenges of Service Delivery

The conversion processes for services and goods are similar in terms of *what* is accomplished—transforming inputs into outputs—but the two differ in *how* the processes are performed (see Exhibit 8.2). That's because the production of goods results in a tangible output—something you can see or touch, such as a jacket, car, or desk—while the production of a service results in an intangible act. Most of the concepts associated

A manufacturer like Vantage Furniture compiles inputs (wood and fabric) and transformation components (such as tools, specialized machinery, and workers). The transformation process is the actual fabrication and assembly of a sofa; the desired output is a flawless piece of furniture ready for consumer purchase. Vantage Furniture sells their finished products in furniture stores across Canada, including The Brick, Leon's, Tanguay, and Brault & Martineau.

| Exhibit 8.2 | **Input-Transformation-Output Relationships for Typical Systems** |

Both goods and services undergo a conversion process, but the components of the process vary to accommodate the differences between tangible and intangible outputs.

SYSTEM	INPUTS	TRANSFORMATION COMPONENTS	TRANSFORMATION FUNCTION	TYPICAL DESIRED OUTPUT
Hospital	Patients, medical supplies	Physicians, nurses, equipment	Health care	Healthy individuals
Restaurant	Hungry customers, food	Chef, waitress, environment	Well-prepared and well-served food	Satisfied customers
Automobile factory	Sheet steel, engine parts	Tools, equipment, workers	Fabrication and assembly of cars	High-quality cars
College or university	High school graduates, books	Teachers, classrooms	Impart knowledge and skills	Educated individuals
Department store	Shoppers, stock of goods	Displays, salesclerks	Attract shoppers, promote products, fill orders	Sales to satisfied customers

Source: Adapted from Mark M. Davis, Nicholas J. Aquilano, and Richard B. Chase, *Fundamentals of Operations Management* (Boston: Irwin McGraw-Hill, 1999), 7.

with goods manufacturing apply to services as well, although service providers do face some unique issues:[3]

- Customers are usually involved in—and can affect the quality of—the service delivery. Personal trainers can instruct clients in the proper way to work out, but if the clients don't follow directions, the result will be unsatisfactory.

- Unlike goods, which can usually be built ahead of time and stored in inventory until customers buy them, most services are consumed at the same time they are produced. For instance, if a 200-seat airline flight takes off half empty, those 100 sales opportunities are lost forever; they can't be stored in inventory for later sale. This attribute can have a dramatic impact on the way service businesses are managed, from staffing (making sure enough people are on hand to help during peak times) to pricing (using discounts to encourage people to buy services when they are available).

- Services are usually people intensive, whether it's manual skills (carpentry, landscaping) or intellectual or creative skills (advertising, freelance writing). Much of the investment in e-commerce in recent years has been aimed at offering services that don't require as much human activity to compete, like Amazon.com in online retailing.

- Customers often dictate when and where services are delivered. The equipment and food ingredients used in a restaurant can be produced just about anywhere, but the restaurant itself needs to be located close to customers and be open when customers want to eat.

- Service quality can be more subjective than goods quality. If you create a pair of scissors, for instance, both you and the customer can measure and agree on the hardness of the steel, the sharpness of the blades, the smoothness of the action, and so on. If you create a haircut using those scissors, however, you and the customer might disagree on the attractiveness of the style or the quality of the salon experience.

With the majority of workers in Canada now involved in the service sector, managers in thousands of companies need to pay close attention to these factors when designing service-delivery systems.

IN-CLASS NOTES

Unique Challenges of Service Delivery

1. Customers are involved in the process
2. No inventory; services are created and consumed simultaneously
3. Services are usually people intensive
4. Customers often dictate when and where services are delivered
5. Service quality tends to be more subjective

_____

_____

_____

_____

_____

_____

Mass Production, Customized Production, and Mass Customization

mass production
The production of uniform products in large quantities

customized production
The production of individual goods and services for individual customers

mass customization
Producing partially customized goods and services by combining mass production techniques with individual customization

Both goods and services can be created through mass production, mass customization, or fully customized production, depending on the nature of the product and the desires of target customers. In **mass production**, identical goods or services are created, usually in large quantities, such as when RIM churns out 100 000 identical BlackBerrys. Although not normally associated with services, mass production is what Air Canada is doing when it offers hundreds of passengers the opportunity to fly from, say, Calgary to Vancouver every day—every customer flying economy gets the exact same service at the same time.

At the other extreme is **customized production**, sometimes called *batch-of-one production* in manufacturing, in which the producer creates a unique good or service for each customer. If you order a piece of furniture from a local craftsperson, for instance, you can specify everything from the size and shape to the types of wood and fabric used. Or you can hire a charter pilot to fly you wherever you want, whenever you want. Both products are customized to your unique needs.

Mass production has the advantage of economies of scale, but it frequently can't deliver the unique goods and services that today's customers demand. On the other hand, fully customized production can offer uniqueness, but usually at a much higher price. An attractive compromise in many cases is **mass customization**, in which part of the product is mass produced, and then the remaining features are customized for each buyer. For instance, it would cost you a small fortune to have someone build you a unique car from scratch, but you can partially customize any manufacturer's model to your needs and tastes by choosing from the available options for engines, colours, seat coverings, stereos, and so on. The manufacturer can mass produce the basic elements of the car, and then partially customize it based on your selections.

Technology continues to increase the options for mass customization. For instance, Meridian Golf mass customizes golf clubs in 1100 different combinations. Customers are fitted by swinging a club on a special in-store platform where computers measure 14 aspects of their golf swing. Thanks to such mass customization, Meridian Golf boasts a 99.5 percent customer satisfaction rate.[4]

Individual craftspeople often engage in customized production, creating a unique product for each customer.

Outsourcing

Chapter 4 introduced the concept of outsourcing as a source of opportunity for small businesses. As we saw in the opening case, nearly all aspects of a business have the potential to be outsourced, from product design and manufacturing to human resources, marketing, and sales. For instance, some companies choose to focus on design and hand some or all of the manufacturing duties off to companies that specialize in that phase of the value chain. DaimlerChrysler's smart car is a good example of this process (see the box entitled "Smart Car, Interesting Process). Outsourcing all or part of the manufacturing function has several potential advantages. For one thing, it allows companies to redirect the capital and resources spent on manufacturing to new product research and development, marketing, and customer service. For another, many contract manufacturers are industry specialists with state-of-the-art facilities and production efficiencies that would be costly to duplicate on an individual scale. In the electronics industry, a number of contract electronic manufacturers (CEMs) now produce all or parts of many products that bear other companies' names. For instance, Solectron, one of the largest of these CEMs, assembles everything from pagers and printers to computers and television decoding boxes for some of the biggest brand names in electronics, including Hewlett-Packard, Cisco, IBM, and Lucent.[6] In some cases, the CEM provides additional services beyond the manufacturing function, including inventory management, delivery, and after-sales service.[7]

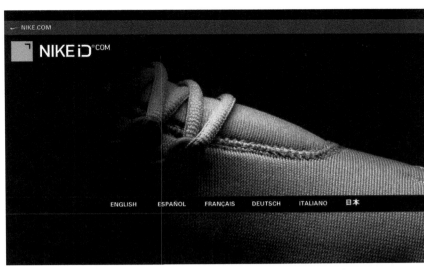

You may not have known the meaning of mass customization until now, but many of you have been served by the practice. The user-friendly Nike iD website allows consumers to custom-design features for their shoes, and enables them to place their own personalized ID on the end product. http://nikeid.nike.com/[5]

IN-CLASS NOTES

Mass Production, Customized Production, and Mass Customization

- *Mass production*: identical goods or services are created, usually in large quantities (typical assembly-line product)
- *Customized production*: unique product for each customer (batch of one)
- *Mass customization*: part of the product is mass produced; the remaining features are customized for each buyer (e.g., Nike iD)

Smart Car, Interesting Process

The smart car is sold in 35 countries and was recently introduced into the Canadian market; it is a unique product that has a very interesting manufacturing process. The vehicle is a glowing example of outsourcing in today's global economy. In some companies, in-house manufacturing operations consist of nothing more than bolting together fabricated chunks that have been manufactured by suppliers. Daimler's smart car is produced in smartville, a production centre in France. Smart car assembly is actually relegated to suppliers—from inventorying nuts and bolts on the assembly line to delivering cars to dealers in Europe and Japan. More than half of the 2000 people working in smartville aren't even on the manufacturer's payroll. The biggest suppliers are on-site, building most of the car in the form of large modules—body, doors, rear section with engine, and so on. Conveyors link major suppliers' plants directly to the assembly building where the cars are bolted together.

Suppliers carry much of the cost of work-in-progress inventory, since they aren't paid until the car comes off the line and is accepted for sale by inspectors—about every 90 seconds, which is quick for the auto industry. Meanwhile, Daimler hopes to incorporate what it has learned about suppliers, modules, pay-on-build, and new technologies into its global operation. "We are getting more and more into learning from others," says one smart plant manager. "We take good things in other places and install them at our plant."[8]

Questions for Critical Thinking

1. What are the advantages and disadvantages of creating such powerful ties with suppliers?
2. Do you believe that the initial success of the smart car in Canada is a short-term response or the beginning of a successful run in this market?

In automotive manufacturing circles, the way the smart car is built has attracted as much attention as the vehicle itself. Outsourcing the manufacturing function integrates the smart car supply chain to the maximum.

Besides outsourcing, another trend sweeping manufacturing organizations is the involvement of suppliers in the manufacturing process. For example, at Volkswagen's factory in Resende, Brazil, seven main suppliers build components and assemble them onto vehicles inside the Volkswagen factory, using the suppliers' own equipment and workers. Volkswagen figures that integrating the suppliers so closely into the production process is a strong incentive for the suppliers to deliver high-quality components in unprecedented time.[9]

With all of the potential financial and technical advantages, however, outsourcing is not without critics or controversy. For a broader look at the implications of outsourcing, see the box entitled "Offshoring: Profits—Yes, but at What Cost?"

Offshoring: Profits—Yes, but at What Cost?

Few business issues in recent years have generated the emotional reaction that outsourcing has stirred up, especially south of the border. Outsourcing has been going on for about as long as businesses have existed, but it has become a hot topic as the outsourcing movement expands from mostly lower-paying assembly positions to higher-paying technical and professional jobs.

When companies outsource any function in the value chain, they often eliminate the jobs associated with that function as well. Increasingly, those jobs aren't going across the street to another local company, but rather around the world, a variation on outsourcing known as *offshoring*. High-tech companies such as IBM, Nortel, Dell, and Microsoft are among the many technology firms that have already moved thousands of technical jobs to India, which has a large pool of educated workers willing to work for far less than North American workers are paid.

Proponents say that offshoring is crucial to the survival of many companies and that it saves other domestic jobs. In addition, offshoring helps raise the standard of living in other countries and thereby expands opportunities for local companies to export their products.

Critics say that companies are selling out the middle class in pursuit of profits and starting a trend that can only harm the domestic economy. When jobs in engineering, medicine, scientific research, architecture, and law can move overseas, they ask, what jobs are going to be left in the nation? Their anger isn't helped by the fact that terminated employees are often forced to train their own overseas replacements, an apparently common practice.

Uncertainty is only fuelling the controversy, because nobody can be entirely certain just how far the offshoring trend will go or what impact it will have on employees, communities, or companies themselves. Estimates vary widely as to the number of jobs that have moved or could move to other countries. Furthermore,

it's often difficult to identify the specific reasons why one country gained jobs or another lost jobs. The emergence of new technology, the phasing out of old technology, shifts in consumer tastes, changes in business strategies, and other factors can all create and destroy jobs.

Traditional economic theory suggests that outsourcing lower-level jobs to countries with lower wages is good for companies because it frees up money and employees to work on more valuable activities. To some degree, this did in fact happen when many manufacturing jobs moved overseas in previous decades. However, when those more valuable activities themselves started to move overseas, quite a few people began to question the theory. Some economists continue to say that short-term pains will lead to long-term gains—that the jobs lost today will once again be replaced by other jobs. Here again, though, there's more uncertainty; no one has yet identified what those jobs are going to be. Paul Craig Roberts, a former assistant treasury secretary in the United States, says the traditional economists are wrong because they're using 200-year-old assumptions about comparative advantage (see Chapter 2) that don't apply to a highly mobile, information-based economy. With companies trying to reduce costs wherever possible, but workers trying to protect as many jobs as possible, offshoring promises to be a hot topic for years to come—not only for businesses and employees but for governments and society as a whole.[10]

Questions for Critical Thinking

1. Are today's outsourced job losses a cause for concern, or is this just a natural part of economic evolution in a global economy? Debate both sides of the argument.
2. Will global labour markets eventually balance out with workers in comparable positions all over the world making roughly the same wages? Explain your answer.

DESIGNING THE PRODUCTION PROCESS

L.O. 3

As Magna executives fully understand, the choice of appropriate operations strategies can dramatically affect a company's ability to deliver quality products. Designing an effective production process is one of the key responsibilities of production and operations managers. It involves six important tasks: identifying the supply chain, forecasting demand, planning for capacity, choosing a facility location, designing a facility layout, and scheduling work.

Establishing the Supply Chain

The value chain and the conversion process that it incorporates rely on supplies every step of the way. Next time you visit a coffeehouse, whether it's a local independent or a chain like Second Cup, take a moment to look around at all the goods and services required to operate it. Even for a relatively simple business the list is long: many different types of coffee beans, flavour additives, chocolate shavings, sugar, sweetener, cream, half-and-half, cow's milk, soy milk, cinnamon, water, electricity, workers' aprons, maintenance for espresso machines, coffee cups, lids, place mats, napkins, stir sticks, and so on. That doesn't include all the goods and services that aren't directly involved in making coffee, such as accounting software to pay taxes and print pay cheques, heating, security systems, advertising, phone service, window washers, paint, rest room supplies, and furniture repair. Now just imagine what it must be like to supply Boeing with the 6 million parts that make up a single 747.[11]

A company's ability to deliver quality products and services is often tied to the dynamics of its suppliers. One faulty part or one late shipment can send rippling effects through the production system and can even bring operations to a grinding halt. When a surge of orders for new Boeing 747s stepped up demand for parts, for instance, Boeing's suppliers were caught offguard. "We had $25 000 engine mounts that couldn't be finished because we were waiting for $40 nuts and bolts," noted one Boeing supplier. As a result, promised aircraft delivery dates were delayed and Boeing suffered huge losses. To avoid such problems in the future, Boeing now works hand in hand with its suppliers to refine products and delivery schedules.[12]

supply chain
The collection of suppliers and systems that provide all of the materials and supplies required to create finished products and deliver them to final customers

The collection of suppliers and systems that provide all the various materials required to make a finished product is called the **supply chain**. (*Supply chain* and *value chain* are sometimes used interchangeably, but it's helpful to distinguish the supply chain as the part of the overall value chain that acquires and manages the goods and services needed to produce goods and then deliver then to the final customer. Everyone in the company is part of the value chain, but not everyone is involved in the supply chain.[13]) The supply chain begins with the provider of raw materials and ends with the company that produces the finished product that is delivered to the customer. The members of the supply chain vary according to the nature of the operation and type of product, but typically include suppliers, manufacturers, distributors, and retailers. For example, if the finished product is a wood table, the supply chain going backward would include the retail store where it was sold, the shipping company that delivered it to the retail store, the furniture manufacturer, the hardware manufacturer, and the lumber company that acquired the wood from the forest.[14]

Supply chain decisions might not sound as glamorous as high-level corporate strategy or innovative e-commerce, but they are every bit as crucial to a company's success. Managers need to identify which materials and other supplies they need, who can supply them, where they should be stored, and a host of other variables. For instance, the public face of Amazon.com is as a website with all the hallmarks of a leading-edge Internet company;

IN-CLASS NOTES

The Supply Chain
- The collection of suppliers and systems that provide all of the materials to create and deliver products to final customers
- The supply chain is part of the overall value chain
- It is crucial to a company's success
- Key decisions include:
  - which materials are needed
  - who can supply them
  - where they should be stored

behind the scenes, though, are some of the world's most sophisticated warehouses and supply-chain technologies. More than a few dot.com pioneers in the 1990s learned a bit too late just how important supply chains are when their razzle-dazzle web company ideas faltered because of nuts-and-bolts supply-chain problems.

Forecasting Demand

A smooth-running supply chain can provide the inputs a company needs, but managers need to figure out how much to buy. To make that decision, they need to forecast demand for the goods they'll be manufacturing or the services they'll be delivering. Using customer feedback, sales orders, market research, past sales figures, industry analyses, and educated guesses about the future behaviour of the economy and competitors, operations managers prepare **production forecasts**, estimates of future demand for the company's products. For example, after years of experience operation managers for Carnival Cruise Lines's Elation ship can now forecast that a one-week Caribbean cruise will require some 10 000 pounds of meat, 10 080 bananas, and 41 600 eggs.[15]

Service companies must also forecast demand. For example, dentists must be able to project approximately how many patients they will treat in a given time period so they can staff their offices properly and have enough dental supplies on hand. These estimates are then used to plan, budget, and schedule the use of resources. Of course, many factors in the business environment cannot be predicted or controlled with certainty. For this reason, managers must regularly review and adjust their forecasts.

Planning for Capacity

Once product demand has been estimated, management must determine the company's capacity to produce the goods or services. The term *capacity* refers to the volume of manufacturing or service capability that an organization can handle. For example, a doctor's office with only one examining room limits the number of patients the doctor can see each day. A cruise ship with 750 staterooms limits the number of passengers the ship can accommodate in any given week. Similarly, a beverage bottling plant with only one conveyor belt and one local warehouse limits the company's ability to manufacture beverage products.

Capacity planning is a long-term strategic decision that establishes the overall level of resources needed to meet customer demand. The neighbourhood convenience store needs to consider traffic volume throughout the day and night to plan staffing levels appropriately. At the other extreme of complexity, when managers at Bombardier plan for the production of a new plane, they have to consider not only the staffing of thousands of people but also factory floor space, material flows from hundreds of suppliers, internal deliveries, cash flow, tools and equipment, and dozens of other factors. Because of the potential impact on finances, customers, and employees, capacity planning involves some of the most difficult decisions that managers have to make. As noted earlier, service businesses have a particular challenge in this respect because they usually can't create their products ahead of time; they need to match capacity and demand simultaneously.

Top management uses long-term capacity planning to make significant decisions about an organization's ability to produce goods and services, such as expanding existing facilities, constructing new facilities, or phasing out unneeded ones. Such decisions involve a great deal of risk for two reasons: (1) Large shifts in demand are difficult to predict accurately, and (2) long-term capacity decisions can be difficult to undo. For example, if a new facility is built to produce a new product that then fails, or if demand for a popular product suddenly declines, the company will find itself with expensive excess capacity. Managers must decide what they should do with this excess capacity. If they keep it, they might try to find an alternate use for this space. If they eliminate it and demand picks up again, the company will have to forgo profits because it is unable to meet customer demand.[16] Service companies face similar problems. Airlines provide transportation, which is a service, but they need facilitating products: airplanes. Purchasing planes to meet demand three, five, or

Many of the newer, larger cruise ships have elegant restaurants, boutiques, luxury spas, high-tech fitness rooms, conference and meeting rooms, theatres, playrooms, ice-skating rinks, and even rock-climbing walls. With passenger counts of 3000 or more, forecasting customer demand for food, supplies, and entertainment is no easy task.

production forecasts
Estimates of how much of a company's goods and services must be produced to meet future demand

capacity planning
A long-term strategic decision that determines the level of resources available to an organization to meet customer demand

ten years down the line is difficult. For example, Air Canada recently announced that it was going to spend $6 billion on 32 airplanes from Boeing. The move was described as a key strategic decision to lower fuel costs and meet specific demand criteria.[17]

Choosing a Facility Location

One long-term issue that management must resolve early when designing the production process for goods and services is the location of production facilities. The goal is to choose a location that minimizes costs while increasing operational efficiencies and product quality. To accomplish this goal management must consider such regional costs as land, construction, labour, local taxes, energy, and local living standards. In addition, management must consider whether the local labour pool has the skills that the firm needs. For example, firms that need highly trained accountants, engineers, or computer scientists often locate in areas near university communities. On the other hand, if most of the jobs can be filled by unskilled or semiskilled employees, firms can choose locations where such labour is available at a relatively low cost. The search for low-cost labour has led many companies to locate their manufacturing operations in countries such as Mexico, Taiwan, India, and China where wages are relatively low.

Also affecting location decisions are transportation costs, which cover the shipping of supplies and finished goods. Almost every company needs easy, low-cost access to ground transportation such as highways and rail lines. Moreover, companies that sell a lot of products overseas must be able to arrange for efficient air or water transportation. Finally, companies must consider raw materials costs. For example, the location of a coal-based power plant must be chosen to minimize the cost of distributing electrical power to customers and to minimize the cost and *lead time* of shipping coal to the plant.

Gildan Activewear has become a global powerhouse in the T-shirt business, capturing about 30 percent of the US imprinted T-shirt business. To remain competitive the company operates manufacturing facilities in the Dominican Republic, Haiti, and Honduras. These locations offer both low-cost labour and shipping. Gildan announced that it was shutting down its two remaining facilities in Canada in 2007. Back in 1998, it had 3000 employees offshore and 1500 in Canada. By the time the decision is executed the company will have 20 000 employees offshore and only 150 at its head offices. This is common in the once powerful employment hub known as the Montreal garment industry. Jack Victor Ltd., a manufacturer of high-end suits, still makes all its suits in the city's downtown core as it has for 94 years. It is the exception rather than the rule, and the company gets away with it because high-end suits have high-end margins that protect the business. But the trend is clear—Peerless Clothing Inc., Parasuco Jeans, and others have moved some production out and many have gone that extra step and followed the Gildan move all the way. The trend in this and many other industries is undeniable.[18]

Location considerations may be different for some service organizations. Although they may also take regional costs into consideration, the main objective for many service firms is to locate where profit potential is greatest. Unlike manufacturing operations, in which low production costs are an important consideration, services tend to focus on more customer-driven factors.[19] Because they often require one-on-one contact with customers, service organizations such as gas stations, restaurants, department stores, and charities must locate where their target market is large and sustainable. Therefore, market research often plays a central role in site selection. However, for service companies that reach customers primarily by telephone, mail, or the Internet, proximity to customers is less of a consideration.

Support from local communities and governments often play a key role in location decisions as well. To provide jobs and expand their income and sales-tax bases, many governments offer companies generous packages of financial relief, from reduced property taxes to free land. When the South Korean automaker Kia recently explored locations for building its first factory in Europe, Slovakia made the most attractive offer, outbidding Poland, the Czech Republic, and Hungary.[20]

Whenever transportation costs are a major expense in the production of a product or service, access to railroads and other means of transport becomes an important consideration.

Designing a Facility Layout

Once a site has been selected managers must turn their attention to *facility layout*, the arrangement of production work centres and other elements (such as materials, equipment, and support departments) needed to process goods and services. Layout includes the efforts involved in selecting specific locations for each department, process, machine, support function, and any other activities required for the operation or service. The need for a new layout design can occur for a number of reasons besides new construction. For instance, a new process or method might become available, the volume of business might change, a new product or service may be offered, an outdated facility may be remodelled, the mix of goods or services offered may change, or an existing product or service may be redesigned.[21]

Facility layout affects the amount of on-hand inventory, the efficiency of materials handling, the use of equipment, and the productivity and morale of employees. In goods manufacturing, the primary concern is the efficient movement of resources and inventory. In the production of services, facility layout controls the flow of customers through the system and influences the customers' satisfaction with the service.[22] In both services and goods operations, the major goals of a good layout design are to minimize materials-handling costs, reduce bottlenecks in moving material or people, provide flexibility, provide ease of supervision, use available space effectively and efficiently, reduce hazards, and facilitate coordination and communications wherever appropriate.[23] (See the box entitled "A Bike That Really Travels.") Four typical facility layouts are *process layout*, *product layout*, *cellular layout*, and *fixed-position layout* (see Exhibit 8.3).[24]

A Bike That Really Travels

When bike-industry veteran Hanz Scholz decided to pedal across Europe in 1987, his vision of packing a folding bike in a suitcase when it was time to board a plane or train soon began to fade. Scholz was disappointed by the quality of folding bikes available. So he set out to build his own: one compact enough to fit into a large suitcase but high-quality enough to tackle steep hills and long, rugged stretches.

Five years later, the first commercial orders for Scholz's Bike Friday were rolling in. Unlike its fold-up predecessors—often one-size-fits-all models available in retail stores—all Bike Fridays are custom made by manufacturer Green Gear Cycling to meet the rider's size and component/colour preference. The bike fits into a car trunk, a tight storage space, or an optional suitcase to travel on a plane like regular baggage.

Green Gear's operations are as distinctive as its product. The relatively small company (US$3 million in sales, 30 employees, and 17 000 square feet of production space) uses advanced manufacturing principles adopted from Toyota Motor and other large manufacturers. Built individually, each Bike Friday begins its life as a bundle of tubes, components, and other structures. These elements are processed through a build-to-order flow-manufacturing configuration organized in a series of cells. The cells are designed so that any one cell can do some of the work of the previous or next cell if production runs behind or ahead.

Once work on a bike has begun, it flows through the process without hesitation at any point. "It works like a track relay with a transition area," says Scholz. "We've set up everything with single-process-specific tools so there is no process changeover time. The flow motto is "touch it once, do it now." When a quality problem is discovered, the operator switches on a red light and all procedures stop until the production cell is adjusted to eliminate the problem.

Operating in a one-at-a-time flow system rather than in batches maximizes the chances for continuous improvement. "For us, every bike is a batch, so we have 150 to 200 chances per month to make process improvements," says Scholz. "A small manufacturer operating in a large-batch mode can be put out of business if he ruins just one. If you can make improvements as you find them, you can survive as a small manufacturer."

Today, Green Gear Cycling builds about 2000 bikes annually. At an average selling price of US$1700, Bike Friday commands a premium price that is primarily paid by North American customers. "We give people what they want, when they want it," says Scholz. "If you do that, people are willing to pay you for it."[25]

Questions for Critical Thinking

1. What are the advantages of using a cellular layout to manufacture Bike Friday?
2. Does Green Gear Cycling mass produce or mass customize folding bikes? Explain your answer.

Types of Facility Layouts

Facility layout is often determined by the type of product an organization is producing.

(A) Process layout: Typically, a process layout is used for an organization producing made-to-order products. A process layout is arranged according to the specialized employees and materials involved in various phases of the production process.

(B) Product layout: A product layout is used when an organization is producing large quantities of just a few products. In a product or assembly-line layout, the developing product moves in a continuous sequence from one workstation to the next.

(C) Cellular layout: A cellular layout works well in organizations that practise mass customization. In a cellular layout, parts with similar shapes or processing requirements are processed together in work centres, an arrangement that facilitates teamwork and flexibility.

(D) Fixed-position layout: A fixed-position layout requires employees and materials to be brought to the product and is used when the product is too large to move.

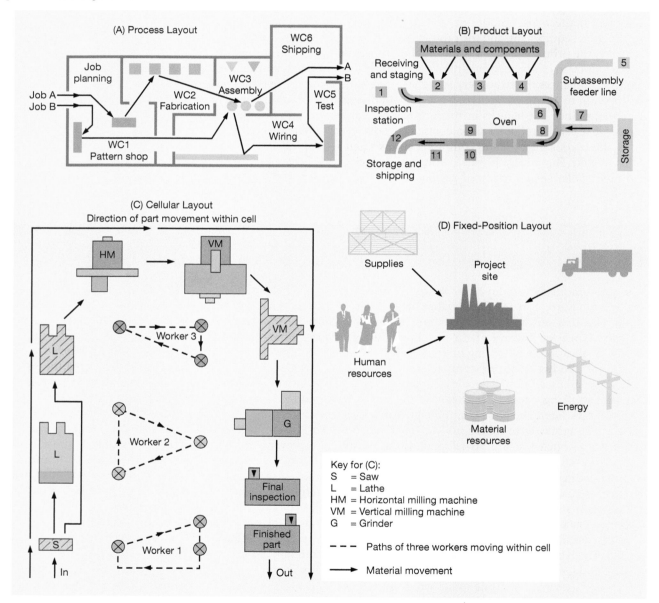

process layout
A method of arranging a facility so that production tasks are carried out in separate departments containing specialized equipment and personnel

A **process layout** is also called a *functional layout* because it concentrates everything needed to complete one phase of the production process in one place. Specific functions, such as drilling or welding, are performed in one location for different products or customers (see Exhibit 8.3A). The process layout is often used in machine shops as well as in service industries. For example, a medical clinic might dedicate one room to X-rays, another room to routine examinations, and still another to outpatient surgery.

An alternative to the process layout is the **product layout**, also called the *assembly-line layout*, in which the main production process occurs along a line, and products in progress move from one workstation to the next. Materials and subassemblies of component parts may feed into the main line at several points, but the flow of production is continuous. Electronics and personal computer manufacturers are just two of many industries that typically use this layout (see Exhibit 8.3B).

Some production of services is also organized by product. For example, when you go to get a driver's licence, you usually go through a series of steps administered by several people: registering, taking a written or computerized test, having an eye exam, paying a cashier, and getting your picture taken. You emerge from this system a licensed driver (unless, of course, you fail one of the tests).

A **cellular layout** groups dissimilar machines into work centres (or cells) to process parts that have similar shapes and processing requirements (see Exhibit 8.3C). Arranging work flow by cells can improve the efficiency of a process layout while maintaining its flexibility. At the same time, grouping smaller numbers of workers in cells facilitates teamwork and joint problem solving. Employees are also able to work on a product from start to finish, and they can move between machines within their cells, thus increasing the flexibility of the team. Cellular layouts are commonly used in computer chip manufacturing and metal fabricating.[26]

Finally, the **fixed-position layout** is a facility layout in which labour, materials, and equipment are brought to the location where the good is being produced or the customer is being served. Buildings, roads, bridges, airplanes, and ships are examples of the types of large products that are typically constructed using a fixed-position layout (see Exhibit 8.3D). Service companies also use fixed-position layouts; for example, a plumber goes to a job site bringing the tools, material, and expertise needed to repair a broken pipe.

Routing is the task of specifying the sequence of operations and the path through the facility that the work will take. The way production is routed depends on the type of product and the layout of the plant. A table-manufacturing company, for instance, uses a process layout because it has three departments, each handling a different phase of the table's manufacturing process and each equipped with specialized tools, machines, and employees. Department 1 cuts wood into tabletops and legs. These pieces are then sent to department 2, where holes are drilled and rough finishing is done. Finally, the individual pieces are routed to department 3, where the tables are assembled and painted.

Scheduling Work

In any production process, managers must use **scheduling**—determining how long each operation takes and setting a start and end time for each. A master schedule, often called a *master production schedule (MPS)*, lists the planned completion order of items. For example, in a health service setting like a doctor's office, the appointment book serves as the master schedule.

When a job has relatively few activities and relationships many production managers keep the process on schedule with a **Gantt chart**. Developed by Henry L. Gantt in the early 1900s, the Gantt chart is a bar chart showing the amount of time required to accomplish each part of a process. It allows managers to see at a glance whether the process is in line with the schedule they had planned (see Exhibit 8.4).

For more complex jobs, the **program evaluation and review technique (PERT)** is helpful. PERT is a planning tool that helps managers identify the optimal sequencing of activities, the expected time for project completion, and the best use of resources within a complex project. To use PERT, the manager must (1) identify the activities to be performed; (2) determine the sequence of activities; (3) establish the time needed to complete each activity; (4) diagram the network of activities; (5) calculate the longest path through the network that leads to project completion; and (6) refine the network's timing or use of resources as activities are completed. The longest path through the network is known as the **critical path** because it represents the minimum amount of time needed to complete the project.

product layout
A method of arranging a facility so that production proceeds along a line of workstations

cellular layout
A method of arranging a facility so that parts with similar shapes or processing requirements are processed together in work centres

fixed-position layout
A method of arranging a facility so that the product is stationary and equipment and personnel come to it

routing
Specifying the sequence of operations and the path the work will take through the production facility

scheduling
The process of determining how long each production operation takes and then setting a start and end time for each

Gantt chart
A bar chart used to control schedules by showing how long each part of a production process should take and when it should take place

program evaluation and review technique (PERT)
A planning tool that managers of complex projects use to determine the optimal order of activities, the expected time for project completion, and the best use of resources

critical path
The sequence of operations that requires the longest time to complete

Exhibit 8.4   **A Gantt Chart**

A chart like this one enables a production manager to see immediately the dates on which production steps must be started and completed if goods are to be delivered on schedule. Some steps may overlap to save time. For instance, after three weeks of cutting table legs, cutting tabletops begins. This overlap ensures that the necessary legs and tops are completed at the same time and can move on together to the next stage in the manufacturing process.

ID	Task Name	Start Date	End Date	Duration	2009
1	Make legs	8/1/09	8/28/09	20d	
2	Cut tops	8/22/09	8/28/09	5d	
3	Drill	8/29/09	9/4/09	5d	
4	Sand	9/5/09	9/11/09	5d	
5	Assemble	9/12/09	9/25/09	10d	
6	Paint	9/19/09	9/25/09	5d	

In place of a single time projection for each task, PERT uses four figures: an *optimistic* estimate (if things go well), a *pessimistic* estimate (if they don't go well), a *most likely* estimate (how long the task usually takes), and an *expected* time estimate (an average of the other three estimates).[27] The expected time is used to diagram the network of activities and determine the length of the critical path.

Consider the manufacturer of shoes in Exhibit 8.5. At the beginning of the process, three paths deal with heels, soles, and tops. All three processes must be finished before the next phase (sewing tops to soles and heels) can be started. However, one of the three paths—the tops—takes 33 days, whereas the other two take only 18 and 12 days. The shoe tops, then, are on the critical path because they will delay the entire operation if they fall behind schedule. In contrast, soles can be started up to 21 days after starting the tops without slowing down production. This free time in the soles schedule is called *slack time* because managers can choose to produce the soles any time during the 33-day period required by the tops.

Exhibit 8.5   **PERT Diagram for Manufacturing Shoes**

In manufacturing these shoes, the critical path involves receiving, cutting the pattern, dyeing the leather, sewing the tops, sewing the tops to soles and heels, finishing, packaging, and shipping—a total of 61 days.

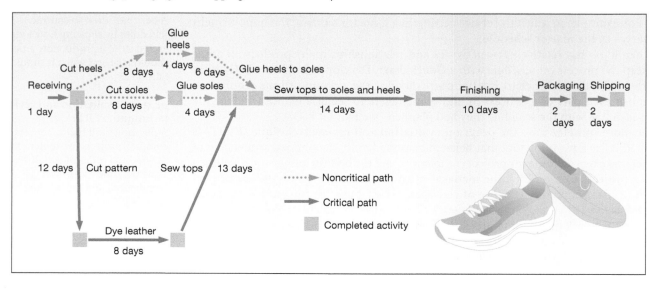

Included in the scheduling process is the **dispatching** function, or the issuing of work orders to department supervisors. These orders specify the work to be done and the schedule for its completion. Work orders also inform department supervisors of their operational priorities and the schedule they must maintain.

Of course, once the schedule has been set and the orders dispatched, a production manager cannot just sit back and assume that the work will get done correctly and on time. Even the best scheduler may misjudge the time needed to complete an operation, and production may be delayed by accidents, mechanical breakdowns, or supplier problems. Therefore, the production manager needs a system for handling delays and preventing a minor disruption from growing into chaos. A successful system is based on good communication between the employees and the production manager.

Suppose a machine breakdown causes department 2 of a manufacturing company to lose half a day of drilling time. If the schedule is not altered to direct other work to department 3 (the next department), the employees and equipment in department 3 will sit idle for some time. However, if department 2 informs the production manager of its machine problem right away, the production manager can immediately reschedule some fill-in work for department 3.

Companies can't afford to waste time. Schedules need to be met to satisfy demand and to stay ahead of the competition. For example, car assembly plants are rated against each other in terms of quality standards and hours per vehicle. Recently, Canadian plants have fared quite well with two GM plants in Oshawa ranking first and second in North America at 15.68 and 16.34 hours per vehicle. As Canadian autoworkers know, companies are constantly looking to consolidate facilities and cut production where they can, so meeting and exceeding standards is vital to survival.[28]

dispatching
Issuing work orders and schedules to department heads and supervisors

---

 IN-CLASS NOTES

Key Steps in Designing an Effective Production Process

1. *Identifying the supply chain*
2. *Forecasting demand*: based on customer feedback, market research, sales figures, industry analysis, etc.
3. *Planning for capacity*: long-term strategic decisions establish the overall level of resources to meet customer demand
4. *Choosing a facility location*: based on land, local taxes, transportation, labour, raw materials, energy, etc.
5. *Designing a facility layout*: process, product, cellular, or fixed position
6. *Scheduling work*

IMPROVING PRODUCTION THROUGH TECHNOLOGY

robots
Programmable machines that can complete a variety of tasks by working with tools and materials

Today, more and more companies are taking advantage of new production technologies to improve their efficiency and productivity. Two of the most visible advances in production technology are computers and **robots**—programmable machines that work with tools and materials to perform various tasks. Although industrial robots may seem exotic, like some science fiction creation, they are quite common and are really nothing more than smart tools. Industrial robots can easily perform precision functions as well as repetitive, strenuous, or hazardous tasks.[29] When equipped with machine vision, or electronic eyes, robots can place doors on cars in precise locations, identify blemished vegetables from frozen-food processing lines, check the wings of aircraft for dangerous ice build-up, make sure that drug capsules of the right colour go into the correct packages before they are shipped to pharmacies, and even assist with surgery.[30]

In addition to robots, other major developments in manufacturing automation include computer-aided design and engineering, computer-aided manufacturing, computer-integrated manufacturing, flexible manufacturing systems, and electronic data interchange.

Computer-Aided Design and Computer-Aided Engineering

computer-aided design (CAD)
Use of computer graphics and mathematical modelling in the development of products

computer-aided engineering (CAE)
Use of computers to test products without building an actual model

computer-aided manufacturing (CAM)
Use of computers to control production equipment

Widely used today is **computer-aided design (CAD)**, the application of computer graphics and mathematical modelling to the design of products. A related process is **computer-aided engineering (CAE)**, in which engineers use computer-generated three-dimensional images and computerized calculations to test products. With CAE, engineers can subject proposed products to changing temperatures, various stresses, and even simulated accidents without ever building preliminary models. Moreover, the *virtual reality* capability of today's computers allows designers to see how finished products will look and operate before physical prototypes are built.

Using computers to aid in design and engineering saves time and money because revising computer designs is much faster than revising hand-drafted designs and building physical models. In fact, computer technology allows companies to perfect a product or abandon a bad idea before production even begins. The result is better overall product quality. For example, when Boeing engineers designed the 777 airplane, they corrected problems and tried out new ideas entirely on their computer screens. Digitally preassembling the 3 million parts of the 777 allowed Boeing to exceed its goals for reducing errors, changes, and rework.[31]

Computer-Aided Manufacturing and Computer-Integrated Manufacturing

The use of computers to control production equipment is called **computer-aided manufacturing (CAM)**. In a CAD/CAM system, computer-aided design data are converted automatically into processing instructions for production equipment to manufacture the part or product. This integration of design and production can increase the output, speed, and precision of assembly lines, as well as make customized production much easier.[32] In addition, the latest CAD/CAM software allows company departments to share designs and data over intranets and the Internet, enabling geographically dispersed departments to work together on complex projects.[33] For example, Ford uses a CAD/CAM/CAE

Robots don't do everything these days. At this Chrysler plant, fine-tuning a limited-edition Viper GTS-R engine is still done by human hands.

system it calls C3P to develop new vehicle prototypes. Whereas it once took two to three months to build, assemble, and test a car chassis prototype, with C3P the entire process can now be completed in less than two weeks. Ford uses C3P to improve engineering efficiency and reduce prototype costs by up to 40 percent. In developing the new Ford F-150 trucks, engineers made extensive use of virtual prototypes, thus saving time and money.[34]

The highest level of computerization in operations management is **computer-integrated manufacturing (CIM)**, in which all elements of production—design, engineering, testing, production, inspection, and materials handling—are integrated into one automated system. Computer-integrated manufacturing is not a specific technology but rather a strategy that uses technology for organizing and controlling a factory. Its role is to link the people, machines, databases, and decisions involved in each step of producing a good.[35]

computer-integrated manufacturing (CIM)
Computer-based systems, including CAD and CAM, that coordinate and control all elements of design and production

Flexible Manufacturing Systems

Advances in design technology have been accompanied by changes in the way the production process is organized. Traditional automated manufacturing equipment is *fixed* or *hard-wired*, meaning it is capable of handling only one specific task. Although fixed automation is efficient when one type or model of good is mass produced, a change in product design requires extensive equipment changes. Such adjustments may involve high **setup costs**, the expenses incurred each time a manufacturer begins a production run of a different type of item. In addition, the initial investment for fixed-automation equipment is high because specialized equipment is required for each of the operations involved in making a single item. Only after much production on a massive scale can a company recoup the cost of that specialized equipment.

setup costs
Expenses incurred each time a producer organizes resources to begin producing goods or services

Technologies That Are Revolutionizing Business

NANOTECHNOLOGY

Think small . . . really small. Think about manufacturing products a molecule or even a single atom at a time. That's the scale of nanotechnology, a rather vague term that covers a wide range of super-tiny research and engineering efforts.

HOW IT'S CHANGING BUSINESS

Nanotechnology is just starting to make a ripple on the front lines of business, but the research projects now in the pipeline could have dramatic impact in the next decade or two. The potential uses of nanotechnology range from the practical—smart materials that can change shape and heal themselves, super-strong and super-light materials for airplanes, smart medical implants, and ultra-small computers—to the somewhat wilder—food-growing machines and microscopic robots that could travel through your body to cure diseases and fix injuries. (Like any new technology with lots of promise, nanotechnology also suffers from lots of hype.)

Also, although they're slightly larger than the generally accepted scale of nanotechnology, *microelectromechanical systems (MEMS)* are already having a major impact in some industries. These tiny machines (pumps, valves, etc.), some no bigger than a grain of pollen, are used in the nozzles of ink-jet printers, air bag sensors, and ultra-precise miniature laboratory devices. MEMS are already a $10 billion industry.[36]

WHERE YOU CAN LEARN MORE

Hundreds of companies and universities are involved with nanotechnology, so you can find information all over the Web. For starters, try IBM (www.research.ibm.com/pics/nanotech), *Small Times* magazine (www.smalltimes.com), and Nanotechnology Now (www.nanotech-now.com). Not everyone supports nanotechnology research, by the way. Check out the Center for Responsible Nanotechnology (www.crnano.org) or search Google for "molecular assembler" or "grey goo."

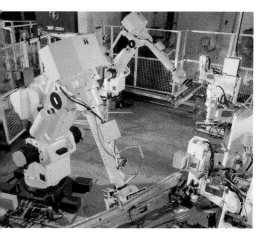

Flexible manufacturing systems make it easy to switch production from one type of product to another.

flexible manufacturing system (FMS)
A production system using computer-controlled machines that can adapt to various versions of the same operation

For example, Harley-Davidson invested US$4.8 million in fixed manufacturing equipment to make a particular motorcycle—only to dismantle the operation when the product faded.[37]

An alternative to a fixed manufacturing system is a **flexible manufacturing system (FMS)**. Such systems link numerous programmable machine tools by an automated materials-handling system of conveyors known as *automatic guided vehicles* (AGVs). These driverless computer-controlled vehicles move materials from any location on the factory floor to any other location. Changing from one product design to another requires only a few signals from a central computer. Each machine changes tools automatically, making appropriate selections from built-in storage carousels that can hold more than 100 tools. In addition, the sequence of events involved in building an item can be completely rearranged.[38] This flexibility saves both time and setup costs. Moreover, producers can outmanoeuvre less agile competitors by moving swiftly into profitable new fields. Flexible manufacturing also allows producers to adapt their products quickly to changing customer needs.[39] For instance, a flexible manufacturing system at Porsche allows 12 different versions of the Porsche 911 to be assembled on the same line.[40] Flexible manufacturing systems are particularly suited for *job shops*, such as small machine shops, which make dissimilar items or produce at so irregular a rate that repetitive operations won't help.

Ford is moving to a flexible manufacturing system. Even its oldest existing plant, which dates back to 1924 and assembled the historic Model T automobile, is part of the revolution. How can a plant that once defined pure mass production make such a move? The simple answer is survival. Ford, GM, and Chrysler are playing catch up to maintain their profitability. Thanks to $100 million in aid from the Ontario government Ford created its first flexible Canadian assembly plant in Oakville. At the newly converted plant, the company can build several models off one, two, or three different platforms. Ford is currently producing the new Ford Edge and Lincoln MKX models at this plant.[41]

IN-CLASS NOTES

Production and Technology

- *Robots*: programmable machines that perform precision functions and increase efficiency
- *CAD, CAE, CAM, CIM and EDI*: design and manufacturing automation tools that are improving all aspects of production
- *Flexible manufacturing systems (FMS)*: link programmable machine tools by an automated materials-handling system of conveyors known as automatic guided vehicles

Electronic Data Interchange

Have you ever had difficulty getting a digital camera to talk to your computer or getting two computers to share files? Multiply that frustration by a few million and you'll have a sense of what it can be like trying to convince the various computers in a complex supply chain to cooperate with one another. To meet this challenge, many businesses rely on **electronic data interchange (EDI)**, a method of electronic communication that simplifies data transfer between computers in a supply chain (think of it as automated email between computers instead of human beings). For instance, when a manufacturer needs more parts from a certain supplier, the manufacturer's inventory software can send an electronic request to the supplier's product database, which then fills the order and sends an electronic invoice back to the manufacturer's accounting system. Roughly one-third of all business documents now travel back and forth electronically using EDI.[42]

EDI has been in use since the 1960s, and like many designs from that era, various companies came up with different and often incompatible schemes. In contrast, the Internet and the World Wide Web are built on universal standards, making them accessible to anyone who follows these standard conventions. One of the newer web standards, a language called **XML** (which stands for *eXtensible Markup Language*), can accomplish the computer-to-computer communication that EDI has been handling for years. (HTML is the basic language for controlling *how* text and graphics are displayed on web pages; XML takes that to another level by also controlling *what* is displayed. Instead of predefining the content, as you have to do with HTML, XML lets you redefine information "on the fly," which means computers can access each other's databases to get whatever information they need.) Because EDI and XML can solve the same problems, supply chain managers in many companies are now faced with the dilemma of which technology to use. XML promises to be less expensive and easier to implement, but EDI is firmly entrenched in thousands of companies around the world. As a result, XML will likely be used in most new systems, but some companies will continue to invest in EDI, and both schemes will coexist in the supply chain for years to come.[43]

MANAGING AND CONTROLLING THE PRODUCTION PROCESS

During the production design phase, operations managers establish the supply chain, forecast demand, plan for capacity, choose facility locations, design facility layouts and configurations, and develop production schedules and sequences. With the process in place, now it's time to "flip the switch" and start producing goods and services. Two major responsibilities at this point are coordinating the supply chain and assuring product quality.

Coordinating the Supply Chain

By now you have a sense of how many pieces must fit together—in the right place, at the right time—for successful production. Unfortunately, you can't just pile up huge quantities of everything you might eventually need because **inventory**, the goods and materials kept in stock for production or sale, costs money to purchase and store. On the other hand, not having an adequate supply of inventory can delay production and result in unhappy customers. That's why more and more companies are changing the way they purchase and handle the materials they use to produce goods and services.

Purchasing is the acquisition of the raw materials, parts, components, supplies, and finished products required to produce goods and services. The goal of purchasing is to make sure that the company has all of the materials it needs, when it needs them, at the lowest possible cost. To accomplish this goal, a company must always have enough supplies on hand to cover a product's **lead time**—the period that elapses between placing the supply order and receiving materials. This

electronic data interchange (EDI) Use of information systems that transmit documents such as invoices and purchase orders between computers, thereby lowering ordering costs and paperwork

XML A standardized web language that goes beyond basic HTML, defining content or data in addition to displaying formatting

inventory Goods kept in stock for the production process or for sales to final customers

purchasing Acquiring the raw materials, parts, components, supplies, and finished products needed to produce goods and services

lead time The period that elapses between the ordering of materials and their arrival from the supplier

L.O. 5

Today's supply chains often span the globe, pulling in parts from multiple countries.

inventory control
A system for determining the right quantity of various items to have on hand and keeping track of their location, use, and condition

just-in-time (JIT) system
A continuous system that pulls materials through the production process, making sure that all materials arrive just when they are needed with minimal inventory and waste

balancing act is the job of **inventory control**, which tries to determine the right quantities of supplies and products to have on hand, then tracks where those items are.

Simply controlling what's in inventory is not enough for many companies, however, and over the years, operations specialists have developed several approaches to coordinating the supply chain, including *just-in-time systems, material requirements planning, manufacturing resource planning*, and *supply-chain management*.

Just-in-Time Systems

Just-in-time (JIT) systems are designed to have only the right amounts of materials arrive at precisely the times they are needed. Because supplies arrive just as they are needed, and no sooner, inventories are theoretically eliminated and waste is reduced.

Reducing stocks of parts to practically nothing also encourages factories to keep production flowing smoothly from beginning to end without any hold-ups, which requires good teamwork. On the other hand, JIT exposes a company to greater risks, as a disruption in the flow of raw materials from suppliers can slow or stop the production process. Shortly after the September 11, 2001, terrorist attacks, for instance, Toyota Motor came within 15 hours of halting production of its Sequoia sport-utility vehicle. One of its suppliers was waiting for steering sensors normally imported by plane from Germany, but the planes weren't flying.[44]

A JIT system also places a heavy burden on suppliers because they must be able to meet the production schedules of their customers. For instance, an increasingly strong demand for electronic and computer components at the beginning of the twenty-first century left many electronic equipment manufacturers battling one another for computer chips and other components. "Just-in-time has become just-in-trouble," said the chief financial officer of one electronics company.[45]

Thus, to be effective, JIT systems must be designed to include multifunctional teamwork, flexible manufacturing, small-batch production, strict production control, quick setups, consistent production levels, preventive maintenance, and reliable supplier networks. Furthermore, poor quality simply cannot be tolerated in a stockless manufacturing environment because one defective part can bring production to a halt. In other words, JIT cannot be implemented without a commitment to total quality control.[46] When all of these factors work in sync, the manufacturer achieves *lean production*; that is, it can do more with less.[47]

Mississauga-based Russel Metals is geared to manage the greatest amount of customers with the least amount of inventory. According to CEO Bud Siegel, inventory decisions have been pushed down the chain to managers. The company's annual compensation package is linked to its return on assets, which makes managers very conscious of inventory levels. According to John Novak of CIBC World Markets, "The company is lean, efficient, and well run."[48] Keep in mind that JIT concepts can also be used to reduce inventory and cycle time for service organizations.

In those cases where it is difficult for manufacturers and suppliers to coordinate their schedules, JIT may not work. For example, shoemaker Allen-Edmonds cannot get its principal raw material whenever it wants because calfskin hides come on the market only at certain times each year.[49] Additional product factors can also affect JIT: seasonality (popularity during specific seasons such as winter), perishability, and unusual handling characteristics such as size or weight.

Material Requirements Planning (MRP)

material requirements planning (MRP)
A method of getting the correct materials where they are needed on time and without carrying unnecessary inventory

perpetual inventory
A system that uses computers to monitor inventory levels and automatically generate purchase orders when supplies are needed

Material requirements planning (MRP) is another inventory control technique that helps a manufacturer get the correct materials where they are needed, when they are needed, and without unnecessary stockpiling. Managers use computer programs to calculate when certain materials will be required, when they should be ordered, and when they should be delivered so that storage costs will be minimal. These systems are so effective at reducing inventory levels that they are used almost universally in both large and small manufacturing firms.

A more automated form of material requirements planning is the **perpetual inventory** system, in which computers monitor inventory levels and automatically generate purchase orders when supplies fall below a certain level. The price scanners found at the checkout

Exhibit 8.6   **MRP II**

An MRP II computer system gives managers and workers in every department easy access to data from all other departments, which in turn makes it easier to generate—and adhere to—the organization's overall plans, forecasts, and schedules.

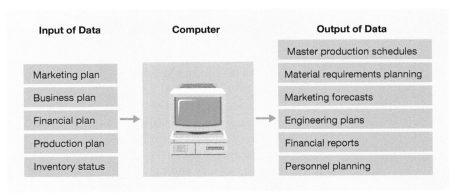

counters of many stores are part of perpetual inventory systems. Every time a product is purchased, the scanner deletes that particular item from the computer system's inventory data. When inventory of the product reaches a predetermined level, the system generates an order for more. Often, the store's system is linked to the supplier's own computer system, which enables the order to be placed with virtually no human involvement.

Manufacturing Resource Planning (MRP II)

The MRP systems on the market today are made up of various modules, including inventory control, purchasing, customer order entry, production planning, shop-floor control, and accounting. With the addition of more and more modules that focus on capacity planning, marketing, and finance, an MRP system evolves into a **manufacturing resource planning (MRP II)** system.

Because it draws together all departments, an MRP II system produces a company-wide game plan that allows everyone to work with the same numbers (see Exhibit 8.6). Employees can now draw on data such as inventory levels, back orders, and unpaid bills once reserved only for top executives. Moreover, the system can track each step of production, allowing managers throughout the company to consult other managers' inventories, schedules, and plans. In addition, MRP II systems are capable of running simulations (models of possible operations systems) that enable managers to plan and test alternative strategies.[50] Many companies have extended the MRP II concept to include functions outside of manufacturing, such as accounting and sales, an approach known as **enterprise resource planning (ERP)**.

The Home Depot Canada uses its ERP system to effectively and efficiently compete. For example, sales activities in each store are logged and measured to understand how business is conducted in each store. Sales are forecast and transactions are continually logged by each store department on a day-to-day and hourly basis. This information is fed into the ERP system and is used to determine, for each location, how many worker hours are needed and where, by type of worker and department.[51]

Supply-Chain Management

Whereas MRP II and ERP systems seek to incorporate more functions with the business, **supply-chain management (SCM)** focuses on the movement and coordination of goods, services, information, and capabilities all the way through the supply chain, from raw materials to finished products delivered to the final consumer.[52] SCM combines business procedures and policies with a comprehensive software solution that integrates the various elements of the supply chain into a cohesive system, even if the supply chain involves a wide variety of outside suppliers and distribution partners. (ERP and SCM are similar in many respects, and the terminology in the industry can be rather confusing; for instance, vendors of ERP software are adding modules that handle SCM tasks.[53])

manufacturing resource planning (MRP II)
A computer-based system that integrates data from all departments to manage inventory and production planning and control

enterprise resource planning (ERP)
A comprehensive database system that expands beyond the production function to include other groups such as sales and accounting

supply-chain management (SCM)
An approach to coordinating and optimizing the flow of goods, services, information, and capabilities throughout the entire supply chain, including outside business partners

Although SCM sounds like basic inventory control on the surface, it has the potential to have a much more important strategic impact on companies in three important ways:[54]

- *Manage risks.* SCM can help companies manage the complex risks involved in a supply chain, risks that include everything from cost and availability to health and safety issues.

- *Manage relationships.* It can also coordinate the numerous relationships in the supply chain and help managers focus their attention on the most important company-to-company relationships. For instance, General Motors buys massive quantities of both steel and aluminium, but the nature of the two markets puts a higher priority on GM's relationship with its aluminium supplier, Alcan. GM uses SCM to forge a close relationship with Alcan, including stabilizing prices in ways that help both companies.

- *Manage trade-offs.* Finally, SCM helps managers address the many trade-offs in the supply chain. These trade-offs can be a source of conflict within the company, and SCM helps balance the competing interests of the various functional areas. This holistic view helps managers balance both capacity and capability along the entire chain. For instance, to deliver a complex, multiple-computer system to a customer, Sun Microsystems used to consolidate all the components at a staging facility then repackage the entire system and have it shipped to the customer. After analyzing the time and cost involved, the company realized it made more sense to have FedEx take care of the consolidation in addition to the shipping.[55]

Successful applications of SCM can lead to increased sales, cost savings, inventory reductions, improved quality, quicker delivery time, and improved customer service.[56] In fact, the potential of SCM is so great that businesses now spend roughly $20 billion a year on SCM software and related technology. Unfortunately, nearly half the companies in one recent survey said they were disappointed with their SCM efforts. Some experts place the blame on the approach people take to SCM, not on the concept itself. To ensure success, managers need to view SCM at a strategic level, look at trade-offs across the entire supply chain, and make sure that the various groups in the chain have the training and tools required to cooperate effectively.[57]

IN-CLASS NOTES

Managing and Controlling the Production Process

- **Coordinating the supply chain**
  - involves balancing inventory levels to reduce cost while ensuring that the supply on hand is enough to cover the product's lead time demands
  - purchasing and inventory control are vital elements of effective coordination
- **Approaches to coordinating the supply chain**
  - just-in-time systems
  - material requirements planning
  - manufacturing resource planning

_____

_____

_____

_____

_____

_____

_____

_____

_____

_____

OOPS

A freelance medical transcriptionist (someone who types doctors' notes from audiotapes) in Pakistan recently threatened to post confidential medical records from patients at the University of California at San Francisco Medical Center on the Internet unless the hospital paid her for her transcription work. The hospital had never heard of her and had no idea how someone in Pakistan got her hands on their medical records. The solution to this mystery? It was a case of outsourcing gone mad. The hospital first outsourced the project to a company called Transcription, stat! which outsourced it to a woman in Florida, who outsourced it to a man in Texas, who then outsourced it to the woman in Pakistan (who was supposed to be paid one-sixth of the amount Transcription, stat! was to be paid by the hospital, by the way).

WHAT YOU CAN LEARN

Whenever work is outsourced, particularly when it involves something as sensitive as medical records, make sure you know where it's going and who's going to perform the work. Many outsourcers put clauses in their contracts that specifically prohibit the work from being re-outsourced to a third party.[58]

Assuring Product Quality

L.O. 7

Besides maintaining optimal inventory levels, companies today must produce high-quality goods as efficiently as possible. In almost every industry you can name this global challenge has caused companies to re-examine their definition of quality and re-engineer their production processes. Still, adopting high-quality standards is not an easy task, because the manufacture of complex goods is not simply a matter of adding part A to part B to part C and so forth until a product emerges ready to ship. For example, the Mercedes M-Class sport-utility vehicle is assembled from subunits built by 65 major suppliers and many other smaller ones.[59] Ensuring that all the pieces are put together in the proper sequence and at the proper time requires large-scale planning and scheduling. The same is true for the production of complex services.

The traditional means of maintaining quality is called **quality control**—measuring quality against established standards after the good or service has been produced and weeding out any defects. A more comprehensive approach is **quality assurance**, a system of companywide policies, practices, and procedures to ensure that every product meets pre-set quality standards. Quality assurance includes quality control as well as doing the job right the first time by designing tools and machinery properly, demanding quality parts from suppliers, encouraging customer feedback, training employees, empowering them, and encouraging them to take pride in their work. When Hunter Harrison, CN's CEO, announced that he was going to push a zero-tolerance policy on safety issues people thought he was crazy. But the priority was put in motion a few years ago and has made a real difference. Leadership starts at the top and the company needed to prioritize the problem.[60] As discussed in Chapter 6, total quality management takes things to an even higher level by building quality into every activity within an organization.

Companies approach quality assurance in various ways. As a builder of sheet-metal components and electromechanical assemblies, Trident Precision Manufacturing empowers workers to make decisions on the shop floor and spends 4.7 percent of payroll on employee training.[61] High-end computer maker Sequent Computer Systems has a "customer process engineering manager" whose primary responsibility is to continually communicate with customers and identify any recurring problems. These companies know that eliminating inefficiency, such as a defect or an excessively complex process, can reduce total product costs because less money is spent on inspection, complaints, and product service.[62]

quality control
Routine checking and testing of a finished product for quality against an established standard

quality assurance
A system of policies, practices, and procedures implemented throughout a company to create and produce quality goods and services

Statistical Quality Control and Continuous Improvement

Quality assurance also includes the now widely used concept of **statistical quality control (SQC)**, in which all aspects of the production process are monitored so that

statistical quality control (SQC)
Monitoring all aspects of the production process to see whether the process is operating as it should be

statistical process control (SPC)
Use of random sampling and control charts to monitor the production process

managers can see whether the process is operating as it should be. The primary tool of SQC is **statistical process control (SPC)**, which involves periodically taking samples from the process and plotting observations of the samples on a *control chart*. A large enough sample provides a reasonable estimate of the entire process. By observing the random fluctuations graphed on the chart, managers and workers can identify whether such changes are normal or whether they indicate that some corrective action is required in the process. In this way, SPC can prevent poor quality.[63]

Statistical quality control is not limited to goods-producing industries. For example, financial services provider GE Capital uses statistical control methods to make sure the bills it sends to customers are correct. The company's use of SQC lowers the cost of making adjustments while improving customer satisfaction.[64]

In addition to using SQC, companies can empower each employee to continuously improve the quality of goods production or service delivery. The Japanese word for continuous improvement is *kaizen.* Japanese manufacturers learned long before many North American manufacturers that continuous improvement is not something that can be delegated to one or a few people. Instead, it requires the full participation of every employee. This means encouraging all workers to spot quality problems, halt production when necessary, generate ideas for improvement, and adjust work routines as needed.[65]

Global Quality Standards

ISO 9000
Global standards set by the International Organization for Standardization establishing a minimum level of acceptable quality

Many manufacturers and service providers in North America, Europe, and around the world require that suppliers comply with standards set by the International Organization for Standardization (ISO), a non-government entity based in Geneva, Switzerland. Recently revised into a family of quality-management-system standards and guidelines known as **ISO 9000**, ISO 9001, and ISO 9004, such standards are voluntary by definition. Companies may choose to comply with these standards and, if met, promote their certification to gain recognition for their quality achievements.

In the past, ISO 9000 standards applied mostly to products that had health and safety-related features. However, the newer 9001 and 9004 standards maintain a greater focus on customer satisfaction, user needs, and continuous improvement.[66] The standards are

| Exhibit 8.7 | **Canada Awards for Excellence (CAE) Quality Award Framework** |

More than 300 CAE Quality Awards have been handed out to model companies since 1984. They are awarded to small, medium, and large organizations in both the private and public sectors. Awards are distributed in the areas of quality, healthy workplace, and education. Recent recipients include DaimlerChrysler Canada and the Canadian Auto Workers, M&M Meat Shops, and Delta Hotels. The following diagram illustrates the framework for the awards.

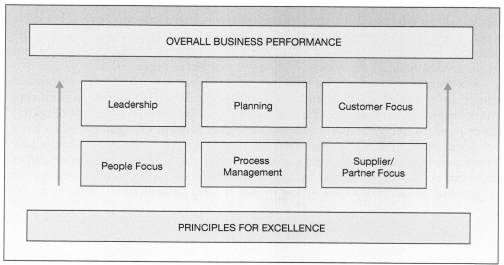

Source: Courtesy of CAE, taken from www.nqi.ca/caeawards/categories.aspx

| Exhibit 8.8 | **Criteria for the Malcolm Baldrige National Quality Award** |

The Malcolm Baldrige National Quality Award is given annually to companies that demonstrate an outstanding commitment to quality. The awards are given to companies in each of four categories: manufacturing, services, small businesses, and universities and hospitals. This chart lists the criteria on which companies are judged for the award.

Leadership. Have senior leaders clearly defined the company's values, goals, and ways to achieve the goals? Is the company a model "corporate citizen"?

Information and analysis. Does the company effectively use data and information to support customer-driven performance excellence and marketplace success?

Strategic planning. How does the company develop strategies and business plans to strengthen its performance and competitive position?

Human resources development and management. How does the company develop the full potential of its workforce? How are its human resource capabilities and work systems aligned with its strategic and business plans?

Process management. How does the company design, manage, and improve key processes, such as customer-focused design and product and service delivery?

Business results. How does the company address performance and improvement in key business areas—product and service quality, productivity and operational effectiveness, supply quality, and financial performance indicators linked to these areas?

Customer focus and satisfaction. How does the company determine requirements, expectations, and preferences of customers? What are its customer satisfaction results?

recognized in more than 158 countries by approximately 634 000 companies. About one-quarter of the world's corporations insist that all their suppliers be ISO certified.[67]

ISO standards help companies become *world-class manufacturers*, a term used to describe the level of quality and operational effectiveness that puts a company among the top performers in the world. Some companies view ISO standards as a starting point to achieving other national quality awards such as Japan's Deming Prize, the Canada Awards for Excellence (CAE; see Exhibit 8.7), or the US Malcolm Baldrige National Quality Award (see Exhibit 8.8). Of course, even if an organization doesn't want to apply for an award, it can improve quality by measuring its performance against an award's standards and working to overcome any problems uncovered by this process.

IN-CLASS NOTES

Assuring Product Quality

- *Quality control*: measuring quality against pre-set standards in search of defects
- *Quality assurance*: policies, practices, and procedures aimed at solving companywide quality issues. Includes quality control as well as:
  - designing tools and machinery properly
  - demanding quality parts from suppliers
  - encouraging customer feedback
  - training employees and empowering them

_____

_____

_____

_____

_____

_____

_____

Behind the Scenes

Planning Capacity and Exploring New Opportunities

What happens when a highly profitable outsourcing agreement gets "in-sourced"? Are you following the technical terms, or should we just get to the facts? As you read in the opening case, BMW is a key customer for Magna's Austrian subsidiary, Magna Steyr. With BMW selling over 110 000 X3's annually, this relationship accounts for almost half of Magna Steyr's assembly capacity. But in 2007, BMW announced that it was going to bring the next generation of the X3 SUV in-house and build them at their Spartanburg, South Carolina facility. Magna expects to continue producing X3s until 2010 when the next generation is launched. This leaves quite a capacity hole to fill, and this announcement was additional bad news that followed the loss of a Chrysler minivan contract. Of course, this is the auto industry and nothing lasts forever. Just ask employees at the various Canadian plants and they can tell you a thing or two about stability and security—it's quite elusive.

Capacity planning involves long-term strategic decisions that establish the overall level of resources needed to meet company demand. With Magna searching for new deals and updating old relationships, the business news began to focus on stories that linked Magna with Chrysler in a more important way. Magna was in talks to develop and manufacture more cars for the company, and news was also being released that Magna planned to take an ownership position in Chrysler or attempt to buy the company with other investment partners. Despite its bid, the decision was announced by DaimlerChrysler (now called Daimler) that Cerberus Capital Management had won the bid to buy Chrysler. Despite the decision, Magna and its various divisions will continue to pursue a closer arrangement with Chrysler and other automotive players.

Magna's New Russian Adventure

Magna's footprint stretches far beyond the Canadian borders and across five continents with product development and engineering centres in places like Japan, China, India, the Czech Republic, and Austria; and manufacturing operations in places like Brazil, South Africa, Poland, and Spain. In all, there are facilities located in 23 countries around the world. More recently, Russia became a major priority. With sales increasing at a rate of approximately 20 percent annually and estimates of 3.4 million annual car sales in Russia by 2010, Magna made a move. In 2007, Frank Stronach, who has been described as a control freak, decided to give up part of the control of his company when he sold 20 million shares to Oleg Deripaska for $1.54 billion. The new bond was established to help Magna take advantage of the potentially rich Russian market. Magna expects a big piece of the pie; it is very optimistic that its average content per car will exceed $1000 in Russia, or about 20 percent more than its North American–operations average. If the company reaches such targets, by 2010 it could mean an additional $2 billion in annual revenue. While Stronach won't speculate on this figure, he did make quite a bold statement when he announced the potential for 300 Magna plants to be built in Russia within 10 years. So will this statement become reality? Will Frank Stronach be happy with a partner after 50 years of building his vision? Only time will tell. One thing is certain—the latest restructuring process will have plenty of implications for the current facilities and for the various independently operated divisions within the company.[68]

Critical Thinking Questions

1. How does BMW's decision to move the X3's production in-house affect Magna's short-, medium-, and long-term operations?
2. Magna's attempt to purchase Chrysler did not succeed; however, it was still a sign of Magna's ambitious growth plans. What impact, if any, could this move have on its relationship with other automobile manufacturers?
3. How will Magna's Russian expansion positively and negatively impact its various divisions around the world?

Learn More Online

Go to Chapter 8 of this text's website at www.pearsoned.ca/bovee and click on the Magna hotlink. Locate the section with company and investor information and read the company's latest annual report. Then look at the current and historical production and sales statistics posted on the site. How many vehicles did Magna produce in the most recent year? What is the output trend? Has the company signed any deals with other manufacturers? Have they lost any additional clients? What is the progress with the Russian expansion?

TEST YOUR KNOWLEDGE

Questions for Review

1. What is meant by the value chain?
2. What are the unique challenges of service delivery?
3. What factors need to be considered when selecting a site for a production facility?
4. What is the purpose of capacity planning?
5. Why might a company want to outsource its manufacturing function? What is meant by offshoring?

Questions for Analysis

6. What are the steps involved in forecasting demand? How would an unexpected economic recession impact such forecasts?
7. How do JIT systems go beyond simply controlling inventory?
8. Why have companies moved beyond quality control to quality assurance?
9. How can supply-chain management help a company establish a competitive advantage?
10. **Ethical Considerations.** How does society's concern for the environment affect a company's decisions about facility location and layout?

Questions for Application

11. Assume you are the production manager for a small machine shop that manufactures precision parts for industrial equipment. How can you use CAD, CAE, CAM, CIM, FMS, and EDI or XML to manufacture better parts more easily?
12. If your final product requires several unique subunits that are all produced with different machinery and in differing lengths of time, what facility layout will you choose and why?
13. **Integrated.** Review the discussion of franchises in Chapter 4. From an operational perspective, why is purchasing a franchise such as Tim Hortons an attractive alternative for starting a business?
14. **Integrated.** Review the discussion of corporate cultures in Chapter 6. What things could you learn about a company's culture by observing the layout and design of its production facility? Discuss both goods and services operations.

PRACTISE YOUR KNOWLEDGE

SHARPENING YOUR COMMUNICATION SKILLS

As the newly hired manager of Campus Athletics, a shop featuring athletic wear bearing logos of colleges and universities, you are responsible for selecting the store's suppliers. Merchandise with team logos and brands can be very trendy. When a college team is hot, you've got to have merchandise ready to sell. You know that selecting the right supplier is a task that requires careful consideration, so you have decided to host a series of selection interviews. Think about all of the qualities you would want in a supplier and develop a list of interview questions that will help you assess whether that supplier possesses those qualities.

BUILDING YOUR TEAM SKILLS

Facility layout is one of the most critical decisions production managers must make. In this exercise, you and your team are playing the role of production managers for the following companies, some producing a specific good and some producing a specific service:

- Cott—soft drinks
- H&R Block—tax consultation
- Bob Mackie—custom-made clothing
- Burger King—fast food
- Bombardier—commercial jets
- Halifax General Hospital—medical services
- Brother—fax machines
- General Motors—sport-utility vehicles

For each company on the list, discuss and recommend a specific facility layout, referring to Exhibit 8.3 for an overview of the four layouts. Why does your team believe the recommended layout is best suited to the product or service each company produces? How would the recommended layouts affect the movement of resources and inventory for the manufacturers on the list? How would the layouts affect customer interaction for the service providers on the list?

EXPAND YOUR KNOWLEDGE

DISCOVERING CAREER OPPORTUNITIES

Whether you prefer to work with products or services, many possible careers await you in production and operations. From input to transformation to output, companies are looking for resourceful, results-oriented employees able to meet the demands of ever-changing schedules and specifications. Start your research by scanning the classifieds and display ads in your local newspaper and in the *Globe and Mail*; also check help-wanted ads in business magazines like *IndustryWeek*. Access Monster.ca and search for production and manufacturing jobs, www.monster.ca

1. As you read through these want ads, note all the production-related job titles you find. How many of these jobs include quality or technology (or both) among the duties and responsibilities?

2. Select two job openings that interest you. Reread the ads for those jobs to find out what kind of work experience and educational background are required. What further preparation will you need to qualify for these jobs?

3. Assume you have the qualifications for the two jobs you have selected. What key words should you include on your electronic resumé to show the employers that you are a good job candidate?

DEVELOPING YOUR RESEARCH SKILLS

Seeking increased efficiency and productivity, a growing number of producers of goods and services are applying technology to improve the production process. Find an article in business journals or newspapers (print or online editions) that discusses how one company used CAD, CAE, robots, electronic information systems, or other technological innovations to refit or reorganize its production operations.

1. What problems led the company to rethink its production process? What kind of technology did it choose to address these problems? What goals did the company set for applying technology in this way?

2. Before adding the new technology, what did the company do to analyze its existing production process? What changes, if any, were made as a result of this analysis?

3. How did technology-enhanced production help the company achieve its goals for financial performance? For customer service? For growth or expansion?

STUDY GUIDE

SUMMARY OF LEARNING OBJECTIVES

1. Explain what production and operations managers do

Production and operations managers design and oversee an efficient conversion process—the sequence of events that convert resources into goods and services. To do this, they must coordinate a firm's resources and optimize output from each resource. Additionally, production and operations managers perform the four basic functions of planning, organizing, leading, and controlling, but the focus of these activities is on the production of a company's goods and services.

2. Highlight the unique challenges of providing efficient and effective service-delivery systems

Most of the concepts associated with goods manufacturing apply to services as well, but there are some unique challenges: (1) Customers are usually involved in—and can affect the quality of—the service delivery; (2) There is no inventory—most services are consumed at the same time they are produced; (3) Services are usually people intensive; (4) Customers often dictate when and where services are delivered; (5) Service quality can be more subjective than goods quality.

3. Explain the role of the supply chain and identify key tasks in designing a production process

The supply chain consists of all companies involved in making a finished product. Today, more and more companies are managing their supply chains to be more responsive to the changing needs of their customers by reducing the number of firms in their supply chain and developing long-term relationships with remaining members.

Designing an effective production process is one of the key responsibilities of production and operations managers. It involves six important tasks: identifying the supply chain, forecasting demand, planning for capacity, choosing a facility location, designing a facility layout, and scheduling work. Managers prepare production forecasts, or estimates of future demand for the company's products. Next they must consider capacity, which is a business's volume of manufacturing or service delivery. The next step is to find a facility location that minimizes regional costs, transportation costs, and raw materials costs. Once a location has been selected, managers need to consider facility layout—the arrangement of production work centres and other facilities (such as material, equipment, and support departments) needed for the processing of goods and services. Finally, managers must develop a master production schedule.

4. Discuss the role of computers and automation technology in production

Computers and automation technology improve the production process in several ways: (1) Robots perform repetitive or mundane tasks quickly and with great precision; (2) CAD and CAE systems allow engineers to design and test virtual models of products; (3) CAM systems easily translate CAD data into production instructions; (4) CIM systems link the people, machines, databases, and decisions involved in each step of producing a good; and (5) flexible manufacturing systems (FMS) reduce setup costs and time by linking programmable, multifunctional machine tools through a computer network and an automated materials-handling system.

5. Explain the strategic importance of coordinating the supply chain and managing inventory

Efficiently coordinating the supply chain is a vital issue; it can help reduce costs and it is essential for the proper flow of inputs and outputs. The goods and materials kept in stock for production or sale make up inventory, which must be managed to minimize costs and ensure that the right supplies are in the right place at the right time. Having too much inventory is costly and increases the risk that products will become obsolete; having too little inventory can result in production delays and unfilled orders.

6. Distinguish among JIT, MRP, and MRP II inventory management systems

Just-in-time (JIT) systems reduce waste and improve quality by producing only enough to fill orders when they are due, thus eliminating finished-goods inventory. Furthermore, under the JIT system, parts or materials are ordered only when they are needed, thus eliminating supplies inventories. Material requirements planning (MRP) and perpetual inventory systems are used to determine when materials are needed, when they should be ordered, and when they should be delivered. A more advanced system is manufacturing resource planning (MRP II), which brings together data from all parts of a company (including financial, design, and engineering departments) to better manage inventory and production planning and control.

7. Highlight the differences between quality control and quality assurance

Quality control focuses on measuring finished products against a pre-set standard and weeding out any defects. On the other hand, quality assurance is a system of companywide policies, practices, and procedures that build quality into a product and ensure that each product meets quality standards.

KEY TERMS

analytic system   (230)
capacity planning   (237)
cellular layout   (241)
computer-aided design (CAD)   (244)
computer-aided engineering
   (CAE)   (244)
computer-aided manufacturing
   (CAM)   (244)
computer-integrated manufacturing
   (CIM)   (245)
critical path   (241)
customized production   (232)
dispatching   (243)
electronic data interchange
   (EDI)   (247)
enterprise resource planning
   (ERP)   (249)
fixed-position layout   (241)
flexible manufacturing system
   (FMS)   (246)

Gantt chart   (241)
inventory   (247)
inventory control   (248)
ISO 9000   (252)
just-in-time (JIT) system   (248)
lead time   (247)
manufacturing resource planning
   (MRP II)   (248)
mass customization   (232)
mass production   (232)
material requirements planning
   (MRP)   (248)
perpetual inventory   (248)
process layout   (240)
product layout   (241)
production   (229)
production and operations
   management (POM)   (229)
production forecasts   (237)

program evaluation and review
   technique (PERT)   (241)
purchasing   (247)
quality assurance   (251)
quality control   (251)
robots   (244)
routing   (241)
scheduling   (241)
setup costs   (245)
statistical process control (SPC)   (252)
statistical quality control (SQC)   (251)
supply chain   (236)
supply-chain management
   (SCM)   (248)
synthetic system   (230)
value chain   (230)
XML   (247)

QUESTIONS

Multiple Choice   Circle the correct answer and then check the answers in the back of the book to chart your progress.

1. What is the main advantage of outsourcing?

   a. Products produced by other companies have higher quality than goods produced in-house.
   b. Many contract manufacturers have better facilities and production efficiencies that would be costly to duplicate.
   c. Outsourcing is one example of being socially responsible and helping other companies.
   d. More jobs are created in-house through outsourcing.

2. What is the main advantage of mass customization?

   a. It uses the efficiency of mass production with the marketing advantages of giving each customer what he or she wants.

   b. It can be more efficient, thus products can be less expensive.
   c. It adds modern technology to mass production.
   d. It is mass production using custom-made machines.

3. Why is demand forecasting so important when planning the production process?

   a. The company must plan to sell the output.
   b. The company must decide which advertising media to use.
   c. The company must plan the best way to produce the level of production they expect to sell.
   d. Capacity can usually be changed from day to day.

4. Which of the following is *not* usually a consideration when choosing a facility location?

   a. Access to well-trained workers
   b. Access to truck, water, or rail transportation
   c. Location in a prestigious area
   d. Energy costs are important, especially for heavy industries like steel or aluminium manufacturing

5. A medical clinic is most likely to use which type of facility layout?

   a. Product layout
   b. Process layout
   c. Cellular layout
   d. Fixed-position layout

6. What is a comprehensive database system that includes information about the firm's suppliers and customers as well as data generated internally called?

   a. SPC
   b. ERP
   c. ISO 9000
   d. CAD

7. Making a movie is a complicated, expensive project that requires many tasks to be completed in the proper order. Which technique would be most appropriate to help the producer ensure the movie is completed on time and on budget?

   a. Gantt chart
   b. PERT
   c. JIT
   d. EDI

8. At some home building centres, the customer and salesperson can use software that helps them design a wooden deck. When the homeowner agrees to the design, the software prints out the parts list and the total cost. What type of system is this?

   a. CAD
   b. CAE
   c. CAD/CAM
   d. CIM/FMS

9. Porsche enables 12 different versions of the Porsche 911 to be assembled on the same production line using what manufacturing concept?

   a. Flexible manufacturing system (FMS)
   b. Fixed manufacturing equipment
   c. Process layout
   d. Just-in-time inventory (JIT)

10. _____ is a seal that refers to global standards set by the International Organization for Standards establishing a minimum level of acceptable quality.

    a. ISO 9000
    b. Gantt
    c. PERT
    d. JIT

True/False

1. True or false? Batch-of-one production is another term for mass production.

2. True or false? Using computer systems like CAD/CAM allows designers to adjust or modify designs.

3. True or false? The main advantage of a just-in-time (JIT) system is that it reduces the amount of money the company maintains in inventory.

4. True or false? To ensure quality, manufacturers have to check every item as it comes off the production line.

5. True or false? The traditional assembly-line process is often called a flexible manufacturing system.

Fill-in-the-Blank

1. A(n) _____ system beaks raw material into one or more distinct products that may or may not resemble the original material in form or function.

2. Under a _____ layout, parts with similar shapes or processing requirements are processed together in work centres.

3. In a _____ network diagram, the sequence of operations that requires the most time is known as the *critical path.*

4. Daimler's smart car is produced at a plant in France, which is divided into various sections or buildings where individual components are assembled. More than half of the workers are not employed by Daimler but rather they are employed by suppliers. Daimler has _____ most of the jobs.

5. The _____ refers to all of the functions required to transform inputs into outputs (goods and services) along with the business functions that support the transformation process.

6. _____ planning is a long-term strategic decision that establishes the overall level of resources needed to meet customer demand.

7. _____ is the task of specifying the sequence of operations and the path through the facility that the work will take.

8. Included in the scheduling process is the _____ function, or the issuing of work orders to department supervisors.

9. The highest level of computerization in operations management is _____, in which all elements of production—design, engineering, testing, production, inspection, and materials handling—are integrated into one automated system.

10. Purchasing tries to ensure that the company has all of the materials it needs when it needs them at the lowest possible cost. To accomplish this goal, a company must always have enough supplies on hand to cover a product's _____, the period that elapses between placing the supply order and receiving materials.

See It on the WEB

Visit the Companion Website at **www.pearsoned.ca/bovee**, review the exercises, and complete the following assignments for Chapter 8:

1. Make Quality Count
2. Follow the Path to Continuous Improvement
3. Step Inside ISO Online

Companion Website

The Big Switcheroo: Vancity

LEARNING OBJECTIVES

The purpose of this video is to help you

1. Understand the complex, non-routine nature of managing a large organization

2. Examine the work expectations and human resource interactions at various levels of the organization

3. Demonstrate important lessons that an executive manager can learn from briefly getting involved in or paying attention to the daily routines of regular employees.

SYNOPSIS

So you think that your boss has an easy job. Are you willing to trade places? Of course you would love to trade bank accounts, but are you willing to put in the long hours? CBC's *Big Switcheroo* series allows the viewer to tag along as employees get their wish and have a chance to sit in the executive chair. The program also forces the CEO to leave the comforts of the head office and get a taste of what their employees would call "real work." Both individuals usually get a new appreciation for what it takes to succeed at the opposite end of the spectrum. In this video we are taken behind the scenes at Vancity, Canada's largest credit union with 50 branches and $10.5 billion in assets, as CEO Dave Mowat and financial services officer Lisa Paille switch places.

Lisa is thrilled to get Dave's fancy car and comfortable office, but she soon realizes that there is a lot more to the CEO's job than playing golf and attending functions. She stumbles in an early speech, is bombarded by communications and is shocked to realize that her days fly by without the chance to sit and eat a proper meal or chat with her family.

Dave on the other hand loves his new short hours and the fact that he is able to eat a family dinner at a reasonable hour, but his work performance is not exactly exemplary. He shows up to work without a tie, spends too much time with each customer, and uses some overly casual, somewhat unprofessional expressions when conversing with the clients. At the end of the experiment, both Dave and Lisa have a new appreciation for the day-to-day job at the other end of the spectrum. Dave recently left Vancity to take a job as president CEO at ATB Financial in Alberta; the *Big Switcheroo* may have taught him a few new tricks and surely gave him a long-term appreciation for front-line workers.

Discussion Questions

1. *For analysis*: Was this experiment just an interesting gimmick or can a CEO take advantage of such lessons?

2. *For application*: What types of programs can Vancity create internally to allow employees to get a taste of different levels of the hierarchy or other departments at the same level?

3. *For debate*: Do you think that Dave Mowat was more effective in his move down the chain of command, or do you believe that Lisa Paille made the transition more effectively? Build your arguments and debate a classmate.

ONLINE EXPLORATION

Visit the Vancity website at www.vancity.com and find out more about the credit union. Also visit the CBC at www.cbc.ca or www.cbclearning.ca and search for the *Big Switcheroo* to see some of the latest employee management switches.

ON LOCATION VIDEO CASE

Feeling like Part of the Family: Kingston Technology

LEARNING OBJECTIVES

The purpose of this video is to help you

1. Understand the importance of motivating employees.

2. Consider how financial and non-financial rewards can motivate employees.

3. Explain how high morale can affect organizational performance.

SYNOPSIS

Kingston Technology, based in California, is the world's largest independent manufacturer of computer memory products. Founded by John Tu and David Sun, Kingston employs more than 2400 people, but makes each employee feel like part of the family. The company returns 10 percent of its company profits to employees every year through a profit-sharing program. Just as important, it fosters mutual trust and respect between employees and management. Senior managers stay in touch with employees at all levels and conduct surveys to obtain employee feedback. For their part, employees report high job satisfaction and develop both personal and professional connections with their colleagues—boosting morale and motivation.

Discussion Questions

1. *For analysis*: After the sale to SoftBank employees learned from news reports that Kingston's US$100 million profit-sharing distribution was one of the largest in history. What was the likely effect of this publicity on employee morale?

2. *For application*: What kinds of questions should Kingston ask to measure satisfaction and morale through employee surveys?

3. *For debate*: Do you agree with Kingston's policy of giving new employees profit-sharing bonuses even when they join the company just one week before profits are distributed? Support your position.

ONLINE EXPLORATION

Visit Kingston Technology's website at www.kingston.com and follow the links to browse company information and read about its awards. From the company information page, follow the link to learn about the organization's values. How do these values support the founders' intention to create a family feeling within the company? How do they support employees' achievement of higher-level needs? Why would Kingston post this listing of milestones on its website, starting with the company's founding and continuing with honours bestowed by *Fortune* and others?

Of all the innovative ideas that bubbled up in the heady days of the dot.com boom, online business-to-business (B2B) exchanges seemed like one of the few that actually made economic sense. The idea behind these exchanges was to bring buyers and sellers together in huge online trading hubs where purchasing, selling, and other supply-chain transactions for the entire industry could take place under one virtual roof—it would all be fast, efficient, and good for just about anybody. This wasn't some crazy dot.com scheme, like giving people free computers in return for watching online advertising. This sounded like a real business opportunity, complete with paying customers.

It sounded so good, in fact, that some 37 000 B2B exchanges opened for business by the end of 2000, serving just about every industry imaginable. Some were run by independent third parties; others were set up by industry players who joined forces to form new ventures. The two most common types of B2B exchanges are *buyer exchanges* and *supplier exchanges*. Buyer exchanges are marketplaces formed by large groups of buyers (including competitors) who purchase similar items. By joining forces and aggregating demand for a product, they can achieve economies of scale that are not possible individually. Supplier exchanges are formed by suppliers who band together to create marketplaces to sell their goods online. These groups of suppliers typically sell complementary products, offering buyers one-stop shopping for most of their needs.

Another Dot.Com Dream Up in Smoke?

B2B exchanges promised to save members billions of dollars annually in reduced supply-chain costs and to transform overnight the way companies bought and sold. Unfortunately, nearly all of them went out of business—95 percent of them by one estimate—and only a few of the survivors have serious backing from major global corporations. Among the casualties were small exchanges like Foodusa.com, which tried to link slaughterhouses, distributors, and brokers of beef and poultry; big exchanges like PetroCosm, an online buying site formed by Chevron and Texaco for the petroleum industry; and Zoho.com, a B2B marketplace formed by Starwood Hotels for the hotel industry. These start-ups learned that the path to B2B prosperity was full of unanticipated roadblocks:

- *Member rivalry.* For large, public B2B exchanges to work effectively, competitors must be willing to expose business processes—processes that often give them a competitive advantage. Some companies were concerned that participation in public exchanges would put sales information

and other critical data in the hands of customers and competitors. For instance, using a public exchange to purchase goods could tip a company's hand to competitors who were monitoring buying patterns, giving them valuable competitive information.

- *Supplier resistance.* It was easy to see how buyers would benefit by joining forces, but suppliers worried that online marketplaces, auction-like pricing, and easy access to cheaper goods would drive down the prices of their goods. Many refused to join.

- *Customer resistance.* Many companies were unwilling to dump the network of suppliers they'd built up over the years and make all their purchases through a new, unfamiliar exchange. Larger companies such as Dell, Intel, and Wal-Mart, for example, already get the best prices possible from suppliers and have no plans to join the public marketplaces that operate in their industry. Moreover, many manufacturers have long-term buying contracts and didn't see how the exchanges would get them lower prices or offer additional benefits. As a result, the anticipated droves of customers never showed up.

- *Incompatible systems.* One of the biggest challenges facing B2B exchanges was the need to seamlessly blend the operating systems used by exchange members. This included dozens of software packages, accounting systems, data management systems, and manufacturing schedules. Different customs, languages, and laws from country to country further complicated the endeavours. For the truly giant endeavours, such as Covisint.com, set up by the major North American automakers, this proved an insurmountable hurdle. As one participant put it, "Relationship behaviour is more important than people thought."

To Be or Not To Be?

Despite these roadblocks, a few public B2B exchanges are making progress, such as exchanges for health care supplies (Broadlane.com), steel and metals (e-Steel.com), chemicals (ChemConnect.com), and shipping (LevelSeas.com).

The real news, however, might be in a new generation of B2B exchanges based on the concept of "one-to-many." Instead of having many buyers and many sellers in the exchange, this new format connects a single buyer with multiple sellers. For instance, IBM Canada has a private B2B exchange with a number of travel-related suppliers, including

American Express, Air Canada, Hertz, and Delta Hotels. Because the suppliers don't compete with one another, and there's only one buyer to coordinate technology with, the system works quite well.

Are the mighty public B2B exchanges a thing of the past, though? Some observers believe the economic benefits are still there, if only people would cooperate. Until that glorious day arrives, private exchanges such as IBM Canada's and smaller public exchanges in niche markets will keep the dream alive.[69]

Questions for Critical Thinking

1. Why would a buyer want to participate in a B2B exchange?

2. Would sellers ever have any incentive to participate? Explain your answer.

3. Why does a private B2B exchange such as IBM Canada's work?

BUSINESS PLANPRO EXERCISES

Managing a Business

Review Appendix B, Your Business Plan, to learn how to use Business PlanPro Software so you can complete these exercises.

Think Like a Pro

Objective: By completing these exercises you will become acquainted with the sections of a business plan that address a company's mission, goals and objectives, and management team. You will use the sample business plan for JavaNet (listed as "Internet cafe" in the Sample Plan Browser) in this exercise.

1. Evaluate JavaNet's mission statement. Does it summarize why the organization exists, what it seeks to accomplish, and the principles that the company will adhere to as it tries to reach its goals? How might you improve this mission statement?

2. Evaluate JavaNet's objectives. Are they clearly stated? Are they measurable? Do they seem realistic? Which objectives might need some refining?

3. Assess the risks facing JavaNet. How do you expect these threats to affect the company's ability to compete?

4. Read about the company's management structure and personnel plan. What challenges might JavaNet face as a result of its chosen structure and personnel plan?

Create Your Own Business Plan

Return to the plan you are creating for your own business. List your company's goals and objectives, and be sure they are clearly stated and measurable. How will you reach these goals and objectives? What might prevent you from achieving them? What information should you include about your management team? Should you mention the team's weaknesses in addition to its strengths? Why?

PART 4

MANAGING
EMPLOYEES

CHAPTER 9
Managing Human Resources

CHAPTER 10
Motivating Today's Workforce and
Handling Employee-Management
Relations

CHAPTER 9

MANAGING HUMAN RESOURCES

LEARNING OBJECTIVES
After studying this chapter, you will be able to

1 List six main functions of human resources departments

2 Cite seven methods recruiters use to find job candidates

3 Identify the six stages in the hiring process

4 Discuss how companies incorporate objectivity into employee performance appraisals

5 Highlight five popular employee benefits

6 Describe four ways an employee's status may change and discuss why many employers like to fill job vacancies from within

BEHIND THE SCENES

From formal policies to television ads, it's clear that human resources are at the front lines of WestJet's corporate strategy. Service with a smile is the official company line.

www.westjet.com

WestJet's advertisements emphasize in-flight live TV, smiling staff members, and attendants telling jokes. *Message number one*: WestJet and its valued employees take a different approach to the airline experience. WestJet attendants won't water your lawn, pick up the mail, or check up on old Aunt Martha while you're away, as their ads seem to indicate, but these exaggerated scenarios are a cute way of making a point. *Message number two*: Our employees own a piece of the company, which is why they go that extra mile to get the job done.

WestJet was founded in 1996 by four Calgary entrepreneurs who saw an opportunity to provide low-rate airfare travel to western Canadians. The inspiration for the company came from observing the successful approach of companies like Southwest Airlines in the United States. With that model in mind, WestJet began operations with three 737 Boeing planes and a big idea. Today, WestJet has expanded across the country and now has a workforce (owner-force) of approximately 6000 employees. The company now flies to 35 cities, and the fleet has expanded to 65 planes, with plans to add another 20 planes in the next two years.

As a company like WestJet grows, it becomes more challenging to maintain that entrepreneurial identity. The human resources department has to become an even greater strategic partner to ensure that the spirit lives on. Human resources managers must maintain and improve policies to address the organizational evolution. From planning the company's staffing needs to executing the hiring process to administering benefits, everything must mesh together. The question over the next decade will be how the continued growth will impact human resources at the company. WestJet is no longer the surprising underdog; it will need to keep its eyes on their valued assets to ensure that the smiles and jokes keep coming in the long-term future.[1]

TEST YOURSELF

Answers to these questions can be found on the website: www.pearsoned.ca/bovee.

1. If you were a member of WestJet's management team, how would you continue to attract, train, and compensate a diverse workforce?

2. What human resources policies and practices would you implement to motivate employees to give top notch service?

3. What is meant by performance appraisal and how does it impact a company like WestJet?

UNDERSTANDING WHAT HUMAN RESOURCES MANAGERS DO

L.O. 1

WestJet seems to understand that motivated employees are vital to an organization's success and cannot be treated as an afterthought, but rather as partners in the overall mission. **Human resources management (HRM)** is a term that describes all the tasks involved in acquiring, maintaining, and developing an organization's employees. Because of the accelerating rate at which today's workforce, economy, and corporate cultures are being transformed, the role of HRM is increasingly viewed as a strategic one.

Human resources (HR) managers must figure out how to attract qualified employees from a pool of entry-level candidates; how to train less-educated, poorly skilled employees; how to keep experienced employees when they have few opportunities for advancement; and how to lay off employees equitably when downsizing is necessary. They must also retrain employees to cope with increasing automation and computerization, manage increasingly complex (and expensive) employee benefits programs, shape workplace policies to address changing workforce demographics and employee needs (discussed in Chapter 10), and cope with the challenge of meeting government regulations in hiring practices and equal opportunity employment. In short, human resources managers and staff members help keep the organization running smoothly at every level.

human resources management (HRM)
A specialized function of planning that focuses on obtaining employees, overseeing their training, and evaluating and compensating them

PLANNING FOR A COMPANY'S STAFFING NEEDS

Proper human resources planning is critical because a miscalculation could leave a company without enough employees to keep up with demand, resulting in customer dissatisfaction and lost business. Yet if a company expands its staff too rapidly, profits may be eaten up by payroll or the firm may have to lay off people who were just recruited and trained at considerable expense. The planning function consists of two steps: (1) forecasting supply and demand; and (2) evaluating job requirements (see Exhibit 9.1).

Forecasting Supply and Demand

Planning begins with forecasting *demand*, the numbers and types of employees who will be needed at various times. HR managers consider a number of variables when estimating demand, including (1) predicted sales of the company's goods and services;

IN-CLASS NOTES

The Six Functions of Human Resources Departments
- Planning for staffing needs
- Recruiting and hiring
- Training and development
- Appraising performance
- Managing compensation and benefits
- Overseeing employment status

_____

_____

_____

_____

_____

Exhibit 9.1   **Steps in Human Resources Planning**

Careful attention to each phase of this sequence helps ensure that a company will have the right human resources when it needs them.

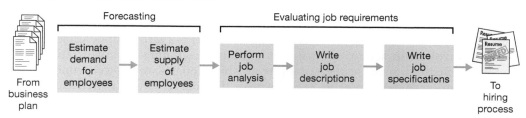

succession planning
Workforce planning efforts that identify possible replacements for key employees, usually senior executives

replacement chart
A planning tool that identifies the most vital employees in the organization and any available information related to their potential replacement

employee retention
Efforts to keep current employees

(2) the expected *turnover rate*, the percentage of the workforce that leave every year; (3) the current workforce's skill level, relative to the company's future needs; (4) upcoming strategic decisions that might affect the number and type of workers needed; (5) changes in technology or other business factors that could affect the number and type of workers needed; and (6) the company's current and projected financial status.[2] Juggling all these variables in a dynamic business environment can get so complex that many HR managers, particularly in larger companies, rely on computer models to help predict workforce demands.

In addition to overall workforce levels, every company has a number of employees and managers who are considered so critical to the company's ongoing operations that HR managers work with top executives to identify potential substitutes in the event any of these people need to be replaced, a process known as **succession planning**. These plans can cover owners, senior executives, researchers, top sales staff, and other vital members of the organization.[3] A **replacement chart** identifies these key employees and lists potential replacements, along with any current vacancies in key positions and other planning details (such as the number of years before the CEO is expected to retire, for instance).

With some idea of future workforce demands, the HR staff then tries to estimate the *supply* of available employees. In many cases, that supply is within the company already—perhaps just needing training to fill future requirements. For example, Clive Beddoe, WestJet's chair and CEO, is not going anywhere yet, but he has begun the succession plan by letting go of his position as president and promoting Sean Durfy, the company's former vice-president of marketing, sales, and airports.[4]

To ensure a steady supply of experienced employees for new opportunities and to maintain existing operations, successful companies focus heavily on **employee retention**, the degree to which they are able to keep desired employees. A good way to understand the retention challenge is to look carefully at Frederick Herzberg's two-factor theory, which is described in detail in Chapter 10. Both hygiene factors (dissatisfiers) and motivators contribute to retention. For instance, both better pay (removing a dissatisfier) and the opportunity to lead a new project (adding a motivator) are steps that could increase employee retention. The steps employers take to retain employees also change with the economy. In contrast to the on-site massage therapists, free espresso, game rooms, and other sometimes frivolous perks from the past, many employers now emphasize more meaningful work-life benefits that help employees balance their work and home lives, including flexible work schedules, telecommuting, and career planning assistance.[5]

If existing employees cannot be tapped for new positions, the HR team must determine how to find people outside the company who have the necessary skills. In addition to hiring permanent employees, either part time or full time, companies have several other options for meeting workforce needs, including temporary employees and outsourcing.

Clive Beddoe named Sean Durfy as president of WestJet as part of his succession plan. Make no mistake about it, though, Beddoe is still in control of the company with his CEO and chair titles.

Temporary Employees

More and more businesses try to save money and increase flexibility by adding to their main workforces with temporary employees, or "temps," whose schedules can be rearranged to suit the company's needs. As a result, this segment of the labour force has increased significantly in recent years.[6] The temporary ranks include computer systems analysts, human resources managers, accountants, doctors, and even CEOs, with technical fields making up the fastest-growing segment of temporary employment.

Companies are incorporating temporary workers in long-term plans, whereas 15 years ago they used temps to fill occasional vacancies. The use of temps is an excellent recruiting technique because it allows companies to try out employees before hiring them permanently. Thus, what often begins as a temp assignment can turn into multiyear employment. Some 29 percent of workers employed by temp agencies remain on the job assignment for one year or more. Many of these "perma-temps" hold high-prestige, high-skilled technology jobs at leading firms. In fact, they often do the same work as the company's permanent employees, but because they are temps, they do not qualify for the benefits enjoyed by regular workers. However, some perma-temps have sued companies, saying that they are, in fact, full-time employees and as such deserve employee benefits.[7] The guidelines for determining whether a worker is an employee or an independent contractor are complicated and not always clear but have significant tax issues for both the worker and the company.[8]

Retired workers are another great resource for HR managers looking for qualified temporary and part-time workers. This segment has historically been downplayed and ignored by some recruiters. However, with seniors living longer, healthier lives and with an unprecedented pool of potential baby-boomer retirees on the horizon, attitudes are quickly changing. A recent *Globe and Mail* report unofficially named four companies (Merck Frosst Canada, Royal Bank of Canada, The Home Depot Canada, and Avis) as the "best employers of people over 50." These companies are actively pursuing this growing segment of the workforce.[9]

Outsourcing

Just as companies can opt to outsource parts of the production function (as discussed in Chapter 8), they can also use outsourcing as a way to meet staffing needs in the

Technologies That Are Revolutionizing Business

ASSISTIVE TECHNOLOGIES

The term "assistive technologies" covers a broad range of devices and systems that help people with disabilities perform activities that might otherwise be difficult or impossible. These include technologies that help people communicate orally and visually, interact with computers and other equipment, and enjoy greater mobility, along with numerous other specific functions.

HOW THEY'RE CHANGING BUSINESS

Assistive technologies create a vital link for thousands of employees with disabilities, giving them the opportunity to pursue a greater range of career paths and giving employers access to a broader base of talent. With Canada heading for a potentially serious shortage of workers in a few years, the economy will benefit from everyone who can make a contribution, and assistive technologies will be an important part of the solution.[10]

WHERE YOU CAN LEARN MORE

AssistiveTech.net, www.assistivetech.net, is a great place to search for the categories of assistive technologies available. If you'd like to explore a career in assistive technology, visit the Rehabilitation Engineering & Assistive Technology Society of North America, www.resna.org. Technology companies such as IBM and Microsoft also devote significant resources to developing assistive technologies and making information technology more accessible.

organization without hiring permanent employees. Some companies outsource an entire function, such as sales or human resources, whereas others outsource selected jobs or projects. In general, outsourcing is used to take advantage of outside expertise, to increase flexibility, or to benefit from the cost-efficiencies offered by firms that specialize in a single business function. Many companies even outsource work to former employees who have set themselves up as independent contractors or started companies that perform the same functions they used to perform for employers.[11]

Outsourcing has many advantages: It gives companies access to new resources and world-class capabilities; it shares the risk of getting the work done; and it frees up company resources for other purposes. Still, outsourcing has its share of risks, including loss of control, greater dependency on suppliers, and loss of in-house skills. Some companies have also experienced work delays, unhappy customers, and labour union battles as a result of outsourcing.[12]

Evaluating Job Requirements

job analysis
The process by which jobs are studied to determine the tasks and dynamics involved in performing them

The second step of the planning function is to evaluate job requirements. If you were the owner of a small business, you might have a good grasp of the requirements of all the jobs in your company. However, in large organizations where hundreds or thousands of employees are performing a wide variety of jobs, management needs a more formal and objective method of evaluating job requirements. That method is called **job analysis**.

To obtain the information needed for a job analysis, HR staff asks employees or supervisors several questions: What is the purpose of the job? What tasks are involved in the job? What qualifications and skills are needed to do the job effectively? In what kind of setting does the job take place? Is there much public contact involved? Does the job entail much time pressure? Sometimes they obtain job information by observing employees directly; other times they ask employees to keep daily diaries describing exactly what they do during the workday.

job description
A statement of the tasks involved in a given job and the conditions under which the holder of the job will work

job specification
A statement describing the kind of person who would best fit the job, including skills, education, and previous experience required

Once a job analysis has been completed, HR develops a **job description**, which is a formal statement summarizing the tasks involved in the job and the conditions under which the employee will work. In most cases, the staff will also develop a **job specification**, a statement describing the skills, education, previous experience, and personal attributes that candidates need to possess to do the job effectively.[13]

RECRUITING, HIRING, AND TRAINING NEW EMPLOYEES

Having forecast a company's supply and demand for employees and evaluated job requirements, the HR manager's next step is to match the job specification with an actual person or selection of people. This task is accomplished through **recruiting**—attracting suitable candidates for an organization's jobs. One recent study shows that companies with excellent recruiting and retention policies provide a nearly 8 percent higher return to shareholders than those that do not have such policies.[14]

recruiting
The process of attracting appropriate applicants for an organization's jobs

Recruiters are specialists on the HR staff who are responsible for locating job candidates. They use a variety of methods and resources, including internal searches, newspaper and Internet advertising, public and private employment agencies, campuses and career offices, trade shows, corporate "headhunters" (people who try to attract workers at other companies), and referrals from employees or colleagues in the industry (see Exhibit 9.2). Companies have strategic preferences; for example, Business Objects recruits more than 30 percent of its new hires from employee referrals and pays referral bonuses ranging from $1000 to $2500 as an incentive to its current employees. Business Objects is a business-intelligence software company that was recently named one of British Columbia's top 30 employers.[15] One of the fastest-growing recruitment resources for both large and small businesses is the Internet. Today, many companies recruit online

Exhibit 9.2 **How Employers and Job Seekers Approach the Recruiting Process**

Studies show that employers prefer to fill job openings with people from within their organization or from an employee's recommendation. Placing want ads is often viewed as a last resort. In contrast, typical job seekers begin their job-search process from the opposite direction (starting with reading newspaper or Internet ads).

Employers

Look for someone inside the organization	Rely on networking contacts and personal recommendations	Hire an employment agency or search firm	Review/send unsolicited resumés	Place/read a newspaper or an Internet ad

Job Seekers

through their websites in addition to using popular online recruiting services, as the "E-Business in Action" feature at the end of this part discusses (see pages 329–330).

The Hiring Process

L.O. 3

After exploring at least one—but usually more—of the available recruitment channels to assemble a pool of applicants, the human resources department may spend weeks and sometimes months on the hiring process. Most companies go through the same basic stages as they look through applications to find the person they want.

The first stage is to select a small number of qualified candidates from all the applications received. Finalists may be chosen on the basis of a standard application form or based on a resumé—a summary of education, experience, and personal data compiled by each applicant (see "Preparing Your Resumé" in Appendix C on the website for further details). Sometimes both sources of information are used. Many organizations use computer scanners to help them quickly sort through resumés and weed out those that don't match the requirements of the job. While it is good to stand out from the crowd, it is important to use common sense when writing your resumé. A recent resumé stunt led to the evacuation of an office building and a hotel and a call to the bomb squad. The actual

IN-CLASS NOTES

Recruiting New Employees
- Companies must compete to find the best possible candidates
- **Internal recruitment resources:** Many positions are filled by current employees (promotions) or through employee referrals
- **External recruitment options:** Ads (newspaper, Internet), employment agencies, campuses and career offices, trade shows, corporate "headhunters"

package delivered was harmless, but it was designed to look like a bomb. Needless to say, recruiters at Cossette Communication Group were not impressed with the candidate.[16]

The second stage in the hiring process is to interview candidates to clarify qualifications and fill in any missing information (see "Interviewing with Potential Employers" in Appendix C for further details). Another goal of the interview is to get an idea of the applicant's personality and ability to work well with others. Depending on the type of job at stake, candidates may also be asked to take a test or a series of tests.

After the initial pre-screening interviews comes the third stage, when the best candidates may be asked to meet with someone in the HR department who will conduct a more probing interview. For higher-level positions, candidates may go through a series of interviews with managers, potential co-workers, and the employees who will make up the successful candidate's staff. For many positions, candidates undergo a tough interview process that can take weeks before they are hired (see the box entitled "New Age Job Interviews: Are you Camera Friendly?").

New-Age Job Interviews: Are you Camera Friendly?

Smile for the camera and make sure to practise your delivery! Many initial interviews today are being conducted via videoconferencing.

Have you taken a drama course? How are your acting skills? Do you come across well on screen? Are you afraid of the lights of a camera? You may be wondering where we're going with this line of questioning. Let's begin with some new-age human resource trends. According to Gordon Orlikow, a senior partner in the Toronto office of the executive recruiting company Korn/Ferry International, "approximately 30 percent of initial job interviews are conducted using a video link between candidates and human resources managers. This figure is up dramatically from about 2 percent just two years earlier."

A few years ago, Donald Trump packaged his extended interview into a TV program meant to entertain and provide some indication of a bizarre version of

the hiring process—*The Apprentice*. The show faded but the use of the camera lens is not far-fetched or unrealistic; real practitioners are seeing the merits of using video equipment to manage their increasing time demands and to decrease costs. This video approach appears to be especially important for high-end executive positions, which tend to extend candidate searches over long distances to other parts of Canada and the world.

Many firms have used unconventional techniques for years, such as asking employees to perform improvisational skits to demonstrate their reactions to a fabricated situation. These approaches force candidates out of their comfort zone and put them under the spotlight. Now human resources managers are truly placing the spotlight on interviewees. So what can a candidate do to prepare for a video interview? A personal face-to-face interview allows the HR manager to focus on what the interviewee is saying, however, in a video interview on-screen appearance and presentation style tend to be more memorable. You can't approach this type of interview with the same mindset.

Will this method continue to grow in popularity? We'll find out. In the meantime, remember that you must tailor your interview preparation to the type of company, organizational culture, industry expectations and now the medium of delivery to be truly effective in any given situation.[17]

Questions for Critical Thinking

1. What are the advantages and disadvantages of the video interview? Debate the issue with a classmate.
2. How would you prepare for a video interview? What additional steps should you take beyond what you would do to prepare for a regular face-to-face interview?

After all interviews have been completed, the process moves to the final stages. In the fourth stage, the department supervisor evaluates the candidates, sometimes in consultation with a higher-level manager, the HR department, and staff. During the fifth stage, the employer checks the references of the top few candidates. The employer may also research the candidates' education or previous employment. In the sixth stage, the supervisor selects the most suitable person for the job. Now the search is over—provided the candidate accepts the offer.

Background Checks

Violence in the workplace is an increasing threat that can harm employees and customers, hurt productivity, and lead to expensive lawsuits and higher health care costs. More than 1 million physical assaults occur at work each year. If an employer fails to address "preventable violence," that employer can be found liable. This means that companies need to be especially careful about negligent hiring.

As Exhibit 9.3 shows,[18] employers conduct a variety of background checks on job applicants to ensure accuracy and fight fraud by verifying all educational credentials and previous jobs, accounting for any large time gaps between jobs, and checking references. Background checks are particularly important for jobs in which employees are in a position to possibly harm others. For example, a trucking company must check applicants' driving records to avoid hiring a new trucker with numerous traffic violations.

The Internet has provided recruiters with a great additional tool to get information on candidates. According to one recent survey, 75 percent of executive recruiters use search engines to check out candidates and about 26 percent said that they eliminated candidates based on information they found online.[19]

Hiring and the Law

Employment labour regulations cover all employers and employees in Canada. Those who fall under federal jurisdiction are covered by the *Canada Labour Code*. All ten provinces and three territories have an employment (or labour) standards act. During the hiring process interviewers must be sure to respect human rights legislation.[20]

Exhibit 9.3   **Checking Out New Hires**

Today's employers are scrutinizing new employees more closely.

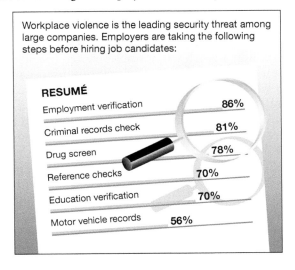

Workplace violence is the leading security threat among large companies. Employers are taking the following steps before hiring job candidates:

RESUMÉ

Employment verification	86%
Criminal records check	81%
Drug screen	78%
Reference checks	70%
Education verification	70%
Motor vehicle records	56%

In particular, employers must be careful to avoid discrimination in the wording of their application forms and when interviewing and testing potential applicants. Asking questions about unrelated factors such as marital status, age, and religion violate regulations because such questions may lead to discrimination. In addition, employers are not allowed to ask questions about whether a person has children or what caused a physical disability. The exception is when such information is related to a bona fide occupational requirement for the specific job.

Employers must also be careful in their hiring practices to ensure that they are not found liable for illegal recruitment practices. For example, a judge in British Columbia awarded RBC Dominion Securities $2.25 million after Merrill Lynch Canada lured away a dozen investment advisers. The defection practically led to the collapse of RBC's Cranbrook office and was challenged because of the manner in which the exodus took place. Individual brokers can switch organizations and bring their client lists to their new employer, but the judge in this case ruled that the recruitment was deceitful, covert, and deliberately executed over a seven-month period.[21]

Testing

One much-debated aspect of the hiring process is testing—using not only the tests that prospective employers give job applicants but any devices that can evaluate employees when making job decisions. Tests are used to evaluate abilities, intelligence, interests, and sometimes even physical condition and personality.

Many companies rely on pre-employment testing to determine whether applicants are suited to the job and whether they'll be worth the expense of hiring and training. Companies use three main procedures: job-skills testing, psychological testing, and drug testing. Job-skills tests are the most common type, designed to assess competency or specific abilities needed to perform a job. Psychological tests usually take the form of questionnaires. These tests can be used to assess overall intellectual ability, attitudes toward work, interests, managerial potential, or personality characteristics—including dependability, commitment, and motivation. When Brigitte Catellier applied for the post of vice-president of legal affairs at Astral Media she was put to the test. She chuckled at one of the first questions that asked whether she would prefer to be an astronaut, an acrobat, or a research technician. But the test was no laughing matter. The gruelling eight tests in seven hours contained hundreds of questions and was a final hurdle in her job search. She also spent two hours with an industrial psychologist before a decision was made between her and another candidate.[22] People who favour psychological testing say that it can predict how well employees will actually perform on the job. However, critics say that such tests are ineffective and potentially discriminatory.

To avoid the increased costs and reduced productivity associated with drug abuse in the workplace (estimated to cost industry some US$100 billion a year), many employers require applicants to be tested for drug use. Studies show that substance abusers have two to four times as many workplace accidents as people who do not use drugs. Moreover, drug use can be linked to more than 40 percent of industry fatalities. Companies with mandatory testing have found real advantages, including lower accident rates, fewer disability claims, and decreased violence and absenteeism. In Canada, employers are not permitted to screen candidates for substance abuse because "alcohol and drug abuse are considered to be a handicap and are covered under human rights codes; an employee cannot be discriminated against during the selection process based on a handicap. In addition, random testing after selection is generally not permitted with the exception of certain safety sensitive positions."[23]

Yasuko Ishikawa, a Delta Air Lines flight attendant, was fired after a random urine test showed her sample had been tampered with. Ishikawa took her case to court. The jury found that the lab conducting the drug test was negligent and awarded Ishikawa US$400 000. Delta also offered to reinstate her.

IN-CLASS NOTES

The Hiring Process
1. Select qualified candidates
2. Screen candidates
3. Conduct interviews
4. Evaluate candidates
5. Check references
6. Select the best candidate

_____

_____

_____

_____

_____

Training and Development

Even the best applicants rarely begin a job knowing everything they need to know or possessing all the skills they need to have to succeed in a specific position, company, or industry. Moreover, with the pace of change in everything from government regulations to consumer tastes to technology, knowledge and skills need to be constantly updated. Consequently, the most successful companies place a heavy emphasis on employee training and development efforts, for everyone from entry-level workers to the CEO.

Most companies begin the training process as soon as new employees join the workforce. These **orientation** programs usually include information about the company's background and structure, equal opportunity practices, safety regulations, standards of employee conduct, company culture, employee compensation and benefits plans, work times, and other topics that newly hired employees might have questions about.[24] Orientation programs help new employees understand their role in the organization and feel more comfortable.

At Intel, for instance, all new hires participate in a six-month "integration" curriculum. Day One begins when new hires receive a package at home. The package contains material about the company's culture and values, along with some forms to fill out. During the first month, all new hires attend a class called "Working at Intel," a formal eight-hour introduction to the company's corporate culture. At the end of the six-month period, each new hire participates in a two-hour structured question-and-answer session in which an executive reviews the employee's transition into Intel and then asks a final long-term question: "What do you think it will take to succeed at Intel?"[25]

In most cases, training and other forms of employee development continue throughout the employee's career. Many HR departments maintain a skills inventory, which identifies both the current skill levels of all the employees and the skills the company needs employees to acquire to succeed. Depending on the industry, some of the most common subjects for ongoing training include problem solving, new products, sales, customer service, safety, sexual harassment, supervision, quality control, strategic planning, communication, time management, and team building.[26]

Training can take place at the work site, where an experienced employee oversees the trainee's on-the-job efforts, or in a classroom, where an expert lectures groups of employees. Employee training may also involve a self-study component using training manuals, computers, tests, and interactive modules. For additional information see the box entitled "Click and Learn: E-Training Today's Employees".

orientation
A session or program to introduce a new employee to the organization and its procedures

At Irving Oil the commitment between the employees and the company is spelled out in the Mutual Values Promise (MVP).

Click and Learn: E-Training Today's Employees

According to the Conference Board of Canada, 77 percent of all Canadian employers now offer some form of e-training to their employees. At Rogers Communications, sales representatives can learn how to deal with routine inquiries and difficult customers with their interactive online role-play scenarios. Employers from automakers and software firms to hospitals and pharmaceutical companies are turning to computers to train their employees. Electronic training, or e-training (also known as e-learning), uses computers and live or taped webcasts, web-based self-paced tutorials, and other forms of electronic media such as CD-ROMs to instruct employees on new products, customer service, sales techniques, and more. What makes e-training possible are the technological advances in today's workplace—more desktop computers, increased Internet access, and more bandwidth.

Dell Computer expects 90 percent of its learning solutions to be totally or partially technology enabled. General Motors University uses interactive satellite broadcasts to teach salespeople the best way to highlight features on new cars. Pharmaceutical companies like Merck use live, interactive Internet classes to instruct sales reps on the latest product information rather than fly them to a conference centre. IBM has moved virtually all content of the first three phases of management training online for its first-line managers, eliminating the need to send them to offsite locations over the course of a training period that stretches over six months.

As these companies have learned, e-training has many benefits:

■ *Reduced costs.* Much of the cost savings comes from reduced travel expenses and time savings. Intel has saved more than US$1 million annually by using e-training programs. "If we save our 70 000 employees just 20 minutes a year, that alone is $1 million in savings," says one Intel training manager.

■ *Increased productivity.* "Our sales force can't come in for three-day conferences anymore," says one Black & Decker vice-president. "But they still need to understand the company's new products and features." So the company has instituted online

training courses—which means the company's 700-person sales force can spend a combined 12 000 more days a year with customers.

■ *Individualized pace.* E-training allows you to learn at your own pace—skipping over material you already know and spending more time on material that meets your specific needs. Canadian Tire offers a very diverse product line. Through e-training, employees are able to focus on specific areas where they lack knowledge.

■ *Increased consistency.* Companies can create one set of instructional materials that is used consistently by everyone in the organization. Thus, all employees are learning the same thing—regardless of their location.

■ *Improved information sharing.* E-training is effectively changing the way companies transfer knowledge and information to employees and customers.

Like many other Internet-related efforts in recent years, e-training saw a rapid rise followed by a period of rethinking when corporate trainers moved past the "gee-whiz" factor and took a more objective look at what training technology really could—and couldn't—offer. They began to appreciate the value of e-training, but also realized it wasn't the solution to every training challenge and that impressive technology was no substitute for good instructional planning. As a result, many companies now emphasize *blended learning*, which is a combination of delivery methods. Wendy O'Brien of 3Com, a computer networking firm, says her team examines the content and audience of each training effort, along with parameters such as budgets and deadlines, before they choose a delivery method. By combining the best available methods in each individual case, 3Com keeps the focus on the learner rather than on the technology while still using e-training to its fullest potential.[27]

Questions for Critical Thinking

1. Why is e-training an increasingly popular approach for companies?
2. How might an economic slowdown affect e-training?

The Bank of Montreal takes employee development seriously, which is evident when you examine the company's training and education initiatives. The company built the BMO Institute for Learning, a place where employees receive standard instruction and dabble in experiential learning. The bank's "university" comes complete with 12 fully wired classrooms, 8 role-play rooms, 20 break-out rooms, and a 250-seat presentation hall. The institute is also geared toward experiential learning and includes an obstacle course that contains an eight-metre wall designed for employees to experience the challenge of

The Bank of Montreal has made a commitment to its employees to address lifelong learning and corporate retraining. The BMO Institute for Learning is a venue for both traditional classrooms and experiential activities.

rappelling and to test their physical limitations.[28] Although some employers worry that employees who develop new or improved skills might leave them for higher-paying jobs, studies show that the contrary is true. The more training given to employees, the more likely they will want to stay, because training gives them a sense that they are going somewhere in their careers, even if they're not getting a promotion.[29]

Janice Wismer, former senior vice-president of human resources at Canadian Tire, was identified as one of Canada's most innovative executives by *Canadian Business.* When she assumed her position in HR, employee product knowledge was identified as a major problem. According to Wismer, "Many employees would walk away from customers instead of approaching them to provide advice." Her solution was to create an Internet-based e-learning initiative rather than a traditional training model. Just three years after the implementation of the program, 98 percent of Canadian Tire stores had adopted the e-learning tool and 948 000 interactive lessons had been completed. These figures are quite impressive considering the fact that Canadian Tire stores are independently owned and operated and that each dealer had to pay an up-front charge to join the program. The initiative is credited with boosting sales and improving customer satisfaction.[30]

IN-CLASS NOTES

Training and Development
- **Employee competence** has a direct effect on productivity and profits
- **Proper training** can help motivate employees and aid in goal achievement
- An orientation session is important, but companies should offer training (and retraining) to support employee growth through **regular courses, workshops, and e-courses**

L.O. 4

APPRAISING EMPLOYEE PERFORMANCE

performance appraisal
The evaluation of an employee's work according to specific criteria

How do employees (and their managers) know whether they are doing a good job? How can they improve their performance? What new skills should they learn? Most human resources managers attempt to answer these questions by developing **performance appraisals** to objectively evaluate employees according to set criteria. Well-designed appraisals promote both fairness and improvement by focusing on job-related performance standards.

The ultimate goal of performance appraisals is not to judge employees, but rather to improve their performance. Thus, experts recommend that performance reviews be an ongoing discipline—not just a once-a-year event linked to employee raises. Periodic evaluations are especially important in today's project-driven, results-oriented workplace. Employees need fast feedback so they can correct problems quickly; more importantly, managers must also emphasize future actions (feedforward) rather than dwelling on the past.[31]

Most companies require regular written evaluations of each employee's work. To ensure objectivity and consistency, firms generally use a standard company performance appraisal form to evaluate employees. The evaluation criteria are in writing so that both employee and supervisor understand what is expected and are therefore able to determine whether the work is being done adequately. Written evaluations also provide a record of the employee's performance, which may protect the company in cases of disputed terminations. An increasing number of companies now conduct evaluations online, using password-protected websites to record and analyze information.[32]

The specific measures of employee performance vary widely by job, company, and industry. Most jobs are evaluated in several areas, including tasks specific to the position, contribution to the company's overall success, and interaction with colleagues and customers. A production-line technician might be evaluated on such factors as work quality, productivity, innovation and problem solving, teamwork, job knowledge, and reliability. In contrast, the production manager might be evaluated on the basis of communication skills, people management, leadership, teamwork, recruiting and employee development, delegation, financial management, planning, and organizational skills.[33]

Many performance appraisals require the employee to be rated by several people (including more than one supervisor and perhaps several co-workers). This practice further promotes fairness by correcting for possible biases. One appraisal format that moves the review process from a one-dimensional perspective to a multidimensional format is the *360-degree review*. Designed to provide employees with a broader range of perspectives, the 360-degree review gets feedback from colleagues above, below, and around the employee to provide observations of the person's performance in several skill and behavioural categories. This means that employees rate the performance of their superiors as well as that of their peers.[34]

One of the biggest problems with any employee appraisal system is finding a way to measure productivity. In a production job, the person who types the most pages of acceptable copy or who assembles the most defect-free microprocessors in a given amount of time is clearly the most productive. But how does an employer evaluate the productivity of a registration clerk at a hotel, a programming manager at a large television station, or a research scientist? Although the organization's overall productivity can be measured (number of rooms booked per night, number of viewers per hour, number of patents or new products), often the employer can't directly relate the results to any one employee's efforts. Evaluating productivity becomes an even greater challenge in organizations where employees work in teams.

electronic performance monitoring (EPM)
Real-time, computer-based, continuous evaluation of employee performance

In addition to formal, periodic performance evaluations, many companies evaluate some workers' performance continuously using **electronic performance monitoring (EPM)**, sometimes called *computer activity monitoring*. For instance, customer service and telephone sales representatives are often evaluated by the number of calls they complete per hour and other variables. Newer software products extend this monitoring capability, from measuring data input accuracy to scanning for suspicious words in employee emails. As you can imagine, EPM efforts can generate controversy in the workplace, elevating employee stress levels and raising concerns about invasion of privacy.[35]

In-Class Notes

Performance Appraisal

- **Performance reviews** should not be a once-a-year event linked to employee raises
- For objectivity and consistency, a **standard appraisal form** should be used
- Many performance appraisal systems require the employee to be **rated by several people**
  - **360-degree reviews** get feedback from colleagues above, below, and around the employee
- **Electronic performance monitoring** (EPM) can provide limited real-time stats on employee performance

_____
_____
_____
_____
_____
_____
_____
_____

Administering Compensation and Employee Benefits

L.O. 5

Pay and benefits are of vital interest to all employees, of course, and these subjects also consume considerable time and attention in HR departments. In many companies, payroll is the single biggest expense in the entire company, and the cost of benefits, particularly health care, continues to climb. Consequently, **compensation**, the combination of direct payments such as wages or salary and indirect payments through employee benefits, is one of the HR manager's most significant responsibilities.

compensation
Money, benefits, and services paid to employees for their work

Wages and Salaries

Many blue-collar (production) and some white-collar (management and clerical) employees receive compensation in the form of **wages**, which are based on calculating the number of hours worked, the number of units produced, or a combination of both time and productivity. Wages provide a direct incentive to an employee: the more hours worked or the more pieces completed, the higher the employee's paycheque. While administering wages, employers in Canada must comply with federal and provincial labour laws that determine issues such as minimum hourly wages and overtime pay for employees.

wages
A cash payment based on the number of hours the employee has worked or the number of units the employee has produced

Employees whose output is not always directly related to the number of hours worked or the number of pieces produced are paid **salaries**. As with wages, salaries base compensation on time, but the unit of time is a week, two weeks, a month, or a year. Salaried employees like managers normally receive no pay for the extra hours they sometimes put in; overtime is simply part of their obligation. However, they do get a certain amount of flexibility in their schedules.

salaries
Fixed weekly, monthly, or yearly cash compensation for work

Both wages and salaries are, in principle, based on the contribution of a particular job to the company. Thus, a sales manager, who is responsible for bringing in sales revenue, is paid more than a secretary, who handles administrative tasks but doesn't sell or supervise. However, pay often varies widely by position, industry, and location. Among the best-paid employees in the world are chief executive officers of large corporations (see the box entitled "Show Me the Money: A Tale of Two Compensation Scales").

Show Me the Money: A Tale of Two Compensation Scales

Compensation has become a hot topic in recent years, at both ends of the pay scale. At the low end, many businesses, employees, and unions are wrestling with the downward pressure on wages, while at the top end, executive compensation has been in the headlines for the opposite reason.

Wal-Mart's huge influence on the economy is undeniable. The company's cost-conscious strategy indirectly affects thousands of people who have never even worked there. In addition to offering lower wages than many traditional grocery and retail stores, Wal-Mart squeezes every possible penny out of operating costs and is quick to import goods from China and other lower-cost countries when domestic suppliers can't meet its demands. As a result, many companies now feel forced to lower their own costs to compete. For instance, as Loblaw, Sobeys, Zellers, and other stores try to compete with Wal-Mart, these retailers feel they have no choice but to cut costs in any way they can (including lower pay and/or fewer benefits). Consumers, particularly low-income shoppers, benefit from Wal-Mart's lower prices, and so do the company's shareholders. However, lower wages also mean Wal-Mart employees are unable to spend more on consumer goods and services, and consumer spending is a major factor in the strength of the economy. As one researcher put it, "You can't have every company adopt a Wal-Mart strategy. It isn't sustainable." Not all of Wal-Mart's competitors are engaging in the "race to the bottom." For example,

Costco is succeeding with a different approach to compensation. Costco offers higher wages and better benefits—and yet still generates better financial results than Wal-Mart's Sam's Club. Costco attributes much of its success to satisfied, motivated employees who are more productive and more eager to help customers.

At the upper end of the pay scale, executive compensation, and the pay of CEOs in particular, has generated its own controversy. CEOs typically receive complex compensation packages that include a base salary plus a wide range of benefits and bonuses, including *golden handshakes* when they join a company and *golden parachutes* when they leave. Part of the controversy stems from the widening gap between CEOs and their employees. A second aspect of the controversy can be traced to the lack of relationship between results and compensation. However, the boards of directors who grant these large packages generally defend them as necessary to retain key executives, but critics respond that many other CEOs earn far less and don't leave in search of greener pastures.[36]

Questions for Critical Thinking

1. How do companies justify decreasing lower-end employee compensation packages while maintaining or even increasing executive compensation packages?

2. What do you think of the "Wal-Mart effect" on the economy? List the positive and negative contributions this company has made.

Incentive Programs

incentives
Cash payments to employees who produce at a desired level or whose unit (often the company as a whole) produces at a desired level

To encourage employees to be more productive, innovative, and committed to their work, many companies provide managers and employees with **incentives**, cash payments that are linked to specific individual, group, or companywide goals; overall productivity; and company success. In other words, achievements, not just activities, become the basis for payment. The success of these programs often depends on how closely incentives are linked to actions within the employee's control.

bonus
A cash payment, in addition to the regular wage or salary, that serves as a reward for achievement

■ *Bonuses.* For both salaried and wage-earning employees, one type of incentive compensation is the **bonus**, a payment in addition to the regular wage or salary. As an incentive to reduce turnover during the year, some firms pay an annual year-end bonus, amounting to a certain percentage of each employee's wages. Other cash bonuses are tied to company performance.

commissions
Payments to employees equal to a certain percentage of sales made

■ *Commissions.* In contrast to bonuses, **commissions** are a form of compensation that pays employees a percentage of sales made. Used mainly for sales staff, they may be either the sole compensation or an incentive payment in addition to a regular salary.

profit sharing
A system for distributing a portion of the company's profits to employees

■ *Profit sharing.* Employees may be rewarded for staying with a company and encouraged to work harder through **profit sharing**, a system in which employees receive a portion of the company's profits. Depending on the company, profits may be distributed quarterly, semiannually, or annually.

These incentive programs are so popular in today's workplace that many employees consider their dollar value as part of their overall salary package.

Employee Benefits and Services

Companies also regularly provide **employee benefits**—financial benefits other than wages, salaries, and incentives. For example, Starbucks offers dental insurance, vacation and holiday pay, stock options, discounts on products, and a free pound of coffee every week. The benefits package is available to part-time as well as full-time employees, which helps the company attract and retain good people at every level.

Companies may offer employee benefits either as a pre-set package—that is, the employee gets whatever insurance, paid holidays, pension plan, and other benefits the company sets up—or as flexible benefits, recognizing that people have different priorities and needs at different stages of their lives. Flexible plans allow employees to pick their benefits—up to a certain dollar amount—to create a benefit package tailored to their individual needs. Moreover, they smooth out imbalances in benefits received by single employees and workers with families.[37] An employee with a young family might want extra life or health insurance, whereas a single employee might choose to "buy" an extra week or two of vacation time by giving up some other benefit.

The benefits most commonly provided by employers are insurance, retirement benefits, employee share-ownership plans, stock options, and family benefits. In the following sections, we will explore how these benefits and services are undergoing considerable change to meet the needs of today's workforce.

employee benefits
Compensation other than wages, salaries, and incentive programs

Insurance

Insurance is the most popular employee benefit. Many businesses offer substantial compensation in the form of life and health insurance, dental and vision plans, disability insurance, and long-term–care insurance. In the past, a company would negotiate a group insurance plan for employees and pay most of the premium costs. However, with insurance premiums and other costs rising faster than employers can raise their own prices, many companies are searching for ways to reduce the financial impact. Perhaps no other issue illustrates the challenging economics of business today than health insurance. Companies are taking a variety of steps, including forcing employees to pick up more of the cost, capping or reducing coverage for retired employees, auditing employees' health claims more carefully, inquiring into employees' health and habits more closely, or dropping spouses from insurance plans. However, workers' earnings aren't increasing fast enough to cover these new expenses, either. The tension is likely to continue, prompting calls for more government intervention, spurring unionizing efforts, and even pitting healthy employees against their less-healthy colleagues.[38] This is especially true in the United States, where universal health care does not exist. Health care costs are also changing the way some employers structure their workforces. More companies are hiring part-time and temporary workers, who typically receive few company benefits, if any. Nonetheless, some companies provide insurance coverage because doing so discourages employee turnover.

Retirement Benefits

The Canada Pension Plan (QPP in Quebec), the Old Age Security program, and the Guaranteed Income Supplement (GIS) were all created by governments to provide basic support to those who could not accumulate the retirement money they would need later in life. The Canada and Quebec Pension Plan is funded by employee contributions and matching employer contributions. If you are self-employed, you pay both portions. The Old Age Security program is funded by the government of Canada from general tax revenues.[39]

In addition to government pension plans, many employees receive company-sponsored retirement benefits. Studies show that 72 percent of workers at large firms (those with more than 500 employees) have some form of company-sponsored retirement coverage.[40] The most popular type of retirement coverage is the **pension plan**, which is funded by company contributions. Each year, enough money is theoretically set aside in a separate pension account to cover employees' future retirement benefits. Unfortunately, that is not always the case (see the Learning from Business Blunders box).

pension plan
A company-sponsored program for providing retirees with income

Defined Contribution Plans versus Defined Benefit Plans In *defined benefit plans* employers typically promise to pay their employees a fixed dollar amount upon retirement,

Learning from Business Blunders

OOPS

Alcan, Nortel, and BCE were all in the top 10 list. Unfortunately, it was not a list they wanted to be associated with. Moody's Investors Service singled out these Canadian companies for having disturbing pension deficits of $3.1, $2.9, and $2.4 billion, respectively. However, these firms were not alone; a study conducted by the Certified General Accountants of Canada indicated that 59 percent of pension plans were running deficits that required $160 billion to cover the difference. In some instances, this dangerous practice has led to some heart-wrenching results when companies go under and employees realize that the pensions they were relying on have disappeared as well.

The growing underfunding problem was receiving headlines from mid-2002 until mid-2005, when ratios of plan assets to liabilities were in the 85 percent range. By 2007, ratios were improving steadily and approaching the 100 percent mark, thanks to improved stock markets

and bond yields and public pressure. For example, Toronto-Dominion Bank turned a $71 million deficit into a $36 million surplus in one year. However, on average the results were still far below previous levels.[41]

WHAT YOU CAN LEARN

Company pension plans will fluctuate with the markets, but many companies have been reminded that they need to be cautious and not get carried away in the good times so they can prepare for the bad times. The spotlight has placed more restrictions on companies, but employees must remember the old saying: "Don't put all your eggs in one basket." Your pension plan is a great potential source of retirement income, but be a wise investor—you still need to make sure that you have a diversified portfolio of your own. There are far too many stories of people who lost it all because of company errors. Don't add your name to the list.

---

based on the employee's retirement age, final average salary, and years of service.[42] For example, a formula could award 2.5 percent of a person's average salary (based on the five best years) to a maximum of 30 years. Based on this formula, an employee would be entitled to 75 percent of his or her salary at the end of 30 years. Defined benefit plans, however, are falling out of favour.[43]

Defined contribution plans are similar to savings plans that provide a future benefit based on annual employer contributions, voluntary employee matching contributions, and accumulated investment earnings. Since securities markets can be unpredictable, the pension amount is more uncertain than in a defined benefit plan. In this case, funds contributed on the employee's behalf along with investment gains are used to buy an annuity that pays the employee a fixed income upon retirement. In recent years, other defined contribution plans have been gaining popularity, such as group RRSPs and deferred profit-sharing plans.[44]

Richard Tucker (left) of Renous, New Brunswick, and Fred Gallant of St. Louis-de-Kent, New Brunswick, walk to their car after protesting the closure of the St. Anne Nackawic pulp mill. Unfortunately, the mill's 400 employees lost their jobs, and many were also shocked to find out that they had lost their pensions after the mill declared bankruptcy and revealed that the pension plan was in financial disarray.[45]

Plans have evolved to accommodate a more mobile workforce, but the shift toward the increased use of defined contribution plans does have some drawbacks. First, they increase the burden on workers to set aside money for retirement and invest it wisely. Second, many employees fail to diversify and instead invest heavily in the employer's stock—subjecting their retirement savings to the fate of one company. Ask former Nortel employees about how millions on paper can be reduced to almost nothing in reality; there are far too many tales to be told.

Registered Retirement Savings Plan   The Registered Retirement Savings Plan (RRSP) was designed as an investment vehicle by the Canadian government to provide individuals added incentive to save their money. Under this plan, the contributor receives tax advantages upon making the purchase. RRSPs entitle investors to deduct their contributions from their taxable income. For example, if Phil earns $60 000 per year and he invests $7000 in an RRSP, he will pay the same amount of taxes as someone in an identical situation who earns $53 000 but does not invest in an RRSP. This investment tool also permits Phil, a 35-year-old man, to watch his savings grow tax free until retirement (likely in about 30 years). RRSPs provide some of the same advantages as company pensions while providing flexibility for the employee.

Employee Share-Ownership Plans

Another employee benefit being offered by a number of companies is the **employee share-ownership plan (ESOP)**, under which a company places a certain amount of its stock in trust for some or all of its employees, with each employee entitled to a certain share. These plans allow employees to later purchase the shares at a fixed price. If the company does well, the ESOP may provide a substantial employee benefit. At Telus, employees are able to invest up to 6 percent of their salaries in company shares, which are then increased by employer contributions. Telus adds $2 for every $5 contributed by an employee. When phone stocks fall, employees feel the pinch, but regardless of the economic trends the goal remains the same: to earn increased equity for the firm and for these very important contributing members of the company.[46] Of course, linking the financial success of employees to the success of the company is indeed a worthy goal, but some say that in the long run ESOPs are not effective performance motivators.

employee share-ownership plan (ESOP)
A program enabling employees to become partial owners of a company

Stock Options

A related method for tying employee compensation to company performance is the stock option plan. **Stock options** grant employees the right to purchase a set number of shares of the employer's stock at a specific price, called the *grant* or *exercise price,* during a certain time period. Options typically "vest" over five years at a rate of 20 percent annually. This means that at the end of one year employees can purchase up to 20 percent of the shares in the original grant, at the end of two years up to 40 percent, and so on. If the stock's market price exceeds the exercise price, the option holder can exercise the option and sell the stock at a profit. If the stock's price falls below the exercise price, the options become worthless, at least temporarily (such options are often referred to as being "under water").

stock options
A contract allowing the holder to purchase or sell a certain number of shares of a particular stock at a given price by a certain date

Stock options can be a win-win situation for employers and employees. From the employer's perspective, stock options cost little, provide long-term incentives for good people to stay with the company, and encourage employees to work harder because they have a vested interest in the company doing well. For example, CIBC World Markets is providing stocks and options to "young performers" to encourage employee loyalty.[47] From the employee's perspective, stock options can generate a handsome profit if the stock's market price exceeds the grant price. But stock options lose their appeal when the stock does not perform as expected. Employees could lose considerable profits if the stock's price falls below the option grant price.[48] Options are particularly common in executive compensation packages where they offer an incentive for effective corporate management. They were also quite popular during the technology boom, when start-ups would frequently lure new employees away with low salaries but thousands of stock options. In the cases where those stocks enjoyed healthy growth, some employees became quite wealthy.

Family Benefits

Government programs have been designed to protect workers and provide mechanisms for meeting family obligations. In Canada, women are entitled to a maternity leave period of one year, whereas American women only receive on average 12 weeks.[49] In Quebec, this benefit is further supported by subsidized daycare that enables parents to have access to $7-a-day childcare centres. In response to growing demands, the federal government created the Universal Child Care Benefit (UCCB) entitling parents with children under six to receive a taxable benefit of $1200 per year per child.[50]

Regardless of current government programs, companies have an important role to play in providing employees with family benefits. For example, the Ford Motor Company plans to open more than a dozen daycare centres providing employees with

CEO Jim Goodnight of SAS Institute (a software development firm) takes a snack break with children at the company's on-site daycare centre.

24-hour childcare—part of a sweeping plan to provide family-related services in more than 30 locations. "Not only will the centres attract and retain the best, but employees, when they're at work, don't have to worry about their children and where they are," says one company spokesperson.[51] Approximately 10 percent of companies provide daycare facilities on their premises, but 86 percent of companies surveyed by Hewitt Associates offer some form of childcare assistance. Types of assistance include dependant-care spending accounts and resource and referral (R&R) services, which help employees find suitable childcare. Firms estimate that they save anywhere from $2.00 to $6.75 in lost productivity and employee absenteeism for every $1.00 they spend on R&R programs.[52]

A related family issue is care for aging parents. An estimated 50 percent of employers offer some form of eldercare assistance, ranging from referral services that help find care providers to dependant-care allowances. Some companies will even agree to move elderly relatives when they transfer an employee to another location.[53]

Other Employee Benefits

Although sometimes overlooked, paid holidays, sick pay, premium pay for working overtime or unusual hours, and paid vacations are important benefits. Companies handle holiday pay in various ways. To provide incentives for employee loyalty, most companies grant employees longer paid vacations after they've been with the organization for a prescribed number of years. Some companies let employees buy additional vacation time or sell unused days back to the employer. Sick-day allowances also vary from company to company and from industry to industry. Some companies have begun offering paid-time-off banks that combine vacation, personal use, and sick days into one package. Employees can then take a certain number of days off each year for whatever reason necessary, with no questions asked.[54]

Companies offer a variety of additional benefits, including sabbaticals, tuition loans and reimbursements, professional development opportunities, personal computers, financial counselling and legal services, assistance with buying a home, paid expenses for spouses who travel with employees, employee assistance programs, nap time, and wellness programs. Typical wellness programs include health screenings, wellness education programs, and fitness programs. Canada Awards for Excellence (handed out by the National Quality Institute) were given to the following companies for providing a healthy workplace: The College of Physicians and Surgeons of Nova Scotia, Pfizer Consumer Healthcare from Markham, Ontario, and Calian Technologies from Ottawa. M&M Meat Shops credits its formal wellness program with keeping employee turnover and absenteeism to a minimum.[55] Company rewards for implementing such programs include reduced absenteeism, health care costs, sickness, and work-related accidents.[56]

employee assistance programs (EAPs)

Company-sponsored counselling or referral plans for employees with personal problems

Employee assistance programs (EAPs) offer private and confidential counselling to employees. EAPs are designed to help with issues related to drugs, alcohol, finances, stress, family, and other personal problems. Studies show that the average annual cost for EAP services runs from $12 to $20 per employee. However, these services save between $5 and $16 for each dollar spent as a result of improved safety and productivity, as well as reduced employee turnover.[57] Magna Corporation offers an EAP to all employees in its family of companies. Its EAP is part of a portfolio of support programs that also includes an Employee Equity Program, a Profit Participation Program, as well as pension and RRSP plans.[58]

Benefits such as company cars, paid country club memberships, free parking, and expanded casual-dress days are often referred to as perks. In a tight job market many companies offer perks to attract the best managers.[59] "But recruitment perks only go so

IN-CLASS NOTES

Administering Compensation and Employee Benefits

- **Compensation:** payments in the form of wages, salaries, incentives, benefits, and services
  - **Wages:** based on the number of hours worked, units produced, etc.
  - **Salaries:** fixed weekly, monthly, or yearly amount; salaried workers normally don't receive overtime pay
  - **Incentives:** payments linked to specific goals (commissions, bonuses, profit sharing)
  - **Employee benefits:** insurance, family and retirement benefits, ESOPs, stock options, etc.

_____

_____

_____

_____

_____

_____

_____

_____

_____

far," says one compensation expert. "Organizations must offer the total work experience to attract talent." To keep talent from leaving, they must offer workers challenging jobs and training, more family-related benefits, and better management supervision.[60]

OVERSEEING CHANGES IN EMPLOYMENT STATUS

L.O. 6

Of course, providing competitive compensation and good employee benefits is no guarantee that employees will stay with the company. Every company experiences some level of **attrition**, when employees leave for reasons other than termination, including retirement, new job opportunities, long-term disability, or death. Virtually all companies also find themselves with the need to terminate employment of selected workers from time to time. When a vacancy occurs, companies must go to the trouble and expense of finding a replacement, whether from inside or outside the company. Overseeing changes in employment status is another responsibility of the human resources department.

attrition
Loss of employees for reasons other than termination

Promoting and Reassigning Employees

As Exhibit 9.3 shows, many companies prefer to look within the organization to fill job vacancies. In part, this "promote from within" policy allows a company to benefit from the training and experience of its own workforce. This policy also rewards employees who have worked hard and demonstrated the ability to handle more challenging tasks. In addition, morale is usually better when a company promotes from within because employees see that they can advance.

However, a potential pitfall of internal promotion is that a person may be given a job beyond his or her competence. As discussed in Chapter 6, a common practice is for someone who is good at one kind of job to be made a manager. Yet managing often requires a completely different set of skills. Someone who consistently racks up the most sales in the company, for example, is not necessarily a good candidate for sales manager. If the promotion is a mistake, the company not only loses its sales leader but also risks losing the employee altogether. People who can't perform well in a new job generally lose confidence in the abilities they do have. At the very least, support and training are needed to help promoted employees perform well.

Terminating Employees

termination
The act of removing an employee through layoff or firing

A company invests time, effort, and money in each new employee it recruits and trains. This investment is lost when an employee is removed by **termination**—permanently laying the employee off because of cutbacks or firing the employee for poor performance. Many companies facing a downturn in business have avoided large-scale layoffs by cutting administrative costs (curtailing travel, seminars, and so on), freezing wages, postponing new hiring, implementing job-sharing programs, or encouraging early retirement. However, sometimes a company has no choice but to reduce the size of its workforce, leaving the human resources department to handle layoffs and their resulting effects on both the terminated and the remaining employees.

layoffs
Termination of employees for economic or business reasons

Layoffs are the termination of employees for economic or business reasons unrelated to employee performance. Companies are free to make layoffs in any manner they choose, just as long as certain demographic groups are not disproportionately affected. But as Michael Dell puts it, making cuts "is one of the hardest, most gut-wrenching decisions you can make as a leader." Layoffs are "an admission that we screwed up" by overhiring, admits Dell. If there's a lesson, says Dell, it's that "when things heat up quite a bit, we should take some pause."[61]

To help ease the pain of layoffs, many companies provide laid-off employees with job-hunting assistance. *Outplacement* aids such as resumé-writing courses, career counselling, office space, and secretarial help are offered to laid-off executives and blue-collar employees alike. Moreover, outplacement centres offer courses and tests to help employees decide what types of jobs are best suited for them.[62] When Levi Strauss & Co. decided to shut down their North American production plants, 1100 Canadian workers in Edmonton and at two Ontario plants, Stoney Creek and Brantford, were left without work. Despite the devastating decision, the company made significant efforts to cushion the impact. Employees were given significant severance packages as well as a transitional payment for job retraining. The company donated $1 million to local educational institutions and community agencies to deal with the layoffs. Self-esteem workshops were heavily attended by both former workers and managers. In Edmonton, concerted organized efforts enabled 105 workers to find new jobs between the time the announcement was made and the day the plant closed. Another 137 were enrolled in retraining programs, 51 retired, 66 were actively seeking a job, and 129 were weighing their options. Despite the decision to move offshore to match its competitor's production costs, Levi acknowledged the contribution of its former employees and showed some compassion.[63] Other companies don't quite send the same message—see the box entitled "You're e-Fired!"

Some companies adopt no-layoff, or guaranteed-employment, policies. This means that in an economic downturn, employees may be shifted to other types of jobs, perhaps at reduced pay, or given the chance to participate in work-sharing programs. Such no-layoff policies help promote employee loyalty and motivation, which benefit the company over the long run.

Retiring Employees

The population is aging rapidly. For the business community, an aging population presents two challenges. The first is to give job opportunities to people who are willing and able to work but who happen to be past the traditional retirement age. Many older citizens are concerned about their ability to live comfortably on fixed retirement incomes. Others simply prefer to work. The second challenge posed by an aging workforce is to find ways to encourage older employees to retire early. Older employees that want to work past 65 have the freedom to do so. Five provinces and three territories in Canada have abolished the mandatory retirement age and pressure is mounting on the

You're e-Fired!

Imagine this scenario: You are sipping your morning coffee and get a message from human resources telling you that you are being let go. It could be followed by a message stating: "Please log off and remove your personal belongings." To add a little insult to injury, there might be a smiley or sad face attached to the end of the message, with words like "Good luck" or "You have been a valuable contributing member" This chapter describes, in great length, the important role of human resources. Company websites are filled with pages that emphasize how much organizations care for the needs of their employees ("People are our number one asset," "Employees are our partners," etc.) The practice of getting the e-boot would seem to indicate otherwise.

That is exactly what happened to 400 employees at Radio Shack, and they're not alone. Some managers who have been overwhelmed with major cuts have taken the short route. In Radio Shack's defence, the company

claimed that they had made announcements at meetings so employees were not caught off guard. The employees themselves used words like "dehumanizing," "cowardly," and "disrespectful." Some things are better said in person, and there is probably nothing more insensitive than receiving bad news via email. Trends catch on quickly in the world of human resources; hopefully this is one that is soon forgotten. Companies must practise what they preach if they are to maintain a good reputation in the long run.[64]

Questions for Critical Thinking

1. How does emailing termination notices affect a company's long-term reputation? Why do you think employees were so upset with Radio Shack for their message?
2. How should companies handle mass layoffs?

---

other provinces to follow.[65] One method a company may use to encourage retirement is to offer older employees financial incentives to resign, such as enhanced retirement benefits or one-time cash payments, called a **worker buyout**. This method can be a lot more expensive than firing or laying off employees. However, it does have several advantages: the morale of the remaining employees is preserved because they feel less threatened about their own security, younger employees see increased chances for promotion, and the risk of age-discrimination lawsuits is minimized.

worker buyout
Distribution of financial incentives to employees who voluntarily depart; usually undertaken to reduce payroll

BEHIND THE SCENES
HR Policies Designed to Avoid Turbulent Labour Issues

WestJet's official mission is to "enrich the lives of everyone in WestJet's world by providing safe, friendly, and affordable air travel." Their vision is to become "one of the five most successful airlines in the world by 2016." Long-term wishes need short-term actions and the right mix of human resources to execute plans. If you examine the company's website, the picture of the ideal job candidate is clearly defined. "WestJetters" are described by terms like fun yet professional; dynamic; cooperative team players with can-do attitudes; or individuals willing to learn and adapt. All of this is summarized in one phrase that describes WestJet's corporate culture: "Not Your Typical Airline—Not Your Typical Job."

Based on their distinct employment expectations it should not be surprising to find out that WestJet believes

strongly in using peer evaluations during the selection process. Choosing the right mix of individuals to join the team is vital to long-term goal attainment. The process often includes group interviews and panel interviews. The panel interview is a pretty standard industry approach in which more than one recruiter interviews a candidate. However, WestJet's group interview process really captures the essence of the company's values. Various candidates are invited to a fun interactive session to enable the company to discover which applicants have what it takes to become a WestJetter.

It is one thing to talk about the important role of employees, but actions and policies speak louder than words. At WestJet, employees enjoy many benefits such as unlimited travel at significantly reduced rates, reduced fares for dependents, and reduced fares with other airlines. These are standard benefits in the airline business. In addition, though, WestJet offers its employees the opportunity to buy a piece of the company's present and future success with its employee share-purchase plan. WestJetters are allowed to contribute up to 20 percent of their wages to the plan, and the company matches every dollar spent by the employees. In other words, an employee buying $10 000 worth of shares is actually getting $20 000 worth. When the company succeeds, the employees benefit greatly and vice versa. As indicated in the opening case, WestJetters won't water your lawn when you are out of town, but they do have an extra incentive to help the company grow. In addition, profit sharing enables employees to get an extra taste of the company's success and can also help reinforce positive behaviour.

Different companies reward their employees in many different ways. To properly recognize employee achievement WestJet created WestJet CARES (CARE stands for "Create a Remarkable Experience"). This program helps managers reward and recognize teams and individuals and is essential for this organization since it aims to create an enthusiastic experience for all of its guests. In addition, WestJet encourages employees to get involved in community initiatives and supports their employees in giving back to society with projects supporting Big Brothers and

Big Sisters of Canada and the CIBC Run for the Cure, to name just two.

WestJet has managed to create a good formula to value employees while simultaneously generating growth. It must not forget the fuel of its founding formula—its employees—as it reaches for even more lofty goals in the future.[66]

Critical Thinking Questions

1. Why would WestJet's human resources managers need to be aware, well in advance, of the company's plans to purchase more planes and open new offices in the upcoming year?

2. What do you think of WestJet's group interview process? Would this approach fit a company like IBM? What are the advantages and disadvantages of the group interview approach?

3. Why does WestJet offer an employee share-purchase plan? What are the disadvantages of this policy?

Learn More Online

Go to Chapter 9 of this text's website at www.pearsoned.ca/bovee and click on the WestJet hotlink. Find the company's latest annual report. How are the results? Did the company continue its growth this year? What does the report say about its workforce initiatives?

TEST YOUR KNOWLEDGE

Questions for Review

1. What are the steps in human resources planning? What are some of the key issues at each stage?

2. What is the purpose of a job description? How is a job description different from a job specification?

3. Describe three forms of incentives commonly offered by employers.

4. What is succession planning?

5. What function does an orientation program serve in both the short and long term?

Questions for Analysis

6. Why is employee retention important to companies? What steps can an organization take to improve its retention rates?

7. Overseeing changes in employment status is an important function of a human resources employee. What is the difference between attrition, layoffs, and worker buyouts?

8. What are the advantages and disadvantages of registered retirement savings plans (RRSP)?

9. **Ethical Considerations.** Corporate headhunters have been known to raid other companies for their top

talent to fill vacant or new positions for their clients. Is it ethical to contact the CEO of one company and lure him or her away to join the management team of another company?

Questions for Application

10. If you were on the human resources staff at a large health care organization that was looking for a new manager of information systems, what recruiting method(s) would you use and why?

11. Assume you are the manager of human resources at a manufacturing company that employs about 500 people. A recent cyclical downturn in your industry has led to financial losses, and top management is talking about laying off workers. Several supervisors have come to you with creative ways of keeping employees on the payroll, such as exchanging workers with other local companies. Why might you want to consider this option? What other options exist besides layoffs?

12. **Integrated.** What are some of the human resources issues managers are likely to encounter when two companies (in the same industry) merge?

PRACTISE YOUR KNOWLEDGE

SHARPENING YOUR COMMUNICATION SKILLS

Visit the HRSDC website (Human Resources and Social Development Canada) at www.hrsdc.gc.ca/en/gateways/topics/yze-gxr.shtml to learn about youth employment. Look through the site in detail and then use the information on this website to write a short memo to your instructor summarizing what you've learned.

BUILDING YOUR TEAM SKILLS

Team up with a classmate to practise your responses to interview questions. Use the list of common interview questions provided in Appendix C (Exhibit C.8) on the website and take turns posing and responding to those questions. Which questions did you find most difficult to answer? What insights did you gain about your strengths and weaknesses by answering these questions? Why is it a good idea to rehearse your answers before going to an interview?

EXPAND YOUR KNOWLEDGE

DISCOVERING CAREER OPPORTUNITIES

If you pursue a career in human resources, you'll be deeply involved in helping organizations find, select, train, evaluate, and retain employees. You have to like people and be a good communicator to succeed in HR. Is this field for you? Using your local newspaper, the *Globe and Mail*, the *National Post*, and online sources such as Monster (www.monster.ca), find ads seeking applicants for positions in the field of human resources.

1. What educational qualifications, technical knowledge, or specialized skills are applicants for these jobs expected to have? How do these requirements fit with your background and educational plans?

2. Next, look at the duties mentioned in the ad for each job. What do you think you would be doing on an average day in these jobs? Does the work in each job sound interesting and challenging?

3. Now think about how you might fit into one of these positions. Do you prefer to work alone, or do you enjoy teamwork? How much paperwork are you willing to do? Do you communicate better in person, on paper, or by phone? Considering your answers to these questions, which of the HR jobs you found seems to be the closest match for your personal style?

DEVELOPING YOUR RESEARCH SKILLS

Locate one or more articles in business journals or newspapers (print or online editions) that illustrate how a company or industry is adapting to changes in its workforce. (Examples include retraining, literacy or basic-skills training, flexible benefits, and benefits aimed at working parents or people who care for aging relatives.)

1. What changes in the workforce or employee needs caused the company to adapt? What did the company do to respond to these changes? Was the company's response voluntary or legally mandated?

2. Is the company alone in facing these changes, or is the entire industry trying to adapt? What are other companies in the industry doing to adapt to the changes?

3. What other changes in the workforce or in employee needs do you think this company is likely to face in the next few years? Why?

STUDY GUIDE

SUMMARY OF LEARNING OBJECTIVES

1. List six main functions of human resources departments

Human resources departments plan for a company's staffing needs, recruit and hire new employees, train and develop employees, appraise employee performance, administer compensation and employee benefits, and oversee changes in employment status.

2. Cite seven methods recruiters use to find job candidates

Recruiters find job candidates by (1) promoting internal candidates; (2) advertising in newspapers and on the Internet; (3) using public and private employment agencies; (4) recruiting at college and university campuses and career placement offices; (5) attending trade shows; (6) hiring corporate "headhunters"; and (7) soliciting referrals from employees or colleagues in the industry.

3. Identify the six stages in the hiring process

The stages in the hiring process are (1) narrowing down the number of qualified candidates; (2) performing initial screening interviews; (3) administering a series of follow-up interviews; (4) evaluating candidates; (5) conducting reference checks; and (6) selecting the right candidate.

4. Discuss how companies incorporate objectivity into employee performance appraisals

Employee performance appraisals are an effective way to inform employees whether they are doing a good job and how they can improve their performance. To ensure objectivity and fairness, most firms use a standard, companywide format, provide a written record of appraisals for future reference, and solicit several perspectives by engaging superiors, peers, and colleagues at different levels in the organization in the review process.

5. Highlight five popular employee benefits

The two most popular employee benefits are insurance (health, life, disability, and long-term care) and retirement benefits like pension plans. Employee share-ownership plans and stock options, two additional benefits, allow employees to receive or purchase shares in the company and thus obtain a stake in the company. Family benefits programs are also popular and include maternity and paternity leave, childcare assistance, and eldercare assistance.

6. Describe four ways an employee's status may change and discuss why many employers like to fill job vacancies from within

An employee's status may change through promotion or reassignment to a different position, termination, voluntary resignation, or retirement. Employers like to fill vacancies created from such changes by promoting from within for these reasons: The employee has been trained by the company and knows the ropes, it boosts employee morale, and it sends a message to other employees that good performance will be rewarded.

KEY TERMS

attrition (285)
bonus (280)
commissions (280)
compensation (279)
electronic performance monitoring (EPM) (278)
employee assistance programs (EAPs) (284)
employee benefits (281)
employee retention (268)
employee share-ownership plan (ESOP) (283)

human resources management (HRM) (267)
incentives (280)
job analysis (270)
job description (270)
job specification (270)
layoffs (286)
orientation (275)
pension plan (281)
performance appraisal (278)
profit sharing (280)

recruiting (270)
replacement chart (268)
salaries (279)
succession planning (268)
stock options (283)
termination (286)
wages (279)
worker buyout (287)

QUESTIONS

Multiple Choice   Circle the correct answer and then check the answers in the back of the book to chart your progress.

1. Which of the following is *not* one of the functions of the human resources department?

   a. Designing new products
   b. Recruiting and hiring the right people
   c. Providing training and development programs for the employees
   d. Developing compensation and other motivational programs

2. Which of the following is *not* an advantage of hiring part-time or temporary workers?

   a. Part-timers or temps can bring flexibility to cover busy periods.
   b. Part-timers are more committed to the long-term success of the company.
   c. Part-time or temp work gives the company and the worker much more information with which to make a permanent hiring decision.
   d. Part-timers and temps generally cost less than full-time, permanent workers.

3. Which document is used in newspaper or Internet advertising so that the job applicants know what they are expected to do?

   a. Job analysis
   b. Job description
   c. Job specification
   d. Job evaluation

4. Which of the following is the least effective source for recruiting new employees?

   a. Promoting from within the company
   b. Hiring from competitors
   c. Hiring recent graduates
   d. Hiring cousins, nieces, or nephews of the president

5. Which of the following is the first step human resources managers take in the human resources planning process?

   a. Estimate the supply and demand for employees
   b. Write job descriptions and job specifications
   c. Place want ads in newspapers and online
   d. Select the best candidate from the individuals that are interviewed

6. Which of the following is *not* an appropriate way to select candidates from the many that may respond to an ad?

   a. A standardized application sheet requiring all candidates to answer the same questions
   b. The hiring manager can interview several candidates, selecting the best
   c. The hiring manager gives the job to the first available candidate that meets the minimum criteria
   d. The human resources specialist checks the references presented by the candidate

7. Which of the following information is *not* typically presented in orientation programs?

   a. Technical skills
   b. Company background
   c. Employee benefit plans
   d. Culture and history

8. Where is the first place an HR manager should look to fill a new job opening?

   a. Online job boards
   b. Resumés received in the last year
   c. Job fairs
   d. Employees

9. Which program enables employees to become partial owners of the company, but it is not shown to be an effective performance motivator?

   a. EAP
   b. ESOP
   c. MRP
   d. RRSP

10. What is the distribution of financial incentives to employees who voluntarily depart called?

    a. Termination
    b. Early retirement
    c. Worker buyout
    d. Employee compensation package

True/False

1. True or False? To ensure a steady supply of experienced employees for new opportunities and to maintain existing operations, successful companies focus heavily on lowering employee turnover.

2. True or False? A job analysis is a document that is given to all potential job candidates and lists the particular tasks involved in the position.

3. True or False? A major problem in any appraisal system is how to calculate the productivity of individual workers when they work together in teams.

4. True or False? To ease the pain of layoffs, many companies provide outplacement services like career counselling.

5. True or False? Some companies use unconventional techniques such as role-play or theatrical improv to test employees.

Fill-in-the-Blank

1. Each company has a number of key employees who are considered critical to the company's operations. HR managers work with top executives to identify potential replacements in the event any of these people need to be replaced, a process known as _____.

2. A _____ is a statement describing the skills, education, previous experience, and personal attributes that job candidates need to possess.

3. _____ are used to objectively evaluate employees according to a specific set of criteria.

4. The _____ process is designed to provide employees with a broader range of perspectives; the process gets feedback from colleagues above, below, and around the employee to provide observations of the person's performance in several skill and behavioural categories.

5. _____, sometimes called *computer activity monitoring*, is used to evaluate customer service and telephone sales representatives by measuring the number of calls they complete per hour and other variables.

6. A _____ is a fixed cash payment for work, usually by yearly amount, that is independent of the number of hours worked.

7. In _____ benefit plans employers typically promise to pay their employees a fixed dollar amount upon retirement based on the employee's retirement age, final average salary, and years of service.

8. _____ grant employees the right to purchase a set number of the employer's shares at a specific price, called the *grant* or *exercise price*, during a certain time period.

9. _____ offer private and confidential counselling to employees; they are designed to help with issues related to drugs, alcohol, finances, stress, family, and other personal problems.

10. Every company experiences some level of _____, when employees leave for reasons other than termination, including retirement, new job opportunities, long-term disability, and so on.

See It on the **WEB**

Visit the Companion Website at **www.pearsoned.ca/bovee**, review the exercises, and complete the following assignments for Chapter 9:
1. Explore the Latest Workforce Management Ideas
2. Staying on Top of the World
3. Maximizing Your Earning Potential

Companion Website

CHAPTER 10

MOTIVATING TODAY'S WORKFORCE AND HANDLING EMPLOYEE-MANAGEMENT RELATIONS

LEARNING OBJECTIVES

After studying this chapter, you will be able to

1   Identify the importance of maintaining a motivated workforce and the key elements behind the various motivational theories

2   Compare Maslow's hierarchy of needs and Herzberg's two-factor theory and explain their application to employee motivation

3   Understand expectancy theory, which is considered by some to be the best description of employee behaviour

4   Discuss three staffing challenges employers are facing in today's workplace

5   Explain the challenges and advantages of a diverse workforce

6   Discuss three popular alternative work arrangements companies are offering their employees

7   Understand the role of unions and the challenges of reaching a collective bargaining agreement in the modern era

8   Cite three options unions can exercise when negotiations with management break down

9   Cite three options management can exercise when negotiations with a union break down

BEHIND THE SCENES

Bombardier: Employee Relations in Good Times and Bad Times

In 1942, J. Armand Bombardier founded a modest company to manufacture tracked transportation vehicles for snow-covered terrain. From these humble beginnings the seeds were planted to create one of the world's largest and most respected transportation companies. Following an initial period of growth that saw the company develop and consolidate its business in the snowmobile industry, Bombardier took a major step forward in 1974 when it expanded its scope of operations—the firm landed a contract to build subway cars for the Montreal metro system. In 1986 the bold move to purchase Canadair launched the firm into the glamorous but tricky aerospace industry. The rise of a Canadian legend was only just beginning, however. The maker of planes, trains, and recreational products enjoyed massive growth from 1985 to 2000 as revenues and profits soared. For example, an investor who bought 1000 shares in Bombardier in 1982 at $10.25 each ($10 250 total) owned 128 000 shares by the end of 2000 after all stock splits were accounted for. When the shares peaked in the $26 range, that initial investment was worth approximately $3.3 million.

Employee Benefits and Demands

Employees were direct beneficiaries of the rise in share price since they were encouraged to participate in generous share ownership plans. Additionally, many assembly workers benefited with systematic overtime pay that allowed shop workers to supplement their income to help the company deal with a huge backlog of aircraft orders. Employees shared in the success of the firm as massive hiring campaigns saw the global employee roster increase to 75 000. This was also achieved through several acquisitions, particularly that of Adtranz, a railcar and engine design company. Despite these perks and because of the rapid growth of the firm, unions began to flex their muscles, eager to earn a larger piece of the growing pie. When times are prosperous, employees are able to put pressure on and succeed in earning concessions from an employer that has time-sensitive orders to fill. However, one question remained: Could wages continue to rise when Bombardier's main rival, Embraer from Brazil, was able to maintain a much lower cost structure and while other low-cost locations like China were battling for a piece of the aerospace assembly business?

Bombardier has come a long way from its humble origins as a manufacturer of Ski-Doos. It is now a powerful global transportation company that produces planes and trains for customers around the world.

Change in the Winds

The next few years would dash the unchecked optimism. The reality check began back in 2000, when financial analysts and investors started asking questions about whether the company could continue to grow at the same rate. Within a year, the September 11, 2001, terrorist attacks occurred and the airline industry fell into a state of depression. This was later compounded by the SARS outbreak. Many airlines faced severe cash problems, leading some to bankruptcy. Bombardier, which makes the majority of its profits from airplane sales, saw its share price fall into a tailspin. The economic crunch forced the company to make drastic changes since it was caught off guard.

By mid-2007 the workforce had been reduced from 75 000 to 56 000 employees with additional employee movement hidden in the total numbers. For example, the electrical harness assembly had moved to Mexico with plans of a new plant and more jobs to follow in the near future. This was a key moment since it signalled the start of a dangerous era for current assembly employees in high-wage countries like Canada, the United States, and the United Kingdom. Bombardier also signed a deal with China Aviation Industry Corporation, which was another symbolic move linked to a low-cost manufacturing shift.

Employee-management relations is a complex topic and extremely difficult to predict in an industry where new products can take a decade to develop but airline demand can change in a matter of months, weeks, or even overnight. For Bombardier to continue to grow for decades to come, it will need to make the right strategic decisions and reconcile with its employee base to recapture the enthusiasm and belief that they all shared just a few years ago.[1]

TEST YOURSELF

Answers to these questions can be found on the website: www.pearsoned.ca/bovee.

1. Why is it so important for Bombardier to maintain positive relations with its employees?

2. What steps can Bombardier take to help maintain morale at its existing North American plants?

3. Bombardier's unions have lost a great deal of their power in recent years. How does this impact their negotiations approach during future collective bargaining rounds?

UNDERSTANDING HUMAN RELATIONS

Employees who maintain high **morale** or a positive attitude toward both their job and organization perform better.[2] But cultivating high morale is an ongoing challenge, in good times and bad. Morale is particularly challenging in a depressed economy or when a specific industry is suffering. Declining share values, plummeting sales, and workforce cutbacks, such as the ones described in the opening case at Bombardier, can result in employee turnover, unscheduled absenteeism, and low morale—all of which can negatively affect a company's productivity and bottom line.[3]

In organizations, the goal of **human relations**—interactions among people within the organization—is to balance the diverse needs of employees with those of management. For instance, employers must motivate employees and keep them satisfied. But they must also remain competitive in the marketplace to ensure the organization's long-term success. Bombardier's decision to lay off about 25 percent of its aerospace workforce was directly related to the near collapse of the airline industry. Achieving this balance becomes increasingly difficult as companies face many staffing and demographic challenges. In this chapter we'll explore these issues.

morale
The attitude an individual has toward his or her job and employer

human relations
The interaction among people within an organization for the purpose of achieving organizational and personal goals

MOTIVATING EMPLOYEES

L.O. 1

Both common sense and formal research suggest that motivated employees are a key to success in every business. You've probably experienced this as a consumer yourself. For instance, when an employee in a retail store seems motivated to make sure you're a satisfied customer, you're likely to keep returning to that store—and to encourage friends and family to shop there as well. Conversely, when employees just don't seem to care, the effect on customers can be just as dramatic in the negative direction, leading to the decline or even collapse of the business.

In fact, making sure that employees are motivated is one of the most important challenges facing every manager. It's also one of the most complex; human beings are complicated creatures to begin with, and today's demanding business environment makes the challenge that much greater. You can start to appreciate the challenge by first exploring what motivation is, then by considering some of the many theories proposed over the years to explain motivation in the workplace.

What Is Motivation?

Motivation is the combination of forces that moves individuals to take certain actions and avoid others in pursuit of individual objectives. The notion of movement is vital here; motivational strategies have little value if they don't translate into action that helps the business enterprise. As you'll see in the following section, a diverse range of

motivation
The force that moves someone to take action

Satisfied, motivated employees tend to be more productive and more effective, leading to higher rates of customer satisfaction and repeat business.

theories attempt to explain motivation. However, every theory or motivational approach needs to consider three key factors:

1. *Need.* The employee senses a need of some sort, from the basic need to earn enough money to buy food, to a need for recognition or self-respect. We are all born with certain needs but can acquire other needs as we grow up, such as a need for achievement, a need for power, or a need to affiliate with compatible friends and colleagues.[4]

2. *Action.* To fulfill the need, the employee engages in actions or behaviours that he or she believes will result in the need being satisfied.

3. *Outcome.* The employee observes the outcome of the action (sometimes called the *reward*) and determines whether the effort was worthwhile. Actions that result in positive outcomes are likely to be repeated; those that result in negative outcomes are less likely to be repeated.

These three factors are an extremely simplified look at the complex issue of motivation, but even from this simple model you can start to grasp the challenges involved. For instance, what if two or more needs conflict, leading to incompatible actions? It's hard to balance the need to relax and have fun with the need to get enough money to pay the rent. Or what if an employee's need for recognition motivates him or her to work hard in the hopes of getting a promotion, but thanks to a tough economy, the company isn't growing and can't offer the promotion? Or what if top management doesn't notice the hard work—or worse yet, credits it to someone else? Think about these three factors the next time you encounter an employee in action. Maybe that customer service representative who wouldn't take the time to help you actually started the job full of desire to help people but soon learned that management rewarded productivity more than customer satisfaction.

Before moving into specific theories, it's important to consider the role of money as a motivator. Money obviously plays a critical role in most everyone's work life, but it is not the ultimate motivator for many people because money often can't compensate for the lack of other satisfying factors. "There's an increasing interest in people finding meaning in their lives and in their work," notes Don Kuhn, the executive director of the International University Consortium for Executive Education. "People are no longer content with income alone. They are looking for personal satisfaction."[5] They want to be part of something they can believe in, something that confers meaning on their work and on their lives. They want to be motivated.[6] This notion seems to be confirmed by a recent poll from Accenture Ltd. that was conducted in 21 countries covering six continents. Challenging and interesting work was the number one criteria listed by candidates seeking a new position.[7]

IN-CLASS NOTES

Motivation and the Workplace

- Maintaining high employee *morale* is key to business success
- *Motivation*: the forces that move people to take certain actions and avoid others
- Motivating employees is a key challenge for every manager
- Motivational theories consider three key elements: *need, action, and outcome*

_____

_____

_____

_____

_____

_____

_____

Theories of Motivation

Motivation has been a topic of interest to managers for more than a hundred years. Frederick W. Taylor was a machinist and engineer who became interested in employee efficiency and motivation in the late nineteenth century. Taylor developed the theory of **scientific management**, an approach that aimed to improve employee efficiency through the scientific study of work. In Taylor's view, people were motivated almost entirely by money, so he set up pay systems that rewarded employees when they were productive. Under Taylor's piecework system, for example, employees who just met or fell short of the quota were paid a certain amount for each unit produced. Those who produced more were paid a higher rate for *all* units produced, not just for those that exceeded the quota; this pay system gave employees a strong incentive to boost productivity.

Although money has always been a powerful motivator, scientific management fails to take into account other motivational elements, such as opportunities for personal satisfaction or individual initiative. Thus, scientific management can't explain why someone still wants to work even though that person's spouse already makes a good living or why a Wall Street lawyer or a Bay Street executive will take a hefty pay cut to serve in government. For example, John McCallum, former minister of national revenue, held the position of chief economist and senior vice-president at the Royal Bank of Canada before entering the political arena.[8] Money was not the driving force behind his decision to enter politics; in fact, it was a deterrent (since he was making much more at the Royal Bank than he could in public service). Therefore, other researchers have looked beyond money to discover what else motivates people. The most widely recognized theories include Maslow's hierarchy of needs, Herzberg's two-factor theory, Theory X and Theory Y, Theory Z, equity theory, and expectancy theory. We'll begin by examining a phenomenon known as the Hawthorne effect.

Like many politicians, John McCallum put aside a lucrative career in order to enter the political arena. His list of experience is lengthy but before this move he was the Chief Economist and Senior Vice-President at the Royal Bank of Canada.

scientific management
A management approach designed to improve employee efficiency by scientifically studying their work

The Hawthorne Effect

A major discovery on human motivation was uncovered in a study initiated in 1924 by Elton Mayo and his colleagues. This famous experiment attempted to measure worker performance at the Hawthorne Western Electric plant, located near Chicago. The initial goal of the study was to examine the effects of lighting, ventilation, and fatigue on employee productivity in the plant.

In one part of the study the researchers selected two groups of employees that were doing similar work under similar conditions and tracked their productivity. After a while they began to increase the lighting in the work environment of one group while keeping the lighting constant for the other group. Each time they increased the level of lighting, worker productivity improved. To determine whether brighter lighting levels led to increased productivity, they began to lower the lighting to measure the reverse effect. *Much to their surprise, the employee productivity continued to rise as the lighting levels were lowered.* The study concluded that the workers were not responding to the lighting variations; instead, they were motivated by the attention they were getting. Test conditions made them feel special and also gave them more freedom from supervisor control. The group was inspired to improve performance by an internal feeling of importance and the feedback and interactions associated with the experiment.[9]

Maslow's Hierarchy of Needs

L.O. 2

In 1943, psychologist Abraham Maslow proposed the theory that behaviour is determined by a variety of needs. He organized these needs into five categories and then arranged the categories in a hierarchy. As Exhibit 10.1 shows, the most basic needs are at the bottom of this hierarchy and the more advanced needs are toward the top. In Maslow's hierarchy, all of the requirements for basic survival—food, clothing, shelter, and the like—fall into the category of *physiological needs.* These basic needs must

Exhibit 10.1   **Maslow's Hierarchy of Needs**

According to Maslow, needs on the lower levels of the hierarchy must be satisfied before higher-level needs can be addressed.

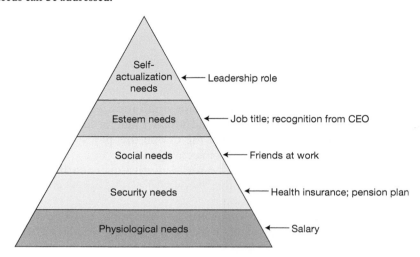

be satisfied before the person can consider higher-level needs such as *safety needs*, *social needs* (the need to give and receive love and to feel a sense of belonging), and *esteem needs* (the need for a sense of self-worth and integrity).

At the top of Maslow's hierarchy is *self-actualization*—the need to achieve one's ultimate potential. This need is also the most difficult to fulfill. Employees who reach this point work not only to make money or to impress others but also because they feel their work is worthwhile and satisfying in itself. Self-actualization needs partially explain why some people make radical career changes or strike out on their own as entrepreneurs.

Although Maslow's hierarchy is a convenient way to classify human needs, it would be a mistake to view it as a rigid sequence. A person need not completely satisfy each level of needs before being motivated by a higher need. Indeed, at any one time, most people are motivated by a combination of needs.

Herzberg's Two-Factor Theory

As briefly discussed in Chapter 9, Frederick Herzberg's two-factor theory was developed in the 1960s after he and his associates undertook their own study of human needs. They asked accountants and engineers to describe specific aspects of their jobs that made them feel satisfied or dissatisfied. Upon analyzing the results, they found that two entirely different sets of factors were associated with satisfying and dissatisfying work experiences: *hygiene factors* and *motivators* (see Exhibit 10.2).

hygiene factors
Aspects of the work environment that are associated with dissatisfaction

motivators
Factors of human relations in business that may increase motivation

What Herzberg called **hygiene factors** are associated with *dissatisfying* experiences. The potential sources of dissatisfaction include working conditions, company policies, and job security. Management can lessen worker dissatisfaction by improving hygiene factors that concern employees, but such improvements seldom influence satisfaction. On the other hand, managers can help employees feel more motivated and, ultimately, more satisfied by paying attention to **motivators**, such as achievement, recognition, responsibility, and other personally rewarding factors. Herzberg's theory is related to Maslow's hierarchy of needs: The motivators closely resemble the higher-level needs, and the hygiene factors resemble the lower-level needs.

According to Herzberg's model, managers need to focus on removing dissatisfying elements (such as unpleasant working conditions or low pay) and adding satisfying elements (such as interesting work and professional recognition). The specific areas to address vary from one situation to the next. A skilled, well-paid, middle-aged employee may be motivated to perform better if motivators are supplied. However, a young, unskilled worker who earns low wages or an employee who is insecure will probably still need the support of strong hygiene factors to reduce dissatisfaction before the motivators can be effective.

Exhibit 10.2   **Two-Factor Theory**

Hygiene factors, such as working conditions and company policies, can influence employee dissatisfaction. On the other hand, motivators, such as opportunities for achievement and recognition, can influence employee satisfaction.

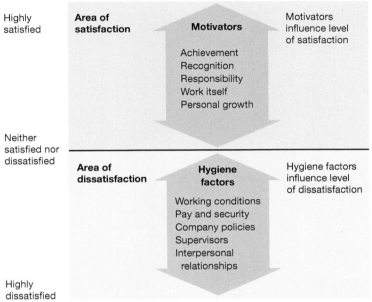

Source: Management, 4th ed., by Richard L. Daft copyright © 1997 by Harcourt Inc., reproduced by permission of the publisher.

McGregor's Theory X and Theory Y

In the 1960s, psychologist Douglas McGregor identified two radically different sets of assumptions that underlie most management thinking. He classified these sets of assumptions into two categories: *Theory X* and *Theory Y* (see Exhibit 10.3).

According to McGregor, **Theory X**–oriented managers believe that employees dislike work and can be motivated only by the fear of losing their jobs or by *extrinsic rewards* such as money, promotions, and tenure. This management style emphasizes physiological and safety needs and tends to ignore the higher-level needs in Maslow's hierarchy. In contrast, **Theory Y**–oriented managers believe that employees like work and can be motivated by working for goals that promote creativity or for causes they believe in. Thus, Theory Y–oriented managers seek to motivate employees through *intrinsic rewards.*

Theory X
A managerial assumption that employees are irresponsible, unambitious, and dislike work; therefore, managers must use force, control, or threats to motivate them

Theory Y
A managerial assumption that employees like work, are naturally committed to certain goals, are capable of creativity, and seek out responsibility under the right conditions

Exhibit 10.3   **Theory X and Theory Y**

McGregor proposed two distinct views of human nature. The assumptions of Theory X are basically negative, whereas those of Theory Y are basically positive.

THEORY X	THEORY Y
1. Employees inherently dislike work and will avoid it whenever possible.	1. Employees like work and consider it as natural as play and rest
2. Because employees dislike work, they must be threatened with punishment to achieve goals.	2. People naturally work towardgoals they are committed to.
3. Employees will avoid responsibilities whenever possible.	3. The average person can learn to accept and even seek responsibility.
4. Employees value security above all other job factors.	4. The average person's intellectual potential is only partially realized.

Source: Douglas McGregor, *The Human Side of Enterprise* (New York: McGraw-Hill, 1960).

IN-CLASS NOTES

Theories of Motivation

- *Maslow's hierarchy of needs*: lower-level needs must be satisfied before shifting focus to higher-level needs
- *Herzberg's two-factor theory*: *hygiene factors* and *motivators* are associated with dissatisfying and satisfying work experiences, respectively
- *Theory X and Theory Y*: managers approach employees based on assumptions. Theory X: negative view/focus on extrinsic rewards; Theory Y: positive view/focus on intrinsic rewards

---

The assumptions behind Theory X emphasize authority; the assumptions behind Theory Y emphasize growth and self-direction. It was McGregor's belief that although some employees need the strong direction demanded by Theory X, those who are ready to realize their social, esteem, and self-actualization needs will not work well under Theory X assumptions.[10]

Ouchi's Theory Z

In the 1980s, when North American businesses began to feel a strong competitive threat from Japanese companies, William Ouchi proposed another approach to motivation that was based on his comparative study of Japanese and North American management practices. His **Theory Z** claims that employees are more motivated if managers involve them in all aspects of company decision making, give them greater responsibility for their own work efforts, and treat them like family. Managers who adopt these practices believe that employees with a sense of identity and belonging are more likely to perform their jobs conscientiously and will try more enthusiastically to achieve company goals.[11]

Equity Theory

Equity theory contributes to the understanding of motivation by suggesting that employee satisfaction depends on the perceived ratio of inputs to outputs. If you work side by side with someone, doing the same job and giving the same amount of effort, only to learn that your colleague earns more money than you, would you be satisfied in your work and motivated to continue working hard? You perceive a state of *inequity*, so you probably won't be happy with the situation. In response, you might ask for a raise, decide not to work as hard, try to change perceptions of your efforts or their outcomes, or simply quit and find a new job; any one of these steps could bring your perceived input/output ratio back into balance.[12] In the aftermath of large-scale layoffs in many sectors of the economy in the past few years, many of the employees left behind feel a sense of inequity in being asked to handle extra work, without getting paid more for the extra effort.[13] Equity also plays a central role in many unionizing

Theory Z
A human relations approach that emphasizes involving employees at all levels and treating them like family

equity theory
A theory that suggests employees base their level of satisfaction on the ratio of their inputs to the job and the outputs or rewards they receive from it

Learning from Business Blunders

OOPS

In a move that is not unusual when a company is struggling, American Airlines CEO Donald Carty asked the company's unions for $1.8 billion in wage and benefit sacrifices, explaining that the company was on the edge of bankruptcy. His plea was successful—until the unions learned that at the same time Carty was asking them to accept pay cuts, he had arranged generous bonuses for top executives and a $40 million plan that would protect their pensions in case the company did in fact slide into bankruptcy. Union leader John Ward expressed what many union members probably felt: "It's the equivalent of an obscene gesture from management." The unions agreed to the pay cuts on the condition that Carty resign, which he did.

WHAT YOU CAN LEARN

The American Airlines pay situation is a classic example of equity theory in action. When most employees know the company is in trouble, they're willing to accept some short-term pain in exchange for keeping their jobs, but they expect everyone in the company to suffer equally. (In contrast to Carty's actions, executives in several other companies in recent financial trouble have reduced or even eliminated their own salaries, and a few have even given back bonuses previously earned.) Carty landed on his feet and was recently named vice-chairman and chief financial officer of Dell; but the lesson from his former employees was clearly delivered.[14]

efforts, whenever employees feel they aren't getting a fair share of corporate profits or are being asked to shoulder more than their fair share of hardships (see the Learning from Business Blunders box).

Expectancy Theory

L.O. 3

Expectancy theory, considered by many experts to offer the best available explanation of employee motivation, links an employee's efforts with the outcome he or she expects from that effort. Like equity theory, expectancy theory focuses less on the specific forces that motivate employees and more on the process they follow to seek satisfaction in their jobs. Expectancy theory expands on earlier theories in several important ways, including linking effort to performance and linking rewards to individual goals (see Exhibit 10.4). The effort employees will put forth depends on (1) their expectations about their own ability to perform; (2) their expectations about the rewards that the organization will give in response to that performance; and (3) the attractiveness of those rewards relative to their individual goals.[15]

expectancy theory
A theory suggesting that employees effort depends on expectations about their own ability to perform, expectations about the rewards that the organization will provide, and the attractiveness of those rewards relative to individual goals

Exhibit 10.4   Expectancy Theory

Expectancy theory suggests that employees base their efforts on expectations of their own performance, expectations of rewards for that performance, and the value of those rewards.

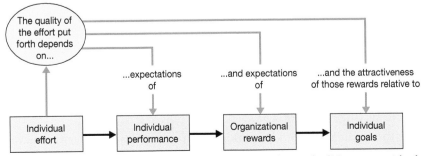

Source: Adapted from Stephen P. Robbins and David A. DeCenzo, *Fundamentals of Management*, 4th ed. (Upper Saddle River, NJ: Prentice Hall, 2004), 289.

IN-CLASS NOTES

Theories of Motivation

■ **Theory Z:** emphasizes treating employees like family and on employee involvement

■ **Equity theory:** employee satisfaction is based on the perceived ratio of inputs to outputs. Key question: Am I being treated fairly?

■ **Expectancy theory:** links employee effort with outcomes. Effort depends on (1) ability to perform, (2) expected rewards, (3) attractiveness of rewards

_____

_____

_____

_____

_____

_____

_____

Imagine that you're a carpenter assigned to a home remodelling project. If you don't think you have the skills necessary to do an absolutely perfect job on the kitchen cabinets (maybe you specialize in framing, not finish work), or you do have the skills but you don't think your boss will reward you for putting in the extra effort, or you don't know what level of performance is expected from you, your motivation may suffer. Or perhaps you do have the skills and the boss will recognize your efforts with a cash bonus, but you'd rather receive an extra day off to spend with your family. Expectancy theory points out several areas in which motivation can suffer and so gives managers more insight into how to successfully motivate employees.

Motivational Strategies

Once managers have some idea of what motivates—or demotivates—employees, they can create policies and procedures that attempt to keep workforce morale at a productive level. The range of motivational decisions managers face is almost endless, from redesigning jobs to making them more interesting to offering recognition programs for high achievers. (You'll read more about some of these decisions later in this chapter, in the section on alternative work arrangements.) Even in professions that have a reputation for poorly motivated workers, creative and committed managers can foster environments that motivate employees and contribute to business success. DIRECTV, the US–based satellite service provider, exceeds the industry average rate of customer satisfaction. The strong results are based on a motivational strategy that emphasizes seven key points:[16]

■ Encouraging enthusiasm for the products the company sells

■ Listening to employees' complaints and suggestions

■ Giving workers the tools they need and the authority to make decisions

■ Making the job seem cool (including inviting celebrities into the customer service centre)

■ Keeping workers busy (for instance, computer-based training lessons pop up on their screens when they don't have customer calls to answer)

■ Giving them some freedom in working with customers rather than making them follow rigid procedures

■ Helping employees reach personal goals (such as offering tuition reimbursement)

Being good to employees is good for business. Higher customer satisfaction scores translate to greater customer loyalty. Whether it's a basic award program for salespeople or an entirely new way to structure the workforce, though, every motivational strategy needs to consider two critical aspects: setting goals and reinforcing behaviour.

Setting Goals

As mentioned earlier, successful motivation involves action. To be successful, that action needs to be directed toward a meaningful goal. Accordingly, **goal-setting theory** suggests that goals can motivate employees. The process of setting goals is often embodied in a technique known as **management by objectives (MBO)**, a companywide process that empowers employees and involves them in goal setting and decision making. This process consists of four steps: setting goals, planning actions, implementing plans, and reviewing performance (see Exhibit 10.5). Because employees at all levels are involved in all four steps, they learn more about company objectives and feel that they are an important part of the companywide team. Furthermore, they understand how even their small job function contributes to the organization's long-term success.

One of the key elements of MBO is a collaborative goal-setting process. Together, a manager and employee define the employee's goals, the responsibilities for achieving those goals, and the means of evaluating individual and group performance so that the employee's activities are directly linked to achieving the organization's long-term goals. Jointly setting clear and challenging—but achievable—goals can encourage employees to reach higher levels of performance.

goal-setting theory
A motivational theory suggesting that setting goals can be an effective way to motivate employees

management by objectives (MBO)
A motivational approach in which managers and employees work together to structure personal goals and objectives for every individual, department, and project to mesh with the organization's goals

Exhibit 10.5   **Management by Objectives**

The MBO process has four steps. This cycle is refined and repeated as managers and employees at all levels work toward establishing goals and objectives, thereby accomplishing the organization's strategic goals.

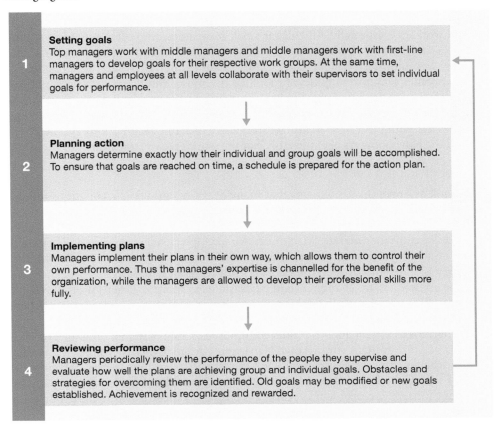

1 **Setting goals**
Top managers work with middle managers and middle managers work with first-line managers to develop goals for their respective work groups. At the same time, managers and employees at all levels collaborate with their supervisors to set individual goals for performance.

2 **Planning action**
Managers determine exactly how their individual and group goals will be accomplished. To ensure that goals are reached on time, a schedule is prepared for the action plan.

3 **Implementing plans**
Managers implement their plans in their own way, which allows them to control their own performance. Thus the managers' expertise is channelled for the benefit of the organization, while the managers are allowed to develop their professional skills more fully.

4 **Reviewing performance**
Managers periodically review the performance of the people they supervise and evaluate how well the plans are achieving group and individual goals. Obstacles and strategies for overcoming them are identified. Old goals may be modified or new goals established. Achievement is recognized and rewarded.

reinforcement theory
A motivational approach based on the idea that managers can motivate employees by influencing their behaviours with positive and negative reinforcement

behaviour modification
The systematic use of rewards and punishments to change human behaviour

Reinforcing Behaviour

Employees in the workplace, like human beings in all aspects of life, tend to repeat behaviours that create positive outcomes. **Reinforcement theory** suggests that managers can motivate employees by controlling or changing their actions through **behaviour modification**. Managers systematically encourage those actions that are desirable by providing pleasant consequences, and discourage those that are undesirable by providing unpleasant consequences.

Positive reinforcement offers pleasant consequences (such as a gift, praise, public recognition, bonus, dinner, or trip) for completing or repeating a desired action. Experts recommend the use of positive reinforcement because it emphasizes the desired behaviour rather than the unwanted behaviour. By contrast, *negative reinforcement* allows people to avoid unpleasant consequences by behaving in the desired way. For example, fear of losing a job (unpleasant consequences) may move an employee to finish a project on time (desired behaviour). Such negative motivation, however, is much less effective than encouraging an individual's own sense of direction, creativity, and pride in doing a good job.

Managers and the organizations they represent in today's global economy take a variety of approaches to motivation, some more enlightened than others. However, all these managers face the challenge of motivating a workforce that is diverse, dynamic, and at times demanding, as you'll see in the following section.

KEEPING PACE WITH TODAY'S WORKFORCE

Today's managers lead the efforts of diverse groups of individuals and recognize that all employees have interests and obligations outside of work, such as family, volunteer activities, and hobbies. Addressing employees' many needs becomes even more critical in a work environment plagued with a number of staffing challenges.

L.O. 4

Staffing Challenges

If you ask business leaders what their biggest challenges are today, you will most likely get the following answers: finding, attracting, and keeping talented people; rightsizing their workforces; and satisfying employees' desire for a work–life balance.[17] Finding and keeping good workers is especially difficult for small companies, who often trail bigger companies in salary, benefits, job security, and other criteria that lead workers to choose one company over another. This is exactly the situation facing Polywheels Manufacturing Ltd., an Oakville, Ontario, supplier, of moulded thermoset and thermoplastic reinforced composite products for a variety of industries including the auto sector. The company is having a difficult time attracting robotics technicians. The supply is limited and potential employees are going to larger manufacturers like Ford and Magna. This problem will worsen if the baby boomers begin to truly exit the workforce in large numbers.[18]

Shortage of Skilled Labour

A close look at Appendix C confirms that many of today's growing occupations require specialized skills or training, whereas the shrinking occupations involve activities that require fewer skills or ones that are increasingly being automated. In fact, nearly all jobs today require computer literacy. Machinists, for example, need computer skills to operate chip-controlled equipment. Even package delivery involves data entry. But finding technology-literate employees is difficult for most companies today.

Some companies are changing rigid pay systems to make it easier for employees to move laterally and enhance their skills. Others are installing new career development programs to help employees plan their career moves. Still others are instituting educational programs to attract and keep skilled employees. Cisco Systems, a manufacturer of computer network routers, runs its own Networking Academy. This in-house vocational program teaches students how to build and manage the computer-server networks the company sells. Cisco hopes that eventually the students will return to the company for permanent jobs.[19] The problem is real and companies must learn to cope. For more information on this topic, see the box entitled "Too Many Workers? Not For Long."

Too Many Workers? Not For Long

Focused on today's labour problems, most companies aren't looking too far around the bend. But when they do, they're in for some big surprises. According to demographers and economists, labour shortages—especially of skilled employees—will become a central issue for companies looking to acquire and retain staff. Companies in Canada and the rest of the industrialized world will face an unprecedented problem. As the baby boomers (people born between 1947 and 1966) retire, the labour pool will have trouble keeping up. In 2001, a report by the Conference Board of Canada indicated that the baby-boom generation made up 47 percent of the labour force. By 2010 the projected retirements will create shortages, especially in areas of technology, health care, and manufacturing.

The problems become clearer when we examine specific scenarios. John Murphy, executive vice-president of human resources at Ontario Power Generation (OPG), faced the following issue: the average age of his workforce was 45 and he projected that the organization would need to replace more than a quarter of its 11 000 staff members within five years. Many of these individuals were top-level engineers and managers who would be taking valuable skill sets with them.

Japan, with one-fifth of the population already over 65, has already begun to feel the effects of this demographic nightmare. The government is stepping up its campaign to maintain the workforce with initiatives to increase the retirement age from 60 to 65 and with programs to encourage more women to join the workforce or to stay home and have more babies. Improved maternity benefits and tax breaks for growing families appear to be just the beginning.

While a labour shortage presents tremendous hurdles for employers, it brings opportunity for employees. A slower-growing workforce could indeed shift the balance of power to workers, forcing employers to hike wages, add daycare centres, increase flexible work hours, provide more training, and develop innovative ways to attract and retrain existing employees. RBC Financial Group accommodates its diverse employees by promoting growth initiatives; each year 12 000 members of the 70 000 workforce move to new positions they find through internal postings. Additionally, as the projected shortages become clearer, older workers could suddenly take on value as a skilled pool of labour. At RBC Financial Group, retirees can work part time for up to 30 months without incurring a penalty on their pension.

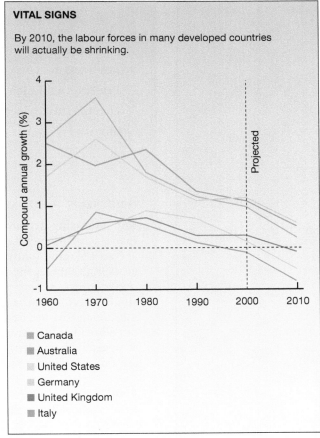

VITAL SIGNS

By 2010, the labour forces in many developed countries will actually be shrinking.

- Canada
- Australia
- United States
- Germany
- United Kingdom
- Italy

Source: Data taken from Watson Wyatt Worldwide.

In Canada, the problem is compounded when you consider that about 40 000 skilled individuals leave the country every year for other opportunities or better pay in the United States or abroad. Bottom line: Employers that refit the work environment to appeal to both young and old, experienced and inexperienced, native and immigrant workers will end up in the best position. But they must begin making such changes now by training and recruiting valuable human resources.[20]

Questions for Critical Thinking

1. Why do experts predict a skilled-labour shortage in the near future?
2. What can employers do to prepare for a future skilled-labour shortage?

Exhibit 10.6	The Committed Employee—Then and Now

Employee loyalty isn't what it used to be. A survey confirmed that even today's most valuable committed workers often put career development and life and family issues ahead of company goals. This chart illustrates this shift in workforce commitment.

CHARACTERISTIC	THEN	NOW
Attachment to employer	Long term	Near term
Readiness to change jobs	Not interested	Not looking (but will listen)
Priorities on the job	The firm and its goals	Personal life and career
Devotion to employer goals	Follows orders	Buys in (usually)
Motto	Always faithful	Seize the day

Rightsizing

The increasing demand for educated workers and the continuing conversion from a manufacturing-based economy to a service-based economy (as discussed in Chapter 1) are also forcing many companies to adjust their workforces into business growth areas, a practice generally known as *rightsizing*. Although rightsizing often involves *downsizing*—reducing the workforce, sometimes by thousands of employees in a single move—companies often add other workers even while they eliminate some jobs. Such was the case at Hewlett-Packard when the company shed marketing jobs but added new positions in consulting and sales. "In many cases, companies are trying to upgrade their talent," says one human resources expert.[21] In a few cases, companies are simply trying to reduce costs.

Employee Loyalty As you can imagine, rightsizing is a contributing factor to declining employee loyalty. Devastated by the lack of job security, employees quickly learn to "do what's best for me," as Exhibit 10.6 shows.[22] For some, that means putting job security and a long-term financial future ahead of finding challenging work. Public affairs specialist Yara Lizarraga didn't even consider looking for another job when her employer Agilent Technologies asked her to take a 10 percent pay cut. "If I said it didn't hurt, I'd be lying," says Lizarraga, "but I'm just so grateful to have a job."[23]

Today's employees have more realistic expectations. They recognize that the old idea of a paternal company taking care of employees has, for the most part, died. Despite these altered expectations, job uncertainty is a major source of stress and employees are challenged to deal with the ambiguities of the modern work environment.[24] They realize that companies are going to do whatever they have to do to succeed and survive. This may mean manufacturing in South America, eliminating three layers of management, closing down plants, or cutting salaries and perks.[25] Even the Japanese tradition of lifetime employment is under attack. After years of severe economic recession and intense global competition, the Japanese are realizing that unconditional loyalty is becoming too expensive to justify. To remain competitive, Japanese companies are chipping away at their seniority-based management system and are forcing executives to perform or go—bringing Japan a little closer to the North American model.[26]

While many individuals acknowledge the forces of the global economy, not all employees are willing to look at the company's bottom line and be understanding when they are losing a job that they worked hard to establish. As Bombardier continued to announce layoff after layoff, many remaining employees were looking at seniority lists and becoming concerned, frustrated, angry, or depressed. This sort of situation can lead to bizarre behaviour regardless of the business environment. For some individuals this can lead to a lessened sense of belonging and frequent surfing of job sites like Monster.ca. For others faced with uncertainty, employee loyalty crosses the lines of ethics and leads to minor criminal activity. Many people begin to believe that they are entitled to take something of value to compensate for their loss. The theft can range from minor office supplies to inventory to misappropriated funds.[27]

Employee Burnout   Rightsizing is also putting pressure on remaining employees to work longer hours. When 3M spun off its data storage and medical imaging divisions, some employees began working 80-hour weeks. One 3M customer service consultant summed up the feelings of many employees when he said, "I always perceived work to be a means to an end, but not *the* end."[28] Others are working longer hours just to keep up. "It seems like you work, work, work," says one chemist.[29]

On average, workers are putting in 260 more hours a year than a decade ago—many without overtime pay.[30] Such long hours can lead to *employee burnout*, which is characterized by emotional exhaustion, depersonalization, and lower levels of achievement. Severe burnout or stress may even lead to clinical depression.[31] Other sources of employee burnout are job insecurity, technological advancements, and information overload:

- *Job insecurity.* Workers anxious about job security feel they have to give more or risk being seen as expendable. Practices that were once considered crises-mode workloads have now become business as usual. These extra hours, which don't always bring extra pay, can leave employees feeling burned out and resentful.[32]

- *Technological advancements.* New technology allows employees to work from home, but being wired to the office 24 hours a day can add extra pressure. Employees feel compelled to answer that voice mail or email whatever the hour. "We have all these great tools to save our time," notes one career expert, "instead, it just extends our week. We're never out of touch anymore."[33]

- *Information overload.* Managers claim they're unable to handle the vast amounts of information they now receive. In fact, more information has been produced in the last 30 years than in the previous 5000, and the total quantity of printed material is doubling every five years—and accelerating.[34]

How does burnout affect the ability of workers to do their jobs? "When you feel under stress, you find your mental wheels spinning and you work mechanically rather than creatively," says one human resources expert. "The tasks that normally would take a few minutes sit unfinished for days because you lose the capacity to prioritize and you put off larger, important projects that take more energy and concentration."[35]

Quality of Work Life

A recent survey found that 42 percent of all job seekers identified work–life issues as the most important consideration in their choice of a new job. For some employees the primary work–life issue is caring for an elderly parent; for others it is childcare, rising college tuition costs, or a desire to return to school part time.[36] Regardless, achieving a work–life balance is especially difficult when both parents work or in situations where downsizing and restructuring have left remaining employees with heavier workloads than in the past.

To help employees balance the demands of work and family, businesses are offering childcare assistance, family leave, flexible work schedules, telecommuting, and other solutions that are explored later in this chapter. Many companies are also focusing on improving the **quality of work life (QWL)**, the environment created by work and job conditions. Dofasco is going the extra mile and providing mental wellness questionnaires to address work-related stress and improve QWL.[37] Hewlett-Packard is addressing the fundamental problems of how much time a job really demands and how to build a life beyond work by encouraging employees to set leisure goals and focus on developing their personal lives. As Hewlett-Packard knows, an improved QWL benefits both the individual and the organization. Employees gain the chance to use their specialized abilities, improve their skills, and balance their lives. The organization gains a more motivated and loyal employee.[38]

Two common ways of improving QWL are through **job enrichment**, which reduces specialization and makes work more meaningful by expanding each job's responsibilities, and **job redesign**, which restructures work to provide a better fit between employees'

quality of work life (QWL)
The overall environment that results from job and work conditions

job enrichment
Reducing work specialization and making work more meaningful by adding to the responsibilities of each job

job redesign
Designing a better fit between employees' skills and their work to increase job satisfaction

skills and their jobs. Quality of work life can be improved in other ways, too. Many organizations are providing their employees with a number of benefits designed to help them balance their work with personal responsibilities. Pepsi has an on-site dry cleaning drop-off at its New York headquarters, and Hewlett-Packard has sponsored schools at company sites that allow employees to visit their children during lunchtime and after school. All of these measures can improve employees' lives by freeing up their time and by making work a more enjoyable place to be.[39] See the box entitled "Chuckle While You Work" for another way companies are trying to make the workplace more enjoyable.

Demographic Challenges

The workforce is always in a state of demographic change, whether from a shift in global immigration patterns or from the changing balance of age groups within a country's population. The companies that are most successful at managing and motivating their employees take great care to (1) understand the diversity of their workforces and (2) establish programs and policies that both embrace that diversity and help employers take full advantage of diversity's benefits.

L.O. 5

Workforce Diversity

The Canadian workforce is diverse in race, gender, age, culture, family structures, religion, sexual orientation, mental and physical ability, and educational background—and will become even more diverse in the years ahead. Smart business leaders recognize the competitive advantages of diverse workforces: They bring a broader range of

Chuckle While You Work

Lighten up. Let loose. Laugh a little. Experts are now advising managers to make company-sponsored fun a fundamental part of work. That's because after experiencing more than a decade of restructuring, downsizing, and re-engineering, employees could use a laugh or two. In fact, a recent survey of 1300 corporate managers showed that more than 60 percent disagreed with the statement "I have fun at work these days."

"Because we spend more of our waking hours working than doing anything else, fun should be a very fundamental part of work," notes one expert on human behaviour. In fact, workplace fun is increasingly important because today's jobs are more insecure and more competitive than they once were. Furthermore, camaraderie is diminishing as employees spend more and more time relating to machines than to each other; they often eat lunch at their desks, or they work from home.

Although traditional business wisdom says that people having fun on the job are probably slacking off, studies show that a happy workforce is also a productive one. For one thing, a little wisecracking and laughs can go a long way toward relieving stress. Moreover, fun can raise a company's bottom line by improving health, reducing absenteeism, boosting morale, building teamwork, releasing creativity, improving productivity, and increasing enthusiasm. So while the pursuit of fun may seem frivolous to the serious-minded, more and more

companies are beginning to see the value of a good hearty laugh or a little giggle now and then.

Take Sprint, for example. Recent company-sponsored fun days encouraged employees to wear clothes backwards and to go on a photo safari with disposable cameras, taking candid photos of other employees. At Lands' End—voted as one of the best places to work—employees can participate in the company's "Cruise Room," where reps can enjoy calypso music and fruit punch on their breaks. Other companies have organized employee costume parties, hosted goofy birthday celebrations, and sponsored fun-filled weekends at hotels. Still others are lifting the workplace spirit by hanging funny signs and posters in offices, holding a messiest desk contest with prizes, and posting comic strips and snapshots on company bulletin boards. These companies and others recognize that if work is fun, people will want to come to work. "Our people are our most important assets," says one executive. "We try to make work a fun place where they can stay as long as they want and get excellent benefits."[40]

Questions for Critical Thinking

1. Under which level of Maslow's hierarchy of needs would you place having fun at work?
2. Would a manager who promoted workplace fun be Theory X– or Theory Y–oriented?

viewpoints and ideas, they help companies understand and identify with diverse markets, and they enable companies to tap into the broadest possible pool of talent. On the other hand this diversity means that employees have a wide range of traditions, backgrounds, experiences, outlooks, and attitudes toward work—all of which can affect employee behaviour on the job. Supervisors face the challenge of communicating with these diverse employees, motivating them, and fostering cooperation and harmony. Teams face the challenge of working together closely, and companies are challenged to coexist peacefully with business partners and with the community as a whole. Some of the most important diversity issues include the globalization of the workforce, the aging workforce, gender equality, and sexual harassment.

The Globalization of the Workforce   For many companies, both large and small, managing the workforce is now an international challenge, whether it involves offshoring work to other countries (see Chapter 8) and hiring employees to establish operations in other countries, or hiring workers who have immigrated to Canada from other countries. The western and northern Europeans who made up the bulk of immigrants during the nation's early years now share space with people from across Asia, Africa, Eastern Europe, and other parts of the world. Nor is this pattern of immigration unique to Canada. Workers from Africa, Asia, and the Middle East are moving to Europe in search of new opportunities, while workers from India, the Philippines, and Southeast Asia contribute to the employment base of the Middle East.[41]

Canada has been a nation of immigrants from the beginning, and that trend continues today. Thirteen to fourteen percent of the Canadian population are visible minorities. This figure is expected to increase to 20 percent by 2017. Approximately 37 percent of Toronto and Vancouver citizens are visible minorities. Calgary is next on the list at 17 percent, with Edmonton, Winnipeg, Ottawa, and Montreal in the 12 to 14 percent range. Seventy-three percent of new immigrants are visible minorities. Stats like these make it is easy to see the importance of these various groups to the continued growth of the nation. Many of these individuals come to Canada with tremendous academic and work experience but face an uphill battle to find employment equivalent to their skills.[42]

Aging Population   As previously described, the population is aging. This situation creates new challenges and concerns for employers and employees alike. Working Canadians between 60 and 79 already contribute more than $2.2 billion in income tax payments each year.[43] Experts predict that because of inadequate pensions and a general desire to stay active, many baby boomers will put off retirement until they are in their seventies. While this could help solve the problems of upcoming labour shortages, there are other issues to be considered. Older, more experienced employees command higher salaries. "For my salary, the company could hire two twenty-somethings," says a 41-year-old worker. "I'm good at what I do. But am I better than two people? Even I know that's not true." Not only do older employees earn more, but the costs of employee benefits such as medical insurance and pensions rise with age as well.[44] Furthermore, as the rate of change speeds up, it can be difficult for older employees to keep up unless they have the stamina of a 25 year old.

On the other hand, older employees provide certain advantages to employers. They have more experience and are usually more seasoned decision makers. They are also more likely to show up on time and less likely to quit. But these traits pale by comparison with the highly desired traits characteristic of younger workers, who appear more flexible, more adaptable, more accepting of new technology, and better at learning new skills.[45]

As baby boomers reach retirement age, the role of mature employees will grow in all aspects of the labour force from part-time positions as retail clerks to corporate career extensions.

glass ceiling
An invisible barrier attributable to subtle discrimination that keeps women (and minorities) out of the top positions in business

sexism
Discrimination on the basis of gender

sexual harassment
Unwelcome sexual advances, requests for sexual favours, or other verbal or physical conduct of a sexual nature within the workplace

Gender Equality   One of the most significant diversity issues in gender equality is avoiding sexism by assuring equal opportunities and equal pay for women in the work-force. Even though women have made tremendous advances, only seven heads of Fortune 500 companies are women.[46] In Canada, only 19 of the top 500 companies have female leaders and only 14.4 percent of corporate officer positions are occupied by women.[47] Canadian women ranked gender as the number-one factor hindering their career advancement, while men placed it thirteenth out of 15.[48] Some attribute this inequality to the *glass ceiling.*

The Glass Ceiling   An invisible barrier that keeps women and minorities from reaching the highest-level positions in organizations is referred to as the **glass ceiling**. One theory suggests that top management has long been dominated by white males who tend to hire and promote employees who look, act, and think as they do. Another theory holds that stereotyping by male middle managers leads them to believe that family life will interfere with a woman's work. As a result, women are relegated to less visible assignments in the company, so their work goes unnoticed by top executives and their careers stagnate.[49] Many women, like many men, decide to self-impose career limitations to address family concerns and quality of life. However, unlike men, the remaining female labour pool has been stereotyped into a companywide limiting mindset.[50] Legislation such as the *Employment Equity Act* is placing legal parameters on companies to eliminate systematic discrimination.

At a recent summit to celebrate Canada's most powerful women, Rose Patten, senior executive vice-president of human resources and head of office strategic management at BMO, was honoured. In the banking sector, BMO leads the way in this regard with women now comprising 35 percent of the company's executives. This represents a dramatic change since 1990 when only 9 percent of these positions were held by women. But despite these gains the Canadian banking industry has yet to see its first female CEO.[51]

In recent years women have made significant strides toward overcoming **sexism**, or job discrimination on the basis of gender. These steps have been achieved thanks to a combination of changing societal attitudes and company commitments to workplace diversity. Such initiatives include long-term commitments to hiring more women, company-sponsored networking and career planning for women, diversity training and workshops, and mentoring programs designed to help female employees move more quickly through the ranks. Pitney Bowes's long-term commitment to diversity, for instance, has resulted in women holding 5 of the top 11 jobs at the company. The initial appointment of Carly Fiorina as CEO of Hewlett-Packard (HP) was hailed by many as a milestone for women. Despite her departure, women account for more than a quarter of HP's managers; it seems that the glass ceiling at this company has been shattered.[52]

Sexual Harassment   Another sensitive issue that women and men face in the workplace is **sexual harassment**, which takes two forms: the obvious request for sexual favours with an implicit reward or punishment related to work, and the more subtle creation of a sexist environment in which employees are made to feel uncomfortable by off-colour jokes, remarks, and posturing. Even though male employees may also be targets of these practices and both male and female employees may experience same-sex harassment, sexual harassment of female employees by male colleagues continues to make up the majority of reported cases.

With all the focus on this issue in recent years, you might think that the problem is diminishing. However, according to the Canadian Human Rights Commission the numbers of complaints are actually increasing.[53] Is this because more people are stepping forward? Is this a sign that many people still don't get the message? To put an end to sexual harassment, companies are now enforcing strict harassment policies. Recent court rulings explain how all employers—large and small—can protect themselves from potential sexual harassment lawsuits. In short, a company can defend itself successfully if it can prove that it had an effective policy against sexual harassment in place and that the employee alleging harassment failed to take advantage of this policy. To be effective, the policy must be in writing, must be communicated to all employees, and must be

enforced.[54] This means that the company must train all employees on the policy, and the company must have clear procedures for reporting such behaviour—including allowing employees access to management beyond their supervisors. Without such policies, companies can be held indirectly responsible for a harasser's actions even when top managers had no idea that such practices were going on.[55]

Diversity Initiatives   To cope with increasing workforce diversity, many companies offer employees sensitivity or awareness training to help them understand the various attitudes and beliefs that minorities and immigrants bring to their jobs. These classes also help managers become more sensitive to the behaviour and communication patterns of employees with diverse backgrounds.

Besides the immigrant populations, Aboriginal peoples are an important segment with unique needs to be considered. In Saskatchewan, Aboriginal people will account for 20 percent of the population by 2015.[56] The Canadian Imperial Bank of Commerce (CIBC) is supporting the creation of an employee-driven diversity network designed to support its 400 native staff members across the country. Procter & Gamble offers a two-day "diversity training" course to all its employees. "Their 2000 Canadian-based employees are actively encouraged to participate in a dozen or so cultural events produced each year for the employees." P&G also offers a prayer room to accommodate people of various faiths on-site.[57]

Although encouraging sensitivity to employee differences is important, a company stands to benefit most when it incorporates its employees' diverse perspectives into the organization's work. This enables the company to uncover new opportunities by rethinking primary tasks and redefining markets, products, strategies, missions, business practices, and even cultures. Western Union's Canadian marketing team is a prime example of a firm that has embraced diversity and gone well beyond inclusion. In fact, among the key members of this national marketing team are individuals from China, India, Colombia, Poland, the Philippines, and one natural-born Canadian. These individuals bring valuable knowledge of their communities and support a network

---

 IN-CLASS NOTES

Workforce Diversity

- **Globalization of the workforce** is a result of offshoring, hiring employees to establish operations in other countries, and new immigrants
- **The aging population** creates challenges as many baby boomers are set for retirement, which may lead to severe worker shortages
- **Gender equality** includes avoiding *sexism* by assuring equal opportunities and equal pay for women in the workforce while addressing the *glass ceiling* and *sexual harassment*

of 3000 "ethnic agents." Diversity can be an important asset, and one challenge of corporate human relations is to make the most of this asset. Companies are starting to get the message. For example, the Royal Bank of Canada has created a Diversity Leadership Council, led by the company's CEO, to move the issue forward.[58]

Alternative Work Arrangements

L.O. 6

To meet today's staffing and demographic challenges, many companies are adopting alternative work arrangements. Three of the most popular arrangements are flextime, telecommuting, and job sharing. Many organizations find that a mix of these arrangements and other employee benefits works better than a one-size-fits-all approach.[59]

Flextime

flextime
A scheduling system in which employees are allowed certain options regarding time of arrival and departure

An increasingly important alternative work arrangement, **flextime** is a scheduling system that allows employees to choose their own hours within certain limits. For instance, a company may require everyone to be at work between 10:00 a.m. and 2:00 p.m., but employees may arrive or depart whenever they want as long as they work a total of eight hours every day. Another popular flextime schedule is to work four, 10-hour days each week, taking one prearranged day off (see Exhibit 10.7).[60] Of course, flextime is more feasible in white-collar businesses that do not have to maintain standard customer service hours. For this reason, it is not usually an option for employees on production teams, in retail stores, or in many offices where employees have to be on hand to wait on customers or answer calls.

The sense of control employees get from arranging their own work schedules is motivating for many. Companies have found that flextime reduces turnover, enables the company to adapt to business cycles, allows operation of a round-the-clock business, and helps maintain morale and performance after re-engineering or downsizing. Still, flextime is not without drawbacks. They include supervisors who feel uncomfortable and less in control when employees are coming and going, and co-workers who resent flextimers because they assume that people who work flexible hours don't take their jobs seriously enough.[61]

Telecommuting

telecommuting
Working from home and communicating with the company's main office via computer and communication devices

Telecommuting, or *telework*—working from home or another location using computers and telecommunications equipment to stay in touch with colleagues, suppliers,

---

Exhibit 10.7   **Nine-to-Five Is Not for Everyone**

For many full-time employees and independent contractors, their degree of job satisfaction is closely linked to the availability of the following job conditions or attributes.

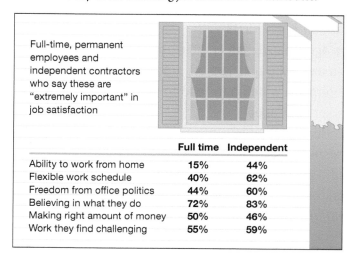

Full-time, permanent employees and independent contractors who say these are "extremely important" in job satisfaction

	Full time	Independent
Ability to work from home	15%	44%
Flexible work schedule	40%	62%
Freedom from office politics	44%	60%
Believing in what they do	72%	83%
Making right amount of money	50%	46%
Work they find challenging	55%	59%

and customers—provides another dimension of flexibility. Approximately 10 percent of Canadians telecommute, but many of them are only able to do so one or two days a week.[62] Some two-thirds of Fortune 1000 companies now offer telecommuting arrangements to at least some of their employees.[63] Telecommuting is on the rise around the world; Europe is now home to over 20 million teleworkers as well.[64]

Companies such as AT&T, IBM, and Lucent Technologies provide employees with laptops, dedicated phone lines, software support, fax-printer units, help lines, and full technical backup at the nearest corporate facility. Some even provide employees who work at home with a generous allowance for furnishings and equipment to be used at their discretion.[65] Still, some company operations clearly are not designed for telecommuting. For example, a printer who runs giant colour presses cannot run the presses from home. But for other jobs that can be performed from remote sites, telecommuting helps meet employees' needs for flexibility while boosting their productivity as much as 20 percent.[66]

Telecommuting offers many advantages. For one thing, it can save companies money by eliminating offices people don't need, consolidating others, and reducing related overhead costs.[67] Telecommuting also enables a company to hire talented people in distant areas without requiring them to relocate. This benefit expands the company's pool of potential job candidates because employees who have an employed spouse, children in school, or elderly parents to care for are reluctant to move.[68] Employees also like telecommuting because they can set their own hours, reduce job-related expenses like commuting costs, and spend more time with their families. Telecommuting can also raise outputs and morale by disconnecting employees from unproductive environments in the office, such as noisy working conditions.

Telecommuting does have potential limitations. One of the most commonly expressed concerns is work–life balance, with employees struggling to shut down their work lives so they can participate in their home lives. Some managers struggle with a perceived loss of control over employees they can't see. Others are concerned that people working at home will slack off (although some studies show that telecommuters actually work *more* hours, not fewer) or that telecommuting could cause resentment among office-bound colleagues or weaken company loyalty.[69] Some companies find that the lack of face-to-face communication hurts decision making, in spite of the best technology available. Accel, a venture-capital firm based in London, England, has cut down on its use of telecommuting because "we were becoming dysfunctional," in the words of one partner.[70]

To see if employees are truly compatible with this style of working, and to prepare them and their managers for the transition, Merrill Lynch requires prospective telecommuters to submit a detailed proposal that covers when and how they're going to work at home and even what their home office will look like. Next, they participate in a series of meetings. Finally, they spend two weeks in a simulation lab that lets employees and their managers experience the change. Once at home, telecommuters are required to document their at-home working hours and submit weekly progress reports.[71]

Genius Babies, seller of educational toys, allows workers like Michelle Donahue-Arpas to telecommute so she can spend more time with her daughter.

Job Sharing

Job sharing, which lets two employees share a single full-time job and split the salary and benefits, has been slowly gaining acceptance as a way to work part-time in a full-time position. According to a survey by Hewitt Associates, a firm specializing in employee benefits, 37 percent of employers offer job-sharing arrangements to their employees.[72] But such arrangements are usually offered to people who already work for the company and who need to cut back their hours. Rather than lose a good employee or have to find and train someone new, the company finds a way to split responsibilities.

job sharing
Splitting a single full-time job between two employees for their convenience

Technologies That Are Revolutionizing Business

TELECOMMUTING TECHNOLOGIES

In its simplest form, telecommuting doesn't require much more than a computer, a telephone, and access to the Internet and email. However, most corporate employees need a more comprehensive connection to their offices, with such features as secure access to confidential files, groupware (see Chapter 5), and web-based virtual meetings that let people communicate and share information over the Internet. Some of the other technologies you'll encounter in telecommuting include broadband Internet connections (cable, DSL, or satellite), some form of file access (including shared workspaces), security (including user authentication and access control), Internet-based telephones, and wireless networking.

HOW THEY'RE CHANGING BUSINESS

When they're used successfully, telecommuting technologies can reduce real estate costs, put employees closer to customers, reduce traffic and air pollution in congested cities, give companies access to a wide range of independent talent, and let employees work in higher-salary jobs while living in lower-cost areas of the country. In the future, these technologies have the potential to change business so radically they could even influence the design of entire cities. With less need to pull millions of workers into central business districts, business executives, urban planners, and political leaders have the opportunity to explore such new ideas as *telecities*—virtual cities populated by people and organizations who are connected technologically rather than physically.[73]

WHERE YOU CAN LEARN MORE

Start with the Telework Coalition, www.telecommute .org. Companies that supply hardware, software, and services for telecommuting often have information as well; see Cisco Systems (www.cisco.com), AT&T (www.att.com), and AgilQuest (www.agilquest.com) for examples.

In addition to alternative work arrangements, companies are looking for new ways to motivate employees and retain quality individuals. At Merck Frosst Canada, new mothers get their maternity benefits topped up to 100 percent by the company for the first 18 weeks. Some companies let moms on maternity keep the company car. With labour shortages looming, it pays to be creative.[74]

IN-CLASS NOTES

Alternative Work Arrangements

- *Alternative work arrangements* can help reduce turnover, recruit new candidates, and reduce overhead costs
- *Flextime* allows employees to choose their own hours within certain limits
- *Telecommuting* allows employees to work from home or communicate through a home office
- *Job sharing* is the splitting of a full-time job between two or more employees

WORKING WITH LABOUR UNIONS

L.O. 7

Today's employees want alternative work arrangements in addition to safe and comfortable working conditions and sufficient pay. At the same time, however, business owners must focus on using company resources to increase productivity and profits. In the best of times and in the most enlightened companies, these two sets of needs can often be met simultaneously. However, when the economy slows down and competition speeds up, balancing the needs of employees with those of management can be a challenge.

Because of this potential for conflict, many employees join **labour unions**, organizations that seek to protect employee interests by negotiating with employers for better wages and benefits, improved working conditions, and increased job security. Historically, labour unions have played an important role in Canadian employee-management relations and are largely responsible for the establishment of worker's compensation, child-labour laws, overtime rules, minimum-wage laws, severance pay, and more. Employees are most likely to turn to unions if they are deeply dissatisfied with their current job conditions and if they believe that unionization can be helpful in improving those conditions.

One advantage of joining labour unions is that it gives employees stronger bargaining power. By combining forces, union employees can put more pressure on management than they could as individuals. During the most prosperous years at Bombardier, unions were able to pressure the company into providing various wage- and work-related concessions. Still, not all employees support labour unions. Many believe that unions hurt employee initiative and are not necessary to ensure fair treatment from employers.

Many companies that have successfully resisted unionization seem to have adopted participative management styles and an enhanced sense of responsibility toward employees. Others have used every legally available tactic to avoid unionization (see the box entitled "Wal-Mart and the U-Word"). Marriott International has recognized that the primary reasons employees consider unionizing is because they feel they are not treated well by management. To demonstrate to workers that they are valued, Marriott offers its employees stock options, social service referral networks, daycare, training classes, and opportunities for advancement. As a result, Marriott's employee turnover is well below that of most companies, and its employees' enthusiasm is high.[75] But even good working conditions are no guarantee that employees won't seek union representation. For instance, although Starbucks is renowned for its generous employee benefit programs and supportive work environment, employees of stores in Vancouver, British Columbia, organized and successfully bargained for higher wages.[76]

labour unions
Organizations of employees formed to protect and advance their members' interests

The Collective Bargaining Process

As long as a union has been recognized as the exclusive bargaining agent for a group of employees, its main job is to negotiate employment contracts with management. In a process known as **collective bargaining**, union and management negotiators work together to create the human resources policies that will apply to the unionized employees—and other employees covered by the contract—for a certain period, usually three years.

Most labour contracts are a compromise between the desires of union members and those of management. The union pushes for the best possible deal for its members, and management tries to negotiate agreements that are best for the company (and the shareholders, if a corporation is publicly held). Exhibit 10.8 illustrates the collective bargaining process.

collective bargaining
A process used by unions and management to negotiate work contracts

Meeting and Reaching an Agreement

When the negotiating teams made up of representatives of the union and management actually sit down together, they state their opening positions and each side discusses its

Wal-Mart and the U-Word

Wal-Mart—the world's largest company—has long resisted unionization. Sam Walton, who founded the firm, believed that unions are divisive and unnecessary, especially in light of Wal-Mart's benefits and open-door policy. All Wal-Mart employees are encouraged to voice their complaints and recommendations to management. Additionally, Wal-Mart keeps on top of workplace issues by conducting regular surveys to measure employee contentment. To keep employees motivated, store managers are given authority to solve problems, stock clerks are promoted to managerial positions, and all workers are encouraged to participate in the company's stock ownership plan. Of course, this is the company's perspective.

On the other side of the debate, many would argue that Wal-Mart simply wants to control its employees and will do anything in its power to destroy union initiatives and keep wages low. Canadian outlets are leading the fight to unionize the company in North America. A store in Jonquière, Quebec, was the first Wal-Mart outlet in North America to unionize. The company began negotiations on the first contract with the union, but Wal-Mart warned that the store was unprofitable and that an unfavourable deal would force the company to close it.

A few months later, after some initial talks, Wal-Mart announced that it was closing the outlet. To thwart other unionization attempts, the company has gone to the Quebec Court of Appeal to fight a certification in Gatineau, and a store in Saint-Hyacinthe shortly after that.

In Weyburn, Saskatchewan, a drive to unionize an outlet has led to a lengthy fight in court and a promise by the company to take its appeal all the way to the Supreme Court of Canada if necessary. It followed through on the promise, but the Supreme Court sided with previous rulings. This after the Saskatchewan Labour Relations Board decided to force Wal-Mart to hand over certain documents that were used to squash union drives. Among the controversial papers was an internal managerial manual entitled "Toolbox to Remaining Union Free."[77]

Questions for Critical Thinking

1. Why are Wal-Mart executives so concerned about the potential unionization of a couple of stores in Canada?
2. What can employers do to help reduce the chances that their employees will unionize?

Exhibit 10.8   **The Collective Bargaining Process**

Contract negotiations go through the four basic steps shown here.

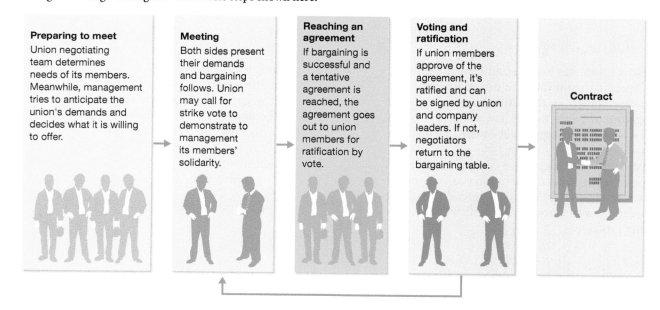

Preparing to meet
Union negotiating team determines needs of its members. Meanwhile, management tries to anticipate the union's demands and decides what it is willing to offer.

Meeting
Both sides present their demands and bargaining follows. Union may call for strike vote to demonstrate to management its members' solidarity.

Reaching an agreement
If bargaining is successful and a tentative agreement is reached, the agreement goes out to union members for ratification by vote.

Voting and ratification
If union members approve of the agreement, it's ratified and can be signed by union and company leaders. If not, negotiators return to the bargaining table.

Contract

position point by point. Unions usually want additions to the current contract. In a cooperative atmosphere, the real issues behind the demands gradually come to light. For example, management may begin by demanding the right to determine the sizes of work crews when all it really wants is smaller work crews; the union, however, wants to protect the jobs of its members and keep crew sizes as large as possible, but may agree to certain reductions in exchange for, say, higher pay. After many stages of bargaining, each party presents its package of terms, and any gaps between labour and management demands are then dealt with.

If negotiations reach an impasse, outside help may be needed. The most common alternative is **mediation**—bringing in an impartial third party to study the situation and make recommendations for resolution of the differences. Mediators are generally well-respected community leaders whom both sides will listen to. However, mediators can only offer suggestions, and their solutions are not binding. When a legally binding settlement is needed, the negotiators may submit to **arbitration**—a process in which an impartial referee listens to both sides and then makes a judgment by accepting one side's view. In *compulsory arbitration*, the parties are required by a government agency to submit to arbitration; in *voluntary arbitration*, the parties agree on their own to use arbitration to settle their differences.

Exercising Options When Negotiations Break Down

The vast majority of management-union negotiations are settled quickly, easily, and in a businesslike manner. Nevertheless, sometimes negotiations reach an impasse when neither side is willing to compromise. Both labour and management are able to draw on many powerful options when negotiations or mediation procedures break down.

Labour's Options Strikes and picket lines are perhaps labour's best-known tactics, but other options are also used.

- *Strike.* The most powerful weapon that organized labour can use is a **strike**, which refers to a temporary work stoppage aimed at forcing management to accept union demands. The basic idea behind a strike is that, in the long run, it costs management more in lost earnings to resist union demands than to give in. If the union has leverage, the tool can be effective. UPS's 3800 Canadian workers went on strike, effectively halting operations in the country and disrupting operations in the United States right before the holiday rush. Two days later the company and the union reached an agreement.[78] However, strikes are a risky proposition and can lead to lengthy, costly disputes. Workers at a Quebec-based aluminium smelter refinery, jointly owned by Alcoa and Alcan, learned that lesson the hard way. The work stoppage lasted for more than five months, even though the strike was costing employees valuable wages and the owners $21.5 million per month.[79] An essential part of any strike is **picketing**, in which union members positioned at entrances to company premises march back and forth with signs and leaflets, trying to persuade non-striking employees to join them and to persuade customers and others to stop doing business with the company.

- *Boycott.* A less direct union weapon is the **boycott**, in which union members and sympathizers refuse to buy or handle the product of a target company. Millions of union members form an enormous bloc of purchasing power, which may be able to pressure management into making concessions.

- *Publicity.* Increasingly, labour is pressing its case by launching publicity campaigns, often called *corporate campaigns*, against the target company and companies affiliated with it.

mediation
A process for resolving a labour contract dispute in which a neutral third party meets with both sides and attempts to steer them toward a solution

arbitration
A process for resolving a labour contract dispute in which an impartial third party studies the issues and makes a binding decision

L.O. 8

strike
A temporary work stoppage to pressure management to accept the union's demands

picketing
A strike activity in which union members march in front of company entrances to protest against an employer

boycott
A union activity in which members and sympathizers refuse to buy or handle the product of a target company

Aliant workers demonstrate their displeasure with management by chanting and picketing to get attention and rally support for their demands in a recent work dispute.

These campaigns might include sending investors alerts that question the firm's solvency, staging rallies during peak business hours, sending letters to charitable groups questioning executives' motives, handing out leaflets that describe safety and health code violations, and stimulating negative stories in the press.

Labour's other options include *slowdowns*, in which employees continue to do their jobs but at a snail's pace, and *sickouts*, in which employees fake being sick and stay home. Both can cripple a company. On one occasion, United Airlines was forced to cancel more than 20 000 flights during the peak summer travel months because company pilots refused to fly overtime hours and called in sick to protest the slow pace of contract negotiations.[80]

L.O. 9

Management's Options   As powerful as the union's tactics are, companies are not helpless when it comes to fighting back. Management can use a number of legal methods to pressure unions when negotiations stall:

■ *Strike-breakers.* In most jurisdictions, when union members walk off their jobs management can legally replace them with **strike-breakers**, non-union workers hired to do the jobs of striking workers (union members brand them as "scabs"). British Columbia and Quebec are the only two jurisdictions in North America that make this practice illegal. Although managers can take on the responsibilities of unionized workers, the firm cannot hire strike-breakers. Newfoundland and Labrador is currently considering adopting a similar law, whereas Ontario instituted and quickly overturned an anti-scab law in the 1990s.[81]

strike-breakers
Non-union workers hired to replace striking workers

lockouts
A management tactic in which union members are prevented from entering a business to force union acceptance of management's last contract proposal

■ *Lockouts.* During a **lockout**, management prevents union employees from entering the workplace to pressure the union to accept a contract proposal. A lockout is management's version of a strike. It is a pre-emptive measure designed to force a union to accept management's demands. Lockouts are legal only if the union and management have come to an impasse in negotiations and the employer is defending a legitimate bargaining position. Hockey fans are all too familiar with this tactic. Despite billionaire owners and millionaire players, an entire NHL season was cancelled because of a lockout.[82]

 IN-CLASS NOTES

Meeting and Reaching and Agreement

■ *Collective bargaining* usually results in a signed agreement without major headlines

■ When negotiations break down, each side has options:
  ■ *Union options*: strike, boycott, publicity, slowdowns, sickouts
  ■ *Management options*: strike-breakers, lockouts, injunctions

■ If negotiations are at an impasse, the parties may need the help of an *arbitrator* or a *mediator*

■ *Injunctions.* An **injunction** is a court order prohibiting union workers from taking certain actions. Management used this weapon without restriction in the early days of unionism, when companies typically sought injunctions to order striking employees back to work on the grounds that the strikers were interfering with business. Today, injunctions are legal only in certain cases. Union-government negotiations have often ended with court proceedings ordering workers back to work under threat of severe consequences such as lost seniority or dismissal.

injunction
A court order prohibiting certain actions by striking workers

The Labour Movement Today

Unions remain a significant force in employee-management relations in Canada. However, the shift from a manufacturing-based economy to one dominated by service industries has created challenges for unions that have watched manufacturing jobs outsourced to other low-cost nations, thus weakening their traditional base. Women, young workers, and highly skilled workers have been harder to organize with traditional methods, as have workers in less hierarchical organizations.[83] Even though unions are sticking to their traditional causes—good wages, safe working conditions, and comprehensive benefits—some progressive, realistic labour leaders are pursuing new workplace issues such as job security, increasing health care costs, labour involvement in management decisions, childcare, and more job training.[84]

The current climate contains some interesting contrasts. According to the Conference Board of Canada, in the next few years we will see more collaboration between management and labour in the private sector. A case in point, at Bombardier unions have been forced to deal with labour cuts as the industry suffers. However, the unions are acting as important lobbyists to gain government aid for the new C-Series line of planes. At the other extreme, public-sector negotiations between unions and governments are expected to be quite confrontational.[85] What does the future hold for employee-management relations? It is difficult to make predictions. But many experts agree that today's global economic conditions severely limit the ability of unions to regain the strength they once had. This is the case both in Canada and in other industrialized countries. Two major issues that have changed the relationships are the rising costs of health care and the threat of international competition.

■ *Health care costs.* By just about any measure, health care costs are spiralling out of control, climbing much faster than the general inflation rate, which has a huge impact on insurance premiums and overall company payments. These costs have become a major point of contention in labour negotiations, with employers saying that employees need to pay a larger share of health care costs and employees saying they can't afford to. This has been a huge issue in the auto sector, with companies like GM suffering from a heavy expense load as a result of an aging workforce and massive roster of retired employees. Ford recently reached an agreement with the Canadian Auto Workers in which it offered up to $125 000 plus a $30 000 voucher for a new Ford vehicle to buyout workers who also agreed to give up future health benefits. The move was aimed at keeping layoffs to a minimum, but it helps highlight the issue of health care costs.[86]

■ *International competition.* In industries that face vigorous international competition, such as the auto sector, steel, and aircraft, some union and business leaders are trying to work more cooperatively than they have in the past. In the steel industry, for instance, union leaders have made significant concessions and even helped arrange the consolidation of battered steel companies in the hopes of competing more effectively with overseas suppliers.[87]

Both health care costs and international competition are staggeringly complex challenges with no clear solutions, but attempts to solve them may well influence the progress of unions in the coming years.

Ford offered a buyout plan to workers who retire; the company was aiming to eliminate health care costs for those employees who took the deal.

IN-CLASS NOTES

The Labour Movement Today

- The shift from a manufacturing-based to a service-based economy has hurt unions
  - Manufacturing jobs have been outsourced to low-cost nations
  - Female, young, and highly skilled workers are harder to organize
- More collaboration between management and unions is expected, especially in the private sector
- Two major issues going forward are health care costs and international competition

_____

_____

_____

_____

_____

_____

_____

_____

BEHIND THE SCENES

Bombardier's Adjusted Flight Plans

On again, off again, on again . . . In mid-2007, after years of restructuring and adjusting to a new market order, Bombardier still had important decisions to make. Management, employees, and union leaders were facing a new challenge that would have major repercussions on staff, investors, suppliers, and government officials. The decision was still up in the air whether or not Bombardier would build its long promised (110–130 seat) C-Series planes with an estimated price tag of $2 billion in development and an additional $1 billion in other launch costs. The proposed target date had shifted from 2010 to 2013. In addition, other questions remained: Where would the planes be built? Could Bombardier compete with its main competitor, Embraer, without this series of planes? Was it risking a fight with Boeing and Airbus if it began building larger airplanes?

While important questions awaited answers one thing was certain: employee-management relations had long ago lost the joyful innocence that came with massive plane backlogs, overtime pay, and rising share prices. How could the company maintain morale with its long-established

employees? What did the future hold for established workers in places like Montreal, Toronto, Belfast, and Wichita? Would they benefit from projected growth in larger regional jets, or would it just mean that the workforce would stabilize while new jobs shifted to Mexico and eventually China?

Between 2003 and 2005 the string of cuts seemed endless across the various established plants. More recently the news has not been any more pleasant. At the end of 2006, with sales of its 70–90 seat regional jets slumping, the company announced that it was laying off another 1330 employees in 2007–08 as it lowered production from 75 to 65 and eventually to 50 units per year for this line. In essence production was reduced from one plane every three days to one plane every five days.

Optimistic Partners?

After seeing the electrical harness division shift to Mexico it must have been a difficult moment for employees and union leaders to watch the company sign a deal with state-owned China Aviation Industry Corporation (AVIC). The deal provides AVIC with $100 million to build its five-abreast ARJ21-900 project. It was a symbolic move that, upon closer examination, gave a shot in the arm to the long-promised C-Series project, which could greatly benefit current employees. As part of the deal, $400 million was pledged by AVIC for research and development, and new equipment and facilities for the proposed C-Series plane. The new facilities were worrisome but, in the same speech, CEO Laurent Beaudoin announced that the final assembly would still take place in Canada and that the Canadian, Quebec, and British governments would still support the project—with a few additional negotiations to come.

This case demonstrates the complicated issues in employee-management relations, especially in the world of aerospace. How can unions protect jobs and the company remain profitable? Is it a good idea to partner with a state-owned Chinese company? Beyond the investment, we are talking about a huge potential market that could lead to important business for years to come. If Bombardier avoids this move, a competitor may jump at the opportunity and Bombardier risks becoming an outsider in an incredible market. But what message does it send to employees? The answer is: a mixed one. An important step was taken to fund the C-Series project (a big launch order from a major airline is the long-awaited final step), which will help assembly workers here in Canada—about 2500 jobs are projected in the Montreal plant alone. But the fear of Chinese manufacturing outsourcing is still very real. However, with governments providing funds to keep jobs in the economy, boost the image of the nation, and help support sub-industries like plane parts suppliers, those manufacturing jobs are probably

secure. Are you confused yet? If you like black-and-white questions with clear solutions you will not be happy trying to analyze this one. However, now you understand a bit more about the complicated world of employee-management relations in the global market. Read newspaper headlines for the latest twists as this saga continues.[88]

Critical Thinking Questions

1. In this chapter we have examined employee loyalty and burnout. How do these concepts apply to Bombardier's recent staffing policies?

2. Do you believe that it is inevitable that many or most of the assembly jobs will end up being outsourced to China or other locations abroad?

3. Bombardier's decision to build the C-Series is a major issue for its workforce. As key stakeholders, what role can the firm's employees play in the process?

4. Do you think Bombardier should proceed with the C-Series project? List the pros and cons. How do you think Boeing and Airbus will respond if Bombardier moves forward with the C-Series project?

Learn More Online

Log on to the Bombardier website at www.bombardier.com. How many workers does Bombardier currently employ? Have any additional cuts been made? How is the C-Series project progressing? Have there been any recent employee-management issues? Has Bombardier engaged in any collective bargaining with its unions in the past year? What were the results? How much are Bombardier's shares worth today?

TEST YOUR KNOWLEDGE

Questions for Review

1. Herzberg's two-factor theory identifies two entirely different sets of factors that lead to satisfying and dissatisfying work experiences. What are they? Explain.

2. How can an organization improve the overall quality of work life (QWL) to improve employee motivation?

3. What is meant by telecommuting? What are the advantages and disadvantages of this practice from an employer's perspective? From an employee's perspective?

4. What tactics can management use to put pressure on a union?

5. What factors lead to employee burnout?

Questions for Analysis

6. There are various motivational theories, but they all consider three key elements: needs, actions, and outcomes. Explain Maslow's hierarchy of needs with these three elements in mind.

7. Compare and contrast equity theory and expectancy theory. Which theory seems to make the most sense from your point of view? Discuss this with a classmate.

8. What is the difference between mediation and arbitration?

9. Why do employees choose to join labour unions? Why would they not want to join a labour union?

10. **Ethical Considerations.** You have a golf game scheduled for Sunday afternoon, and you've worked all weekend to write a proposal that will be presented on Monday morning. The proposal is more or less finished, but a few more hours of work would make it polished and persuasive. Do you cancel the game?

Questions for Application

11. Some of your talented and hardworking employees come to you one day and say they do not feel challenged. They want to be able to diversify their skills more and take on greater responsibility than they currently have. How do you respond?

12. Assume you are the plant manager for a company that manufactures tires for cars and light trucks. To compete more economically in the global marketplace, the company is seriously considering closing the plant within the next year and moving manufacturing operations to Southeast Asia. Upon hearing about the possible plant closing, the union votes to launch a strike in one week if its demands for job security aren't met. Because of a recent surge in orders, the company is not in a position to close the plant yet. What are your options as you continue to negotiate with union representatives? Which option would you choose and why?

13. **Integrated.** How do economic concepts such as profit motive and competitive advantage (see Chapter 1) affect today's workforce?

14. **Integrated.** Why is it difficult for small businesses to allow employees to telecommute, share jobs, and work flexible hours?

PRACTISE YOUR KNOWLEDGE

SHARPENING YOUR COMMUNICATION SKILLS

As the director of public relations for a major airline on aspect of your job is to prepare news releases should the pilots decide to strike. This is a challenging task because many people will be affected by a strike. Being a good communicator, you know that one of the first things you must do before preparing a message is to analyze the audience. Think about an airline strike and answer these questions to practise this important communication technique:

1. What groups of people do you think would be interested in the information about the airline strike?

2. What information do you think each of these groups would want to know about most?

3. How might they react to the information you will provide?

Summarize your answers to these three questions in a short memo to your instructor.

BUILDING YOUR TEAM SKILLS

Debate the pros and cons of telecommuting for an accounting, computer programming, or graphics design firm. Break into groups of four, with two students taking the employees' pro side and the other two taking management's con side. As you prepare for this debate, consider the following factors: employee motivation, staffing challenges, quality of work life, costs, control, and feasibility.

During your team's debate, let one side present its arguments while the other side takes notes on the major points. After both sides have completed their presentations, discuss all of the supporting points and try to reach a consensus as to whether your firm will support telecommuting. Draft a one-page statement outlining your team's conclusion and reasoning, and then share it during a class discussion.

Compare your team's conclusion and reasoning with those of other teams. Do most teams believe telecommuting is a good or a bad idea? What issues do most teams agree on? What issues do they disagree on?

EXPAND YOUR KNOWLEDGE

DISCOVERING CAREER OPPORTUNITIES

Is an alternative work arrangement such as flextime, job sharing, or telecommuting in your future? This exercise will help you think about whether these work arrangements fit into your career plans.

1. Look at the list of possible business careers in Appendix C (Exhibit C.1) on the website. Of the careers that interest you, which seem best suited to flextime? To job sharing? To telecommuting?

2. Select one of the careers that seems suited to telecommuting. What job functions do you think could be performed at home or from another remote location?

3. Thinking about the same career, do you think it would be possible to split the job's responsibilities with a co-worker under a job-sharing arrangement? What issues, if any, might you need to resolve first?

DEVELOPING YOUR RESEARCH SKILLS

Select one or two articles from recent issues of business journals or newspapers (print or online editions) that relate to employee motivation or morale.

1. What is the problem or trend discussed in the article(s) and how is it influencing employee attitudes or motivation?

2. Is this problem unique to this company, or does it have broader implications? Who is affected by it now, and who do you think might be affected by it in the future?

3. What challenges and opportunities does this situation present to the company or industry? The employees? Management?

STUDY GUIDE

SUMMARY OF LEARNING OBJECTIVES

1. Identity the importance of maintaining a motivated workforce and the key elements behind the various motivational theories

Organizations must balance the diverse needs of employees with those of management. Maintaining high employee morale is a key element to competing because the employees are on the front line of client interactions and motivated employees are more likely to be positive and productive. In this chapter, various theories were examined to shed light on what it takes to motivate people. These theories focus on three primary elements: needs, actions, and outcomes.

2. Compare Maslow's hierarchy of needs and Herzberg's two-factor theory and explain their application to employee motivation

Maslow's hierarchy organizes individual needs into five categories and proposes that the individual must satisfy the most basic needs before being able to address higher-level needs. Based on the assumption that employees want to "climb to the top" of Maslow's pyramid, managers should provide opportunities to satisfy those higher-level needs. Herzberg's two-factor theory covers the same general set of employee needs but divides them into two distinct groups. His theory suggests that hygiene factors—such as working conditions, company policies, and job security—can influence employee dissatisfaction, but an improvement in these factors will not motivate employees. Only motivational factors such as recognition and responsibility can improve employee performance.

3. Explain why expectancy theory is considered by some to be the best description of employee behaviour

Expectancy theory suggests that the effort employees put into their work depends on expectations about their own ability to perform, expectations about the rewards that the organization will give in response to that performance, and the attractiveness of those rewards relative to their individual goals. This is considered by many to be a good model of employee behaviour because it considers the linkages between effort and outcome. For instance, if employees think a linkage is "broken," such as having doubts that their efforts will yield acceptable performance or worries that they will perform well but no one will notice, they're likely to put less effort into their work.

4. Discuss three staffing challenges employers are facing in today's workplace

A shortage of skilled labour, rightsizing the workforce, and an increasing employee desire to balance work and life responsibilities are making it difficult for employers to find and keep talented people. The factors contributing to these staffing challenges are the increasing use of technology in the workplace, a robust economy, the conversion of a manufacturing-based economy to a service-based economy, a general mismatch between employee job skills and job demands, declining employee loyalty, and increasing employee burnout.

5. Explain the challenges and advantages of a diverse workforce

Smart business leaders recognize that diverse workforces bring a broader range of viewpoints and ideas, they help companies understand and identify with diverse markets, and they enable companies to tap into the broadest possible pool of talent. Supervisors face the challenge of communicating with these diverse employees, motivating them, and fostering cooperation and harmony among them. Teams face the challenge of working together closely, and companies are challenged to coexist peacefully with business partners and with the community as a whole.

6. Discuss three popular alternative work arrangements companies are offering their employees

To meet today's staffing and demographic challenges, companies are offering their employees alternative work arrangements. Three of the most popular are flextime (the ability to vary their work hours), telecommuting (the ability to work from home or another location), and job sharing (the ability to share a single full-time job with a co-worker).

7. Understand the role of unions and the challenges of reaching a collective bargaining agreement in the modern era

After years of corporate rightsizing and outsourcing, the role of the modern union has changed—even if some union leaders refuse to accept it. Competing in a global economy has forced many firms to abandon former practices and reduce cost structures with dramatic moves. Unions will still flex their muscles in times of prosperity, but economic downturns and intense competition have forced many bargaining units to re-evaluate their goals and negotiate under new terms.

8. Cite three options unions can exercise when negotiations with management break down

Unions can conduct strikes, organize boycotts, and use publicity to pressure management into complying with union proposals. A strike is a temporary work stoppage, which the union hopes will cost management enough in lost earnings so that they will be forced to accept union demands. A boycott is a union tactic designed to pressure management into making concessions by convincing sympathizers to refuse to buy or handle the product of the target company. A negative publicity campaign

against the target company is a pressure tactic designed to smear the reputation of the company in hopes of spurring management into action.

9. Cite three options management can exercise when negotiations with a union break down

To pressure a union into accepting its proposals, management may continue running the business with strike-breakers (non-union workers hired to do the jobs of striking workers), institute a lockout by preventing union employees from entering the workplace, or seek an injunction against a strike or other union activity. Strike-breakers are not permitted by law in British Columbia and Quebec.

KEY TERMS

arbitration   (317)
behaviour modification   (304)
boycott   (317)
collective bargaining   (315)
equity theory   (300)
expectancy theory   (301)
flextime   (312)
glass ceiling   (310)
goal-setting theory   (303)
human relations   (295)
hygiene factors   (298)
injunction   (319)

job enrichment   (307)
job redesign   (307)
job sharing   (313)
labour unions   (315)
lockouts   (318)
management by objectives
    (MBO)   (303)
mediation   (317)
morale   (295)
motivation   (295)
motivators   (298)
picketing   (317)

quality of work life (QWL)   (307)
reinforcement theory   (304)
scientific management   (297)
sexism   (310)
sexual harassment   (310)
strike   (317)
strike-breakers   (318)
telecommuting   (312)
Theory X   (299)
Theory Y   (299)
Theory Z   (300)

QUESTIONS

Multiple Choice   Circle the correct answer and then check the answers in the back of the book to chart your progress.

1. What is the inner force that moves individuals to take action?

   a. Positive reinforcement
   b. Morale
   c. Motivation
   d. Analysis

2. Which of the following is *not* one of the four primary steps in the management by objectives approach?

   a. Setting goals
   b. Planning actions
   c. Correcting errors
   d. Implementing plans

3. Which of the following would be considered a hygiene factor under Herzberg's two-factor theory?

   a. Opportunity for achievement
   b. Recognition by peers
   c. Personal responsibility
   d. Working conditions

4. Which of the following represents the philosophy employed by a Theory Y manager?

   a. Bosses should encourage workers to take classes to improve their skills.
   b. Bosses should immediately dock the pay of workers who arrive late.

c. Bosses should yell at employees when their production slips.

d. Bosses should pay more money to those workers who produce more output.

5. Which of the following is *not* a major issue facing managers of today's workforce?

a. Most of today's jobs require considerable skills, including computer skills.

b. Employers must choose from among hundreds of well-qualified applicants for each job opening.

c. Companies have to decide which employees to lay off or fire.

d. Workers are working more hours than a generation ago.

6. Companies try to improve quality of work life by reducing work specialization, by making work more meaningful, and by adding to the responsibilities of each job. What is this approach called?

a. Job description

b. Job-work analysis

c. Job enrichment

d. Job specification

7. Which of the following is an advantage of hiring older workers?

a. Older workers require lower salaries.

b. Older workers are stronger and have more energy.

c. Older workers use less medical coverage.

d. Older workers have more experience and tend to be more seasoned decision makers.

8. In recent years, many great strides have been made in the fight to overcome sexism. What has caused much of this change?

a. Companies are trying to hire more female professionals.

b. Companies and professional associations help women form business networks.

c. Companies have formal or informal arrangements where experienced women can "mentor" less-experienced workers.

d. All of the above have contributed to overcoming sexism in the workplace.

9. Which of the following is a disadvantage of flextime?

a. Flextime reduces turnover.

b. Flextime makes it easier for the company to supply their services around the clock.

c. Flextime may mean supervisors and workers are not at work at the same time.

d. Flextime makes it easier for the company to provide more staffing at busy periods.

10. Which of the following is *not* a union tactic used when the collective bargaining process is not proceeding as planned?

a. Lockout

b. Boycott

c. Negative publicity

d. Strike

True/False

1. True or false? Frederick W. Taylor's scientific management theory is based on the assumption that workers respond primarily to money.

2. True or false? Technological advances like email and cell phones allow employees to work anytime during a 24-hour period, but may increase worker stress.

3. True or false? There are fewer visible minorities in the Canadian workforce today than there were a decade ago.

4. True or false? If a union agrees to submit their salary dispute to binding arbitration and the arbitrator decides on an agreement that provides lower wages and more hours, the union can go on strike for better terms.

5. True or false? Employment rates among older workers have been increasing in recent years.

Fill-in-the-Blank

1. _____ needs are at the top of Maslow's hierarchy of needs.

2. According to Herzberg's two-factor theory, managers can help employees feel more focused and satisfied by paying attention to _____, such as achievement, recognition, responsibility, and other personally rewarding factors.

3. _____ is a human relations approach that emphasizes involving employees at all levels and treating them like family.

4. _____, considered by many experts to offer the best available explanation of employee motivation, links an employee's efforts with the outcome he or she expects from that effort.

5. _____ is a companywide four-step process that empowers employees and involves them in goal setting and decision making.

6. _____ allows people to avoid unpleasant consequences by behaving in the desired way.

7. Job enrichment reduces specialization and makes work more meaningful by expanding each job's responsibilities, whereas _____ restructures work to provide a better fit between employees' skills and their jobs.

8. The _____ is an invisible barrier attributable to subtle discrimination that keeps women (and minorities) out of top business positions.

9. A(n) _____ is an impartial third party that is brought in when negotiations are not moving forward. The _____ studies the situation and attempts to steer the parties toward a solution.

10. Splitting a single full-time job between two workers is called _____.

See It on the **WEB**

Visit the Companion Website at **www.pearsoned.ca/bovee**, review the exercises, and complete the following assignments for Chapter 10:

1. Working Hard on the Web
2. Learn the Language of Equal Opportunity
3. Telecommuting Your Way to Success
4. Spreading the Union Message

Companion Website

CBC VIDEO CASE

Work–Life Special: Voices of Canadians

LEARNING OBJECTIVES

The purpose of this video is to help you

1. Understand the various challenges facing today's workforce.

2. Recognize sources of stress and identify policies designed to relieve the mounting pressure on employees.

3. Identify sources of motivation in the workplace and factors that diminish employee morale.

SYNOPSIS

How many times have you heard a friend, colleague, or family member utter these words: "I am so stressed." This common bond can be linked to long hours, unreachable deadlines, unwritten rules, difficult bosses, overtime, downsizing, or rightsizing. One recent survey of 33 000 Canadians shed some light on the topic. The subject clearly struck a nerve, as after answering all of the detailed questions more than 10 000 people went a step further and added written comments. People are starting work early, working late, and coming in on the weekends. Fifty- to sixty-hour weeks are the norm for many workers; in some industries a 50-hour week is equated with "slacking off." This pressure to perform and to go above and beyond the standard work week has created various side effects. Companies are paying millions in insurance claims for antidepressant drugs, and absenteeism is costing the Canadian economy $3 billion each year. Corporate Canada is opening its eyes to the problem; many companies have created flex hours, telecommuting, and other programs. However, many employees believe that their employers talk about quality of work life and family-friendly policies but don't actually encourage them.

Bob Howe heads up a small law firm in Toronto. In most big law firms, face time (time spent in the office between 8:00 a.m. and 8:00 p.m.) is a vital element. Many lawyers work 12 or more hours per day regularly. At Davies Howe, employees have more flexible work hours and work in a more considerate environment, yet they have not sacrificed their pay. How? The firm traded its fancy office for a lower-rent location and passes the savings on to lawyers in the form of more reasonable workloads. With more and more employees feeling overwhelmed by the pressure to perform it is clear that companies that can effectively deal with this problem will be in a better position to excel in the future.

Discussion Questions

1. *For analysis*: Why are so many workers raising the white flag and complaining about their working conditions? What has changed in the last decade or two?
2. *For analysis*: How does low employee morale affect worker productivity?
3. *For application*: Using Herzberg's two-factor theory, explain the apparent satisfaction being experienced by the lawyers at the Davies Howe law firm.
4. *For debate*: In many countries employees enjoy a shorter work week. Should the Canadian government shorten the official work week? Will this help reduce absenteeism and lead to a more motivated workforce? Or would such a move lead to a lazier workforce?

ONLINE EXPLORATION

Visit the Human Resources and Social Development Canada (HRSDC) web page on work–life balance at www.hrsdc.gc.ca/en/lp/spila/wlb/02whats_new.shtml. Read Linda Duxbury's research findings under the heading "Voices of Canadians: Seeking Work–Life Balance." What are some of the key issues being addressed by the article? Does it support the claims that were made in the video?

ON LOCATION VIDEO CASE

Recruitment and Placement

LEARNING OBJECTIVES

The purpose of this video is to help you

1. Recognize how human resource management contributes to organizational performance.

2. Identify some of the ways in which HR managers handle staff evaluation and development.

3. Understand how and why HR managers provide feedback and identify useful techniques they use to do so.

SYNOPSIS

This video provides a unique look at the recruitment, selection, and placement procedures of the human resources department at Bertelsmann BMG. This discussion takes place after the hiring process and looks back at what went wrong with the hiring of one particular employee. The two participants are having a Monday-morning quarterback debate. The video allows us to see how HR departments interact with various other organizational departments to coordinate the hiring process. Despite the obvious tension (and maybe because of it) we can identify some of the expectations on both sides as well as important issues that can lead to problems. This case gives us an interesting glimpse at two different perspectives on the hiring process at Bertelsmann.

Discussion Questions

1. *For analysis*: Do you think running an ad in *Rolling Stone* magazine was a wise choice for drawing an outside candidate to fill the position that Sylvie had in her department? What are some other sources they could

have used to attract qualified people? When considering alternatives, remember that you have a limited budget.

2. *For analysis*: Paul Fiolek's conversation revealed a great deal about the formal structure of Bertelsmann BMG's HR department. Bertelsmann is a giant in the music and entertainment industry. Analyze how this might have both a positive and a negative influence on hiring practices.

3. *For application*: Describe the steps that Bertelsmann BMG would need to take to rewrite the job specifications for this opening. Why might this be useful to you as an HR manager? If you feel it would not be useful, explain why.

4. *For application*: What type of interview do you feel would be best suited to this dynamic music placement department? Why?

5. *For debate*: Do you agree with Cheryl Brie that Sylvie Aronson is "looking to place blame" on the HR department? If you do agree, how would you have reacted to Sylvie's accusations? If you do not agree, explain why you feel Sylvie is justified in her view of the HR department's role in this situation.

ONLINE EXPLORATION

Visit Bertelsmann BMG's website at www.bertelsmann.com. Follow the "Jobs & Careers" link to look at career opportunities and company benefits. What kinds of jobs are being featured on the website? How does the firm make it convenient for applicants to submit resumés online?

E-cruiting (recruiting over the Internet) has become an integral part of HR strategy for companies of all sizes. Companies have discovered that the Internet is a fast, convenient, and inexpensive way to find prospective job candidates. Job candidates are finding that the Internet is a convenient way to gather company information, search for job vacancies, and post resumés on both high-volume career websites such as Monster.ca, Workopolis.com, Hotjobs.ca, and Jobpostings.ca, and on more focused websites like Dice (for high-tech jobs).

The Traditional Path versus E-Cruiting

Before the advent of the Internet, recruiting followed a traditional path: A company "announced" a job opening to the marketplace (through a classified ad, an executive recruiter, employee referral incentives, a job fair, or other medium), and recruiters made endless rounds of cold calls to identify potential job candidates. Then, after a lengthy process of sorting through faxed and mailed resumés, someone from human resources called the most promising candidates and interviewed them.

This process, however, is expensive and inefficient. For one thing, communication by regular mail is slow. By the time a phone call is made or snail mail is received, a good candidate may have accepted another job. Plus, the cost of placing classified ads in newspapers is high, so most ads contain brief job descriptions and appear for only a few days or weeks. Furthermore, the traditional process operates mostly in one direction. Most applicants do not place ads announcing their availability—although some job seekers do send unsolicited letters with resumés.

Thanks to the Internet, however, the recruiting process is changing. Companies are using the Internet to search for resumés of promising candidates, take online applications, accept electronic resumés, conduct interviews, and administer tests. Recruiters at Amazon.com, for example, post ads on job boards and actively search the Web for resumés. "To be a recruiter at Amazon.com, you have to like the thrill of the hunt," says Amazon's manager of technical recruiting. Amazon's recruiters sort through hundreds of candidates they consider for every position by using a tool to pre-sort and categorize resumés. Like Amazon, many companies now advertise job vacancies on their company websites and on third-party job boards. From entry-level positions to chief executive officers, no job is outside the Internet's reach.

Benefits and Drawbacks of E-Cruiting

In comparison to traditional recruiting methods, the benefits of Internet recruiting are many:

- *Speed.* The Internet allows job seekers to search for jobs quickly, from any place and at any time, and to communicate via email with potential employers. Companies can also save time in the hiring process by using the Internet to become a 24/7 recruiter and give applicants quick responses to their queries. Determined nocturnal headhunters can snap up hot resumés posted on the Internet before dawn and contact candidates immediately by email. Some companies report receiving responses and resumés only minutes after posting a job opening.

- *Reach.* The Internet allows employers to contact a broader selection of applicants more quickly, target specific types of applicants more easily, and reach highly skilled applicants more efficiently. Some company websites bring in thousands of resumés in one week, a volume that would be far too cumbersome to manage through traditional means.

- *Cost savings.* Electronic ads typically cost much less than traditional print ads, career fairs, or open houses. Moreover, processing electronic application forms is more efficient than processing paper forms. Intelligent automated search agents can filter or pre-screen potential applicants and find resumés that match job descriptions and specific employer criteria.

Of course, e-cruiting is not without drawbacks. The biggest complaint voiced by companies is that the Internet produces more job applicants than ever before. The number of resumés one company received went from 6000 to 24 000 annually after going online. The increased volume of resumés makes it more difficult to separate promising candidates from unqualified ones. Companies get resumés from faraway places such as Albania and Timbuktu. "People will send their resumé because it's very simple to cut and paste. But, they're in no way qualified for the position," notes one HR director. Another drawback is that not everyone has Internet access or uses the Internet to search for jobs.

The Future of E-Cruiting

In spite of these drawbacks, the future of e-cruiting looks promising. The transfer to e-cruiting will be more attractive as new screening and matching tools are developed to manage the volume of resumés and to weed out inappropriate ones. "There is still a large window of opportunity for companies to leverage the Internet and other technologies as part of their recruiting strategies," notes Gordon Bingham, senior vice-president at Olsten, a strategic staffing firm. But the e-cruiting bandwagon is rolling and picking up steam.[89]

Questions for Critical Thinking

1. How are job seekers and employers using the Internet in the recruiting process?

2. What are the benefits and drawbacks of Internet recruiting?

3. What steps would you take to make your resumé stand out among the thousands that are transmitted electronically? (Hint: Think of content.)

BUSINESS PLANPRO EXERCISES

Managing Human Resources and Employee Relations

Review Appendix B, Your Business Plan to learn how to use Business PlanPro Software so you can complete these exercises.

Think Like a Pro

Objective: By completing these exercises you will become acquainted with the sections of a business plan that address staffing the enterprise and managing employees. You will use the sample business plan for Sagebrush Sam's (listed as Restaurant-Steak Buffet in the Sample Plan Browser) in this exercise.

1. What do the mission statement and keys to success sections say about Sagebrush Sam's approach to employee relations? Why are good relations with employees so important to the success of this type of business?

2. What workforce challenges are Sagebrush Sam's likely to encounter as it grows?

3. What are the company's estimates for manager and employee compensation, and how do these estimates change over the years covered by the plan?

4. According to the business plan, Sagebrush Sam's will need a director of store operations when it has more than five units. How might the company recruit a manager with the appropriate experience and background for this position?

Create Your Own Business Plan

The success of your business depends on hiring, training, and motivating the right employees. Answer the following questions as you continue to develop your own business plan. How many employees will your business require? Of these, how many will be managers? How will you motivate your staff? Will you pay them a salary or a commission? Will you offer alternative work arrangements? If so, which ones? Will you use part-time and temporary employees? Will you provide your employees with benefits? If so, which ones?

DEVELOPING MARKETING STRATEGIES TO SATISFY CUSTOMERS

CHAPTER 11
Developing Product and Pricing Strategies

CHAPTER 12
Developing Distribution and Promotional Strategies

CHAPTER 11

DEVELOPING PRODUCT AND PRICING STRATEGIES

LEARNING OBJECTIVES

After studying this chapter, you will be able to

1 Explain what marketing is and describe the four utilities created by marketing

2 Explain why and how companies learn about their customers

3 Describe how the organizational-customer decision process differs from the consumer process

4 Outline the three steps in the strategic marketing planning process

5 Define market segmentation and cite six factors used to identify segments

6 List the steps involved in developing new products

7 Highlight the four stages in the life cycle of a product and the marketing focus of each stage

8 Understand the important role of branding and the strategies used to build and maintain brand equity

9 Discuss the functions of packaging and labelling

10 Identify four ways of expanding a product line and discuss two risks that product-line extensions pose

11 List seven factors that influence pricing decisions and cite five common pricing methods

Behind the Scenes

Shoppers Drug Mart is updating its image to improve service and bolster the bottom line. Key initiatives in this phase include bigger stores in more central locations; more private-label brand sales; and the expansion of the cosmetics lines to include upscale brands.

www.shoppersdrugmart.ca

Shoppers Drug Mart (Pharmaprix in Quebec) faces many new challenges. Wal-Mart and Loblaw have increased their pharmacy businesses and are offering clients the ability to fill prescriptions while shopping. Shoppers is feeling the heat from traditional competitors like the Edmonton-based Katz Group, which has 1800 stores under such banners as Rexall, IDA, and Pharma Plus. Jean Coutu has a dominant share in Quebec and has stores in Ontario and New Brunswick as well. In addition, Jean Coutu will soon own a 32 percent stake in Rite Aid, the third-largest pharmacy chain in the United States. The competitors each have their own strategies that will likely result in more intense competition ahead.

Shoppers Drug Mart was founded in 1962 by Murray Koffler. At the time, he wanted to build a national chain that could provide the personalized service available at independent local pharmacies. Today there are more than 1000 Shoppers Drug Mart outlets and 58 Shoppers HomeHealthCare centres across the country. Mission accomplished. However, to continue its success the firm will need to make some changes.

Faced with new competitive threats and a consumer that is constantly looking for a fresh, appealing retail experience, Shoppers Drug Mart has embarked on a plan to distinguish itself from the competition. The company has set very specific interrelated marketing objectives and strategies to achieve their goals.

Step 1: Retail Outlet Face Lift. Shoppers is making some important changes to compete. New products have been added to the shelves and the chain is carrying more convenience goods. Stores are being renovated and or replaced by updated outlets. New central locations are getting bigger—the average size of new outlets is 12 000 to 14 000 square feet, nearly double the average size of traditional locations. In addition, Shoppers has turned their attention to university campuses. They already have a new store at UBC and are in conversation with other educational and health institutions.

Step 2: Increased Emphasis on Private-Label Brands. Shoppers is increasing its private-label brand presence with its "Life" and "Quo Cosmetics" brands. Currently, 14 percent of all revenues come from private-label sales. The goal, under new CEO Jurgen Schreiber, is to earn 20 to 25 percent of all revenues from private labels.

These house brands provide obvious cost advantages for customers (they are about 25 percent cheaper than national brands) and profit advantages for retailers (there is an approximately 15 percent better profit margin). In addition, retailers like Shoppers hope to achieve brand loyalty similar to what Loblaw has achieved with its President's Choice label. If consumers identify with a brand that is only available in their stores, the retail chain will benefit.

Step 3: Re-launch the Loyalty Card. The Shoppers Optimum program counts over 7.7 million active members. More than 50 percent of them are women and they spend 57 percent more per average shopping basket compared to non-card holders. The card enables the company to track purchase histories and send specific promotions to their customers who, for example, are in the habit of buying baby products. The re-launch will include a VIP program to provide additional incentives to current and potential members alike.

Step 4: Expand the Cosmetics Line. In particular, Shoppers has focused on acquiring the rights to sell higher-end brands. They have invested in store improvements to acquire the rights to sell brands previously reserved for department stores and boutiques.

The chain now generates about $8 billion in annual revenue and $400 million in net earnings and is growing at a rate of 7 to 10 percent annually. Shoppers is setting a clear direction. It plans to add another 275 to 300 big-box outlets by 2011. It remains to be seen whether or not the strategy continues to pay off in the long term, but the initial returns are very promising.[1]

TEST YOURSELF

Answers to these questions can be found on the website: www.pearsoned.ca/bovee.

1. What is the difference between a private-label brand and a national brand?

2. Why are private-label brands so important for retailers?

3. What are the benefits of the Optimum card for consumers? For Shoppers Drug Mart?

4. What do you think of the changes at Shoppers Drug Mart? Can they fend off direct and indirect competitors with their updated approach?

WHAT IS MARKETING?

L.O. 1

Your experiences as a consumer may have not provided you with many insights into accounting and production, but they have definitely contributed to your knowledge of marketing. Companies like Shoppers Drug Mart have been trying to sell you products for years, and you've learned something about their techniques—contests, advertisements, fancy displays of merchandise, price markdowns, and product giveaways, to name just a few. Molson, for example, has a tremendous variety of approaches to gain your attention. They range from its interactive website to the "House of Blues" concert series to sponsorships of amateur sports. Molson also sponsors the CFL and five of its teams: the Saskatchewan Roughriders, Edmonton Eskimos, Calgary Stampeders, Hamilton Tiger-Cats, and Montreal Alouettes. Their long standing association with the NHL spreads to all six Canadian teams as well as two important cross-border US teams: the Buffalo Sabres and Detroit Red Wings. Marketing involves much more than a fancy display of merchandise, a clever commercial, or a special contest, though. In fact, a lot of planning and execution are needed to develop a new product, set its price, get it into stores, and convince people to buy it.

Think about all the decisions you would have to make if you were involved in the decision-making process at Shoppers Drug Mart: Which new product lines are potentially the most profitable? Which product lines should be expanded or reduced? How can we increase brand loyalty? How many private-label brands should we add this year? How can we take advantage of the marketing data that is collected from the Optimum card client records? These are just a few of the many marketing decisions that all companies make to be successful.

The American Marketing Association (AMA) defines **marketing** as planning and executing the conception, pricing, promotion, and distribution of ideas, goods, and services to create exchanges that satisfy individual and organizational objectives.[2] With respect to products, marketing involves all decisions related to determining a product's characteristics, price, production specifications, market-entry date, distribution, promotion, and sales. With respect to customers, marketing involves understanding customers' needs and their buying behaviour, creating consumer awareness, providing **customer service**—which is everything a company does to satisfy its customers—and maintaining relationships with customers long after the sales transaction is complete (see Exhibit 11.1). At Holt Renfrew a recent evaluation of client perceptions led to the realization that although the retailer had a clear upscale brand image, many customers found the sales staff to be distant or snobby. In the past two years, Holt Renfrew has made efforts to correct this problem, starting with an emphasis on friendlier interactions with customers, supported by investments in technology to avoid stock-outs and to better address customer feedback. Holt Renfrew also provides great services, like their popular personal shoppers, to address specific needs of clients.[3]

marketing
The process of planning and executing the conception, pricing, promotion, and distribution of ideas, goods, and services to create and maintain relationships that satisfy individual and organizational objectives

customer service
Efforts a company makes to satisfy its customers and help them realize the greatest possible value from the products they are purchasing

Exhibit 11.1   **What Is Marketing?**

Each of the core marketing concepts—needs, wants, demands, products, services, value, satisfaction, quality, exchanges, transactions, relationships, and markets—builds on the ones before it.

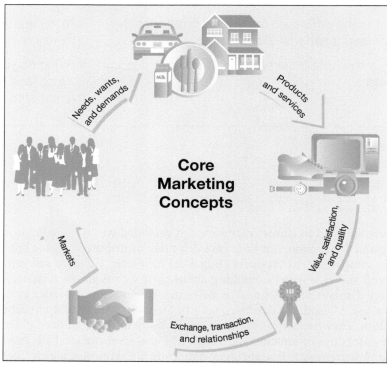

Source: Gary Armstrong and Philip Kotler, *Marketing: An Introduction*, 5th ed. (Upper Saddle River, NJ: Prentice Hall, 2000), 5 (Figure 1.1—Core marketing concepts).

place marketing
Marketing efforts to attract people and organizations to a particular geographic area

cause-related marketing
Identification and marketing of a social issue, cause, or idea to selected target markets

Special Olympics Canada advertisements provide an effective example of cause-related marketing. They are not selling a shiny new product, but rather are looking to gain attention and inspire support for the games and the organization.

Most people think of marketing in connection with selling tangible goods for a profit (the term *product* refers to any "bundle of value" that can be exchanged in a marketing transaction). But marketing applies to services, non-profit organizations, people, places, and causes, too. Politicians always market themselves. Election campaigns involve positioning, brand names (the respective political parties), slogans, large promotion campaigns (TV/radio ads, posters, signs, billboards, etc.), personal selling (door-to-door canvassing), and event planning (political rallies), to name just a few marketing activities politicians undertake. Places (such as Paris, Poland, or a local municipality) that want to attract residents, tourists, and business investment also promote their respective strengths. **Place marketing** describes efforts to market geographic areas ranging from neighbourhoods to entire countries. **Cause-related marketing** promotes a cause or a social issue, such as physical fitness, cancer awareness, recycling, or highway safety. Special Olympics Canada urges support by reminding us of the athlete's oath: "Winning at Life." The aim is to inspire financial support, volunteers, and fans to this very worthy cause.[4]

The Role of Marketing in Society

Take another look at the AMA definition of marketing. Notice that marketing involves an exchange between two parties—the buyer and the selling organization—both of whom must obtain satisfaction from the transaction.

This definition suggests that marketing plays an important role in society by helping people satisfy their needs and wants and by helping organizations determine what to produce.

Needs and Wants

To survive, people need food, water, air, shelter, and clothing. A **need** represents a difference between your actual state and your ideal state. You're hungry and you don't want to be hungry; you need to eat. Needs create the motivation to buy products and are therefore at the core of any discussion of marketing.

Your **wants** are based on your needs but are more specific. Producers do not create needs, but they do shape your wants by exposing you to alternatives. For instance, when you need some food, you may want a Snickers bar or an orange. A fundamental goal of marketing is to direct the customer's basic need for various products into the desire to purchase specific brands. Al Ries and Jack Trout, co-authors of *The 22 Immutable Laws of Marketing*, note that customers' wants are directed by changing people's perception of products.[5] After all, what's the real difference between Scott and Bounty paper towels? Is one actually more absorbent than the other, or do you only perceive it that way?

Exchanges and Transactions

When you participate in the **exchange process**, you trade something of value (usually money) for something else of value, whether you're buying an airline ticket, a car, or a college education. When you make a purchase, you cast your vote for that item and encourage the producer of that item to make more of it. In this way, supply and demand are balanced, and society obtains the goods and services that are most satisfying.

When the exchange actually occurs, it takes the form of a **transaction**. Party A gives Party B $1.79 and gets a medium Coke in return. A trade of values takes place. Most transactions in today's society involve money, but money is not necessarily required. When you were a child, you may have traded your peanut butter sandwich for a friend's bologna and cheese in a transaction that involved no money. Bartering, which pre-dates the use of cash, is making a comeback thanks to the Internet. The dot.com boom, which saw many cash-poor start-ups pay for goods and services with company shares instead of cash, seemed to open up many eyes to trading possibilities. A number of online exchanges now facilitate bartering using a trade credit system; members trade everything from office space to website design.[6]

need
The difference between a person's actual state and his or her ideal state; provides the basic motivation to make a purchase

wants
Objects that are desirable in light of a person's experiences, culture, personality and perspective

exchange process
The act of obtaining a desired object from another party by offering something of value in return

transaction
An exchange between parties

 ## IN-CLASS NOTES

The Role of Marketing in Society
- **Needs and wants:** consumers *need* water, marketers help consumers choose (*want*) Propel over Dasani
- **Exchange process:** obtaining an object by trading something of value for it (money vs. bartering)

Exhibit 11.2   **Examples of the Four Utilities**

The utility of a good or service has four aspects, each of which enhances the product's value to the consumer.

UTILITY	EXAMPLE
Form utility	Gummy Bears appeal to youngsters because of their shapes and colours.
Time utility	LensCrafters has captured a big chunk of the market for eyeglasses by providing on-the-spot, one-hour service.
Place utility	La Senza offers convenient worldwide home delivery of their latest apparel, lingerie, and accessories.
Possession utility	RealNetworks, a producer of software for listening to music from the Internet, allows customers to download and install its programs directly from the company's website.

utility
The power of a good or service to satisfy a human need

form utility
Consumer value created by converting raw materials and other inputs into finished goods and services

time utility
Consumer value created by making a product available at a convenient time

place utility
Consumer value created by making a product available in a convenient location

possession utility
Consumer value created when someone takes ownership of a product

marketing concept
An approach to business management that stresses customer needs and wants, seeks long-term profitability, and integrates marketing with other functional units within the organization

The Four Utilities

To encourage the exchange process, marketers enhance the appeal of their products and services by adding **utility**, something of value to customers (see Exhibit 11.2). When organizations change raw materials into finished goods, they are creating **form utility** desired by consumers. For example, when Nokia combines plastic, computer chips, and other materials to make digital phones, the company is providing form utility. In other cases, marketers try to make their products available when and where customers want to buy them, creating **time utility** and **place utility**. Overnight couriers like Purolator create time utility, whereas ATM machines in shopping malls create place utility. The final form of utility is **possession utility**—the satisfaction that buyers get when they actually possess a product, both legally and physically. The Royal Bank, for example, creates possession utility by offering loans that allow people to buy homes they could otherwise not afford.

The Marketing Concept

The underlying philosophy that guides all marketing decisions and activities is known as the **marketing concept**, the idea that companies should stress customers' needs and wants while seeking long-term profitability and coordinating their own marketing efforts to achieve the company's long-term goals. The Bay, Costco, Telus, Hyatt Hotels, and hundreds of well-known, successful companies have adopted the marketing concept. These customer-focused companies modify their marketing strategies and product offerings to satisfy customer needs and wants.

For example, at The Bay, sales associates enhance their knowledge and improve their customer service through workshops, online learning, and the "HBC University." Employees can log on to the Online Personal Approach to Learning (OPAL) and access more than 200 online courses that range from health and safety issues to product knowledge. OPAL keeps track of courses that associates have taken. "HBC University provides associates with a centralized resource and support for learning and development."[7]

Understanding Today's Customers

To implement the marketing concept, companies must have good information about what customers want. They must "know and understand the customer so well that the product or service fits him and sells itself," said management consultant and author Peter Drucker.[8] This is a challenge because today's customers are not easy to understand. Customers are sophisticated, price sensitive, and demanding. They live time-compressed lifestyles and have little patience for retailers who do not understand them or will not adapt business practices to meet their needs. They expect products and services

Exhibit 11.3   The Consumer Decision Process

Consumers go through a decision-making process that can include up to five steps.

1	2	3	4	5
Need recognition	Information search	Evaluation of alternatives	Purchase	Postpurchase evaluation

to be delivered faster and more conveniently. They have no problem switching to competitors if their demands are not met. Armed with facts, prices, data, product reviews, advice, how-to guides, and databases, today's customers are informed, which places them in an unprecedented position of control.[9]

Home buyers, for example, use real estate websites like MLS.ca to gain more control over the house-hunting process. Home descriptions, room dimensions, photographs, virtual tours, property tax information, and school and town information are all provided on the website. Customers are informed before even entering the real estate office.[10] The same is true for car buyers. They walk into car dealerships reading spec sheets obtained from websites that disclose the dealer's invoice cost, dealer rebates, and other purchasing incentives.[11] From travel agents to supermarkets to auto dealers to furniture stores to realtors—today's customers are calling the shots, which is why it is increasingly important for businesses to understand how buyers think and what buyers want.

The Buyers' Decision Process Suppose you want to buy a car. Do you rush to the dealer and buy the first car you see? Of course not. Like most buyers, you go through a decision process (outlined in Exhibit 11.3) that begins with identifying a problem, which in this case is the need for a car. Your next step is to look for a solution to your problem. Possibilities occur to you on the basis of your experience (perhaps you recently drove a certain make or model) and on your exposure to marketing messages. If none of the obvious solutions seems satisfying, you gather additional information. The more complex the problem, the more information you are likely to seek from friends or relatives, magazines, salespeople, store displays, and sales literature.

cognitive dissonance
Anxiety following a purchase that prompts buyers to seek reassurance about the purchase; commonly known as buyer's remorse

Once you have all the information in hand, you are ready to make a choice. You may select one of the alternatives, such as a new Volvo C30 or a MINI Cooper. You might even postpone the decision or decide against making any purchase at all, depending on the magnitude of your desire, the outside pressure to buy, and your financial resources. If you decide to buy, you will evaluate the wisdom of your choice. If the item you bought is satisfying, you might buy the same product again under similar circumstances, thus developing a loyalty to the brand. If it is not satisfying, you will probably not repeat the purchase.

If the purchase was a major one, you will sometimes suffer from **cognitive dissonance**, commonly known as buyer's remorse. You will think about all the alternatives you rejected and wonder whether one of them might have been a better choice. At this stage, you're likely to seek reassurance that you have done the right thing. Realizing this tendency, many marketers try to reinforce their sales with guarantees, phone calls to check on the customer's satisfaction, user hotlines, follow-up letters, and so on. Such efforts help pave the way for repeat business.

Saturn uses a "No Hassle, No Haggle" policy to help relieve the stress of negotiating for a new car. They also offer an exchange policy to customers

Infiniti's website allows customers to choose different colours, features, and packages while pricing the models, all from the convenience of their own home. This sort of easy access to information is expected by consumers today. It also provides a great resource for leads for the company.

who change their mind within 30 days or 2500 kilometres. The extended customer service is evident the moment the client picks up the car. Customers are greeted by the staff and sent off to music and a drumbeat as they unveil their car and ride off. Phone calls to ensure satisfaction are also part of the Saturn touch.[12]

Factors that Influence the Buyer's Decision Process Throughout the buying process, various factors may influence a buyer's purchase decision. An awareness of the following factors and consumer preferences enables companies to appeal to the right group:

- *Culture.* The cultures and subcultures that people belong to shape their values, attitudes, and beliefs and influence the way they respond to the world around them. Understanding culture is therefore an increasingly important step in international business and in marketing to diverse populations, especially in a rich multicultural country. Specifically, the Canadian marketer must pay careful attention to the French-Canadian population, especially in Quebec and New Brunswick. Additionally, certain ethnic groups have a powerful identity that marketers may wish to access. Cleve Lu, founder of Era Integrated Marketing Communications, helps AIM Trimark and other major companies tailor and adapt messages geared toward the unique Chinese-Canadian culture.[13]

- *Social class.* In addition to being members of a particular culture, people also belong to a certain social class—be it upper, middle, lower, or somewhere in between. In general, members of various classes pursue different activities, buy different goods, shop in different places, and react to different media. Companies tailor their images to appeal directly to different social classes. Porsche, by virtue of its product features and pricing scheme, sells almost exclusively to the upper class. They produce very few cars compared to a company like GM, but manage to earn great profits. What would happen if Porsche began to produce a $20 000 model for the North American market? Porsche would surely sell a lot of these cars. So why do they resist the temptation? Quite simply, they would lose their exclusive image and many of their profitable core customers. Porsche has expanded in recent years, but they are being very careful to maintain this image.[14]

- *Reference groups.* A reference group consists of people who have a good deal in common: family members, friends, co-workers, sports enthusiasts, music lovers, computer buffs, and so on. Individuals are members of many such reference groups, and they use the opinions of the appropriate group as a benchmark when they buy certain types of goods or services. You surely have many such groups that influence your buying behaviour whether you admit it or not. For example, most students immediately conform to the power of their work environment once they enter the workforce. The school bag is replaced by a briefcase; jeans give way to business attire; hairstyles tend to become more conservative. There aren't too many mohawks in the corporate world.

- *Self-image.* The tendency to believe that "you are what you buy" is especially popular among young people. Marketers capitalize on people's need to express their identity through their purchases by emphasizing the image value of goods and services. Just take a look at any of the latest advertisements for Miss Sixty, Calvin Klein, or Parasuco Jeans. It's also why professional athletes and celebrities frequently appear as product endorsers—so that consumers will incorporate part of the celebrity's public image into their own self-image (see the Learning from Business Blunders box). Jarome Iginla is a hockey hero who celebrates his birthday on Canada Day. He has become an appealing celebrity for endorsements, and his notable exploits in the Olympics and World Cup Hockey have increased his power as a promotional spokesperson.[15]

Parasuco Jeans are sold in locations across Canada and are targeted at a high-end, fashion-forward clientele that identifies with images of youth and glamour.

Learning from Business Blunders

OOPS

On the surface, it looked like Hallmark Cards did about everything you're supposed to do. Its researchers, monitoring the demographic bulge of the baby-boom generation, created the Time of Your Life product line to appeal specifically to people reaching the 50-year milestone in life. Their careful customer research showed that while boomers might be aging, they don't want to think of themselves as old. In response, the product line featured youthful, healthy images of people in the prime of life. The products were displayed in a special Time of Your Life section in Hallmark stores. Great idea? It sounded like another winner, but the product line was a flop.

WHAT YOU CAN LEARN

While the products themselves may have been right on the mark in terms of customer wants and needs, the final piece of the puzzle—the retail presentation—put people off. Boomers who didn't want to think of themselves as old weren't about to shop in the "old people's" section of the card store. Marketers need to consider the entire consumer experience; a mistake at any stage can doom the entire effort.[16]

■ *Situational factors.* These factors include events or circumstances in people's lives that are more circumstantial but that can influence buying patterns. Such factors might include having a coupon, being in a hurry, celebrating a holiday, being in a bad mood, current social surroundings, and so on. If you've ever practiced "retail therapy" to cheer yourself up, you know all about situational factors. The social surroundings also serve to influence the buying situation. For example, a crowded beach may serve to create a negative experience for a vacationer that was promised an exclusive getaway in a brochure, but a crowded bar is required to satisfy customer expectations. Nobody likes an empty night club.

The Organizational-Customer Decision Process   In a sense, the purchasing behaviour of organizations (including businesses, non-profit organizations, and governments) is easier to understand because it's more clearly driven by economics and influenced less by emotional factors. Here are some of the significant ways in which organizational purchasing differs from consumer purchasing:[17]   L.O. 3

■ *An emphasis on economic payback and other rational factors.* Most organizational purchases are carefully evaluated for financial impact, technical compatibility,

---

 IN-CLASS NOTES

Factors That Influence the Buyer's Decision

- ■ Culture
- ■ Social class
- ■ Reference groups
- ■ Self-image
- ■ Situational factors

reliability, and so on. Businesses and other organizations don't always make the best choices, but their choices are usually based on a more rational analysis of needs and alternatives. However, some business-to-business marketers make the mistake of assuming that customer emotions play little or no role in the purchase decision, forgetting that organizations don't make decisions, people do. Fear of change, fear of failure, excitement over new technologies, and the pride of being associated with world-class suppliers are just a few of the emotions that can influence organizational purchases.

- *A formal buying process.* From office supplies to new factories, most organizational purchases follow a formal buying process, particularly in government agencies and in mid- to large-size companies. In fact, the model in Exhibit 11.3 is a better representation of organizational purchasing than it is of consumer purchasing, although organizational purchasing often includes additional steps such as establishing budgets, analyzing potential suppliers, and requesting proposals.

- *The participation and influence of multiple people.* Except in the very smallest businesses, where the owner may make all the purchasing decisions, the purchase process usually involves a number of people. This team can include end users, technical experts, the manager with ultimate purchasing authority, and a professional purchasing agent (whose job includes researching suppliers, negotiating prices, and evaluating supplier performance).

- *Closer relationships between buyers and sellers.* Close and long-lasting relationships between buyers and sellers are common in organizational purchasing. A company may use the same advertising agency, accounting firm, and raw materials suppliers for decades. In some cases, employees from the seller have offices inside the buyer's facility to promote close interaction.

Marketing Research and Customer Databases

marketing research
The collection and analysis of information for making marketing decisions

database marketing
The process of building, maintaining, and using customer databases for the purpose of contacting customers and transacting business

Many companies obtain information about customers' changing needs by engaging in **marketing research**—the process of gathering and analyzing information about customers, markets, and related marketing issues. Popular marketing research tools include personal observation, customer surveys and questionnaires, experiments, telephone or personal interviews, studies of small samples of the consumer population, and focused interviews of 6 to 10 people (called *focus groups*). Thanks to their low costs and rapid delivery of results, online surveys have become quite popular in recent years, although they do suffer from the potential flaw of not representing a true cross-section of the population.[18]

Another way to learn about customer preferences is to gather and analyze customer-related data. **Database marketing** is the process of recording and analyzing customer interactions, preferences, and buying behaviour for the purpose of contacting and transacting with customers (see the box entitled "Your Right to Privacy versus the Marketing Databases"). Companies gather information about customers by engaging in two-way, ongoing dialogue with customers through email, web pages, fax machines, and toll-free telephone numbers. In addition, frequent-shopper card programs, good for a wealth of discounts at checkouts, have convinced customers to share some of the most intimate details about their lives. For instance, customer grocery purchases reveal preferences for everything from hygiene products to junk food to magazines. If you receive a targeted email from Shoppers Drug Mart offering you a coupon for your favourite hair products, it is probably not a coincidence. All of your purchases are linked to your loyalty card number and sharp retailers like Shoppers Drug Mart, Best Buy, and M&M Meat Shops are already tailoring messages to your needs.[19]

Online research tools, such as this survey system available from Zoomerang, help marketers learn more about their customers.

Your Right to Privacy versus the Marketing Databases

Are all the details of your personal life really private? Consider this: Your bank knows your account balance, your credit history, and your Social Insurance Number. Government agencies know how much money you made last year, the kind of car you own, and how many parking tickets you've had. Credit agencies know to whom you owe money and how much you owe. The list goes on and on, from video stores to insurance companies. Every time you register online, or even click on a website, all sorts of data are being collected about you. By depositing "cookies" on your hard drive, web marketers can follow your path and track the sites you visit.

Of course, there's nothing unethical about collecting data or maintaining a database. The ethical problems arise when marketers buy, borrow, rent, or exchange information, usually without your knowledge or permission. Who should have the right to see your records? The answer depends on where you live. In Europe, strict privacy regulations prevent companies from using data about individuals without asking permission and explaining how the data will be used. But in Canada and most other countries, marketers can easily buy information about who you are, where you live, how much you earn, and what you buy—for as little as a nickel.

Many web marketers post privacy policies showing how they use personal data. Since January 1, 2001, the *Personal Information Protection and Electronic Documents Act* (*PIPEDA*) has applied to all federal businesses. "It gives the individual control over personal information by requiring organizations to obtain consent to collect, use, or disclose information." The law indicates the obligations of organizations, the rules of conduct, as well as the rights of individuals. If a person feels as though their rights have been violated and they are unable to resolve them directly, they can submit a formal complaint to the Office of the Privacy Commissioner of Canada (1-800-282-1376).

As you can imagine, the consumer's right to privacy is an ongoing debate. Privacy advocates argue that people should have the right to be left alone, whereas marketers argue that they should have the right to freedom of speech—the right to inform customers about their offers, that is. Thus, the ultimate dilemma is whether a marketer's needs and freedom of speech outweigh the consumer's right to privacy. What's your opinion?[20]

Questions for Critical Thinking

1. Should a marketer selling long-distance telephone service be allowed to see your telephone records without your knowledge or permission?

2. Should web marketers be required to conspicuously post their privacy policies and ask consent before collecting and using visitors' personal data?

Capital One, for example, has become a leading North American credit card company by collecting extensive records on millions of consumers and using that information to plan its marketing strategies. Ritz-Carlton records all customer requests, comments, and complaints in a worldwide database that now contains individual profiles of more than 500 000 guests. By accessing these profiles, employees at any Ritz-Carlton hotel can accommodate the individual tastes of its customers from anywhere in the world.[21]

Building Relationships with Customers

Another way that companies remain customer-focused is by building long-term, satisfying relationships with key parties—customers, suppliers, distributors—to retain their long-term business. This practice, commonly referred to as **relationship marketing**, focuses on establishing a learning relationship with each customer. Thus, the relationship between customer and company does not end with the sales transaction; instead, it is viewed as an ongoing process.[22] This relationship gets smarter with each customer interaction—you learn something about your customer and change your product or service to meet their needs. To help manage customer

relationship marketing
A focus on developing and maintaining long-term relationships with customers, suppliers, and distributors for mutual benefit

Technologies That Are Revolutionizing Business

DATA MINING

To find a few ounces of precious gold, you dig through a mountain of earth. To find a few ounces of precious information, you dig through mountains of data using data mining, a combination of technologies and techniques that extract important customer insights buried within thousands or millions of transaction records.

HOW IT'S CHANGING BUSINESS

Data mining is an essential part of business intelligence (see Chapter 6) because it helps transform millions of pieces of individual data (including demographics, purchase histories, customer-service records, and research results) accumulating in super-sized databases known as *data warehouses* or department-specific subsections known as *data marts*. Data mining helps marketers identify who their most profitable customers are, which goods and services are in highest demand, how to structure promotional campaigns, where to target upcoming sales efforts, and which customers are likely to be high credit risks, among many other benefits.[23]

WHERE YOU CAN LEARN MORE

Intelligent Enterprise magazine, www.intelligententerprise .com, offers numerous articles and news updates on data mining, data warehousing, and other business intelligence topics. You can also learn about specific solutions from the companies that either offer stand-alone data mining products or incorporate the technology into databases and other prospects, including Angoss (www.angoss.com), Insightful (www.insightful.com), SAS (www.sas.com), IBM (www.ibm.com), and Microsoft (www.microsoft .com).

---

customer relationship management
A computer-based method for collecting information and coordinating activities related to a company's interactions with each of its customers

information and coordinate multiple interactions between the company and its customers, companies have turned to **customer relationship management (CRM)** systems for help.

Maintaining long-term relationships with customers has many benefits:[24]

- Acquiring a new customer can cost up to five times as much as keeping an existing one.
- Long-term customers buy more, take less of a company's time, bring in new customers, and are less price sensitive.
- Satisfied customers are the best advertisement for a product.
- Firms perceived to offer superior customer service find that they can charge as much as 10 percent more than their competitors.
- Research shows that dissatisfied customers may tell as many as 20 other people about their bad experiences.

But keeping customers satisfied in an environment where they have more product information available than ever before is a challenge. So some companies try to gain a competitive edge by differentiating the customer experience—making it more personal and compelling.

One-to-one marketing involves individualizing a firm's marketing efforts for a single customer to accommodate the specific customer's needs. Starbucks lets you order coffee drinks in more than 19 000 individualized varieties, for instance.[25] Industrial and technology companies have been customizing multimillion-dollar systems and facilities for the unique demands of individual buyers for years, but thanks to e-commerce and mass customization in more and more industries, consumers can now customize everything from makeup and shoes to cars and furniture.[26] The four key steps to putting an effective one-to-one marketing program in place are (1) identifying your customers; (2) differentiating among them; (3) interacting with them; and (4) customizing your product or service to fit each individual customer's needs.[27]

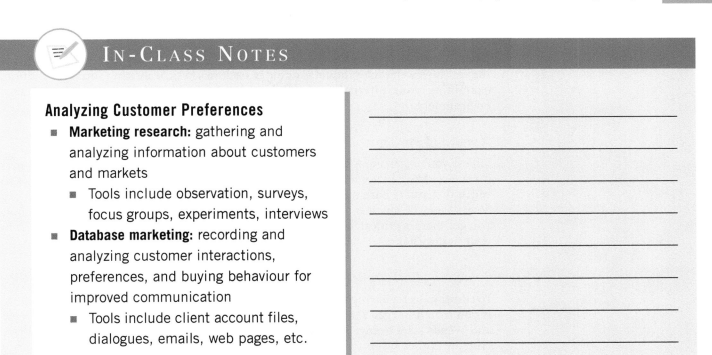

IN-CLASS NOTES

Analyzing Customer Preferences

- **Marketing research:** gathering and analyzing information about customers and markets
    - Tools include observation, surveys, focus groups, experiments, interviews
- **Database marketing:** recording and analyzing customer interactions, preferences, and buying behaviour for improved communication
    - Tools include client account files, dialogues, emails, web pages, etc.

PLANNING YOUR MARKETING STRATEGIES

L.O. 4

By now you can see why successful marketing rarely happens without carefully analyzing and understanding your customers. Once you have learned about your customers, you're ready to begin planning your marketing strategies. *Strategic marketing planning* is a process that involves three steps: (1) examining your current marketing situation; (2) assessing your opportunities and setting your objectives; and (3) developing a marketing strategy to reach those objectives (see Exhibit 11.4). The purpose of strategic marketing planning is to help you identify and create a competitive advantage, something that sets you apart from your rivals and makes your product more appealing to customers.[28] Most companies record the results of their planning efforts in a document called the *marketing plan*. Here's a closer look at the three steps in the process.

Exhibit 11.4 **The Strategic Marketing Planning Process**

Strategic marketing planning comprises three steps: (1) examining your current marketing situation, (2) assessing your opportunities and setting objectives, and (3) developing your marketing strategy.

Examine Current Marketing Situation	**Assess Opportunities and Set Objectives**	**Develop Marketing Strategy**
✓ Review past/current performance	✓ Assess product and market opportunities	✓ Segment market
✓ Evaluate competition	✓ Set specific and measurable objectives	✓ Choose target market
✓ Examine internal strengths and weaknesses		✓ Position product
✓ Analyze external environment		✓ Develop marketing mix

Step 1: Examining Your Current Marketing Situation

Examining your current marketing situation includes reviewing your past performance (how well each product is doing in each market), evaluating your competition, examining your internal strengths and weaknesses, and analyzing the external environment.

Reviewing Performance

Unless you're starting a new business, your company has a history of marketing performance. Maybe sales have slowed in the past year; maybe you've had to cut prices so much that you're barely earning a profit; or maybe sales are going quite well and you have money to invest in new marketing activities. Reviewing where you are and how you got there is critical, because you will want to repeat your successes and learn from your past mistakes.

Evaluating Competition

In addition to reviewing past performance, you must also evaluate your competition. If you own a Burger King franchise, you need to watch what McDonald's, Harvey's, and Wendy's are doing. You also have to keep an eye on Swiss Chalet, Subway, Pizza Hut, and other restaurants in addition to paying attention to any number of ways your customers might satisfy their hunger—including fixing a sandwich at home. Furthermore, you need to watch out for competitors that do not yet exist, like the next big food craze. For instance, when low-carbohydrate diets caught on, established food companies such as Kraft and General Mills found themselves suddenly losing business to competitors they'd never heard of before, like Atkins Nutritionals.[29]

Examining Internal Strengths and Weaknesses

Successful marketers try to identify sources of competitive advantage and areas that need improvement. They look at such things as management, financial resources, production capabilities, distribution networks, managerial expertise, and promotional capabilities. This step is important because you can't develop a successful marketing strategy if you don't know your strengths as well as your limitations. On the basis of your internal analysis, you will be able to decide whether your business should (1) limit itself to those opportunities for which it possesses the required strengths, or (2) challenge itself to reach higher goals by acquiring and developing new strengths.

Understanding your strengths and weaknesses is especially important when evaluating the merits of global expansion. Selling products overseas requires managerial expertise, financial resources and the ability to adjust operations to different cultures, customs, legal requirements, and product specifications (see Chapter 2). Even selling on the Internet requires technological expertise and commitment as well as a solid understanding of customer buying behaviour.

Analyzing the External Environment

Marketers must also analyze a number of external environmental factors when planning their marketing strategies:

- *Economic conditions.* The Bank of Canada's policies cannot be controlled by an organization. Marketers are greatly affected by trends in interest rates, inflation, unemployment, personal income, and savings rates. In tough times, consumers put off buying expensive items such as major appliances, new cars, new furniture, or homes. They cut back on travel, entertainment, and luxury goods. When the economy is good, consumers open their wallets and satisfy their demand for higher-priced goods and services.

■ *Natural environment.* Changes in the natural environment can affect marketers, both positively and negatively. Interruptions in the supply of raw materials can upset even the most carefully put together marketing plans. Floods, droughts, and cold weather can affect the price and availability of many products as well as the behaviour of target customers. For example, ski resorts are highly dependent on the weather. Extreme cold spells or a very mild winter can have a huge negative impact. The results can be devastating for a small ski operator, but even major companies like Vancouver, British Columbia's Intrawest are not immune to the uncontrollable impact of Mother Nature. Each individual mountain has to face these challenges. In Intrawest's case, the effects are lessened by the geographic dispersion of their locations. They have resorts spread out across North America—from Mont-Tremblant in Quebec to Whistler Blackcomb in British Columbia to US locations like Copper Mountain in Colorado.[30]

Ski resort operators have a tenuous relationship with Mother Nature, since uncontrollable weather patterns often reduce potential profits by driving skiers and snowboarders away.

■ *Social and cultural trends.* Planners also study the social and cultural environment to determine shifts in consumer values. If social trends are running against a product, the producer might need more advertising to educate consumers about the product's benefits or alter the product to make it more appealing. When beef consumption fell out of favour, marketers used ads to educate consumers on the benefits of including more beef in their diet. Today's consumers are becoming more and more health conscious. Even Coca-Cola has turned to pushing a portfolio of water brands to take advantage of this trend and deal with the fact that more and more people are reducing their consumption of their flagship brand, Coke. The company recently bought Energy Brands for US$4.1 billion, which is the number-two player (behind Pepsi's Propel Fitness Water) in the enhanced-vitamin-water business.[31] Who would have expected 20 years ago that the cola wars would turn to water? The answer is people who were observing social trends.

■ *Laws and regulations.* Like every other function in business today, marketing is controlled by laws at the local, provincial, federal, and international levels. From product design to pricing to advertising, virtually every task you'll encounter in marketing is affected in some way by laws and regulations. The Food and Drug Regulations force marketers to put standardized nutritional labels on food products. Although these regulations cost manufacturers millions of dollars, they have a huge positive impact for food-testing laboratories.[32] Government laws can also affect competition. Recent regulations give a big boost to cars that meet certain fuel-efficiency requirements and punish those that don't. As of March 20, 2007, the ecoAUTO Rebate Program entitles car buyers to earn rebates of between $1000 to $2000 for buying fuel-efficient vehicles such as the Toyota Prius or the Honda Civic Hybrid.[33]

The federal government provides an incentive for people to purchase vehicles like the environmentally friendly Toyota Prius through the ecoAUTO Rebate Program. Prius buyers will receive a rebate of up to $2000.

■ *Technology.* When technology changes, so must your marketing approaches. Encyclopedia Britannica presents a classic case of how changing technology can turn an industry upside down—almost overnight. The 235-year-old publisher cruised into the 1990s with record sales of its flagship product—an encyclopedia set that cost over $1400, weighed 118 pounds, and consumed four-and-a-half feet of shelf space. But then along came CD-ROMs and the Internet, which enabled much cheaper—and sometimes free—solutions from competitors. Even though most of these alternatives couldn't deliver the comprehensive quality of Britannica, they quickly ate into the company's sales. After a stumble or two, Britannica now has 200 000 paid subscribers online.[34]

Marketers must not only keep on top of today's external environment, they must also think about tomorrow's changes.

Step 2: Assessing Your Opportunities and Setting Your Objectives

Once you've examined your current marketing situation, you're ready to assess your marketing opportunities and set your objectives. Successful companies are always on the lookout for new marketing opportunities, which can be classified into four options: selling more of your existing products in current markets (market penetration), creating new products for your current markets (new product development), selling your existing products in new markets (geographic expansion), or creating new products for new markets (diversification).[35] These options are listed in order of increasing risk; trying new products in unfamiliar markets is usually the riskiest choice of all.

market share
A firm's portion of the total sales in a market

With opportunities in mind, you are ready to set your marketing objectives. A common marketing objective is to achieve a certain **market share**, which is a firm's portion of the total sales within a market. Objectives must be specific and measurable. Establishing a goal to "increase sales in the future" is not a good objective; it doesn't say by how much or by what date. On the other hand, a goal to "increase sales by 25 percent by the end of next year" provides a clear target and a reference against which progress can be measured. Objectives should also be challenging enough to be motivating. Whatever objectives you set, be sure all employees know and understand what the organization wants to accomplish. Every Ritz-Carlton employee, for example, attends a daily 15-minute meeting in which managers repeat the hotel chain's business goals and commitment to customer service.[36]

Step 3: Developing Your Marketing Strategy

marketing strategy
The overall plan for marketing a product

Using your current marketing situation and your objectives as your guide, you're ready to move to the third step. This is where you develop your **marketing strategy**, which consists of dividing your market into *segments* and *niches,* choosing your *target markets* and the *position* you'd like to establish in those markets, and then developing a *marketing mix* to help you get there.

Dividing Markets into Segments

L.O. 5

market
People or businesses that need or want a product and have the money to buy it

market segmentation
The division of the total market into smaller, relatively homogeneous groups

A **market** contains all the customers or businesses that might be interested in a product and can pay for it. Most companies subdivide the market in an economical manner by identifying *market segments*, or homogeneous groups of customers within a market that are significantly different from each other. This process is called **market segmentation**; its objective is to group customers with similar characteristics, behaviours, and needs. Each of these market segments can then be targeted by offering products that are priced, distributed, and promoted differently.

The goal of market segmentation is to understand why certain customers buy what they buy so that you can sell them your products and services by targeting their needs. Here are six factors marketers frequently use to identify market segments:

demographics
The study of statistical characteristics of a population

- *Demographics.* When you segment a market using **demographics**, the statistical analysis of a population, you subdivide your customers according to characteristics such as age, gender, income, race, occupation, or ethnicity. The baby-boomer population—people born after World War II until the mid-1960s—has been receiving a vast amount of attention for quite some time as the dominant group in our economy. But one segment catching the eye of marketers in recent years is the evolving "tween" market, which consists of children (ages 7 to 14) who are growing up quicker than ever. According to YTV, there are 2.5 million tweens in Canada, and they account for $2.9 billion in retail purchases. No surprise, then, that US-based Tween Brands Inc. is planning to expand into Canada with approximately 100 stores of its Limited Too and Justice outlets to give La Senza Girl some competition.[37] Be aware, however, that according to some recent studies, demographic variables are poor predictors of behaviour. For instance, not all Canadian men aged 35 to 44 making $100 000 per year buy a Mercedes. In fact, some don't even buy a luxury car, and those who do may not purchase such cars for the same reasons.[38]

Questionable Marketing Tactics on Campus

Alarmed by how quickly university and college students can bury themselves in debt and fed up with aggressive sales tactics, a growing number of universities are banning or restricting credit card marketing on campus.

Administrators complain that students are bombarded with credit card offers from the moment they step on campus. Marketers have shown up on campuses unannounced and without permission to hawk cards; they stuff applications into bags at campus bookstores and entice students to apply for cards and take on debt with free T-shirts, music CDs, and promises of an easy way to pay for spring break vacations. Some yell at students to get their attention and follow them through hallways to make a sale; they even get student organizations to work for them so that friends pressure friends.

Students are, of course, a prized target for the credit card industry because consumers tend to be loyal to their first credit card. Even though students often have little or no income, they are not considered high-risk borrowers because parents generally bail them out if they get into trouble. As a result, roughly 63 percent of full-time students now have a credit card in their own name. But only about half of those students pay their bills in full each month, and the number of students who usually make just the minimum payment is rising.

While some schools have banned credit card marketers from campus to protect students from their own potentially destructive credit practices, many students say it's unfair for schools to do so. After all, marketers don't give up. They just move across the street or to other locations frequented by students.[39]

Questions for Critical Thinking

1. Should credit card companies be prohibited from soliciting on campuses? Why or why not?
2. Why do credit card companies target students even though they have little or no income?

■ *Geographics.* When differences in buying behaviour are influenced by where people live, it makes sense to use **geographic segmentation**. Segmenting the market into different geographic units such as regions, cities, towns, or neighbourhoods allows companies to customize and sell products that meet the needs of specific markets. For instance, car rental agencies stock more four-wheel-drive vehicles in mountainous regions. The Canadian market can be divided into five regions: Maritimes, Quebec, Ontario, Prairies, and Western Canada.[40]

geographic segmentation
The categorization of customers according to their geographic location

■ *Psychographics.* Whereas demographic segmentation is the study of people from the outside, **psychographics** is the analysis of people from the inside, focusing on their psychological makeup, including attitudes, interests, opinions, and lifestyles. Psychographic analysis focuses on why people behave the way they do by examining such issues as brand preferences, media preferences, reading habits, values, and self-concept. It attempts to understand consumer habits by looking beyond simple statistical data profiles.

psychographics
The classification of customers on the basis of their psychological makeup

■ *Geodemographics.* Dividing markets into distinct neighbourhoods by combining geographic and demographic data is the goal of **geodemographics**. "Systems like PRIZM, developed by Claritas Corporation, and Compusearch's Psyte neighbourhood classification system can link census data with market potential at the level of postal codes and neighbourhoods."[41]

geodemographics
A method of combining geographic data with demographic data to develop profiles of neighbourhood segments

■ *Behaviour.* Markets can also be segmented according to customers' knowledge of, attitude toward, use of, or response to products or product characteristics. This approach is known as **behavioural segmentation**. Many web-based companies ask first-time visitors to fill out a personal profile so they can gear product recommendations and even display customized web pages that appeal to certain behavioural segments.

behavioural segmentation
The categorization of customers according to their relationship with products or response to product characteristics

■ *Usage.* All customers are not created equal. That may sound like a controversial statement, but in terms of marketing it is vital that firms identify and target individuals that are heavy users. Rewards, special financing, and focused promotions are common. It is estimated that for most firms 80 percent of sales come from 20 percent of the consumers (the 80/20 rule).[42] This also helps explain why it seems like every second commercial during a broadcast of *Hockey Night in Canada* is for beer, whereas during a CBC drama airing at the same time on another night this is not the case.

An increasingly popular way to segment e-commerce customers is by Internet usage patterns. Companies are finding that categorizing web users by their session length, time per page, category concentration, and so on helps define the types of marketing that are best suited for each type of user.[43]

When you segment your market, you end up with several customer groups, each representing a potentially productive focus for marketing efforts. However, keep in mind that marketers also segment customers using multiple variables to produce more narrowly defined target groups known as *micro-segments* or *niches*.[44]

Choosing Your Target Markets

target markets
Specific customer groups or
segments to whom a company
wants to sell a particular product

Once you have segmented your market, the next step is to find appropriate target segments or **target markets** to focus your efforts on. Deciding exactly which segment to target—and when—is not an easy task. Sometimes the answer will be obvious, such as when you lack the necessary technological skills or financial power to enter a particular market segment. At other times, you'll have the resources to compete in several segments but not enough resources to compete in all of them. In general, marketers use a variety of criteria to narrow their focus to a few suitable segments. These criteria include size of segment, competition, sales and profit potential, compatibility with company resources and strengths, costs, growth potential, and risks.[45]

Targeting is such a critical part of strategic marketing that missteps can be costly. Reaching a specific target requires careful strategy and expertise. Even with their tremendous knowledge and resources, Bell Mobility decided to team up with British-based Virgin Group to launch a wireless, no-contract service aimed at the under-25 crowd. Features geared toward this market include simplified email as well as music content from MTV. Virgin made a similar successful deal in the United States and managed to sign up 1.75 million subscribers.[46]

Exhibit 11.5 diagrams three popular strategies for reaching target markets. Companies that practise *undifferentiated marketing* (or mass marketing) ignore differences among buyers and offer only one product or product line to satisfy the entire market. This strategy, which concludes that all buyers have similar needs that can be served with the same standardized product, was more popular in the past than it is today. Initially, Henry Ford sold only one type of car (the Model T Ford) in one colour (black) to the entire market.

By contrast, companies that manufacture or sell a variety of products to several target customer groups practise *differentiated marketing*. General Motors, for instance, manufactures a car for every personality, and Nike produces a shoe for every athlete. Canadian fashion retailer Michael Gold continues to add stores across the country under the following banners: Sirens, Suzy Shier, Stitches, Urban Planet, and Bluenotes. His various stores cater to different client needs. Suzy Shier caters more to career women; Sirens is trendier and offers casual fashions and accessories; Urban Planet sells clothing, shoes, and costume jewellery to men and women.[47] Differentiated marketing is a popular approach, but it requires substantial resources because you have to tailor products, prices, promotional efforts, and distribution arrangements for each customer group.

When company resources are limited, *concentrated (niche) marketing* may be the best marketing strategy. You acknowledge that different market segments exist and choose to target just one. WestJet was created by four Calgary entrepreneurs who saw an opportunity to provide low-fare air travel across western Canada.[48] The biggest

Exhibit 11.5 **Market-Coverage Strategies**

Three alternative market-coverage strategies are undifferentiated marketing, differentiated marketing, and concentrated marketing.

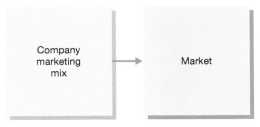

1. Undifferentiated marketing

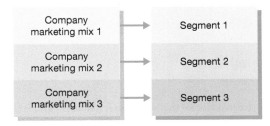

2. Differentiated marketing

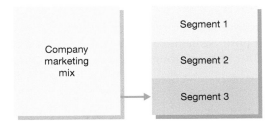

3. Concentrated marketing

Source: Gary Armstrong and Philip Kotler, *Marketing An Introduction*, 5th ed. (Upper Saddle River, NJ: Prentice Hall 2000), 201.

advantage of concentrated marketing is that it allows you to focus all of your time and resources on a single type of customer. The strategy can be risky, however, because you've staked your company's fortune on just one segment. For that reason many firms turn to companies like Youthography, a Toronto-based youth-marketing consultancy that provides expertise on people aged 13 to 29.[49]

Positioning Your Product

Once a company has decided which segments of the market it will enter, it must then decide what position it wants to occupy within those segments. **Positioning** your product is the act of designing your company's offering and image so that it occupies a meaningful and distinct competitive position in your target customers' minds.

Even though consumers position products with or without the help of marketers, marketers do not want to leave their product's position to chance. Instead, they choose positions that will give their products the greatest advantage in selected target markets.[50] They can position their products on specific product features or attributes (size, ease of use, style, performance, quality, durability, design), on the services that accompany the product (convenient delivery, lifetime customer support, installation methods), on the product's image (reliability or sophistication), on price (low cost or premium), on category leadership (the leading online bookseller), and so forth. For example, BMW and Porsche associate their products with performance, Mercedes-Benz

positioning
Using promotion, product, distribution, and price to differentiate a good or service from those of competitors in the minds of prospective buyers

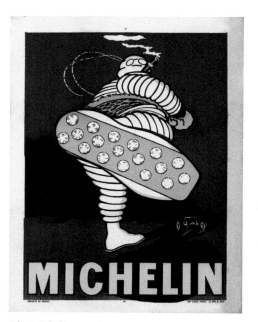

The Michelin Man is a 110-year-old lovable character that has changed over time to meet the needs of society. To make sure that his image reflects the evolution and strength of their tires, Michelin has slimmed down the icon over the years to reflect a positive image to today's more health-conscious consumers.

with luxury, and Volvo with safety. Organizing products and services into categories based on the perceived position helps consumers simplify the buying process. Instead of test-driving all cars, for instance, they may focus on those they perceive to be high-performance vehicles.

Developing the Marketing Mix

marketing mix
The four key elements of marketing strategy: product, price, distribution (place), and promotion

After you've segmented your market, selected your target market, and positioned your product, your next task is to develop a marketing mix. A firm's **marketing mix** (often called the *four Ps*) consists of product, price, place (or distribution), and promotion (see Exhibit 11.6).

product
A good or service used as the basis of commerce

Products The most basic marketing mix element is *product*, which covers the product itself plus brand name, design, packaging, services, quality, and warranty. From a marketing standpoint, a **product** is anything offered for the purpose of satisfying a want or a need in a marketing exchange. If you were asked to name three popular products off the top of your head, you might think of McCain's French Fries, the Porsche 911, or Mac Cosmetics. You might not think of the Ottawa Senators, Marineland, or *Hockey Night in Canada*. That's because we tend to think of products as *tangible* objects, or things that we can actually touch and possess. Hockey teams, amusement parks, and television programs provide an *intangible* service for our use or enjoyment, not for our ownership. Nevertheless, these and other services are products just the same. In fact, broadly defined, products can be persons, places, physical objects, ideas, services, and organizations.

price
The amount of money charged for a product or service

Pricing **Price**, the amount of money customers pay for the product (including any discounts), is the second major component of a firm's marketing mix. Developing a product's price is one of the most critical decisions a company must make, because price is the only element in a company's marketing mix that produces revenue—all other elements represent costs. Thus, setting a product's price not only determines the amount of income your company will generate from sales of that product, but it can also differentiate the product from the competition. As you can imagine, determining the right price is not an easy task. If a company charges too much, it will generate fewer sales, if it charges too little, it will sacrifice potential profits.

Exhibit 11.6 **Positioning and the Marketing Environment**

When positioning products for target markets, you need to consider the four marketing mix elements plus the external environment.

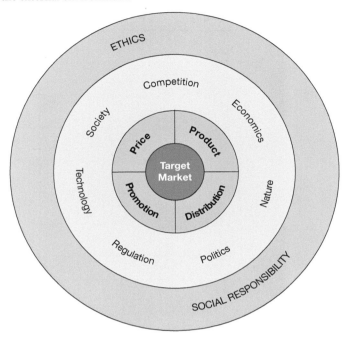

distribution channels
Systems for moving goods and services from producers to customers; also known as marketing channels

Distribution or Place *Place* (commonly referred to as *distribution*) is the third marketing mix element. It covers the organized network of firms that move goods and services from the producer to the consumer. This network is also known as *marketing channels* or **distribution channels**. A company's channel decisions directly affect all other marketing decisions. For instance, a company's pricing depends on whether it uses mass merchandisers or high-quality specialty stores. A firm's sales force and advertising decisions depend on how much training, motivation, and support the dealers need.[51]

promotion
The wide variety of persuasive techniques used by companies to communicate with their target markets and the general public

Promotional Strategies **Promotion**, the fourth marketing mix element, includes all activities the firm undertakes to communicate its products to the target market: advertising, personal selling, public relations, and sales promotion. Promotion may take the form of direct, face-to-face communication or indirect communication through such media as television, radio, magazines, newspapers, direct mail, billboards, bus ads, the Internet, and other channels. Of the four components in a firm's marketing mix, promotion is perhaps the one most often associated with marketing. Although it is no guarantee of success, promotion does have a profound impact on a product's performance in the marketplace.

The remainder of this chapter takes a closer look at what's involved in developing product and pricing strategies. Chapter 12 discusses the steps involved in developing a firm's distribution and promotional strategies.

Marineland ads are ever-present during the summer season; the catchy jingle and repeated ads plant Marineland in the minds of Canadians.

In-Class Notes

Planning Marketing Strategies

- **Step 1: Examine current marketing situation:** review performance, evaluate the competition, examine your strengths and weaknesses, analyze the external environment
- **Step 2: Assess opportunities and set objectives:** market penetration, new product development, geographic expansion, diversification
- **Step 3: Develop marketing strategies:** segments, target market, positioning, marketing mix

_____

_____

_____

_____

_____

_____

_____

L.O. 6

DEVELOPING PRODUCT STRATEGIES

Why does General Motors offer a product in nearly every category of automobile, from economy cars to SUVs, whereas Ferrari offers only a handful of models, all of which are ultra-expensive sports cars? Why is Nokia now an electronics company and not a paper or tire company? Why can't you buy a burger and fries at Starbucks or fettuccine alfredo at McDonald's? The answers to these questions might seem obvious to consumers, but every company needs to address *product strategy* questions at some point to maintain competitiveness.

Product strategies are among the most difficult and important decisions managers need to make, since products can take months or years and millions of dollars to develop and introduce to the marketplace. Most companies have survived the occasional flop, but few can survive a sustained series of product mistakes. To maximize the chances of success, companies should follow a clear process for developing new products:[52]

1. *Generate new ideas.* New product ideas can come from a variety of sources, including customers, salespeople, research engineers, and even competitors. Some consumer-product companies employ thousands of teenagers to report back on what's hot and what's not all over the world.[53] Of course, many "new" product ideas are simply improvements to or variations on existing products, but even those slight alterations can generate big revenues.

2. *Develop and screen product concepts.* Many of these ideas need to be explored further and expanded into realistic product concepts, then managers need to screen these concepts to see which are compatible with the company's overall strategy and resources and which stand the best chance of success in the marketplace.

3. *Develop marketing strategies.* At this stage, marketing specialists create a preliminary marketing plan that identifies potential customers, pricing options, distribution channels, and so on.

4. *Analyze business potential.* With a clearer idea of what the product will be and who might buy it, financial experts can then compare the cost of designing and manufacturing the product (or delivering the service) with the price the company

hopes to charge for it. If the *business case* doesn't look promising, most companies will either drop the idea or find ways to improve it.

5. *Design and develop the products.* If the product idea makes financial sense, the next step is to devote time and resources to completing the design and getting it ready for production. Depending on the product, this could take anywhere from many months to many years. Companies that are fast and efficient have a considerable advantage over their competitors.

6. *Test market.* Have you ever seen a new menu item show up in your favourite fast-food restaurant only to disappear a few weeks later? Chances are the company was *test marketing* it, trying to gauge marketplace reaction before investing in wide-spread marketing efforts.

7. *Commercialize.* When the chances of success look good, the company then ramps up production and markets the product on a wide scale.

This process doesn't guarantee success, of course, but it does improve the chances. Cutting corners on any of these seven steps can dramatically increase the chance of failure.

Types of Products

Although some products are predominantly tangible and others are mostly intangible, most products fall somewhere between these two extremes. When you buy software like Adobe's Acrobat, for example, you get service features along with the product—such as product updates and customer assistance. The *product continuum* indicates the relative amounts of tangible and intangible components in a product (see Exhibit 11.7). Education is a product at the intangible extreme, whereas salt and shoes are at the tangible extreme. A chain like Pizza Delight falls in the middle because it involves both tangible (food) and intangible (service) components.

Service products have some special characteristics that affect the way they are marketed. As we have seen, *intangibility* is one fundamental characteristic. You can't usually show a service in an ad, demonstrate it before customers buy, mass produce it, or give customers anything tangible to show for their purchase. Services marketers often compensate for intangibility by using tangible symbols or by adding tangible components to their products. Prudential Insurance, for example, uses the Rock of Gibraltar as a symbol of stability.

Another unique aspect of service products is *perishability*. Because services cannot usually be created in advance or held in storage until people are ready to buy, services are time sensitive. For instance, if WestJet doesn't sell seats on a particular flight, once the flight takes off an unsold seat can never produce revenue. Hotel rooms, movie theatre seats, and restaurants are similar. For this reason, many services try to shift customer demand by offering discounts or promotions during slow periods.

Another way that marketers categorize products is by use. Both organizations and consumers use many of the same products, but they use them for different reasons and in different ways. Individual consumers or households generally purchase smaller quantities of goods and services for personal use. Products that are primarily sold to consumers are

Exhibit 11.7   **The Product Continuum**

Products contain both tangible and intangible components; predominantly tangible products are categorized as goods, whereas predominantly intangible products are categorized as services.

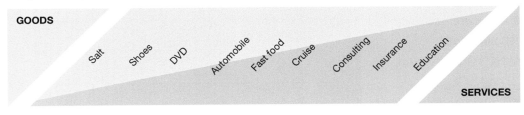

GOODS — Salt, Shoes, DVD, Automobile, Fast food, Cruise, Consulting, Insurance, Education — SERVICES

Tangible dominant   Intangible dominant

known as *consumer products*. Consumer products can be classified into four subgroups, depending on how people shop for them:

- *Convenience products* are the goods and services that people buy frequently, without much conscious thought, such as toothpaste, dry cleaning, and photocopying.
- *Shopping products* are fairly important goods and services that people buy less frequently: a stereo, a computer, a refrigerator, or a university education. Such purchases require more thought and comparison shopping to check on price, features, quality, and reputation.
- *Specialty products* include CK perfume or Armani suits—particular brands that the buyer especially wants and will seek out, regardless of location or price. Specialty products are not necessarily expensive, but they are products that customers go out of their way to buy and rarely accept substitutes for. Even through a recent recession, the Danish firm Bang & Olufsen fared well selling its world-renowned home entertainment gear, which includes $20 000 TV sets and $8000 speakers.[54]
- *Unsought goods* are products that people do not normally think of buying, such as life insurance, cemetery plots, and new products they must be made aware of through promotion.[55]

By contrast, *organizational products*, or products sold to firms, are generally purchased in large quantities and are not for personal use. Two categories of organizational products are expense items and capital items. *Expense items* are relatively inexpensive goods and services that organizations generally use within a year of purchase (e.g., pencils and printer cartridges). *Capital items*, by contrast, are more expensive organizational products and have a longer useful life (e.g., desks, photocopiers, and computers).

Aside from dividing products into expense and capital items, organizational buyers and sellers often classify products according to their intended usage.

- *Raw materials* like iron ore, crude petroleum, lumber, and chemicals are used in the production of final products.
- *Components* like spark plugs and printer cartridges are similar to raw materials. They also become part of the manufacturer's final products.
- *Supplies* such as pencils, nails, and light bulbs that are used in a firm's daily operations are considered expense items.
- *Installations* such as factories, power plants, airports, production lines, and semiconductor fabrication machinery are major capital projects.
- *Equipment* includes less-expensive capital items such as desks, telephones, and fax machines that are shorter-lived than installations.
- *Business services* range from simple and fairly risk-free services such as landscaping and cleaning to complex services such as management consulting and auditing.

In-Class Notes

Products
- **Development process:** seven key steps from idea to commercialization
- **Services:** intangible and perishable
- **Classification of consumer goods:** convenience, shopping, specialty, and unsought
- **Organizational products:** capital vs. expense

_____

_____

_____

_____

_____

Exhibit 11.8   **The Product Life Cycle**

Exhibit 11.8   **The Product Life Cycle**

Most products and product categories move through a life cycle similar to the one represented by the curve in this diagram. However, the duration of each stage varies widely from product to product.

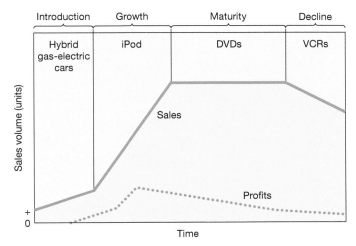

The Product Life Cycle

L.O. 7

Regardless of a product's classification, few products last forever. Most products go through a **product life cycle**, passing through four distinct stages in sales and profits: introduction, growth, maturity, and decline (see Exhibit 11.8). As the product passes from stage to stage, various marketing approaches become appropriate.

product life cycle
Four basic stages through which a product progresses: introduction, growth, maturity, and decline

The product life cycle can describe a product class (gasoline-powered automobiles), a product form (sport-utility vehicles), or a brand (Ford Explorer). Product classes and forms tend to have the longest life cycles, whereas specific brands tend to have shorter life cycles. The amount of time that a product remains in any one stage depends on customer needs and preferences, economic conditions, the nature of the product, and the marketer's strategy. Still, the increase in new products, changing technology, globalization, and the ability to quickly imitate competitors is pushing product forms and brands through their life cycles much faster.

Consider electronics, where product life is now a matter of months. Why? Smart companies know that if they don't keep innovating, competitors who do will capture the business. Such was the case with Polaroid, a company that failed to properly respond to digital technology. One by one, Polaroid customers defected to digital cameras or other technologies. Polaroid missed the opportunity to leverage its name and take advantage of new technologies.[56]

Introduction

The first stage in the product life cycle is the *introductory stage*, during which producers launch a new product and stimulate demand. In this stage, companies typically spend heavily on conducting research and development efforts to create the new product, on developing promotions to build awareness of the product, and on establishing the distribution system to get the product into the marketplace. Every product—from personal computers to digital cameras—gets its start in this stage. The producer makes little profit during the introduction; however, these start-up costs are a necessary investment if the new product is to succeed.

Growth

After the introductory stage comes the *growth stage*, marked by a rapid jump in sales and, usually, an increase in the number of competitors and distribution outlets. As competition increases, so does the struggle for market share. This situation creates pressure to introduce new product features and to maintain large promotional budgets and competitive prices. In fact, marketing in this stage is so expensive that it can drive out smaller, weaker firms. With enough growth, however, a firm can often produce and deliver its products more economically than in the introduction phase. Thus, the growth stage can bring handsome profits for those who survive.

Maturity

During the *maturity stage,* the longest in the product life cycle, sales begin to level off or show a slight decline. Most products are in the maturity stage of the life cycle when competition increases and market share is maximized—making further expansion difficult. Because the costs of introduction and growth have diminished in this stage, most companies try to keep mature products alive so they can use the resulting profits to fund development of new products. Some companies extend the life of a mature product by modifying the product's characteristics to improve the product's quality and performance. Keebler, for instance, has extended the life of its popular cookies by selling them in convenient mini-versions. Packaged in resealable cans, the mini-cookies are sold at convenience stores to appeal to consumers on the run.[57]

Decline

Although maturity can be extended for many years, most products eventually enter the *decline stage,* when sales and profits slip and then fade away. Declines occur for several reasons: changing demographics, shifts in popular taste, product competition, and advances in technology. When a product reaches this point in the life cycle, the company must decide whether to keep it and reduce the product's costs to compensate for declining sales or discontinue it and focus on developing newer products. Companies are not scrambling to invest money to create new and improved VCRs, for instance. The life cycle is at an end. Many retailers and manufacturers no longer sell or produce new VCRs. The manufacturers that are still in the market are just trying to milk any last sales at this point in time. DVDs will follow as new technologies continue to improve and gain acceptance.

Product Identities

Creating an identity for your products is an important part of developing effective product strategies. Companies create product identities by assigning their products a **brand** identity—a unique name or design that sets the product apart from those offered by competitors—and by designing and producing an attractive package and label for the product.

Branding

Jeep, Levi's, and Labatt are **brand names**, the portion of a brand that can be spoken, including letters, words, or numbers. McDonald's golden arches symbol is an example of a **brand mark**, the portion of a brand that cannot be expressed verbally. The choice of a brand name and any associated brand marks can be a critical success factor. A well-known brand name, for instance, can generate more sales than an unknown name. As a result, manufacturers aggressively protect their names. Sometimes companies like Warner Brothers *license* or sell the rights to specific well-known names and symbols—such as Looney Tunes cartoon characters—to manufacturers that use the licensed items to help sell products.

Brand names and brand symbols may be registered with the Trade-marks Office in Gatineau, Quebec.[58] As Appendix A explains, a **trademark** is a brand that has been given legal protection so that its owner has exclusive rights to its use. Keep in mind, however, that when a name becomes too widely used it no longer qualifies for protection under trademark laws. Cellophane, kerosene, linoleum, escalator, zipper, shredded wheat, and raisin bran are just a few of the many brand names that have passed into public domain, much to their creators' dismay.

Brand names may be owned by manufacturers, retailers, wholesalers, and a variety of business types. Brands offered and promoted by a national manufacturer, such as Procter & Gamble's Tide detergent and Pampers disposable diapers, are called **national brands**. **Private brands** are not linked to a manufacturer but instead carry a wholesaler's or a retailer's brand. Shoppers Drug Mart promotes private-label brands like Life and Quo.

---

brand
A name, term, sign, symbol, design, or combination of these used to identify the products of a firm and to differentiate them from competing products

L.O. 8

brand names
The portion of a brand that can be expressed orally, including letters, words, or numbers

brand mark
The portion of a brand that cannot be expressed verbally

trademark
A brand that has been given legal protection so that its owner has exclusive rights to its use

national brands
Brands owned by manufacturers and that are distributed nationally

private brands
Brands that carry the label of a retailer or a wholesaler rather than a manufacturer

President's Choice and Motomaster are private brands sold by Loblaw and Canadian Tire, respectively. As an alternative to branded products, some retailers also offer **generic products**, which are packaged in plain containers that bear only the name of the product. Generic products can cost up to 40 percent less than brand-name products because of uneven quality, plain packaging, and lack of promotion. Yet generic goods have found a definite market niche, as a look at your local supermarket shelves will confirm.

Co-branding is another way to strengthen brands and products. **Co-branding** occurs when two or more companies team up to closely link their names in a single product. It can help change a product's image. In an attempt to associate the Kodak brand with the output side of digital photography, the company has been co-branding its name with all things digital. The Kodak name sits above Lexmark's logo on an ink-jet printer and it's all over the websites of companies that trumpet their use of Kodak processing and photo paper.[59]

Brand equity is a term used to describe the extra value a brand name provides to a product beyond its functional benefits.[60] It can be loosely compared to stock value. Stock price variations are usually based on economic performance and the company's future prospects. On the other hand, *brand equity* is based on reputation and perception among target groups. It is directly linked to issues like customer satisfaction, value, and long-term integrated marketing communication effects. It is established by the consumers' experiences and views of the brand name. Therefore, if a company launches a poorly manufactured product that fails miserably and leaves a lot of unhappy customers, brand equity may be damaged. Similarly, if a brand is associated with a crisis (e.g., food poisoning, unfair labour practices) all products carrying the brand name are affected. At the opposite extreme, all positive coverage (e.g., corporate responsibility, good product reviews, positive word of mouth) are reflected on all products that carry a particular brand name. In practical terms, strong brand equity helps a company take advantage of consumer perceptions to maintain and increase market share, set or maintain premium prices, launch new readily acceptable products, and fight competitively for consumer business.

Packaging

L.O. 9

Another way that marketers create an identity for their products is through packaging. Most products need some form of packaging to protect the product from damage or tampering and to make it convenient for customers to purchase. In some cases, packaging is an essential part of the product itself, like microwave popcorn. Besides function, however, packaging plays an important role in a product's marketing strategy. Packaging makes products easier to display, facilitates the sale of smaller products, serves as a means of product differentiation, and enhances the product's overall appeal and convenience.

Companies spend a lot of money on packaging to attract consumer attention and to promote a product's benefits through the package's shape, composition, and design. Gatorade's ergonomically designed bottle, Quaker Oats cereal in bags, and Coca-Cola's 12-pack refrigerator dispenser box are examples of innovative packaging with strong consumer appeal.

generic products
Products characterized by a plain label, with no advertising and no brand name

co-branding
A partnership between two or more companies to closely link their brand names together for a single product

brand equity
The extra value a brand name provides to a product beyond its functional benefits

IN-CLASS NOTES

Branding Products
- **Branding:** brand marks and trademarks
- **Brand equity:** the perceived value derived beyond the products functional value
- **Private-label vs. national brands:** category based on type of owner

Labelling

Labelling is an important part of packaging. Whether the label is a separate element attached to the package or a printed part of the container, it serves to identify a brand. Labels also provide grading information about the product and information about ingredients, operating procedures, shelf life, or risks. The labelling of foods, drugs, cosmetics, and many health products is regulated under various federal laws, which often require disclosures about potential dangers, benefits, and other issues consumers need to consider when making a buying decision.

Labels do more than communicate with consumers. They are also used by manufacturers and retailers as a tool for monitoring product performance and inventory. **Universal Product Codes (UPCs)**, those black stripes (bar codes) on packages, give companies a cost-effective method of tracking the movement of goods. Store checkout scanners read UPC codes and relay the identity, sales, and prices of all products to the retailer's computer system. Such data can help retailers and manufacturers measure the effectiveness of promotions such as coupons and in-store displays. They are also helpful for inventory control.

Universal Product Codes (UPCs)
A bar code on a product's package that provides information read by optical scanners

L.O. 10

Product-Line and Product-Mix Strategies

In addition to developing branding, packaging, and labelling strategies, a company must decide how many products it will offer. To stay competitive, most companies continually add and drop products to ensure that declining items will be replaced by growth products. A **product line** is a group of products that are similar in terms of use or characteristics. The General Mills Canada snack-food product line, for example, includes Bugles, Fruit Roll-Ups, Nature Valley Granola Bars, and Pop Secret popcorn. Within each product line, a company confronts decisions about the number of goods and services to offer.

An organization with several product lines has a **product mix**, a collection of goods or services offered for sale. For example, the General Mills product mix consists of cereals, baking products, desserts, snack foods, main meals, and so on (see Exhibit 11.9[61]). Three

product line
A series of related products offered by a firm

product mix
The complete list of all products that a company offers for sale

---

Exhibit 11.9   **The Product Mix at General Mills Canada**

Selected products from General Mills Canada show a product mix that is fairly wide but that varies in length and depth within each product line.

PRODUCT LINES	READY-TO-EAT CEREALS	MAIN MEALS AND SIDE DISHES	BAKING PRODUCTS AND DESSERTS	SNACKS	FROZEN SNACKS
	Cheerios	Green Giant Create A Meal	Bisquick	Bugles	Pillsbury Pizza Minis
	Oatmeal Crisp	Hamburger Helper	Betty Crocker angel food cakes	Nature Valley Crunchy Granola Bars	Pillsbury Mini Pops
	Golden Grahams	Chicken Helper	Betty Crocker brownie mixes	Nature Valley Chewy Trail Mix Bars	Pillsbury Pizza Pops
	Lucky Charms	Tuna Helper	Betty Crocker SuperMoist cake mixes	Pop Secret popcorn	
	Count Chocula	Bowl Appétit!	Betty Crocker Snackin' Cake mixes	Fruit Roll-Ups	
	Chex	Green Giant canned vegetables	Betty Crocker frosting	Fruit by the Foot	
	Trix	Specialty potatoes (mashed and sliced)		Dunkaroos	
	Fibre 1	Old El Paso meals			

| Exhibit 11.10 | **Expanding the Product Line** |

Knowing that no product or category has an unlimited life cycle, companies use one or more of these product-line expansion methods to keep sales strong.

METHOD OF EXPANSION	HOW IT WORKS	EXAMPLE
Line filling	Developing items to fill gaps in the market that have been overlooked by competitors or have emerged as consumers' tastes and needs shift	Alka-Seltzer Plus Cold Medicine
Line extension	Creating a new variation of a basic product	Oatmeal Crisp – Maple Nut
Brand extension	Putting the brand for an existing product category into a new category	Nestlé Smarties Ice Cream
Line stretching	Adding higher- or lower-priced items at either end of the product line to extend its appeal to new economic groups	Volkswagen Phaeton; Mercedes C230 Sport Coupe

important dimensions of a company's product mix are *width*, *length*, and *depth*. A company's product mix is *wide* if it has several different product lines. General Mills Canada's product mix, for instance, is fairly wide with five or more product lines. A company's product mix is *long* if it carries several items in its product lines, as General Mills Canada does. A product mix is *deep* if it has a number of versions of *each* product in a product line. General Mills Canada, for example, produces several different versions of Cheerios—frosted, multigrain, and honey nut, to name a few. The same is true for many other products in the company's other product lines.

When deciding on the dimensions of a product mix, a company must weigh the risks and rewards associated with various approaches. Some companies limit the number of product offerings and focus on selling a few selected items to be economical: Doing so keeps the production costs per unit down and limits selling expenses to a single sales force. Other companies adopt a full-line strategy as a protection against shifts in technology, taste, and economic conditions.

As Exhibit 11.10 shows, you can expand your product line in a number of ways. You can introduce additional items in a given product category under the same brand name—such as new flavours, forms, colours, ingredients, or package sizes (line extension). You can also develop new items to fill gaps in the marketplace (line filling), extend the brand to new product categories (brand extension), and stretch the line to include lower- or higher-priced items (line stretching).[62] These approaches are quite popular; only about 5 percent of new product launches are new brands. CEO of Nestlé Canada, Bob Leonidas, says that the company will continue to add line extensions for the number-one chocolate bar in the country: Kit Kat. In recent years, we have seen the addition of Kit Kat Dark, Kit Kat Peanut Butter, as well as single and chunky sizes, and of course the brand extension of Kit Kat ice cream. Building on the name recognition of an existing brand cuts the costs and risks of introducing new products.

Of course, taking a respected brand into new territory must be handled with care. Two of the biggest risks with product-line extensions include a loss of brand identity (weakening of the brand's meaning) and cannibalization of sales of other products in the product line. There are limits to how far a brand name can be stretched to accommodate new products, as Nestlé learned in Britain. The Kit Kat brand was stretched too far with 10 new flavours in one year, including lemon, yogurt, mango, passion fruit, tiramisu, and lime Crush. Sales initially spiked but consumers became exhausted and confused by all the flavours. Sales dropped by 17 percent within one year of this brand abuse.[63]

Nestlé Canada is creating new extensions of Kit Kat to capitalize on the brand equity in Canada's number-one chocolate bar. One of the latest additions is Kit Kat Peanut Butter.

IN-CLASS NOTES

Product-Line and Product-Mix Decisions

- **Product line:** line filling, line extension, brand filling, brand extension
- **Product mix:** width, length, depth, risks, and rewards

_____

_____

_____

_____

L.O. 11

DEVELOPING PRICING STRATEGIES

A company's pricing decisions are determined by manufacturing and selling costs, competition, and the needs of wholesalers and retailers who distribute the product to the final customer. In addition, pricing is influenced by a firm's marketing objectives, government regulations, consumer perceptions, and consumer demand.

- *Marketing objectives.* The first step in setting a price is to match it to the objectives you set in your strategic marketing plan. Is your goal to increase market share, increase sales, improve profits, project a particular image, or combat competition? For example, Rolex uses premium pricing along with other marketing mix elements to give its watches a luxury position.

- *Government regulations.* Government plays a big role in pricing in many countries. To protect consumers and encourage fair competition, governments have enacted various price-related laws over the years. Three important classes of pricing are regulated: (1) *price fixing*—an agreement among two or more companies supplying the same type of products as to the prices they will charge; (2) *price discrimination*—the practice of unfairly offering attractive discounts to some customers but not to others; and (3) *deceptive pricing*—pricing schemes that are considered misleading.

- *Consumer perceptions.* Another consideration is the perception of quality that your price will elicit from your customers. When people shop, they usually have a rough price range in mind. An unexpectedly low price triggers fear that the item is of low quality.

- *Consumer demand.* Whereas a company's costs establish a floor for prices, demand for a product establishes a ceiling. Theoretically, if the price for an item is too high, demand falls and the producers reduce their prices to stimulate demand. Conversely, if the price for an item is too low, demand increases and the producers are motivated to raise prices. As prices climb and profits improve, producers boost their output until supply and demand are in balance and prices stabilize. Nonetheless, the relationship between price and demand isn't always this perfect. Some goods and services are relatively insensitive to changes in price; others are highly responsive. Marketers refer to sensitivity as **price elasticity**—how responsive demand will be to a change in price.

price elasticity
A measure of the sensitivity of demand to changes in price

When companies set their prices they take these factors—among others—into account before choosing a general pricing approach. Common pricing approaches include cost-based pricing, price-based pricing, skimming, penetration pricing, and discounting.

Cost-Based and Price-Based Pricing

Many companies simplify the pricing task by using *cost-based pricing* (also known as cost-plus pricing). They price by starting with the cost of producing a good or a service and then add a mark-up to the cost of the product. This form of pricing, while simple, makes little sense. First, any pricing that ignores demand and competitor prices is not likely to lead to the best price. Second, although cost-based pricing may ensure a certain profit, companies using this strategy tend to sacrifice profit opportunity.

Recent thinking holds that cost should be the last item analyzed in the pricing formula, not the first. Companies that use *price-based pricing* can maximize their profit by first establishing an optimal price for a product or service. The product's price is based on an analysis of a product's competitive advantages, the user's perception of the item, and the market being targeted. Once the desired price has been established, the firm focuses its energies on keeping costs at a level that will allow for a healthy profit. Although few businesses fail from overpricing their products, many more will fail from underpricing them.[64]

Price Skimming

A product's price seldom remains constant and will vary depending on the product's stage in its life cycle. During the introductory phase, for example, the objective might be to recover product development costs as quickly as possible. To achieve this goal, the manufacturer might charge a high initial price—a practice known as **skimming**—and then drop the price later when the product is no longer a novelty and competition heats up. Products such as HDTV and flat-screen monitors are perfect examples of this practice. Price skimming makes sense under two conditions: (1) if the product's quality and image support a higher price, and (2) if competitors cannot easily enter the market with competing products and undercut the price.

skimming
Charging a high price for a new product during the introductory stage and lowering the price later

Penetration Pricing

Rather than setting a high initial price to skim off a small but profitable market segment, a company might try to build sales volume by charging a low initial price, a practice known as **penetration pricing**. This approach has the added advantage of discouraging competition because the low price (which competitors would be pressured to match) limits the profit potential for everyone.

Penetration pricing can also help expand the entire product category by attracting customers who wouldn't have purchased at higher, skim-pricing levels. Furthermore, if a company is new to a category pioneered by another company, this strategy can help take customers away from the pioneer.[65] Still, the strategy makes most sense when the market is highly price sensitive so that a low price generates additional sales and the company can maintain its low-price position long enough to keep out competition.

penetration pricing
Introducing a new product at a low price in hopes of building sales volume quickly

Price Discounts

Once a company has set a product's price, it may choose to adjust that price from time to time to account for changing market situations or changing customer preferences. When you use **discount pricing**, you offer various types of temporary price reductions, depending on the type of customer being targeted and the type of item being offered. You may decide to offer a trade discount to wholesalers or retailers as a way of encouraging orders, or you may offer cash discounts to reward customers who pay cash or pay promptly. You may offer a quantity discount to buyers who buy large volumes, or you may offer a seasonal discount to buyers who buy merchandise or services out of season.

discount pricing
Offering a reduction in price

Another way to discount products is by *value pricing* them, charging a fairly affordable price for a high-quality offering. Many restaurants offer value menus for certain times of the day or certain customer segments, such as seniors. This strategy builds loyalty among price-conscious customers without damaging a product's quality image.

Although discounts are a popular way to boost the sales of a product, the downside is that they can touch off price wars among competitors. Price wars encourage customers to focus only on a product's pricing, and not on its value or benefits. Thus, they can hurt a business—even an entire industry—for years.

IN-CLASS NOTES

Pricing
- **Strategic pricing considerations:** marketing objectives, consumer perceptions, consumer demand, and government regulations
- **Pricing approaches:**
  - Cost based vs. price based
  - Skimming vs. penetration pricing
  - Discounting

_____

_____

_____

_____

_____

_____

BEHIND THE SCENES

Shoppers Cosmetics: Makeup Beautifies the Bottom Line

Can you remember the last time that you walked into a new or newly renovated Shoppers Drug Mart big-box pharmacy? Close your eyes for a second. What is the first thing that you see as you enter the store? Cosmetics! A few years ago Shoppers decided to increase their cosmetics lines and try to capture the upscale cosmetics market, which was traditionally controlled by department stores. They had tried, for some time, to convince companies like Estée Lauder to bring high-end brands like Clinique into their stores without success. Why the big emphasis in this area? Profits! High-end cosmetics can carry margins of 40 percent or more. That is significant in the competitive retail industry. Compare that to the 3 to 4 percent margins typically earned by grocery stores and the strategic leap of faith is easy to understand.

Why would a manufacturer resist the opportunity to be sold in 1000 additional outlets in Canada? As you have read in this chapter, the answer is quite simple: Companies, especially high-end cosmetics firms like Estée Lauder, protect their brands and try to ensure that they are sold in outlets that reflect their image and respect the expectations of their core customers. High-end brands need to ensure that their target market consumer does not get alienated. Clearly, the traditional drugstore model was ideal for lower-end brands

like Revlon and Maybelline—consumers flocked to purchase reasonably priced makeup in drugstores—but they were traditionally no place for the likes of Chanel, Clinique, and other higher-end names.

Despite being denied in the past, Shoppers Drug Mart was unwilling to accept this rejection. Rather, they decided to take appropriate measures to make Shoppers a destination worthy of the lucrative business from high-end cosmetics. But how could they do it? Remember the old saying: You have to spend money to make money. As you saw in the opening case, Shoppers was investing heavily in building new locations and improving or moving older locations. These updated stores have dedicated primary space that directs traffic flow to the cosmetics section. Appealing layouts and improved service is changing the image of pharmacy shopping, and Shoppers is at the front of the pack—and has the cosmetics sales to prove it.

All of the work paid off. A recent announcement sent shivers up the spines of department store executives in 2007 when Shoppers became the first North American drugstore chain to carry Clinique. Initially only a handful of locations earned the right to carry the line, but within a year about 150 updated or well-designed locations were expected to carry the brand. This deal helped turn Shoppers into a destination.

Customers who buy their Clinique cosmetics at the corner pharmacy will also most likely buy a few other items during their visit. Furthermore, most of these purchases can be tracked through customer Optimum cards and targeted information can be used to provide additional customer service to Shoppers customers. According to Estée Lauder, maker of Clinique, Shoppers' investments in customer service and new beauty boutiques is what sealed the deal.

In addition to these premium brands, Shoppers has been expanding their own in-house (private-label) cosmetics brand called Quo. Makeup has beautified the bottom line at Shoppers Drug Mart, and the company is continuing to invest in this area for continued long-term growth.[66]

Critical Thinking Questions

1. Do you believe that customers are ready to pay premium prices for cosmetics bought in a drugstore? Explain.

2. What key demographic groups are Shoppers tapping into with the addition of high-end cosmetics brands? How can the Optimum card help Shoppers Drug Mart target this key customer segment?

3. In this chapter you learned about the concept of brand equity. Explain the relationship between this term and Estée Lauder's hesitation to sign the deal with Shoppers Drug Mart. What made Estée Lauder change its mind?

Learn More Online

Go to Chapter 11 of this text's website at www.pearsoned.ca/bovee and click on the hotlink to the Shoppers Drug Mart website. Find the company's most recent financial results, both for the last year and the last quarter. Analyze and discuss the results. Next, read some of the latest press releases. Is there any more news about Shoppers' cosmetics lines?

TEST YOUR KNOWLEDGE

Questions for Review

1. Explain what is meant by the marketing concept.
2. Describe the product development process.
3. How can legal and regulatory factors affect a company's short-term marketing objectives?
4. Describe the four stages of the product life cycle.
5. Explain what is meant by niche marketing and provide an example of a company that is using this approach effectively.

Questions for Analysis

6. How have new techniques in database marketing revolutionized the way companies communicate with their core customers? What tools have enabled them to improve their data collection processes?

7. How do consumer purchases differ from organizational purchases? Describe the difference between the processes of a consumer buying an automobile for personal use versus an organization purchasing a fleet of delivery cars.

8. What is meant by brand equity? What can companies do to maintain or improve brand equity?

9. Why is it important to review the objectives of a strategic marketing plan before setting a product's price?

10. **Ethical Considerations**. Why might an employee with high personal ethical standards act less ethically when developing packaging, labelling, or pricing strategies?

Questions for Application

11. How does a hotel chain like Holiday Inn deal with the specific challenges of the service industry (intangibility and perishability)? What impact do these factors play in pricing?

12. Think of a product you recently purchased and review your decision process. Why did you need or want that product? How did the product's marketing influence your purchase decision? How did you investigate the product before making your purchase decision? Did you experience cognitive dissonance after your purchase?

13. A technology firm has just developed a new Internet browsing device that is designed for practical home use and can free up the problem parents have with children fighting over the computer—not to mention the parents' lack of access. The product can be produced at a very low manufacturing cost. What pricing approach should they use—skimming or price penetration? Explain.

14. **Integrated**. Why is it important to analyze a firm's marketing plan before designing the production process for a service or a good? (Production processes were discussed in Chapter 8.) What kinds of information are generally included in a marketing plan that might affect the design of the production process?

15. **Integrated**. Discuss how the following economic indicators discussed in Chapter 1 might affect a company's marketing decisions: consumer price index, inflation, unemployment.

PRACTISE YOUR KNOWLEDGE

SHARPENING YOUR COMMUNICATION SKILLS

Collect some examples of mail communications you have received from companies trying to sell you something. How do these communications try to get your attention? Highlight all instances in which these communications use the word *you* or even your personal name. How is using the word *you* an effective way to communicate with customers? Does the communication appeal to your emotions or to your logic? How does the company highlight the benefits of its products or services? How does the company approach price? Finally, how does the company motivate you to act? Bring samples to class and be prepared to present your analysis to your classmates.

BUILDING YOUR TEAM SKILLS

In the course of planning a marketing strategy, marketers need to analyze the external environment to consider how forces outside the firm may create new opportunities and challenges. One important environmental factor for merchandise buyers at Canadian Tire is weather conditions. For example, when merchandise buyers for lawn and garden products think about the assortment and number of products to purchase for the chain's stores, they don't place any orders without first poring over long-range weather forecasts for each market.

In particular, temperature and precipitation predictions are critical to the company's marketing plan, because they offer clues to consumer demand for barbecues, lawn furniture, gardening tools, and other merchandise. What other products would benefit from examining weather forecasts? With your team, brainstorm to identify at least three types of products (in addition to lawn and garden items) for which Canadian Tire should examine the weather as part of its analysis of the external environment. Share your recommendations with the entire class. How many teams identified the same products your team did?

EXPAND YOUR KNOWLEDGE

DISCOVERING CAREER OPPORTUNITIES

Jobs in the four P's of marketing cover a wide range of activities, including personal selling, advertising, marketing research, product management, and public relations. You can get more information about various marketing positions by consulting your local job bank, as well as online job search websites like Monster.ca.

1. Select a specific marketing job that interests you. Using one or more of the preceding resources, find out more about this chosen job. What specific duties and responsibilities do people in this position typically handle?

2. Search through help-wanted ads in newspapers, specialized magazines, or websites to find two openings in the field you are researching. What educational background and work experience are employers seeking in candidates for this position? What kind of work assignments are mentioned in these ads?

3. Now think about your talents, interests, and goals. How do your strengths fit with the requirements, duties, and responsibilities of this job? Do you think you would find this field enjoyable and rewarding? Why?

DEVELOPING YOUR RESEARCH SKILLS

From recent issues of business journals and newspapers (print or online editions), select an article that describes in some detail a particular company's attempt to build relationships with its customers (either in general or for a particular product or product line).

1. Describe the company's market. What geographic, demographic, behavioural, or psychographic segments of the market is the company targeting?

2. How does the company hold a dialogue with its customers? Does the company maintain a customer database? If so, what kinds of information does it gather?

3. According to the article, how successful has the company been in understanding its customers?

STUDY GUIDE

SUMMARY OF LEARNING OBJECTIVES

1. Explain what marketing is and describe the four utilities created by marketing

Marketing is the process of planning and executing the conception, pricing, promotion, and distribution of ideas, goods, and services to create exchanges that satisfy individual and organizational objectives. Marketers enhance the appeal of their products and services by adding utility. Form utility is created when companies turn raw materials into finished goods desired by consumers. Time utility is created by making the product available when the consumer wants to buy it. Place utility is created when a product is made available at a location that is convenient for the consumer. Possession utility is created by facilitating the transfer of ownership from seller to buyer.

2. Explain why and how companies learn about their customers

Companies learn about their customers so they can stay in touch with their current needs and wants, deliver quality products, and provide good customer service. Such attention tends to keep customers satisfied and helps build long-term loyalty. Moreover, studies show that sales to repeat customers are more profitable. Most companies learn about their customers by studying consumer behaviour, conducting marketing research, and capturing and analyzing customer data.

3. Describe how the organizational-customer decision process differs from the consumer process

Purchasing behaviour of organizations (which includes businesses, non-profit organizations, and governments) is easier to understand because it's driven by monetary issues, not emotions. There tends to be a formal buying process within organizations and there are many people involved in analyzing a major purchase decision. There is also a closer relationship with buyers and sellers that have been built over time.

4. Outline the three steps in the strategic marketing planning process

The three steps in the strategic marketing planning process are (1) examining your current marketing situation, which includes reviewing your past performance, evaluating your competition, examining your internal strengths and weaknesses, and analyzing the external environment; (2) assessing your opportunities and setting your objectives; and (3) developing your marketing strategy, which covers segmenting your market, choosing your target markets, positioning your product, and creating a marketing mix to satisfy the target market.

5. Define market segmentation and cite six factors used to identify segments

Market segmentation is the process of subdividing a market into homogeneous groups to identify potential customers and to devise marketing approaches geared to their needs and interests. The six most common factors used to identify segments are demographics, geographics, psychographics, geodemographics, behaviour, and usage.

6. List the steps involved in developing new products

Product strategies are among the most difficult and important decisions managers need to make, since products can take months or years and millions of dollars to introduce to the marketplace. To maximize the chances of success, companies will usually take a careful seven-step approach: (1) Generate new ideas; (2) Develop and screen product concepts; (3) Develop marketing strategies; (4) Analyze business potential; (5) Design and develop the products; (6) Test the market; (7) Commercialize.

7. Highlight the four stages in the life cycle of a product and the marketing focus of each stage

Products start in the introductory stage where marketers focus on stimulating demand for the new product. As the product progresses through the growth stage, marketers focus on increasing the product's market share. During the maturity stage, marketers try to extend the life of the product by highlighting improvements or by repackaging the product in different sizes. Eventually, all products move to a decline stage, where the marketer must decide whether to keep the product and reduce its costs to compensate for declining sales or discontinue the product altogether.

8. Understand the important role of branding and the strategies used to build and maintain brand equity

Creating a recognized and respected brand name with consumers is a central goal of all firms. Brand names may be owned by manufacturers, retailers, wholesalers, and a variety of business types. Brand equity is a term used to describe the extra value a brand name provides to a product beyond its functional benefits. It can be loosely compared to stock value. It is directly linked to issues like customer satisfaction, value, and long-term integrated marketing communication effects. It is established by the consumers' experiences and views of the brand name.

9. Discuss the functions of packaging and labelling

Packaging provides protection for the product, makes products easier to display, and attracts attention. In addition, packaging enhances the convenience of the product and communicates its attributes to the buyer. Labels help identify and distinguish the brand and product. They provide information about the product—including ingredients, risks, shelf life, and operating procedures, and they contain UPC codes, which are used for scanning sales information and monitoring inventory and pricing.

10. Identify four ways of expanding a product line and discuss two risks that product-line extensions pose

A product line can be expanded by filling gaps in the market, extending the line to include new varieties of existing products, extending the brand to new product categories, and stretching the line to include lower- or higher-priced items. Two of the biggest risks with product line extensions include a loss of brand identity (weakening of the brand's meaning) and cannibalization of sales of other products in the product line.

11. List seven factors that influence pricing decisions and cite five common pricing methods

Pricing decisions are influenced by manufacturing and selling costs, competition, the needs of wholesalers and retailers who distribute the product to the final customer, a firm's marketing objectives, government regulations, consumer perceptions, and consumer demand. Five common pricing methods are cost-based pricing, price-based pricing, skimming, penetration pricing, and discounting.

KEY TERMS

behavioural segmentation   (347)
brand   (356)
brand equity   (357)
brand mark   (356)
brand names   (356)
cause-related marketing   (334)
co-branding   (357)
cognitive dissonance   (337)
customer service   (333)
customer relationship management   (CRM)   (342)
database marketing   (340)
demographics   (346)
discount pricing   (361)
distribution channels   (351)
exchange process   (335)
form utility   (336)
generic products   (357)

geodemographics   (347)
geographic segmentation   (347)
market   (346)
market segmentation   (346)
market share   (346)
marketing   (333)
marketing concept   (336)
marketing mix   (350)
marketing research   (340)
marketing strategy   (346)
national brands   (356)
need   (335)
penetration pricing   (361)
place marketing   (334)
place utility   (336)
positioning   (349)
possession utility   (336)
price   (350)

price elasticity   (360)
private brands   (356)
product   (350)
product life cycle   (355)
product line   (358)
product mix   (358)
promotion   (351)
psychographics   (347)
relationship marketing   (341)
skimming   (361)
target markets   (348)
time utility   (336)
trademark   (356)
transaction   (335)
utility   (336)
Universal Product Codes (UPCs)   (358)
wants   (335)

QUESTIONS

Multiple Choice   Circle the correct answer and then check the answers in the back of the book to chart your progress.

1. What is a group of six to ten people who are interviewed for the purpose of improving a product called?

   a. Reference group
   b. Focus group
   c. Permission marketing meeting
   d. Relationship marketing team

2. Which of the following is *not* one of the fundamental needs?

   a. Food
   b. Money
   c. Shelter
   d. Clothing

3. Marketers enhance the appeal of their product by adding "utility." Which of the following is *not* one of the four utilities?

   a. Form utility
   b. Time utility
   c. Place utility
   d. Worth utility

4. Which of the following is an important final step in the consumer decision process?

   a. Need recognition
   b. Evaluation of alternatives
   c. Purchase decision
   d. Postpurchase evaluation

5. Which of the following is *not* a personal factor that can influence the consumer decision process?

   a. Culture
   b. Social class
   c. Self-image
   d. Advertising

6. What is the last step in strategic marketing planning?

   a. Examining the current marketing situation
   b. Assessing the opportunities
   c. Setting objectives
   d. Developing a strategy to reach the objectives

7. Which of the following is *not* one of the external environmental factors that could impact the marketing strategy?

   a. Economic conditions
   b. Social and cultural trends
   c. Technological developments
   d. Management skills

8. Markets are often subdivided into market segments. Which of the following is *not* a common way to group together similar consumers?

   a. Demographics
   b. Geographics
   c. Geodemographics
   d. Perceptual graphics

9. Which of the following is *not* one of the methods of targeting specific market segments?

   a. Undifferentiated marketing
   b. Differentiated marketing
   c. Unfocused marketing
   d. Concentrated marketing

10. Which of the following terms is used to describe how sensitive demand is to price changes?

    a. Price fixing
    b. Price elasticity
    c. Price control
    d. Price regulating

True/False

1. True or false? A successful brand name can be used to stretch a brand into any market.

2. True or false? Buyer's remorse, or cognitive dissonance, is the feeling of unease buyers often experience after making an important purchase.

3. True or false? Marketers need to understand the consumer decision process to provide information consumers need at every step.

4. True or false? Private brands or generic products are always lower in quality than their nationally branded counterparts.

5. True or false? When company resources are limited, concentrated marketing may be the best marketing strategy.

Fill-in-the-Blank

1. _____ occurs when two or more companies team up to link their names on a new product.

2. _____ describes efforts to market geographic areas ranging from neighbourhoods to entire countries.

3. When organizations change raw materials into finished goods, they are creating _____ desired by consumers.

4. The extra value a brand name provides to a product beyond its functional benefits is known as _____.

5. The process of gathering and analyzing information about customers and markets is called _____.

6. To help manage customer information and coordinate multiple interactions between the company and its customers, companies have turned to _____ systems.

7. Your _____ consists of dividing your market into *segments* and *niches*, choosing your *target markets* and the *position* you'd like to establish in those markets, and then developing a *marketing mix* to help you get there.

8. When differences in buying behaviour are influenced by where people live, it makes sense to use _____.

9. Services such as education, insurance, and consulting are at one end of the product continuum and are distinguished by their _____ nature.

10. _____ pricing is used when introducing a new product at a low price in hopes of building sales volume quickly.

See It on the **WEB**

Visit the Companion Website at **www.pearsoned.ca/bovee**, review the exercises, and complete the following assignments for Chapter 11:

1. Protect Your Trademarks
2. Sign Up For Electronic Commerce

CHAPTER 12

DEVELOPING DISTRIBUTION AND PROMOTIONAL STRATEGIES

LEARNING OBJECTIVES
After studying this chapter, you will be able to

1 Explain what marketing intermediaries do and list their seven primary functions

2 Explain how wholesalers and retailers function as intermediaries

3 Discuss the key factors that influence channel design and selection

4 Differentiate between intensive, selective, and exclusive distribution strategies

5 Discuss the Internet's effect on the distribution function

6 Identify the five basic categories of promotion

7 Distinguish between the two main types of sales promotion and give examples of each

8 Discuss the use of integrated marketing communications

BEHIND THE SCENES

MEC: Climbing Toward the 3 Million Member Mark

Mountain Equipment Co-operative has grown into a top supplier of specialty outdoor gear, selling through its retail outlets across Canada and by direct sales via the Internet, telephone and, mail.

www.mec.ca

Mountain Equipment Co-operative (MEC) has been serving the recreational outdoor needs of Canadians since 1971. Originally founded by a group of students from the University of British Columbia, MEC has grown into Canada's largest retail cooperative by membership statistics. Expanding from its roots in Vancouver, MEC has established a retail footprint across the various regions of the country and also serves Canadians through catalogue, telephone, and Internet sales. By mid-2007, the company had 2.6 million members in over 100 countries and will most likely reach 3 million members soon.

From the beginning, MEC demonstrated a pattern of socially responsible behaviour. The co-op sends a portion of its gross sales to environmental initiatives and has also incorporated the philosophy into the physical structure of its retail outlets. For example, the new 17 000-square-foot location in Victoria received an extensive green renovation and is estimated to use about 35 percent less energy than conventional buildings. The location in Montreal can boast to be the "most energy efficient retail building in the province, incorporating geothermal energy, radiant heating and cooling, and a natural ventilation system that reduces energy consumption by approximately 50 percent. Additionally, a roof water collection system reuses the roof water runoff for the landscape irrigation system."

The retail outlets range in size from 10 000 to 45 000 square feet and offer a wide variety of outdoor equipment, including camping gear, hiking gear, cycling accessories, and equipment for snow sports. The shopping experience at MEC is accentuated by a customer-centred approach. From rock climbing walls to demo stations, it is easy to see why more than 2.6 million people have said yes to MEC membership; the company tries to ensure that the client needs are met and that the retail outing is an experience.

In spite of its successful climb during its first three decades of operation, MEC was aware that it could provide improved access to its products by going online. It was servicing its customers from its traditional retail outlets and supplementing that with catalogue and phone sales, but MEC executives knew that the long-term growth of the company would require an effective website. If MEC ignored this channel it could leave room for current and potential competitors to gain advantage. One concern with launching the site was that the Internet retail arm could replace sales from existing retail channels. The careful coordination of the system was vital to ensure that the full potential was achieved. The official launch dates back to May 2001, and like most companies at the time, some trial-and-error learning occurred as they redefined their multichannel mixes. MEC has made continuous attempts to improve the client experience. Since the initial launch the site has undergone two major revisions in 2003 and 2006, and MEC also created a French site in 2006. The initial decision to go online and the subsequent adjustments were important strategic moments and required careful planning and implementation to allow MEC to enhance its solid customer-centred image.[1]

TEST YOURSELF

Answers to these questions can be found on the website: www.pearsoned.ca/bovee.

1. What were some of the concerns MEC had when they originally launched their website?

2. Why is it important for a company to maintain a consistent message between its traditional outlets and its Internet retail arm?

3. How can a company effectively cross-promote its website and its retail outlets?

Developing Distribution Strategies

Getting products to consumers is the role of distribution, the third element of a firm's marketing mix—also known as *place*. As Chapter 11 pointed out, distribution channels, or *marketing channels*, are an organized network of firms that work together to get goods and services from producer to consumer. A company's **distribution strategy**, which is its overall plan for moving products to buyers, plays a major role in the firm's success. Producers use intermediaries like Mountain Equipment Co-operative, a retailer, to get their products to market in an efficient manner.

How many products do you buy directly from the producer? From clothing to sports equipment to toiletries and DVDs, you are probably interacting with other intermediaries. Most companies do not sell their goods directly to the final users, even though the Internet is making it easier to do so these days. Instead, producers in many industries work with **marketing intermediaries** (also called *middlemen*) to bring their products to market.

distribution strategy
A firm's overall plan for moving products to intermediaries and final customers

marketing intermediaries
Businesspeople and organizations that channel goods and services from producers to consumers

Understanding the Role of Marketing Intermediaries

Two main types of marketing intermediaries are wholesalers and retailers. **Wholesalers** sell primarily to retailers, to other wholesalers, and to organizational users such as government agencies, institutions, and commercial operations. In turn, the customers of wholesalers either resell the products or use them to make products of their own. For example, fruit and vegetable wholesalers such as F.G. Lister and Canadawide help to increase efficiency, reduce transactions, and ensure that these perishable products reach a variety of locations. From small mom-and-pop fruit stores to large grocery chains and restaurants, the system needs to be efficient to ensure timely delivery and avoid produce loss.

By contrast, **retailers** sell products to the final consumer for personal use. Retailers can operate out of a physical facility (supermarket, gas station, kiosk), through vending equipment (soft-drink machine, newspaper box, automated teller), or from a virtual store (via telephone, catalogue, or website). Most retailers today reach shoppers through a carefully balanced blend of store and non-store retail outlets. The major types of retailers are described in Exhibit 12.1.

Wholesalers and retailers are instrumental in creating three of the four forms of utility mentioned in Chapter 11: place utility, time utility, and possession utility. They provide an efficient process for transferring products from the producer to the customer, they reduce the number of transactions, and they ensure that goods and services are available at a convenient time and place for consumers. In short, wholesalers and retailers perform a number of specific distribution functions that make life easier for both producers and customers:

L.O. 1, 2

wholesalers
Firms that sell products to other firms for resale or for organizational use

retailers
Firms that sell goods and services to final consumers for their own use rather than for resale

- *Match buyers and sellers.* By making sellers' products available to multiple buyers, intermediaries like MEC reduce the number of transactions between producers and customers.
- *Provide market information.* Intermediaries like MEC collect valuable data about customer purchases: who buys, how often, and how much. Collecting such data allows them to spot buying patterns and to share marketplace information with producers.
- *Provide promotional and sales support.* Many intermediaries, like Pepsi distributors, create advertising, produce eye-catching displays, and use other promotional devices for some or all of the products they sell. Some employ a sales force, which can perform a number of selling functions.
- *Gather an assortment of goods.* MEC, Roots, Staples, and other intermediaries receive bulk shipments from producers and break them into more convenient units by sorting, standardizing, and dividing bulk quantities into smaller packages.

Exhibit 12.1   **Types of Retail Stores**

The definition of retailer covers many types of outlets. This table shows some of the most common types.

TYPE OF RETAILER	DESCRIPTION	EXAMPLES
Category killer	A specialty store that focuses on specific products on a giant scale and dominates retail sales in the product categories	Staples (Bureau en Gros); Toys "R" Us
Convenience store	Offers staple convenience goods, long service hours, quick checkouts	Couche-Tard; Mac's; Becker's
Department store	Offers a wide variety of merchandise, in departmentalized sections, with many customer services all under one roof	The Bay; Sears
Discount store	Offers a wide variety of merchandise at low prices with few services	Wal-Mart
Factory/retail outlet	Large outlet store selling discontinued items, overruns, and factory seconds	Nike outlet store
Hypermarket	Giant store offering food and general merchandise at discount prices	Wal-Mart
Off-price store	Offers designer and brand-name merchandise at low prices with few services	Winners
Online retailers	Web-based stores offering anything from a single product line to comprehensive selections in many product areas; can be web-only (Amazon.com) or integrated with physical stores (MEC.ca)	Amazon.ca, MEC.ca
Specialty store	Offers a complete selection in a narrow range of merchandise	Aldo Shoes
Supermarket	Large, self-service store offering a wide selection of food and non-food merchandise	Loblaw; Sobeys
Warehouse club	Large, warehouse-style store that sells food and general merchandise at discount prices; most require club membership	Costco; Sam's Club

- *Transport and store the product.* Intermediaries such as Future Shop and The Brick maintain an inventory of merchandise that they acquire from producers so they can quickly fill customer orders. In many cases, retailers purchase this merchandise from wholesalers who, in addition to breaking bulk, may also transport the goods from the producer to the retail outlets.

- *Assume risks.* When intermediaries accept goods from manufacturers, they take on the risks associated with damage, theft, product perishability, and obsolescence. For example, if products stocked or displayed at The Bay are stolen or become obsolete, The Bay assumes responsibility for the loss.

- *Provide financing.* Large intermediaries sometimes provide loans to smaller producers.

As Exhibit 12.2 shows, without marketing intermediaries, the buying and selling process would be expensive and time consuming.

Selecting Your Marketing Channels

distribution mix
The combination of intermediaries and channels a producer uses to get a product to end users

Distribution channels come in all shapes and sizes. Some channels are short and simple; others are complex and involve many people and organizations. A company's decision about the number and type of intermediaries to use—its **distribution mix**—depends

Exhibit 12.2   **How Intermediaries Simplify Commerce**

Intermediaries actually reduce the price customers pay for many goods and services because they reduce the number of contacts between producers and consumers that would otherwise be necessary. They also create place, time, and possession utility.

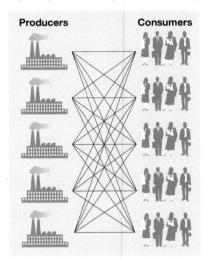

Number of transactions required when consumers buy directly from manufacturers

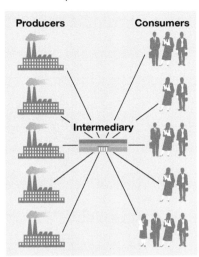

Number of transactions required when buying is conducted via an intermediary

Source: Adapted from Philip Kotler, *Marketing Management*, 10th ed. (Upper Saddle River, NJ: Prentice Hall, 2000), 491.

on the kind of product being sold and the marketing practices of the industry. An arrangement that works well for a power tool and appliance manufacturer like Black & Decker or a book publisher like Pearson Canada would not necessarily work for an insurance company like Sun Life. In general, consumer products and business products tend to move through different channels (see Exhibit 12.3).

IN-CLASS NOTES

Distributing Products
- **Distribution strategy**
  - Overall plan for moving products to buyers
  - Most firms don't sell directly to final users
- **Marketing intermediaries**
  - Middlemen that facilitate movement of goods from producers to consumers (retailers, wholesalers, agents, brokers, etc.)

Exhibit 12.3   **Alternative Channels of Distribution**

Producers of consumer and business goods and services must analyze the alternative channels of distribution available for their products so they can select the channels that best meet their marketing objectives and their customers' needs.

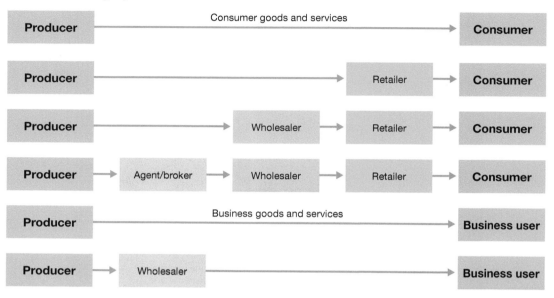

Length of Distribution Channels

Most businesses purchase goods they use in their operations directly from producers, so the distribution channel is short. Bombardier, for example, purchases more than 10 000 kilograms of parts to build airplanes from hundreds of large and small companies. For example, Pratt & Whitney Canada and GE supply aircraft engines, Alcoa provides primary aluminium, and Héroux-Devtek provides sub-assemblies and main machined parts.[2]

In contrast, the channels for consumer goods are usually longer and more complex. The four primary channels for consumer goods are as follows:

- *Producer to consumer.* Producers who sell directly to consumers through catalogues, telemarketing, infomercials, and the Internet are using the shortest, simplest distribution channel. Dell Computer and other companies that sell directly to consumers are seeking closer relationships with customers and more control over pricing, promotion, service, and delivery.[3] Although this approach eliminates payments to channel members, it also forces producers to handle distribution functions such as storing inventory and delivering products.

- *Producer to retailer to consumer.* Some producers create longer channels by selling their products to retailers such as Rona or Canadian Tire, which then resell them to consumers. Sico Paint, Scotts "Turf Builder" fertilizer, and GE light bulbs are examples of products distributed in this way.

- *Producer to wholesaler to retailer to consumer.* Most manufacturers of supermarket and drugstore items rely on even longer channels. They sell their products to wholesalers, who in turn sell to the retailers. This approach works particularly well for small producers who lack the resources to sell or deliver merchandise to individual retail sites.

Each Bombardier airplane contains thousands of parts that are purchased directly from hundreds of small-, medium-, and large-sized suppliers.

- *Producer to agent/broker to wholesaler to retailer to consumer.* Additional channel levels are common in certain industries, such as agriculture, where specialists are required to negotiate transactions or to perform functions such as sorting, grading, or subdividing the goods.

Factors That Influence Channel Selection

Should you sell directly to end users or rely on intermediaries? Which intermediaries should you choose? Should you try to sell your product in every available outlet, or limit distribution to a few exclusive outlets? Should you use more than one channel? These are some of the critical decisions that managers face when designing and selecting marketing channels for any product.

Building an effective channel system takes years and, like all marketing relationships, requires commitment. Thus, companies take extra care when establishing their initial marketing channels because changing distribution arrangements at a later date may prove difficult. As Chris Denove, a channel expert, puts it, "It's much more difficult to modify an existing system than to start with a clean slate." Citing the automobile industry, for example, Denove points out that "if an auto maker could start over now, none of them would create a franchise distribution system that looks like the existing one."[4]

When establishing marketing channels, companies must consider four key factors: market coverage, cost, control, and channel conflict.

Market Coverage The appropriate *market coverage*—the number of wholesalers or retailers that will carry a product—varies by type of product. Inexpensive convenience goods or organizational supplies such as computer paper and pens sell best if they are available in as many outlets as possible. Such **intensive distribution** requires wholesalers and retailers of many types. In contrast, shopping goods (goods that require some thought before being purchased) like Sub-Zero refrigerators require different market coverage, because customers shop for such products by comparing features and prices. For these items, the best strategy is usually **selective distribution**, selling through a limited number of outlets that can give the product adequate sales and service support.

If producers of expensive specialty or technical products do not sell directly to customers, they may choose **exclusive distribution**, offering products in only one outlet in each market area. High-end vehicle manufacturers like Porsche have traditionally relied on exclusive distribution agreements to sell through one dealership in each viable local area. By contrast, other firms use multiple channels to increase their market coverage and reach several target markets. Apparel manufacturers like Gildan Activewear frequently sell through a combination of channels, including department stores, specialty stores, the Internet, and catalogues.

Cost Costs play a major role in determining a firm's channel selection. It takes money to perform all of the functions that are handled by intermediaries. Small or new companies often cannot afford to hire a sales force large enough to sell directly to end users or to call on a host of retail outlets. Neither can they afford to build large warehouses and distribution centres or to buy trucks to transport their goods. These firms need the help of intermediaries who can spread the cost of such activities across a number of non-competing products. With time and a larger sales base, a producer may build enough strength to take over some of these functions and reduce the length of its distribution channel.

Control A third issue to consider when selecting distribution channels is control of how, where, when, and for how much your product is sold. Longer distribution channels mean less control for producers, who become increasingly distant from sellers and buyers as

intensive distribution
A market coverage strategy that tries to place a product in as many outlets as possible

selective distribution
A market coverage strategy that uses a limited number of outlets to distribute products

exclusive distribution
A market coverage strategy that gives intermediaries exclusive rights to sell a product in a specific geographic area

Marketers of luxury products often use exclusive distribution through carefully selected stores to ensure an optimum shopping experience for their customers.

Holt Renfrew is an upscale retail outlet that carries many high-end brand names like Burberry. Its 10 outlets serve many major Canadian cities, including Vancouver, Edmonton, Calgary, Winnipeg, Toronto, Ottawa, Montreal, and Quebec City.

the number of intermediaries multiplies. On the other hand, companies may not want to concentrate too many distribution functions in the hands of too few intermediaries. Control becomes critical when a firm's reputation is at stake. For instance, high-priced fashion brands, such as Burberry or Louis Vuitton, generally limit distribution to exclusive boutiques or high-end retail stores like Holt Renfrew. Otherwise, their brands could lose some of their appeal if they were available at mid-priced retailers like Sears Canada. A brand's reputation is also linked to the success and image of the retailers it selects. As we saw in Chapter 11, Shoppers Drug Mart had tremendous difficulty convincing high-end cosmetics manufacturers to allow their elite brands to be sold in Shoppers' stores. The drugstore retailer already offered a tremendous market presence with prime locations. However, the company was only able to start landing brands like Clinique after Shoppers committed significant funds to build attractive in-store sections and kiosks with trained personnel. Producers of complex technical products like X-ray machines use limited distribution for more practical reasons. They don't want their products handled by unqualified intermediaries that can't provide adequate customer service.

Channel Conflict   Because the success of individual channel members depends on the overall channel success, ideally all channel members should work together smoothly. However, individual channel members must also run their own businesses profitably, which means that they often disagree on the roles each member should play. Such disagreements create *channel conflict*.[5] Channel conflict may arise when suppliers provide inadequate product support, when markets are oversaturated with intermediaries, or when companies sell products via multiple channels, each of which is competing for the same customers. For instance, Hallmark's decision to sell cards to mass-market outlets such as discount stores, supermarkets, and drugstores angered its 8200 independent dealers, who were forced to compete with large chains.[6]

Similarly, when producers choose to sell direct to consumers via the Internet, they run the risk of damaging their existing relationships with other channel members. Such was the case when Avon decided to sell their cosmetics online. Avon has had a presence in Canada since 1914 and can boast an extensive network of more than 65 000 sales dealers across the country, and 5 million representatives worldwide. The heart and soul of Avon Canada, and by extension Avon International, are these loyal dealers. The introduction of the online distribution channel initially angered many representatives, who saw this as a threat to their existing markets. Many agents were also concerned that Avon's push into retail outlets would further hurt their business. Through a concerted effort by Avon headquarters, many reps eventually embraced the slightly more upscale line as an advertisement for the lower-end product lines they traditionally carry.[7]

Channel conflict can also occur as members of the chain deal with various competitors simultaneously. A retailer often sells brands from direct competitors and must be conscious of that rivalry in making various decisions. For example, in nearly every convenience store you will find Coke and Pepsi products side by side. This is not a problem in itself, but favourable product placement of one brand over the other can lead to conflict. Conflict can also occur when a special relationship is threatened. Coke has been the preferred supplier for McDonald's for 51 years in the United States and 40 years in Canada. This relationship and the huge sales volumes attached to it have been a major force enabling Coke to maintain its status as the number-one beverage company with an estimated 42.9 percent share over Pepsi's 31.2 percent. When McDonald's recently announced that it would experiment with offering its consumers the choice between the two brands in a few US markets it was a major source of conflict for these long-time partners. Coke earns approximately 10 percent of its North American profits from sales in McDonald's outlets.[8]

In-Class Notes

Channel Selection Factors

- **Market coverage:** the number of wholesalers or retailers varies by type of product (e.g., convenience goods use *intensive distribution*)
- **Costs:** small or new companies often cannot afford to hire a sales force large enough to sell directly to end users
- **Control:** longer distribution channels mean less control for producers
- **Channel conflict:** occurs when members disagree on roles and expectations

---

Managing Physical Distribution

Developing a distribution strategy involves more than selecting the most effective channels for selling a product. Companies must also decide on the best way to move their products and services through the channels so that they are available to the customers at the right place, at the right time, and in the right amount. **Physical distribution** encompasses all activities required to move finished products from the producer to the consumer, including order processing, inventory control, warehousing, materials handling, and outbound transportation (see Exhibit 12.4).

physical distribution
All activities required to move finished products from the producer to the consumer

Exhibit 12.4   **Steps in the Physical Distribution Process**

The phases of a distribution system should mesh as smoothly as the cogs in a machine. Because the steps are interrelated, a change in one phase can affect the other phases. The objective of the process is to provide a target level of customer service at the lowest overall cost.

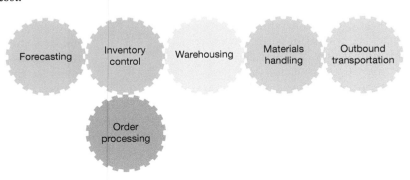

Forecasting — Inventory control — Warehousing — Materials handling — Outbound transportation

Order processing

logistics
The planning and movement of goods and related information throughout the supply chain

The physical movement of goods may not appear glamorous or exciting, but it is vital to a company's success. To illustrate the importance of physical distribution, consider this: A typical box of breakfast cereal can spend as long as 104 days getting from factory to supermarket, moving haltingly through a series of wholesalers and distributors, each of which has a warehouse. In fact, so many physical distribution systems are hurt by duplication and inefficiency that in industry after industry executives have been placing one item near the top of the corporate agenda: **logistics**—the planning and movement of goods and information throughout the supply chain.

Hard pressed to knock out competitors on quality or price, companies are trying to gain an edge by streamlining processes that extend beyond companies and continents—no easy task, although the payoff can be enormous.

In the past few years, Zara, a Spanish clothing retailer, has been expanding its operations; it now accounts for 1026 locations around the world. It has begun to make an imprint on the Canadian clothing landscape with stores in Montreal, Quebec City, Calgary, Toronto, Edmonton, and Vancouver. One of the secrets to its success is a lightning-fast distribution system that allows it to transform an idea or design into a product and have it on its shelves within three weeks. While this system required substantial upfront costs to implement, it helped the firm to spot the latest trends and reduce inventory costs. Some of its competitors still plan and produce their goods as much as five months in advance. Zara's system produces at least 10 000 designs annually and creates a sense of urgency among its regular clientele since no style lasts for more than four weeks.[9]

The key to success in managing physical distribution is to achieve a competitive level of customer service at the lowest total cost. Doing so requires trade-offs, because as the level of service improves, the cost of distribution increases. For instance, if you reduce the level of inventory to cut your storage costs, you run the risk of being unable to fill orders in a timely fashion. Or if you use slower forms of transportation you reduce your shipping costs, but you probably increase your storage costs. The trick is to optimize the *total* cost of achieving the desired level of service. This optimization requires a careful analysis of each step in the distribution process in relation to every other step. Let's take a closer look at each of these steps.

Order Processing

Order processing involves preparing orders for shipment and receiving orders when shipments arrive. It includes a number of activities, such as checking the customer's credit, recording the sale, making the appropriate accounting entries, arranging for the item to be shipped, adjusting the inventory records, and billing the customer. Because order processing involves direct interaction with the customer, it affects a company's reputation for customer service. Most companies establish standards for filling orders within a specific time period.

Inventory Control

As Chapter 8 discussed, in an ideal world a company would always have just the right amount of goods on hand to fill the orders it receives. In reality, however, inventory and sales are seldom in perfect balance. Most firms like to build a supply of finished goods so that they can fill orders in a timely fashion. But how much inventory is enough? If your inventory is too large, you pay extra expenses for storage space, handling, insurance, and taxes; you also run the risk of product obsolescence. On the other hand, if your inventory is too low, you may lose sales when the product is not in stock. The objective of *inventory control* is to resolve these issues. Inventory managers decide how much product to keep on hand and when to replenish the supply of goods in inventory. They also decide how to distribute products to customers if orders exceed supply.

Warehousing

Products held in inventory are physically stored in a **warehouse**, which may be owned by the manufacturer, by an intermediary, or by a private company that leases space to others. Some warehouses are almost purely holding facilities in which goods are stored for relatively long periods. Other warehouses, known as **distribution centres**, serve as command posts for moving products to customers. In a typical distribution centre, goods produced at a company's various locations are collected, sorted, coded, and redistributed to fill customer orders.

Some of today's most advanced physical distribution centres employ satellite navigation and communication, voice-input computers, machine vision, robots, onboard computer logbooks, and planning software that relies on artificial intelligence. FedEx, for instance, runs a fully automated distribution centre. The company's US$180 million small-package sorting system processes more than 400 000 packages an hour. Each parcel is scanned four times, weighed, and measured, and its digital image is recorded in the computer. In addition, the company's world shipping software streamlines customer billing, reduces shipping paperwork, and allows customers to track their shipments on the Internet.[10]

Even the national carriers have come a long way from their traditional delivery systems. Canada Post has been serving Canadians for more than 150 years. As transportation and communications have evolved, so have their operating methods. Canada Post now processes approximately 11.6 billion articles of mail each year. It is increasingly moving into providing integrated solutions for business-to-business needs, like its merchandise return service aimed particularly at retailers and e-tailers. Canada Post accomplishes this with 25 major plants and a sophisticated national control centre that oversees the system.[11]

Canada Post's national control centre serves to coordinate the mail/parcel distribution system and ensures prompt delivery. Along with regional centres, it anticipates problems such as weather conditions and highway closures and sets contingency plans into action.

warehouse
A facility for storing inventory

distribution centres
Warehouse facilities that specialize in collecting and shipping merchandise

Materials Handling

An important part of warehousing activities is **materials handling**, the movement of goods within and between physical distribution facilities. One main area of concern is storage method—whether to keep supplies and finished goods in individual packages, in large boxes, or in sealed shipping containers. The choice of storage method depends on how the product is shipped, in what quantities, and to which locations. For example, a firm that typically sends small quantities of goods to widely scattered customers would not want to use large containers. Materials handling also involves keeping track of inventory so that the company knows where in the distribution process its goods are located and when they need to be moved.

materials handling
The movement of goods within a firm's warehouse terminal, factory, or store

Outbound Transportation

For any business, the cost of transportation is normally the largest single item in the overall cost of physical distribution. Five common types of outbound transportation are rail, truck, water (ships), air (planes), and pipeline. When choosing among these five modes of transportation, managers weigh the advantages and disadvantages of each. In particular, they consider such factors as storage, financing, sales, inventory size, speed, product perishability, dependability, flexibility, and convenience—to name a few. The goal is to maximize the efficiency of the entire distribution process while minimizing overall cost.

IN-CLASS NOTES

Managing Physical Distribution

- **Order processing:** preparing orders for shipment and receiving orders when they arrive
- **Inventory control:** deciding how much inventory to keep on hand and when to replenish supply
- **Warehouses:** either pure holding facilities or distribution centres; a key part of warehousing activities is *materials handling*, movement of goods within and between facilities
- **Outbound transportation:** normally the largest cost of physical distribution; five common types (rail, truck, water, air, or pipeline)

_____

_____

_____

_____

_____

_____

_____

_____

_____

_____

L.O. 5

Incorporating the Internet into Your Distribution Strategies

The Internet's efficient and effective global reach is revolutionizing the way goods and services are sold and distributed. Amazon.com's Jeff Bezos was a pioneer in recognizing the Internet's potential for making goods and services available to buyers. He reasoned that, given a choice, many people would prefer the ease and convenience of online shopping to visiting a store every time they wanted to buy a book. He also believed that publishers would welcome Amazon.com as yet another way to get their books into the hands of readers. Today, a growing number of businesses sell a huge selection of goods and services online. For some, like Amazon, the Internet is their only marketing channel. But for others, like Future Shop, the Internet offers an additional way to sell to customers and provide product information.

An increasing number of businesses are using the Internet to improve the efficiency of their distribution systems and to expand their market reach. Some are using the Internet to eliminate intermediaries, whereas others are incorporating Internet intermediaries into their distribution system. For example, Kanetix labels itself as Canada's insurance marketplace. It allows shoppers to obtain multiple quotes from various insurance providers such as RBC Insurance and Standard Life. Consumers can purchase directly online or can be connected directly to their insurer of choice.[12]

In short, the Internet is a powerful force that is changing the role of traditional intermediaries. The livelihoods of travel agents, retailers, real estate agents, and independent sales representatives are threatened as never before, as the Internet increasingly allows sellers and buyers to find each other and do business directly or differently.

PROMOTIONAL STRATEGIES

Although distribution is a critical element in the marketing mix, promotion is perhaps the one element you associate most with the marketing function. That's because promotion is highly visible to consumers. In Chapter 11 we defined promotion as a form of persuasive communication that motivates people to buy whatever an organization is selling—goods, services, or ideas. Promotion may take the form of direct, face-to-face communication or indirect communication through such media as television, radio, magazines, newspapers, direct mail, billboards, the Internet, floor ads, and other channels. How do you decide on which forms of promotion to use? Many firms develop a **promotional strategy**; that is, they define the direction and scope of the promotional activities their companies will take to meet their marketing objectives.

Developing a promotional strategy encompasses several steps. You begin by setting your promotional goals. Next you take several product variables into consideration and decide on the best market approach before selecting your promotional mix. Finally, you fine-tune your product mix to make sure that all of your promotional elements communicate the same message.

promotional strategy
A statement or document that defines the direction and scope of the promotional activities that a company will use to meet its marketing objectives

Setting Your Promotional Goals

You can use promotion to achieve three basic goals: to inform, to persuade, and to remind. *Informing* is the first promotional priority, because people cannot buy something until they are aware of it and know what it can do for them. Potential customers need to know where the item can be purchased, how much it costs, and how to use it. *Persuading* is also an important priority, because most people need to be encouraged to purchase something new or to switch brands. Advertising that meets this goal is classified as **persuasive advertising**. *Reminding* the customer of the product's availability and benefits is also important, because such reminders stimulate additional purchases. The term for such promotional efforts is **reminder advertising**.

Beyond these general objectives, your promotional strategy should accomplish specific objectives: It should attract new customers, increase usage among existing customers, aid distributors, stabilize sales, boost brand-name recognition, create sales leads, differentiate the product, and influence decision makers.

persuasive advertising
Advertising designed to encourage product sampling and brand switching

reminder advertising
Advertising intended to remind existing customers of a product's availability and benefits

Analyzing Product Variables

Before selecting your promotional mix, you must consider a number of product and market factors. To begin with, you have to take into consideration the nature of your product. Various types of products lend themselves better to different forms of promotion. Simple, familiar items like laundry detergent can be explained adequately through advertising, but personal selling is generally required to communicate the features of unfamiliar and sophisticated goods and services such as office-automation equipment or municipal waste–treatment facilities. Direct, personal contact is particularly important in promoting customized services such as interior design, financial advice, or legal counsel. In general, consumer and organizational goods usually require different promotional mixes.

The product's price is also a factor in the selection of the promotional mix. Inexpensive items such as shaving cream or breakfast cereal sold to a mass market are well suited to advertising and sales promotion, which have a relatively low per-unit cost. At the other extreme, products with a high unit price like in-ground swimming pools lend themselves to personal selling because the high cost of a sales call is justified by the price of the product. Furthermore, the nature of the selling process often demands face-to-face interaction between the buyer and seller.

Another factor that influences both the level and mix of promotional activity is the product's position in its life cycle. Early on, when the seller is trying to inform the customer about the product and build the distribution network, promotional efforts are in high gear. Selective advertising, sales promotion, and public relations are used

Learning from Business Blunders

OOPS

Advertising is an important tool that helps a brand gain awareness and recognition while differentiating it from the competition. Companies spend millions of dollars pursuing these goals and positioning their products in the minds of consumers. These advertising costs are just part of building a strong brand. Unfortunately for McCain, the correlation between advertising dollars spent and long-term brand recognition, and eventual sales, for their Rising Crust Pizza was corrupted.

A few years ago, both McCain and Kraft came out with major campaigns to promote their frozen pizza brands. Kraft promoted their Delissio brand with the slogan "It's Not delivery—It's Delissio," while McCain's used the slogan "Who can tell it from takeout?" Both campaigns had similar themes. Unfortunately for McCain, the message was filtering back to Kraft; in essence McCain was supplementing Kraft's advertising budget. Customers were watching McCain ads but remembering Kraft's Delissio—their campaign was helping the competition! After a couple of years of flat sales, McCain conducted research and identified the depressing truth. After that point, McCain totally changed their slogan and the company also created the Crescendo brand to develop a unique identity for the new ads. The company also focused on a new target: teens.

They did not ignore their original market (moms), but they made a clear effort to reach the teen end user. Teens may not purchase frozen pizza in large quantities, but they influence their parent's decisions. Some people loved the new campaign, which featured young people getting tan lines from watching their Crescendo Pizza's crust rising in the oven, while others disliked it. Bottom line—nobody confused these ads for Delissio ads. The Crescendo brand was established and sales were up 25 percent in the first month alone.

WHAT YOU CAN LEARN

If you are going to spend millions of dollars on an ad campaign, try to make sure that it is original or at the very least that the brand is clearly associated with the ad. Perhaps the greatest difference between these two ad campaigns was that Kraft created a unique brand and incorporated the Delissio name into its slogan. Kraft managed to establish the Delissio brand name in consumer's minds. This example demonstrates the power of branding and also shows us the importance of follow-up market research. McCain eventually discovered the startling truth, but only after years and market share had already been lost. Had they discovered these truths early on, the company would have corrected the problem much sooner than they did.[13]

---

to build awareness and to encourage early adopters to try the product; personal selling is used to gain the cooperation of intermediaries. Gillette, for example, spent US\$300 million to promote the launch of the Mach3 razor during its first year—on top of more than US\$750 million in development costs—to accelerate the Mach3's transition from the costly introduction stage to the profitable growth stage faster than any previous Gillette razor. Just 18 months after the Mach3 was launched, sales for the product hit US\$1 billion, making it the company's most successful new product ever.[14] As the Mach3 product moved along the product life cycle, Gillette launched the Mach3 Turbo, Mach3 Turbo champion, and M3Power. More recently, Gillette launched Fusion, which has five blades and is aimed at answering the threat from Schick's four-bladed Quattro.[15]

As the market expands during the growth phase, the seller broadens its advertising and sales promotion activities to reach a wider audience and continues to use personal selling to expand the distribution network. When the product reaches maturity and competition is at its peak, the seller's primary goal is to differentiate the product from rival brands. Advertising generally dominates the promotional mix during this phase, but sales promotion is an important supplemental tool, particularly for low-priced consumer products. As the product begins to decline, the level of promotion generally tapers off. Advertising and selling efforts are carefully targeted toward loyal, steady customers.

A mature product like blue jeans requires a different promotional strategy than a product in the introductory or growth stages of the product life cycle.

Deciding on Your Market Approach

The selection of your promotional mix also depends on whether you plan to focus your marketing effort on intermediaries or on final customers. If the focus is on intermediaries, the producer uses a **push strategy** to persuade wholesalers and retailers to carry the item. Producers may, for instance, offer wholesalers or retailers special discounts or incentives for purchasing larger quantities. You would expect to see personal selling and sales promotions to dominate the promotional mix aimed at intermediaries. If the marketing focus is on end users, the producer uses a **pull strategy** to appeal directly to the ultimate customer, using advertising, direct mail, contests, discount coupons, and so on. With this approach, consumers learn about the product through promotion and request it from retailers, who respond by asking their wholesalers for it or by going directly to the producer (see Exhibit 12.5).

The power of the "pull strategy" is very evident around the Christmas holidays when Canadian shoppers flock to retail outlets like The Bay or Toys "R" Us and desperately search for that heavily promoted "hot toy" of the season. Retailers seize the opportunity and attempt to reorder large quantities when frenzied customers come to them in desperate need of satisfying their child's wishes.

Most companies use both push and pull tactics to increase the impact of their promotional efforts. For example, when Schering-Plough introduced Claritin antihistamine, it used push tactics to educate physicians about the prescription drug's use and effectiveness, while it used pull tactics such as television and print advertising to increase market awareness and encourage consumers to ask for the new medication. This diverse, high-powered promotional mix helped Claritin capture a whopping 54 percent of the antihistamine drug market within a short time.[16] Unfortunately for Schering-Plough, competitors also caught on to the power of push-pull marketing and the patent on Claritin ran out (meaning that competitors could make lower-cost generic versions), adding up to a short-lived advantage in the marketplace.[17]

push strategy
A promotional approach designed to motivate wholesalers and retailers to push a producer's products to end users

pull strategy
A promotional strategy that stimulates consumer demand, which in turn exerts pressure on wholesalers and retailers to carry a product

---

Exhibit 12.5 **Push and Pull Strategies**

In a push strategy, the manufacturer "pushes" products through the distribution channel, first promoting and distributing them to wholesalers, who then push them to retailers, who then push them to consumers. In a pull strategy, the manufacturer promotes its products directly to consumers, who then "pull" the products through the distribution channel by requesting them from retailers, who then request them from wholesalers, who then request them from the manufacturer. Many companies use a combination of push and pull strategies.

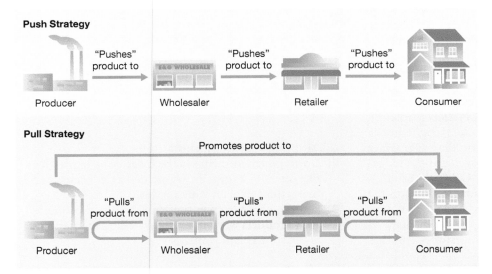

Push Strategy

Producer → "Pushes" product to → Wholesaler → "Pushes" product to → Retailer → "Pushes" product to → Consumer

Pull Strategy

Promotes product to

Producer ← "Pulls" product from ← Wholesaler ← "Pulls" product from ← Retailer ← "Pulls" product from ← Consumer

The promotional mix is also influenced by the size and concentration of the market. In markets with many widely dispersed buyers, advertising is generally the most economical way of communicating the product's features. In markets with relatively few customers, particularly when they are clustered in a limited area, personal selling is a practical promotional alternative. Many marketers use a combination of methods, often relying on advertising and public relations to build awareness and interest, following up with personal selling to complete the sale.

Where Did the Audience Go?

Looking around at today's media-saturated world, it's hard to imagine a time when "mass media" consisted of a couple of nationwide television networks, radio, local newspapers, and a handful of popular magazines. If you wanted to launch a new product nationwide, you simply bought commercial time on CTV or CBC in Canada (CBS, ABC, or NBC in the United States) and you would have had a pretty good chance of reaching your target market. Advertisers didn't have to look very far to find consumers, because consumers didn't have anywhere else to turn (and they didn't even have remote controls to mute commercials or change the channel).

Fast-forward to the twenty-first century when advertisers wonder where everybody went. Consumers are still around, of course, but now they're scattered in smaller, isolated pockets all over the media landscape, from blogs to Internet radio to online e-zines to digital cable systems with hundreds of channels. With personal video recorders (PVRs) they can zoom right past commercials they once had to sit through. Many people, particularly younger consumers, are spending less time watching regular TV and more time playing video games or enjoying DVDs. According to one study, a national US advertiser in 1995 could reach 80 percent of American women aged 18 to 49 by running a commercial just three times. To reach that same group a decade later required 97 ads, and these figures are climbing as the media fragments further.

How can advertisers reach audiences that won't sit still and won't pay attention when they are sitting still? Nobody has the answer for every situation, but advertisers are trying plenty of possibilities. *Product placement*, in which advertisers put their products right into a TV show or movie, is more common than ever. Have you noticed those Coke-logo beverage cups the judges drink from on *American Idol*? Coca-Cola paid $20 million to put them there. That program also features the Coca-Cola interview room, with red and white bottles appearing in the background on digital displays as Ryan Seacrest asks the contestants questions. Another

common move is taking the ads to wherever the customers are, from posters in rest rooms to TV screens positioned near checkout lines, gas pumps, and other places people are forced to wait. Highway billboards have gone high tech, too, with flashy electronic displays that can be altered by remote control to catch the eye of drivers stuck in traffic. One company pays college students to wear company logos on their foreheads. Tremor, a promotions company started by consumer giant Procter & Gamble, has recruited several hundred thousand teenagers to help promote its products—without pay. These boys and girls are treated to sneak previews and inside information about various products, and they're only too happy to share the news with their friends.

Television commercials aren't going away, of course, but advertisers are working harder to make them more entertaining and more memorable, if sometimes more risqué or even disgusting in some viewers' opinions. If you don't like these new ads, don't think you can get away by switching off the TV to play a video game instead; many games now have ads built right into them (and if you play networked games over the Internet, somebody's probably measuring your response to these ads, too).

Of course, every new solution seems to create another round of problems. With ads everywhere, consumers are now complaining that there's nowhere to hide. Until somebody dreams up a better way to reach consumers, though, chances are that wherever you go you'll find an ad waiting for you—and it might be delivered by your best friend.[18]

Questions for Critical Thinking

1. Do fragmented media make it easier or harder for marketers to engage in segmented or concentrated marketing? Explain your answer.
2. Is it ethical to engage consumers to help promote your products without explicitly telling them you're doing so? Explain your answer.

IN-CLASS NOTES

Promotional Strategies

- Promotion can be used to achieve three basic goals: to *inform*, to *persuade*, and to *remind*
- Before selecting a promotional mix consider the *nature of your product*, the *product's price*, and the *product's position in its life cycle*
- Focusing marketing efforts on the end user is called a *pull strategy*; focusing on intermediaries is called a *push strategy*

_____

_____

_____

_____

_____

_____

_____

_____

_____

Selecting Your Promotional Mix

Within the framework of a company's promotional goals, product variables, and market approach, marketers use a mix of five activities to achieve their promotional objectives: personal selling, advertising, direct marketing, sales promotion, and public relations. These elements can be combined in various ways to create a **promotional mix** for a particular product or idea (see Exhibit 12.6).

L.O.6

promotional mix
The particular blend of personal selling, advertising, direct marketing, sales promotion, and public relations that a company uses to reach potential customers

Exhibit 12.6　**The Five Elements of Promotion**

The promotional mix typically includes a blend of various elements. The most effective mix depends on the nature of the market and the characteristics of the good or service being marketed. Over time, the mix for a particular product may change.

ACTIVITY	REACH	TIMING	FLEXIBILITY	COST/EXPOSURE
Personal Selling	Direct personal interaction with limited reach	Regular, recurrent contact	Message tailored to customer and adjusted to reflect feedback	Relatively high
Advertising	Indirect interaction with large reach	Regular, recurrent contact	Standard, unvarying message	Low to moderate
Direct Marketing	Direct personal interaction with large reach	Intermittent, based on short-term sales objectives	Customized, varying message	Relatively high
Sales Promotion	Indirect interaction with large reach	Intermittent, based on short-term sales objectives	Standard, unvarying message	Varies
Public Relations	Indirect interaction with large reach	Intermittent, as newsworthy events occur	Standard, unvarying message	No direct cost

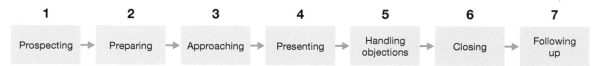

Exhibit 12.7   The Personal Selling Process

The personal selling process can involve up to seven steps, starting with prospecting for sales leads and ending with following up after the sale has been closed.

1		2		3		4		5		6		7
Prospecting	→	Preparing	→	Approaching	→	Presenting	→	Handling objections	→	Closing	→	Following up

Personal Selling

personal selling
In-person communication between a seller and one or more potential buyers

Personal selling is the interpersonal aspect of the promotional mix. It involves person-to-person presentation—face to face, by phone, or by interactive media such as video-conferencing or customized websites—for the purpose of making sales and building customer relationships. Personal selling allows for immediate interaction between the buyer and seller. It also enables the seller to adjust the message to the specific needs, interests, and reactions of the individual customer. The chief disadvantage of face-to-face personal selling is its relatively high cost—about US$170 per sales call, according to one recent study.[19]

Although it may look easy, personal selling is not a simple task. Some sales, of course, are made in a matter of minutes. However, other sales, particularly for large organizational purchases, can take months to complete. Many salespeople follow a carefully planned seven-step process from start to finish, as illustrated in Exhibit 12.7.

- *Prospecting.* Finding and qualifying potential buyers of the product or service.
- *Preparing.* Considering various options for approaching the prospect and preparing for the sales call.
- *Approaching.* Contacting the prospect, getting his or her attention, and building interest in the product or service.
- *Presenting.* Communicating a message that persuades a prospect to buy.
- *Handling objections.* Countering the buyer's objections with convincing claims.
- *Closing.* Asking the prospect to buy the product.
- *Following up.* Checking customer satisfaction following the sale and building goodwill.

Technological advances are facilitating these steps and the entire selling process. Some companies are using custom software to provide online proposal-generation and order-management systems. The software relieves salespeople of non-productive tasks and allows sales reps to spend more time attending to customers' specific needs. Sales reps at Owens Corning use laptops, the Internet, and a custom software package called Field Automation Sales Team system (FAST) to inquire about customers' backgrounds and sales histories, resolve customer service issues on the spot, modify pricing information as needed, print customized sales material, and more. Such technology empowers Owens Corning reps: "They become the real managers of their own business and their own territories," says Owens Corning's regional general manager.[20] For all its power, sales-force automation involves more engineering and maintenance work than some companies want to take on, but these firms can turn to web-based solutions such as Salesforce.com. Some 32 300 companies in dozens of industries now use the company's sales and customer service solutions that are available in fourteen languages.[21]

advertising
Paid, non-personal communication to a target market from an identified sponsor using mass communication channels

Advertising and Direct Marketing

Advertising and direct marketing are the two elements of a firm's promotional mix with which consumers are most familiar. **Advertising** consists of messages paid for by an identified sponsor and transmitted through a mass communication medium such as television, radio, or newspapers. **Direct marketing** is defined by the Direct

direct marketing
Direct communication other than personal sales contacts designed to bring about a measurable response

Marketing Association as distributing promotional materials directly to a consumer or business recipient for the purpose of generating (1) a response in the form of an order, (2) a request for further information, or (3) a visit to a store or other place of business for purchase of a specific product or service.[22]

All forms of advertising and direct marketing have three objectives: to create product awareness, to create and maintain the image of a product, and to stimulate consumer demand. Advertising and direct marketing are also the promotional approaches that best reach mass audiences quickly at a relatively low per-person cost. But to be effective, your messages must be persuasive, stand out from the competition's, and motivate your target audience—a lofty goal considering the fact that Canadian consumers are bombarded by ads. As a recent article in *Marketing* magazine pointed out, Canadians are exposed to thousands of messages each day. When you include television, radio ads, bus and subway ads, billboards, and ads on varied objects from T-shirts to coffee mugs, this figure is put into context.[23] Basically, advertisers can say whatever they want, just as long as they stay within the boundaries of the law and conform to the moral and ethical standards of the advertising medium and trade associations.

Celebrity endorsers frequently license their names and images for use in advertising and direct marketing. Some endorsers also allow their names to be used as part of a product name, as boxer George Foreman did with the George Foreman Grill.

To limit promotional abuses, the Canadian Radio-television and Telecommunications Commission (CRTC) regulates broadcasted advertisements, while Advertising Standards Canada administers codes of practice that are voluntarily established.[24] For example, the CRTC limits broadcasters to 12 minutes of advertising time per hour. But with the ad game changing and **product placement** (placing a product directly into a television program or movie) gaining in importance, the CRTC is reassessing its approach.[25] Certain industries fall under additional authority; for example, pharmaceutical advertisements fall under the domain of Health Canada. Recently some groups have accused Health Canada of dropping the ball by relaxing regulations and allowing two types of ads: reminder ads (that focus on the drug but not the disease), and help-seeking ads (that discuss the disease but not the drug). Critics argue that drugs should

product placement
The practice of paying to place branded products directly into a program

Technologies That Are Revolutionizing Business

INDIVIDUALIZED ADVERTISING

Don't be surprised if you look out the window one morning to see clouds in the sky arranged in letters that spell out your name and invite you to try a refreshing bottle of Coke or remind you to have a Harvey's burger for lunch.

HOW IT'S CHANGING BUSINESS

Maybe it won't get quite that far, but advertisers are perfecting a variety of technologies that allow them to pinpoint individual audience members with customized messages. Given the continuing fragmentation of mainstream media and advertisers' growing disappointment in mass advertising that no longer brings in the results it used to, individualized advertising promises to be the next big thing in promotional strategies. A few examples are personalized magazine covers (including one that showed an aerial photograph of each subscriber's neighbourhood with his or her home or office circled in red), commercials on digital cable systems that can be targeted to viewers in an individual neighbourhood or even an individual household (with messages shaped by the demographics of the residents of the house), narrowly focused audio messages that can be aimed at a single shopper in a retail store, and Google's Gmail service, which serves up ads based on specific words in your email messages (if you invite a colleague out for sushi, for instance, ads for local sushi restaurants could appear next to your message).[26]

WHERE YOU CAN LEARN MORE

Individualized advertising is still a young technology, so the key players and information sources are likely to change frequently in the coming months and years. In the meantime, database and search engine queries for "personalized advertising," "customized advertising," and "individualized advertising," as well as variations on those terms, should yield interesting results.

direct mail
Advertising sent directly to
potential customers

permission marketing
Promotional campaigns that send
information only to those people
who have specifically asked to
receive it

telemarketing
Selling or supporting the sales
process over the telephone

product advertising
Advertising that tries to sell specific
goods or services, generally by
describing features, benefits, and
occasionally price

institutional advertising
Advertising that seeks to create
goodwill and to build a desired
image for a company rather than to
sell specific products

*Advertisers pay a premium to be viewed at a
major event like the Grey Cup. While not taking
in the $2.6 million per spot that the Super Bowl
earns, the Grey Cup is a significant event that
has clients lining up to pay about $75 000 per
30-second spot to associate themselves with the
game and the annual spectacle of artists like
Timmins, Ontario, native Shania Twain.*

not be promoted in the same way as cola or toothpaste. They point to the string of
Viagra ads that focus solely on the end result: men and women are shown singing in the
shower, skipping to work, and smiling from ear to ear. By giving the audience a wink and
a nod these ads avoid the origins of the situation and the side effects of the drug.[27]

On the other hand, when governments step in they can sometimes create a politically dangerous backlash. When anti-tobacco legislation restricted tobacco companies
from sponsoring public events, people worried that some events would suffer (or be
cancelled altogether) as promoters scrambled to fill the void. Few people disputed the
positive intention of the laws, but when large, well-attended events like the Canadian
Grand Prix were put in danger, federal and provincial governments scrambled to save
them.[28] The legislation went through, but most events were able to find other sponsors so the events could continue.

Direct-Marketing Vehicles

Direct marketing is an effective promotional tool for many companies because
it enables them to more precisely target and personalize messages to specific consumer
and business segments and build long-term customer relationships.[29] The most popular direct marketing vehicles are direct mail, targeted email, telemarketing, and the
Internet.

- *Direct mail.* The principal vehicle for direct marketing is **direct mail**, which includes
  catalogues, brochures, DVDs, and other promotional materials delivered through
  Canada Post and private carriers.

- *Targeted email.* As millions of consumers and business employees got connected
  to email in recent years, email appeared to be a promising medium for advertising.
  The ability to reach millions of people inexpensively and direct them to an
  e-commerce website was an interesting combination. As anyone with an email
  account knows, however, legitimate email campaigns are now getting buried
  in a sea of spam campaigns that vary from the suspicious to the down-and-
  out illegal. Mike Gilbert of Three a.m. Advertising has clients like Microsoft
  and has abandoned mass emailing for his clients because it risks tainting a
  valuable brand by associating it with spammers.[30] To avoid that problem and
  to help potential customers get the information they really do want, many
  mainstream companies now emphasize **permission marketing**, in which they
  first ask for permission before sending email messages (usually through "opt-
  in" choices that are displayed on their websites).

- *Telemarketing.* Another popular form of direct marketing is **telemarketing**,
  or selling over the telephone. Telemarketing is a low-cost way to efficiently
  reach many people. Unfortunately, it has a spotted reputation because of
  some shady practitioners. "The Canadian Government has taken aim at tele-
  marketers with the *Competition Act* (Bill C-20) and a further amendment,
  Bill C-51, that defines new offences as 'enterprise crimes' and brings them
  within the scope of the *Criminal Code* scheme for seizure and forfeiture of
  proceeds."[31]

Advertising Categories

Advertising is commonly classified by type. **Product advertising** is the most common type, designed to sell specific goods or services, such as Tim Hortons
Timbits, Kellogg's cereals, or MAC cosmetics. Product advertising generally
describes the product's features and may mention its price. **Institutional
advertising** is designed to create goodwill and build a desired image for a
company rather than to sell specific products. As discussed in Chapter 3, many companies are now spending large sums for institutional advertising that focuses on
green marketing, creating an image of companies as corporate conservationists.
Institutional advertisers point out their actions, contributions, and philosophies
not only as supporting the environmental movement but as leading the way.

When used as *corporate advertising*, institutional advertising often promotes an entire line of a company's products. Institutional ads can also be used to remind investors that the company is doing well.

Advertising can also be classified according to the sponsor. **National advertising** is sponsored by companies that sell trademarked products on a nationwide basis. The term *national* refers to the level of the advertiser, not the geographic coverage of the ad. If a national manufacturer places an ad in only one city, the ad is still classified as a national ad. By contrast, **local advertising** is sponsored by a local merchant. Grocery store ads in the local newspaper are a good example. **Cooperative advertising** is a financial arrangement whereby companies with products sold nationally share the costs of local advertising with local merchants and wholesalers. As a result, it is a cross between local and national advertising. A national furniture manufacture like Palliser may share costs with local furniture shops.

Regardless of which type of advertising you use, you must get your message to your target audience by using suitable **media**, or channels of communication. Advertising media fall into seven major categories, each with its own strengths and weaknesses, as highlighted in Exhibit 12.8. Your goal as a marketer is to select

national advertising
Advertising sponsored by companies that sell products on a nationwide basis; refers to the geographic reach of the advertiser, not the geographic coverage of the ad

local advertising
Advertising sponsored by local merchants

cooperative advertising
Joint efforts between local and national advertisers in which producers of nationally sold products share the costs of local advertising with local merchants and wholesalers

media
Communications channels such as newspapers, radio, and television

---

Exhibit 12.8 **Advantages and Disadvantages of Major Advertising Media**

When selecting the media mix, companies attempt to match the characteristics of the media audiences with the characteristics of the customer segments being targeted. A typical advertising campaign involves the use of several media.

MEDIUM	ADVANTAGES	DISADVANTAGES
Newspapers	Extensive market coverage; low cost; short lead time for placing ads; good local market coverage; geographic selectivity	Poor graphic quality; short life span; cluttered pages; visual competition from other ads
Television	Great impact; broad reach; appealing to senses of sight, sound, and motion; creative opportunities for demonstration; high attention; entertainment carryover	High cost for production and air time; less audience selectivity; long preparation time; commercial clutter; short life for message; vulnerability to remote controls; losing ground to new media options
Direct mail	Can deliver large amounts of information to narrowly selected audiences; excellent control over quality of message; personalization	High cost per contact; delivery delays; difficulty of obtaining desired mailing lists; customer resistance; generally poor image (junk mail)
Email	Extremely low cost; fast preparation and delivery; ability to customize and to provide links back to websites	Deluge of spam, much of it illegal or offensive, has tainted this medium for general advertising use, possibly beyond repair; many legitimate marketers use only permission-based (opt-in) email now
Radio	Low cost; high frequency; immediacy; highly portable; high geographic and demographic selectivity	No visual possibilities; short life for message; commercial clutter; lower attention than television; lower level of engagement makes it easier to switch stations
Magazines	Good production quality; long life; local and regional market selectivity; authority and credibility; multiple readers	Limited demonstration possibilities; long lead time between placing and publishing ads; high cost; less compelling than other major media
Internet	Rich media options and creative flexibility can make ads more compelling and more effective; changes and additions can be made quickly and easily in most cases; web pages can provide an almost unlimited amount of information; can be personalized more than any other medium	Customer resistance; increasing clutter (such as pop-up ads); extreme fragmentation (millions of websites)

media mix
The combination of various media options that a company uses in an advertising campaign

a **media mix**—the combination of print, broadcast, and other media that maximizes the return of your advertising dollar. The box entitled "Zoom Media: A Good Place for an Ad" describes an unconventional but successful advertising approach.

Zoom Media: A Good Place for an Ad

Consumers are faced with an endless string of ads on television, in magazines, on the radio, and in other traditional media outlets. It is difficult for sponsors to get a message through to the current ad-weary generation. Once upon a time, a firm could advertise on a local station and feel confident that it would reach a significant portion of the targeted community. Today, satellite and digital cable are providing countless stations and fragmenting the market. Personal video recorders are reducing the ad impressions as consumers are able to skip ads like never before. Furthermore, traditional media are competing for our leisure time with alternatives like the Internet. What can a savvy marketer do? Zoom Media offers a solution by enabling sponsors to place strategically integrated messages into consumers' everyday work and play environments.

You may or may not be familiar with Zoom Media, but you have undoubtedly seen its ads. They are located in washrooms across the country, from your local school campus to the bar you frequent to sports and medical complexes in your community. What began in 1991 as a university project to raise awareness and reduce the spread of sexually transmitted diseases eventually grew into Zoom Media. This company now boasts 30 000 billboard locations in more than 4000 venues. Carl Grenier and his team pioneered this advertising approach; they began by acquiring the rights to display ads in restaurants and bars. The Zoom resto-bar division now serves close to 2000 different outlets. If a sponsor is targeting a specific youth segment it can reach them directly in their favourite bar or restaurant. Zoom also serves 70 educational institutions, 320 sports clubs, 375 medical facilities, and 230 golf courses across Canada and the United States. According to research, consumers are at peace with the invasion of their washrooms: "80% of students appreciate the ads and 54% of students recall the advertisements."

Zoom Media continues to expand its reach. With its recent acquisition of Parkad Media Ltd. it has branched out to serve parking lots. In addition to its extensive network of restaurants, Zoom Media has forged an alliance with McDonald's and serves 558 franchise locations. One thing is clear: washrooms

Zoom Media pioneered the concept of bathroom ads; however, the idea spread quickly as marketers immediately identified the targeting possibilities offered by this approach.

across the nation have become a new permanent outlet to access your mind and influence your perception of products.[32]

Questions for Critical Thinking

1. One of the benefits of Zoom Media's approach is the opportunity for sponsors to target specific groups.
   a. Name a product/brand that would be a good candidate to promote in Zoom's golf network. Explain.
   b. Which products/brands would fit in better in Zoom's McDonald's network? Explain.
2. How do Zoom's washroom ads fulfill the three principle objectives of advertising?

Sales Promotion

Sales promotion, which includes a wide range of events and activities designed to stimulate immediate interest in and encourage the purchase of your product or service, is the fourth element of the promotional mix. The impact of sales promotion activities is often short term; thus, sales promotions are not as effective as advertising or personal selling in building long-term brand preference.[33] Sales promotion consists of two basic categories: consumer promotion and trade promotion.

Consumer Promotion   **Consumer promotion** is aimed directly at final users of the product. Companies use a variety of promotional tools and incentives to stimulate repeat purchases and to entice new users:

- *Coupons.* The biggest category of consumer promotion—and the most popular with consumers—is **coupons**, certificates that spur sales by giving buyers a discount when they purchase specified products. Customers redeem their coupons at the time of purchase. Companies offer coupons on packages, in print ads, in direct mail, at the checkout, and on the Internet to encourage trial of new products, reach out to non-users of mature products, encourage repeat buying, and temporarily lower a product's price.[34]

- *Rebates.* Similar to coupons, rebates are another popular promotional tool. Instead of receiving the discount at the time of purchase, buyers generally get reimbursement cheques from the manufacturer by submitting proofs of purchase along with a prepared manufacturer's rebate form. Because many buyers neglect to redeem the rebates, the cost of running such programs remains relatively low. Moreover, rebates allow the manufacturer to promote the reduced price even though customers pay the full price at checkout.[35]

- *Point-of-purchase.* Another widely used consumer promotion technique is the **point-of-purchase (POP) display**, a device for showing a product in a way that stimulates immediate sales. It may be simple, such as the end-of-aisle stacks of cola in a supermarket or the racks of gum and mints at checkout counters, or it may be more elaborate, such as digital displays or ad decals strategically placed on floor aisles. Simple or elaborate, point-of-purchase displays really do work. Studies show that in almost every instance, such displays significantly increase sales.[36]

- *Special-event sponsorship.* Sponsoring special events has become one of the most popular sales promotion tactics. Thousands of companies spend billions of dollars to sponsor events ranging from golf to opera. The organizers of the upcoming Vancouver 2010 Winter Olympics are banking on receiving about $600 million to help finance the games.[37] They are off to a good start; Bell Canada secured the rights as the official telecommunications sponsor in a $200 million deal.[38] Air Canada is close to signing a deal estimated to be worth between $15–30 million as well.[39]

- *Cross-promotion.* Another popular sales promotion vehicle is **cross-promotion**, which involves using one brand to advertise another non-competing brand. One of the most successful cross-promotion campaigns ever is "Intel Inside." Just two years following the campaign's inception, awareness of the Intel chip went from roughly 22 percent of PC buyers to more than 80 percent.[40] Like most blockbuster movie releases, *Spider-Man 3* was promoted using many cross-promotion partners. Burger King flooded the various media with contests and ads focused on the superhero.

- *Samples.* Samples are an effective way to introduce a new product, encourage non-users to try an existing product, encourage current buyers to use the product in a new way, or expand distribution into new areas. Sampling has been around for decades, but it's alive and well in the computer age, too; many software companies let potential customers try their products for a limited period of time before making a purchase decision.

sales promotion
The wide range of events and activities (including coupons, rebates, contests, in-store demonstrations, free samples, trade shows, and point-of-purchase displays) designed to stimulate interest in a product

consumer promotion
A sales promotion aimed at final consumers

coupons
Certificates that offer discounts on particular items and are redeemed at the time of purchase

point-of-purchase (POP) display
Advertising or other display materials set up at retail locations to promote products to potential customers as they are making their purchase decisions

cross-promotion
Jointly advertising two or more non-competing brands

Spider-Man 3 was cross-promoted with various corporate partners. BURGER KING® was one company that got on the bandwagon in a major way by featuring the hero in mass-promoted ads, holding Spider-Man contests and giveaways, and distributing premiums.

Air Canada created quite a buzz a few years ago when it used Céline Dion to usher in the new post–bankruptcy protection era and launch its new uniforms. Céline Dion performed in front of 2000 employees in a cavernous airport hangar at Pearson Airport in Toronto. Love her or hate her, the pop diva managed to attract the type of buzz that Air Canada was looking for.

premiums
Free or bargain-priced items offered to encourage consumers to buy a product

specialty advertising
Advertising that appears on various items such as coffee mugs, pens, and calendars, designed to help keep a company's name in front of customers

trade promotions
Sales promotion efforts aimed at convincing distributors or retailers to push a producer's products

trade allowance
A discount offered by producers to wholesalers and retailers

public relations
Non-sales communication that businesses have with their various audiences (includes both communication with the general public and press relations)

Other popular consumer sales promotion techniques include in-store demonstrations, loyalty and frequency programs such as frequent-flyer miles, and **premiums**, which are free or bargain-priced items offered to encourage the consumer to buy a product. Contests, sweepstakes, and games are also quite popular in some industries and can generate a great deal of public attention, particularly when valuable or unusual prizes are offered. **Specialty advertising** (on pens, calendars, T-shirts, and so on) helps keep a company's name in front of customers for a long period of time.

Trade Promotion   Although shoppers are more aware of consumer promotion, trade promotions actually account for the largest share of promotional spending. **Trade promotions** are aimed at convincing distributors or retailers to sell a company's products by offering them a discount on the product's price, or a **trade allowance**. The distributor or retailer can pocket the savings and increase company profits or can pass the savings on to the consumer to generate additional sales. Besides discounts, other popular trade allowance programs are display premiums, dealer contests or sweepstakes, and travel bonus programs. All are designed to motivate distributors or retailers to push particular merchandise.

Public Relations

Public relations encompasses all of the non-sales communications that businesses have with their many stakeholders—communities, investors, industry analysts, government agencies and officials, and the news media. Companies rely on public relations to build a favourable corporate image and foster positive relations with these groups.

In fact, successful companies recognize that a good reputation is one of a business's most important assets. A recent study shows that companies with a good public image have a big edge over less-respected companies. Customers are more than twice as likely to buy new products from companies they admire, which is why smart companies work hard to build and protect their reputations. Smart executives not only work to build a positive public image, but also prepare a *crisis communication plan* to make sure they're ready to communicate in the event of accidents, financial stumbles, product tampering, or any disaster.

Two standard public relations tools are the news release and the news conference. A **news release** is a short memo sent to the media covering topics that are of potential news interest; a *video news release* is a brief video clip sent to television stations. Companies use news releases to get favourable news coverage about themselves and their products. Richard Branson is a master at this game. During the initial Canadian launch of Virgin Mobile he swept through the country with spectacles that were covered by local and national media.[41] When a business has significant news to announce, it will often arrange a **news conference**. Both tools are used when the company's news is of widespread interest, when products need to be demonstrated, or when company officials want to be available to answer questions from the media.

Integrating Your Marketing Communications

With five major promotional methods available—personal selling, advertising, direct marketing, sales promotion, and public relations—how do you decide on the right mix for your product? There are no easy answers, because you must take many factors into account. In fact, when you consider all the ways that audiences can receive marketing messages today, the potential for confusion is not all that surprising. Besides the traditional media—radio, television, billboards, print ads, and direct-mail promotions—marketers are using websites, email, faxes, kiosks, sponsorships, and a number of clever vehicles to deliver messages to targeted audiences. Coordinating promotional and communication efforts is becoming vital if a company is to send a consistent effective message.

Exhibit 12.9 **Integrated Marketing Communications**

Coordinating the five elements of promotion delivers a consistent message to the marketplace.

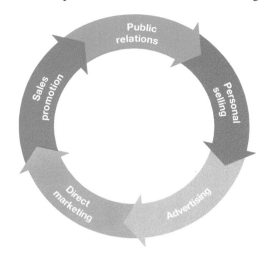

news release
A brief statement or video program released to the press announcing new products, management changes, sales performance, and other potential news items

news conference
A gathering of media representatives at which companies announce new information; also called a press briefing

integrated marketing communications (IMC)
The strategy of coordinating and integrating communications and promotional efforts with customers to ensure greater efficiency and effectiveness

Integrated marketing communications (IMC) is a strategy of coordinating and integrating all one's communications and promotional efforts to provide customers with clarity, consistency, and maximum communications impact. "It's everything from running ads to developing new media, to creating custom media, licensing, promotion, sweepstakes—every aspect of communicating to consumers," says one media expert.[42] The basics of IMC are quite simple: communicating with one voice and one message to the marketplace, as Exhibit 12.9 suggests.

The need for communicating with one voice is even greater today. Consumers are exposed to a greater variety of marketing communications and don't necessarily distinguish among message sources the way that marketers do. In the consumer's mind, messages from different sources blur into one single message about the company. Thus, conflicting messages from different sources can result in confused company images and brand positions.[43]

Properly implemented, IMC increases marketing and promotional effectiveness. According to Bell Canada, the campaign featuring Frank and Gordon, the Bell Beavers, has helped the company in three key growth areas: Internet, TV, and mobile services. According to Léger Marketing, Bells's ads rank near the top of the "least-liked ads" list, but they also rank near the top of the most-loved list (with a ratio of 3:1 in favour). Bottom line: the campaign has created tremendous market awareness. The results were not a chance occurrence. Bell has coordinated a deliberate message across media. Someone in a car can hear Frank and Gordon on the radio or zoom by a billboard ad, for a second or two, while driving down the highway, and immediately remember the message. A good integrated marketing campaign is able to reinforce the message with minimal effort from the consumer if it maintains consistent themes. Frank and Gordon help Bell effectively achieve these goals.[44]

While integrating your communications and promotional efforts may seem logical and relatively simple, many organizations find IMC difficult to implement. They discover that over time their promotional mixes develop into collections of disconnected efforts. Organizational resistance is the primary cause for IMC failure. Many marketing departments are accustomed to autonomy and see IMC as a threat to their resources and decision-making power. Besides, moving to an IMC approach requires new ways of organizing, planning, and managing all marketing functions, and some marketing departments are not up to the task.[45]

Frank and Gordon, the Bell Canada "Spokesbeavers," are both loved and hated. The integrated marketing campaign has been tremendously successful on an awareness level. While their future is unclear, some ad experts predict that the duo may in fact be in place all the way until the 2010 Vancouver Winter Olympics.

IN-CLASS NOTES

Integrated Marketing Communications (IMC)

- IMC is a strategy of coordinating all communications and promotional efforts to provide customers with *clarity*, *consistency*, and *maximum communications impact*
- Properly implemented, IMC increases marketing and promotional effectiveness

_____

_____

_____

_____

_____

_____

BEHIND THE SCENES

MEC's Effective Blend of Retail and E-tail Channels

After carefully evaluating the advantages and disadvantages of establishing an online presence, MEC moved forward with a clear purpose. From the beginning, MEC concentrated on creating a "multichannel" approach to its system that harmoniously blends its online and offline outlets. MEC built functionality into its operating methods to improve member services. It offers in-store shipping pickup and store-level stock checks. It also made an effort to integrate its marketing communications messages. As a customer-centred organization, MEC did not simply rest on its initial online efforts. Important upgrades were made in 2003 and 2006 to address inefficiencies and improve the site's user friendliness. As a testament to these efforts, MEC was recognized by the Retail Council of Canada as Multi-Channel Retailer of the year in 2005. Additionally, US-based *Internet Retailer* recognized MEC as one of the top 50 Internet retailers. MEC was the only Canadian company to receive this distinction from the online magazine.

The company also continues to mail approximately 750 000 English-language catalogues and 75 000 French-language catalogues twice a year (Fall/Winter, Spring/Summer). Most are sent out directly to members, who are encouraged to shop on the Internet. Recently, MEC created a specialty catalogue geared toward snow sports. The company expected to send out approximately 50 000 catalogues to members in 2007. The various retail channels

serve to reinforce each other. The website often serves an information-gathering purpose that leads to online, telephone, or in-store sales. The basic idea is that the more product information available at the consumer's fingertips, the better.

Overall, MEC's blend of bricks and clicks has proven to be quite successful. The MEC website receives about 450 000 unique site visits each month and saw a 16.7 percent increase in 2006. MEC's sales were more than $221.6 million, of which web sales accounted for $10.6 million. The multichannel approach is an integral part of MEC's future growth; it creates purchase synergy because consumers have access to a variety of information sources that lead them to an MEC channel.[46]

Critical Thinking Questions

1. How did MEC blend its online and offline channels?
2. How has MEC's success as a traditional retailer benefited its online business?

Learn More Online

Go to Chapter 12 of this text's website at www.pearsoned.ca/bovee, and click on the hotlink to the MEC website. After reviewing the site, answer the following questions: What are MEC's return policies for online customers? How does MEC promote its physical stores?

TEST YOUR KNOWLEDGE

Questions for Review

1. What is meant by channel conflict and how can companies reduce the likelihood of conflict within the chain?
2. What factors have an influence on channel selection?
3. What is the difference between product advertising and institutional advertising?
4. What are the seven steps in the personal selling process?
5. What is meant by the term integrated marketing communications?

Questions for Analysis

6. What is the difference between a category killer and a department store?
7. What trade-offs must you consider when adopting a physical distribution system?
8. If a manufacturer starts to sell its goods on its company website, why might this arouse channel conflict?
9. Describe the relationship between a push and a pull strategy and the corresponding level of use of consumer or trade promotions.
10. **Ethical Considerations.** Direct-mail marketers often publish different prices in different catalogues targeted at different market segments. When you call to order, the sales representative first asks for your customer or catalogue number or postal code so that the rep knows which price to charge you. Is this practice ethical?

Questions for Application

11. Scan your local papers and highlight or clip ads that could possibly mislead the public. What do you find misleading about the ad? How would you improve it?
12. Find three newspaper or magazine ads that you think are particularly effective and three more that you think are ineffective. What do you like about the effective ads? How might you improve the ineffective ads?
13. **Integrated.** In Chapter 8 we discussed the fact that supply chain management integrates all of the activities involved in the production of goods and services from suppliers to customers. What are the benefits of involving distributors in the design, manufacturing, or sale of a company's product or service?
14. **Integrated.** Which of the four basic functions of management discussed in Chapter 6 would be involved in decisions that establish or change a company's channels of distribution? Explain your answer.

PRACTISE YOUR KNOWLEDGE

SHARPENING YOUR COMMUNICATION SKILLS

Select a product you're familiar with and examine the strategies used to advertise and promote that product. Identify the media (website, print, television, radio, billboards, and so on) used to advertise the product. Consider the following:

- Where do the ads appear?
- Who is the target audience? Does the company attempt to appeal to a wide variety of people with different ads?
- What creative theme or appeal is being used?
- Is the company taking advantage of any Internet technologies for promotion?

Prepare a brief summary of your findings as directed by your instructor. Compare your findings with those of other students and note any differences or similarities in the promotion of your selected products.

BUILDING YOUR TEAM SKILLS

In small groups, discuss three or four recent ads or consumer promotions that you think were particularly effective. Using the knowledge you've gained from this chapter, try to come to a consensus on what attributes contributed to the success of each ad or promotion. For instance, was it persuasive? Informative? Competitive? Creative? Did it stimulate you to buy the product? Why? Compare your results with those of other teams. Did any teams mention the same ads? Did you list the same attributes?

EXPAND YOUR KNOWLEDGE

DISCOVERING CAREER OPPORTUNITIES

Retailing is a dynamic, fast-paced field with many career opportunities in both store and non-store settings. In addition to hiring full-time employees when needed, retailers of all types often hire extra employees on a temporary basis for peak selling periods like the year-end holidays. You can find out about seasonal and year-round job openings by checking newspaper classified ads, looking for signs in store windows, and browsing the websites of online retailers.

1. Select a major retailer, such as a chain store in your area or a retailer on the Internet. Is this a specialty store, discount store, department store, or another type of retailer?

2. Visit the website of the retailer you selected. Does the site discuss the company's hiring procedures? If so, what are they? What qualifications are required for a position with the company?

3. Research your chosen retailer using library sources or online resources. Is this retailer expanding? Is it profitable? Has it recently acquired or been acquired by another firm? What are the implications of this acquisition for job opportunities?

DEVELOPING YOUR RESEARCH SKILLS

Find an article in a business journal or newspaper (online or print editions) discussing changes a company is making to its distribution strategy or channels. For example, is a manufacturer selling products direct to consumers? Is a physical retailer offering goods via a company website? Is a company eliminating the intermediary? Has a non-store retailer decided to open a physical store? Is a category killer opening smaller stores? Has a major retail tenant closed its stores in a mall?

1. What changes in the company's distribution structure or strategy have taken place? What additional changes, if any, are planned?

2. What were the reasons for the changes? What role, if any, did electronic commerce play in the changes?

3. If you were a shareholder in this company, would you view these changes as positive or negative? What, if anything, might you do differently?

STUDY GUIDE

SUMMARY OF LEARNING OBJECTIVES

1. Explain what marketing intermediaries do and list their seven primary functions

Marketing intermediaries, or middlemen, bring producers' products to market and help ensure that the goods and services are available in the right time, place, and amount. More specifically, intermediaries match buyers and sellers; provide market information; provide promotional and sales support; sort, standardize, and divide merchandise; transport and store the product; assume risks; and provide financing.

2. Explain how wholesalers and retailers function as intermediaries

Wholesalers buy from producers and sell to retailers, to other wholesalers, and to organizational customers such as businesses, government agencies, and institutions. Retailers buy from producers or wholesalers and sell the products to the final consumers.

3. Discuss the key factors that influence channel design and selection

Channel design and selection are influenced by the type of product and industry practices. They are also influenced by a firm's desired market coverage (intensive, selective, or exclusive), financial ability, desire for control, and potential for channel conflict.

4. Differentiate between intensive, selective, and exclusive distribution strategies

With an intensive distribution strategy, a company attempts to saturate the market with its products by offering them in every available outlet. Companies that use a more selective approach to distribution choose a limited number of retailers that can adequately support the product. Firms that use exclusive distribution grant a single wholesaler or retailer the exclusive right to sell the product within a given geographic area.

5. Discuss the Internet's effect on the distribution function

Companies are using the Internet to enhance their existing channel structures, expand their market reach, and add efficiencies to their channel structures. Some are eliminating layers of intermediaries from a marketing channel and transferring the eliminated intermediary functions to the Internet. In many cases, these changes—especially the bypassing of a channel—are causing channel conflict.

6. Identify the five basic categories of promotion

The five basic categories of promotion are (1) personal selling, which involves contacting customers by phone, interactive media, or in person to make a sale; (2) advertising, which is a paid sponsored message transmitted by mass media; (3) direct marketing, which is the distribution of promotional material to consumers via direct mail, email, telemarketing, or the Internet to generate an order or other consumer response; (4) sales promotion, which includes a number of consumer and promotional tools designed to stimulate consumer interest in a product and encourage a purchase; and (5) public relations, which includes non-sales communications between businesses and their stakeholders to foster positive relationships.

7. Distinguish between the two main types of sales promotion and give examples of each

The two main types of sales promotion are consumer promotion and trade promotion. Consumer promotions are intended to motivate the final consumer to try new products or to experiment with the company's brands. Examples include coupons, cross-promotion, specialty advertising, premiums, point-of-purchase displays, and special events sponsorship. Trade promotions are designed to induce wholesalers and retailers to stimulate sales of a producer's products. Examples include trade allowances, display premiums, dealer contests, and travel bonus programs.

8. Discuss the use of integrated marketing communications

The likelihood of sending conflicting marketing messages to consumers increases when companies use a greater variety of marketing communications. Integrated marketing communications (IMC) is a process of coordinating all of a company's communications and promotional efforts so that they present only one consistent message to the marketplace. Properly implemented, IMC increases marketing and promotional effectiveness.

KEY TERMS

advertising (386)
consumer promotion (391)
cooperative advertising (389)
coupons (391)
cross-promotion (391)
direct mail (388)
direct marketing (386)
distribution centres (379)
distribution mix (372)
distribution strategy (371)
exclusive distribution (375)
institutional advertising (388)
integrated marketing
    communications (IMC) (393)
intensive distribution (375)
local advertising (389)

logistics (378)
marketing intermediaries (371)
materials handling (379)
media (389)
media mix (390)
national advertising (389)
news conference (393)
news release (393)
permission marketing (388)
personal selling (386)
persuasive advertising (381)
physical distribution (377)
point-of-purchase (POP)
    display (391)
premiums (392)
product advertising (388)

product placement (387)
promotional mix (385)
promotional strategy (381)
public relations (392)
pull strategy (383)
push strategy (383)
reminder advertising (381)
retailers (371)
sales promotion (391)
selective distribution (375)
specialty advertising (392)
telemarketing (388)
trade allowance (392)
trade promotions (392)
warehouse (379)
wholesalers (371)

QUESTIONS

Multiple Choice   Circle the correct answer and then check the answers in the back of the book to chart your progress.

1. Which of the following are *not* considered marketing intermediaries?

   a. Retailers
   b. Wholesalers
   c. Consumers
   d. All of the above

2. Which of the following retailers offer a complete selection in a narrow range of merchandise?

   a. Convenience stores
   b. Department stores
   c. Hypermarkets
   d. Specialty stores

3. Which of the following is a type of specialty store on a giant scale?

   a. Category killer
   b. Convenience store
   c. Department store
   d. Supermarket

4. Marketing intermediaries perform a number of distribution functions. Which of the following is *not* one of the common distribution functions?

   a. Match buyers and sellers
   b. Gather an assortment of goods
   c. Provide financing
   d. Manufacture the product

5. Which of the following forms of market coverage is most appropriate for selling chocolate bars?

   a. Intensive distribution
   b. Selective distribution
   c. Exclusive distribution
   d. Elitist distribution

6. Which of the following forms of market coverage would you choose if you were producing a high-priced prestige item?

   a. Intensive distribution
   b. Selective distribution
   c. Exclusive distribution
   d. None of the above

7. Which of the following is *not* one of the basic goals of promotion?

   a. To inform
   b. To persuade
   c. To remind
   d. To manufacture

8. Which of the following products is best sold face to face?

   a. Mars chocolate bars
   b. Industrial machines
   c. Popular novels
   d. Ice cream

9. Which of the following is the best strategy for a company selling a new pharmaceutical product?

   a. Push strategy
   b. Pull strategy
   c. Both push and pull strategies
   d. Neither push nor pull strategies

10. Which of the following has the highest cost per customer?

    a. Personal selling
    b. Advertising
    c. Direct marketing
    d. Sales promotion

True/False

1. True or false? The distribution channels used for business products are generally shorter than the distribution channels used for consumer products.

2. True or false? Institutional advertising attempts to sell trademarked products on a national basis.

3. True or false? Giving out samples is a good way to get consumers to try the product, especially new products.

4. True or false? Coupons are only used when a company wants to offer savings to its steady customers who have bought the product for many years.

5. True or false? In recent years many companies have moved away from the idea of using an integrated marketing communications approach.

Fill-in-the-Blank

1. _____ sell products to the final consumer for personal use.

2. Companies that use _____ are using a market coverage strategy that tries to place a product in as many outlets as possible.

3. An important part of warehousing activities is _____, the movement of goods within and between physical distribution facilities.

4. _____ is a financial arrangement whereby companies with products sold nationally share the costs of local advertising with local merchants and wholesalers.

5. A _____ strategy is a promotional approach designed to motivate wholesalers and retailers to promote a producer's product to the end user.

6. The _____ promotional approach can be described by the following statement: There are no direct costs when using this approach.

7. _____ are free or bargain-priced items offered to encourage the consumer to buy a product.

8. _____ is the final step of the personal selling process.

9. _____ are sales promotion efforts aimed at convincing distributors or retailers to push a producer's products.

10. A widely used consumer promotion technique is the _____, a device for showing a product in a way that stimulates immediate sales. It may be simple, such as racks of gum and mints at checkout counters, or it may be more elaborate, such as ad decals strategically placed on aisle floors.

See It on the WEB

Visit the Companion Website at **www.pearsoned.ca/bovee**, review the exercises, and complete the following assignments for Chapter 12:

1. Explore the World of Wholesaling
2. Learn the Consumer Marketing Laws
3. See How the Pros Put Marketing to Work

CBC ✸ VIDEO CASE

The Bay's Wishlist: Redefining a Retail Giant

LEARNING OBJECTIVES

The purpose of this video is to help you

1. Understand the competitive landscape in the Canadian retail sector.

2. Identify important segmentation variables that retailers must consider when setting corporate marketing strategies and positioning a retail brand.

3. Identify important trends in the marketplace and techniques to successfully navigate challenges.

SYNOPSIS

The Hudson's Bay Company has been in operation since 1670 and has overcome all types of challenges and competitors. Despite an interesting history of courageous adventurers, The Bay has fallen victim to its own traditional model and faces tremendous challenges today. Will this Canadian icon last another 300 plus years? Most retail consultants aren't looking that far ahead; many have doubts about the company's survival in the next 20, 10, or even 2–5 years. Competition is coming from all sources as the generalist department store is no longer a formula for guaranteed success. That point was clearly made a few years ago when Eaton's ceased operations. Today, The Bay is losing important business to category killers such as Future Shop and Toys "R" Us, from specialty stores like Sleep Country Canada, and from low-cost competition like Wal-Mart. The landscape is changing and The Bay needs to clearly redefine itself to move forward with strength. In this video, analysts provide a list of seven tips to help redefine The Bay and help it reconnect with consumers to improve the bottom line. What does the future hold? Only time will tell, however, this video provides clear opinions on how to save this Canadian icon.

Discussion Questions

1. *For analysis*: Describe the major shifts in the marketplace that have placed The Bay in a vulnerable position.

2. *For analysis*: From your own perspective and experience as a Canadian consumer, what are The Bay's biggest challenges?

3. *For application*: Which of the seven tips would you implement if you were in charge of setting The Bay's marketing strategy? Which would you ignore? Explain your answers.

4. *For debate*: The Bay is a Canadian institution that has long historical roots in this country despite the fact that it was recently acquired by an American billionaire named Jerry Zucker. Some analysts in the video had a pessimistic tone to their opinions, but they all provided some important and clear advice. Using the arguments in the video as well as you own observations, debate the future of the company: Long, continued success vs. short-term peril.

ONLINE EXPLORATION

Visit The Bay's website at www.hbc.com and take a look at the corporate information section. Read through the press releases and identify any new strategies that the company has implemented. Take a look at the website. Does the site appeal to people in your age group?

ON LOCATION VIDEO CASE

In Consumers' Shoes: Skechers

LEARNING OBJECTIVES

The purpose of this video is to help you

1. Describe the role of the "four P's" in a company's marketing mix.

2. Explain how a company uses marketing research to learn about customer needs.

3. Discuss how and why a company uses market segmentation.

SYNOPSIS

Skechers enjoys a reputation for producing fashionable footwear that combines comfort with innovative design. The Manhattan Beach, California, firm distributes its product line in more than 110 countries and territories throughout the world. Since its start in 1992, Skechers has nurtured its image as a marketer of "cool shoes for cool people"— men, women, and children in the 12-to-24-year-old market segment, as well as older consumers who want to feel young. Rather than try to influence the market with its products, Skechers carefully researches customer needs and attitudes, then uses this information to shape its product, promotion, distribution, and pricing activities. Skechers has gained market share while competing against some powerful players in the shoe industry by building a mega-brand with integrity and a distinctly youthful personality.

Discussion Questions

1. *For analysis:* Which of the "four P's" of the marketing mix seems to govern Skechers' marketing strategy? Why?

In what ways do you think Skechers alters elements of its domestic marketing mix for international markets?

2. *For analysis:* How does Skechers gather data about its customers' needs and preferences through marketing research? Why does this approach to marketing research suit the company's marketing goals as well as its customer base?

3. *For application:* Describe how Skechers segments the market for shoes. What other demographic, geographic, psychographic, and product usage variables would you suggest the company use in segmenting its market? Why?

4. *For application:* Building brand loyalty is a major effort that presents both opportunities and challenges. What are some of the opportunities and challenges encountered by the marketing managers at Skechers?

5. *For debate:* Kelly O'Connor stresses that the youth market will drop a brand if it loses its "street credibility." Should Skechers invest more heavily in edgy new products or in novel promotion to maintain its brand's credibility? Support your chosen position.

ONLINE EXPLORATION

Visit the Skechers website at www.skechers.com to see how it presents its product lines and reaches out to its targeted market segments. Then visit the websites of competitors Nike (www.nike.com) and Reebok (www.reebok.com). Are these rivals targeting the same segments as Skechers? How do their marketing mix strategies compare with those of Skechers? To continue differentiating itself from Nike and Reebok, what new product lines should Skechers consider researching?

When established retailers started to consider a move to the web a few years ago, many experts advised them to keep their new e-businesses separate. The thinking was that the creation of separate e-businesses would allow the web entity to speed up decision making, be more flexible, be more entrepreneurial, act independently, and thus compete more effectively with pure-play e-businesses (those that exist only on the Internet, like Amazon.ca). While some retailers embraced this approach, others debated whether to sell online at all. They worried about spreading their human and financial resources too thin. They worried about competing with their existing distributors, their competitors, and themselves (because their e-sales could cannibalize their physical-store sales).

Mixing Clicks with Bricks

In hindsight, the experts were wrong. Although financially the separate e-businesses promised considerable shareholder potential, running separate online and offline operations did not work.

Consider Barnes & Noble, a major bookstore chain in the United States. To compete with Amazon.com, the company established a completely separate division—Barnes & Noble.com (www.bn.com)—and later spun the division off as a stand-alone company. But unlike pure-plays, Barnes & Noble.com lacked a sense of urgency about the web and let Amazon capture the lion's share of initial e-business and publicity. Moreover, customers did not care that the two were separate entities. Web customers became confused and angry when they tried to return books purchased online to the physical Barnes & Noble bookstores, only to be turned away. Furthermore, the strategy forced the physical stores to compete with their online sibling and prevented them from sharing management teams, combining marketing programs, or achieving economies of scale.

It didn't take long for Barnes & Noble to realize its decision to separate its online and physical stores was a mistake and decide to combine the two operations. This move made it possible for web customers to return purchases at a company's physical stores. Other companies have since followed Barnes & Noble's lead by reeling in their separate e-businesses or launching websites that are seamless additions to the company. Indigo Books and Music Inc. provides another example of the importance of mixing clicks and bricks. In a recent holiday season, during a period when in-store sales were being hurt by severe winter storms, the online site managed to surpass expectations as shoppers turned to the company's website in greater numbers and helped make up for some of the lost business.

Creating the Perfect Blend

After much debate, experts now agree that integrating a retailer's physical stores with its web operation is the most effective approach to e-commerce. Mixing clicks with bricks (also known as *clicks-and-bricks* or *clicks-and-mortar*) makes a store's physical and web operations transparent to the customer. A Sears customer, for instance, can gather product information from Sears.ca before heading to the outlet at the local mall. Salespeople can then add value by doing things the website can't—such as answering specific product questions and demonstrating products. At Future Shop, customers who purchase online can only receive their shipment at home; however, the company plans to allow for in-store pickup in the near future. But online customers are able to return merchandise directly to a physical Future Shop location within 30 days of purchase.

A clicks-and-bricks strategy is beneficial for retailers. Multichannel customers who shop both online and in stores tend to be more loyal and spend more. Eddie Bauer (which sells products through catalogues, retail stores, and its website) reports that shoppers who use all three methods to purchase from the company spend five times more than those who shop only by catalogue. Moreover, clicks-and-bricks retailers can use their websites to advertise, test merchandise, suggest gifts, increase product awareness, cross-promote online and offline products, and drive traffic to their physical stores or vice versa. Some are even using their websites to provide specialty items not available in stores. "We don't have the same real estate issues," says one spokesperson for the Gap, which offers plus sizes for men and women exclusively online. "It's an easy, lower-cost way to get merchandise out there quickly."

But there are limitations to mixing clicks with bricks. Not all retailers, especially those that don't have a catalogue business, are able to offer their entire inventories online because of the expense of photographing and describing every item. This confuses customers. Delivery fees continue to be a barrier to online purchases, which is why so many companies offer free delivery when you spend a certain amount of money. Still, if you don't mix clicks with bricks, "you literally won't exist as a retailer," declares one e-commerce expert. The web is where most consumers do their initial phases of shopping—whether it's as basic as price comparison or searching for store locations. However, unlike the early naïve days of the Internet, it is not enough to set up a site and hope for the best. According to one expert, companies need to focus on three basic elements: (1) have a goal; (2) design your site to be measurable; and (3) treat your site like an ongoing experiment (a work in progress). In short, sites need to be managed, maintained, and measured to offer the e-shopper an optimal experience.[47]

Questions for Critical Thinking

1. Why did retailers initially separate their physical and web stores?

2. Why did the strategy to separate online and offline stores fail?

3. What are the benefits of a clicks-and-bricks strategy?

BUSINESS PLANPRO EXERCISES

Developing Marketing Strategies to Satisfy Customers

Review Appendix B, "Your Business Plan" to learn how to use Business Plan Pro Software so you can complete these exercises.

Think Like a Pro

Objective: By completing these exercises you will become acquainted with the sections of a business plan that address a firm's product, pricing, promotion, and distribution strategies. You will use the sample business plan for Boulder Stop (listed as Sports Equipment-Café in the Sample Plan Browser) in this exercise.

1. Define the target market for Boulder Stop. How will the company differentiate its products and services from its competitors?

2. Describe the company's pricing, promotion, sales, and distribution strategies. Which distribution channels will the company use to deliver its products?

3. Rank the company's three market segmentation categories according to their importance.

4. According to the Keys to Success section, what must Boulder Stop do to be successful?

Create Your Own Business Plan

Consider your own target market and customers as you continue working on the business plan you are creating. How will you segment your target market? Which customers are likely to buy your product or service? Describe your product, pricing, promotion, and distribution strategies. Now make some preliminary sales forecasts. Under which section headings will you present this information?

PART 6

MANAGING
FINANCIAL
INFORMATION AND
RESOURCES

CHAPTER 13
Analyzing and Using Financial
Information

CHAPTER 14
Understanding Banking and Securities

CHAPTER 13

ANALYZING AND USING FINANCIAL INFORMATION

LEARNING OBJECTIVES

After studying this chapter, you will be able to

1 Discuss how managers and outsiders use financial information

2 Describe what accountants do

3 Summarize the impact of the *Sarbanes-Oxley Act* in the United States and Bill C-198 in Canada

4 State the basic accounting equation and explain the purpose of double-entry bookkeeping and the matching principle

5 Differentiate between accrual-basis and cash-basis accounting

6 Explain the purpose of the balance sheet and identify its three main sections

7 Explain the purpose of the income statement

8 Explain the purpose of the statement of cash flows

9 Explain the purpose of ratio analysis and list the four main categories of financial ratios

10 Identify the responsibilities of a financial manager

This photo, taken in front of a Nortel building in Ottawa, seems peaceful with people walking in front of a still lake. The environment at Canada's former high-tech poster child has been anything but calm and peaceful in recent years, but the company is slowly trying to put this difficult period in the past.

www.nortel.com

The Nortel brand was tremendously well-respected and had instant credibility in business circles back in the 1990s. But something changed all that positive sentiment. Years of expansion and acquisitions enabled Nortel to grow. At the close of the 1990s, an estimated 75 percent of Internet traffic was moving through Nortel equipment. As it moved into the new millennium, Nortel was over 100 years old and yet it had successfully transformed into the poster child for the new Internet economy. Investors and corporate partners considered Nortel a solid blue-chip company that could be trusted without hesitation.

When the Internet bubble burst it had a devastating effect on all telecom companies, and Nortel's sales fell along with the value of its new acquisitions. However, this difficult time should have led to some major cost cutting and job losses (which it did) and a slow recovery. After all, the Internet bubble had an impact on all firms to some extent. What has truly hurt Nortel's reputation is their string of financial restatements. When investors read balance sheets, income statements, and statements of cash flows they believed that these figures, examined and audited by major accounting firms, were true representations. Nortel's track record in the past seven years has been nothing short of embarrassing and disgraceful in this regard.

Nortel's current problem of inaccurate financial statements came to light when then-CEO Frank Dunn informed the board of directors that the company would lose approximately $112 million in the first part of 2003. However, by March he reported a profit of $40 million based on an accounting manoeuvre known as cookie jar accounting. The board of directors eventually realized that the profits were based on false accounting and terminated Dunn along with the company's chief financial officer and top controller. Cookie jar accounting is the process of establishing a pool of money that the company can use in the future to refund customers who may be unhappy because of a missed deadline, poor service, or product defects. For example, if Nortel sells a customer $10 million of goods it may put $1 million of this amount away to offset any future problems with that customer. The $1 million becomes an expense on the income statement for that year and reduces the company's net income. In the 1990s, Nortel appeared to be putting more money away than it would ever need to pay unsatisfied customers. When the market slowed, Nortel continuously raided this cookie jar, taking out money and counting it as revenue so investors would never know that sales were declining.

Bill Owens replaced Dunn as Nortel's CEO and worked to repair investor confidence in the troubled company. But he had to postpone the restatement of revenues and net profits several times, and customers became concerned about the long-term viability of the company. He was later replaced by Mike Zafirovski, a former executive at Motorola.

In 2005, the 2003 financials were restated and profit was reduced from US$732 to US$434 million. The 2004 figures actually showed a loss of US$51 million. Unfortunately, this was not the end. In March of 2006, Nortel announced that it was once again delaying its results and it would once again restate financials from 2003, 2004, and 2005. These announcements were beginning to sound like the words of a lying third grader telling a friend, "this is the truth, I really, really, really mean it this time." More troubles followed in 2007, with the US Securities and Exchange Commission and the Ontario Securities Commission announcing legal proceedings against former CEO Frank Dunn and three former senior executives.

Many investors have lost faith; even corporate partners and suppliers, which once considered Nortel as a rock-solid partner, are a bit more careful because the golden child was on the brink of financial destruction not so long ago. What does the future hold? It's still not clear. One thing is certain, though—Nortel needs to get its accounting in order if it wants to be taken seriously again.[1]

TEST YOURSELF

Answers to these questions can be found on the website: www.pearsoned.ca/bovee.

1. What will it take for Nortel to regain the respect it once had from investors and customers?

2. Do you think that customers and suppliers should avoid doing business with Nortel until it gets its house in order?

3. What can governments do to protect investors and other stakeholders from unethical or illegal practices?

4. How does the Nortel case relate to the tighter new laws and regulations that fall under the *Sarbanes-Oxley Act* in the United States and Bill C-198 in Canada?

WHAT IS ACCOUNTING?

L.O. 1

It's difficult to manage a business today without accurate and up-to-date financial information. **Accounting** is the system a business uses to identify, measure, and communicate financial information to others inside and outside the organization. Financial information is important to businesses like Nortel for two reasons. First, it helps managers and owners plan and control a company's operation and make informed business decisions. Second, it helps outsiders evaluate a business. Suppliers, banks, and other lenders want to know whether a business is creditworthy; investors and shareholders are concerned with a company's profit potential; government agencies are interested in a business's tax accounting.

Because outsiders and insiders use accounting information for different purposes, accounting has two distinct facets. **Financial accounting** is concerned with preparing financial statements and other information for outsiders such as *shareholders* and *creditors* (people or organizations that have loaned a company money or have extended credit). Nortel's adjustment of old financial statements has cast doubt over all of their recent figures. If customers and investors are unsure of the validity of these figures they can't make informed decisions with confidence. **Management accounting** is concerned with preparing cost analyses, profitability reports, budgets, and other information for insiders such as management and other company decision makers. To be useful, all accounting information must be accurate, objective, consistent over time, and comparable to information supplied by other companies.

What Accountants Do

L.O. 2

Some people confuse the work accountants do with **bookkeeping**, which is the clerical function of recording the economic activities of a business. Although some accountants do perform bookkeeping functions, their work generally goes well beyond the scope of this activity. Accountants design accounting systems, prepare financial statements, analyze and interpret financial information, prepare financial forecasts and budgets, and prepare tax returns. Some accountants specialize in certain areas of accounting, such as **cost accounting** (calculating and analyzing production costs), **tax accounting** (preparing tax returns and interpreting tax law), or **financial analysis** (evaluating a company's performance and the financial implications of strategic decisions such as product pricing, employee benefits, and business acquisitions).

In addition to traditional accounting work, accountants may also help clients improve business processes, plan for the future, evaluate product performance, analyze

accounting
Measuring, interpreting, and communicating financial information to support internal and external decision making

financial accounting
The area of accounting concerned with preparing financial information for users outside the organization

management accounting
The area of accounting concerned with preparing data for use by managers within the organization

bookkeeping
Record keeping; the clerical aspect of accounting

cost accounting
An area of accounting focusing on the calculation of manufacturing and storage costs of products for use or sale in a business

tax accounting
An area of accounting focusing on tax preparation and tax planning

financial analysis
The process of evaluating a company's performance and analyzing the costs and benefits of strategic actions

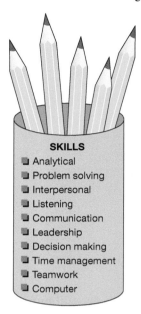

Exhibit 13.1 **Ten Most Important Skills for Accountants**

Besides having a thorough knowledge of accounting, today's accountants need the right mix of personal and business skills to increase their chances of having a successful career.

SKILLS
- Analytical
- Problem solving
- Interpersonal
- Listening
- Communication
- Leadership
- Decision making
- Time management
- Teamwork
- Computer

private accountants
In-house accountants employed by organizations and businesses other than a public accounting firm; also called *corporate accountants*

controller
The highest-ranking accountant in a company, responsible for overseeing all accounting functions

chartered accountants (CAs)
Professionally licensed accountants who meet certain requirements for education and experience and who pass a comprehensive examination

certified management accountants (CMAs)
Accountants who have fulfilled the requirements for certification as a specialist in management accounting

certified general accountants (CGAs)
Accountants who have fulfilled the requirements for certification as a general accountant

profitability by customer and product groups, design and install new computer systems, assist companies with decision making, and provide a variety of other management consulting services. Performing these functions requires a strong business background and a variety of business skills beyond accounting (see Exhibit 13.1).

Most accountants are **private accountants** (sometimes called *corporate accountants*). Private accountants work for a business, a government agency (such as the Canada Revenue Agency, a school, or a local police department), or a non-profit corporation (such as a church, charity, or hospital).[2] Private accountants generally work together as a team under the supervision of the organization's **controller**, who reports to the vice-president of finance. Exhibit 13.2 shows the typical finance department of a large company. In smaller organizations, the controller may be in charge of the company's entire finance operation and report directly to the president.

Although certification is not required of private accountants, many are licensed **chartered accounts (CAs)**, which means they have passed a rigorous licensing exam. To become eligible to sit for the exam, candidates must earn a university degree, complete prerequisite courses in accounting and information systems, and complete 24 to 30 months of training in a public accounting firm. A growing number of private accountants are becoming **certified management accountants (CMAs)**; to do so they must earn a university degree (except in British Columbia), complete prerequisite course work, pass an entrance exam prior to admission, complete a two-year professional component called Strategic Leadership, and complete 24 months of relevant work experience. People interested in another professional designation in Canada may opt for the **certified general accountant (CGA)** designation, which requires a university degree, work experience, and the successful completion of an examination. The main difference between the three designations is the focus of their educational program and training: the CA educational program emphasizes auditing and is generally considered the most prestigious of the three designations, CMAs focus on combining management and accounting training, while CGAs learn about completing financial statements and taxes.

Exhibit 13.2 **Typical Finance Department**

Here is a typical finance department of a large company. In smaller companies, the controller may report directly to the president.

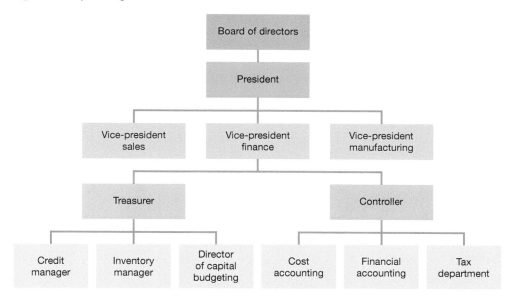

Public accountants, by contrast, are independent of the businesses, organizations, and individuals they serve. Most public accountants are employed by public accounting firms that provide a variety of accounting and consulting services for their clients. Members of the firm are generally CAs and must obtain the CA designation before they are eligible to conduct an **audit**—a formal evaluation of a company's accounting records and processes to ensure the integrity and reliability of a company's financial statements.

Companies whose shares are publicly traded in Canada are required to file audited financial statements with the stock exchange on which they trade. During an audit, CAs who work for an independent accounting firm (also known as *external auditors*) review a client's financial records to determine whether the statements that summarize these records have been prepared in accordance with **generally accepted accounting principles (GAAP)**, basic accounting standards and procedures that have been agreed upon by regulators, auditors, and companies over decades. GAAP aims to give a fair and true picture of a company's financial position.

Once the auditors have completed an audit, they attach a report summarizing their findings to the client's published financial statements. Sometimes these reports disclose information that might materially affect the client's financial position, such as the bankruptcy of a major supplier, a large obsolete inventory, costly environmental problems, or questionable accounting practices. Most companies, however, receive a clean audit report, which means that to the best of the auditors' knowledge the company's financial statements are accurate.

To assist with the auditing process, many large organizations employ **internal auditors**—employees who investigate and evaluate the organization's internal operations and data to determine whether they are accurate and whether they comply with GAAP, federal laws, and industry regulations. Although this self-checking process is vital to an organization's financial health, an internal audit is not a substitute for having an independent auditor look things over and provide an unbiased opinion. Many people, such as creditors, shareholders, investors, and government

public accountants
Professionals who provide accounting services to other businesses and individuals for a fee

audit
The formal evaluation of the fairness and reliability of an organization's financial statements

generally accepted accounting principles (GAAP)
Professionally approved Canadian standards and practices used by accountants in the preparation of financial statements

internal auditors
Employees who analyze and evaluate a company's operations and data to determine their accuracy

IN-CLASS NOTES

What Is Accounting?

- Accountants design accounting systems, prepare financial statements, analyze and interpret financial information, prepare forecasts and budgets, and prepare tax returns
- Accountants can specialize in **cost accounting, tax accounting,** or **financial analysis**
- Designations in Canada: **CAs, CMAs,** and **CGAs**
- **Private accountants** work for a business, a government agency, or a non-profit organization
- Most **public accountants** are employed by accounting firms, are independent of their clients, and are generally CAs

_____

_____

_____

_____

_____

_____

_____

_____

_____

_____

agencies, rely on the integrity of a company's financial statements and place great trust and confidence in the independence of auditors whose detached position allows them to be objective and, when necessary, critical.

L.O. 3

The Rules of Accounting

All Canadian companies must create their financial statements in accordance with GAAP. This requirement makes it possible for external users to compare the financial results of public companies to gain a general idea of a firm's relative effectiveness and its standing within a particular industry.

GAAP

In Canada, the Canadian Institute of Chartered Accountants (CICA) is responsible for developing and monitoring GAAP. Other countries have similar governing boards. In the United States, the Financial Accounting Standards Board (FASB) establishes GAAP. Therefore, American companies such as GE and Adobe report accounting data using rules that are different from those used in Canada. Some large companies that list their securities on more than one stock exchange must convert financial statements prepared under foreign accounting rules to the GAAP of the country in which the exchange is listed. So a company that trades on both the TSX and the NYSE exchanges will have to produce two separate sets of financial statements. This requirement ensures that all companies listed on a particular stock exchange are on even ground. Since some Canadian companies report their earnings using both Canadian and American GAAP, their results can differ depending on which GAAP they use. For example, Talisman Energy, a Canadian oil company, reported a net income of $2005 million in 2006 using Canadian GAAP, but when it applied American GAAP its net income shrunk to $1920 million.[3]

Recent proposals to develop a uniform set of global accounting rules known as international accounting standards (IAS) could help eliminate such differences and simplify the bookkeeping process for multinational companies. But such global rules are meeting strong resistance from the US Securities and Exchange Commission (SEC) and other regulators, who are concerned that many of the international accounting standards are not as strict as their GAAP.[4]

Accountants perform a variety of services for their clients beyond tax preparation and auditing. Many serve on strategic planning teams and help companies plan for the future.

How Strict Is GAAP?

GAAP sets forth the principles and guidelines that companies and accountants must follow when preparing financial reports or recording accounting transactions (which we will discuss later in this chapter). But, as with any set of rules, GAAP can be interpreted aggressively or conservatively. In other words, GAAP gives executives the freedom to use their judgment in areas that can dramatically affect the company's bottom line without breaking any rules. Unfortunately, some companies take advantage of this flexibility by resorting to a number of accounting tricks that overstate expenses, puff up income, and hide problems from the public. Bombardier has long been criticized by investors for using programmed accounting that sees the company generously estimate the number of planes that will be sold and base production costs on this estimate. Financial analysts note that while this form of accounting is allowed under GAAP, it is quite aggressive and if the company fails to sell as many planes as it estimates, the profit per plane could change dramatically from what was recorded. For example, when Bombardier makes a new plane, it estimates how many it will sell over a 20-year period and base production costs on the economics of scale realized from producing that many planes. If, however, it fails to sell that number of planes, the cost structure could be much higher than previously recorded and profits would have to be changed.

It's hard to tell just how many companies are crossing the line. What is clear, however, is that in most cases "accounting irregularities don't start with dishonesty; rather they start with pressure for financial performance," says one financial expert.[5] Such pressure comes from employee shareholders whose life savings are invested in company shares, executives whose bonuses are tied to a company's bottom line, and financial managers who must meet Bay and Wall Street estimates or pump up a company's share price. The box entitled "Putting Accountability Back into Public Accounting" describes some of the recent efforts to fix the problems.

New Rules: *Sarbanes-Oxley* and Bill C-198

L.O. 3

GAAP sets forth the principles and guidelines for companies and accountants to follow when preparing financial reports or recording accounting transactions, but high-profile scandals involving Enron, Nortel, WorldCom, and other big corporations prove that it is still possible to get around the rules and deceive investors. To repair investor confidence, the US Congress passed the *Public Company Accounting Reform and Investor Protection Act*, usually referred to as the **Sarbanes-Oxley Act**. This Act had a direct impact on some Canadian companies when it was first introduced.

Sarbanes-Oxley Act
Comprehensive US legislation passed in the wake of business scandals like Enron that is designed to improve integrity and accountability of financial information.

Putting Accountability Back into Public Accounting

For a profession that is supposed to be all about trust and financial responsibility, public accounting seems to be sliding from one scandal to another: billions of dollars in accounting fraud slipped past auditors, multimillion-dollar fines for selling shady tax shelters, accountants arrested for destroying documents, accusations of overbilling, an endless parade of lawsuits from investors and clients—and the biggest black eye of them all, the collapse of the once-mighty accounting firm Arthur Andersen. How did all this happen over the past decade, and how can the profession restore public confidence?

No situation this complex has a simple explanation, but observers point out several issues that have contributed to many of the recent problems:

- *Deliberate deception by corporate clients.* Auditors maintain that in many cases it's impossible to detect deliberately misleading bookkeeping, and it's unfair to hold them accountable when they don't see it. An auditor "cannot provide 100 percent guarantee against fraud," says Chuck Landes, director of auditing for the American Institute of Certified Public Accountants (AICPA).

- *Changes in accounting practices.* Some claim that auditors aren't looking in the right places. In the past, auditors used a labour-intensive process of sifting through thousands of transactions to determine if bookkeeping entries were correct. Now they focus on analyzing the computerized bookkeeping programs and internal controls. While this

approach prevents low-level employees from swiping petty cash, it can't always catch executives who shift millions or billions around using creative accounting schemes.

- *Conflict of interest.* Others blame the conflict of interest that exists when an accounting firm earns millions performing consulting work for an audit client. "If you are auditing your own creations, it is very difficult to criticize them," says one accounting expert. Critics say these cozy relationships discourage some auditors from examining corporate books closely enough or challenging CEOs when potential irregularities surface.

With billions of dollars and the financial health of millions of people on the line, this new attention is a good thing. The past few years have given everyone a clear and important reminder: Auditing is a vital function upon which free enterprise and the health of the global economy depend.[6]

Questions for Critical Thinking

1. Examine the reasons given in this feature to explain why auditors sometimes don't detect accounting irregularities and discuss why these problems exist and what else can be done to eliminate or curb these problems.
2. Why is the auditing function of such vital importance to the global economy?

However, the new Canadian-made Bill C-198 now makes compliance everyone's business. Let's take a brief look at both pieces of legislation.

The *Sarbanes-Oxley Act* aims to stop abuses and errors in several important areas. The Act:[7]

- outlaws most loans by corporations to their own directors and executives
- creates the Public Company Accounting Oversight Board (PCAOB) to oversee external auditors
- requires corporate lawyers to report evidence of financial wrongdoing
- prohibits external auditors from providing some non-audit services
- requires that audit committees on the board of directors have at least one financial expert and that the majority of board members be independent (not employed by the company in an executive position)
- prohibits investment bankers from influencing stock analysts

- requires CEOs and CFOs to sign statements attesting to the accuracy of their financial statements

- requires companies to document and test their internal financial controls and processes

The last two items in particular have generated lots of interest and some controversy among businesses. In a few of the recent scandals, top executives claimed not to know what was going on in their own companies, although "the idea that a CEO doesn't know what's going on in his company is ridiculous," according to United Technologies CEO George David. In any event, signing their financial statements under oath should have the intended effect of ensuring close attention to the details. However, the requirement to document and test financial controls has generated perhaps the most widespread discussion. Estimates of the cost of compliance vary widely, from a few hundred thousand dollars to several million, depending on the size of the company and initial state of its financial systems. According to one study, US companies will need to spend a total of $7 billion to get into compliance initially.[8]

Bill C-198 is a Canadian law, but it embraces the principles of the *Sarbanes-Oxley Act* and follows its lead in both wording and regulatory requirements. It has placed pressure on Canadian firms to focus on compliance issues.[9] Do regulators have the right idea? Is all of this necessary? As you might expect with anything this complex and far-reaching, opinions vary widely. Most investors will surely welcome the changes. Firms must move forward in this new open spirit. According to a recent study by Deloitte, "wholeheartedly embracing the law can actually be less expensive in the long run than begrudgingly accepting it." In another recent survey, 54 percent of top executives felt it was unnecessary, and only 10 percent thought it was "very necessary." As the rules are implemented and evolve, businesses will respond and the true costs and benefits of the *Sarbanes-Oxley Act* and Bill C-198 should become more visible. Like it or not, the errors of the past decade have forced government authorities to move in this direction and it is now a part of doing business.[10]

Bill C-198
Legislation (under the *Ontario Securities Act*) that applies to all TSX-listed companies and aims for more accountability in financial information (embraces the same principles as the US *Sarbanes-Oxley Act*)

Technologies That Are Revolutionizing Business

COMPLIANCE MANAGEMENT SOFTWARE

The *Sarbanes-Oxley Act* and Bill C-198 require publicly traded companies to regularly verify their internal accounting controls. To assist in this recurring task, a number of software companies now offer *compliance management software*.

HOW IT'S CHANGING BUSINESS

Verifying accounting controls can be a considerable task for large or decentralized companies with multiple accounting systems. For instance, one recent study found that the average billion-dollar public company has 48 separate financial systems. Rather than creating their own software solutions to the problem or adapting existing accounting software, many companies now turn to ready-made compliance management software. The costs can be considerable (up to $100 000 or more just to purchase the software and possibly many times more than that to have it customized and installed. The companies buying these solutions say it's cheaper and faster than building their own, plus they can take advantage of the compliance knowledge programmed into the software. Whether they build or buy, a number of firms are also using the new reporting requirements as an opportunity to streamline and improve their business operations.[11]

WHERE YOU CAN LEARN MORE

Several professional publications are keeping an eye on the compliance software market, including *Computerworld* (www.computerworld.com), *CIO* (www.cio.com), *InformationWeek* (www.informationweek.com), *eWeek* (www.eweek.com), and *CFO* and *CFO IT* (www.cfo.com). Search each website for "compliance software" to get the latest news.

In-Class Notes

The Rules of Accounting

- Public companies publish their financial statements in accordance with **generally accepted accounting principles (GAAP)**
- The **Canadian Institute of Chartered Accountants (CICA)** is responsible for developing and monitoring GAAP in Canada
- *Sarbanes-Oxley* in the US and **Bill C-198** in Canada were created to address the high number of accounting scandals; they contain new rules to improve integrity and accountability of financial information

_____

_____

_____

_____

_____

_____

_____

_____

L.O. 4

FUNDAMENTAL ACCOUNTING CONCEPTS

As pressure mounts for companies to produce cleaner financial statements and to disclose material information promptly, the need increases for all businesspeople—not just accountants—to understand basic accounting concepts. In the next sections we discuss the fundamental accounting concepts, explore the key elements of financial statements, and explain how managers and investors analyze a company's financial statements to make decisions.

In working with financial data, accountants are guided by three basic concepts: the *fundamental accounting equation, double-entry bookkeeping,* and the *matching principle.* Let's take a closer look at each of these concepts.

The Accounting Equation

assets
Any things of value owned or leased by a business

liabilities
Claims against a firm's assets by creditors

owners' equity
The portion of a company's assets that belongs to the owners after obligations to all creditors have been met

accounting equation
The basic accounting equation that assets equal liabilities plus owners' equity

For thousands of years, businesses and governments have kept records of their **assets**—valuable items they own or lease, such as equipment, cash, land, buildings, inventory, and investments. Claims against those assets are **liabilities**, or what the business owes to its creditors, such as banks and suppliers. For example, when a company borrows money to purchase a building, the lender or creditor has a claim against the company's assets. What remains after liabilities have been deducted from assets is **owners' equity**:

$$\text{Assets} - \text{Liabilities} = \text{Owners' Equity}$$

Using the principles of algebra, this equation can be restated in a variety of formats. The most common is the simple **accounting equation**, which serves as the framework for the entire accounting process:

$$\text{Assets} = \text{Liabilities} + \text{Owners' Equity}$$

This equation suggests that either creditors or owners provide all of the assets in a corporation. Think of it this way: If you were starting a new business, you could contribute cash to the company to buy the assets you need to run your business or you could borrow money from a bank (the creditor) or you could do both. The company's liabilities are placed before owners' equity in the accounting equation because creditors are paid first. After liabilities have been paid, anything left over belongs to the owners or, in the case of a corporation, to the shareholders. As a business engages in economic activity, the dollar amounts and composition of its assets, liabilities, and owners' equity change. However, the equation must always be in balance; in other words, one side of the equation must always equal the other side.

Double-Entry Bookkeeping and the Matching Principle

To keep the accounting equation in balance, companies use a **double-entry bookkeeping** system that records every transaction affecting assets, liabilities, or owners' equity. For example, if Manitoba Telecom Services (MTS) purchased a $50 000 computer system on credit, assets would increase by $50 000 (the cost of the system) and liabilities would also increase by $50 000 (the amount the company owes the vendor), keeping the accounting equation in balance. But if MTS paid cash outright for the equipment (instead of arranging for credit), the company's total assets and total liabilities would not change because the $50 000 increase in equipment would be offset by an equal $50 000 reduction in cash. In fact, the company would just be switching assets—cash for equipment.

double-entry bookkeeping
A way of recording financial transactions that requires two entries for every transaction so that the accounting equation is always kept in balance

Software Simplifies Accounting Tasks

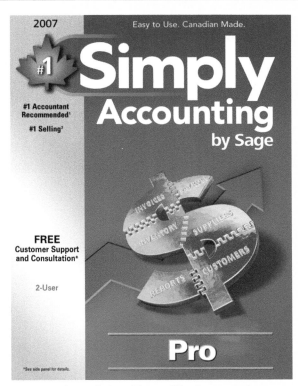

Accounting software designed for small businesses, such as QuickBooks from Intuit or Simply Accounting from Sage, simplify bookkeeping and financial planning for small business owners.

Most small business owners love the idea of building their dream into a real business. Unfortunately, many of them forget that for the business to be viable in the long run they must keep their financial books in order. Many small business owners dread the nuts and bolts of accounting and focus on building sales. But to ensure a solid financial footing, to keep the government off their

backs, and to attain proper financing from banking institutions and investors, entrepreneurs need to pay attention to accounting matters. Thankfully, the process of maintaining the books has become a lot easier in recent years with the continued development and improvement of software accounting packages like Simply Accounting and QuickBooks. These software programs can range from $50 to a few thousand dollars. More advanced software packages like ACCPAC can range from the low thousands to over $100 000.

Simply Accounting, for example, has various product lines to meet the different needs of small businesses. The Entrepreneur version provides basic services like preparing invoices and tracking GST/PST. The Basic version enables users to manage inventory, track projects, and handle payroll in-house. The Pro version enables departmental accounting and is multiple-user ready. The Premium version can produce enhanced financial reports and enables the user to prepare forecasts. For more information on the differences between the packages you can visit www.simplyaccounting.com.

The bottom line: these programs are improving efficiency and enabling individuals with a limited accounting background, but a willingness to learn, to perform basic accounting functions effectively.

Questions for Critical Thinking

1. List some of the practical ways that accounting software can help a small business owner develop his or her business.
2. Selecting a specific software package that is right for a firm's particular needs can be difficult. What criteria should a small business owner consider before making a selection?

matching principle
A fundamental accounting principle requiring that expenses incurred in producing revenue be deducted from the revenues they generate during an accounting period

accrual basis
An accounting method in which revenue is recorded when a sale is made and an expense is recorded when it is incurred

cash basis
An accounting method in which revenue is recorded when payment is received and an expense is recorded when cash is paid

amortization
An accounting procedure for systematically spreading the cost of an asset over its estimated useful life

The **matching principle** requires that expenses incurred in producing revenues be deducted from the revenue they generated during the same accounting period. This matching of expenses and revenue is necessary if the company's financial statements are to present an accurate picture of the profitability of a business. Accountants match revenue to expenses by adopting the **accrual basis** of accounting, which states that revenue is recognized when you make a sale or provide a service, not when you are paid. Similarly, your expenses are recorded when you receive the benefit of a service or when you use an asset to produce revenue—not when you pay for it. Accrual accounting focuses on the economic substance of the event instead of on the movement of cash. It's a way of recognizing that revenue can be earned either before or after cash is received and that expenses can be incurred when you receive a benefit (such as a shipment of supplies), whether it's before or after you pay for it.

If a business runs on a **cash basis**, the company records revenue only when money from the sale is actually received. Your chequebook is an easy-to-understand cash-based accounting system: You record cheques at the time of purchase and deposits at the time of receipt. Revenue thus equals cash received, and expenses equal cash paid. The trouble with cash-based accounting, however, is that it can be misleading. You can misrepresent expenses and income by the way you time payments. It's easy to inflate income, for example, by delaying the payment of bills. For that reason, public companies are required to keep their books on an accrual basis.

Amortization, or the allocation of the cost of a long-term asset over a period of time, is another way that companies match expenses with revenues. During the normal course of business, a company enters into many transactions that benefit more than one accounting period—such as the purchase of buildings, inventory, and equipment. When you buy a piece of real estate or equipment, instead of deducting the entire cost of the item at the time of purchase you amortize it, or spread its cost over the asset's useful life (because the asset will likely generate income for years to come). If the company were to expense long-term assets at the time of purchase, the financial performance of the company would be distorted in the year of purchase as well as in all future years when these assets generate revenue.

IN-CLASS NOTES

Fundamental Accounting Concepts
- **Assets = Liabilities + Owners' equity**
- To keep the accounting equation in balance, companies use **double-entry bookkeeping**
- Under the **matching principle**, expenses are deducted during the same accounting period as revenues are generated
- Under the **accrual basis** of accounting, revenue is recognized when you make a sale and expenses are recorded when you receive the benefit (required for public companies)
- Under the **cash basis**, the company records revenue only when money from the sale is received

_____
_____
_____
_____
_____
_____
_____
_____
_____
_____
_____

Using Financial Statements

A typical corporate accounting system is made up of thousands or even millions of individual transactions—debits and credits, to be exact. During the accounting process, sales, purchases, and other transactions are recorded and classified into individual accounts. Once these individual transactions are recorded and then summarized, accountants must review the resulting transaction summaries and adjust or correct all errors or discrepancies before they can **close the books**, or transfer net revenue and expense items to retained earnings. Exhibit 13.3 presents the process for putting all of a company's financial data into standardized formats that can be used for decision making, analysis, and planning. To make sense of these individual transactions, accountants summarize them by preparing financial statements.

close the books
The act of transferring net revenue and expense account balances to retained earnings for the period

Understanding Financial Statements

Financial statements consist of three separate yet interrelated reports: the *balance sheet*, the *income statement*, and the *statement of cash flows*. Together these statements provide information about an organization's financial strength and ability to meet current obligations, the effectiveness of its sales and collection efforts, and its effectiveness in managing its assets. Organizations and individuals use financial statements to spot opportunities and problems, to make business decisions, and to evaluate a company's past performance, present condition, and future prospects. Whether the company is a one-person consulting firm or a multinational with 100 000 employees, financial statements are vital.

   In the following sections we will examine the financial statements of Computer Central, a fictional company engaged in direct sales and distribution of brand-name personal computers (such as HP, Toshiba, and Macintosh) and related computer products (such as software, printer cartridges, and scanners). The company conducts its primary business from a combined telemarketing/corporate office/warehouse/showroom facility in Halifax, Nova Scotia. There, Computer Central's 600-plus account executives service more than 634 000 customers annually. In 2008 the company shipped more than 2.3 million orders, amounting to more than $1.7 billion in sales—a 35 percent increase in sales from the prior year. The company's daily sales volume has grown exponentially over the last decade—from $232 000 to $6.8 million. Because of this tremendous growth

Exhibit 13.3 **The Accounting Process**

The traditional printed accounting forms are shown here. Today, nearly all companies use the computer equivalents of these forms.

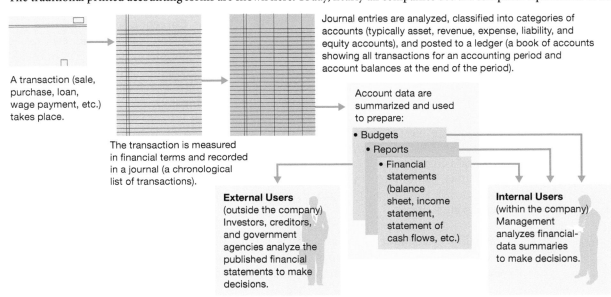

and the increasing demand for new computer products, the company recently purchased an 84 125-square-metre building. Keep these points in mind as we discuss Computer Central's financial statements in the following sections.

Balance Sheet

balance sheet
Statement of a firm's financial position on a particular date; also known as a *statement of financial position*

The **balance sheet**, also known as the *statement of financial position,* is a snapshot of a company's financial position on a particular date, such as December 31, 2008. In effect, it freezes all business actions and provides a baseline from which a company can measure change. This statement is called a balance sheet because it includes all elements in the accounting equation and shows the balance between assets on one side of the equation and liabilities and owners' equity on the other side. In other words, as in the accounting equation, a change on one side of the balance sheet means changes must be made elsewhere. Exhibit 13.4 is the balance sheet for Computer Central as of December 31, 2008.

In reality, however, no business can stand still while its financial condition is being examined. A business may make hundreds of transactions of various kinds every working day. Even during a holiday, office fixtures grow older and decrease in value and interest on savings accounts accumulates. Yet the accountant must set up a balance sheet so that managers and other interested parties can evaluate the business's financial position as if it were static rather than ever-changing.

calendar year
A 12-month accounting period that begins on January 1 and ends on December 31

fiscal year
Any 12 consecutive months used as an accounting period

Every company prepares a balance sheet at least once a year, most often at the end of the **calendar year**, covering January 1 to December 31. However, many business and government bodies use a **fiscal year**, which may be any 12 consecutive months. For example, a company may use a fiscal year of June 1 to May 31 because its peak selling season ends in May. Its fiscal year would then correspond to its full annual cycle of manufacturing and selling. Some companies prepare a balance sheet more often than once a year, perhaps at the end of each month or quarter. Thus, every balance sheet is dated to show the exact date when the financial snapshot was taken.

By reading a company's balance sheet and comparing it to previous periods, you should be able to determine the size of the company, the major assets owned, any asset changes that occurred in recent periods, how the company's assets are financed, and any major changes that have occurred in the company's debt and equity in recent periods. Most companies classify assets, liabilities, and owners' equity into categories like those shown in the Computer Central balance sheet.

current assets
Cash and items that can be turned into cash within one year

fixed assets
Assets retained for long-term use, such as land, buildings, machinery, and equipment; also referred to as *property, plant, and equipment*

Assets   As discussed earlier in this chapter, an asset is something owned by a company that will be used to generate income. Assets can consist of cash, things that can be converted into cash (such as investments), and equipment needed to make products or to provide services. For example, Computer Central needs a warehouse and a sizable inventory to sell computer products to its customers. Most often, the assets section of the balance sheet is divided into current assets and fixed assets. **Current assets** include cash and other items that will or can become cash within the following year. **Fixed assets** (sometimes referred to as *property, plant, and equipment*) are long-term investments in buildings, equipment, furniture and fixtures, transportation equipment, land, and other tangible property used in running the business. Fixed assets have a useful life of more than one year. Computer Central's principal fixed asset is the company's warehouse facility.

Assets are listed in descending order by *liquidity,* or the ease with which they can be converted into cash. Thus, current assets are listed before fixed assets. The balance sheet gives a subtotal for each type of asset and then a grand total for all assets. Computer Central's current assets consist primarily of cash, investments in short-term marketable securities like money-market funds, accounts receivable (or amounts due from customers), and inventory (such as computers, software, and other items the company sells to customers).

Liabilities   Liabilities come after assets because they represent claims against the company's assets, as shown in the basic accounting equation: Assets = Liabilities + Owners' Equity. Liabilities may be current or long term, and they are listed in the order in which

Exhibit 13.4   **Balance Sheet for Computer Central**

The categories used on Computer Central's year-end balance sheet are typical.

Computer Central

Balance Sheet
As of December 31, 2008
(in thousands)

ASSETS

Current Assets		
Cash	$4 230	
Marketable Securities	36 458	
Accounts Receivable	158 204	
Inventory	64 392	
Miscellaneous Prepaid and Deferred Items	6 504	
Total Current Assets		$269 788
Fixed Assets		
Property and Equipment	53 188	
Less: Accumulated Depreciation	−16 132	
Total Fixed Assets		37 056
Other Assets		4 977
Total Assets		$311 821

LIABILITIES AND SHAREHOLDERS' EQUITY

Current Liabilities		
Accounts Payable	$41 358	
Accrued Expenses	29 700	
Total Current Liabilities		$71 058
Long-Term Liabilities		
Loans Payable	$15 000	
Total Long-Term Liabilities		15 000
Total Liabilities		86 058
Shareholders' Equity		
Common Stock		
(21571 shares @ $.01 par value)	$216	
Less: Treasury Stock (50000 shares)	−2 089	
Paid-in Capital	81 352	
Retained Earnings	146 284	
Total Shareholders' Equity		225 763
Total Liabilities and Shareholders' Equity		$311 821

Current Assets
Cash and other items that will or can be converted to cash within one year.

Fixed Assets
Long-term investments in buildings, equipment, furniture, and any other tangible property expected to be used in running the business for a period longer than one year.

Current Liabilities
Amounts owed by the company that are to be repaid within one year.

Long-Term Liabilities
Debts that are due a year or more after the date of the balance.

Shareholders' Equity
Money contributed to the company for ownership interests, as well as the accumulation of profits that have not been paid out as dividends (retained earnings).

they will come due. The balance sheet gives subtotals for **current liabilities** (obligations that will have to be met within one year of the date of the balance sheet) and **long-term liabilities** (obligations that are due one year or more after the date of the balance sheet), and then it gives a grand total for all liabilities.

Current liabilities include accounts payable, short-term financing, and accrued expenses. *Accounts payable* includes the money the company owes its suppliers (such as Hewlett-Packard or Toshiba) as well as money it owes vendors for miscellaneous services (such as electricity and telephone charges). *Short-term financing* consists of trade credit—the amount owed to suppliers for products purchased but not yet paid

current liabilities
Obligations that must be met within one year

long-term liabilities
Obligations that fall due more than one year from the date of the balance sheet

Businesses rely on bank loans as a chief source of long-term financing. Here bankers review a company's financial statements to determine whether the firm is creditworthy.

for—and commercial paper—short-term promissory notes of major corporations sold in denominations of $100 000 or more, with maturities of up to 270 days (the maximum allowed by law without registration). *Accrued expenses* are expenses that have been incurred but for which bills have not yet been received. For example, because Computer Central's account executives earn commissions on computer sales to customers, the company has a liability to its account executives once the sale is made—regardless of when a cheque is issued to the employee. Thus, the company must record this liability because it represents a claim against company assets. If such expenses and their associated liabilities were not recorded, the company's financial statements would be misleading and would violate the matching principle (because the commission expenses that were earned at the time of sale would not be matched to the revenue generated from the sale).

Long-term liabilities include loans, leases, and bonds. As Chapter 4 points out, bank loans may be secured or unsecured. The borrowing company makes principal and interest payments to the bank over the term of the loan, and its obligation is limited to these payments (see "Debt versus Equity Financing" in Chapter 4). Leases are an alternative to loans. Rather than borrowing money to buy a piece of equipment, a firm may enter into a long-term **lease**, under which the owner of an item allows another party to use it in exchange for regular payments. Bonds are certificates that obligate the company to repay a certain sum, plus interest, to the bondholder on a specific date. Bonds are traded on organized securities exchanges and are discussed in detail in Chapter 14.

Computer Central's long-term liabilities are relatively small for a company its size. In 2008, the company purchased a new $30 million warehouse facility with $15 million in cash it had saved over many years and a five-year $15 million bank loan. The company invests its excess cash in short-term marketable securities so it can earn interest on these funds until they are needed for future projects.

Owners' Equity The owners' investment in a business is listed on the balance sheet under owners' equity (or shareholders' equity for a corporation like Computer Central). Sole proprietorships list owner's equity under the owner's name with the amount (assets minus liabilities). Small partnerships list each partner's share of the business separately, and large partnerships list the total of all partners' shares. Shareholders' equity for a corporation is presented in terms of the amount of common shares that are outstanding, meaning the amount that is in the hands of the shareholders. The combined amount of the assigned or par value of the common shares plus the amount paid over the par value (paid-in capital) represents the shareholders' total investment. Roughly $81 million was paid into the corporation by Computer Central shareholders at the time the company's shares were issued. In 2008, the company repurchased 50 000 shares of the company's own stock in the open market for $2 089 000. The company will use this *treasury stock* for its employee stock option plan and other general corporate purposes.

Shareholders' equity also includes a corporation's **retained earnings**—the portion of shareholders' equity that is not distributed to its owners in the form of dividends or the income to date that has been retained by the corporation. Computer Central's retained earnings amount to $146 million. The company did not pay dividends. Instead, it is building its cash reserves for future asset purchases and to finance future growth.

Income Statement

If the balance sheet is a snapshot; the income statement is a movie. The **income statement** shows an organization's profit performance over a specific period of time, typically one year. It summarizes all **revenues** (or sales), the amounts that have been or are to be received from customers for goods or services delivered to them, and all **expenses**, the costs that have arisen from generating revenues. Expenses and income taxes are then subtracted from revenues to show the actual profit or loss of a company, a figure known as **net income**—profit, or the *bottom line*. By briefly reviewing a company's income statement you should have a general sense of the company's size, its

lease
A legal agreement that obligates the user of an asset to make payments to the owner of the asset in exchange for using it

retained earnings
The portion of shareholders' equity earned by the company but not distributed to its owners in the form of dividends

income statement
The financial record of a company's revenues, expenses, and profits over a given period of time

revenues
Amounts earned from sales of goods or services and inflow from miscellaneous sources such as interest, rent, and royalties

L.O. 7

expenses
Costs incurred in the process of generating revenues

net income
The profit earned or lost by a firm, determined by subtracting expenses from revenues; also called the *bottom line*

Exhibit 13.5　**Income Statement for Computer Central**

An income statement summarizes the company's financial operations over a particular accounting period, usually a year.

Revenues
Funds received from sales of goods and services to customers, as well as other items such as rent, interest, and dividends. Net sales are gross sales less returns and allowances.

Cost of Goods Sold
Cost of merchandise or services that generate a company's income by adding purchases to beginning inventory and then subtracting ending inventory.

Operating Expenses
Generally classified as selling and general expenses. Selling expenses are those incurred through the marketing and distributing of the company's products. General expenses are operating expenses incurred in the overall administration of a business.

Net Income After Taxes
Profit or loss over a specific period determined by subtracting all expenses and taxes from revenues.

Computer Central

Income Statement
Year ended December 31, 2008
(in thousands)

Revenues		
Gross Sales	$1 991 489	
Less Sales Returns and Allowances	−258 000	
Net Sales		$1 733 489
Cost of Goods Sold		
Beginning Inventory	$61 941	
Add: Purchases During the Year	1 515 765	
Cost of Goods Available for Sale	1 577 706	
Less: Ending Inventory	−64 392	
Total Cost of Goods Sold		−1 513 314
Gross Profit		$220 175
Operating Expenses		
Selling Expenses	$75 523	
General Expenses	40 014	
Total Operating Expenses		115 537
Net Operating Income (Gross Profit Less Operating Expenses)		104 638
Other Income		4 373
Net Income Before Income Taxes		109 011
Less: Income Taxes		−43 170
Net Income After Taxes		**$65 841**

trend in sales, its major expenses, and the resulting net income or loss. Owners, creditors, and investors can evaluate the company's past performance and future prospects by comparing net income for one year with net income from previous years. Exhibit 13.5 is the 2008 income statement for Computer Central, showing net income of almost $66 million. This is a 32 percent increase over the company's net income of $50 million from the previous year.

Expenses—the costs of doing business—include both the direct costs associated with creating or purchasing products for sale and the indirect costs associated with operating the business. Whether a company manufactures or purchases its inventory, the cost of storing the product for sale (such as heating the warehouse, paying the rent, and buying insurance on the storage facility) is added to the difference between the cost of the beginning inventory and the cost of the ending inventory to calculate the actual cost of items that were sold during a period—or the **cost of goods sold**. The calculation can be summarized as follows:

Cost of goods sold = Beginning inventory + Net purchases − Ending inventory

As shown in Exhibit 13.5, cost of goods sold is deducted from sales to obtain a company's **gross profit**—a key figure used in financial statement analysis. In addition to the costs directly associated with producing goods, companies deduct **operating expenses**, which include both *selling expenses* and *general expenses*, to calculate a firm's *net operating income*, or the income that is generated from business operations. **Selling expenses** are operating expenses incurred through marketing and distributing the product (such as wages or salaries of salespeople, advertising, supplies, insurance for the sales operation, amortization for the store and sales equipment, and other sales department

cost of goods sold
The cost of producing or acquiring a company's products for sale during a given period

gross profit
The amount remaining when the cost of goods sold is deducted from net sales; also known as *gross margin*

operating expenses
All costs of operation that are not included under cost of goods sold

selling expenses
All operating expenses associated with marketing goods or services

Exhibit 13.6 **Statement of Cash Flows for Computer Central**

A statement of cash flows shows a firm's cash receipts and cash payments as a result of three main activities—operating, investing, and financing—for a period of time, usually one year.

Cash flows from operations
How much cash a company's business generates or uses; contains clues to how healthy earnings are. Most companies start with net income from the income statement and detail items that cause income to differ from cash.

Cash flows from investments
Cash used to buy or received from selling stock, assets, and businesses, plus capital expenditures.

Cash flows from financing
Cash from or paid to outsiders—such as banks or stockholders. If positive, the company relied on outsiders for funds. If negative, the company may have paid down debt or bought back stock.

Computer Central
Statement of Cash Flows
Year ended December 31, 2008
(in thousands)

Cash Flows from Operating Activities:*		
Net Income	$ 65 841	
Adjustments to Reconcile Net Income to		
Net Cash Provided by Operating Activities	–61 317	
Net Cash Provided by or Used in Operating Activities		$4 524
Cash Flows from Investing Activities:		
Purchase of Property and Equipment	–30 110	
Purchase of Securities	–114 932	
Redemptions of Securities	112 463	
Net Cash Provided by or Used in Investing Activities		–32 579
Cash Flows from Financing Activities		
Loan Proceeds	15 000	
Purchase of Treasury Stock	–2 089	
Proceeds from Exercise of Stock Options	1 141	
Net Cash Provided by or Used in Financing Activities		14 052
Net Increase (Decrease) in Cash		–14 003
Cash and Cash Equivalents at Beginning of Year		$18 233
Cash and Cash Equivalents at End of Year		$4 230

* Note: Numbers preceded by a minus sign indicate cash outflows

general expenses
Operating expenses like office and administrative expenses that are not directly associated with creating or marketing a good or a service

expenses like telephone charges). **General expenses** are operating expenses incurred in the overall administration of a business. They include professional services (accounting and legal fees), office salaries, amortization of office equipment, insurance for office operations, supplies, and so on.

A firm's net operating income is then adjusted by the amount of any non-operating income or expense items like the gain or loss on the sale of a building. The result is the firm's net income or loss before income taxes (losses are shown in parentheses), a key figure used in budgeting, cash-flow analysis, and a variety of other financial calculations. Finally, income taxes are deducted to calculate the company's net income or loss for the period.

L.O. 8

statement of cash flows
A statement of a firm's cash receipts and cash payments that presents information on its sources and uses of cash

Statement of Cash Flows

In addition to preparing a balance sheet and an income statement, all public companies and many privately owned companies prepare a **statement of cash flows** to show how much cash the company generated over time and where it went (see Exhibit 13.6). The statement of cash flows tracks the cash coming into and flowing out of a company's bank accounts. It reveals the increase or decrease in the company's cash for the period and summarizes (by category) the sources of that change. From a brief review of this statement you should have a general sense of the amount of cash created or consumed by daily operations, the amount of cash invested in fixed or other assets, the amount of debt borrowed or repaid, and the proceeds from the sale of shares or payments for dividends. In addition, an analysis of cash flows provides a good idea of a company's ability to pay its short-term obligations when they become due.

As Exhibit 13.6 shows, the statement of cash flows is organized into three parts: operating activities, investing activities, and financing activities. Computer Central's statement of cash flows shows that the company used $15 million of its cash reserves and the proceeds of a $15 million bank loan in 2008 to pay for its new facility.

IN-CLASS NOTES

Understanding Financial Statements

- **Financial statements** are used to identify opportunities and problems, make business decisions, and evaluate a company's past, present, and future
- The **balance sheet** shows assets on one side and liabilities and owners' equity on the other; it's a snapshot of financial position on a specific date
- The **income statement** shows profit performance over a specific period of time (usually one year)
- The **statement of cash flows** shows how much cash was generated over time and where it went; (categories: *operations*, *investments*, *financing*)

_____

_____

_____

_____

_____

_____

_____

_____

_____

_____

Analyzing Financial Statements

Once financial statements have been prepared, managers and outsiders use these statements to evaluate the financial health of the organization, make business decisions, and spot opportunities for improvements by looking at the company's performance in relation to its past performance, the economy as a whole, and the performance of its competitors.

Trend Analysis

The process of comparing financial data from year to year to see how they have changed is known as *trend analysis*. You can use trend analysis to uncover shifts in the nature of the business over time. Most large companies provide data for trend analysis in their annual reports. Their balance sheets and income statements typically show three to five years or more of data (making comparative statement analysis possible). Changes in other key items—such as revenues, income, earnings per share, and dividends per share—are usually presented in tables and graphs.

Of course, when you are comparing one period with another, it's important to take into account the effects of extraordinary or unusual items such as the sale of major assets, the purchase of a new line of products from another company, weather-related disturbances, or economic conditions that may have affected the company in one period but not the next. These extraordinary items are usually disclosed in the text portion of a company's annual report or in the notes to the financial statements. For example, airline companies referred to the events of September 11, 2001, as an extraordinary event that made comparing trends problematic over sequential time periods. This tragic event is properly described by such a notation. However, a problem for investors is determining whether an extraordinary event is going to become ordinary. Many airline companies in Canada and around the world, for example, are noting the spike in oil prices as an event that is affecting their income statements and making trend comparison difficult. These companies are saying that the downward pressure on their earnings caused by the high price of oil will ease off as oil returns to normal levels, so any trend downward should be discounted. Recently, however, financial analysts have stated they expect oil prices to remain high and perhaps continue to rise dramatically, causing investors to wonder whether the so-called reversible trend downward in earnings is in fact reversible. Airline companies are at the mercy of this uncontrollable factor.

Ratio Analysis

Managers and others calculate financial ratios to facilitate the comparison of one company's financial results with those of competing firms and with industry averages. **Ratio analysis** compares two elements from the same year's financial figures. They are called *ratios* because they are calculated by dividing one element of a financial statement by another. The advantage of using ratios is that it puts companies on the same footing; that is, it makes it possible to compare different-sized companies and changing dollar amounts. For example, by using ratios you can easily compare a large supermarket's ability to generate profits from sales with a similar statistic for a small grocery store.

The benefit of converting numbers into ratios can be explained by the following example: Suppose you wanted to know how well your favourite baseball player is performing this year. To find out, you would check the player's statistics—batting average, runs batted in (RBIs), hits, and home runs. In other words, you would look at data that have been arranged into meaningful statistics that allow you to compare present performance with past performance and with the performance of other players in the league. Financial ratios do the same thing. They convert the raw numbers from the current and prior years' financial statements into ratios that highlight important relationships or measures of performance.[12]

Just as baseball statistics focus on various aspects of performance (such as hitting or pitching), financial ratios help companies understand their current operations and answer key questions: Is inventory too large? Are credit customers paying too slowly? Can the company pay its bills? Ratios also set standards and benchmarks for gauging future business by comparing a company's scores with industry averages that show the performance of competition. Every industry tends to have its own "normal" ratios, which act as yardsticks for individual companies. Dun & Bradstreet, a credit-rating firm, and Robert Morris Associates publish average financial figures and ratios for a variety of industries and company sizes.

Before reviewing specific ratios, consider two rules of thumb: First, avoid drawing too strong a conclusion from any one ratio. For instance, even with a low batting average, a baseball player's RBIs may prove valuable to the team's line-up. Second, once ratios have presented a general indication, refer back to the specific data involved to see whether the numbers confirm what the ratios suggest. In other words, do a little investigating, because statistics can be misleading. Remember, a baseball player who has been at bat only two times and has one hit has a batting average of .500.

Types of Financial Ratios

Financial ratios can be organized into the following groups, as Exhibit 13.7 shows: profitability, liquidity, activity, and debt (or leverage).

Profitability Ratios   You can analyze how well a company is conducting its ongoing operations by calculating **profitability ratios**, which show the state of the company's financial performance or how well it's generating profits. Three of the most common profitability ratios are **return on sales**, or profit margin (the net income a business makes per unit of sales); **return on investment (ROI)**, or return on equity (the income earned on the owner's investment); and **earnings per share** (the profit earned for each share outstanding). Exhibit 13.7 shows how to calculate these profitability ratios by using the financial information from Computer Central.

Liquidity Ratios   **Liquidity ratios** measure the ability of the firm to pay its short-term obligations. As you might expect, lenders and creditors are very interested in liquidity measures. Liquidity can be judged on the basis of *working capital*, the *current ratio*, or

L.O. 9

ratio analysis
The use of quantitative measures to evaluate a firm's financial performance

profitability ratios
Ratios that measure the overall financial performance of a firm

return on sales
The ratio between net income after taxes and net sales; also known as *profit margin*

return on investment (ROI)
The ratio between net income after taxes and total owners' equity; also known as *return on equity*

earnings per share
The measure of a firm's profitability for each outstanding share, calculated by dividing net income after taxes by the average number of common shares outstanding

liquidity ratios
Ratios that measure a firm's ability to meet its short-term obligations when they are due

Exhibit 13.7 **How Well Does This Company Stack Up?**

Nearly all companies use ratios to evaluate how well the company is performing in relation to prior performance, the economy as a whole, and the company's competitors.

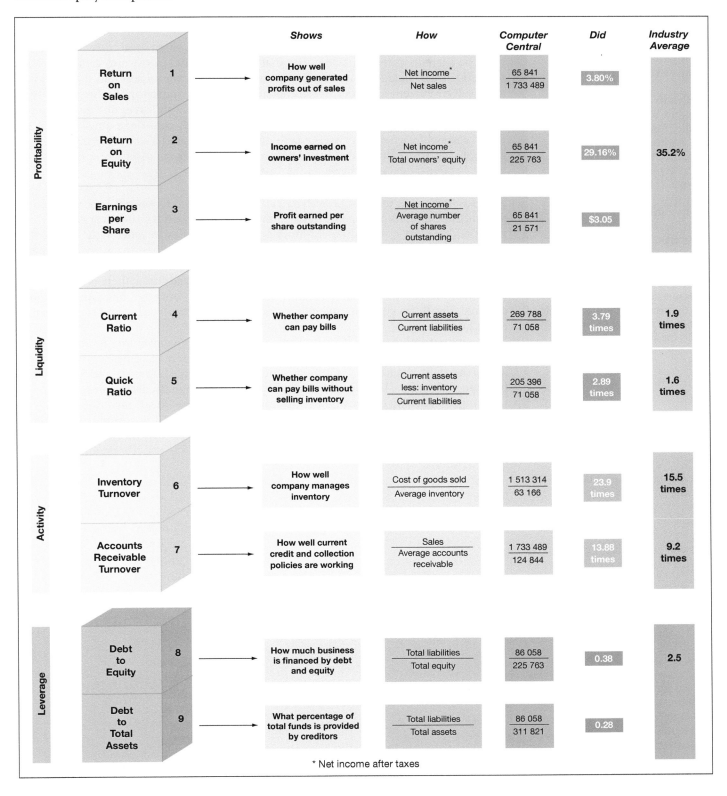

		Shows	How	Computer Central	Did	Industry Average
Profitability	Return on Sales — 1	How well company generated profits out of sales	Net income* / Net sales	65 841 / 1 733 489	3.80%	35.2%
	Return on Equity — 2	Income earned on owners' investment	Net income* / Total owners' equity	65 841 / 225 763	29.16%	
	Earnings per Share — 3	Profit earned per share outstanding	Net income* / Average number of shares outstanding	65 841 / 21 571	$3.05	
Liquidity	Current Ratio — 4	Whether company can pay bills	Current assets / Current liabilities	269 788 / 71 058	3.79 times	1.9 times
	Quick Ratio — 5	Whether company can pay bills without selling inventory	Current assets less: inventory / Current liabilities	205 396 / 71 058	2.89 times	1.6 times
Activity	Inventory Turnover — 6	How well company manages inventory	Cost of goods sold / Average inventory	1 513 314 / 63 166	23.9 times	15.5 times
	Accounts Receivable Turnover — 7	How well current credit and collection policies are working	Sales / Average accounts receivable	1 733 489 / 124 844	13.88 times	9.2 times
Leverage	Debt to Equity — 8	How much business is financed by debt and equity	Total liabilities / Total equity	86 058 / 225 763	0.38	2.5
	Debt to Total Assets — 9	What percentage of total funds is provided by creditors	Total liabilities / Total assets	86 058 / 311 821	0.28	

* Net income after taxes

working capital
Current assets minus current liabilities

current ratio
A measure of a firm's short-term liquidity, calculated by dividing current assets by current liabilities

quick ratio
A measure of a firm's short-term liquidity, calculated by adding cash, marketable securities, and receivables, then dividing that sum by current liabilities; also known as the *acid-test ratio*

activity ratios
Ratios that measure the effectiveness of the firm's use of its resources

inventory turnover ratio
A measure of the time a company takes to turn its inventory into sales, calculated by dividing cost of goods sold by the average value of inventory for a period

accounts receivable turnover ratio
A measure of time a company takes to turn its accounts receivable into cash, calculated by dividing sales by the average value of accounts receivable for a period

debt ratios
Ratios that measure a firm's reliance on debt financing of its operations (sometimes called *leverage ratios*)

debt-to-equity ratio
A measure of the extent to which a business is financed by debt as opposed to invested capital; calculated by dividing the company's total liabilities by owners' equity

the *quick ratio*. A company's **working capital** (current assets minus current liabilities) is an indicator of liquidity because it represents current assets remaining after the payment of all current liabilities. The dollar amount of working capital can be misleading, however. For example, it may include the value of slow-moving inventory items that cannot be used to help pay a company's short-term debts.

A different picture of the company's liquidity is provided by the **current ratio**—current assets divided by current liabilities. This figure compares the current debt owed with the current assets available to pay that debt. The **quick ratio**, also called the *acid-test ratio*, is calculated by subtracting inventory from current assets and then dividing the result by current liabilities. This ratio is often a better indicator of a firm's ability to pay creditors than the current ratio because the quick ratio leaves out inventories—which can sometimes be difficult to sell. Analysts generally consider a quick ratio of 1.0 to be reasonable, whereas a current ratio of 2.0 is considered a safe risk for short-term credit. Exhibit 13.7 shows that both the current and quick ratios of Computer Central are well above these benchmarks and industry averages.

Activity Ratios   A number of **activity ratios** may be used to analyze how well a company is managing its assets. The most common is the **inventory turnover ratio**, which measures how fast a company's inventory is turned into sales; in general, the quicker the better, because holding excess inventory can be expensive. When inventory sits on the shelf, money is tied up without earning interest; furthermore, the company incurs expenses for its storage, handling, insurance, and taxes. In addition, there is always a risk that the inventory will become obsolete before it can be converted into finished goods and sold. The firm's goal is to maintain enough inventory to fill orders in a timely fashion at the lowest cost.

Keep in mind that it's difficult to judge a company by its inventory level. For example, lower inventories might mean one of many things: you're running an efficient operation, the right inventory is not being stocked, or sales are booming and you need to increase your orders. Likewise, higher inventories could signal a decline in sales, careless ordering, or stocking up because of favourable pricing. The "ideal" turnover ratio varies with the type of operation. In 2008, Computer Central turned its inventory 23.9 times (see Exhibit 13.7). This rate is unusually high when compared with industry averages, and it suggests that the company stocks only enough inventory to fill current orders and cover a product's reorder time, as discussed in Chapter 8.

Another popular activity ratio is the **accounts receivable turnover ratio**, which measures how well a company's credit and collection policies are working by indicating how frequently accounts receivable are converted to cash. The volume of receivables outstanding depends on the financial manager's decisions regarding several issues, such as who qualifies for credit and who does not, how long customers are given to pay their bills, and how aggressive the firm is in collecting its debts. Be careful here as well. If the ratio is going up, you need to determine whether the company is doing a better job of collecting or if sales are rising. If the ratio is going down, it may be because sales are decreasing or because collection efforts are sagging. In 2008, Computer Central turned its accounts receivable 13.88 times—considerably higher than the industry average (see Exhibit 13.7).

Debt, or Leverage, Ratios   You can measure a company's ability to pay its long-term debts by calculating its **debt ratios**, or leverage ratios. Lenders look at these ratios to determine whether the potential borrower has put enough money into the business to serve as a protective cushion for the loan. The **debt-to-equity ratio** (total liabilities divided by total equity) indicates the extent to which a business is financed by debt as opposed to invested capital (equity). From the lender's standpoint, the lower this ratio, the safer the company, because the company has less existing debt and may be able to repay additional money it wants to borrow. However, a company that is conservative in its long-term borrowing is not necessarily well managed; often a low level of debt is associated with a low growth rate. Computer Central's low debt-to-equity ratio of 38 percent (as shown in Exhibit 13.7) reflects the company's practice of financing its growth by using excess cash flow from operations and by selling common shares to the public.

IN-CLASS NOTES

Analyzing Financial Statements

- **Trend analysis:** comparing data from year to year to find shifts in business over time
- **Ratio analysis:** compares two elements from the same year's financial figures; makes it possible to compare different-sized companies
- **Profitability ratios** show how a firm is generating profits
- **Liquidity ratios** measure the company's ability to pay short-term obligations
- **Activity ratios** show how well a company is managing its assets
- **Debt ratios** measure its ability to pay long-term debts; also known as *leverage ratios*

Rogers Communications, owner of Rogers Cable, Rogers Wireless, and a host of other companies, takes a much more aggressive approach to debt management than Computer Central. After purchasing Microcell, a rival telecommunications company, almost entirely through the use of debt the company had a very high debt-to-equity ratio of 2.8. While there is no ideal debt-to-equity ratio, anything above 2 is considered aggressive. As of August 2007, Rogers's debt-to-equity ratio has been reduced to 1.6, but this ratio is still well above the industry average of 0.8.[13]

The **debt-to-total-assets ratio** (total liabilities divided by total assets) also serves as a simple measure of a company's ability to carry long-term debt. As a rule of thumb, the amount of debt should not exceed 50 percent of the value of total assets. For Computer Central, this ratio is very low at 28 percent and again reflects the company's policy of using retained earnings to finance its growth (see Exhibit 13.7). However, this ratio, too, is not a magic formula. Like grades on a report card, ratios are clues to performance. Managers, creditors, lenders, and investors can use them to get a fairly accurate idea of how a company is doing. But remember, one ratio by itself doesn't tell the whole story.

debt-to-total-assets ratio
A measure of a firm's ability to carry long-term debt, calculated by dividing total liabilities by total assets

WHAT DOES FINANCIAL MANAGEMENT INVOLVE?

L.O. 10

Planning for a firm's current and future money needs is the foundation of **financial management**, or finance. This area of concern involves making decisions about alternative sources and uses of funds with the goal of maximizing a company's value (see Exhibit 13.8). To achieve this goal, financial managers develop and implement a firm's financial plan, monitor a firm's cash flow and decide how to create or use excess funds, budget for current and future expenditures, recommend specific investments, develop a plan to finance the enterprise for future growth, and interact with banks and capital markets.

financial management
The effective acquisition and use of money

Exhibit 13.8   **Sources and Uses of a Company's Funds**

Financial management involves finding suitable sources of funds and deciding on the most appropriate uses for those funds.

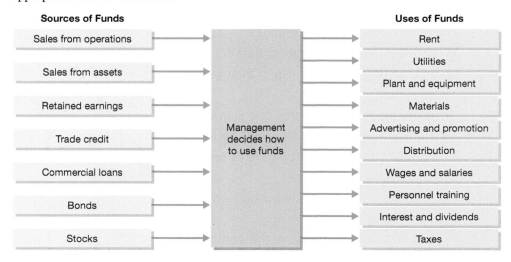

Developing and Implementing a Financial Plan

financial plan
A forecast of financial requirements and the financing sources to be used

One way in which companies like Domtar make sure they have enough money is by developing a *financial plan*. Normally in the form of a budget, a **financial plan** is a document that shows the funds a firm will need for a period of time as well as the sources and uses of those funds. When you prepare a financial plan for a company, you have two objectives: achieving a positive cash flow and efficiently investing excess cash to make your company grow. Financial planning requires looking beyond the four walls of the company to answer some key questions: Is the company introducing a new product in the near future or expanding its market? Is the industry growing? Is the national economy declining? Is inflation heating up? Would an investment in new technology improve productivity?[14] Even small businesses depend on financial planning to assist them in moving the company forward. Michael Duck, owner of SureShot Dispensing Systems, a small but growing Nova Scotia company that sells cream dispensers to McDonald's, Tim Hortons, and Starbucks, has noted in speeches that his company's close attention to sound financial planning is one of the main reasons why it has been able to grow so quickly.[15]On a larger scale, Canadian National (CN) budgeted $1.6 billion in capital spending in 2007; more than $1 billion was spent on improving railway track infrastructure.[16]

Monitoring Cash Flow

An underlying concept of any financial plan is that all money should be used productively. This concept is important because without cash a company cannot purchase the assets and supplies it needs to operate. In accounting, you prepare income statements to determine the net income of a firm. In finance, however, you focus on cash flows. Although the firm's income is important, cash flows are even more important because cash is necessary to purchase the assets required to continue operations and pay dividends to shareholders. Cash flows are generally related to net income; that is, companies with relatively high profits generally have relatively high cash flows, but the relationship is not precise.

One way financial managers improve a company's cash flow is by monitoring its *working capital accounts*: cash, inventory, accounts receivable, and accounts payable. They use common sense procedures such as shrinking accounts receivable collection periods, dispatching bills on a timely basis without paying bills earlier than necessary, controlling the level of inventory, and investing excess cash so the company can earn as much interest as possible. Aggressive financial managers use electronic cash management (the ability to access bank account information online) to move cash between accounts and pay bills on a daily basis; they also invest excess cash on hand in short-term investments called

marketable securities. These interest-bearing or dividend-paying investments include money-market funds or publicly traded stocks such as Bombardier or RBC. They are said to be "marketable" because they can be easily converted back to cash. Because marketable securities are generally used as contingency funds, however, most financial managers invest these funds in government securities or securities of solid companies—ones perceived to have the least amount of risk. (Securities are discussed in detail in Chapter 14.) To see the results of these decisions, you may want to read a company's annual report, which details all of the company's cash and non-cash activities for a year. For information on how to read an annual report, see the box entitled "How to Read an Annual Report."

marketable securities
Stocks, bonds, and other investments that can be turned into cash quickly

Developing a Budget

In addition to developing a financial plan and monitoring cash flow, financial managers are responsible for developing a **budget**, a financial blueprint for a given period (often one year). Master (or operating) budgets help financial managers estimate the flow of money into and out of the business by structuring financial plans in a framework of a firm's total estimated revenues, expenses, and cash flows. Accountants provide much of the data required for budgets and are important members of the budget development team because they have a complete understanding of the company's operating costs.

budget
A planning and control tool that reflects expected revenues, operating expenses, and cash receipts and outlays

How to Read an Annual Report

Whether you're thinking of investing in companies, becoming a supplier for them, or applying for a job with them, you'll need to know how to read annual reports in your career. Thus, it's worth your while to consider the advice of *Newsweek* columnist Jane Bryant Quinn, who provided the following pointers.

READ THE LETTERS

First, turn to the auditor's report. This third-party statement will tell you right off the bat if the report conforms to generally accepted accounting principles. Now turn to the letter from the chair. This letter should tell you how the company fared this year, but more important, the letter should tell you why. Keep an eye out for sentences that start with "Except for . . ." and "Despite the. . . ." They're clues to problems. The chair's letter should also give you insights into the company's future. For example, look for what's new in each line of business. Is management getting the company in good shape to weather the tough and competitive years ahead?

DIG INTO THE NUMBERS

Check out the trend in the company's working capital (the difference between current assets and current liabilities). If working capital is shrinking, it could mean trouble. One possibility: The company may not be able to keep dividends growing rapidly.

Another important number to analyze is earnings per share. Management can boost earnings by selling off a plant or by cutting the budget for research and advertising. Read the accompanying notes to the financial statements; they often tell the whole story.

If earnings are down only because of a change in accounting, maybe that's good. The company owes less tax and has more money in its pocket. If earnings are up, maybe that's bad. They may be up because of a special windfall that won't happen again next year. One good indicator is the trend in net sales. If sales increases are starting to slow, the company may be in trouble.

GET OUT YOUR CALCULATOR AND COMPARE

High and rising debt, relative to equity, may be no problem for a growing business. But it shows weakness in a company that's levelling out. So get out your calculator and divide long-term liabilities by shareholders' equity (the debt-to-equity ratio). A high ratio means the company borrows a lot of money to fund its growth. That's okay—if sales grow too, and if there's enough cash on hand to meet the payments. But if sales fall, watch out. The whole enterprise may slowly sink.

Remember, one ratio, one annual report, one chairman's letter won't tell you much. You have to compare. Is the company's debt-to-equity ratio better or worse than it used to be? Better or worse than the industry norms? In company watching, comparisons are everything. They tell you whether management is staying on top of things.[17]

Questions for Critical Thinking

1. Why might a job seeker want to read a company's annual report before applying for a job with that company?
2. What types of valuable non-financial information might an annual report disclose to a potential supplier?

Learning from Business Blunders

OOPS

With a nationwide advertising campaign and free financing, Mitsubishi Motors went all out to entice young drivers to buy an Eclipse. The strategy worked—worked so well in fact that it cost the company nearly a billion dollars. Those young drivers took Mitsubishi up on the offer, and then thousands of them defaulted on their loans when they couldn't make the payments. The bad debts cost the company $469 million. After fixing the credit problem, Mitsubishi then watched sales drop by half and had to spend $432 million more to buy back unsold inventory.

WHAT YOU CAN LEARN

Two lessons: Credit can be as dangerous for buyers as it for sellers, and there is such a thing as a bad customer. Companies that go overboard in efforts to attract customers can find themselves in Mitsubishi's shoes—losing money on customers who couldn't afford their products in the first place.[18]

financial control
The process of analyzing and adjusting the basic financial plan to correct for forecasted events that do not materialize

capital investments
Money paid to acquire something of permanent value in a business

capital budgeting
The process of evaluating proposed investments in select projects that provide the best long-term financial return

The master operating budget sets a standard for expenditures, provides guidelines for controlling costs, and offers an integrated and detailed plan for the future. For example, by reviewing the budget of any airline you can determine whether the company plans to increase its fleet of aircraft, add more routes, hire more employees, increase employees' pay, or continue or abandon any discounts for travellers. No wonder companies like to keep their budgets confidential. Once a budget has been developed, the finance manager compares actual results with projections to discover variances and recommends corrective action—a process known as **financial control**.

In addition to developing operating budgets, financial managers develop capital budgets to forecast and plan for a firm's **capital investments**, such as major expenditures on buildings or equipment. Capital investments generally cover a period of several years and help the company grow. Before investments can be made, however, a firm must decide on which of the many possible capital investments to make, how to finance those that are undertaken, and even whether to make any capital investments at all. This process is called **capital budgeting**.

The process generally begins by having all divisions within a company submit their capital requests—essentially, "wish lists" of investments that would make the company more profitable and thus more valuable to its owners over time. Next, the financial manager decides which investments need evaluating and which don't. For example, the routine replacement of old equipment probably wouldn't need evaluating; however, the construction of a new manufacturing facility would. Finally, a financial evaluation is performed to determine whether the amount of money required for a particular investment will be greater than, equal to, or less than the amount of revenue it will generate. On the basis of this analysis, the financial manager can determine which projects to recommend to senior management for purchase approval. This process of capital budgeting is crucial to business, as the wrong investment can cost a company millions of dollars—not only in trying to recoup the investment dollars but in lost opportunity, as an investment in one project often means failing to invest in another project. In August 2007, for example, Paramount Energy Trust decided to invest the remainder of its $125 million capital budget for 2007 despite tough results in the previous quarter. The organization evaluated the future opportunities and made the conscious choice to push ahead with its plans while other companies in the industry cut back on previously announced plans.[19]

Companies plan for construction projects like this one years in advance and reflect the costs of such long-term projects in their capital budgets.

IN-CLASS NOTES

What Does Financial Management Involve?

■ **Developing and implementing a financial plan**

   ■ Evaluating the amount of funds, sources of funds, uses of funds

■ **Monitoring cash flow**

   ■ Looking at cash, inventory, accounts receivable, and accounts payable

■ **Developing a budget**

   ■ Including financial control, capital investments, capital budgeting

_____

_____

_____

_____

_____

_____

_____

_____

BEHIND THE SCENES

How Long Will It Take? Nortel's Troubles Resurface

By mid-2007, Nortel executives were putting on a brave face as CEO, Mike Zafirovski, announced that Nortel was "once again ready to be a leader in a massive market that will define a new era in communications." At the company's annual meeting, he addressed shareholders and added that "Nortel is back in the game." After watching Nortel trip over its own actions and words for a few years, many analysts were not overly enthusiastic or ready to put their blind faith in the words of a Nortel executive.

Basic Facts: The Anchored Ship

As 2006 came to a close, Nortel, famous for its many two-for-one stock splits (where shareholders get an additional share for every share they own, which brings down the per share price without diluting owners' investments) that characterized the boom in share value and pushed the shares to a high of $124.50, went ahead with a reverse one-for-ten stock split. Share prices rose by a factor of 10 times to $24, but total shares were reduced to 433 million from 4.33 billion. In other words, if you held 1000 shares at $2.40 before the split you now only had 100 shares

at $24. Companies try to avoid reverse stock splits since this manoeuvre is not seen as positive; it is employed as a necessity when share values diminish and don't recover, as was the case with Nortel.

In mid-2007, the Nortel employee roster stood at about 34 000 employees, down from approximately 94 500 at the end of 2000. Despite throwing 60 000 people off the once-powerful ship, another 2900 job cuts were announced at the beginning of 2007 and another 1000 jobs were being relocated to low-cost places like China, India, and Mexico. While the company's new executives were talking about calm seas ahead and great new expeditions, the company's past was still anchoring its potential.

In addition, former CEO Frank Dunn, along with three senior executives, were facing charges of civil fraud from the US Securities and Exchange Commission for their creative accounting and restatements. The Ontario Securities Commission was charging them with knowingly making "material misstatements." The charges make it clear that these executives knew what they were doing or should have known that their statements were misleading.

The Importance of Sound Accounting

Nortel's rise and fall were based on market factors. Nortel was courageous in its attempts to redefine itself and take advantage of the new Internet economy. As such it received the benefits of its actions and rightfully earned its high-tech poster-child status. Of course, its efforts to redefine itself made it more vulnerable to the Internet bubble and it paid the price when the bubble burst. This is the world of business: You are rewarded when your strategies are in tune with a rising market, but you are punished when the markets tumble.

Nortel's current problems, however, are made much more complicated by their accounting problems. The market understands risks and can forgive Nortel for getting caught and being a leader in the Internet craze. The technology boom was quite a period of enthusiasm. However, Nortel's future ability to raise capital and attract investors is based on the trust that markets have in the company. The accounting errors and fraud in recent years continue to cast doubts on Nortel. At this point, all it can do is continue to come clean and slowly rebuild confidence by being a model citizen from this point on. It will take many years before confidence is restored—there is no more room for error.[20]

Critical Thinking Questions

1. What impact do the current charges against former CEO Frank Dunn have on Nortel's future?
2. In this chapter we have discussed the importance of financial figures and the ability of analysts and investors to crunch numbers. How do accounting irregularities affect this process? In particular, discuss the impact on the process of ratio analysis.
3. After taking major cost-cutting initiatives and laying-off approximately 65 000 people to save the company, what does Nortel need to do to recapture some of its status?

Learn More Online

Visit and review Nortel's website at www.nortel.com. Have there been any changes to upper management since this case was written? What are they? Search the site for the company's news releases and see what reasons they gave for these changes. Do you think Nortel will ever return to its former glory days?

TEST YOUR KNOWLEDGE

Questions for Review

1. What is the difference between a private and a public accountant?
2. What is the purpose of the *Sarbanes-Oxley Act* and Bill C-198?
3. What are the primary elements of an income statement?
4. What is meant by the term "closing the books?"
5. What is the primary goal of capital budgeting?

Questions for Analysis

6. GAAP is monitored and developed by the Canadian Institute of Chartered Accountants (CICA). Why is GAAP important to company stakeholders?
7. Why do some companies resort to accounting tricks, and what steps are being taken to clamp down on such wrongdoings?
8. What is the main purpose of calculating the various liquidity ratios?
9. What information can a stakeholder learn by reading a company's balance sheet?
10. **Ethical Considerations.** In the process of closing the company books, you encounter a problematic transaction. One of the company's customers was charged twice for the same project materials, resulting in a $1000 overcharge. You immediately notify the con-

troller, whose response is, "Let it go, it happens often." What should you do?

Questions for Application

11. The senior partner of an accounting firm is looking for ways to increase the firm's business. What other services besides traditional accounting can the firm offer to its clients? What new challenges might this additional work create?
12. Log on to the Toronto Stock Exchange website at www.tsx.com and click on "Listed Company Directory." Search for Royal Bank and Canadian Tire. Using these financials, calculate the working capital, current ratio, and quick ratio for each company. Does one company appear to be more liquid than the other? Why?
13. **Integrated.** Review Chapter 3. Then review this chapter's discussion of Bombardier. Do you think the concept of program accounting is ethical even though it may be legal? Is it ethical for the Bombardier family to control so many voting shares but own very little common stock?
14. **Integrated.** Your appliance manufacturing company recently implemented a just-in-time inventory system for all parts used in the manufacturing process. How might you expect this move to affect the company's inventory turnover rate, current ratio, and quick ratio?

PRACTISE YOUR KNOWLEDGE

SHARPENING YOUR COMMUNICATION SKILLS

Obtain a copy of the annual report of a business and examine what the report shows about finances and current operations. In addition to other chapter material, use the information in the box entitled "How to Read an Annual Report" on page 429 as a guideline for understanding the annual report's content.

- Consider the statements made by the CEO regarding the past year. Did the company do well, or are changes in operations necessary to its future well-being? What are the projections for future growth in sales and profits?

- Examine the financial summaries for information about the fiscal condition of the company. Did the company show a profit?

- If possible, obtain a copy of the company's annual report from the previous year and compare it with the current report to determine whether past projections were accurate.

- Prepare a brief written summary of your conclusions.

BUILDING YOUR TEAM SKILLS

Divide into small groups and calculate the following financial ratios for Pacific Manufacturing using the company's balance sheet and income statement provided. Compare your answers to those of your classmates.

- Profitability ratios: return on sales; return on equity; earnings per share

- Liquidity ratios: current ratio; quick ratio

- Activity ratios: inventory turnover; accounts receivable turnover

- Leverage ratios: debt to equity; debt to total assets

PACIFIC MANUFACTURING INCOME STATEMENT YEAR ENDED DECEMBER 31, 2008	
Sales	$25 000
Less: Cost of Goods Sold	11 600
Gross Profit	$13 400
Less: Total Operating Expenses	6 450
Net Operating Income Before Income Taxes	6 950
Less: Income Taxes	1 350
NET INCOME AFTER INCOME TAXES	$ 5 600

PACIFIC MANUFACTURING BALANCE SHEET DECEMBER 31, 2008	
ASSETS	
Cash	$ 2 000
Accounts Receivable (beginning balance $1 500)	3 500
Inventory (beginning balance $1 500)	2 700
Current Assets	$ 8 200
Fixed Assets	33 000
Total Assets	$41 200
LIABILITIES AND SHAREHOLDERS' EQUITY	
Current Liabilities (beginning balance $4 000)	5 000
Long-Term Debts	28 200
Shareholders' Equity (500 common shares outstanding valued at $16 each)	8 000
Total Liabilities and Shareholders' Equity	$41 200

EXPAND YOUR KNOWLEDGE

DISCOVERING CAREER OPPORTUNITIES

People interested in entering the field of accounting can choose among a wide variety of careers with diverse responsibilities and challenges. Select one of the occupations mentioned in this chapter. Using library sources, Internet websites from one of the major accounting firms, or the websites for CICA (CAs), CMAs, or CGAs, dig deeper to learn more about your chosen occupation.

1. What are the day-to-day duties of this occupation? How would these duties contribute to the financial success of a company?

2. What skills and educational qualifications would you need to enter this occupation? How do these qualifications fit with your current plans, skills, and interests?

3. What kinds of employers hire people for this position? According to your research, does the number of employers seem to be increasing or decreasing? How do you think this trend will affect your employment possibilities if you choose this career?

DEVELOPING YOUR RESEARCH SKILLS

Select an article from a business journal or newspaper (print or online editions) that discusses the quarterly or year-end performance of a company that industry analysts consider notable for either positive or negative reasons.

1. Did the company report a profit or a loss for this accounting period? What other performance indicators were reported? Did the company's performance improve or decline over previous accounting periods?

2. Did the company's performance match industry analysts' expectations, or was it a surprise? How did analysts or other experts respond to the firm's actual quarterly or year-end results?

3. What reasons were given for the company's improvement or decline in performance?

STUDY GUIDE

SUMMARY OF LEARNING OBJECTIVES

1. **Discuss how managers and outsiders use financial information**

   Managers use financial information to control a company's operations and to make informed business decisions. Outsiders use financial information to evaluate whether a business is creditworthy or a good investment. Specifically, banks want to know if a business is able to pay back a loan, investors want to know if the company is earning a profit, and governments want to be assured that the company is paying the proper amount of taxes.

2. **Describe what accountants do**

   Accountants design and install accounting systems, prepare financial statements, analyze and interpret financial information, prepare financial forecasts and budgets, prepare tax returns, interpret tax law, calculate and analyze production costs, evaluate a company's performance, and analyze the financial implications of business decisions. In addition to these functions, accountants help managers improve business procedures, plan for the future, evaluate product performance, and analyze the firm's profitability. Auditors are licensed certified public accountants who review accounting records and processes to assess whether they conform to generally accepted accounting principles (GAAP) and whether the company's financial statements fairly present the company's financial position and operating results.

3. **Summarize the impact of the *Sarbanes-Oxley Act* in the United States and Bill C-198 in Canada**

   The *Sarbanes-Oxley Act* introduced a number of rules covering the way publicly traded companies manage and report their finances, including restricting loans to directors and executives, creating a new board to oversee public auditors, requiring corporate lawyers to report financial wrongdoing, requiring CEOs and CFOs to sign-off on financial statements under oath, and requiring companies to document their financial systems. These rules had a direct impact on many firms based in Canada as well. Bill C-198 has taken the basic sentiment of *Sarbanes-Oxley* and brought tough compliance rules north of the border.

4. **State the basic accounting equation and explain the purpose of double-entry bookkeeping and the matching principle**

   Assets = Liabilities + Owners' Equity is the basic accounting equation. Double-entry bookkeeping is a system of recording financial transactions to keep the accounting equation in balance. The matching principle makes sure that expenses incurred in producing revenues are deducted from the revenue they generated during the same accounting period.

5. **Differentiate between accrual-basis and cash-basis accounting**

   Accrual-basis accounting recognizes revenue at the time of sale, even if payment is not made. Similarly, expenses are recorded when you receive the benefit of a service or when you use an asset to produce revenue. Cash-basis accounting recognizes revenues at the time payment is received and expenses when cash is paid. Public companies are required to keep their books on an accrual basis.

6. **Explain the purpose of the balance sheet and identify its three main sections**

   The balance sheet provides a snapshot of the business at a particular point in time. It shows the size of the company, the major assets owned, how the assets are financed, and the amount of owners' investment in the business. Its three main sections are assets, liabilities, and owners' equity.

7. **Explain the purpose of the income statement**

   The income statement reflects the results of operations over a period of time. It gives a general sense of a company's size and performance.

8. **Explain the purpose of the statement of cash flows**

   The statement of cash flows shows how a company's cash was received and spent in three areas: operations, investments, and financing. It gives a general sense of the amount of cash created or consumed by daily operations, fixed assets, investments, and debt over a period of time.

9. Explain the purpose of ratio analysis and list the four main categories of financial ratios

Financial ratios provide information for analyzing the health and future prospects of a business. Ratios facilitate financial comparisons among different-sized companies and between a company and industry averages. Most of the important ratios fall into one of four categories: profitability ratios, which show how well the company generates profits; liquidity ratios, which measure the company's ability to pay its short-term obligations; activity ratios, which analyze how well a company is managing its assets; and debt ratios, which measure a company's ability to pay its long-term debt.

10. Identify the responsibilities of a financial manager

The responsibilities of a financial manager include developing and implementing a firm's financial plan, monitoring a firm's cash flow and deciding how to create or use excess funds, budgeting for current and future expenditures, recommending specific investments, raising capital to finance the enterprise for future growth, and interacting with banks and capital markets.

KEY TERMS

accounting   (407)
accounting equation   (414)
accounts receivable turnover
   ratio   (426)
accrual basis   (416)
activity ratios   (426)
amortization   (416)
assets   (414)
audit   (409)
balance sheet   (418)
Bill C-198   (413)
bookkeeping   (407)
budget   (429)
calendar year   (418)
capital budgeting   (430)
capital investments   (430)
cash basis   (416)
certified general accountants
   (CGAs)   (408)
certified management
   accountants (CMAs)   (408)
chartered accountants (CAs)   (408)
close the books   (417)
controller   (408)
cost accounting   (407)

cost of goods sold   (421)
current assets   (418)
current liabilities   (419)
current ratio   (426)
debt ratios   (426)
debt-to-equity ratio   (426)
debt-to-total-assets ratio   (427)
double-entry bookkeeping   (415)
earnings per share   (424)
expenses   (420)
financial accounting   (407)
financial analysis   (407)
financial control   (430)
financial management   (427)
financial plan   (428)
fiscal year   (418)
fixed assets   (418)
general expenses   (422)
generally accepted accounting
      principles (GAAP)   (409)
gross profit   (421)
income statement   (420)
internal auditors   (409)
inventory turnover ratio   (426)
lease   (420)

liabilities   (414)
liquidity ratios   (424)
long-term liabilities   (419)
management accounting   (407)
marketable securities   (429)
matching principle   (416)
net income   (420)
operating expenses   (421)
owners' equity   (414)
private accountants   (408)
profitability ratios   (424)
public accountants   (409)
quick ratio   (426)
ratio analysis   (424)
retained earnings   (420)
return on investment (ROI)   (424)
return on sales   (424)
revenues   (420)
Sarbanes-Oxley Act   (411)
selling expenses   (421)
statement of cash flows   (422)
tax accounting   (407)
working capital   (426)

QUESTIONS

Multiple Choice   Circle the correct answer and then check the answers in the back of the book to chart your progress.

1. Which of the following is *not* one of the new requirements established to prevent accounting fraud?

   a. Tougher criminal penalties for executives convicted of fraud

   b. Banning accounting firms from selling various forms of consulting services

   c. Creating a time period for the rotation of company auditors

   d. Requiring all CEOs and CFOs to go through credit checks

2. Which of the following is the most popular job for people trained as accountants?

   a. Private accountant
   b. Public accountant
   c. Government accountant
   d. Bookkeeper

3. Which of the following is *not* one of the three basic concepts of accounting?

   a. The accounting equation
   b. Double-entry bookkeeping
   c. Profitability
   d. The matching principle

4. Which of the following is *not* one of the three major items on a balance sheet?

   a. Assets
   b. Net Income
   c. Liabilities
   d. Owners' Equity

5. Which is the final step of the accounting process?

   a. A transaction occurs
   b. The transaction is recorded (journal entry)
   c. The journal entries are classified and summarized (posted)
   d. Financial statements are prepared for internal and external users

6. Which of the following cannot be determined from examining a company's balance sheet?

   a. The size of the company
   b. Changes in the company's liabilities
   c. The net profits for the period
   d. How the assets are financed

7. Which of the following increases retained earnings from year to year?

   a. Purchase of equipment
   b. Net profits
   c. Payment of dividends
   d. Labour expenses

8. Which of the following cannot be determined from the income statement?

   a. The size and composition of the company's assets
   b. The company's sales
   c. The company's major expenses
   d. Whether the company made a profit or a loss

9. Which of the following types of financial ratios indicate how quickly the company can pay its short-term debts?

   a. Profitability ratios
   b. Liquidity ratios
   c. Activity ratios
   d. Leverage ratios

10. Which of the following is *not* a subdivision of fixed assets?

    a. Property
    b. Factory
    c. Inventory
    d. Equipment

True/False

1. True or false? The cash-basis accounting method records revenue when a sale is made and records an expense when it is incurred.

2. True or false? The balance sheet, or statement of financial position, shows the revenues and expenses for a 12-month period.

3. True or false? The inventory turnover ratio shows how well the company is using its investment in inventory.

4. True or false? Companies invest in marketable securities to earn extra income on cash not needed immediately.

5. True or false? Liabilities are defined by the following statement: "Anything of value owned or leased by a business."

Fill-in-the-Blank

1. A _____ is required to certify that the financial statements of a public company are prepared according to GAAP.

2. In Canada, the _____ is responsible for developing and monitoring GAAP.

3. Some people confuse the work accountants do with _____, which is the clerical function of recording the economic activities of a business.

4. The process of evaluating a company's performance and analyzing the costs and benefits of a strategic action is known as _____.

5. Private accountants generally work together as a team under the supervision of the organization's _____, who reports to the vice-president of finance.

6. CA is one professional designation in Canada; some accountants opt for the _____ designation, which requires a university degree, work experience, and the successful completion of an examination.

7. _____ are basic accounting standards and procedures that have been agreed upon by regulators, auditors, and companies over decades.

8. Under the basic accounting equation, assets equal liabilities plus _____.

9. Accountants match revenue to expenses by adopting the _____ of accounting, which states that revenue is recognized when you make a sale or provide a service, not when you are paid.

10. _____ is the process for evaluating proposed investments in select projects that provide the best long-term financial return.

Companion Website

See It on the **WEB**

Visit the Companion Website at **www.pearsoned.ca/bovee**, review the exercises, and complete the following assignments for Chapter 13:

1. Link Your Way to the World of Accounting
2. Sharpen Your Pencil
3. Think Like an Accountant

CHAPTER 14

UNDERSTANDING BANKING AND SECURITIES

LEARNING OBJECTIVES

After studying this chapter, you will be able to

1 Highlight the functions, characteristics, and common forms of money

2 Discuss the responsibilities and insurance methods of the Canadian Deposit Insurance Corporation (CDIC)

3 Discuss the Canadian banking industry

4 Differentiate among a share's par value, its market value, and its book value

5 Highlight the distinguishing features of common shares, preferred shares, bonds, and mutual funds

6 Differentiate among an auction exchange, dealer exchange, and electronic communication network (ECN)

7 Explain how government regulation of securities trading tries to protect investors

Behind the Scenes

Retooling Canada's Banks: Despite Merger Restrictions, Some Positive Results

The disappointing merger restrictions that stopped the major Canadian banks from joining forces a decade ago are still in place. However, the banks have managed to earn some tremendous results by looking inward and improving efficiency.

www.bmo.com, www.rbc.com, www.cibc.com, www.scotiabank.com, www.td.com, www.nbc.ca

Back in Chapter 1 we looked at the various types of economic systems and referred to Canada as a mixed economy. In a pure capitalist state the government does not get involved in business activities. When it comes to banking, the government has a tremendous impact in Canada. Government policies have helped provide stability and peace of mind to consumers by creating general restrictions on how the financial institutions can invest their funds; creating mechanisms to insure accounts (CDIC); placing limits on foreign ownership, and so on. All of these actions help to secure the public's confidence in the Canadian banking system.

However, the decision to halt bank mergers about a decade ago also had a major impact on the Canadian banks. Back in 1998 it appeared as though the big six Canadian banks—Royal Bank of Canada, Bank of Montreal, Canadian Imperial Bank of Commerce, Toronto Dominion, Scotiabank, and the National Bank—were set to turn into the big four or three. The rush to create these marriages was being pushed in the name of global competition. Canadian banks had traditionally been respected powerful figures on the world scene, but with major bank mergers creating giant competitors around the world the Canadian banks were feeling less significant and feared for their long-term strength. Even after RBC and BMO announced that a merged bank would cut service charges and expand the number of branches, the public remained firm in its opposition and the government heard the message loud and clear.

Shortly after denying the mergers, the Canadian government announced it would work with banking officials, businesses, and public interest groups to study the issue and establish clear guidelines concerning the question of

bank mergers. As of 2007, Canadian chartered banks are still waiting for clear guidance from the government on the matter. Some financial analysts claim that it is too late since Canadian banks, which were once mid-sized players on the world stage, have shrunk in status so much that mergers might not even enable them to climb back to their previous positions.

Despite the major fears, the banks have managed to perform extremely well given their limitations. In spite of the restrictions and partially because of them the banks were forced to look within to improve their current systems. The efforts in recent years have paid off. According to a major study by the Boston Consulting Group, Canadian banks collectively provided the highest shareholder return at 15.5 percent. This figure was nearly three times as high as for the US institutions, which collectively ranked fifth. In addition, three Canadian banks ranked in the top-ten list of performers: Bank of Nova Scotia, Royal Bank, and Bank of Montreal.

The merger issue is not going away. While they're waiting, the Canadian banks are doing everything they can to function under the current system while preparing for a more open market.[1]

TEST YOURSELF

Answers to these questions can be found on the website: www.pearsoned.ca/bovee.

1. How does the government's position on mergers relate to their historical actions in creating the CDIC, enacting the *Bank Act*, and establishing the Bank of Canada?

2. Why has the Canadian government avoided the temptation to allow the Canadian banks to merge?

3. Why were consumers so opposed to bank mergers when the issue became public knowledge? Do you think the fears are legitimate?

MONEY AND FINANCIAL INSTITUTIONS

Where should you invest your hard-earned money? Businesses and individuals have many choices when it comes to investing money. They can deposit funds in a bank account, purchase company shares or bonds, or acquire real estate, artwork, or other assets that they hope will appreciate over time. This chapter discusses two investment options: banking and securities markets. We begin by explaining some of the characteristics and types of money. Next, we look at common types of financial institutions, the services they provide, and the changing nature of the Canadian banking environment. In the second half of the chapter we explore three principal types of securities investments—shares, bonds, and mutual funds—and discuss the types of securities markets in which such investments are traded. Finally, we conclude the chapter by looking at securities trading procedures, performance barometers, and regulations.

Characteristics and Types of Money

L.O. 1

Money is anything generally accepted as a means of paying for goods and services. Before it was invented, people got what they needed by trading their services or possessions; in some societies, this system of trading, or bartering, still exists. However, barter is inconvenient and impractical in a global economy, where many of the things we want are intangible, come from places all over the world, and require the combined work of many people. To be an effective medium of exchange, money must have these important characteristics: It must be divisible, portable (easy to carry), durable, and difficult to counterfeit, and it should have a stable value. In addition, money must perform three basic functions: First, it must serve as a medium of exchange—a tool for simplifying transactions between buyers and sellers. Second, it must serve as a measure of value so that you don't have to negotiate the relative worth of dissimilar items every time you buy something. Finally, money must serve as a temporary store of value—a way of accumulating your wealth until you need it.

Paper money and coins are the most visible types of money, but money exists in a variety of forms, including:

- **Currency**: Coins, bills, traveller's cheques, cashier's cheques, and money orders
- **Demand deposit**: Money available immediately on demand, such as from chequing accounts
- **Time deposits**: Accounts that pay interest and restrict the owner's right to withdraw funds on short notice, such as savings accounts, certificates of deposit, and money-market deposit accounts

money
Anything generally accepted as a means of paying for goods and services

currency
Bills and coins that make up a country's cash money

demand deposits
Money that can be used by the customer at any time, like chequing accounts

time deposits
Bank accounts that pay interest and require advance notice before money can be withdrawn

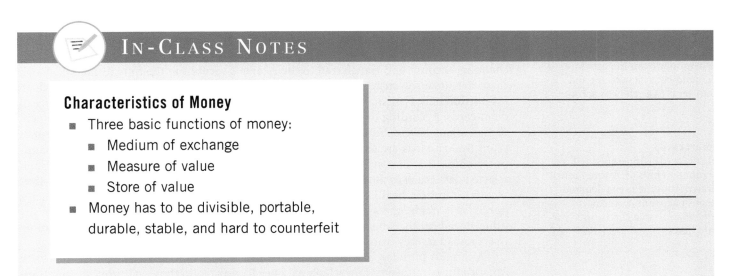

IN-CLASS NOTES

Characteristics of Money
- Three basic functions of money:
  - Medium of exchange
  - Measure of value
  - Store of value
- Money has to be divisible, portable, durable, stable, and hard to counterfeit

Chequing and Savings Accounts

Money you put into your chequing account is a *demand deposit*, or *near money*, available immediately (on demand) through the use of **cheques**, written orders that direct your bank to pay the stated amount of money to you or to someone else. Several types of chequing accounts exist, each offering benefits in exchange for monthly fees, minimum account balances, or other requirements. For example, high-interest-paying chequing accounts pay interest but limit the number of cheques customers can write and impose a fee if the account balance falls below a minimum level.

You can also earn interest on the money you put in savings accounts. Originally, these accounts were known as *passbook savings accounts* because customers received a small passbook in which the bank recorded all deposits, withdrawals, and interest. Today, most banks send out statements instead of passbooks, so these accounts have become known as *statement savings accounts*. In general, money in savings accounts can be withdrawn at any time, but certain types of savings accounts may require advanced notice or impose withdrawal limits. For example, money in a *money-market deposit account* earns more interest, but you are allowed only a limited number of monthly withdrawals. Money held in a *guaranteed investment certificate (GIC) account* earns an even higher interest rate, but you cannot withdraw the funds for a stated period, such as six months or more. If you want to make an early withdrawal from a GIC, you will lose some or all of the interest you've earned.

Credit, Debit, and Smart Cards

You are probably quite familiar with the basics of the plastic credit world. For everyday access to short-term credit, banks and other institutions issue **credit cards**, cards that entitle customers to make purchases now and repay the amount later. Credit cards are a popular substitute for currency and cheques. Many credit card issuers charge an annual fee for Visa and MasterCard credit cards, and all charge interest on any unpaid balance. Credit cards have become immensely popular with consumers because they are convenient and allow people to postpone payment on the purchases they make. They also help people manage their finances by either choosing to repay the full amount when they are billed or making small payments month by month until the debt has been repaid. Credit card companies make money by charging customers interest on their unpaid account balances and by charging businesses a processing fee, which can range from 2 to 5 percent of the value of each sales transaction paid by credit card. Nearly every store accepts credit cards, and mail-order merchants and Internet retailers are especially dependent on credit cards to facilitate purchases.

While credit cards provide tremendous convenience, many consumers fall victim to the credit card "treadmill trap." They charge large amounts and then have to work harder and harder just to meet their minimum monthly payments. The CBC Video Case at the end of this chapter, "Card Tricks: The Credit Card Web of Rules," gives some important life lessons for managing your credit; see page 473.

In addition to credit cards, many banks offer **debit cards**, plastic cards that function like cheques in that the amount of a purchase is electronically deducted from the user's chequing account and transferred to the retailer's account at the time of the sale. Debit cards are ideal for customers who must control their spending or stick to a budget. Proportionately, Canadians are the world leaders in terms of the availability and usage of debit cards. According to the Canadian Bankers Association, approximately 86 percent of Canadians have debit cards and 83 percent have used them at least once in the past year.[2] **Smart cards** are similar to debit cards, but these plastic cards contain tiny computer chips that can store amounts of money (from the user's bank account) and selected data (such as the user's shipping address, credit card information, frequent-flyer account numbers, health and insurance details, or other personal information). When a purchase is made, the store's equipment electronically deducts the amount from the value stored on the smart card and reads and verifies requisite customer information. Users reload money from their bank accounts to their smart cards as needed.

Although popular in Europe, smart cards have been slow to catch on in North America for two reasons: Low telephone rates (compared to those in European countries)

Technologies That Are Revolutionizing Business

CREDIT SCORING SOFTWARE

Credit scoring software is a type of business intelligence software (see Chapter 6) that measures the creditworthiness of applicants for credit cards, mortgages, and other forms of credit. It has the dual objective of filtering out applicants that don't meet a lender's criteria while speeding up the process for those that do. Most of these packages use variations on a scoring system originally developed by the Fair Isaac Corporation (abbreviated as FICO).

HOW IT'S CHANGING BUSINESS

Using sophisticated mathematical models based on historical records, credit scoring software helps lenders decide which applicants to accept and how much credit to extend to each one. In addition, software with *predictive modelling* or *predictive analytics* helps a company analyze which applicants will make the best customers (lowest risk and highest profit potential) for a given lender. For instance, customers who receive credit cards but never use them or who pay off their balance every month are less profitable than customers who tend to carry a balance and therefore pay interest charges every month. The software can also help detect fraudulent credit card applications, which cost card issuers $1 billion a year—a cost that gets passed on to consumers and businesses in the form of higher interest rates, higher fees, and tighter credit availability. Variations on credit scoring software are also used in the insurance industry to predict the likelihood that an applicant will file a claim in the future.[3]

WHERE YOU CAN LEARN MORE

The details of the FICO model are confidential, but you can read more about the products offered by Fair Isaac at www.fairisaac.com. If you'd like to see what your own credit score is, you can buy a report at www.equifax.ca.

---

make it affordable to verify credit card transactions over the phone, and it is not cost-effective for most North American businesses to replace current debit and credit card infrastructures with smart card readers and computer chip technology. Nevertheless, American Express has made inroads with its combination smart card and credit card, Blue. Designed to appeal to online shoppers, Blue comes with software and a small smart card reader that plugs into the user's serial port. Customers who purchase online simply insert Blue into the reader and type in a password, and the digital information stored on the smart card tells the vendor the customer's credit card number, expiration date, and shipping address.[4] See the box entitled "Surprise! You've Been Swiped" to learn about some of the current threats to various electronic payment systems.

Financial Institutions and Services

As a businessperson, you may or may not be responsible for writing company cheques or investing a firm's money, but you will be receiving a paycheque and you will need to deposit that cheque into a financial institution or cash it so that you can pay your bills. In fact, no matter where in the world you live, work, or travel, today's businesses and individuals require a wide range of financial services.

Deposit and Non-Deposit Financial Institutions

The types of services provided by a financial institution are generally governed by whether it is a *deposit institution* or *non-deposit institution*. Deposit institutions accept deposits from customers or members and offer chequing and savings accounts, loans, and other banking services. Among the many deposit institutions are the following:

- *Chartered banks*: profit-oriented financial institutions federally regulated and chartered under the *Bank Act*. Chartered banks make money by charging customers fees and higher interest rates on loans than the interest rates they pay on customers' deposits.

- *Trust companies*: incorporated by either the federal or the provincial governments. Trust companies serve both individuals and businesses by acting as safeguards for funds and estates entrusted to them, serve as a trustee in bond sales, and often provide banking services.

Surprise! You've Been Swiped

Skimming is the fastest-growing area of credit and debit card fraud. A skimmer is someone who steals customer account information by swiping a credit card through a handheld magnetic card reader—about the size of a pager. The reader copies the cardholder's name, account number, and even the card validation code—stored on the magnetic strip—giving the counterfeiter all the data needed to create a perfect clone of the credit card. Debit card skimming is almost identical, but because of the need for the user's personal identification number (PIN) to gain access to funds, thieves have set up hidden cameras to record the PINs of unsuspecting users. Recently in Halifax, Nova Scotia, thieves took debit card skimming a step further by placing a clear plastic sleeve over the keypad on debit machines. The sleeve was linked to a computer and every time someone typed in his or her PIN the information was transferred directly to a PC. Card readers can be purchased for as little as US$100 over the Internet and are intended for legitimate use by banks, restaurants, retailers, and hotels. Unfortunately, some end up in the wrong hands.

Thieves and, increasingly, organized crime groups pay waiters and store clerks to steal information from credit cards using the concealed devices. By skimming 14 to 20 accounts, crooks can generate $50 000 to $60 000 worth of fraud that will probably go undiscovered until the victims get their bills—30 to 60 days after the crime. Moreover, skimmed data from, say, a customer in Winnipeg, Quebec City, or Ottawa can be emailed to Taiwan, Japan, or Europe and used for mail-order, telephone-order, or e-commerce overseas transactions within 24 to 48 hours of the theft. Professionals can even encode the stolen codes into a strip and use equipment to produce an electronically indistinguishable counterfeit card.

While credit and debit card issuers decline to say how much they are losing to skimmers—in part because they don't want to scare consumers out of using their plastic—industry analysts estimate skimmers reap more than US$125 million annually. To curb this fraud, major card issuers are cooperating with the RCMP to pool information about fraudulent transactions. For example, issuers can generate computer analyses that flag locations where numerous cards may have been skimmed. Or if someone in Hong Kong tries to buy something with a credit card that was used two hours earlier in Toronto, the computer will reject the transaction.

What can you do to prevent your cards from getting skimmed? Not much, say experts, besides covering up the keypad when entering your PIN, using PINs that are unrelated to personal characteristics and events, reading your bills closely, checking your accounts on the web or by phone during the month to make sure there are no surprises, and reporting improper charges promptly. Although you're not liable for fraudulent credit card charges made to your accounts by skimmers or other scam artists, you do have to face the hassle of getting the unauthorized transactions removed from your bills. To date, banks have been willing to cover debit card losses, though some are now doing so only if the PIN is not easily detectable by knowing some of the user's personal information such as important birthdays or telephone numbers. Of course, you can always pay with old-fashioned cash. But if you carry a lot of that around, you may have to worry about the old-fashioned robber.[5]

Questions for Critical Thinking

1. To curb the abuse, why don't credit or debit card issuers require customers to present additional personal validation data at the time of sale?
2. Why won't skimming increase the demand for smart cards?

- *Credit unions and caisses populaires*: non-profit, member-owned organizations that take deposits only from members, such as one company's employees or one union's members or another designated group. The provinces and the Credit Union Central of Canada, which operates as the central finance facility for credit unions, regulate these organizations. Credit unions and caisses populaires offer the same services as chartered banks.

Non-deposit institutions offer specific financial services but do not accept deposits. Non-deposit financial institutions include the following:

- *Insurance companies* provide insurance coverage for life, property, and other potential losses; they invest payments they receive in real estate, construction projects, etc.

IN-CLASS NOTES

Financial Institutions

- **Deposit institutions** accept deposits from customers or members and offer chequing and savings accounts, loans, and other banking services
  - Chartered banks, trust companies, credit unions, and caisses populaires
- **Non-deposit institutions** offer specific financial services but do not accept deposits
  - Insurance companies, pension funds, finance companies, brokerage firms

_____
_____
_____
_____
_____
_____
_____

- *Pension funds* are set up by companies to provide retirement benefits for employees; money contributed by the company and its employees is put into securities and other investments.
- *Finance companies* lend money to consumers and businesses for home improvements, expansion, purchases, and other purposes.
- *Brokerage firms or security dealers* allow investors to buy and sell shares, bonds, and other investments; many also offer chequing accounts, high-paying savings accounts, and loans to buy securities.

The rules governing financial institutions have been altered. In the past, each financial institution focused on offering a particular set of financial services for specific customer groups. However, the competitive situation has evolved over the past 10 years as legislation has been passed allowing both deposit and non-deposit institutions to offer similar services. This blurring of the line between banks and other financial organizations has resulted in increased competition in the industry, which is designed to benefit consumers.

Loans

Personal and business loans are vital tools that help fuel commerce in the modern economy. Individuals usually apply for mortgage loans when they want to buy a home. They also look to banks and financial services firms for auto loans, home improvement loans, student loans, and many other types of loans. Businesses rely on banks to provide loans for expansion, purchases of new equipment, construction or renovation of plants and facilities, or other large-scale projects. Some businesses obtain a working capital **line of credit**, which is an agreed upon maximum amount of money a bank is willing to lend to a business during a specific period of time, usually one year. Once a line of credit has been established, the business may obtain unsecured loans for any amount up to that limit, provided the bank has funds. The line of credit can be cancelled at any time, so companies that want to be sure to obtain credit when needed should arrange a revolving line of credit, which guarantees that the bank will honour the line of credit up to the stated amount. A line of credit is not limited to businesses; individuals can also obtain a line of credit for personal use.

line of credit
An arrangement in which the financial institution makes money available for use at any time after a loan has been approved

IN-CLASS NOTES

Common Reasons for Taking Out Loans

- **Consumer loans**
  - Mortgage
  - Automobile
  - Home improvement
  - Student
- **Business loans**
  - Expansion
  - New equipment
  - Construction
  - Line of credit

_____

_____

_____

_____

_____

_____

_____

---

automated teller machines (ATMs)
Electronic terminals that permit people to perform basic banking transactions 24 hours a day without a human teller

electronic funds transfer systems (EFTS)
Computerized systems for completing financial transactions

Electronic banking options like ATMs offer speed and convenience, but many banks find that customers still want the personal communication offered by branches.

Electronic Banking

Most deposit institutions offer electronic banking services that may be conducted from sites other than the bank's physical location. For instance, all over the world customers rely on **automated teller machines (ATMs)** to withdraw money from their demand-deposit accounts at any hour. Look around and you'll see that ATMs are everywhere, from banks, malls, and supermarkets to airports, resorts, and tourist attractions. Canada actually has the highest number of bank machines per capita in the world. By linking with regional, national, and international ATM networks, banks let customers withdraw cash far from home, make deposits, and handle other transactions. To compete, more banks are jazzing up their ATMs. The latest ATMs are wired to the web and allow customers to pay insurance premiums and utility bills, print cashier's cheques, and purchase stamps, movie tickets, ski-lift tickets, DVDs, and even foreign currency.

Electronic funds transfer systems (EFTS) are another form of electronic banking. These computerized systems allow users to conduct financial transactions efficiently from remote locations. Today many employers are using EFTS to deposit employees' cheques directly into their bank accounts. This procedure saves employers and employees the worry and headache of handling large amounts of cash. Even the Canadian government uses EFTS for regular payments like employment insurance benefits.

In addition to ATM and EFTS, banks and many insurance companies now offer Internet or online banking to accommodate the growing number of individuals and businesses that want to transfer money between accounts, check account balances, pay bills, apply for loans, and handle other transactions at any hour. Online banking is not only fast and easy for customers, but also extremely cost-efficient for banks.[6] To read more about cyberbanks (Internet-only banks) take a look at the "E-Business in Action" feature at the end of this chapter (see page 475).

Bank Safety

L.O. 2

The Canadian Deposit Insurance Corporation (CDIC) is a Crown corporation that was founded in 1967 to bring deposit insurance to the Canadian banking system. The insurance covers deposits at banks, trust companies, and loan companies up to $100 000, and reimburses clients when a member institution fails. Since the CDIC was formed in 1967, 43 member institutions have failed; the last time it occurred was back in 1996 when Security Home Mortgage Corporation went under.[7] Money deposited at credit unions and caisses populaires is protected by provincial insurance.

The Evolving Canadian Banking Environment

L.O. 3

The current banking system is a direct result of the Great Depression in the 1930s, when prime minister Richard Bennett was facing criticism about the current financial structure along with the lack of direct means for settling international accounts. Bennett appointed a Royal Commission to study Canada's monetary and financial system and it concluded that the country would benefit from a national bank. In 1935 the *Bank Act* was passed, officially bringing the Bank of Canada into existence. Originally, the bank was to be a private institution with shareholders, but in 1938 the new prime minister, William Lyon Mackenzie King, nationalized the Bank of Canada. It immediately became the lone issuer of currency and manager of credit in the country. Today the Bank of Canada is in charge of setting interest rates; controlling the supply of money; administering the public debt, including the maintenance of records and making payments on the government's behalf; and providing a host central banking service, including setting regulations and acting as a bank for other Canadian financial institutions by accepting their deposits.[8]

Canada's banking system was originally founded on the principles of branch banking, in which large national banks would open regional branches in rural communities. Since the population of Canada was quite small and spread out, this branch system enabled banks to open across the country with a limited amount of capital. For most of the twentieth century, Canada's finance industry was dominated by six unique participants: chartered banks, credit unions/caisses populaires, trust companies, insurance agencies, brokers, and other lending agencies. Each institution, with the exception of banks and credit unions/caisses populaires, operated in different markets offering Canadians diverse financial services. This began to change in the 1980s and 1990s when several amendments were made to the *Bank Act* to increase the amount of competition in the financial services industry. For example, banks were permitted to sell securities, insurance companies could compete in some areas with banks, and foreign banks were introduced to Canada.

As a result of these changes, Canadian banks became the dominant players in the financial services industry, holding more than 76 percent of domestic assets. The remaining 24 percent is spread out over credit unions/caisses populaires, trust companies, insurance companies, and other financial institutions. Of the 69 banks operating in Canada, the Big Six—Royal Bank of Canada, Bank of Montreal, Toronto Dominion Bank, Scotiabank, Canadian Imperial Bank of Commerce, and National Bank—account for 90 percent of the money controlled by banks and operate in excess of 8000 branches across the country.[9] As mentioned in the opening case, the Big Six banks are pushing for bank mergers among themselves and with large insurance companies as an expansion strategy, but the Canadian government has blocked any merger activity to date because of public concern.

Branch bankers excel at personal service. They will meet with small business owners and work with them on their business plan, and they will loan them money to help them grow their business to the next level.

In-Class Notes

Bank Safety and Regulation

■ In 1935, the *Bank Act* was officially passed, bringing the Bank of Canada into existence

■ The **Bank of Canada** sets interest rates, controls the money supply, administers public debt, and acts as a bank for Canadian financial institutions by accepting their deposits

■ The **Canadian Deposit Insurance Corporation (CDIC)** covers deposits at banks, trust companies, and loan companies for up to $100 000 if an institution fails

_____

_____

_____

_____

_____

_____

_____

_____

L.O. 4, 5

securities
Investments such as shares, bonds, options, futures, and commodities

authorized shares
Maximum number of ownership shares into which a corporation's board of directors decides the business can be divided

issued shares
The portion of authorized shares sold to and held by shareholders

unissued shares
The portion of authorized shares not yet sold to shareholders

stock split
An increase in the number of shares of ownership that each share certificate represents with a proportionate drop in each share's value

TYPES OF SECURITIES INVESTMENTS

With the line between banks and brokerage houses blurring, consumers now have more options as to where they can purchase **securities**—shares, bonds, and other investments—to meet their investment goals. Securities are traded in organized markets. Corporations sell shares or bonds to finance their operations or expansion, while governments and provinces issue bonds to raise money for building or public expenses—from national defence to road improvements. Here's a closer look at these three principal types of securities investments.

Shares

As discussed in Chapter 5, a share represents ownership in a corporation and is evidenced by a share certificate. The number of shares a company sells depends on the amount of equity capital the company will require and on the price of each share it sells. A corporation's board of directors sets a maximum number of shares into which the business can be divided. In theory, all of these shares—called **authorized shares**— may be sold at once. In practice, however, the company sells only a part of its authorized shares. The part sold and held by shareholders is called **issued shares**; the unsold portion is called **unissued shares**.

From time to time a company may announce a **stock split**, in which it increases the number of shares that each share certificate represents while proportionately lowering the value of each share. Companies generally use a stock split to make the share price more affordable. When a company with 1 million shares outstanding and a share price of $50 per share announces a two-for-one split, it is doubling the number of shares. After the split, the company will have 2 million shares outstanding, and each original share will become two shares worth $25 each. For example, Research in Motion, maker of the famous BlackBerry, trades shares on the Toronto Stock Exchange (TSX) under the symbol RIM.TO and on Nasdaq under the symbol RIMM. The company completed a three-for-one stock split in August 2007, tripling the number of common shares from 186 million to more than 568 million and reducing the individual share price to one third the value. Interestingly, while many companies willingly split their shares as a means of making it more attractive and to create more value for shareholders, Warren Buffet, who is regarded as the greatest investor over the past century, dislikes stock splits and has never split the shares of his company, Berkshire Hathaway. As a result of Buffet's stance, the company's class "A" common shares recently traded in excess of US$112 500 per share on the New York Stock Exchange.[10]

When shares are first issued, the company assigns a **par value**, or dollar value, to the shares primarily for bookkeeping purposes. Par value is also used to calculate dividends (for certain kinds of shares). Keep in mind that par value is not the same as the share's *market value*, the price at which a share currently sells, or its *book value*, the amount of net assets of a corporation represented by one common share.

par value
As shown on the share certificate, a value assigned to a share for use in bookkeeping and in calculating dividends

Common Shares

Most investors buy common shares, which represent an ownership interest in a corporation. As Chapter 5 points out, shareholders of this class vote to elect the company's board of directors, vote on other important corporate issues, and receive dividend payments from the company's profits. But they have no say in day-to-day business activities. Still, common shareholders have the advantage of limited liability if the corporation gets into trouble, and as part owners they share in the fortunes of the business and are eligible to receive dividends as long as they hold the shares. In addition, common shareholders stand to make a profit if the share price goes up and they sell their shares for more than the purchase price. The reverse is also true: common shareholders can lose money if the market price drops and they sell the shares for less than they paid for them.

Preferred Shares

Investors who own preferred shares, the second major class of shares, usually enjoy higher dividends and a better claim (after creditors) on assets if the corporation fails. The amount of the dividend on preferred shares is printed on the share certificate and set when the shares are first issued. If interest rates fluctuate, the market price of preferred shares will go up or down to adjust for the difference between the market interest rate and the share's dividend. Preferred shares often come with special privileges. *Convertible preferred shares* can be exchanged, if the shareholder chooses, for a certain number of common shares issued by the company. *Cumulative preferred shares* has an additional advantage: If the issuing company stops paying dividends for any reason, the dividends on these shares will be held (accumulate) until preferred shareholders have been paid in full—before common shareholders are paid anything.

bond
A method of funding in which the issuer borrows from an investor and provides a written promise to make regular interest payments and repay the borrowed amount in the future

principal
The amount of money a corporation borrows from an investor through the sale of a bond

Bonds

Unlike shares, which give the investor an ownership stake in the corporation, bonds are debt financing. A **bond** is a method of raising money in which the issuing organization borrows from an investor and issues a written pledge to make regular interest payments and then repay the borrowed amount later. When you invest in this type of security, you are lending money to the company or government that issued the bond. Bonds are usually issued in multiples of $1000, such as $5000, $10 000, or $50 000. Also, like shares, bonds are evidenced by a certificate, which shows the issuer's name, the amount borrowed (the **principal**), the date this principal amount will be repaid, and the annual interest rate investors receive.

The interest is stated in terms of an annual percentage rate but is usually paid at six-month intervals. For example, the holder of a $1000 bond that pays 8 percent interest due January 15 and July 15 could expect to receive $40 on each of those dates. A look at the financial section of any newspaper will show that some corporations sell new bonds at an interest rate two to three percentage points higher that that offered by

Share certificates represent a share of ownership of a company.

Exhibit 14.1   **Corporate Bond Ratings**

Standard & Poor's (S&P) and Moody's Investors Service are two companies that rate the safety of corporate bonds. When its bonds receive a low rating, a company must pay a higher interest rate to compensate investors for the higher risk.

S&P	INTERPRETATION	MOODY'S	INTERPRETATION
AAA	Highest rating	Aaa	Prime quality
AA	Very strong capacity to pay	Aa	High grade
A	Strong capacity to pay; somewhat susceptible to changing business conditions	A	Upper-medium grade
BBB	More susceptible than A-rated bonds	Baa	Medium grade
BB	Somewhat speculative	Ba	Somewhat speculative
B	Speculative	B	Speculative
CCC	Vulnerable to non-payment	Caa	Poor standing; may be in default
CC	Highly vulnerable to non-payment	Ca	Highly speculative; often in default
C	Bankruptcy petition filed or similar action taken	C	Lowest rated; extremely poor chance of ever attaining real investment standing
D	In default		

other companies, yet the terms of the bonds seem similar. Why? Because bonds are not guaranteed investments. The variations in interest rates reflect the degree of risk associated with the bond, which is closely tied to the financial stability of the issuing company. Agencies such as Standard & Poor's (S&P) and Moody's rate bonds on the basis of the issuers' financial strength. Exhibit 14.1 shows that the safest corporate bonds are rated AAA (S&P) and Aaa (Moody's). Low-rated bonds, known as *junk bonds*, pay higher interest rates to compensate investors for the higher risk.

Corporate Bonds

secured bonds
Bonds backed by specific assets that will be given to bondholders if the borrowed amount is not repaid

debentures
Corporate bonds backed only by the reputation of the issuer

convertible bonds
Corporate bonds that can be exchanged at the owner's discretion into the issuing company's common shares

Companies issue a variety of corporate bonds. **Secured bonds** are backed by company-owned property (such as airplanes or plant equipment) that will pass to the bondholders if the issuer does not repay the amount borrowed. *Mortgage bonds,* one type of secured bond, are backed by real property owned by the issuing corporation. **Debentures** are unsecured bonds, backed only by the corporation's promise to pay. Because debentures are riskier than other types of bonds, investors who buy these bonds receive higher interest rates. **Convertible bonds** can be exchanged at the investor's option for a certain number of the corporation's common shares. Because of this feature, convertible bonds generally pay lower interest rates.

Canadian Government Securities Bonds

Just as corporations raise money by issuing bonds, so too do municipal, provincial, and federal governments. As an investor, you can buy a variety of Canadian government securities, including Canada Savings Bonds, T-bills, and bonds issued by various municipalities and provinces.

Treasury bills
Short-term debt securities issued by the Bank of Canada; also referred to as *T-bills*

    Treasury bills (also referred to as *T-bills*) are short-term debt obligations issued by the Bank of Canada that are repaid in less than one year. Treasury bills are sold at a discount and redeemed at face value. The difference between the purchase price and the redemption price is, in effect, the interest earned.

Canada Savings Bonds
Debt securities issued by the Bank of Canada that are usually held in excess of one year

    Canada Savings Bonds are Canadian government bonds that investors can purchase and redeem at any time, although most are used as long-term investment devices. In general, Canadian government securities pay lower interest than corporate bonds because they are considered safer: There is very little risk that the government will fail to repay bondholders as promised. A traditional choice for many individual investors, Canada Savings Bonds are issued by the Canadian government in amounts ranging from $50 to $10 000.

Mutual Funds

Mutual funds are financial organizations that pool money from many investors to buy a diversified mix of shares, bonds, or other securities. The Canadian government made this type of investment popular by encouraging people to invest for their retirement by contributing to Registered Retirement Savings Plans (RRSPs). Canadians receive a tax credit for each dollar they invest in their RRSP. The contribution limit is set at 18 percent of gross income per year, but cannot exceed the maximum cap, which is set at $19 000 in 2007, $20 000 in 2008, $21 000 in 2009, and $22 000 in 2010. This type of investment also became fashionable during the bull market of the late 1990s and when banks started to offer investment advice as part of their regular services to customers. Mutual funds are particularly well-suited for investors, like those saving for their

Canadian Savings Bond certificates have been a popular investment choice with risk-averse investors that like the security of the CSB. However, the low interest rate environment in recent years has forced many to look at other options.

retirement, who wish to spread a fixed amount of money over a variety of investments and do not have the time or experience to search out and manage investment opportunities. Investors hope to benefit from the purchase of mutual funds and other securities by receiving dividends, which are profits distributed to shareholders, and earning capital gains, which occur when an investor sells a security for a higher price than the purchase price. *No-load* funds charge no fee to buy or sell shares, whereas *load funds* charge investors a commission to buy or sell. The most common types of loads are front end (assessed when you purchase the fund) and back end (assessed when you sell the fund).

Investment companies offer two types of mutual funds. An *open-end fund* issues additional shares as new investors ask to buy them. In essence, the fund's books never close. The number of shares outstanding changes daily, as investors buy new shares or redeem old ones. These shares aren't traded in a separate market. *Closed-end funds,* on the other hand, raise all of their money at once by distributing a fixed number of shares that trade much like shares on major security exchanges. As soon as a certain number of shares are sold, the fund closes its books.

Various mutual funds have different investment priorities. Among the most popular mutual funds are **money-market funds**, which invest in short-term securities and other liquid investments. *Growth funds* invest in shares of rapidly growing companies. *Income funds* invest in securities that pay high dividends and interest. *Balanced funds* invest in a carefully chosen mix of shares and bonds. *Sector funds* (also known as *specialty* or *industry funds*) invest in companies within a particular industry. *Global funds* invest in foreign and Canadian securities, whereas *international funds* invest strictly in foreign securities. And *index funds* buy shares in companies included in specific market averages, such as the S&P/TSE 300. You can buy shares in mutual funds through your broker or directly from the mutual fund company.

For years, individual investors viewed mutual funds as a safe and easy way to invest in the stock market, but that perception took a significant hit when two types of widespread trading abuses came to light. The first is called *market timing*, in which a large shareholder in a mutual fund jumps in and out of the fund, trying to profit from short-term movements in the price. While this practice isn't illegal, it's unfair to smaller investors because fund managers can't manage their assets as effectively when huge sums of money are moving in and out of the fund on short notice. Moreover, although many mutual fund companies officially forbid market timing, the SEC discovered that half of the 88 largest fund companies were allowing it for selected customers.[11]

The second abuse, known as either *late trading* or *stale pricing*, occurs when fund managers let favoured clients (usually wealthy individuals or institutions) essentially buy or sell shares in a fund after 4:00 p.m., when

mutual funds
Financial organizations pooling money to invest in diversified blends of shares, bonds, or other securities

money-market funds
Mutual funds that invest in short-term securities and other liquid investments

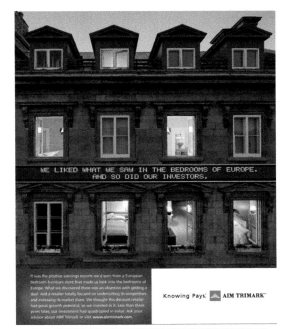

WE LIKED WHAT WE SAW IN THE BEDROOMS OF EUROPE. AND SO DID OUR INVESTORS.

Knowing Pays: AIM TRIMARK

Aim Trimark is a leading investment management company. Their ads focus on the importance of digging deep and understanding what companies do: "Knowing pays." The theme revolves around their fund managers and their willingness to go the extra mile to select companies with the potential to succeed.

IN-CLASS NOTES

Types of Security Investments

- **Common shares:** ownership interest in a corporation (voting rights, limited liability, profit if share value increases, receive dividends)
- **Preferred shares:** holders enjoy a better claim (after creditors) on assets if the corporation fails
- **Bonds:** issuers make interest payments to investors and repay borrowed amount later; allow firms to raise money without giving up ownership
- **Mutual funds:** financial organizations that pool money from investors to buy a diversified mix of shares, bonds, or other securities

trading officially stops and the fund's price is fixed until the following day. The reason such moves are illegal and unfair to other investors in the fund is that these late traders can act on financial news that breaks after the 4:00 p.m. deadline, while still getting that day's price. In other words, these late traders can act on events that happen in the evening, while everyday investors are locked out until markets open the next day. The mutual fund industry as a whole enjoyed six decades of fairly loose oversight from authorities, but it is likely to find itself under much closer scrutiny in the future.[12] The recent sub-prime mortgage scandal in the United States will only make things worse. Now, even relatively safe funds have lost their status as virtual no-risk investments.

Income Trusts

income trusts
Legal entities that hold cash-generating assets in trust and distribute the majority of income to unitholders in the form of dividends

Income trusts represent a unique type of company structure and investment opportunity that has captured headlines in recent years. As discussed in Chapter 5, in the past decade and in particular between 2002 and 2006 income trusts grew exponentially in Canada. The combined worth of income trusts went from $20 billion in 2000 to $200 billion in 2006; companies worth $70 billion in market capitalization switched or had announced plans to convert to income trusts in 2006 alone. Under this frenzied environment the government felt as though it needed to act quickly to address the situation. Finance Minister Jim Flaherty announced a new Tax Fairness Plan near the end of the year that placed a 34 percent tax levy on trusts and effectively poured cold water on the movement to convert. Many companies that had made the announcement retreated from the move.[13]

What does this all mean from an investor's point of view? Trust companies closely resemble corporations in that they have investors who own shares of the company and these shares trade on stock exchanges (trust companies include .UN after their stock symbol to indicate they are trusts). Just like common shares, the shareholders in a trust vote at annual meetings and have rights to dividend. However, the shares are referred to as *units* and the owners are called unitholders. Where a trust traditionally differs most from corporations is that it is a legal entity that holds cash-generating assets (a business) in a holding company, and the business does not reinvest any of its net income. Rather, it allows the majority of income to flow to the owners of the trust company through dividends. As a result, the income trust traditionally avoided paying tax and income was only taxed in the hands of the unitholders. Since income trusts paid out the majority of their net income to unitholders, their dividends were usually much higher than traditional common shares. Investors who purchase income trust units want to see their value or unit price appreciate while earning a high dividend yield.

Part of the attractiveness of income trusts are the current low interest rates in Canada, which make it difficult for investors to earn high interest from bonds. It is not uncommon to see trust companies pay dividend yields in excess of 7 percent, whereas most common shares pay dividends under 3 percent. Critics of trusts worry about their ability to sustain high dividend payouts with little money being reinvested in the company; that some restaurant companies like The Keg and A&W, which are income trusts, do not represent businesses with consistent cash flows; and that, if interest rates start to rise sharply, the price of the units may fall substantially, offsetting any income earned from the dividend.

The recent rule changes have calmed the fears of many critics and forced investors to re-evaluate this investment choice. However, for investors that were already heavily invested in income trusts the move was a bitter pill to swallow (see the box entitled "Income Trusts: Playing the Blame Game").

Income Trusts: Playing the Blame Game

In mid-2006 it seemed as though every company in Canada had either converted, announced intentions, or was thinking of converting to an income trust. Okay, that might be an exaggeration but you get the point. A snowball effect was in place and the government was stuck at the bottom of the hill trying to find a way to make sure that it did not get snowed under by the movement. The tipping point probably came when major players like Telus and BCE joined the ranks and announced their conversion plans. There are legitimate long-term business concerns of company's converting, and in addition the government feared major tax revenue losses if the trend was not stopped. However, the government would be changing the rules of the tax game in a major way, and the move would have a punishing effect on investors already committed to this investment vehicle. The Conservative government's official policy is to avoid government intervention if at all possible. However, in October of 2006, the Tax Fairness Plan came into effect and the income trust bubble burst. Investors lost as the value of income trust investments diminished.

Although there were signs along the way, angry investors felt cheated. Some even went as far as to make irrational threats toward Finance Minister Jim Flaherty. A Louisiana stockbroker was charged with uttering death threats for two emails that he sent. The stockbroker claims that the Tax Fairness Plan ruined his business and his client's portfolios. He faces up to five years in prison and a $250 000 fine. While this example is extreme, it does illustrate the difficult nature of the decision. As the poster boy for the move, Flaherty has taken praise from some and a lot of grief from others. Many experts believe that this move should have been made a couple of years earlier, and yet others are totally against government intervention and were not pleased by the decision.

Key lesson: Whether you are investing in shares, bonds, income trusts or any other vehicle, get all the facts, get professional advice, and stay informed. Despite some claims, this decision did not come out of nowhere. Perhaps it was more devastating than expected, but a possible move had been hinted at for quite some time. Nobody should have been shocked by the decision, because the same old rules apply: Keep a diversified portfolio and look for signs. Investors sometimes have a hard time seeing beyond today's successes and don't believe that the good times will end. When the other shoe drops, emotions are hard to keep in check, especially when financial nest eggs are at stake.[14]

Questions for Critical Thinking

1. Do you think that the government made the right choice? Did they level the playing field or did they unnecessarily interfere?
2. Every government decision affects multiple stakeholders and has a positive effect on some and a negative effect on others. Create two columns and list the winners and losers in this situation.

primary market
A market where firms sell new securities issued publicly for the first time

secondary market
A market where subsequent owners trade previously issued shares and bonds

stock exchanges
The location where traders buy and sell shares and bonds

over-the-counter (OTC) market
Network of dealers who trade securities on computerized linkups rather than a trading floor

NASDAQ (National Association of Securities Dealers Automated Quotations)
A national over-the-counter securities trading network

auction exchange
A centralized marketplace where securities are traded by specialists on behalf of investors

L.O. 6

stock specialist
An intermediary who trades in a particular security on the floor of an auction exchange; "buyer of last resort"

dealer exchanges
Decentralized marketplaces where securities are bought and sold by dealers out of their own inventories

SECURITIES MARKETS

Where can you purchase bonds, shares, and other securities? Shares and bonds are bought and sold in two kinds of marketplaces: primary markets and secondary markets.

Newly issued shares or initial public offerings (IPOs) are sold in the **primary market**. Once these shares have been issued, subsequent investors can buy and sell them in the organized **secondary market**, known as **stock exchanges** (or *securities exchanges*).

Securities Exchanges

The Toronto Stock Exchange (TSX) is the largest securities exchange in Canada, with more than 1500 companies trading approximately 351 million shares per day.[15] The New York Stock Exchange (NYSE), also known as the "Big Board," is the world's largest securities exchange. The stocks and bonds of about 2750 companies, with a combined market value topping US$25.1 trillion, are traded on the exchange's floor.[16] After the NYSE, some of the largest stock exchanges are located in Tokyo, London, Frankfurt, and Paris. Many companies list their securities on more than one securities exchange. Thus, some TSX-listed shares can also be bought and sold on the NYSE.

The **over-the-counter (OTC) market** consists of a network of registered stock and bond representatives who are spread out across North America—and in some cases around the world. Most use a nationwide computer network owned by the National Association of Securities Dealers (NASD). This network is called **NASDAQ (National Association of Securities Dealers Automated Quotations)** and it is the second-largest stock market in the United States. In 1998, NASD (owners of NASDAQ) acquired the American Stock Exchange (the world's third-largest auction exchange), making NASDAQ an even stronger competitor to the New York Stock Exchange.[17] In Canada, the OTC market is referred to as the Canadian Unlisted Board (CUB).

How to Buy and Sell Securities

The process for buying and selling securities varies according to the type of exchange. As Exhibit 14.2 depicts, in an **auction exchange**, such as the New York Stock Exchange, all buy and sell orders (and all information concerning companies traded on that exchange) are funnelled onto an auction floor. There, buyers and sellers are matched by a **stock specialist**, a broker who occupies a post on the trading floor and conducts all trades in specific stocks via a central clearinghouse. If buying or selling imbalances occur in that stock, a specialist can halt trading to prevent the price from plunging without adequate cause. Specialists can also sell stock to customers out of their own inventory.[18]

In Canada, the TSX and TSX Venture Exchanges buy and sell securities using an electronic trading system. While the NASDAQ is a **dealer exchange**, it has no central marketplace for making transactions. Instead, all buy and sell orders are executed through computers by **market makers**, registered stock and bond representatives who sell securities out of their own inventories.

Electronic communication networks (ECNs) use the Internet to link buyers and sellers. Frequently referred to as a virtual stock market or cybermarket, ECNs have no exchange floors, specialists, or market makers. In fact, they are nothing more than computer networks with software programs that match buy and sell orders directly, cutting out the once-dominant market makers and specialists. Keep in mind that even though a company's shares are listed on an auction or dealer exchange, its shares may also be traded on an ECN. For instance, many brokerage firms use a combination of auction exchanges, dealer exchanges, and ECNs to execute their trades. In fact, more than 38 percent of NASDAQ shares are traded on ECNs.[19]

Like other securities marketplaces, ECNs aim to make money by providing a place where shares can be traded and by collecting

More than 3000 companies trade their shares on the NASDAQ exchange, including such well-known firms as Merrill Lynch, Microsoft, Apple Computer, and RIM.

Exhibit 14.2   Old and New Ways to Buy Shares

Some think that floor trading will become a thing of the past as electronic communication networks become increasingly popular.

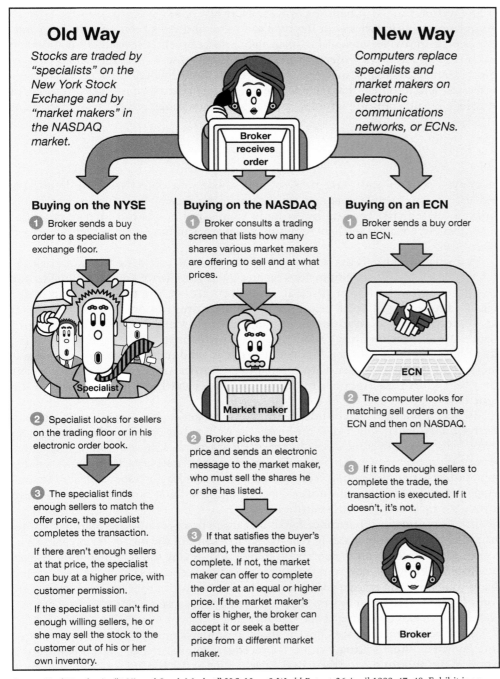

Old Way

Stocks are traded by "specialists" on the New York Stock Exchange and by "market makers" in the NASDAQ market.

New Way

Computers replace specialists and market makers on electronic communications networks, or ECNs.

Broker receives order

Buying on the NYSE

1. Broker sends a buy order to a specialist on the exchange floor.

Specialist

2. Specialist looks for sellers on the trading floor or in his electronic order book.

3. The specialist finds enough sellers to match the offer price, the specialist completes the transaction.

If there aren't enough sellers at that price, the specialist can buy at a higher price, with customer permission.

If the specialist still can't find enough willing sellers, he or she may sell the stock to the customer out of his or her own inventory.

Buying on the NASDAQ

1. Broker consults a trading screen that lists how many shares various market makers are offering to sell and at what prices.

Market maker

2. Broker picks the best price and sends an electronic message to the market maker, who must sell the shares he or she has listed.

3. If that satisfies the buyer's demand, the transaction is complete. If not, the market maker can offer to complete the order at an equal or higher price. If the market maker's offer is higher, the broker can accept it or seek a better price from a different market maker.

Buying on an ECN

1. Broker sends a buy order to an ECN.

ECN

2. The computer looks for matching sell orders on the ECN and then on NASDAQ.

3. If it finds enough sellers to complete the trade, the transaction is executed. If it doesn't, it's not.

Broker

Source: Fred Vogelstein, "A Virtual Stock Market," *U.S. News & World Report*, 26 April 1999, 47–48; Exhibit is on page 48—Robert Kemp *U.S. News & World Report*

commissions on each trade. Most ECNs operate globally and economically—which is why they are becoming increasingly popular.

Securities Brokers

Regardless of when, where, or how you trade securities, you must execute all trades by using a securities broker. Currently, individuals cannot interact with securities

market makers
Registered representatives who trade securities from their own inventories on dealer exchanges, making a ready market for buyers and sellers

electronic communication networks (ECNs)
Internet-based networks that match up buy and sell orders without using an intermediary

marketplaces or ECNs directly; purchases must be made through traditional stockbrokers—although some hope this will change soon.[20]

A **broker** is an expert who has passed a series of formal examinations and is legally registered to buy and sell securities on behalf of individual and institutional investors. As an investor, you pay *transaction costs* for every buy or sell order to cover the broker's commission, which varies with the type of broker and the size of your trade. A *full-service broker* provides financial management services such as investment counselling and planning; a *discount broker* provides fewer or limited services and generally charges lower commissions than a full-service broker. Still, some discount brokers offer a range of services and resources that include free or low-cost research, customized tracking of securities, emails confirming trades, and electronic newsletters packed with investment advice.

Orders to Buy and Sell Securities

Before you start to trade, take time to think about your objectives, both long-term and short-term. Next, look at how various securities match your objectives and your attitude toward risk, because investing in shares and bonds can involve potential losses. Finally, consider the many ways in which you can have your broker buy or sell securities.

A **market order** tells the broker to buy or sell at the best price that can be negotiated at the moment. A **limit order** specifies the highest price you are willing to pay when buying or the lowest price at which you are willing to sell. A **stop order** tells the broker to sell if the price of your security drops to or below the price you set, protecting you from losing more money if prices are dropping. You can also place a time limit on your orders. An **open order** instructs the broker to leave the order open until you cancel it. A **day order** is valid only on the day you place it and should not be confused with a *day trader*, a stock trader who holds positions for a very short time (minutes to hours) and closes out these positions within the same day.

If you have special confidence in your broker's ability, you may place a **discretionary order,** which gives the broker the right to buy or sell your securities at the broker's discretion. In some cases, discretionary orders can save you from taking a loss, because the broker may have a better sense of when to sell a security. If the broker's judgment proves wrong, however, you cannot hold the broker legally responsible for the consequences, so investigate your broker's background and think carefully before you give anyone the right to trade your securities.

Investors sometimes borrow cash to buy shares, a practice known as **margin trading**. Instead of paying for the shares in full, you borrow some of the money from your stockbroker, paying interest on the borrowed money and leaving the shares with the broker as collateral. Be aware, however, that margin trading increases risk. If the price of the shares you bought on margin goes down, you will have to give your broker more money or the broker will sell your shares. Such forced sales can cause prices to fall even further, triggering a vicious cycle of sales and margin calls.[21]

If you believe that a share's price is about to drop, you may choose a trading procedure known as **short selling**. With this procedure, you sell shares you borrow from a broker in the hope of buying them back later at a lower price. After you return the borrowed shares to the broker, you keep the price difference. For example, you might decide to borrow 25 shares that are selling for $30 per share and sell short because you think the share price is going to plummet. When the share's price declines to $15, you buy 25 shares on the open market and make $15 profit on every share (minus transaction costs). Selling short is risky. If the shares had climbed to $32, you would have had to buy shares at that higher price, even though you would be losing money. For example, many investors thought shares of WestJet were overvalued in the fall of 2004 and early winter of 2005 as the company faced increasing competition from Air Canada, CanJet and Jetsgo. As a result, many investors sold their shares short hoping that the

---

broker
An expert who has passed specific tests and is registered to trade securities for investors

market order
Authorization for a broker to buy or sell securities at the best price that can be negotiated at the moment

limit order
A market order that stipulates the highest or lowest price at which the customer is willing to trade securities

stop order
An order to sell a security when its price falls to a particular point to limit an investor's losses

open order
A limit order that does not expire at the end of a trading day

day order
Any order to buy or sell a security that automatically expires if not executed on the day the order is placed

discretionary order
A market order that allows the broker to decide when to trade a security

margin trading
Borrowing money from brokers to buy shares, paying interest on the borrowed money, and leaving the shares with the broker as collateral

short selling
Selling shares borrowed from a broker with the intention of buying them back later at a lower price, repaying the broker, and keeping the profit

IN-CLASS NOTES

Securities Markets

- Initial public offerings (IPOs) are sold in the **primary market**; investors can then buy and sell the shares in the **secondary market** known as *stock exchanges*
- Major **securities exchanges** include the NYSE in New York and the TSX in Toronto
- **Brokers** pass formal exams and are legally registered to buy and sell securities for investors

share price would drop. But when Jetsgo unexpectedly went out of business, WestJet shares rose more than 20 percent in one day, causing many short sellers to lose significant amounts of money.

How to Analyze Financial News

Regardless of which trading procedures you use, you will want to monitor financial news sources to see how your investments are doing. Start with daily newspaper reports on securities markets. Other sources include newspapers aimed specifically at investors (such as the investment sections of the *Globe and Mail* and the *National Post, Investor's Business Daily,* and *Barron's*) and general-interest business publications that follow the *Globe and Mail* and the *National Post*'s investment sections as well as the corporate world and give hints about investing (such as the *Wall Street Journal, Forbes, Fortune, Report on Business* and *Canadian Business*). Standard & Poor's, Moody's Investors Service, and Value Line also publish newsletters and special reports on securities. Online sources include your brokerage firm's website plus a growing number of excellent financial websites listed in the box entitled "Put Your Money Where Your Mouse Is!"

What types of financial information should you be looking for? First, you want to determine the general direction of share prices. If prices have been rising over a long period, the industry and the media will often describe this situation as a **bull market**. The reverse is a **bear market**, one characterized by a long-term trend of falling prices. Once you have the general picture, look at the timing. Has a bull market lasted for too long, suggesting that shares are overvalued and a *correction* (tumbling prices) might be around the corner? Also watch the volume of shares traded each day. If the stock market is down on heavy volume (that is, if prices are moving downward and a lot of trading is going on), investors may be trying to sell before prices go down further—a bearish sign.

bull market
A rising stock market

bear market
A falling stock market

Put Your Money Where Your Mouse Is!

The Internet has been hailed as the great equalizer between individual investors and the experts on Bay and Wall Streets. Today's investors have access to a large amount of valuable information and investment tools—many of which are used by professionals. But having access to information is one thing; using it wisely is another. So before you put a dollar (or a euro) into any investment, learn as much as possible about the market, the security, its issuer, and its potential. Here are some tips to point you in the right direction.

For "how-to" advice, try Globe Investor (www .globeinvesetor.ca), Globe Fund (www.globefund .com), Business News Network (www.bnn.ca), the Motley Fool (www.fool.com), or CNN/Money's website (http://money.cnn.com). For the latest online news and commentary about shares, check out The Street (www .thestreet.com) and MarketWatch (www.marketwatch .com). Then research individual securities using Yahoo! (www.yahoo.com) or another Internet search tool. Plug in the company name and click to see the latest news. Go to Hoovers Online (www.hoovers.com) to read a little about the company's history and recent results. Be sure to stop by the company's website to read its press releases and financial statements. You can dig even further into potential investments using the following websites:

- Corporate financial data filed for Canadian companies (www.sedar.com)
- Corporate financial data filed with the SEC (www.freeedgar.com)
- Toronto Stock Exchange (www.tsx.ca)

Construct a hypothetical portfolio on Quicken, Yahoo!, or another financial website and watch how your investments fare. Track your favourite market index on MSN Money (http://money.msn.com) and compare it to your personal investment portfolio. Are your proposed investments meeting, missing, or beating the market index?

Now you're in a better position to buy securities, but your research shouldn't end here. Even after you start trading, you need to stay on top of the latest news and industry developments that can affect the securities in which you have invested. If a potential investment seems too good to be true, point your web browser to the North American Securities Administrators Association (www.nasaa.org) and get some tips on investment fraud. When it comes to investments, your web surfing can really pay off.

Questions for Critical Thinking

1. Why is it important to learn about a company's financial results and background before buying its shares or bonds?
2. What are the disadvantages of searching for investment information on the Internet?

Watching Market Indexes and Averages

market indexes
Measures of market activity calculated from the prices of a selection of securities

One way to determine whether the market is bullish or bearish is to watch **market indexes** and averages, which use the performance of a representative sample of shares, bonds, or commodities as a guide to broader market activity. The most famous Canadian index is the S&P/TSX Composite Index, which measures the performance of the largest companies in the country; another well-known index is the TSX Venture Exchange, which consists of smaller and/or new companies.

The best-known American index is the Dow Jones Industrial Average (DJIA), which tracks the prices of 30 *blue-chip* or well-established stocks, each representing a particular sector of the US economy. Critics say the Dow is too narrow and too vulnerable to short-term swings, lacks the right shares, and gives too much weight to higher-priced shares. But advocates say the Dow's 30 shares serve as a general barometer of market conditions. In 1999 the *Wall Street Journal* editors (guardians of the Dow) replaced time-honoured blue-chip companies Chevron, Goodyear, Sears Roebuck, and Union Carbide with Microsoft, Intel, The Home Depot, and SBC Communications. More recently, in 2004, long-time components AT&T, Eastman Kodak, and International Paper were dropped for Verizon, American International Group, and Pfizer.[22] These changes should make the DJIA more representative of the "new economy."

Another widely watched index in Canada is the S&P/TSX 60 Index, which tracks the performance of 60 corporate shares, fewer than the S&P/TSX Composite Index. This index is weighted by market value, not by share price, so large companies carry far more weight than small ones.[23] A widely watched index in the United States is the Standard & Poor's 500 Stock Index (S&P 500), which tracks the performances of 500 corporate shares, many more than the DJIA. The Wilshire 5000 Index, which actually covers some 7000 shares, is the broadest index measuring US market performance. To get a sense of how technology shares are doing, check the NASDAQ Composite Index, covering more than 3000 over-the-counter shares, including many high-tech firms. You can also look at indexes to learn about the performance of foreign markets, such as Japan's Nikkei 225 Index and the United Kingdom's FTSE 100 Index.

Interpreting the Financial News

In addition to watching market trends, you will want to follow the securities you own and others that look like promising investments. For shares, you can turn to the stock exchange report in major daily newspapers. Exhibit 14.3 shows how to read this report, which includes high and low prices for the past 52 weeks, the number of shares

---

Exhibit 14.3   How to Read a Newspaper Stock Quotation

Even before you invest, you will want to follow the latest quotations for your stock. This table shows you how to read the newspaper stock quotation tables.

(1) 52-WEEK HIGH	(2) 52-WEEK LOW	STOCK	(3) SYM	(4) DIV	(5) YLD %	(6) PE	(7) VOL 000$	(8) HI	LOW	(9) LAST	(10) NET CHG
72.75	62.61	Bank of Montreal	BMO	2.72	4.10	12.30	2295.3	65.49	64.11	65.4	−1.97
101.76	76.69	Magna International	MG.A.	1.11	1.30	15.9	637.9	92	84.25	90.22	+5.48

1. **52-week high/low:** Indicates the highest and lowest trading price of the stock in the past 52 weeks plus the most recent week but not the most recent trading day (adjusted for splits). Stocks are quoted in dollars and cents. In most newspapers, boldfaced entries indicate stocks whose price changed by at least 4 percent, but only if the change was at least 75 cents a share.

2. **Stock:** The company's name may be abbreviated. A capital letter usually means a new word.

3. **Symbol:** Symbol under which this stock is traded on stock exchanges.

4. **Dividend:** Dividends are usually annual payments based on the last quarterly or semiannual declaration, although not all stocks pay dividends. Special or extra dividends or payments are identified in footnotes.

5. **Yield:** The percentage yield shows dividends as a percentage of the share price.

6. **PE:** Price-to-earnings ratio, calculated by dividing the stock's closing price by the earnings per share for the latest four quarters.

7. **Volume:** Daily total of shares traded, in hundreds. A listing of 888 indicates 88 800 shares were traded during that day.

8. **High/Low:** The stock's highest and lowest price for that day.

9. **Close:** Closing price of the stock that day.

10. **Net change:** Change in share price from the close of the previous trading day.

Common Stock Footnotes: d—new 52-week low; n—new; pf—preferred; s—stock split or stock dividend of 25 percent or more in previous 52 weeks; u—new 52-week high; v—trading halted on primary market; vi—in bankruptcy; x—ex dividend (the buyer won't receive a recently declared dividend, but the seller will)

traded (volume), and the change from the previous day's closing price. Canada started using decimals in 1996. Prior to that year, prices were quoted in fractions as small as 1/16. Using decimals in trading makes share prices easier for many investors to understand. Moreover, quoting shares down to the penny permits shares to be priced in smaller increments.[24]

price-earnings ratio
A ratio calculated by dividing a share's market price by its prior year's earnings per share

Included in the stock exchange report is the **price-earnings ratio**, or *p/e ratio* (also known as the *price-earnings multiple*), which is calculated by dividing a share's market price by its *prior* year's earnings per share. Some investors also calculate a forward p/e ratio using *expected* year earnings in the ratio's denominator. Bear in mind that if a share's p/e ratio is well below the industry norm, either the company is in trouble or it's an undiscovered gem with a relatively low share price. For more detailed data on a stock, consult the company's annual reports or documents filed with the TSX in Canada or with the Securities and Exchange Commission (SEC) in the United States.

To follow specific bonds, check the bond quotation tables in major newspapers (see Exhibit 14.4). When reading these tables, remember that the price is quoted as a percentage of the bond's value. For example, a $1000 bond shown closing at 65 actually sold at $650.

Newspapers and business publications also include tables of price quotations for investments such as mutual funds, commodities, options, and government securities (see Exhibit 14.5). These same publications also carry news about current challenges the securities industry is facing, securities regulations, reported frauds, and proposals to improve investor protection.

L.O. 7

Industry Challenges

The Canadian markets are facing numerous challenges. One of the largest complaints in Canada is the lack of a national securities regulator like the SEC in the United States. In Canada, the regulation of securities falls under the jurisdiction of the provinces, and laws can differ from province to province. The International Monetary Fund (IMF) has called on Canada to scrap the provincial system in favour of a national body. The Ontario Securities Commission (OSC) has emerged as the most powerful player of the 13 commissions and it regulates the largest markets in the country. Recently, Alberta Finance Minister Lyle Oberg made the following statement: "The current system of 13 provincial and territorial regulators is out of step with market participants and the rest

---

Exhibit 14.4   **How to Read a Newspaper Bond Quotation**

Newspapers often carry bond quotations in slightly different formats. They sometimes provide very basic information, noting the issuer, the coupon rate (interest paid on the bonds), and the price yield (what interest rates the bonds are paying now). Other formats include much more detail, as illustrated below. Please note that newspapers show prices as a percentage of the bond's value, which is typically $1000.

ISSUER	COUPON	MATURITY	BID PRICE	ASK PRICE (1)	BID YLD	ASK YLD (2)	YLD	CHG (3)	DATE
Royal Bank	5.000	2014-JAN-20	101.93		102.23	4.73	4.69	−0.042	
Bombardier	6.400	2010-DEC-22	101.15		101.88	5.67	5.22	−0.060	

1. **Company:** Name of company issuing the bond, such as Royal Bank, and bond description, such as 5.0 percent bond maturing in 2014.

2. **Coupon:** Interest the bond pays.

3. **Ask Yield:** Annual interest of $1000 bond divided by the closing price shown. The ask yield for the Royal Bank is approximately 4.75 percent.

Volume: Number of bonds traded (in thousands) that day.

Yield change: Change in bond price from the close of the previous trading day.

Exhibit 14.5 **How to Read a Newspaper Mutual Fund Quotation**

A mutual fund listing shows the new asset value of one share (the price at which one share is trading) and the change in trading price from one day to the next.

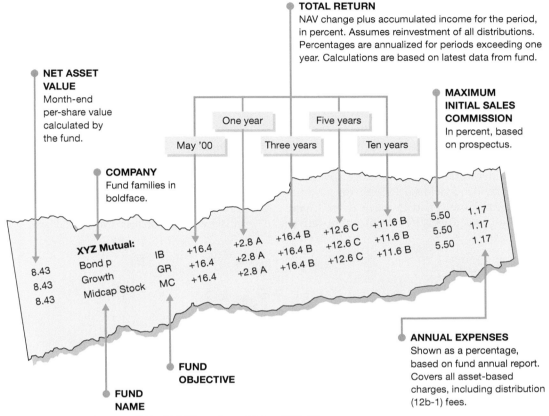

TOTAL RETURN
NAV change plus accumulated income for the period, in percent. Assumes reinvestment of all distributions. Percentages are annualized for periods exceeding one year. Calculations are based on latest data from fund.

NET ASSET VALUE
Month-end per-share value calculated by the fund.

MAXIMUM INITIAL SALES COMMISSION
In percent, based on prospectus.

COMPANY
Fund families in boldface.

ANNUAL EXPENSES
Shown as a percentage, based on fund annual report. Covers all asset-based charges, including distribution (12b-1) fees.

FUND OBJECTIVE

FUND NAME

Source: "How to Read the Monthly Performance Tables," *Wall Street Journal*, 5 June 2000, R2.

IN-CLASS NOTES

Analyzing Financial News
- A **bull market** occurs when stock prices have been rising for a long time; a **bear market** is a long-term trend of falling stock prices
- Key market indexes and averages include:
  - S&P/TSX Composite Index
  - Dow Jones Industrial Average (DJIA)
  - NASDAQ Composite Index
- Shares, bonds, mutual funds, commodities, options, and government securities are all quoted in major daily papers

Put the Experts to the Test: Stocks That Can Stand Up to the Storm

As you can understand from reading this section, stocks can rise and fall quickly, but predicting when they will rise, by how much, and when they will fall is no easy task. We have referred to bear markets and bull markets, preferred shares and common shares, and looked at other investments like bonds, debentures, trusts, and a variety of different types of mutual funds. When markets begin to move, investors look to experts for some guidance. During one particularly volatile period in mid-2007, the markets fell into retreat mode and charged back in quick spurts. When market waters are rough, many investors look for comfort. Investors will often turn to dividend yield stocks with low payouts to ride out the storm. However, in an article in the *Globe and Mail*, Yin Luo, executive director of quantitative

strategy at CIBC World Markets, proposed the following portfolio based on a more scientific approach that created defensive scores for stocks.[25]

Questions for Critical Thinking

1. Look up all of the stock symbols on the list and see how stable these predictions have been since July 31, 2007. Which stock performed the best? Which performed the worst? Were these stocks in fact a good choice? Beware of stock splits.
2. Select two of these stocks and visit their websites. Learn as much as you can about the companies. Why do you think that these companies were on the "stand up to the storm" list? Discuss their core businesses and industries in your analysis.

COMPANY	SYM	GICS SECTOR	PRICE $ JULY 31	DEFENSIVE SCORE %[1]
Saputo Inc.	SAP	Consmr Staples	51.10	3.71
CCL Ind., B	CCL.B	Materials	42.05	3.08
Canam Group	CAM	Materials	13.00	3.05
Linamar Corp.	LNR	Consmr Discret.	20.81	2.94
Rothmans Inc.	ROC	Consmr Staples	20.95	2.88
Cdn. Tire Corp.	CTC.A	Consmr Discret.	82.93	2.82
Atco. Ltd., I	ACO.X	Utilities	58.00	2.82
Empire Co., A	EMP.A	Consumer Staples	49.35	2.75
Potash Corp.*	POT	Materials	85.69	2.72
Stantec Inc.	STN	Industrials	34.21	2.64
TransAlta Corp.	TA	Utilities	30.38	2.61
Richelieu Hrdwr	RCH	Industrials	24.10	2.60
Toromont Ind.	TIH	Industrials	25.46	2.59
Atrium Innov.*	ATB	Consmr Staples	26.85	2.58
Indus. Alliance	IAG	Financials	39.52	2.57

Source: BLOOMBERG, COMPUSTAT, CPMS, IBES, AND CIBC WORLD MARKETS QUANTITATIVE STRATEGY

Reporting in USD: *[1] Defensive score is an equally weighted score of five factors: forward P/E, relative strength, trailing ROA, earnings risk, and market beta.

of the world." This was an important step that brings some hope to clearing the logjam since these words go against Alberta's long held position.[26]

The push toward round-the-clock trading is another challenge securities markets are facing. Extending the traditional trading hours of 9:30 a.m. to 4:00 p.m. (Eastern Standard Time) by adding early morning and late-night trading sessions is the next revolution sweeping Bay and Wall Streets. *After-hours trading* or *extended-hours trading* refers to the purchase and sale of publicly traded stocks after the major stock markets, such as the TSX, NYSE, and NASDAQ, close. Many securities exchanges now offer after-hours trading via ECNs that typically operate from 8:00 a.m. to 9:15 a.m. and 4:15 p.m. to 7:00 or 8:00 p.m., although some operate 24 hours a day. The biggest advantage to extended-hours trading is that it accommodates traders who live in regions outside the Eastern

Standard time zone. The biggest disadvantage, however, is lack of volume. Most institutional investors close up shop after the TSX and NYSE close. Nonetheless, to remain competitive, many traditional securities exchanges have already extended their trading hours.

Online trading is another phenomenon that has revolutionized the securities industry. When online trading first became popular in the 1990s, many full-service brokerages like Merrill Lynch resisted offering such services because they worried about losing lucrative commissions. But now, most full-service firms and chartered banks offer some form of online trading to remain competitive in the marketplace. Investors who choose online trading execute their trades via a brokerage firm's website instead of by phoning a firm's brokers. Convenience, control, and lower commissions are the main advantages of online trading. Still, online trading is not for everyone. When you trade online, you trade alone, with no one to check for mistakes or offer advice. Moreover, online trading websites have had their share of problems. The top five consumer complaints filed with the SEC against online brokers are: (1) failure to process orders or delays in executing orders; (2) difficulty in accessing one's account or contacting a broker; (3) errors in processing orders; (4) execution of orders at higher prices than posted on the website; and (5) errors and omissions in account records and documents.[27]

The online trading boom, which peaked along with the markets at the turn of the century, has been dropping ever since.

Regulation of Securities Markets

Whether you buy and sell securities online or use a traditional full-service house, your trades are governed by a network of provincial laws. Combined with industry self-regulation, these laws are designed to ensure that all investors receive accurate information and that no one artificially manipulates the market price of a given security. Trading in shares and bonds is monitored by 13 provincial and territorial exchange commissions, although the OSC dictates policy for the largest Canadian markets. Each participating exchange is a member of the Canadian Securities Administrators (CSA), which seeks to harmonize and regulate Canadian capital markets. The actual equity trading is monitored by the Market Regulations Services (RS), which reviews daily trades and transactions.

Filing Requirements

Companies must meet certain requirements (which include filing a blizzard of registration papers and reports) to be listed on any stock exchange. Similarly, brokers must operate according to the rules of the exchanges—rules that are largely designed to protect investors. Overseeing all of these details keeps the TSX Group, which runs the TSX and the Canadian Venture Exchange, along with the provincial exchange commissions and the RS very busy indeed. Every year it screens thousands of annual reports, handles investor complaints, and reviews prospectuses (a legal statement that describes the objectives of a specific investment) and proxy statements (a shareholder's written authorization giving someone else the authority to cast his or her vote). The different regulatory bodies all maintain websites that contain mountains of public documents that investors can browse, download, or print to learn more about publicly traded companies.[28]

Regulation Fair Disclosure

Regulation Fair Disclosure (FD) is a principal that is supposed to create a level playing field for all investors. Specifically, the regulation mandates that any news with the potential to affect the price of a share must be released to everyone simultaneously. In other words, the regulation prohibits companies from "selectively disclosing" important information (like earnings estimates) to big institutional shareholders and market analysts ahead of regular investors. Otherwise, early news recipients would be able to "make a profit or avoid a loss at the expense of those kept in the dark."[29] In spite of its good intentions, the regulation could have unintended consequences, say critics. Some worry that instead of giving small and large investors equal access to market-sensitive information, the regulation could cut down on the amount of information received by everyone.

Securities Fraud

The combination of a "get-rich" mindset and the huge number of people now investing online has resulted in a rise in the number of Internet stock scams. Today, with just an email address list and a chat-board alias or two, penny-stock promoters can dupe tens of thousands (if not millions) of investors by making false claims about a company, watching investors eager to make a fast profit pump up the company's share price, then selling or dumping their penny shares at inflated prices and pocketing a handsome profit. This practice is getting more difficult to stop as the practice of pump-and-dump spamming has grown over the years. According to Commtouch, an international email security firm, approximately 24 billion unsolicited spam emails are sent each day on the subject of stock scams.[30]

In fact, the problem has become so pervasive that the US Department of Justice, the Federal Trade Commission, the US Attorneys offices, the FBI, and the RCMP have stepped up efforts to police such fraud. Even NASDAQ has developed an Internet search engine to find phrases such as "too good to be true," and it monitors securities' chat forums for fraudulent or misleading information.[31] As an investor, your best defence against fraud is to carefully research securities before you buy and to steer clear of any investment that seems too good to be true (see Exhibit 14.6).

Two particular forms of securities fraud making the headlines today are insider trading and accounting fraud. **Insider trading** occurs when people buy or sell a stock based on information that is not available to the general public, such as a company merger or new discovery. Insider trading can produce big profits for the unscrupulous, but it can also claim many victims. Acquisition companies, for example, are forced to pay higher-than-expected premiums to buy a target company when leaks trigger a run-up in the target's stock price. Shareholders who rely on the integrity of corporate executives can lose billions while friends of loose-lipped company insiders profit from the information. In a very famous case, Martha Stewart sold 4000 shares of ImClone Systems one day

insider trading
Use of material non-public information to make an investment profit

Learning from Business Blunders

OOPS

You know that e-commerce has truly spanned the globe when you can get scammed out of money from halfway around the world. Anyone with an email account has probably seen the Nigerian investment scam. Someone claiming to be connected to somebody connected to the Nigerian government or the national oil company claims to have a way to shuttle millions of dollars out of the country if only you'll provide some up-front money to shake the whole thing loose. Sounds crazy, but the scheme has already defrauded hopeful email recipients out of more than $100 million in the United States alone. One retired man from Florida shelled out more than $300 000 before he realized he'd been had.

WHAT YOU CAN LEARN

If it sounds too good to be true, it is. This rule applies in the stock market, in the grocery market—pretty much anywhere on planet Earth. If you're ever tempted by this or any other investment pitch, stop and ask yourself a couple of questions: (1) Why are they offering this to *me*, out of the 5 or 6 billion people in the world? (2) What would have to happen for me to make any money from this deal? If you can't make the connection between your investment and the promised payoff, that's a good sign there won't be one.[32]

Exhibit 14.6   **Ten Questions to Ask Before You Invest**

You can avoid getting taken in an online stock scam by asking yourself the following 10 questions before you invest.

1. Is the investment registered with the SEC and your province's securities commission?
2. Have you read the company's audited financial statements?
3. Is the person recommending this investment a registered broker?
4. What does the person promoting the investment have to gain?
5. If the tip came from an online bulletin board or email, is the author identifiable or using an alias? Is there any reason to trust that person?
6. Are you being pressured to act before you can evaluate the investment?
7. Does the investment promise you'll get rich quick, using words like "guaranteed," "high return," or "risk free"?
8. Does the investment match your objectives? Could you afford to lose all of the money you invest?
9. How easy would it be to sell the investment later? Remember, stocks with fewer shares are easy for promoters to manipulate and hard for investors to sell if the price starts falling.
10. Does the investment originate overseas? If yes, beware: It is tougher to track money sent abroad and harder for burned investors to have recourse to justice.

Source: Amy Feldman, "The Seedy World of Online Stock Scams," *Money*, February 2000, 143–148.

before the Food and Drug Administration rejected ImClone's application for approval of a cancer drug. The announcement sent ImClone's shares tumbling. Stewart was a close friend of ImClone's former CEO, Samuel D. Waksal, who allegedly used the inside information to tip off his family members, who also sold their ImClone shares.[33] Such insider trading is punishable by a jail term, as Martha Stewart found out.

Accounting trickery is another form of securities fraud, as discussed in Chapter 13. In fact, the unusually high number of companies engaging in accounting tricks and fraud at the turn of this century has not only kept regulators busy but taken its toll on Canadian and US securities markets and the global economy. Individuals who were highly respected are serving jail time or awaiting sentencing for their actions, and a host of respected companies like Nortel have taken away the unquestioned confidence that many investors had for blue-chip companies.

IN-CLASS NOTES

Regulating Security Markets

- There are **13 exchange commissions** in Canada, but the lack of a **central regulator** is a problem
- Equity trading is monitored by the **Market Regulations Services (RS)** who monitor daily trades and transactions
- Under **fair disclosure (FD)** any news that can influence stock prices must be released to everyone simultaneously
- Two forms of securities fraud in the headlines are **insider trading** and **accounting fraud**

BEHIND THE SCENES

Separating Facts from Fiction: Canadian Bank Mergers

There is no doubt that the restriction on bank mergers stopped Canadian banking institutions from quickly increasing their overall size and moving forward under more equal terms with international competitors. These restrictions forced the companies to look inwards instead of outwards to find new ways to improve efficiency. Nearly a decade after the decision, Canadian banks ranked number one in the world in terms of shareholders' return and earned a whopping $19 billion in net profits in fiscal 2006, breaking the previous mark by $6 billion. That's the good news. Under the current tight rules, these banks are maximizing their somewhat reduced opportunities.

The bad news was recently highlighted by former Bank of Canada governor David Dodge: "Unless regulators lift restrictions, Canada could become increasingly less efficient in the financial markets. With the Royal Bank being only one-quarter the size of the world's largest banks, it is ultimately less attractive to international business." While Mr. Dodge is a long-time advocate of allowing Canadian banks to become more globally competitive, he has not been this blunt before on the issue of mergers. This idea was further expressed in mid-2007 in a paper published by the C.D. Howe Institute. Thorsten Koeppl, assistant economics professor at Queen's University, and James MacGee, assistant economics professor at the University of Western Ontario, said that "rules should be changed to let banks merge and allow foreign financial players easier access to the Canadian market." According to the report, mergers would allow some Canadian banks to become bigger international players while allowing others to become more efficient specialized players in the domestic market. There is a sense of urgency to see concrete actions soon. According to the paper, even if the two largest Canadian banks were to merge today they would only barely break into the top 25 largest banks. The message: Act now before it's too late.

Despite these alarming remarks, Canadian banks are using every opportunity at their disposal to grow and compete. TD Banknorth, owned by Toronto-Dominion Bank, recently purchased Commerce Bancorp, Inc. and its 460 US branches for US$8.5 billion. Not bad for a company that has lost some of its international power over the years. The other major Canadian banks are actively looking for and completing deals to open or acquire branches in locations around the world as well.

Consumer fears were a major force in stopping these domestic merger deals last time. Consumer groups and small businesses opposed the mergers, believing that merged banks would reduce expenses by cutting services, employees, and branches. Furthermore, they worried that in some small communities bank mergers would eliminate consumer choice. Opponents argue that Canada is too small a country to host such large banks and the government should stop any mergers while forcing the banks to provide better services. Is this issue truly reborn? Will the doors open? If they do you can be sure that the talks and the mergers will heat up quickly and the Canadian retail banking business will be altered forever.[34]

Critical Thinking Questions

1. Public speeches by high-ranking government officials tend to be very diplomatic and carefully constructed. In his former position as Bank of Canada governor, David Dodge was very aware of the importance of word selection. Why do you think he was so direct in this particular speech?

2. The government seemed to be considering the rights of Canadian citizens as consumers when stopping the mergers. Do you think it gave equal thought to Canadian citizens as bank stakeholders? Why or why not?

3. Do you think the government was right to prevent the bank mergers back in 1998? Why or why not? Based on what you have read, should the government allow bank mergers?

Learn More Online

Visit and review the website of the Canadian Bankers Association (www.cba.ca). What are the association's views on the changes in the marketplace? How do these views differ from those expressed by the Canadian Federation of Independent Business (www.cfib.ca)? Conduct your own search online using various search engines. What additional information can you find?

TEST YOUR KNOWLEDGE

Questions for Review

1. What are the various forms of money? Describe each form in some detail.

2. What purpose does a line of credit serve for a business?

3. Explain the purpose of the bond ratings system. What is the difference between a AAA-rated bond and a B-rated bond?

4. What is meant by an over-the-counter (OTC) market?

5. What is the difference between a bear market and a bull market?

Questions for Analysis

6. How are deposit institutions different from non-deposit financial institutions? Provide examples.

7. Why did income trusts gain such popularity in the Canadian marketplace in recent years? How has the atmosphere changed since the new rules were put in place?

8. When might an investor sell a stock short? What risks are involved in selling short?

9. How does the CDIC help bring stability and calm to the Canadian retail banking market?

10. **Ethical Considerations.** You work in the research and development department of a large corporation and have been involved in a discovery that could lead to a new, profitable product. News of the discovery has not been made public. Is it legal for you to buy shares in the company? Now assume the same scenario, but you talk to your friend about your discovery while dining at a restaurant. The person at the next table overhears the conversation. Is it legal for the eavesdropper to buy the company's shares before the public announcement of the news?

Questions for Application

11. What are the advantages and disadvantages of using cash, cheques, credit cards, and debit cards to pay for goods and services?

12. If you were thinking about buying shares of Bombardier, under what circumstances would you place a market order, a limit order, an open order, and a discretionary order?

13. **Integrated.** Besides watching market indexes, which economic statistics discussed in Chapter 1 might investors want to monitor? Why?

14. **Integrated.** Look back at Chapter 6 and review the discussion of mission statements. Suppose you were thinking about purchasing 100 common shares of General Electric. Why might you want to first review the company's mission statement? What would you be looking for in the company's mission statement that could help you decide whether or not to invest?

PRACTISE YOUR KNOWLEDGE

SHARPENING YOUR COMMUNICATION SKILLS

Interviewing a broker is one of the most important steps you can take before hiring that broker to execute your trades or manage your funds and investment portfolio. Practise your communication skills by developing two sets of questions:

1. Questions you might ask to help you decide whether you would use his or her services.

2. Questions you might pose to help you evaluate the merits of purchasing a specific security.

BUILDING YOUR TEAM SKILLS

You and your team are going to pool your money and invest $5000. Before you plunge into any investments, how can you prepare yourselves to be good investors? First, consider your group's goals. What will you and your teammates do with any profits generated by your investments? Once you have agreed on a goal for your team's profits, think about how much money you will need to achieve this goal and how soon you want to achieve it.

Next, think about how much risk you personally are willing to take to achieve the goal. Bear in mind that safer investments generally offer lower returns than riskier investments—and certain investments, such as shares, can lose money. Now hold a group discussion to find a level of risk that feels comfortable for everyone on your team.

Once your team has decided how much risk to take, consider which investments are best suited to your group's goals and chosen risk level. Will you choose shares, bonds, a combination of both, or other securities? What are the advantages and disadvantages of each type of investment for your team's situation? Then come to a decision about specific investment opportunities—particular shares, for example—that your group would like to investigate further.

Compare your group's goal, risk level, and investment possibilities with those of the other teams in your class and discuss the differences and similarities you see.

EXPAND YOUR KNOWLEDGE

DISCOVERING CAREER OPPORTUNITIES

Think you might be interested in a job in the securities and commodities industry? This industry has one of the most highly educated and skilled workforces of any industry. And the requirements for entry are high—most employees have a university degree plus additional training. Log on to the Investment Dealers Association of Canada at www.ida.ca and read up on educational and employment opportunities available in the field. Then answer the following questions:

1. What are the licensing and continuing education requirements for securities brokers?

2. What is the typical starting position for many people in the securities industry?

3. What factors are expected to contribute to the projected long-term growth of this industry?

DEVELOPING YOUR RESEARCH SKILLS

Since the turn of the century, the shares of several high-profile companies, such as Tyco, Enron, and WorldCom, tumbled following the disclosures of negative company information. Use computer resources or business journals to find a company whose disclosure of negative information dramatically affected its securities. Then perform some research on that company so you can answer the following questions:

1. On what exchanges do the company's shares trade and under what ticker symbol?

2. What negative information did the company disclose? When? Did the company commit a fraudulent act? How did the information affect the company as a whole?

3. How did the negative information affect the company's securities? What was the company's share price prior to the release of the negative information? Following the release of the information? What was the shares' 52-week high and low during the year the disclosure was made?

STUDY GUIDE

SUMMARY OF LEARNING OBJECTIVES

1. Highlight the functions, characteristics, and common forms of money

Money functions as a medium of exchange, a measure of value, and a store of value. It must be divisible, portable, durable, stable, and difficult to counterfeit. Common forms of money include currency, such as coins, bills, traveller's cheques, cashier cheques, and money orders; demand deposits, like chequing accounts; and time deposits, such as savings accounts, certificates of deposit, and money-market deposit accounts.

2. Discuss the responsibilities and insurance methods of the Canadian Deposit Insurance Corporation (CDIC)

The CDIC is a federal insurance program that protects deposits in banks up to $100 000 if a member bank fails.

3. Discuss the Canadian banking industry

The Canadian banking industry consists of large chartered banks operating small branches throughout the country with little influence from foreign competitors and trust companies. The Big Six banks are Royal Bank of Canada, Scotiabank, Canadian Imperial Bank of Commerce, Toronto Dominion Bank, Bank of Montreal, and National Bank. They control the majority of the nation's assets and are currently seeking a mandate from the government to merge with one another so they can compete more effectively on the world stage.

4. Differentiate among a share's par value, its market value, and its book value

Par value is the dollar value assigned to a share for book-keeping and for dividend calculations. Market value is the price at which a share is currently selling. Book value is the portion of a corporation's net assets represented by a single common share.

5. Highlight the distinguishing features of common shares, preferred shares, bonds, and mutual funds

Common shares give shareholders an ownership interest in the company, the right to elect directors and vote on important issues, and the chance to earn dividends and share in the fortunes of the company—while limiting the shareholder's liability to the price paid for the shares. Preferred shares usually provide shareholders a higher dividend than common shares and a preferred claim over common shareholders if the corporation fails. Certain types of preferred shares have special privileges. Bonds are long-term loans investors make to the issuing entity in return for a stated interest amount. The loan or principal is paid back to the bondholder over the life of the bond. Bonds may be secured, unsecured, or convertible. They may be issued by corporations or federal, provincial, and municipal agencies. Mutual funds are pools of money drawn from many investors to buy a variety of shares, bonds, and other marketable securities. The primary benefit of this investment is diversification.

6. Differentiate among an auction exchange, dealer exchange, and electronic communication network (ECN)

Auction exchanges such as the Toronto Stock Exchange and the New York Stock Exchange funnel all buy and sell orders into one centralized location. Dealer exchanges like NASDAQ are decentralized marketplaces in which dealers, known as market makers, are connected electronically to handle buy and sell orders without a single, centralized trading floor. Electronic computerized networks (ECNs) match buy and sell orders directly (cutting out the market makers and specialists); ECNs operate globally, and they operate economically.

7. Explain how government regulation of securities trading tries to protect investors

The government tries to prevent fraud in the securities markets by requiring companies to file registration papers, fulfill certain requirements, and file periodic information reports so that investors receive accurate information. Government regulations also control the listing of companies on stock exchanges and prohibit such fraudulent acts as improper release of information, insider trading, stock scams, and other acts designed to deceive investors.

KEY TERMS

auction exchange   (454)
authorized shares   (448)
automated teller machines
    (ATMs)   (446)
bear market   (457)
bond   (449)
broker   (456)
bull market   (457)
Canada Savings Bonds   (450)
cheques   (442)
convertible bonds   (450)
credit cards   (442)
currency   (441)
day order   (456)
dealer exchanges   (454)
debentures   (450)
debit cards   (442)
demand deposits   (441)
discretionary order   (456)

electronic communication networks
    (ECNs)   (455)
electronic funds transfer systems
    (EFTS)   (446)
income trusts   (452)
insider trading   (464)
issued shares   (448)
limit order   (456)
line of credit   (445)
margin trading   (456)
market indexes   (458)
market makers   (455)
market order   (456)
money   (441)
money-market funds   (451)
mutual funds   (451)
NASDAQ (National Association of
    Securities Dealers Automated
    Quotations)   (454)

open order   (456)
over-the-counter (OTC)
    market   (454)
par value   (449)
price-earnings ratio   (460)
primary market   (454)
principal   (449)
secondary market   (454)
secured bonds   (450)
securities   (448)
short selling   (456)
smart cards   (442)
stock exchanges   (454)
stock specialist   (454)
stock split   (448)
stop order   (456)
time deposits   (441)
Treasury bills   (450)
unissued shares   (448)

QUESTIONS

Multiple Choice   Circle the correct answer and then check the answers in the back of the book to chart your progress.

1. What are corporate bonds that are backed only by the reputation of the insurer called?

   a. T-bills
   b. Debentures
   c. Savings bonds
   d. Convertible bonds

2. Which of the following is *not* one of the important characteristics of money?

   a. Money must be engraved with the picture of famous leaders.
   b. Money must be divisible in units small enough to handle day-to-day purchases.
   c. Money must be easy to carry, even when conveying a great amount of value.
   d. Money must be difficult to produce.

3. Which of the following best describes the difference between credit cards and debit cards?

   a. Credit cards charge an annual fee; debit cards do not.
   b. Debit cards are only available to those customers with the best credit scores.

   c. Credit cards permit the buyer to defer payment, but debit cards immediately deduct the amount of the purchase from the cardholder's chequing account.
   d. Credit cards require immediate payment, but debit cards allow payments to be deferred.

4. Which of the following is the key advantage for consumers using EFTS, or direct deposit of paycheques?

   a. Customers do not have to wait in line to deposit their paycheques.
   b. It is cheaper for banks to process EFTS deposits.
   c. It is easier for employers to pay their workers with EFTS.
   d. Government regulations require businesses to pay their workers using EFTS.

5. Which of the following is an advantage of owning shares in a corporation rather than owning bonds issued by the same corporation?

   a. Shares guarantee both quarterly income and price appreciation.
   b. If the company does well, the dividend on the shares may increase, but the interest on the bond will not.

c. Shareholders get paid first if and when the company disposes of its assets.

d. Common shares are guaranteed by a government agency.

6. Gary notices that IBM's common shares are quoted at a price of $50 per share. How is the price of a common share determined?

   a. The issuing company determines the "par value," which is the amount Gary will have to pay.

   b. Prices are determined in the market with the interaction of buyers and sellers. Gary's broker forwards his order to buy to the stock market, where it interacts with other buyers and sellers.

   c. The various exchange commissions set the prices of every share at the close of business.

   d. Gary must pay the "book value," which the accountants calculate every quarter.

7. Standard & Poor's and Moody's rate bonds based on the issuers' financial strength. Why do some investors choose to invest in low-rated "junk bonds"?

   a. Some investors believe that a higher interest rate is enough compensation to assume a greater risk.

   b. Some investors prefer the low-rated bonds because they are safer.

c. The lower-rated bonds are protected with collateral or guarantees whereas the higher-rated bonds are not.

d. Investors are randomly assigned the bonds by the brokers, without regard to ratings.

8. Which of the following securities has the shortest maturity?

   a. Treasury bills
   b. Corporate bonds
   c. Debentures
   d. Canada Savings Bonds

9. Which of the following terms describes how a small group of people can use the web to convince potential investors to buy and raise the price of a stock?

   a. Convince and crop
   b. Hawk and dove
   c. Pump and dump
   d. Talk up and drop down

10. Which of the following is *not* considered a deposit financial institution?

    a. Chartered banks
    b. Credit unions and caisses populaires
    c. Trust companies
    d. Pension funds

True/False

1. True or false? An *open* order tells the broker to sell if the price of your security drops below the price you set, protecting you from losing more money if prices are dropping.

2. True or false? Banks make their money by charging more interest on loans than the interest they pay on deposits.

3. True or false? The par value of a share refers to the value assigned to a share for use in bookkeeping and in calculating dividends. It is not the same thing as the market value of a share.

4. True or false? Preferred shareholders are paid only after the common shareholders receive their dividends.

5. True or false? When the stock market experiences a long-term period of falling prices it known as a bear market.

Fill-in-the-Blank

1. A _____ account earns a higher interest rate than a regular savings account, but you cannot withdraw the funds for a stated period of time. If you make an early withdrawal you will lose some or all of the interest you've earned.

2. _____ are similar to debit cards; however, these plastic cards contain tiny computer chips that can store amounts of money (from the user's bank

account) and selected data (such as shipping address, credit card information, frequent-flyer account numbers, health and insurance details, or other personal information).

3. When a _____ occurs there is an increase in the number of shares of ownership that each share certificate represents with a proportionate drop in each share's value.

4. _____ are non-profit, member-owned organizations that take deposits from members, such as a company's employees or union members and offers the same services as a chartered bank.

5. A _____ is an arrangement where a bank agrees, for a specified period (usually one year), to lend a specified amount of money as a short-term loan.

6. To help consumers gain peace of mind, the _____ was formed. The insurance covers banks, trust companies, and loan companies for up to $100 000 per depositor.

7. A _____ is a method of raising money in which the issuing organization borrows from an investor and issues a written pledge to make regular interest payments and then repay the borrowed amount later.

8. _____ are financial organizations that pool money from many investors to buy a diversified mix of stocks, bonds, or other securities.

9. _____ invest in a carefully chosen mix of stocks and bonds.

10. If you believe that a share's price is about to drop, you may choose a trading procedure known as _____. With this procedure, you sell shares you borrow from a broker in the hope of buying it back later at a lower price.

Companion Website

See It on the WEB

Visit the Companion Website at **www.pearsoned.ca/bovee**, review the exercises, and complete the following assignments for Chapter 14:

1. Visit the Bank of Canada and US Treasury
2. Stock Up at the TSX and NYSE
3. Invest Wisely, Don't Be a Fool

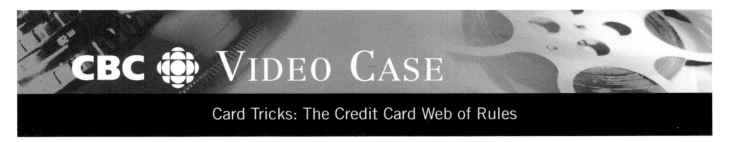

CBC ❖ VIDEO CASE

Card Tricks: The Credit Card Web of Rules

LEARNING OBJECTIVES

The purpose of this video is to help you

1. Understand the fundamental terms and conditions of the typical credit card contract that financial institutions have with consumers.

2. Identify major pitfalls of common credit card practices that consumers are often unaware of.

3. Develop strategies to capitalize on the current system and avoid unnecessary fees.

SYNOPSIS

Many young consumers receive their first credit card and are totally unaware of the consequences of overspending and carrying balances. The terms of credit card agreements are difficult to read and are heavily slanted in favour of the financial lending institution. Some credit card users who make the initial mistake of overspending learn their lesson and eventually come to respect the basic rules. Some people never fully understand the heavy burden of a 20 percent interest rate because they can't be bothered. These consumers simply focus on paying their minimum monthly payment. This is a dangerous practice that eats up funds quickly. It is like running on a treadmill; you need to run fast just to stay in the same place. Unfortunately, in the case of credit card debt, you don't lose weight—you burn financial resources and if you are not careful you may find that the speed of the treadmill is increasing and you are unable to keep up.

This video does not focus on fundamental spending problems associated with credit cards. It digs deeper to expose practices that even some of the most knowledgeable

consumers are unaware of (i.e., hidden exchange fees). The reporters in this clip provide real-life examples of consumers that feel like they have been cheated. Each scenario is clearly described and then the covert rules, written by lawyers for lawyers, are re-written by the CBC reporters in clear, no-nonsense (albeit a bit sarcastic) language. The basic message is that consumers should take a look at their agreement carefully, understand the rules, and also carefully examine their statements each month to avoid unnecessary credit problems. Credit cards provide convenience but they must be used with some caution.

Discussion Questions

1. *For analysis*: Do you believe that the consumers in the video were justified in making formal complaints or lawsuits for their particular issues? Which case surprised you the most?

2. *For application*: Visit two Canadian bank websites and find the current interest rate charged by each institution for their line of credit cards. What was the highest rate at each bank? What was the lowest rate charged? Did they offer low-interest-rate cards? What sort of conditions did they have?

3. *For debate*: Is it ethical for banks and other financial institutions to charge consumers upwards of 20 percent interest on credit cards when the prime rate has been fairly low in recent years?

ONLINE EXPLORATION

Visit the Canadian Bankers Association website at www.cba .ca and type the following into the search area: "interest rates and credit cards." What type of information does the CBA provide? Do they provide any consumer tips? What did you learn about interest rates?

ON LOCATION VIDEO CASE

Accounting for Billions of Burgers: McDonald's

LEARNING OBJECTIVES

The purpose of this video is to help you

1. Understand the challenges a company may face in managing financial information from operations in multiple countries.

2. Consider how management and investors use the financial information reported by a public company.

3. Recognize how different laws and monetary systems can affect the accounting activities of a global corporation.

SYNOPSIS

Collecting, analyzing, and reporting financial data from more than 30 000 restaurants in 119 countries is no easy task, as the accounting experts at McDonald's know all too well. Every month, the individual restaurants send in their sales figures to be consolidated with data from other restaurants at the local or country level. From there, the figures are sent to country-group offices and then to one of three major regional offices before going to their final destination at McDonald's headquarters in Oak Brook, Illinois. In the past, financial information arrived in Illinois in bits and pieces, sent by courier, mail, or fax. Today, local and regional offices log on to a special secure website and enter their month-end figures, enabling the corporate controller to quickly produce financial statements and projections for internal and external use.

Discussion Questions

1. *For analysis*: Why does McDonald's use "constant currency" comparisons when reporting its financial results?

2. *For analysis*: What types of assets might McDonald's list for depreciation in its financial statements?

3. *For application*: What effect do the corporate income tax rates in the countries where McDonald's operates have on the income statements prepared in local offices?

4. *For application*: What problems might arise if individual McDonald's restaurants were required to enter sales data directly into the company's centralized accounting website, instead of following the current procedure of sending it through country and regional channels?

5. *For debate*: To help investors and analysts better assess the company's worldwide financial health, should McDonald's be required to disclose detailed financial results for every country and region? Support your chosen position.

ONLINE EXPLORATION

Visit the McDonald's corporate website at **www.mcdonalds.com/corp.html**, locate the most recent financial report (quarterly or annual), and examine both overall and regional results. What aspects of its results does McDonald's highlight in this report? What does McDonald's say about its use of constant currency reporting? Which regions are doing particularly well? Which are lagging? How does management explain any differences in performance?

Banking tradition hangs on
Even those who bank online still use traditional services.
For example, 46% say they visit a branch in person.

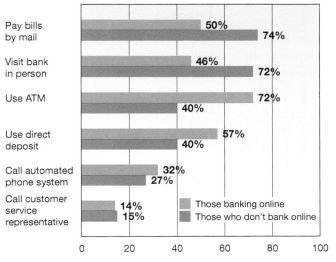

When cyberbanks (Internet-only banks) began popping up in the late 1990s, many believed they would revolutionize retail banking. Lower transactions costs, no physical building costs, and smaller staffs than physical banks meant that Internet banks could afford to offer customers higher interest rates on deposits, little or no transaction fees, and lower interest rates on loans. Furthermore, because they existed in cyberspace, customers could bank at home 24 hours a day, seven days a week. They could move money from a savings account to a chequing account—or even into the stock market—whenever they pleased. But the promise that banking customers would flock to cyberbanks and give traditional banks a run for their money never materialized. Certainly they have a place in the economy, but they have not replaced traditional institutions.

Tough Sell

Why didn't cyberbanks take over? Like most Internet-only start-ups, cyberbanks faced the following roadblocks:

- *Lack of name recognition.* To attract new customers, cyberbanks launched their e-businesses with expensive marketing campaigns, eliminating much of the Internet cost advantage.
- *No friendly banker.* Customers appreciated the cost advantages that cyberbanks offered, but without branches many online banks lacked a concrete place for

customers to resolve problems. Customers wanted the assurance that someone was there (in person) if they needed help.

- *Limited services.* Customers still needed to venture into the physical world to get services cyberbanks did not offer: ATMs, safe deposit boxes, or business loans. Moreover, without a network of ATMs, cyber-customers faced hefty ATM fees and were required to deposit money into their cyberaccounts by mail.

To overcome these challenges, some cyberbanks got physical by opening service centres, setting up kiosks, and establishing ATM networks. Others offered rebates on ATM surcharges their customers paid to other banks. Still others, such as Juniper Financial in the United States, formed alliances with stores like Mail Boxes Etc. so customers could deposit cheques nationwide. But these actions were not enough to fend off the awakening giants.

Bricks-and-Mortar Banks Wake Up

Rather than give traditional (bricks-and-mortar) banks a run for their money, cyberbanks gave them ideas. Some traditional banks established partnerships with key cyberbank players or swallowed them up altogether. Others, such as Bank One in the United States, established their own virtual banks—keeping them separate entities. But in spite of their efforts, few traditional banks generated profits from their online banking ventures. Cyberbanking did not reach the mass appeal needed to justify the huge investment and operating costs involved.

From Competitive Edge to Commodity

The playing field has changed considerably since virtual banking first emerged. Online banking has moved from having a competitive edge to being a commodity. Today, 42 percent of Canadians do at least some of their banking online, and online banking continues to grow rapidly. Almost all banks offer some form of online banking services, such as transferring money, bill payments, loan applications, and account management. Some, such as TD, allow customers to set up a personal account and aggregate all the services they use into one web page interface at **www.TDbank.ca**. But in spite of the rising use of online banking services, there is still a lot of work to be done before pure cyberbanks achieve the potential they once promised.[35]

Questions for Critical Thinking

1. What challenges did cyberbanks face in the competitive banking environment, and what steps did they take to overcome these challenges?

2. Why did most pure Internet banks close up or fold into their parent organizations?

3. What banking services, if any, do you perform online? What do you like and dislike about banking online?

BUSINESS PLANPRO EXERCISES EXERCISES

Review Appendix B, Your Business Plan to learn how to use Business PlanPro Software so you can complete these exercises.

Think Like a Pro

Objective: By completing these exercises you will become acquainted with the sections of a business plan that address a company's financial and operational projections. You will use the sample business plan for Fantastic Florals (listed as Import—Artificial Flowers in the Sample Plan Browser) in this exercise.

1. Identify the source(s) Fantastic Florals will use to fund its start-up costs. Why is it important to indicate how much start-up money will be used to fund assets versus expenses?

2. Review the financial assumptions, sales tables and graphs, and other financial information included in the Fantastic Florals plan. Assuming the financial projections are on target, would an investment of $75 000 for a 20 percent ownership stake in the company be prudent? Explain your answer. Which financial statement(s) did you use to make your decision?

3. Examine the company's projected gross margin for the years covered by the plan. How does Fantastic Florals' gross margin compare with the industry profile? How might a potential investor view this comparison?

Create Your Own Business Plan

Return to the plan you are developing for your own business. How will you categorize your revenue and expense items? Will you break down your sales by product type, by service, or by location? What general operating and product-related expenses will you incur? Set up your basic revenue and expense categories and build the framework for your profit and loss statement. How do the categories in your plan compare to those used by Fantastic Florals?

Appendix A
The Canadian Legal System

THE CANADIAN LEGAL SYSTEM

We have discussed various legal issues throughout this text and referred to a number of regulatory agencies, such as the Competition Bureau, the Ontario Securities Commission (OSC), and the Federal Trade Commission (FTC), whose function is to protect society from the potential abuses of business. In this appendix we explore how the Canadian government protects its citizens from corporate wrongdoing through its legal system. The law protects both businesses and individuals against those who threaten society. It also spells out accepted ways of performing many essential business functions—along with the penalties for failing to comply. In other words, like the average person, companies—no matter how big or small—must obey the law or face the consequences. For example, a small Vancouver-based graphic design company named Dossier fought and won a battle against Staples when the giant company launched a new line of small office stores in Montreal under the Dossier banner. After sending letters and hiring lawyers and investigators, the small 15-person operation with sales of about $1.5 million managed to convince the giant to make a name change. Officially, Staples contends that the change was due to consumer feedback. Regardless, this case demonstrates the power of legal rights. Staples made the right move before investing any more funds in their new retail concept.[1]

As you read this material, keep in mind that many companies conduct business overseas. Thus, in addition to knowing Canadian laws, these companies must also be familiar with **international law**, the principles, customs, and rules that govern the relationships between sovereign states and international organizations and persons.[2] Successful global business requires an understanding of the domestic laws of trading partners as well as those of established international trading standards and legal guidelines.

Dossier, a small Vancouver-based graphic design company, fought and won a battle against Staples when the company launched a new line of small office stores in Montreal under the name Dossier.

Global companies like Coca-Cola must have a firm grasp of international law.

Sources of Law

A *law* is a rule developed by a society to govern the conduct of and relationships among its members. The Canadian constitution is the foundation for Canadian laws and consists of two unique parts. The first part deals with the division of power and clarifies jurisdictions between federal and provincial government, while the second part is the *Charter of Rights and Freedoms*, which enshrines the fundamental rights and freedoms of Canadians. Because the constitution is a general document, laws offering specific answers to specific problems are constantly embellishing its basic principles. However, law is not static; it develops in response to changing conditions and social standards. Individual laws originate in various ways: through legislative action (*statutory law*), through administrative rulings (*administrative law*), and through customs and judicial precedents (*common law*). To one degree or another, all three forms of law affect businesses. Moreover, at times the three forms of law may overlap so that the differences between them become indistinguishable. Nonetheless, in cases where the three forms of law appear to conflict, statutory law generally prevails.

Statutory Law

Statutory law is law written by the federal or provincial governments. One very important part of statutory law affecting businesses is each province's *Sale of Goods Act*, which is based on the English *Sale of Goods Act* that was first enacted in 1893. The Act defines the legal framework for business transactions between producers and consumers and has remained virtually unchanged for the past century.

Administrative Law

Once laws have been passed by the federal or provincial government, an administrative agency or commission may take responsibility for enforcing them. That agency may be called on to clarify a regulation's intent, often by consulting representatives of the affected industry. The administrative agency may then write more specific regulations, which are considered **administrative law**. In Canada, many business activities, including employment standards and labour relations, fall under the control of such regulatory bodies.

Common Law

Common law, the type of law that comes out of courtrooms and judge's decisions, began in England many centuries ago and was brought to Canada by colonists. It is applied in all provinces except Quebec, which has adopted a hybrid type of legal system. Quebec follows Canadian common law when dealing with criminal matters, but in non-criminal matters the civil code is applied. Common law is sometimes called the "unwritten law" to distinguish it from government Acts and administrative regulations, which are written documents. Instead, common law is established through customs and the precedents set in courtroom proceedings.

Despite its unwritten nature, common law has great continuity, which derives from the doctrine of ***stare decisis*** (Latin for "stand by decisions"). What the *stare decisis* doctrine means is that a judge's decisions establish a precedent for deciding future cases of a similar nature. Because common law is based on what has been decided before, the legal framework develops gradually.

In Canada, common law is applied and interpreted in the system of courts. Common law thus develops through the decisions in trial courts, special courts, and appellate courts. The **Supreme Court of Canada** sets precedents for the entire legal system. Lower courts must abide by these precedents as they pertain to similar cases.

Business Law

Although businesses must comply with the full body of laws that apply to individuals, a subset of laws can be defined more precisely as **business law**. This includes those elements of law that directly affect business activities. For example, laws pertaining to business licensing, employee safety, and corporate income taxes can all be considered business law. For the remainder of this appendix, we will examine some of the specific categories of laws affecting businesses, including torts; contracts; agency; property transactions; patents, trademarks, and copyrights; negotiable instruments; and bankruptcy.

Torts

A **tort** is a non-criminal act (other than breach of contract) that results in injury to a person or to property.[3] A tort can be either intentional or the result of negligence. The victim of a tort is legally entitled to some form of financial compensation, or **damages**, for his or her loss and suffering. This compensation is also known as a *compensatory damage award*. In some cases the victim may also receive a *punitive damage award* to punish the wrongdoer and discourage repetition of the act if the misdeed was glaringly bad.

Intentional Torts   An **intentional tort** is a wilful act that results in injury. For example, accidentally hitting a softball through someone's window is a tort, but purposely cutting

Merrill Lynch and after four years RBC won the initial battle and was awarded $2 million compensation. However, in 2007 the court of appeals overturned the ruling. This case may eventually end up at the Supreme Court of Canada. According to some experts, it has created confusion on the issue of employee obligations, for others it has clearly swung the balance in favour of the departing employee—if they give proper notice. Is this the end? The conclusion to this case will be anticipated by many and the results will be used in courts for years to come.[13]

To control the increasing costs of litigation, more and more companies are now experimenting with alternatives to the courtroom. These include independent mediators, who sit down with the two parties and try to hammer out a satisfactory solution to contract problems, and mandatory arbitration, in which an impartial arbitrator or arbitration panel hears evidence from both sides and makes a legally binding decision. However, mandatory arbitration has come under fire by consumer groups because it can wipe out a customer's right to sue. For example, Gateway Computers includes a clause in the purchase agreement documents it ships with every computer stating that any dispute or controversy arising from an agreement to purchase a Gateway product "shall be settled exclusively and finally by arbitration." Moreover, the courts have ruled that failure to read such documents constitutes acceptance of Gateway's terms. Although some consumers prefer to use alternative dispute resolution, those who do not wish to waive their right to sue are advised to read the fine print of all contracts and purchase agreements. The same advice applies to employment and service contracts.[14]

Warranties The *Sale of Goods Act* in each province specifies that everyday sales transactions are a special kind of contract (although this provision applies only to tangible goods, not to services), even though they may not meet all of the exact requirements of regular contracts. Related to the sales contract is the notion of a **warranty**, which is a statement specifying what the producer of a product will do to compensate the buyer if the product is defective or if it malfunctions. Warranties come in several forms. One important distinction is between *express warranties,* which are specific, written statements, and *implied warranties,* which are unwritten but involve certain protections under the law. Also, warranties are either *full* or *limited.* The former obligates the seller to repair or replace the product, without charge, in the event of any defect or malfunction, whereas the latter imposes restrictions on the defects or malfunctions that will be covered. Warranty laws also address a number of other details, including giving consumers instructions on how to exercise their rights under the warranty.[15]

Agency

These days it seems that nearly every celebrity has an agent. Hockey players hire agents to get them commercials and handle their contract negotiations; authors' agents sell manuscripts to the publishers that offer the largest advances; actors' agents try to find choice movie and television roles for their clients. These relationships illustrate a common legal association known as **agency**, which exists when one party, known as the *principal,* authorizes another party, known as the *agent,* to act on his or her behalf in contractual matters.[16]

All contractual obligations come into play in agency relationships. The principal usually creates this relationship by explicit authorization. In some cases—when a transfer of property is involved, for example—the authorization must be written in the form of a document called **power of attorney**, which states that one person may legally act for another (to the extent authorized).

Usually, an agency relationship is terminated when the objective of the relationship has been met or at the end of a period specified in the contract between agent and principal. It may also be ended by a change of circumstances, by the agent's breach of duty or loyalty, or by the death of either party.

Property Transactions

Anyone interested in business must know the basics of property law. Most people think of property as some object they own (a book, a car, a house). However, **property** is actually the relationship between the person having the rights to any tangible or intangible object and all other persons. The law recognizes two primary types of property: real and personal. **Real property** is land and everything permanently attached to it, such as trees, fences, or mineral deposits. **Personal property** is all property that is not real property; it may be tangible (cars, jewellery, or anything having a physical existence) or intangible (bank accounts, stocks, insurance policies, customer lists). A piece of marble in the earth is real property until it is cut and sold as a block, when it becomes personal property. Property rights are subject to various limitations and restrictions. For example, the government monitors the use of real property for the welfare of the public, to the point of explicitly prohibiting some property uses and abuses.[17]

Two types of documents are important in obtaining real property for factory, office, or store space: a deed and a lease. A **deed** is a legal document by which an owner transfers the *title*, or right of ownership, to real property to a new owner. A **lease** is used for a temporary transfer of interest in real property. The party that owns the property is commonly called the *landlord*; the party that occupies or gains the right to occupy the property is the *tenant*. The tenant pays the landlord, usually in periodic instalments, for the use of the property. Generally, a lease may be granted for any length of time on which the two parties agree.

Patents, Trademarks, and Copyrights

If you invent a product, write a book, develop some new software, or simply come up with a unique name for your business, you probably want to prevent other people from using or prospering from your **intellectual property** without fairly compensating you. Several forms of legal protection are available for your creations. They include patents, trademarks, and copyrights. Which one you should use

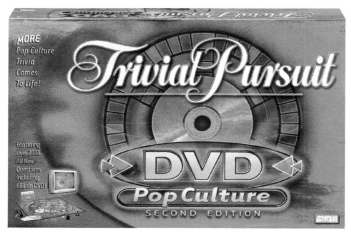

Thirteen years of litigation appear to be over after a Nova Scotia man lost a legal battle in which he claimed that Chris Haney stole his idea to create Trivial Pursuit. In mid-2007 the judge dismissed the case and made a finding that the plaintiff was not credible.

depends on what you have created. Having a patent, copyright, or trademark still doesn't guarantee that your idea or product will not be copied. However, they do provide you with legal recourse if your creations are infringed upon. It is important to note, however, that just because you protect your intellectual property in Canada does not provide it with protection in the United States or the rest of the world. To gain international protection you must register your property in each country separately, with the exception being copyright material that may be protected in some jurisdictions. For additional information visit the Canadian Intellectual Property Office's website at www.cipo.gc.ca.

Intellectual property ownership is a big deal. For example, Trivial Pursuit has been around for more that a quarter century and yet its creators recently won a battle against a man who claims that he told Chris Haney, one of the co-inventors, about an idea for a trivia game while hitching a ride in Cape Breton back in 1979. This court case went on for 13 years with 65 witnesses in five provinces. In mid-2007 a judge ruled that there was no concrete evidence to prove that the idea was stolen and the judge ruled against the man's claims.[18]

Patents   A patent protects the invention or discovery of a new and useful process, an article of manufacture, a machine, a chemical substance, or an improvement on any of these. Issued by the Canadian Intellectual Property Office, a patent grants the owner the right to exclude others from making, using, or selling the invention for 20 years from the date the patent application is filed.[19] After that time, the patented item becomes available for common use. On the one hand, patent law guarantees the originator the right to use the discovery exclusively for a relatively long period of time, thus encouraging people to devise new machines, gadgets, and processes. On the other hand, it also ensures that rights to the new item

will be released eventually, allowing other enterprises to discover even more innovative ways to use it.

Trademarks   A trademark is any word, name, symbol, or device used to distinguish the product of one manufacturer from those made by others. In Canada, trademarks must be registered with the trademarks office and are renewable every 15 years. A service mark is the equivalent for services. McDonald's golden arches are one of the most visible of modern trademarks. Brand names such as Esso or Tim Hortons can also be registered as trademarks. Additionally, the distinct shape of a product or package (called *trade dress*) can also be registered. For example, if you manufacture candy in the shape of a giraffe, you could register this shape. Apple Computer filed suit against Future Power for allegedly infringing on the iMac trade dress with its look-alike E-Power PC. Apple Computer asked the court to prohibit the sale of E-Power in addition to awarding actual and punitive damages. A US District Court granted a preliminary injunction against Future Power from making, distributing, and selling a 15-inch all-in-one computer with a coloured plastic cover while the case was being heard. The two parties settled the lawsuit when Future Power agreed to refrain from producing the look-alike for three more years.[20]

If properly registered and renewed every 15 years, a trademark generally belongs to its owner forever. Among the exceptions are popular brand names that have become generic terms, meaning that they describe a whole class of products. A brand-name trademark can become a generic term if the trademark has been allowed to expire, if it has been incorrectly used by its owner, or if the public comes to equate the name with the class of products, as was the case with zipper, linoleum, aspirin, and many other brand names.

One of the most recognized trademarks in the world is the Nike Swoosh.

Copyrights   Copyrights protect the creators of literary, dramatic, musical, artistic, scientific, and other intellectual works. Any printed, filmed, or recorded material can be copyrighted. The copyright gives its owner the exclusive right to reproduce (copy), sell, or adapt the work he or she has created. Copyright law covers reproduction by photocopying, videotape, and magnetic storage. The Copyright Office will issue a copyright to the creator or to whomever the creator has granted the right to reproduce the work. A book, for example, may be copyrighted by the author or the publisher; the copyright protection lasts until 50 years after the author's death.[21]

Copyright protection on the Internet has become an especially important topic as more businesses and individuals include original material on their websites. Technically, copyright protection exists from the moment material is created. Therefore, anything you post on a website is protected by copyright law. However, loose Internet standards and a history of sharing information has made it difficult for some users to accept this situation.

Negotiable Instruments

Whenever you write a personal cheque, you are creating a **negotiable instrument**, a transferable document that represents a promise to pay a specified amount. (*Negotiable* in this sense means that it can be sold or used as payment of a debt; an *instrument* is simply a written document that expresses a legal agreement.) In addition to cheques, negotiable instruments include certificates of deposit, promissory notes, and commercial paper. To be negotiable, an instrument must meet several criteria:[22]

- It must be in writing and signed by the person who created it.

- It must have an unconditional promise to pay a specified sum of money.

- It must be payable either on demand or at a specified date in the future.

- It must be payable either to some specified person or organization or to the person holding it (the bearer).

You can see how a personal cheque meets these criteria; when you write one, you are agreeing to pay the amount of the cheque to the person or organization to which you're writing it.

Bankruptcy

Even though the Canadian legal system establishes rules of fair play and offers protection from the unscrupulous, it cannot prevent most businesses from taking on too much debt. The legal system does, however, provide help for businesses that find themselves in deep financial trouble. **Bankruptcy** is the legal means of relief for debtors (either individuals or businesses) who are unable to meet their financial obligations, and it is governed by the federal statute called the *Bankruptcy and Insolvency Act*.

Voluntary bankruptcy is initiated by the debtor. *Involuntary bankruptcy* is initiated by creditors. If a company emerges from bankruptcy as a leaner, healthier organization, creditors generally benefit. That's because once a company is back on its financial feet it can resume payments to creditors. Some companies, like Air Canada, emerge from bankruptcy, but others, like Canada 3000, simply cease operations and sell all their assets.

It is important to note that companies that are having trouble paying their debt do not always have to file for bankruptcy. Rather, they can try to work out arrangements with their creditors using either informal or formal negotiation. Informal negotiation involves contacting creditors and trying to work out arrangements in which creditors accept a lesser amount of money or receive payments over a longer period than originally stated in the contract. Unsecured creditors may agree to such negotiated terms because if the business were to file for bankruptcy, they often will receive nothing since secured creditors receive payment first. Secured creditors may be willing to accept different terms when the business does not have many assets and they would receive much less money than originally owed if the company went bankrupt. A formal proposal is one filed with a bankruptcy trustee, a specially trained chartered accountant appointed by the government through the Superintendent of Bankruptcy, and it falls under the *Bankruptcy and Insolvency Act*. In a formal proposal the trustee presents a plan to creditors asking them to accept different repayment terms than originally agreed upon. If the creditors accept the new terms, the company can keep operating as long as they meet these newly negotiated provisions. But if one secured creditor or the majority of unsecured creditors fail to agree to the formal proposal, the company is considered bankrupt. Exhibit A.2 shows the recent statistical history of bankruptcies in Canada.

Exhibit A.2   **Canadian Bankruptcy Statistics 1980–2006**

According to the latest Canadian Bankruptcy statistics there are approximately 2.5 filings per/thousand.

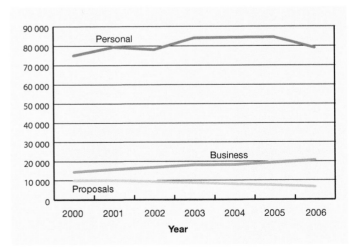

Source: Industry Canada website [accessed August 10 2007] www.ic.gc.ca; BankruptcyCanada.com website [accessed August 10 2007] www.bankruptcycanada.com/bankstats1.htm.

Appendix B
Your Business Plan

GETTING STARTED WITH BUSINESS PLANPRO SOFTWARE

Business PlanPro (BPP) software is a template for crafting a winning business plan. The software is designed to stimulate your thinking about the many tasks and decisions that go into planning and running a business. The software does not do your thinking for you. Instead, it leads you through a thought process by asking you to respond to questions about your business and to provide data for the preformatted tables and charts. Accompanying instructions, examples, and sample business plans provide you with a full range of assistance you can use to draft your own comprehensive business plan. By working through the exercises at the end of each text part, you will gain a practical skill for your business career.

When installing the software be sure to install Adobe Acrobat Reader software so you can view the sample business plans that are included with the disk and downloadable from the web. You can get an overview of the BPP software by clicking on the "Help" menu from the main screen, then selecting "About Business PlanPro." Under the "Help" menu, you can click on contents and then "Getting Help" for operational instructions or to look up business terms in the software's glossary. For quick answers to questions about using the software, look under the "How Do I" menu at the top right of the screen. An overview of the software's features is also on the web at www.paloalto.com/prenticehall.

NAVIGATING THE SOFTWARE

One of the best ways to become familiar with the BPP software is by navigating one of the BPP sample business plans. Launch the BPP software, then click on "Create a New Business Plan" to reach the main screen. Now choose "File" from the menu and click "Open Sample." This brings you to the Sample Plan Browser. An alternate way to get to this screen is by clicking on the "Research It" menu along the left of the screen, then selecting "Sample Plan Browser."

The names of the sample plans are listed on the left, and the first page of plans bundled with the software can be seen on the right. To view a sample plan, double-click on the plan name. To page through a plan, simply click on the arrows on the bottom of the frame in which the plan pages appear. If you have an Internet connection, the software will download the latest version of the sample plan. You can also check the web at www.bplans.com/sp to search through more than 60 sample plans created using BPP software. To see how a sample plan in the BPP software is organized or to move between sections in your order, click the "Show/Hide Navigation" icon to the right of the printer icon on the menu above the sample plan page. When you click on a section name, the plan displays that page.

As you will see when exploring the sample plans, the Executive Summary section provides a brief overview of the business plan. The Company Summary discusses company specifics such as the mission and ownership. The Products and Services section describes exactly what the company is selling. The Market Analysis examines the company's market, including competitors and customers. The Strategy and Implementation section indicates the company's broad course of action in the market, its sales goals, and how it will implement the plan. The Management Summary introduces the organizational structure and management personnel. Finally, the Financial Plan section presents profit-and-loss projections and other financial plans.

You may find it helpful to print out a full copy of the sample plan you have selected and review it as you navigate its contents on your screen. This way you can see how the software uses the information to construct a formal business plan. To print out the sample plan, click on the printer icon and select "Plan." You may also choose to print selected sections or the instructions or examples for a business plan. Once you've finished viewing or printing sample plans, click to close the frame and return to the main screen. You have multiple options for accessing the same information, as shown under the View menu. The Plan Manager option guides you through the process of researching a plan, building it, distributing and delivering it, and making it happen. The Plan Outline option allows you to develop the plan section by section in outline form. To access the text mode option, where you write your business plan's text, select "Text Mode" from the View menu. You can move between sections by selecting from topics in the Topic drop-down menu above the text screen or using the forward and backward arrows at the right of the Topic menu. To view related tables and charts, click the Table mode or the Chart mode under the View menu.

CREATING A WINNING BUSINESS PLAN

The exercises included at the end of each text part use the knowledge you've gained from reading that text part. Each exercise has two tasks: "Think Like a Pro" tasks require you to navigate the software, find and review information in the sample business plans, and evaluate and critique some of the thinking that went behind these plans. By reviewing these sample plans with a critical eye, you will begin to sharpen your own business planning skills. "Create Your Own Business Plan" tasks are an opportunity for you to apply your business planning skills to create your own winning business plan. So begin thinking now about the type of business you'd like to own or manage some day. Then develop and refine your business strategies as you work through the exercises.

Answers to Study Guide Questions

CHAPTER 1

MULTIPLE CHOICE

1. d 2. d 3. c 4. a 5. c 6. d 7. c 8. a 9. b 10. b

TRUE/FALSE

1. F 2. T 3. F 4. F 5. T

FILL-IN-THE-BLANK

1. Non-profit organizations; 2. capital-intensive; 3. Service businesses; 4. barriers to entry; 5. factors of production; 6. Socialism; 7. supply; 8. monopolistic competition; 9. Monetary policy; 10. GDP

CHAPTER 2

MULTIPLE CHOICE

1. d 2. d 3. c 4. b 5. b 6. d 7. d 8. c 9. a 10. c

TRUE/FALSE

1. F 2. T 3. T 4. T 5. F

FILL-IN-THE-BLANK

1. balance of trade; 2. Protectionism; 3. dumping; 4. embargo; 5. The International Monetary Fund (IMF); 6. European Union (EU); 7. floating-exchange; 8. importing; 9. joint venture; 10. multinational corporations (MNCs)

CHAPTER 3

MULTIPLE CHOICE

1. b 2. c 3. d 4. d 5. c 6. d 7. d 8. a 9. b 10. a

TRUE/FALSE

1. F 2. T 3. F 4. T 5. F

FILL-IN-THE-BLANK

1. Insider trading; 2. Kyoto Protocol; 3. social audit; 4. conflict of interest; 5. *Canadian Environmental Protection Act;* 6. code of ethics; 7. ethical lapse; 8. Canadian Standards Association (CSA); 9. diversity initiatives; 10. Philanthropic

CHAPTER 4

MULTIPLE CHOICE

1. a 2. d 3. d 4. c 5. b 6. b 7. a 8. a 9. b 10. a

TRUE/FALSE

1. F 2. F 3. T 4. T 5. T

FILL-IN-THE-BLANK

1. Intrapreneurs; 2. business plan; 3. franchisee; 4. collateral; 5. initial public offering (IPO); 6. Venture capitalists; 7. Angel investors; 8. outsource; 9. Business Development Bank of Canada (BDC); 10. Incubators

CHAPTER 5

MULTIPLE CHOICE

1. d 2. c 3. a 4. b 5. b 6. c 7. d 8. d 9. c 10. b

TRUE/FALSE

1. F 2. T 3. T 4. F 5. F

FILL-IN-THE-BLANK

1. limited liability; 2. Common stock; 3. limited liability partnership (LLP); 4. subsidiary; 5. leveraged buyout (LBO); 6. general partnership; 7. dividends; 8. Preferred stock; 9. liquidity; 10. shark repellent

CHAPTER 6

MULTIPLE CHOICE

1. a 2. b 3. d 4. a 5. b 6. b 7. a 8. c 9. b 10. c

TRUE/FALSE

1. F 2. F 3. T 4. T 5. T

FILL-IN-THE-BLANK

1. Strategic; 2. interpersonal; 3. Quantitative; 4. transformational; 5. Corporate culture; 6. Total quality management (TQM); 7. Contingency; 8. Benchmarking; 9. control cycle; 10. conceptual

CHAPTER 7

MULTIPLE CHOICE

1. c 2. d 3. a 4. c 5. c 6. a 7. b 8. d 9. c 10. b

TRUE/FALSE

1. T 2. F 3. T 4. T 5. F

FILL-IN-THE-BLANK

1. Accountability; 2. Responsibility; 3. matrix; 4. informal organization; 5. chain of command; 6. flat; 7. centralized; 8. task force; 9. Brainstorming; 10. groupthink

CHAPTER 8

MULTIPLE CHOICE

1. b 2. a 3. c 4. c 5. b 6. b 7. b 8. c 9. a 10. a

TRUE/FALSE

1. F 2. T 3. T 4. F 5. F

FILL-IN-THE-BLANK

1. analytic; 2. cellular; 3. PERT; 4. outsourced; 5. value chain; 6. Capacity; 7. Routing; 8. dispatching; 9. computer-integrated manufacturing (CIM); 10. lead time

CHAPTER 9

MULTIPLE CHOICE

1. a 2. b 3. b 4. d 5. a 6. c 7. a 8. d 9. b 10. c

TRUE/FALSE

1. T 2. F 3. T 4. T 5. T

FILL-IN-THE-BLANK

1. succession planning; 2. job specification; 3. Performance appraisals; 4. 360-degree review; 5. Electronic performance monitoring (EPM); 6. salary; 7. defined; 8. Stock options; 9. Employee assistance programs (EAPs); 10. attrition

CHAPTER 10

MULTIPLE CHOICE

1. c 2. c 3. d 4. a 5. b 6. c 7. d 8. d 9. c 10. a

TRUE/FALSE

1. T 2. T 3. F 4. F 5. T

FILL-IN-THE-BLANK

1. Self-actualization; 2. motivators; 3. Theory Z; 4. Expectancy theory; 5. Management by objectives (MBO); 6. Negative reinforcement; 7. job redesign; 8. glass ceiling; 9. mediator; 10. job sharing

CHAPTER 11

MULTIPLE CHOICE

1. b 2. b 3. d 4. d 5. d 6. d 7. d 8. d 9. c 10. b

TRUE/FALSE

1. F 2. T 3. T 4. F 5. T

FILL-IN-THE-BLANK

1. Co-branding; 2. Place marketing; 3. form utility; 4. brand equity; 5. market research; 6. customer relationship marketing (CRM); 7. marketing strategy; 8. geographic segmentation; 9. intangible; 10. Penetration

CHAPTER 12

MULTIPLE CHOICE

1. c 2. d 3. a 4. d 5. a 6. c 7. d 8. b 9. c 10. a

TRUE/FALSE

1. T 2. F 3. T 4. F 5. F

FILL-IN-THE-BLANK

1. Retailers; 2. intensive distribution; 3. materials handling; 4. Cooperative advertising; 5. push; 6. public relations; 7. Premiums; 8. Following up; 9. Trade promotions; 10. point-of-purchase (POP)

CHAPTER 13

MULTIPLE CHOICE

1. d 2. a 3. c 4. b 5. d 6. c 7. b 8. a 9. b 10. c

TRUE/FALSE

1. F 2. F 3. T 4. T 5. F

FILL-IN-THE-BLANK

1. Chartered Accountant (CA); 2. Canadian Institute of Chartered Accountants (CICA); 3. bookkeeping; 4. financial analysis; 5. controller; 6. certified general accountant (CGA); 7. Generally accepted accounting principles (GAAP); 8. owners' equity; 9. accrual basis; 10. Capital budgeting

CHAPTER 14

MULTIPLE CHOICE

1. b 2. a 3. c 4. a 5. b 6. b 7. a 8. a 9. c 10. d

TRUE/FALSE

1. F 2. T 3. T 4. F 5. T

FILL-IN-THE-BLANK

1. Guaranteed investment certificate (GIC); 2. Smart cards; 3. stock split; 4. Credit unions and caises populaires; 5. line of credit; 6. Canadian Deposit Insurance Corporation; 7. bond; 8. Mutual funds; 9. Balanced funds; 10. short selling

References

Chapter 1

1. Joe Castaldo, "RIM's Test of Faith," *Canadian Business*, 9 April 2007, 28–33; RIM's website [accessed 4 July 2007] www.rim.net; Geoffrey York, "RIM Cracks China Market for BlackBerry," *Globe and Mail*, 4 July 2007, B1–B7; Tim Shufelt, "Taking the BlackBerry around the Globe," *Globe and Mail*, 4 July 2007, B7; Simon Avery, "Business as Usual at RIM, Balsillie Says," *Globe and Mail*, 3 June 2007, B1; Catherine McLean, "Soaring RIM Shrugs Off iPhone Threat," *Globe and Mail*, 29 June 2007, B1; Simon Avery, "Opinions on RIM's Future Remain Polarized," *Globe and Mail*, 9 May 2006, B18; Simon Avery, "RIM's Fight to Stay on Top," *Globe and Mail*, 18 September 2004, B11; Simon Avery, "RIM's Profit Soars on Pearl Sales," *Globe and Mail*, 22 December 2006, B11; Barrie McKenna, "Will iPhone Change Everything—or Fall Flat?" *Globe and Mail*, 26 June 2007, B18; Ian Rowley, "BlackBerry in Japan?" 8 June 2007, *BusinessWeek* website [accessed 5 July 2007] http://www.businessweek.com/globalbiz/blog/asiatech/archives/2006/06/blackberry_in_j.html

2. Adam Horowitz, Mark Athitakis, Mark Lasswell, and Owen Thomas, "The 101 Dumbest Moments in Business," *Business 2.0* [accessed 27 March 2004] www.business2.com

3. Richard Blackwell, "Irving Sees Multibillion-Dollar Boost for East," *Globe and Mail*, 6 October 2006, B7.

4. Canadian Red Cross website [accessed 3 July 2007] www.redcross.ca/cmslib/general/crc_annual_report2007eng.pdf

5. Ken Stammen, "Where Big Planes Are Born," *Cincinnati Post*, 12 September 2000, 7C.

6. Richard Paton, "While Factories Close, Governments Sleep," *Globe and Mail*, 21 May 2007, B2.

7. Jefferson Graham, "Instant Messaging Programs Are No Longer Just for Messages," *USA Today*, 20 October 2003, 5D; Todd R. Weiss, "Microsoft Targets Corporate Instant Messaging Customers," *Computerworld*, 18 November 2002, 12; "Banks Adopt Instant Messaging to Create a Global Business Network," *Computer Weekly*, 25 April 2002, 40; Michael D. Osterman, "Instant Messaging in the Enterprise," *Business Communications Review*, January 2003, 56–62; John Pallato, "Instant Messaging Unites Work Groups and Inspires Collaboration," *Internet World*, December 2002, 14+; Mark Gibbs, "Racing to Instant Messaging," *NetworkWorld*, 17 February 2003, 74.

8. *IBM 1997 Annual Report*, Annual Report Gallery [accessed 21 April 1999] www.reportgallery.com

9. Bombardier Annual Report 2003–2004, 53.

10. Statistics Canada website [accessed 22 June 2004] www.statscan.ca

11. "Fortune 1000 Ranked within Industry," *Fortune*, 26 April 1999, F51–F73.

12. "Fortune 500: Largest Corporations," *Fortune*, 5 April 2004, B-1.

13. Michael R. Solomon et al., *Consumer Behaviour: Buying, Having, Being* (Toronto: Prentice Hall, 2005), 451.

14. Statistics Canada website [accessed 16 June 2004] www.statscan.ca; *Statistical Abstract of the United States, 1996* (Washington, DC: GPO, 1996), 56–59, 394, 396.

15. Stephen Baker, "Where Danger Lurks," *BusinessWeek*, 25 August 2003, 114–118; W. Brian Arthur, "Why Tech Is Still the Future," *Fortune*, 24 November 2003, 119–125; Kevev Anderson, "Delivery at Internet Speed," BBC News Online, 22 December 1999 [accessed 30 March 2004] news.bbc.co.uk

16. Heather Scoffield, "A Warning For the Services Sector," *Globe and Mail*, 27 December 2006, B1.

17. Cirque du Soleil website [accessed 19 June 2004] www.cirquedusoleil.com

18. Robert L. Heilbroner and Lester C. Thurow, *Economics Explained* (New York: Simon & Schuster, 1994), 29–30.

19. Ronald M. Ayers and Robert A. Collinge, *Economics: Explore and Apply* (Upper Saddle River, NJ: Pearson Prentice Hall, 2005), 97–103.

20. Heilbroner and Thurow, *Economics Explained*, 250.

21. Ibid.

22. Greg Steinmetz, "Her Majesty May Sell Part of London's Tube, Angering Some in U.K.," *Wall Street Journal*, 14 October 1999, A1, A12; Erik Eckholm, "Chinese Restate Goals to Reorganize State Companies," *New York Times*, 23 September 1999, A10; Dexter Roberts, "China's New Revolution," *BusinessWeek*, 27 September 1999, 72–78.

23. Department of Finance Canada website [accessed 30 March 2005] www.fin.gc.ca/news04/04-052e.html; Peter Verburg, "Fill'er Up," *Canadian Business*, 29 March 2004; Keith Kalawsky, "Sell Low, Hold High," *Canadian Business*, 19 August 2004.

24. Exhibit is adapted from Chris Woodyard, "Firms Stretch Travel Dollars," *USA Today*, 16 March 1999, B1–B2.

25. Air Canada website [accessed 6 July 2007] www.aircanada.com/en/about/media/facts/profile.html#fleet

26. LivePerson website [accessed 6 July 2007] www.liveperson.com, www.liveperson.com/docs/casestudies/BellCanada_CaseStudy.pdf; Mary Wagner, "The Long Road to Online Checkout," *Internet World*, April 2001 [accessed 7 May 2001] www.internetretailer.com; Karen J. Bannan, "Burning Up the Wires," *PSINet eBusiness*, Winter 2001, 48–51; Bruce Horovitz, "Site Untangles E-Customer Service Mess," *USA Today*, 23 November 1999 [accessed 7 May 2001] www.usatoday.com; "LivePerson Reels in $19 Million," *Red Herring*, 10 August 1999 [accessed 7 May 2001] www.redherring.com; Connie Guglielmo, "LivePerson Puts a Pulse into Web Interaction," *ZDNet*, 21 June 1999 [accessed 7 May 2001] www.zdnet.com; Vanessa Geneva Melter, "Closing the Sale with Interactive Chat," *ShopGuide News*, 7 June 1999 [accessed 7 May 2001] www.shopguide.com; Jennifer Gilbert, "LivePerson Focuses on the Human Touch," *Advertising Age*, 1 June 1999 [accessed 7 May 2001] www.adage.com; Craig Bicknell, "Somebody Freakin' Talk to Me!" *Wired*, 1 June 1999 [accessed 7 May 2001] www.wired.com

27. Jeff Wise, "How Skiboarding Became the New Snowboarding," *New York Times Magazine*, 21 March 1999, 58–61.

28. Department of Justice Canada website [accessed 17 June 2004] http://laws.justice.gc.ca/en/C-34/35559.html

29. Susan Monroe, "Canadian Bank Mergers Decision," 14 December 1998, Canada Online website [accessed 17 June 2004] http://canadaonline.about.com/library/weekly/aa121498.htm

30. Paul Waldie, "Central Bank Suggests Mergers No Threat," *Globe and Mail*, 11 June 2004, B3.

31. Paul Viera, "Ottawa Still Cool on Bank Mergers," *Financial Post*, 5 July 2007.

32. "Privatizing BC Hydro Is Already Costing You Money," BC Citizens for Public Power website [accessed 22 June 2004] www.citizensforpublicpower.ca/articles/may04pluggedin.html

33. "Nortel Networks Provides Update on Status of Restatements and Related Matters and Business Performance," 2 June 2004, Nortel Networks website [accessed 22 June 2004] www.nortelnetworks.com

34. Joe Castaldo, "RIM's Test of Faith," *Canadian Business*, 9 April 2007, 28–33.

35. Bank of Canada website [accessed 15 June 2004] www.bankofcanada.ca; Jeannine Aversa, "Fed Ends String of Rate Cuts," *Journal-Gazette*, 31 January 2001, 7B.

36. Bank of Canada website [accessed 17 June 2004] www.bankofcanada.ca/en/faq.htm

37. Budget 2007, Department of Finance Canada website [accessed 6 July 2007] http://www.budget.gc.ca/2007/bp/bpc7e.html

38. Heather Scoffield, "Welcome to a New Economic Cycle," *Globe and Mail*, 10 February 2007, B4; Greg Keenan, "Will Chery Be Detroit's Nightmare?" *Globe and Mail*, 6 July 2007, B4; Greg Keenan, "Chrysler to Axe 2000 Jobs," *Globe and Mail*, 8 February 2007, B4.

39. Richard Blackwell, "Canada Ranks Number 1 for Economic Strength," *Globe and Mail*, 21 December 2006, B5.

40. See Note 1 for case sources.

Chapter 2

1. Fred Lum, "Molson Coors Brews Up Strong Showing," *Globe and Mail*, 9 May 2007, B7; Andy Hoffman, "Molson Coors Ends Ill-Fated Foray into Brazil," *Globe and Mail*, 17 January 2006, B1; 2006 Annual Report/Press Releases, Molson Coors website [accessed 23 May 2007] www.molsoncoors.com; Richard Bloom, "Molson Coors Upbeat on Future; the Street Not So Sure," *Globe and Mail*, 29 April 2005, B1; Keith McArthur, "Coors' Toughest Tasks Are Only Just Beginning," *Globe and Mail*, 2 February 2005, B4; Allan Swift, "Plenty of Hurdles Remain for Merged Beer Giant," *Globe and Mail*, 2 February 2005, B2; Keith McArthur, "Molson's Market Share Sinks," *Globe and Mail*, 29 October 2005, B1.

2. Holley H. Ulbrich and Mellie L. Warner, *Managerial Economics* (New York: Barron's Educational Series, 1990), 190.

3. Strategis website [accessed 16 May 2007] http://strategis.gc.ca/sc_mrkti/tdst/tdo/tdo.php#tag; Jeff Sanford, "How to Cash in on Global Trade," *Canadian Business*, 7–20 June 2004, 69.

4. Ian Austin, "Thomson Adds Reuters in $17 Billion Bid to Be Giant," 16 May 2007, *New York Times Website* [accessed 18 May 2007] http://www.nytimes.com/2007/05/16/business/media/16thomson.html; Grant Robertson and Eric Reguly, "Thomson-Reuters," *Globe and Mail*, 16 May 2007, B3.

5. "Balance of Payments," Government of Canada website [accessed 2 April 2005], http://canadianeconomy.gc.ca/english/economy/balance_payment.html

6. Robert J. Samuelson, "Trading with the Enemy," *Newsweek*, 1 April 1996, 41; Amy Borrus, Pete Engardio, and Dexter Roberts, "The New Trade Superpower," *BusinessWeek*, 16 October 1995, 56–57; David A. Andelman, "Marco Polo Revisited," *American Management Journal*, August 1995, 10–12; John Greenwald, "Get Asia Now, Pay Later," *Time*, 10 October 1994, 61; Lewis M. Simons, "High-Tech Jobs for Sale," *Time*, 22 July 1996, 59.

7. Derek DeCloet, "Protectionism Isn't the Cure for the Hollowing Out of Corporate Canada," *Globe and Mail*, 5 May 2007, B2.

8. WTO website [accessed 18 May 2007] http://www.wto.org/English/tratop_e/dispu_e/dispu_status_e.htm#yr2007; Thomas Watson, "Trade Wars: The U.S. Often Preaches Free Trade—but Often Practices Protectionism," *Canadian Business*, 29 December–18 January 2004, 38, 39.

9. Alberta Beef Producers website [accessed 18 May 2007] http://www.albertabeef.org/news.asp; Sandra Cordon, "Beef Dispute with U.S. Could Hurt Liberals," *Globe and Mail*, 9 June 2004, A7; "Where's the Beef?" *Canadian Business*, 29 March–11 April 2004, 9.

10. Eric Schmitt, "U.S. Backs Off Sanctions, Seeing Poor Effect Abroad," *New York Times*, 31 July 1998, A1, A6; Robert T. Gray, "Book Review," *Nation's Business*, January 1999, 47.

11. "Saudi Arabia Hopes to Join WTO by 2002," *Reuters Business Report*, 3 August 1997.

12. CBC website [accessed 18 May 2007] http://www.cbc.ca/news/background/food/margarine.html; Matthew McClearn, "I Can't Believe It's Not Better," *Canadian Business*, 29 December–18 January 2004, 31–36.

13. Greg Keenan, "NAFTA 'Unreasonable,' Toyota Says," *Globe and Mail*, 28 June 2004, B17.

14. WTO website [accessed 18 May 2007] www.wto.org/English/tratop_e/dispu_e/dispu_status_e.htm#yr2007

15. Steven Chase, "Softwood Deal Is Built to Last, U.S. Trade Envoy Says," *Globe and Mail*, 13 September 2006, B6; Peter Kennedy, "Lumber Payment Duties Are Months Away," *Globe and Mail*, 29 April 2006, B3; Stephen Mertl, "New Faces at Softwood Lumber Talks Won't Mask Long-Standing Differences,"

Canadian Press, 28 March 2005, CBC website [accessed 2 April 2005] www.cbc.ca.

16. WTO website [accessed 18 May 2007] http://www.wto.org/english/thewto_e/whatis_e/tif_e/org6_e.htm; James Cox, "Tariffs Shield Some U.S. Products," *USA Today*, 6 May 1999, 1B, 2B.

17. IMF Annual Report, page 96, IMF website [accessed 18 May 2007] www.imf.org/external/pubs/ft/ar/2006/eng/pdf/file9.pdf

18. Christopher Koch. "It's a Wired, Wired World," *Webmaster*, March 1997, 50–55.

19. APEC website [accessed 18 May 2007] www.apec.org; "APEC Ministers Commit to Sustainable Development," *Xinhau News Agency*, 11 June 1997; Fred C. Bergsten, "An Asian Push for World-Wide Free Trade: The Case for APEC," *The Economist*, 6 January 1996, 62.

20. Masaaki Kotabe and Maria Cecilia Coutinho de Arruda, "South America's Free Trade Gambit," *Marketing Management*, Spring 1998, 3936.

21. Alan Clendenning, "Economic Views Conflict at Mercosur Meet," 19 January 2007, *Washington Post* website [accessed 18 May 2007] www.washingtonpost.com/wp-dyn/content/article/2007/01/19/AR2007011900216.html; "Grand Illusions," *The Economist*, 4 March 1995, 87; Bob Davis, "Global Paradox: Growth of Trade Binds Nations, but It Also Can Spur Separatism," *Wall Street Journal*, 20 June 1994, A1, A6; Barbara Rudolph, "Megamarket," *Time*, 10 August 1992, 43–44; Peter Truell, "Free Trade May Suffer from Regional Blocs," *Wall Street Journal*, 1 July 1991, A1.

22. Patrice M. Jones, "Leaving Trade Pact's Woes Behind," *Chicago Tribune*, 10 May 2000, sec. 3, 42.

23. Rafael A. Lecuona, "Economic Integration: NAFTA and MERCOSUR, A Comparative Analysis," *International Journal on World Peace*, December 1999, 27–49.

24. Emeric Lepourte, "Europe's Challenge to the U.S. in South America's Biggest Market," *Christian Science Monitor*, 8 April 1997, 19; Mario Osava, "Mercosur: Free Trade with Europe More Advantageous than FTAA," *Inter Press English News Wire*, 6 May 1997; Robert Maynard, "At a Crossroads in Latin America," *Nation's Business*, April 1996, 38–39; Gregory L. Miles and Loubna Freih, "Join the Caribbean Revolution," *International Business*, September 1994, 42–54; Matt Moffett, "Spreading the Gospel," *Wall Street Journal*, 28 October 1994, R12.

25. Luiza Ilie and Kremena Miteva, "Romania, Bulgaria Are Newest EU States," *Globe and Mail*, 1 January 2007, B5; Europa website [accessed 18 May 2007] europa.eu/abc/index_en.htm

26. Mary Jacoby, "EU Recommends Charges Against Intel," *Globe and Mail*, 17 January 2007, B13; Brandon Mitchener, "Increasingly Rules of Global Economy Are Set in Brussels," *Wall Street Journal*, 23 April 2002, A1, A10.

27. Europa website [accessed 17 May 2007] ec.europa.eu/economy_finance/euro/our_currency_en.htm; Thomas Kamm, "EU Certifies Participants for Euro," *Wall Street Journal*, 26 March 1998, A14; Mitchener, "Increasingly Rules of Global Economy Are Set in Brussels," A1, A10.

28. Europa website [accessed 6 April 2005] europa.eu.int/abc/12lessons/index7_en.htm#

29. Slobodan Lekic, "Slovenia Today Becomes the 13th State to Adopt Euro," *Globe and Mail*, 1 January 2007, B5.

30. Thane Peterson, "The Euro," *BusinessWeek*, 27 April 1998, 90–94; Joan Warner, "The Great Money Bazaar," *BusinessWeek*, 27 April 1998, 96–98; Gail Edmondson, "Industrial Evolution," *BusinessWeek*, 27 April 1998, 100–101.

31. Doug Sanders, "Budget Crisis Threatens EU," *Globe and Mail*, 16 June 2005, B1, B17; Barrie McKenna, "Euro Plunges as Continental Drift Widens," *Globe and Mail*, 2 June 2005, B18.

32. Lecuona, "Economic Integration: NAFTA and MERCOSUR, A Comparative Analysis."

33. Anthony DePalma, "With the U.S. Economy Slumping, Canada and Mexico Are Reeling," *New York Times*, 17 December 2001, C13.

34. Gildan website [accessed 23 May 2007] gildan.com/corporate/corporateCitizenship/overview.cfm

35. Geri Smith, "Betting on Free Trade," *BusinessWeek*, 23 April 2001, 60–62.

36. Carolyn Leitch, "Fortifying a Portfolio With BRICs," *Globe and Mail*, 14 October 2006, B9.

37. David Parkinson, "Emerging Markets: The Key Words Are Risk and Volatility," *Globe and Mail*, 19 January 2007, B11; Theresa Ebden, "China, India Driving Forces for Growth," *Globe and Mail*, 13 December 2006, E3; Geoffrey York, Sinclair Stewart, Boyd Erman, "China's Market Myths," *Globe and Mail*, 3 March 2007, B4.

38. Theresa Ebden, "Driving through the BRIC Wall," *Globe and Mail*, 21 February 2007, B1.

39. Jeff Hale, "Ask What Another Country Can Do for You," *Globe and Mail*, 22 February 2007, B11.

40. Rick Whiting, "Innovation: Videoconferencing's Virtual Room," *Information Week*, 1 April 2002, 14; Mark Alpert, "Long-Distance Robots," *Scientific American*, December 2001, 94; Teliris website [accessed 8 August 2003] www.teliris.com

41. Shirley Won, "Movie Makers Rolling Back into Canada," *Globe and Mail*, 3 March 2007, B1–B5; 2007 CFTPA report, CFTPA website [accessed 20 May 2007] www.cftpa.ca/PDFs/Profile07_CLEAN.pdf; Denis Seguin, "The Battle for Hollywood North," *Canadian Business*, 15 September 2003, 55–62.

42. UPS website [accessed 20 March 2007] www.pressroom.ups.com/mediakits/factsheet/0,2305,866,00.html; John Alden,

"What in the World Drives UPS?" *International Business*, March/April 1998, 6–7.

43. David A. Ricks, *Blunders in International Business*, 3rd ed. (Oxford, England: Blackwell Business, 1997), 134.

44. "Getting It Right in Japan," *International Business*, May–June 1997, 19.

45. Matt Apuzzo, "Chiquita Pleads Guilty to Paying Terrorists," *Globe and Mail*, 20 March 2007, B10.

46. Martin Crutsinger, "U.S. Turns Up the Heat on Piracy in China," *Globe and Mail*, 10 April 2007, B8; Neil King, Jr., "Chinese Piracy Spat Headed to WTO," *Globe and Mail* (original source WSJ.com), 7 April 2007, B2; Peter Wonacott, Joseph B. White, and Norihiko Shirouz, "$3 Billion Investment by GM Revs Up China's Car Industry," *Globe and Mail* (original source WSJ.com), 8 June 2004, B13.

47. *Corruption of Foreign Public Officials Act*, Department of Justice Canada website [accessed 7 July 2004] www.justice.gc.ca/en/dept/pub/cfpoa/guide5.html

48. "Officially Supported Export Credits," OECD website [accessed 6 July 2004] www.oecd.org

49. James Wilfong and Toni Seger, *Taking Your Business Global* (Franklin Lakes, NJ: Career Press, 1997), 289.

50. Export Development Canada website [accessed 2 July 2004] www.edc.ca

51. Jules Abend, "Jockey Colors Its World," *Bobbin*, February 1999, 50–54.

52. Ricky W. Griffin and Michael W. Pustay, *International Business* (Reading, MA: Addison-Wesley, 1999), 415.

53. Andy Hoffman, "Tims Stays the Course on its U.S. Expansion," *Globe and Mail*, 21 September 2007, B10; Tim Hortons website [accessed 21 May 2007] www.timhortons.com/en/index.html

54. "Padgett Surveys Franchise/Small Business Sectors," *Franchising World*, March–April 1995, 46; John Stansworth, "Penetrating the Myths Surrounding Franchise Failure Rates—Some Old Lessons for New Business," *International Small Business Journal*, January–March 1995, 59–63; Laura Koss-Feder, "Building Better Franchise Relations," *Hotel & Motel Management*, 6 March 1995, 18; Carol Steinberg, "Franchise Fever," *World Trade*, July 1992, 86, 88, 90–91; John O'Dell, "Franchising America," *Los Angeles Times*, 25 June 1989, sec. IV, 1.

55. Dori Jones Yang, "An American (Coffee) in Paris—and Rome," *U.S. News and World Report*, 19 February 2001, 47.

56. Star Alliance website [accessed 21 May 2007] www.staralliance.com

57. "GM to Build New SUV at Ontario Plant," *Reuters*, 4 September 2002.

58. Greg Keenan, "Magna Cum Laude: Stronach to Build Car for Russian Market," *Globe and Mail*, 11 October 2006, B1.

59. Simons, "High-Tech Jobs for Sale."

60. Bertrand Marotte, "China Signs a 20-Year Pact for Bombardier Trains," *Globe and Mail*, 28 June 2005, B4; John Partridge, "Bombardier Holding off on China Plant," *Globe and Mail*, 29 June 2004, B9.

61. David Friend, "Bank of Nova Scotia Eyes India, China," *Globe and Mail*, 28 November 2006, B9.

62. Couche-Tard website [accessed 21 May 2007] www.couche-tard.com/the-network.html; Bertrand Marotte, "Couche-Tard's Head Store Clerk Corners Market by Adaptation," *Globe and Mail*, 2 April 2005, B4; Bertrand Marotte, "Clearing a Direct Path to the Cooler," *Globe and Mail*, 2 April 2005, B4.

63. Ernest Beck and Emily Nelson, "As Wal-Mart Invades Europe, Rivals Rush to Match Its Formula," *Wall Street Journal*, 6 October 1999, A1, A6.

64. Rob Ferguson, "Canada Losing Ground in Foreign Investment," *Toronto Star*, Fall 2003; Press Release, 17 September 2003, A.T. Kearney website [accessed 27 April 2004] www.atkearney.com

65. David Ricks, "How to Avoid Business Blunders Abroad," *Business*, April–June 1984, 3–11; CBC videos, "Field of Seeds," 2002; Spitz Sales Inc. website [accessed 28 June 2004] www.spitzsales.com; Amy Chozick, "Japan Finally Opens Door to BlackBerry," *Globe and Mail*, 26 September 2006, B9.

66. Paulo Prado and Bruce Orwall, "A Certain 'Je Ne Sais Quoi' at Disney's New Park." *Wall Street Journal*, 12 March 2002, B1, B4.

67. Rajesh Mahapatra, "Disney Continues Indian Push with 150 Stores," *Globe and Mail*, 12 October 2006, B17.

68. KFC website [accessed May 22, 2007] www.kfc.com/about/default.asp; Brian O'Keefe, "Global Brands," *Fortune*, 26 November 2001, 102–110.

69. Tara Parket-Pope, "Custom-Made," *Wall Street Journal*, 26 September 1996, R22–R23.

70. Yum! Brands website [accessed 23 May 2007] www.yum.com/investors/annualreport/06annualreport/pdf/yum_ar06.pdf

71. See Note 1 for case sources.

72. Bank of Canada website [accessed 21 December 2007] www.bankofcanada.ca/en/rates/can_us_lookup.html

Chapter 3

1. *Corporate Knights*, 3(1), July 2004, 24–25; Telus Corporate Social Responsibility Report 2006, Telus website [accessed 13 June 2007] http://about.telus.com/csr2006/csr/en/commitment/stakeholder-intro.html

2. Matt Daily, "Enron's Lay Grilled Over Lavish Lifestyle," *Globe and Mail*, 2 May 2006, B17; "From Collapse to Convictions: A Timeline," 23 October 2006, CBC website, [accessed 11 July 2007] http://www.cbc.ca/news/background/enron

3. Ellen Florian, "Scandal Cheat Sheet," *Fortune*, 7 July 2003, 48–49; "Timeline of Enron's Collapse," *Washington Post*, 27 January 2004 [accessed 2 April 2004] www.washingtonpost.com

4. Kurt Eichenwald, "Canadian Bank Agrees to Pay Fine and Drop Unit in Enron Case," 23 December 2003, *New York Times* website [accessed 1 June 2004] www.nytimes.com/2003/12/23/business/23enron.html

5. Carrie Johnson and Peter Behr, "Andersen Guilty of Obstruction: Will End Audit Work," *Washington Post*, 16 June 2002, A1.

6. "Nortel Announces Another Restatement," 1 March 2007, CBC website, [accessed 11 June 2007] http://www.cbc.ca/money/story/2007/03/01/nortelrestate.html; "Nortel Settles Lawsuit for $2.5 Billion US," 1 March 2007, CBC website [accessed 11 June 2007] http://www.cbc.ca/money/story/2006/02/08/nortel-060208.html

7. Ben Klayman, "Tyco to Settle Kozlowski-era Class Action Cases," *National Post*, 15 May 2007.

8. Christopher Stern, "WorldCom Plans New Job Cuts," *Washington Post*, 16 January 2004, E1.

9. "The WorldCom Story," 26 September 2006, CBC website [accessed 11 June 2007] http://www.cbc.ca/news/background/worldcom

10. Paul Waldie, "Court Hears of Emailed Death Threat," *Globe and Mail*, 12 June 2007, A13; Paul Waldie, "Testimony Provides Glimpse of Black's Collectibles and Tomes," *Globe and Mail*, 2 June 2007, A17; Shawn McCarthy, "The Case Against Black," *Globe and Mail*, 18 November 2005, B1; Jacquie McNish, "Black Told to Return Boxes from Hollinger," *Globe and Mail*, 26 May 2005, A3; "Black Wants Verdict Quashed," 28 August 2007, *Toronto Star* website [accessed 16 September 2007] www.thestar.com/News/Canada/article/250490

11. Justin Hyde, "Explorer Owners Seek $2 Billion," *Detroit Free Press*, 31 May 2007 [accessed 11 June 2007] http://www.freep.com/apps/pbcs.dll/article?AID=/20070531/BUSINESS01/705310374/1014

12. "Staying Current: Sarbanes-Oxley Cost," *The Controllers Report*, November 2003, 2–3; Jorge E. Guerra, "The Sarbanes-Oxley Act and Evolution of Corporate Governance," *CPA Journal*, March 2004, 14+.

13. Brent Jang and Paul Waldie, "Late Nights, Hush-Hush E-mails and the 007 Project," *Globe and Mail*, 3 October 2006, B8; Karin Kovalsky, "Spy vs. Spy," *Canadian Business*, 13 February 2005, 33–43; Brent Jang, "Airline Says Trash Data a Treasure," *Globe and Mail*, 25 November 2004, B1.

14. Adam Horowitz, Mark Athitakis, Mark Lasswell, and Owen Thomas, "The 101 Dumbest Moments in Business," *Business 2.0* [accessed 27 March 2004] www.business2.com; Bob Garfield, "KFC Serves Big, Fat Bucket of Nonsense in 'Healthy' Spots," *Advertising Age*, 3 November 2003, 61; "KFC Blunders in Healthy Ads," *Advertising Age*, 3 November 2003, 22.

15. Michael McCarthy, "Recent Crop of Sneaky Ads Backfires," *USA Today*, 17 July 2001, 3B; "Publishers Clearing House Strikes Deceptive-Practices Accord," *New York Times*, 23 August 2000, A16.

16. Aaron Bernstein, Brian Grow, Darnell Little, Stanley Holmes, and Diane Brady, "Bracing for a Backlash," *BusinessWeek*, 4 February 2002, 32–36.

17. Suzanne Wooley, "The Hustlers Queue Up on the Net," *BusinessWeek*, 20 November 1995, 146–148.

18. Wendy Stueck, "Bre-X Geologist Alive? His Widow Says Maybe," *Globe and Mail*, 26 May 2005, B8; Claudia Cattaneo, "Judge Orders Release of Secret Bre-X Report," *Financial Post*, 8 January 1998.

19. National Fraud Information Center website [accessed 12 July 2004] media@nclnet.org

20. John S. McClenahen, "Your Employees Know Better," *Industry Week*, 1 March 1999, 12–14.

21. Betsy Stevens, "Communicating Ethical Values: A Study of Employee Perceptions," *Journal of Business Ethics*, June 1999, 113–120.

22. Petro-Canada website (Corporate Governance section) [accessed 11 June 2007] www.petro-canada.ca

23. Milton Bordwin, "The Three R's of Ethics," *Management Review*, June 1998, 59–61.

24. Craig Dreilinger, "Get Real (and Ethics Will Follow)," *Workforce*, August 1998, 101–102; Louisa Wah, "Workplace Conscience Needs a Boost," *HRFocus*, June 1998, 7.

25. "American Workers Do the Right Thing," *HRFocus*, March 1999, 4.

26. Luma Muhtadie, "Canadians Want Whistle-Blowers Protected," *Globe and Mail*, 28 October 2003.

27. Bank of Montreal website (Code of Conduct) [accessed 12 July 2004] www.bmo.ca

28. Manuel G. Velasquez, *Business Ethics: Concepts and Cases* (Upper Saddle River, NJ: Prentice Hall, 1998), 87; Joseph L. Badaracco, Jr., "Business Ethics: Four Spheres of Executive Responsibility," *California Management Review*, Spring 1992, 64–79; Kenneth Blanchard and Norman Vincent Peale, *The Power of Ethical Management* (Reprint, 1989; New York: Fawcett Crest, 19991), 7–17; John R. Boatright, *Ethics and the Conduct of Business* (Upper Saddle River, NJ: Prentice Hall, 1996), 35–39, 59–64, 79–86.

29. See Vanderbilt's letter in the *New York Times*, 25 August 1918, and *New York Herald*, 1 October 1918.

30. M"Business of Social Responsibility," *Businessline*, 3 August 1999, 1.

31. "Does It Pay to Be Ethical?" *Business Ethics*, March-April 1997, 14–16; Don L. Boroughs, "The Bottom Line on Ethics," *U.S. News & World Report*, 20 March 1995, 61–66.

32. Shawn McCarthy, "So You Want to Bet on the Environment," *Globe and Mail*, 9 June 2007, B4.

33. Weld Royal, "Real Expectations," *IndustryWeek*, 4 September 2000, 32.

34. Ann Graham, "Lynn Sharp Payne: The Thought Leader Interview," *Strategy + Business*, Summer 2003, 97–105.

35. Joseph Weber, "3M's Big Cleanup," *BusinessWeek*, 5 June 2000, 96–98.

36. PeaceWorks website [accessed 11 June 2007] www.peaceworks.com

37. Telus Corporate Social Responsibility Report 2006, Telus website [accessed 13 June 2007] http://about.telus.com/csr2006/csr/en/commitment/stakeholder-intro.html

38. Canadian Tire website [accessed 12 June 2007] www2.canadiantire.ca/CTenglish/foundation.html

39. US Department of Energy website [accessed 3 April 2004] www.energy.gov

40. Environmental Protection Review Canada website [accessed 12 June 2007] www.eprc-rpec.gc.ca

41. Government of Canada (North American Agreement on Environmental Cooperation) website [accessed 12 June 2007] www.naaec.gc.ca/eng/agreement/agreement_e.htm

42. Sydney Tar Ponds Agency website [accessed 12 June 2007] www.tarpondscleanup.ca

43. Danny Hakim, "To Avoid Fuel Limits, Subaru Is Turning a Sedan into a Truck," *New York Times*, 13 January 2004; "Hummer Mania," CBS News website [accessed 3 April 2004] www.cbsnews.com

44. "Kyoto Protocol FAQs," 14 February 2007, CBC website [accessed 15 September 2007] www.cbc.ca/news/background/kyoto/#s7

45. Brian Laghi, "Baird Has Declared Clean-Air Act Dead, Critics Say," *Globe and Mail*, 24 April 2007, A5.

46. Brian Laghi, "Climate Deal Struck—With No Firm Targets," *Globe and Mail*, 8 June 2007, A1; Gwyn Morgan, "It's Up to Bush: Only the US Has Enough Clout to Reduce World's Emissions," *Globe and Mail*, 11 June 2007, B2.

47. Steven Chase and Greg Keenan, "Ottawa Gets Auto Emissions Deal," *Globe and Mail*, 23 March 2005, B1; Patrick Brethour, "Canada's Big Emitters Brace for Investment Climate Change," *Globe and Mail*, 19 February 2005, B4.

48. Bill Curry, "Canada to Ban Traditional Light Bulbs," *Globe and Mail*, 26 April 2007, A11; Shawn McCarthy, "A Light Bulb Came On, and It Was Energy Efficient," *Globe and Mail*, 22 January 2007, B3.

49. Cascades corporate newspaper release, May 2004, 8.

50. HBC website, Social Responsibility Highlights [accessed 12 June 2007] www.hbc.com

51. "The IW Survey: Encouraging Findings," *IndustryWeek*, 19 January 1998, 62.

52. Ben & Jerry's website [accessed 1 April 2004] www.benjerry.com; George F. Will, "Being Green and Ben & Jerry's," *Newsweek*, 6 May 2002, 72; Edward O. Welles, "Ben's Big Flop," *Inc.* September 1998, 40+; Constance L. Hays, "Ben & Jerry's to Unilever, with Attitude," *New York Times*, 13 April 2000, C1, C20; Fred Bayles, "Reviews in on Ben & Jerry's Sweet Deal," *USA Today*, 20 April 2000, 3A.

53. John Markoff, "Technology's Toxic Trash Is Sent to Poor Nations," *New York Times*, 25 February 2002, C1, C4.

54. Canadian Standards Association website [accessed 11 April 2005] www.csa.ca

55. *Consumer Packaging and Labelling Act*, Department of Justice Canada website [accessed 21 July 2004] http://laws.justice.gc.ca/en/c-38/36740.html

56. "Benetton Explains RFID Privacy Flap," *RFID Journal* [accessed 1 April 2004] www.rfidjournal.com; David LaGress, "They Know Where You Are," *U.S. News & World Report*, 8 September 2003, 32–38; Christopher Elliott, "Some Rental Cars Are Keeping Tabs on Drivers," *New York Times*, 13 January 2004, C6.

57. Patrick Bethour and Janet McFarland, "Forzani Agrees to Pay Record Settlement," *Globe and Mail*, 7 July 2004, B1, B22.

58. Marina Strauss and Simon Tuck, "Tribunal Rules Sears Broke Law by Inflating Tire Savings," *Globe and Mail*, 25 January 2005, B1, B8.

59. "New Cigarette Pack Warning Labels Appear," 22 December 2000, Health Canada website [accessed 22 July 2004] www.hc-sc.gc.ca/english/media/releases/2000/2000_21_tob-label.htm

60. Inco website [accessed 13 June 2007] www.inco.com/development/community/profiles/voisey/default.aspx; Wendy Stueck, "Vindication of Voisey's Bay," *Globe and Mail*, 3 September 2005, B4; Wendy Stueck, "Natives Hope for Big Gains from Inco's Nickel Riches," *Globe and Mail*, 17 June 2004, B5; Wendy Stueck, "Voisey's Bay at Last Getting Off the Ground," *Globe and Mail*, 17 June 2004, B1, B4; Peter Kennedy, "Inco Advances Voisey's Startup by Six Months," *Globe and Mail*, 21 July 2004, B4.

61. Bertrand Marotte, "Cinar Shareholders Seek Lawyer's Trust Fund Details," *Globe and Mail*, 31October 2006.

62. John A. Byrne, Leslie Brown, and Joyce Barnathan, "Directors in the Hot Seat," *BusinessWeek*, 8 December 1997, 100, 102, 104.

63. Laura Bogolmy, "The Bar Is Set High," *Canadian Business*, 19 July–15 August 2004, 44–45.

64. *Employment Equity Act*, Department of Justice website [accessed 13 June 2007] http://laws.justice.gc.ca/en/ShowFullDoc/cs/E-5.401///en

65. Valerie Merchant, "The New Face of Work," 29 March 2004, *Canadian Business* website [accessed 22 July 2004] www.canadianbusiness.com

66. Canadian Centre for Occupational Health and Safety website [accessed 13 June 2007] www.ccohs.ca/ccohs.html

67. Sustainability Report Ranking, *Corporate Knights*, 3(1), 30.

68. See Note 1 for case sources.

69. Nathalie Pace, "China Surpasses US in Internet Usage," *Forbes Magazine*, [accessed 24 May 2007] www.forbes.com/2006/03/31/china-internet-usage-cx_nwp_0403china.html; CNNIC website [accessed 24 May 2007] www.cnnic.net.cn/en/index/0O/index.htm; Sumner Lemon, "China's Online Game Market to Top 1.2 Billion," 26 July 2006 [accessed 24 May 2007] www.networkworld.com/news/2006/072506-chinas-online-game-market-to.html; "China Is World's No. 2 Spam Receiver," ChinaTechNews.com, 17 March 2004 [accessed 5 April 2004] www.chinatechnews.com; Bruce Einhorn, "The Net's Second Superpower," *BusinessWeek*, 15 March 2004, 54–56; David J. Lynch, "Surf's Up in China, Where Millions Are Going Online,: *USA Today*, 8 October 2003, B1–2; "China Pulls Plug on Internet Blogs," ChinaTechNews.com, 17 March 2004 [accessed 5 April 2004] www.chinatechnews.com; "China Suspends Registration of New Net Cafés," ChinaTechNews.com, 3 March 2004 [accessed 5 April 2004] www.chinatechnews.com.

Chapter 4

1. Diedre McMurdy, "Opportunity Knocks—Hard," *Canadian Business*, 10 December 2001; InLine Hockey Central website [accessed 10 March 2007] www.inlinehockeycentral.com/article.php?article_id=51111; Randy Burns, Mission-Itech VP of marketing [20 March 2007]; Mission-Itech website [accessed 10 March 2007] www.itech.com; "Mission Hockey Merges with Itech," SkateLog.com website [accessed 30 June 2004] www.skatelog.com/skates/mission/2004-05-itech-merger.htm

2. Small Business Statistics, Industry Canada website [accessed 10 March 2007] http://strategis.ic.gc.ca/epic/site/sbrp-rppe.nsf/en/rd02097e.html

3. Industry Canada website [accessed 14 April 2005] www.ic.gc.ca

4. Jim Hopkins, "Entrepreneur 101: Supervising Employees," *USA Today*, 12 September 2001, 9B; Claudia H. Deutsch, "When a Big Company Hatches a Lot of Little Ideas," *New York Times*, 23 September 1998, D4.

5. Key Small Business Statistics, January 2007, Industry Canada website [accessed 10 March 2007] http://strategis.ic.gc.ca/epic/site/sbrp-rppe.nsf/en/rd02100e.html

6. Small Business Statistics, Industry Canada website [accessed 10 March 2007] http://strategis.ic.gc.ca/epic/site/sbrp-rppe.nsf/en/rd01238e.html

7. Annabelle King, "Hang 'em High," *Montreal Gazette*, 2 July 2004, B1.

8. LeapFrog website [accessed 10 March 2007] www.leapfrog.com

9. "Matters of Fact," *Inc.*, April 1985, 32.

10. Lisa Stephens, "Staying Small—and Loving It," *Globe and Mail*, 19 October, 2005, E11.

11. Annual Report 2006, Magna International website [accessed 10 March 2007] http://media.corporate-ir.net/media_files/irol/86/86334/news/022707EarningsEnglish.pdf

12. Exhibit is adapted from Carrie Dolan, "Entrepreneurs Often Fail as Managers," *Wall Street Journal*, 15 May 1989, B1. Reprinted by permission of *The Wall Street Journal*, © 1989 Dow Jones & Company, Inc. All Reserved Worldwide.

13. Brian O'Reilly, "The New Face of Small Business," *Fortune*, 2 May 1994, 82–88.

14. Simon Avery, "Small Guys Find Their Niche and Prosper," *Globe and Mail*, 21 September 2006, B16.

15. Michael Moeller, Steve Hamm, and Timothy J. Mullaney, "Remaking Microsoft," *BusinessWeek*, 17 May 1999, 106–116.

16. Timothy D. Schelhardt, "David in Goliath," *Wall Street Journal*, 23 May 1996, R14; Deutsch, "When a Big Company Hatches a Lot of Little Ideas."

17. Angela Pacienza, "Job Website Serves Retired Workers," *Globe and Mail*, 9 June 2004, C10.

18. Grant Buckler, "Cybernetworking: Making the Digital Connection," *Globe and Mail*, 22 March 2007, B8; David Pescovitz, "Technology of the Year: Social Network Applications," *Business 2.0*, November 2003, 113–114; Spoke website [accessed 11 April 2004] www.spoke.com; LinkedIn website [accessed 11 April 2004l] www.linkedin.com; Ryze website [accessed 11 April 2004] www.ryze.com

19. Grant Buckler, "The Virtual Reality of Getting Good Help," *Globe and Mail*, 18 October 2006, E5.

20. *Inc. Special Edition—The State of Small Business 1997*, 20 May 1997, 112; James Wilfong and Toni Seger, *Taking Your Business Global* (Franklin Lakes, NJ: Career Press, 1997), 84

21. Michael Ryval, "Making a Statement On-Line," *Globe and Mail*, 17 March 2005, B8; Brian Hurley and Peter Birkwood, *A Small Business Guide to Doing Big Business on the Internet* (Bellingham, Washington: International Self-Counsel Press, 1996),

124–134; "Design a Better Web Site," *Journal of Accountancy*, August 1998, 18; Anita Dennis, "A Home on the Web," *Journal of Accountancy*, August 1998, 29–31.
22. Rob Shaw, "Small Business Driving Growth, and Women Are in Control," *Globe and Mail*, 29 June 2005, B3: Roma Luciw, "Stay-at-Home Moms Stay the Business Course," *Globe and Mail*, 3 March 2007, B10
23. Key Small Business Statistics, July 2006, Industry Canada website [accessed 13 March 2007] www.strategis.gc.ca
24. CIBC World Markets, "Start Me Up: A Look at New Entrepreneurs in Canada," *CanadaOne Magazine* website [accessed 26 July 2004] www.canadaone.com/ezine/july04/small_business_startups.html
25. Anne R. Carey and Grant Jerding, USA Snapshot, *USA Today*, 26 March 1998, B1.
26. Tony Martin, "Home-Business Operator Learns Her Lessons," *Globe and Mail*, 17 July 2004, B8.
27. CIBC World Markets, "Start Me Up: A Look at New Entrepreneurs in Canada."
28. Wilfong and Seger, *Taking Your Business Global*, 78–80; Kelly J. Andrews, "Born or Bred?" *Entrepreneurial Edge*, 3 (1998), 24–28.
29. Jane Applegate, *Succeeding in Small Business* (New York: Plume/Penguin, 1992), 1.
30. Jill Mahoney, "How Running Room's Founder Stays on Track," *Globe and Mail*, 14 July 2004, B1; Running Room website [accessed 13 March 2007] www.runningroom.com/content/?id=124
31. Eve Tahmincioglu, "Even the Best Ideas Don't Sell Themselves," *New York Times*, 9 October 2003, C9.
32. Richard Bloom, "How to Sell Your Idea to the Money Men," *Globe and Mail*, 20 October, 2004, E5: Allison Dunfield, "Failed to Plan? Then Plan to Fail," *Globe and Mail*, 18 October, 2006, E3.
33. J. Tol Broome, Jr., "How to Write a Business Plan," *Nation's Business*, February 1993, 29–30; Albert Richards, "The Ernst & Young Business Plan Guide," *R&D Management*, 1995, 253; David Lanchner, "How Chitchat Became a Valuable Business Plan" *Global Finance*, February 1995, 54–56; Marguerita Ashby-Berger, "My Business Plan—And What Really Happened," *Small Business Forum*, Winter 1994–95, 24–35; Stanley R. Rich and David E. Gumpert, *Business Plans That Win $$$* (New York: Harper Row, 1985).
34. Norm Brodsky, "Caveat Emptor," *Inc.*, August 1998, 31–32; "Why Buy a Business?" CCH Toolkit website [accessed 20 May 1999] aol.toolkit.cch.com/text/PO1_0820.asp
35. "Canadian Franchise Statistics," BeTheBoss.ca [accessed 17 September 2007] http://www.betheboss.ca/general.cfm?page=franchise-statistics.cfm
36. *Montreal Entrepreneur's Guidebook*, 2nd edition, (1999, Youth Employment Services Publication, 1999) 3–58, 3–59;

Canadian Franchise Association website [accessed 29 July 2004] www.cfa.ca
37. Roberta Maynard, "Choosing a Franchise," *Nation's Business*, October 1996, 56–63.
38. Marjo Johne, "Got Guts, and a Good Amount of Capital?" *Globe and Mail*, 18 October, 2006, E8, 1-800-GOT-JUNK? website [accessed 16 March 2007] www.1800gotjunk.com/content/pdf/PRESS_KIT.pdf
39. Second Cup website [accessed 20 March 2007] www.zingbias.com/second_cup/eng/franchising.php?section=4#m1
40. World Franchising website [accessed 16 March 2007] www.worldfranchising.com/profiles/harveys-restaurants/16/1/
41. Cara Operations Limited website [accessed 16 March 2007] www.cara.com
42. Michael Hopkins, "Zen and the Art of the Self-Managed Company," *Inc.*, November 2000, 54–63.
43. Joseph W. Duncan, "The True Failure Rate of Start-Ups," *D&B Reports*, January–February 1994; Maggie Jones, "Smart Cookies," *Working Woman*, April 1995, 50–52; Janice Maloney, "Failure May Not Be So Bad After All," *New York Times*, 23 September 1998, 12.
44. Tony Martin, "Follow the Numbers to Gauge Success," *Globe and Mail*, 18 October 2006, E10.
45. Jerry Useem, "The Secret of My Success," *Inc.*, May 1998, 67–80
46. Maloney, "Failure May Not Be So Bad After All."
47. Loren Fox, "Hatching New Companies," *Upside*, February 2000, 144–152.
48. AgriTECH website [accessed 29 July 2004] www.agritechpark.com/services.html; CEIM website [accessed 16 March 2007] www.ceim.org/english.html; Toronto Fashion Incubator website [accessed 16 March 2007] www.fashionincubator.on.ca
49. Dale Buss, "Bringing New Firms Out of Their Shell," *Nation's Business*, March 1997, 48–50; Fox, "Hatching New Companies."
50. Jonathan Katz, "Hatching Ideas," *Industry Week*, 18 September 2000, 63–65.
51. Andrew Willis, "Scaled-Down Brick IPO Not a Bad Omen," *Globe and Mail*, 20 July 2004, B16.
52. Jim Hopkins, "Corporate Giants Bankroll Start-Ups," *USA Today*, 29 March 2001, B1.
53. Bob Zider, "How Venture Capital Works," *Harvard Business Review*, November/December 1998, 131–139.
54. Shirley Won, "Wooing the Money Men," *Globe and Mail*, 17 March 2005, C1; 2006 Annual Statistics Review, Canadian Venture Capital Association website [accessed 19 March 2007] www.cvca.ca/files/Downloads/Final_English_Q4_2006_VC_Data_Deck.pdf, page 8.
55. Dori Jones Yang, "Venture Capitalists Seek Less Adventure," *U.S. News & World Report*, 4 June 2001, 39.

56. Charles B. Crawford, *Montreal Entrepreneur's Guidebook*, 1999, 7–33.
57. Crazy Plates website [accessed 19 March 2007] www.crazyplates.com
58. Rodney Ho, "Banking on Plastic," *Wall Street Journal*, 9 March 1998, A1, A8.
59. Joel Russell, "Credit Card Capitalism," *Hispanic Business*, March 1998, 40.
60. See Note 1 for case sources.
61. Small Business Statistics, Industry Canada website [accessed 19 March 2007] http://strategis.ic.gc.ca/epic/site/sbrp-rppe.nsf/en/rd02100e.html

Chapter 5
1. Konrad Yakabuski, "The Builder," *Report on Business Magazine*, October 2004, 85–96; Marina Strauss, "Rona Hammers Out Bold Stategy," *Globe and Mail*, 7 June 2006, B1; Marina Strauss, "Investors Hammer Rona Shares Despite Strong Profit Report," *Globe and Mail*, 23 February 2007, B7; Peter Shawn Taylor, "Home Fires Burning," *Canadian Business*, 11–24 October 2004, 77–83; Konrad Yakabuski, "Lowe's Schmoes, Rona Has Eyes on Little Guys," *Globe and Mail*, 16 June 2005, B2; Marina Strauss, "Lowe's Targets Canadian Handywoman," *Globe and Mail*, 7 June 2005, B1, B7; Haris Anwar, "Rona Eyes Continued Canadian Expansion," *Globe and Mail*, 26 March 2005, B6; Patrick Brethour, "Rona Builds Up Alberta Business," *Globe and Mail*, 22 December 2004, B1; Allan Swift, "Expansion Helps Power Rona Profit 77% in 2004," *Globe and Mail*, 24 February 2005, B5; Zena Olijnyk, "Handy Woman," *Canadian Business*, 9 November 2003, 33–36; Rona website [accessed 6 June 2007] www.rona.ca/content/profile_profile_investor-relations; Home Hardware website [accessed 6 June 2007] www.homehardware.ca/en/home-hardware-contact-us.php
2. Norman M. Scarborough and Thomas W. Zimmerer, *Effective Small Business Management* (Upper Saddle River, NJ: Prentice Hall, 2000), 84.
3. "LLP Legislation Proclaimed in Manitoba," *CA Folio Newsletter*, 121, March/April 2003 [accessed 25 November 2004] www.icam.mb.ca/pdf/Folio121.pdf; McGill Legal Information Clinic Hotline [accessed 12 November 2005]; Scott A. Campbell, "Extra-Provincial Limited Liability Partnerships," *Business Beat*, 11(2), May 2001 [accessed 14 November 2004] www.mcleankerr.com/pdfs/LLP.PDF
4. James W. Cortada, "Do You Take this Partner," *Total Quality Review*, November–December 1995, 11.
5. Verne Kopytoff, "YouTube Investors Enjoy 'Storybook: Payday,'" *Globe and Mail*, 9 February 2007, B8.
6. RIM website (Investor Relations) [accessed 17 April 2005] www.rim.com
7. Tony Kontzer, "Learning to Share," *InformationWeek*, 5 May 2003, 28; Jon Udell,

"Uniting Under Groove," *InfoWorld*, 17 February 2003 [accessed 9 September 2003] www.elibrary.com; Alison Overhold, "Virtually There?" *Fast Company*, 15 February 2002, 108.

8. Cirque du Soleil website [accessed 6 June 2007] www.cirquedusoleil.com/CirqueDuSoleil/en/default.htm; Bob Simon, "Inside Cirque du Soleil," *60 Minutes*, 13 December 1999; CBS News, "Fab Four du Soleil," [accessed 25 November 2004] www.cbsnews.com/stories/2004/10/14/entertainment/printable649299.shtml

9. Konrad Yakabuski, "The Builder," *Report on Business Magazine*, October 2004, 85–96.

10. Wendy Stueck, "Pattison Group Eyes More Say at Canfor," *Globe and Mail*, 13 March 2007, B3; Gordon Pitts, "Invisible Billionaire Casts a Huge Shadow," *Globe and Mail*, 18 April 2005, B3; Jim Pattison Group website [accessed 6 June 2007] www.jimpattison.com/divisional_websites.htm

11. Wal-Mart website [accessed 6 June 2007] www.walmartfacts.com/FactSheets/3142007_Corporate_Facts.pdf; "30 Canadian Metropolitan Areas" [accessed 27 November 2004] www.canadainfolink.ca/cities.htm

12. Data for 31 July 2004, Globe Investor website [accessed 27 November 2004] http://investdb.theglobeandmail.com/invest/investSQL/gx.company_prof?company_id=181455&symbol_in=

13. Rana Dogar, "Crony Baloney," *Working Woman*, January 1997; Richard H. Koppes, "Institutional Investors, Now in Control of More than Half the Shares of U.S. Corporations, Demand More Accountability," *National Law Journal*, 14 April 1997, B5; John A. Byrne, "The Best & Worst Boards," *BusinessWeek*, 25 November 1996, 82–84; Anthony Bianco, John Byrne, Richard Melcher, and Mark Maremont, "The Rush to Quality on Corporate Boards," *BusinessWeek*, 3 March 1997, 34–35.

14. "Independence Makes Big Gains in the Boardroom," *Globe and Mail*, 12 October 2004, B1.

15. Elizabeth Church, "Boards Recruit New Faces, New Visions," *Globe and Mail*, 13 October 2004, B1.

16. Andrew Willis, "Mulroney Lands Spot on Blackstone Board," *Globe and Mail*, 5 June 2007, B10.

17. Janet McFarland, "More Women Take Seats in the Boardroom," *Globe and Mail*, 15 January 2007, B1.

18. Gary Strauss, "From Public Service to Private Payday," *USA Today*, 17 April 2000, 1B, 2B.

19. Canada Business Services website [accessed 28 November 2004] www.cbsc.org/english/search/display.cfm?code=4000&Coll=FE_FEDSBIS_E

20. Report On Business, "The Top 1000," 2006 Edition, Globe and Mail website

[accessed 6 June 2007] www.theglobeandmail.com/v5/content/tp1000/index.php?view=financial_cooperatives

21. Canada Business Services website [accessed 28 November 2004] www.cbsc.org/english/search/display.cfm?code=4000&Coll=FE_FEDSBIS_E

22. Ibid.

23. Steven Chase and Leonard Zehr, "Flaherty to Unveil Economic Strategy," *Globe and Mail*, 2 November 2006, B1; Jeff Sanford, "Income Trusts: No Surprises," *Canadian Business*, 25 September–8 October 2006, 49–55; Department of Finance Canada website [accessed 7 June 2007] www.fin.gc.ca/news06/06-061e.html; Steven Chase, "Income Trusts Launch Damage Control," *Globe and Mail*, 23 October 2006, B1.

24. Randy Burns, Mission-Itech VP of Marketing, 3 August 2004; Mission-Itech website [accessed 6 June 2007] www.itech.com; "Mission Hockey Merges with Itech," SkateLog.com website [accessed 30 June 2004] www.skatelog.com/skates/mission/2004-05-itech-merger.htm

25. Alison MacGregor, "Reebok Scores with Acquisition of Hockey Co." *Montreal Gazette*, 9 April 2004, B1.

26. Pizza Delight website, Press Releases [accessed 6 June 2007] www.pizzadelight.ca

27. David A. Nadler, "10 Steps to a Happy Merger," *New York Times*, 15 March 1998, BU14.

28. Peter Passell, "Do Mergers Really Yield Big Benefits?" *New York Times*, 14 May 1998, C1, C2.

29. Andy Holloway, "Wasting Time," *Canadian Business*, 1 March 2004, 95+; John Motavalli, "More AOL Woes for Time Warner," *Television Week*, 5 January 2004, 1+; Andy Kessler, "Here's the Sinking Case of AOL Time Warner," *Wall Street Journal* Online, 8 October 2002; Frank Ahrens, "At AOL and Disney, Uneasy Chairs," *Washington Post*, 18 September 2002, E01; Martin Peers, "Will Steve Case Leave AOL?" *Wall Street Journal*, 12 September 2002, B1, B7; Jeremy Kahn and Bill Powell, "Can These Guys Fix AOL?" *Fortune*, 2 September 2002, 95–100; Tom Lowry, "The Sinkhole of 'Synergy,'" *BusinessWeek*, 26 August 2002, 42; Frank Ahrens, Merissa Marr, "Old-School Media Reassert Control," *Toronto Star*, 30 July 2002; "Big Media Mergers Raise Big Doubts: Is Synergy Achievable—or Even Desirable?" *Washington Post*, 14 May 2002, A01.

30. Merrill Goozner and John Schmeltzer, "Mass Exodus Hits Corporate Names," *Chicago Tribune*, 12 May 1998, sec. 3, 1, 3; Bill Vlasic, "The First Global Car Colossus," *BusinessWeek*, 18 May 1998, 40–43; Abid Aslam, "Exxon-Mobil Merger Could Poison the Well," *Inter Press Service English News Wire*, 2 December 1998, Electric Library [accessed 2 June 1999]; Agis Salpukas, "Do Oil and Bigger Oil Mix?" *New York Times*, 2 December 1998, C1, C4.

31. Steve Lipen, "Concentration: Corporations' Dreams Converge in One Idea: It's Time to Do a Deal," *Wall Street Journal*, 26 February 1997, A1, A8.

32. Matthew McClearn, "Aluminum Foil," *Canadian Business*, 29 September 2003, 29.

33. Larry Selden and Geoffrey Colvin, "M&A Needn't Be a Loser's Game," *Harvard Business Review*, June 2003, 70–79; Amy Kover, "Big Banks Debunked," *Fortune*, 21 February 2000, 187–194; Erick Schonfeld, "Have the Urge to Merge? You Better Think Twice," *Fortune*, 31 March 1997, 114–116; Phillip L. Zweig et al., "The Case against Mergers," *BusinessWeek*, 30 October 1995, 122–130; Kevin Kelly et al., "Mergers Today, Trouble Tomorrow?" *BusinessWeek*, 12 September 1994; "How to Merge," *The Economist*, 9 January 1999, 21–23; "Study Says Mergers Often Don't Aid Investors," *New York Times*, 1 December 1999, C9.

34. Joann S. Lublin, "'Poison Pills' Are Giving Shareholders a Big Headache, Union Proposals Assert," *Wall Street Journal*, 23 May 1997, C1.

35. Martha Groves and Stuart Silverstein, "Levi Strauss Offers Year's Pay as Incentive Bonus," *Los Angeles Times*, 13 June 2006, A1.

36. Michael Hickins, "Searching for Allies," *Management Review*, January 2000, 54–58.

37. Gary Dessler, *Management*, 2nd ed. (Upper Saddle River, NJ: Prentice Hall, 2001), 45.

38. Virgin Mobile website [accessed 7 June 2007] www.virginmobile.ca; BCE website [accessed 29 November 2004] www.bce.ca/en/news/releases/bc/2004/03/30/71061.html

39. See Note 1 for case sources.

40. Charles Mandel, "In the World of B2B, You Can File this Under Oeno-Line," *Globe and Mail*, 10 February 2005, C1, C18; Paulette Thomas, "The Morning After," *Wall Street Journal*, 27 March 2002, R12; "The Internet's Bust Became a Boom (Who Ever Doubted It?)," Mediagrif Interactive Technologies website [accessed 7 June 2007] www.mediagrif.com/html/investors/overview_en.asp; New York Metro.com website [accessed 23 December 2004] www.newyorkmetro.com/nymetro/news/yearinreview/2004/10673/; Michael Totty and Ann Grimes, "If at First You Don't Succeed," *Wall Street Journal*, 11 February 2002, R6–R7; J. William Gurley, "Startups, Beware: Obey the Law of Supply and Demand," *Fortune*, 29 May 2000, 278; William M. Bulkeley and Jim Carlton, "E-Tail Gets Derailed: How Web Upstarts Misjudged the Game," *Wall Street Journal*, 5 April 2000, A1, A6; Leslie Kaufman, "After Taking a Beating, Dot-Coms Now Seek Financial Saviors," *New York Times*, 18 April 2000, C1, C18; Kevin Maney, "Net Start-Ups Pull Out of the Garage," *USA Today*, 1 October 1999, 1B, 2B; Matt Krantz, "E-Retailers Run Low on Fuel," *USA Today*, 26 April 2000, 1B, 2B; "Survival of the

Fastest," *Inc. Tech*, 16 November 1999, 44–58; Darnell Little, "Peapod Is in a Pickle," *BusinessWeek*, 3 April 2000, 41; Heather Green, Nanette Byrnes, Norm Alster, and Arlene Weintraub, "The Dot.Coms Are Falling to Earth," *BusinessWeek*, 17 April 2000, 48–49; John A. Byrne, "The Fall of a Dot-Com," *BusinessWeek*, 1 May 2000, 150–160; Stephanie N. Mehta, "As Investors Play VC, It's Dot-Com Doomsday," *Fortune*, 1 May 2000, 40–41; David P. Hamilton and Mylene Mangalindan, "Angels of Death," *Wall Street Journal*, 25 May 2000, A1, A8; Luisa Kroll, "When the Music Stops," *Forbes*, 15 May 2000, 182; Chris Farrell, "Death of the Dot-Coms?" *BusinessWeek*, 22 May 2000, 104; John Steele Gordon, "The Golden Spike," *Forbes ASAP*, 21 February 2000, 118–122; Eric W. Pfeiffer, "Where Are We in the Revolution?" *Forbes ASAP*, 21 February 2000, 68–70; James Lardner and Paul Sloan, "The Anatomy of Sickly IPOs," *U.S. News and World Report*, 29 May 2000, 42; Hillary Stout, "Crunch Time," *Wall Street Journal*, 7 June 2000, B1; Jerry Useem, "Dot-Coms—What Have We Learned?" *Fortune*, 30 October 2000, 82–104; Heather Green and Norm Alster, "Guess What—Venture Capitalists Aren't Geniuses," *BusinessWeek*, 10 July 2000, 98; Thomas E. Weber, "What Were We Thinking?" *Wall Street Journal*, 18 July 2000, B1, B4.

Chapter 6

1. Jane Wardell, "Online Music Sales Nearly Double Globally," *Globe and Mail*, 18 January 2007, B7; Apple iTunes website [accessed 16 June 2007] www.apple.com/itunes; "iPod Rocks with Users, Rolls to 100 Million in Sales" *Globe and Mail*, 10 April 2007, B14; Keith McArthur, "Is This the Holy Grail of Gadgets?" *Globe and Mail*, 10 January 2007, B1; Bloomberg, "Apple Posts Record Profit on iPod Sales," *Globe and Mail*, 18 January 2007, B14; CNN, "The Steve Jobs Way," 23 April 2004, CNN website [accessed 16 June 2007] www.cnn.com/2004/WORLD/americas/04/16/jobs; Matthew Ingram, "Apple's Really Shiny, but Microsoft's in No Danger Yet," *Globe and Mail*, 8 February 2007, B13; Simon Avery, "Apple Raises Curtain on Movie Service," *Globe and Mail*, 13 September 2007, B1; Jeff Leeds, "Online Song Sales, though Rising Fast, Are at Most a Hopeful Blip," *Los Angeles Times*, 1 February 2004, C1; Pui-Wing Tam and Nick Wingfield, "Apple's iTunes to Fall Short on Song Sales," *Wall Street Journal*, 16 March 2004, B3; Bob Tedeschi, "Music at Your Fingertips, but a Battle among Those Selling It to You," *New York Times*, 1 December 2003, C21; Gloria Goodale, "'Don't Call Me a Pirate, I'm an Online Fan;' One Girl's Downloading Habits Reveal the Gulf between the Music Industry and Teens," *Christian Scince Monitor*, 18 July 2003, 13; John Schwartz and John Markoff, "Power Players: Big Names Are Jumping into the Crowded Online Music Field," *New York Times*, 12 January 2004 [accessed 30 March 2004] www.nytimes.com; Peter Lewis, "Gadgets: Drop a Quarter in the Internet," *Fortune*, 14 March 2004 [accessed 30 March 2004] www.fortune.com

2. Richard L. Daft, *Management*, 4th ed. (Fort Worth, TX: Dryden Press, 1997), 8.

3. Courtland L. Bovée, John V. Thill, Marian Burk Wood, and George P. Dovel, *Management* (New York: McGraw-Hill, 1993), 220; David H. Holt, *Management: Principles and Practices*, 2nd ed. (Upper Saddle River, NJ: Prentice Hall, 1990), 10–12; James A. F. Stoner, *Management*, 4th ed. (Upper Saddle River, NJ: Prentice Hall, 1989), 15–18.

4. Gillian Flynn, "A Flight Plan for Success," *Workforce*, July 1997, 72–128.

5. Stephen P. Robbins, *Managing Today* (Upper Saddle River, NJ: Prentice Hall, 1997), 452.

6. Leonard Goodstein, Timothy Nolan, and J. William Pfeiffer, *Applied Strategic Planning* (New York: McGraw-Hill, 1993), 169–192.

7. Aimee L. Stern, "Management: You Can Keep Your Staff on the Competitive Track If You . . . Inspire Your Team with a Mission Statement," *Your Company*, 1 August 1997, 36.

8. Cornelis A. de Kluyver and John A Pearce II, *Strategy: A View from the Top* (Upper Saddle River, NJ: Prentice-Hall, 2003), 62.

9. Norman M. Scarborough and Thomas W. Zimmerer, *Effective Small Business Management* (Upper Saddle River, NJ: Prentice Hall, 2000), 50.

10. Richard L. Daft, *Management*, 4th ed. (Fort Worth, TX: Dryden Press, 1997), 221–223, 260–262.

11. Judy A. Smith, "Crisis Communications: The War on Two Fronts," *IndustryWeek*, 20 May 1996, 136; John F. Reukus, "Hazard Communication," *Occupational Hazards*, February 1998, 39; Kim M. Gibson and Steven H. Smith, "Do We Understand Each Other?" *Journal of Accountancy*, January 1998, 53.

12. Canadian Press, "Royal Bank Computer Glitch Affects Millions," CTV website [accessed 28 October 2004] www.ctv.ca

13. Michael Moeller, Steve Hamm, and Timothy J. Mullaney, "Remaking Microsoft," *BusinessWeek*, 17 May 1999, 106–116

14. Stephanie Armour, "Once Plagued by Pink Slips, Now They're in Driver's Seat," *USA Today*, 14 May 1998, 1B–2B.

15. Daft, *Management*, 219–221.

16. Harvey Schachter, "Getting Personal with Leadership Traits," *Globe and Mail*, 6 June 2007, C3; Harvey Schachter, "Full of Themselves, Failing Themselves," *Globe and Mail*, 2 May 2007, C3; Jack Welch, "The Best Advice I Ever Got," *Fortune*, 21 March 2005, 101–114; Jacqueline Foley, "Listen Up: Good Leaders Are All Ears," *Globe and Mail*, 8 March 2006, C1; Janet McFarland, "What CEO's Are Made of," *Globe and Mail*, 25 August 2006, B1; Gordon Pitts, "Need a Leader? Just Look for a GE Graduate," *Globe and Mail*, 11 July 2005, B11; Diane Davies, "Meet the Seven Deadly Executive Types," *Globe and Mail*, 4 November 2005, C7; Barb Sawyers, "Managers Must be On the Front Lines of Transparency," *Globe and Mail*, 13 May 2005, C1.

17. Gary A. Yukl, *Leadership in Organizations*, 2nd ed. (Upper Saddle River, NJ: Prentice Hall, 1989), 9, 175–176.

18. Daniel Goleman, "What Makes a Leader?" *Harvard Business Review*, November–December 1998, 92–102; Shari Caudron, "The Hard Case for Soft Skills," *Workforce*, July 1999, 60–66.

19. Daft, *Management*, 498–499.

20. Jenny Anderson, "Al Gets the Chainsaw," *Institutional Investor*, October 1999, 224.

21. David Dotlich, James Noel, and Norman Walker, "Failure Breeds Successful Leaders," *Globe and Mail*, 28 January 2005, C1.

22. Danny King, Bloomberg News, "EBay Chief Whitman Named Most Powerful Businesswoman," *The Gazette* (Montreal), 5 October 2004.

23. Stratford Sherman, "Secrets of HP's 'Muddled' Team," *Fortune*, 18 March 1996, 116–120.

24. Daniel Goleman, "Leadership That Gets Results," *Harvard Business Review*, March–April 2000, 78–90.

25. Daft, *Management*, 526

26. Stephen P. Robbins and David A. DeCenzo, *Fundamentals of Management*, 4th ed. (Upper Saddle River, NJ: Prentice Hall, 2004), 325.

27. Stephen P. Robbins and David A. DeCenzo, *Fundamentals of Management*, 2nd ed. (Upper Saddle River, NJ: Prentice Hall, 1998), 55–56; James Waldroop and Timothy Butler, "The Executive as Coach," *Harvard Business Review*, November–December 1996, 113.

28. "The Advantage of Female Mentoring," *Working Woman*, October 1991, 104.

29. David Welch and Kathleen Kerwin, "Rick Wagoner's Game Plan," *BusinessWeek*, 10 February 2003, 52–60.

30. Eric Reguly, "Latest Ski-Doo Numbers Show Bombardier Didn't Get Best Price," *Globe and Mail*, 28 October 2004, B2; Sean Silcoff, "Tellier's Decision Caused Rift: Book," *Globe and Mail*, 19 October 2004, B6.

31. Daft, *Management*, 382; Robbins and DeCenzo, *Fundamentals of Management*, 4th ed. 209.

32. Michael Been and Nitin Nohria, "Cracking the Code of Change," *Harvard Business Review*, May–June 2000, 133–141.

33. Robbins and DeCenzo, *Fundamentals of Management*, 4th ed. 210–211; Daft, *Management*, 384, 396.

34. Barb Sawyers, "Ten Tips to Help Managers Communicate in Times of

Change," *Globe and Mail*, 15 September 2004, C3; Michael Barrier, "Managing Workers in Times of Change," *Nation's Business*, May 1998, 31–32.

35. Andrew Bird, "Do You Know What Your Corporate Culture Is?" *CPA Insight*, February, March 1999, 25–26; Gail H. Vergara, "Finding a Compatible Corporate Culture," *Healthcare Executive*, January/February 1999, 46–47; Hal Lancaster, "To Avoid a Job Failure, Learn the Culture of a Company First," *Wall Street Journal*, 14 July1998, B1.

36. John A. Byrne, Mike France, and Wendy Zellner, "Enron and Beyond," *BusinessWeek*, 25 February 2002, 118–120.

37. Paul Waldie, "De Zen Cuts Deal, Gives Up Control of Royal Group," *Globe and Mail*, 25 March 2005, B1; John Gray, "Royal Mess," *Canadian Business*, 25 October–7 November, 49.

38. Richard Pérez-Peña and Matthew L. Wald, "Basic Failures by Ohio Utility Set Off Blackout, Report Finds," *New York Times*, 20 November 2003, A1; "US Blackout: Interim Report," *Power Economics*, January 2004, 9; Edward Iwata, "Report: Major Blackout Could Have Been Prevented," *USA Today*, 6 April 2004, A1.

39. Kostas N. Dervitsiotis, "The Challenge of Managing Organizational Change," *Total Quality Management*, February 1998, 109–122.

40. George Taninecz, "BorgWarner Automotive," *IndustryWeek*, 19 October 1998, 44–46.

41. Bovée et al., *Management*, 680.

42. James R. Lackritz, "TQM within Fortune 500 Corporations," *Quality Progress*, February 1997, 69–72.

43. David Sirota, Brian Usilaner, and Michelle S. Weber, "Sustaining Quality Improvement," *Total Quality Review*, March–April 1994, 23; Joe Batten, "A Total Quality Culture," *Management Review*, May 1994, 61; Rahul Jacon, "More than a Dying Fad?" *Fortune*, 18 October 1993, 66–72.

44. Lackritz, "TQM within Fortune 500 Corporations."

45. Courtland L. Bovée and John V. Thill, *Business Communication Today*, 6th ed. (Upper Saddle River, NJ: Prentice Hall, 2000), 4.

46. Daft, *Management*, 128; Kathryn M. Bartol and David C. Martin, *Management* (New York: McGraw-Hill, 1991), 268–272.

47. University of Alberta School of Business press release, "Dominic D'Alessandro: 2007 Canadian Business Leader of the Year," [accessed 17 June 2007] www.business .ualberta.ca/ext-relations/media/releases/2006/20061002.htm

48. Bartol and Martin, *Management*, 268–272; Ricky W. Griffin, *Management*, 3rd ed. (Boston: Houghton Mifflin, 1990), 131–137.

49. Robbins, *Managing Today*, 72.

50. Roma Luciw, "No.1 Employee Not Always Your No.1 Manager," *Globe and Mail*, 17 February 2007, B10; Virginia Galt, "Lousy People Skills are Biggest Hurdle for Leaders," *Globe and Mail*, 15 October 2006, B11.

51. Robert L. Katz, "Skills of an Effective Administrator," *Harvard Business Review*, September–October 1974. Reprinted in *Paths toward Personal Progress: Leaders Are Made, Not Born* (Boston: Harvard Business Review, 1983), 23–35; Mike Dawson, "Leaders versus Managers," *Systems Management*, March 1995, 32; R. S. Dreyer, "Do Good Bosses Make Lousy Leaders?" *Supervision*, March 1995, 19–20; Michael Maccoby, "Teams Need Open Leaders," *Research-Technology Management*, January–February 1995, 57–59.

52. TechEncyclopedia, [accessed 13 April 2004] www.techweb.com/encyclopedia; Business Objects websites [accessed 13 April 2004] www.businessobjects.com; Cognos website [accessed 13 April 2004] www.cognos.com

53. See Note 1 for case sources.

Chapter 7

1. Interview with Jean-François Grenier, Altitude Concepts president, 19 June 2007; Altitude Concepts website [accessed 19 June 2007] www.altitude-concepts.com

2. Richard L. Daft, *Management*, 4th ed. (Fort Worth, TX: Dryden Press, 1997), 358.

3. Rob Goffee and Gareth Jones, "What Holds the Modern Company Together?" *Harvard Business Review*, November–December 1996, 134–145.

4. Peter F. Drucker, "Management's New Paradigms," *Forbes*, 5 October 1998, 152–176.

5. Stephen P. Robbins, *Managing Today*! (Upper Saddle River, NJ: Prentice Hall, 1997), 193; Daft, *Management*, 320.

6. "Tesco Picks Wavelink to Manage Over 5000 Wireless Access Points Across More Than 600 Stores," Wavelink website [accessed 14 April 2004] www.wavelink.com; "University of Wyoming—Rocky Mountain Campus Builds Rock-Solid Wireless Network," Cisco website [accessed 14 April 2004] www.cisco.com; "Wireless Access Point (WLAN) Basics," Caltech Information Technology Services website [accessed 14 April 2004] www.its.caltech.edu

7. Stephen P. Robbins and David A. DeCenzo, *Fundamentals of Management*, 2nd ed. (Upper Saddle River, NJ: Prentice Hall, 1998), 201; Daft, *Management*, 321.

8. BP website [accessed 6 December 2004] www.bp.com/sectiongenericarticle.do?categoryId=3&contentId=2006926; "Sharing Knowledge through BP's Virtual Team Network," *Harvard Business Review*, September–October 1997, 152–153; BP website [accessed 18 June 2007] www.bp.com

9. Alan Webber, "The Best Organization Is No Organization," *USA Today*, 13A; Eve Tahmincioglu, "How GM's Team Approach Works," *Gannett News Service*, 24 April 1996, S11.

10. Fred R. David, *Strategic Management*, 6th ed. (Upper Saddle River, NJ: Prentice Hall, 1997), 225; Kathryn M. Bartol and David C. Martin, *Management* (New York: McGraw-Hill, 1991), 352.

11. GlaxoSmithKline website [accessed 18 June 2007] www.gsk.ca/en; Kevin Kelleher, "The Drug Pipeline Flows Again," *Business 2.0*, April 2004 [accessed 15 April 2004] www.business2.com

12. Magna website [accessed 2 December 2004] www.magna.ca/magnaWeb.nsf/webpages/Magna+Worldwide+Global+Structure?OpenDocument#

13. Clayton M. Christensen and Michael E. Taynor, "Why Hard-Nosed Executives Should Care About Management Theory," *Harvard Business Review*, September 2003, 67–74; Martha McKay, "Lucent Turns Its First Profit in 14 Quarters," *The Record* (Bergen County, NJ), 23 October 2003 [accessed 14 April 2004] www.highbeam .com

14. Daft, *Management*, 325.

15. Courtland L. Bovée, John V. Thill, Marian Wood, and George Dovel, *Management* (New York: McGraw-Hill, 1993), 285.

16. Bartol and Martin, *Management*, 370–371.

17. Gary Izumo, "Teamwork Holds Key to Organization Success," *Los Angeles Times*, 20 August 1996, D9; Daft, *Management*, 328–329; David, *Strategic Management*, 223.

18. Gareth R. Jones, *Organizational Theory, Design, and Change*, 4th ed. (Upper Saddle River, NJ: Prentice Hall, 2004), 167.

19. Rogers website [accessed 18 June 2007] www.rogers.com/english/investorrelations/index.html

20. Steven Burke, "Acer Restructures into Six Divisions," *Computer Reseller News*, 13 July 1998, 10; Acer America website [accessed 20 July 2000] www.acer.com/aac/about/profile.htm

21. Sobeys Annual Report, Sobeys website [accessed 20 June 2007] corporate.sobeys .com/English/Annual_Reports/2006/financialHighlights.html

22. Daft, *Management*, 332, 328–329; David, *Strategic Management*, 223; Bartol and Martin, *Management*, 376.

23. Dan Dimancescu and Kemp Dwenger, "Smoothing the Product Development Path," *Management Review*, 1 January 1996, 36.

24. Dimancescu and Dwenger, "Smoothing the Product Development Path."

25. Robbins, *Managing Today*! 209; Daft, *Management*, 333–336

26. Daft, *Management*, 340–343; Robbins, *Managing Today*! 213–214.

27. Ibid.

28. John A. Byrne, "The Horizontal Corporation," *BusinessWeek*, 20 December 1993, 76–81

29. Daft, *Management*, 352–353; David, *Strategic Management*, 217; Bartol and Martin, *Management*, 357–358.

30. Stephen P. Robbins, *Essentials of Organizational Behavior*, 6th ed. (Upper Saddle River, NJ: Prentice Hall, 2000), 105.

31. Daft, *Management*, 591; Robbins, *Managing Today!* 295.

32. "Canadian Businesses Failing to Meet the Information Sharing Needs of Employees, Finds Ipsos-Reid Poll," Microsoft Canada website [accessed 4 December 2004] www .microsoft.com/canada/media/releases/ 2003_10_21_1.mspx

33. "Top Ranking in Study Boosts Microsoft's College Recruiting Efforts," 25 August 2004, Microsoft website [accessed 4 December 2004] www.microsoft.com/ presspass/features/2004/aug04/08-25college. asp; "Microsoft Teamwork," *Executive Excellence*, 6 July 1996, 6–7.

34. Nicolas Van Praet, "Team Players," *The Gazette* (Montreal), 24 September 2004, B1; Jim Clemmer, "Team Spirit Built from the Top," *Globe and Mail*, 26 November 2004, C1; Mountain Quest website [accessed 5 December 2004] www.mountainquest.ca; Outward Bound Canada website [accessed 5 December 2004] www.outwardbound.ca/ default.asp

35. Daft, *Management*, 594–595; Robbins and DeCenzo, *Fundamentals of Management*, 336; Robbins, *Managing Today!* 309.

36. Jeffrey Pfeffer, "When It Comes to 'Best Practices'—Why Do Smart Organizations Occasionally Do Dumb Things?" *Organizational Dynamics*, 1 June 1996, 33.

37. SEI Canada website [accessed 25 June 2007] www.seic.com; Scott Kirsner, "Total Teamwork: SEI Investments," *Fast Company*, 14, April 1998, 130.

38. Daft, *Management*, 594; Robbins and DeCenzo, *Fundamentals of Management*, 336.

39. Daft, *Management*, 594; Robbins and DeCenzo, *Fundamentals of Management*, 338; Robbins, *Managing Today!* 310–311.

40. Seth Lubove, "Destroying the Old Hierarchies," *Forbes*, 3 June 1996, 62–64.

41. Dantar Oosterwal, "Harley-Davidson's Formula for NPD," Product Development and Management Association website [accessed 4 December 2004] www.pdma.org/ visions/jan04/harley.html; Clyde Fessler, "Rotating Leadership at Harley-Davidson: From Hierarchy to Interdependence," *Strategy & Leadership*, July–August 1997, 42–43; Mark A. Brunelli, "How Harley-Davidson Uses Cross-Functional Teams," *Purchasing*, 4 November 1999, 148.

42. Ellen Neuborne, "Companies Save, but Workers Pay," *USA Today*, 25 February 1997, B1; Daft, *Management*, 594; Robbins and DeCenzo, *Fundamentals of Management*, 338; Robbins, *Managing Today!* 310.

43. "Canada–U.S. Task Force Presents Final Report on Blackout of August 2003," Natural Resources Canada website [accessed 4 December 2004] www.nrcan-rncan.gc.ca/ media/newsreleases/2004/200414_e.htm

44. Daft, *Management*, 594.

45. Robbins, *Essentials of Organizational Behaviour*, 109.

46. Deborah L. Duarte and Nancy Tennant Snyder, *Mastering Virtual Teams* (San Francisco: Jossey-Bass Publishers, 1999), 23.

47. American Express website [accessed 20 April 2002] www.americanexpress.com; Sally Richards, "Make the Most of Your First Job," *Information Week*, 21 June 1999, 183–186; Time Greene, "American Express: Don't Leave Home to Go to Work," *Network World*, 8 March 1999, 25; Mahlon Apgar IV, "The Alternative Workplace: Changing Where and How People Work," *Harvard Business Review*, May/June 1998, 121–130; "How Senior Executives at American Express View the Alternative Workplace," *Harvard Business Review*, May/June 1998, 132–133; Michelle Marchetti, "Master Motivators," *Sales and Marketing Management*, April 1998, 38–44; Carrie Shook, "Leader, Not Boss," *Forbes*, 1 December 1997, 52–54.

48. Alan Price, *Human Resources Management in a Business Context*, HRM Guide website [accessed 4 December 2004] http://hrmguide .net/hrm/chap4/ch4-links5.htm

49. "Sharing Knowledge through BP's Virtual Team Network," *Harvard Business Review*, September–October 1997, 152–153.

50. Daft, *Management*, 612–615.

51. Robbins, *Essentials of Organizational Behavior*, 98.

52. Ross Sherwood, "The Boss's Open Door Means More Time for Employees," *Reuters Business Report*, 30 September 1996.

53. "Customer-Focused Empowerment Pays at Ritz-Carlton" [accessed 5 December 2004] www.serviceexcellence.co.uk/ritz.shtm; Neuborne, "Companies Save, but Workers Pay," B2; Charles L. Parnell, "Teamwork: Not a New Idea, but It's Transforming the Workplace," *Vital Speeches of the Day*, 1 November 1996, 46.

54. Robbins and DeCenzo, *Fundamentals of Management*, 151.

55. Harvey Shachter, "How to Light a Team's Fire," *Globe and Mail*, 7 November, 2006, B9.

56. Jared Sandberg, "Teamwork: When It's a Bad Idea," *Globe and Mail*, 1 October 2004, C7.

57. Larry Cole and Michael Cole, "Why Is the Teamwork Buzz Word Not Working?" *Communication World*, February/March 1999, 29; Patricia Buhler, "Managing in the 90s: Creating Flexibility in Today's Workplace," *Supervision*, January 1997, 241; Allison W. Amason, Allen C. Hochwarter, Wayne A. Thompson, and Kenneth R. Harrison, "Conflict: An Important Dimension in Successful Management Teams," *Organizational Dynamics*, Autumn 1995, 201.

58. "The Saturn Difference," GM Canada website [accessed 5 December 2004] www .gmcanada.com/ssi/static/english_lw/ vehicles/2005/saturn/difference/promise .html; "Team Players," *Executive Excellence*, May 1999, 18.

59. Stephen P. Robbins, David A. DeCenzo, and Robin Stuart-Kotze, *Fundamentals of Management*, 3rd Canadian ed. (Toronto: Pearson Canada/Prentice Hall, 2002), 218; Daft, *Management*, 602–603.

60. Richard Bloom, "Life Lesson: Teamwork Really Means Pulling Together," *Globe and Mail*, 16 February, 2005, C2.

61. Robbins, *Managing Today!* 297–298; Daft, *Management*, 604–607.

62. Thomas K. Capozzoli, "Conflict Resolution—A Key Ingredient in Successful Teams," *Supervision*, November 1999, 14–16.

63. Daft, *Management*, 609–612.

64. Steven Crom and Herbert France, "Teamwork Brings Breakthrough Improvements in Quality and Climate," *Quality Progress*, March 1996, 39–41.

65. Karine Daisy, "Workplace Bullying: It Dismantles Teamwork, Hobbles Productivity—and Costs Money," *Canadian Business*, 13–26 September 2004, 87–88.

66. David, *Strategic Management*, 221.

67. Joseph Koob and Wallace Immen, "Cheek to Cheek—Or Fist to Fist—On the Workplace Dance Floor," *Globe and Mail*, 4 November 2005, C3.

68. Virginia Galt, "Let's Have a Meeting about How to Have a Meeting," *Globe and Mail*, 18 February 2006, B10.

69. "Better Meetings Benefit Everyone: How to Make Yours More Productive," *Working Communicator Bonus Report*, July 1998, 1.

70. Ken Blanchard, "Meetings Can Be Effective," *Supervisory Management*, October 1992, 5.

71. "Better Meetings Benefit Everyone: How to Make Yours More Productive."

72. See Note 1 for case sources.

Chapter 8

1. Greg Keenan, "More Restructuring Ahead for Magna," *Globe and Mail*, 12 January 2007, B5; Derek DeCloet, "Magna's Russian Math Doesn't Add Up," *Globe and Mail*, 5 June 2007, B2; Greg Keenan, "Stronach Says He Can't Be Bought at Any Price," *Globe and Mail*, 12 May 2007, B7; Greg Keenan, "Magna Targets Higher Content in Russia," *Globe and Mail*, 29 May 2007, B3; Magna Annual Report, Magna Corporation website [accessed 23 June 2007] www.magna.com/ magna/en/investors/governance/documents/ pdf/2007_March_29_AIF.pdf; Lori McLeod, "Russia Can't Get Enough of Those Foreign Cars," *Globe and Mail*, 11 May 2007, B4; Greg Keenan, "Magna in Talks on Building Cars for DaimlerChrysler," *Globe and Mail*, 2 February 2007, B1; Greg Keenan, "Magna Loses Bid for Chrysler," *Globe and Mail*,

14 May 2007, A1, A7; Greg Keenan, "Magna Steers into Vehicle Designer Lane," *Globe and Mail*, 2 May 2005, B5; Gail Edmunston, "Look Who's Building Bimmers," *BusinessWeek Online*, 1 December 2003 [accessed 22 December 2004] http://yahoo.businessweek.com/magazine/content/03_48/b3860094.htm

2. Roberta A. Russell and Bernard W. Taylor III, *Operations Management: Focusing on Quality and Competitiveness*, 2nd ed. (Upper Saddle River, NJ: Prentice Hall, 1998), 21.

3. Robert Kreitner, *Management*, 9th ed. (Boston: Houghton-Mifflin, 2004), 576–578.

4. T. J. Becker, "Have It Your Way," *Edward Lowe Report*, February 2002, 1–3, 12.

5. Nike ID website [accessed 3 January 2005] http://nikeid.nike.com/nikeid/index.jhtml?_requestid=303930

6. Gene Bylinsky, "For Sale: Japanese Plants in the U.S.," *Fortune*, 21 February 2000, 240B–240D.

7. Hansell, "Is This the Factory of the Future?"; Pete Engardio, "Souping Up the Supply Chain," *BusinessWeek*, 31 August 1998, 110–112.

8. Greg Keenan, "Tiny Mercedes-Benz Rolls In," *Globe and Mail*, 5 October 2004, B5; Tony Van Alphen, "Smart Sells Out in Canada" [accessed 23 April 2005] www.zapworld.com/about/news/watch_smartcanada.asp; Auto Intelligence website [accessed 22 December 2004] www.autointell.net/nao_companies/daimlerchrysler/smart/thesmart1.htm; Paul Williams, "Smart Cars Ready to Roll," *Backbone Magazine*, September–October 2004, 46–48; Francois Shalom, "Smart Car Is a Go in Canada," *The Gazette* (Montreal), 17 September 2004, B1; Paul Williams, "Driving Smart," *The Gazette* (Montreal), 13 October 2004, E3; Philip Siekman, "The Smart Car Is Looking More So," *Fortune*, 15 April 2002, 310(I)–310(P).

9. Alice Rangel de Paiva Abreu, Huw Beynon, and Jose Ricardo Ramalho, "The Dream Factory: VW's Modular Production System in Resende, Brazil," Sage Publications website [accessed 22 December 2004] http://wes.sagepub.com/cgi/content/abstract/14/2/265; David Woodruff, Ian Katz, and Keith Naughton, "VW's Factory of the Future," *BusinessWeek*, 7 October 1996, 52, 56.

10. Stephanie Amour and Michelle Kessler, "USA's New Money-Saving Export: White-Collar Jobs," *USA Today*, 5 August 2003, B1–B2; Steve Lohr, "Offshore Jobs in Technology: Opportunity or Threat?" *New York Times*, 22 December 2003, C1, C6; Kris Maher, "Next on the Outsourcing List," *Wall Street Journal*, 28 March 2004, B1, B8; Jennifer Reingold, "Into Thin Air," *Fast Company*, April 2004, 76–82; Paul Craig Roberts, "The Harsh Truth About Outsourcing," 22 March 2004, 48; Craig Karmin, "'Offshoring' Can Generate Jobs

in the U.S.," *Wall Street Journal*, 16 March 2004, B1, B7; Bernard J. La Londe, "From Outsourcing to 'Offshoring'—Part 1" *Supply Chain Management Review*, 1 March 2004 [accessed 16 April 2004] www.manufacturing.net; Paul Kaihla, "Straws in the Wind," *Business 2.0*, 27 April 2004 [accessed 22 July 2004] www.business2.com

11. Faye Bowers, "Building a 747: 43 Days and 3 Million Fasteners," *Christian Science Monitor*, 29 October 1997 [accessed 16 April 2004] www.csmonitor.com.

12. Ronald Henkoff, "Boeing's Big Problem," *Fortune*, 12 January 1998, 96–103; James Wallace, "How Boeing Blew It," *Sales and Marketing Management*, February 1998, 52–57; John Greenwald, "Is Boeing out of Its Spin?" *Time*, 13 July 1998, 67–69; John T. Landry, "Supply Chain Management: The Case for Alliances," *Harvard Business Review*, November–December 1998, 24–25.

13. Robert J. Trent, "What Everyone Needs to Know About SCM," *Supply Chain Management Review*, 1 March 2004 [accessed 16 April 2004] www.manufacturing.net

14. Mark M. Davis, Nicholas J. Aquilano, and Richard B. Chase, *Fundamentals of Operations Management* (Boston: Irwin McGraw-Hill, 1999), 382.

15. John Greenwald, "Cruise Lines Go Overboard," *Time*, 11 May 1998, 42–45.

16. Joseph G. Monks, *Operations Management, Theory and Problems* (New York: McGraw-Hill, 1987), 7–8.

17. Bret Jang and Bertrand Marotte, "Air Canada Bets $6 Billion on Future," *Globe and Mail*, 26 April 2005, B1.

18. Bertrand Marotte, "Closing to Compete," *Globe and Mail*, 28 March 2007, B2; Bertrand Marotte, "Gildan Unravels North American Production, Shifts Jobs South," *Globe and Mail*, 28 August 2006, B1; Gordon Pitts, "Hanging by a Quality Thread," *Globe and Mail*, 28 September 2006, B4.

19. Davis et al., *Fundamentals of Operations Management*, 241–242.

20. Mark Landler, "Slovakia No Longer a Laggard in Automaking," *New York Times*, 13 April 2004 [accessed 15 April 2004] www.nytimes.com

21. Jae K. Shim and Joel G. Siegel, *Operations Management* (Hauppauge, NY: Barron's Educational Series, 1999), 206.

22. Monks, *Operations Management, Theory and Problems*, 2–3.

23. Shim and Siegel, *Operations Management*, 206.

24. Monks, *Operations Management, Theory and Problems*, 125.

25. Lisa Marshall, "A Bike That Really Travels," *Boulder Daily Camera*, June 1999; Bike Friday website [accessed 11 August 2000] www.bikefriday.com; Tim Stevens, "Pedal Pushers," *IndustryWeek*, 17 July 2000, 46–52.

26. Davis et al., *Fundamentals of Operations Management*, 254; Richard L. Daft,

Management, 4th ed. (Fort Worth, TX: Dryden Press, 1997), 718.

27. Kathryn M. Bartol and David C. Martin, *Management* (New York: McGraw-Hill, 1991), 307–308.

28. Greg Keenan, "Oshawa GM Plants Lead Industry," *Globe and Mail*, 1 June 2007, B3.

29. Larry E. Long and Nancy Long, *Introduction to Computers and Information Systems*, 5th ed. (Upper Saddle River, NJ: Prentice Hall, 1997), 84.

30. Stuart F. Brown, "Giving More Jobs to Electronic Eyes," *Fortune*, 16 February 1998, 104B–104D.

31. "IBM and Dassault Awarded Boeing CATIA Contract," *CAD/CAM Update*, 1 January 1997, 1–8.

32. Russell and Taylor, *Operations Management*, 211.

33. "CAD/CAM Industry Embracing Intranet-Based Technologies," *Computer Dealer News*, 12 (28 November 1996), 21.

34. 2004 Ford F-150 Special Features, Ford Truck Spec website [accessed 22 January 2005] www.ford-trucks.com/specs/2004/2004_f150_5.html; Drew Winter, "C3P: New Acronym Signals Big Change at Ford," *Ward's Auto World*, 32 (1 August 1996), 34; Thomas Hoffman, "Ford to Cut Its Prototype Costs," *Computerworld*, 30 September 1996, 65; Drew Winter, "Massive Changes Coming in Computer Engineering," *Ward's Auto World*, 32 (1 April 1996), 34.

35. Davis et al., *Fundamentals of Operations Management*, 64; Russell and Taylor, *Operations Management*, 257–258.

36. Barnaby J. Feder, "Technology: Bashful vs. Brash in the New Field of Nanotech," *New York Times*, 15 March 2004 [accessed 15 April 2004]; "Nanotechnology Basics," Nanotechnology Now website [accessed 16 April 2004] www.nanotech-now.com; Center for Responsible Nanotechnology website [accessed 16 April 2004] www.crnano.org; Gary Stix, "Little Big Science," *Scientific American*, 15 September 2001 [accessed 16 April 2004] www.sciam.com; Tim Harper, "Small Wonders," *Business 2.0*, July 2002 [accessed 16 April 2004] www.business2.com; Erick Schonfeld, "A Peek at IBM's Nanotech Research," *Business 2.0*, 5 December 2003 [accessed 15 April 2004] www.business2.com; David Pescovitz, "The Best New Technologies of 2003," *Business 2.0*, November 2003, 109–116.

37. Brian S. Moskal, "Born to Be Real," *IndustryWeek*, 2 August 1993, 14–18.

38. Russell and Taylor, *Operations Management*, 255–256.

39. John H. Sheridan, "Agile Manufacturing: Stepping Beyond Lean Production," *IndustryWeek*, 19 April 1993, 30–46.

40. Porsche website [accessed 21 December 2004] www2.porche.com; Robyn Meredith, "Porsche Goes Soccer Mom," *Forbes*, 4 February 2000, 54.

41. "Changing the Game: New Ford Edge and Lincoln MKX Roll Off Oakville's Flexible Assembly Line," Ford website [accessed 24 June 2007] www.ford.com; Simon Tuck and Greg Keenan, "GM Ups Ante in Bid for Federal Cash," *Globe and Mail*, 20 December 2004, B1; Greg Keenan, "Ford's Chicago Plant Gets Flexible as Firm Chooses a Different Road for Survival," *Globe and Mail*, 19 August 2004, B1; Steve Erwin, "Automakers Seek Production Flexibility," *The Gazette* (Montreal), 21 September 2004, E7.

42. James A. Senn, *Information Technology: Principles, Practices, Opportunities*, 3rd ed. (Upper Saddle River, NJ: Prentice-Hall, 2004), 328.

43. Helen Gurevich, "Surviving the Enterprise Integration War," *Health Management Technology*, February 2004, 66+; Mark Jones, "Ingram Micro: The Trouble with XML and Web Services," *InfoWorld*, 9 November 2001 [accessed 17 April] www.infoworld.com; "Companies Continue to Find Benefit in EDI Investments," *Electronic Commerce News*, 1 March 2004, 1.

44. Greg Ip, "Risky Business," *Wall Street Journal*, 24 October 2001, A1, A4.

45. Jon E. Hilsenrath, "Parts Shortages Hamper Electronics Makers: Surging Demand Shows Flaw in Just-in-Time Chains," *Wall Street Journal*, 7 July 2000, B5.

46. Shim and Siegel, *Operations Management*, 326.

47. Russell and Taylor, *Operations Management*, 712–733.

48. Greg Keenan, "Steel Firm Forges Strategy for Good and Bad Times," *Globe and Mail*, 24 July 2004, B1.

49. Allen-Edmonds website [accessed 21 December 2004] www.allenedmonds.com; Patricia W. Hamilton, "Getting a Grip on Inventory," *D&B Reports*, March–April 1994, 32.

50. Russell and Taylor, *Operations Management*, 652–653.

51. Dan McLean, "Home Depot Wins With IT, Others, Not so Much," *Globe and Mail*, 21 June 2007, B9.

52. Trent, "What Everyone Needs to Know About SCM."

53. David Hughes, "Life-Cycle Software," *Aviation Week & Space Technology*, 18 August 2003 [accessed 17 April 2004] www.ebsco.com

54. Tim Laseter and Keith Oliver, "When Will Supply Chain Management Grow Up?" *strategy+business*, Fall 2003, 32–36; Trent, "What Everyone Needs to Know About SCM."

55. Laura Rock Kopczak and M. Eric Johnson, "The Supply-Chain Management Effect," *MIT Sloan Management Review*, Spring 2003, 27–34

56. George Taninecz, "Forging the Chain," *IndustryWeek*, 15 May 2000, 40–46.

57. Laseter and Oliver, "When Will Supply Chain Management Grow Up?"

58. Adam Horowitz, Mark Athitakis, Mark Lasswell, and Owen Thomas, "The 101 Dumbest Moments in Business," *Business 2.0* [accessed 27 March 2004] www.business2.com; David Lazarus, "Pakistani Threatened UCSF to Get Paid, She Says," *San Francisco Chronicle*, 12 November 2003 [accessed 17 April 2004] www.sfgate.com

59. Karl Ritzler, "A Mercedes Made from Scratch," *Atlanta Journal and Constitution*, 30 May 1997, S1.

60. Brent Jang, "CN Vows to Prevent Costly Derailments," *Globe and Mail*, 25 April 2007, B3.

61. Del Jones, "Training and Service at Top of Winners' List," *USA Today*, 17 October 1996, 5B.

62. John A. Byrne, "Never Mind the Buzzwords. Roll Up Your Sleeves," *BusinessWeek*, 22 January 1996, 84.

63. Davis et al., *Fundamentals of Operations Management*, 177–179; Russell and Taylor, *Operations Management*, 131.

64. William M. Carley, "Charging Ahead: To Keep GE's Profits Rising, Welch Pushes Quality-Control Plan," *Wall Street Journal*, 13 January 1997, A1, A6.

65. Russell and Taylor, *Operations Management*, 131.

66. Gillian Babicz, "ISO 9004: The Other Half of the Consistent Pair," *Quality*, June 2001, 50–53; David Drickhemer, "Standards Shake-Up," *IndustryWeek*, 5 March 2001, 37–40.

67. ISO website [accessed 24 June 2007] www.iso.org; Hugh D. Menzies, "Global Guide: Quality Counts When Wooing Overseas Clients," *Your Company*, 1 June 1997, 64; Michael E. Raynor, "Worldwide Winners," *Total Quality Management*, July–August 1993, 43–48; Greg Bounds, Lyle Yorks, Mel Adams, and Gipsie Ranney, *Beyond Total Quality Management: Toward the Emerging Paradigm* (New York: McGraw-Hill, 1994), 212; Russell and Taylor, *Operations Management*, 115–116.

68. See Note 1 for case sources.

69. Erik Heinrich, "What Can Work: One Buyer, Many Sellers," *Toronto Sun*, 23 October 2003 [accessed 17 April 2004] www.highbeam.com; Peter Loftus, "E-Commerce: Business to Business Exchanges—Making It Work," *Wall Street Journal*, 11 February 2002, R16; Ralph Kisiel, "Automakers Saving by Using Covisint," *Crain's Detroit Business*, 21 January 2002, 12; Eric Young, "Web Marketplaces That Really Work," *Fortune Tech Review*, Winter 2002, 10; J. William Gurley, "Big Company.com: Should You Start a B2B Exchange?" *Fortune*, 3 April 2000, 260; Peter D. Henig, "Revenge of the Bricks," *Red Herring*, August 2000, 121–134; Daniel Lyons, "B2Bluster," *Forbes*, 1 May 2000, 122–126; Steven Kaplan and Mohanbir Sawhney, "E-hubs: The New B2B Marketplaces," *Harvard Business Review*, May–June 2000, 97–100; Robert D. Hof, "Who Will Profit from the Internet Agora?" *BusinessWeek E.Biz*, 5 June 2000, EB56–EB62; Joseph B. White, "Getting Into Gear," *Wall Street Journal*, 17 April 2000, R30–R32; Edward Iwata, "Despite the Hype, B2B Marketplaces Struggle, "*USA Today*, 10 May 2000, 1B–2B; Jack Trout, "Stupid Net Tricks," *Business 2.0*, May 2000, 76–77; John W. Verity, "Invoice? What's an Invoice?" *BusinessWeek*, 10 June 1996, 110–112; Christina Binkley, "Hyatt Plans Internet Firm with Marriott," *Wall Street Journal*, 2 May 2000, A3, A6; Clint Willis, "B2B . . . to Be?" *Forbes ASAP*, 21 August 2000, 125–130; Jason Anders, "Yesterday's Darling," *Wall Street Journal*, 23 October 2000, R8.

Chapter 9

1. WestJet Annual Report, WestJet website [accessed 28 June 2007] www.westjet.com/pdffile/WestJet2006AR.pdf; Brent Jang and Tavia Grant, "Fuller Planes, Cost Cuts Propel Airlines," *Globe and Mail*, 27 October 2006, B1; Richard Blackwell, "WestJet, Air Canada Hit Heights in 2006," *Globe and Mail*, 5 January 2007, B5; Patrick Brethour, "WestJet Showing Strains of Spreading Its Wings," *Globe and Mail*, 8 May 2004, B7; Keith McArthur, "WestJet Hails Taxi for Its New TV Ads," *Globe and Mail*, 8 May 2004, B1.

2. Gary Dessler, *A Framework for Human Resource Management* (Upper Saddle River, NJ: Pearson Prentice Hall, 2004), 74–75.

3. Shari Randall, "Succession Planning Is More Than a Game of Chance," *Workforce Management* [accessed 1 May 2004] www.workforce.com

4. Brent Jang, "Beddoe Makes Move (Again) in WestJet Succession Plan," *Globe and Mail*, 8 September 2006, B1.

5. David Koeppel, "The New Cost of Keeping Workers Happy," *New York Times*, 7 March 2004, 11.

6. Joanne Cole, "Permatemps Pose New Challenges for HR," *HR Focus*, December 1999, 7–8; Sharon R. Cohany, "Workers in Alternative Employment Arrangements: A Second Look," *Monthly Labor Review*, November 1998, 3–21.

7. Steven Greenhouse, "Equal Work, Less-Equal Perks," *New York Times*, 30 March 1998, C1, C6; Aaron Bernstein, "When Is a Temp Not a Temp?" *BusinessWeek*, 7 December 1998, 90–92.

8. "Employee or Independent Contractor? How to Tell," *HR Focus*, January 2004, 7, 10.

9. Virginia Galt, "Firms See Value in Putting Retirees Back to Work," *Globe and Mail*, 8 September 2004, B7.

10. IBM Accessibility Center, www.3.ibm.com/able [accessed 30 April 2004]; AssistiveTech.net, www.assistivetech.net [accessed 30 April 2004]; Business Leadership Network website, www.usbln.com [accessed 30 April 2004]; National Institute on Disability and Rehabilitation

Research website, www.ed.gov/about/offices/list/osers/nidrr [accessed 30 April 2004]; Rehabilitation Engineering and Assistive Technology Society of North America website, www.resna.org [accessed 30 April 2004].

11. Joellen Perry, "Help Wanted," *U.S. News & World Report*, 8 March 2004, 48–54.

12. William J. Stevenson, *Production Operations Management*, 6th ed. (Boston: Irwin McGraw-Hill, 1999), 698; Laurie Edwards, "When Outsourcing Is Appropriate," *Wall Street and Technology*, July 1998, 96–98.

13. Dessler, *A Framework for Human Resource Management*, 72.

14. Stephanie Armour, "Some Companies Choose No-Layoff Policy," *USA Today*, 17 December 2001, 1B.

15. Virginia Galt, "Hiring Firms Employ the Buddy System," *Globe and Mail*, 29 April 2006, B10.

16. Wallace Immen, "Resumé Stunts Can Count You Out, Rather than Make You Stand Out," *Globe and Mail*, 6 November 2004, B11.

17. Wallace Immen, "Lights, Camera . . . Can I Have a Job?" *Globe and Mail*, 9 March 2007, C1; Raizel Robin, "Dreams of the Donald," *Canadian Business*, 12–15 April 2004, 47–49.

18. "Checking Out New Hires," *USA Today*, 18 May 2000, B1.

19. Kevin Marron, "Employers Are Checking You Out On-Line," *Globe and Mail*, 25 January 2006, C1.

20. Gary Dessler, Nina Cole, Patricia M. Goodman, and Virginia L. Sutherland, *Management of Human Resources*, 2nd ed. (Toronto: Pearson Education Canada, 2007).

21. Kirk Makin, "RBC Dominion Awarded $2.25 Million After Merrill Lures Brokers," *Globe and Mail*, 12 November 2004, B4.

22. Wallace Immen, "Prospective Hires Put to the Test," *Globe and Mail*, 26 January 2005, C1.

23. Dessler et al., *Management of Human Resources*, 154.

24. Randall S. Schuler, *Managing Human Resources* (Cincinnati, Ohio: South-Western College Publishing, 1998), 386.

25. Katharine Mieszkowski, "Report from the Future," *Fast Company*, February–March 1998, 28–30

26. Tammy Galvin, "2003 Industry Report," *Training*, October 2003, 21+.

27. Virginia Galt, "Making Performance Reviews Painless," *Globe and Mail*, 6 January 2005, B11; Joe Mullich, "A Second Act for E-Learning," *Workforce Management*, February 2004, 51–55; Gail Johnson, "Brewing the Perfect Blend," *Training*, December 2003, 30; Michael A. Verespej, "Click and Learn," *IndustryWeek*, 15 January 2001, 31–36; Elisabeth Goodridge, "Slowing Economy Sparks Boom in E-Learning," 12 November 2001, 100–104; Cynthia Pantazix, "Maximizing E-Learning to

Train the 21st Century Workforce," *Public Personnel Management*, Spring 2002, 21–26; Mary Lord, "They're Online and on the Job," *U.S. News & World Report*, 15 October 2001, 72–78.

28. "Bank of Montreal Institute for Learning: Case Study," Moriyama & Teshima website [accessed 9 December 2004] www.mtarch.com/bofmcasestudy.html

29. Michael Barrier, "Develop Workers and Your Business," *Nation's Business*, December 1998, 25–27.

30. Laura Bogomolny, "Janice Wismer: Most Innovative Exec," *Canadian Business*, April 26–May 9 2004, 52.

31. Virginia Galt, "Instead of Feedback, How about 'Feedforward'?," *Globe and Mail*, 10 November 2006, C1.

32. Dessler, *A Framework for Human Resource Management*, 198.

33. PerformanceNow.com website [accessed 2 May 2004] www.performancenow.com; Dessler, *A Framework for Human Resource Management*, 199.

34. Kate Ludeman, "How to Conduct Self-Directed 360," *Training and Development*, July 2000, 44–47; Cassandra Hayes, "To Tell the Truth," *Black Enterprise*, December 1998, 55.

35. Jeff St. John, "Kennewick, Wash., 'Snoop' Software Maker Also Protects Privacy," *Tri-City Herald* (Kennewick, Wash.), 17 April 2004 [accessed 2 May 2004] www.highbeam.com; Dessler, *A Framework for Human Resource Management*, 204–205.

36. Elayne Robertson Demby, "Two Stores Refuse to Join the Race to the Bottom for Benefits and Wages," *Workforce Management*, February 2004, 57–59; Stanley Holmes and Wendy Zellner, "The Costco Way," *BusinessWeek*, 12 April 2004, 76–77; Jennifer Reingold, "CEOs Who Should Lose Their Jobs," *Fast Company*, October 2003, 68–80; Louis Lavelle, "Executive Pay," *BusinessWeek*, 21 April 2003, 86–90; Jerry Useem, "Have They No Shame?" *Fortune*, 28 April 2003, 57–64; Matthew Grim, "Wal-Mart Uber Alles," *American Demographics*, October 2003, 38–39; Jeffrey E. Garten, "Wal-Mart Gives Globalism a Bad Name," *BusinessWeek*, 8 March 2004, 24; Jerry Useem, "Should We Admire Wal-Mart?" *Fortune*, 8 March 2004, 118–120.

37. Fiona Jebb, "Flex Appeal," *Management Today* (London), July 1998, 66–69; Milton Zall, "Implementing a Flexible Benefits Plan," *Fleet Equipment*, May 1999.

38. Joseph Pereira, "Parting Shot: To Save on Health-Care Costs, Firms Fire Disabled Workers," *Wall Street Journal*, 14 July 2003, A1, A7; Timothy Aeppel, "Ill Will: Skyrocketing Health Costs Start to Pit Worker vs. Worker," *Wall Street Journal*, 17 July 2003, A1, A6; Vanessa Furhmans, "To Stem Abuses, Employers Audit Workers' Health Claims," *Wall Street Journal*, 31 March 2004, B1, B7; Milt Freudenheim,

"Employees Paying Ever-Bigger Share for Health Care," *New York Times*, A1, C2; Julie Appleby, "Employers Get Nosy About Workers' Health," *USA Today*, 6 March 2003, B1–B2; Ellen E. Schultz and Theo Francis, "Employers' Caps Raise Retirees' Health-Care Costs," *Wall Street Journal*, 25 November 2003, B1, B11; Vanessa Fuhrmans, "Company Health Plans Try to Drop Spouses," *Wall Street Journal*, 9 September 2003, D1, D2.

39. Luis R. Gomez-Mejia, David B. Balkin et al., *Managing Human Resources*, 3rd Canadian ed. (Toronto: Pearson/Prentice Hall, 2004), 332; "Canada and Quebec Pension Plan," [accessed 9 December 2004] http://benefits.org/interface/benefit/cpp.htm; HRSDC website [accessed 9 December 2004] www.hrdsc.gc.ca

40. Richard D. Pearce, "The Small Employer Retirement Plan Void," *Compensation and Benefits Management*, Winter 1999, 51–55.

41. Richard Blackwell, "Pension Plans Staging Strong Recovery, Study Shows," *Globe and Mail*, 12 April 2007, B3.

42. Brian Murray and Minghe Sun, "Selection among Employer-Sponsored Pension Plans: The Role of Individual Differences," *Personal Psychology*, Summer 2000, 405–432.

43. Elizabeth Church, "Defined Benefit Plans Falling Out of Favour," *Globe and Mail*, 3 May 2006, B5; Gomez-Mejia et al., *Managing Human Resources*, 346–347.

44. Gomez-Mejia et al., *Managing Human Resources*, 346–347.

45. CTV News, "Unemployed New Brunswick Mill Workers Lose Their Pensions," [accessed 9 December 2004] www.ctv.ca/servlet/ArticleNews/story/CTVNews/1102462269443_97871469

46. Telus Annual Report 2003, "Notes to Consolidated Financial Statements," 70.

47. Andrew Willis, "CIBC Finds a Way to Reward a Job Well Done and Thwart Deserters at the Same Time," *Globe and Mail*, 10 December 2004, B1.

48. Del Jones, "More Workers Get Options, Too," *USA Today*, 7 April 1999, 3B.

49. Real Women of Canada website [accessed 27 June 2007] www.realwomenca.com/newsletter/2003_jan_feb/article_8.html

50. CBC News, "Canada Day Tax Tweaks," CBC website [accessed 28 June 2007] www.cbc.ca/news/background/cdngovernment/taxchanges.html

51. Stephanie Armour, "Ford Plans Ambitious Child-Care Program for Workers," *USA Today*, 22 November 2000, B1.

52. "Workplace Briefs," Gannett News Service, 24 April 1997; Julia Lawlor, "The Bottom Line," *Working Woman*, July–August 1996, 54–58, 74–76.

53. Stephanie Armour, "Employers Stepping Up in Elder Care," *USA Today*, 3 August 2000, 3B.

54. Del Jones, "Firms Take New Look at Sick Days," *USA Today*, 8 October 1996, 8B.

55. National Quality Institute website [accessed 27 June 2007] http://www.nqi.ca/ NewsEvents/details.aspx?ID=593

56. William Atkinson, "Wellness, Employee Assistance Programs: Investments, Not Costs," *Bobbin*, May 2000, 42–48.

57. Atkinson, "Wellness, Employee Assistance Programs"; Kevin Dobbs, Jack Gordon, and David Stamps, "EAPs Cheap but Popular Perk," *Training*, February 2000, 26.

58. Magna Corporation website [accessed 11 December 2004] www.magna.com

59. "50 Benefits and Perks That Make Employees Want to Stay Forever," *HR Focus*, July 2000, S2–S3.

60. Edward Iwata, "Staff-Hungry Tech Firms Cast Exotic Lures," *USA Today*, 1 February 2000, B1.

61. Adam Cohen and Cathy Booth Thomas, "Inside a Layoff," *Time*, 16 April 2001, 38–40.

62. Rodney Ho, "AT&T's Offer of $10,000 May Test Entrepreneurship of Laid-Off Workers," *Wall Street Journal*, 12 March 1997; David Fischer and Kevin Whitelaw, "A New Way to Shine Up Corporate Profits," *U.S. News & World Report*, 15 April 1996, 55.

63. Virginia Galt, "Jeans Workers Helped to Face Life after Levi," *Globe and Mail*, 11 October 2004, B1, B12.

64. Marjo Johne, "Delete This Practice: Giving Staff the e-Boot," *Globe and Mail*, 8 September 2006, C1.

65. Human Resources and Social Development Canada, "Manadatory Retirement in Canada," HRSDC website [accessed 28 June 2007] www.hrsdc.gc.ca/en/ lp/spila/clli/eslc/19Mandatory_Retirement .shtml

66. See Note 1 for case sources.

Chapter 10

1. Eric Reguly, "Bombardier Partners with China on Jet Plan," *Globe and Mail*, 19 June 2007, B1; Bertrand Marotte, "Bombardier Puts Off C-Series Launch Decision," *Globe and Mail*, 1 February 2007, B8; Bertrand Marotte, "Despite Cuts, Bombardier Sees Bright Future," *Globe and Mail*, 25 October 2006, B1; "Strike Hits Bombardier Wichita Plant," *Globe and Mail*, 3 October 2006, B5; Bertrand Marotte, "New Jet Cleared for Business Takeoff," *Globe and Mail*, 16 March 2005, B1; Allan Swift, "Bombardier, Union Reach Deal," *The Gazette* (Montreal), 3 March 2005, B1; Bombardier website [accessed 2 July 2007] www.bombardier .com; Simon Tuck, "Ottawa Eyes National Aerospace Plan," *Globe and Mail*, 15 December 2004, B1; Brent Jang, "Next Stop: Make-or-Break Decision on Jets," *Globe and Mail*, 14 December 2004, B7; "Bombardier Cuts 2,000 Jobs; Most in Montreal Area," CBC News website [accessed 7 October 2004] www.cbcnews.ca; Jerry Siebenmark, "Bombardier's Toronto Union

Approves Agreement, Layoffs," *Wichita Business Journal*, 17 March 2003; "Pressure Mounts on CAW for Concessions at Bombardier, Air Canada," *Canadian Press*, 11 March 2003; Bertrand Marotte and Simon Tuck, "Kansas Vying for Assembly of New Bombardier Jet," *Globe and Mail*, 16 October 2004, B5; Bertrand Marotte, "Bombardier Axes 2000, Warns More Jobs May Go," *Globe and Mail*, 8 October, B1; Francois Shalom, "We'll Cut 2000," *The Gazette* (Montreal), 8 October 2004, A1; Eric Reguly, "Lobbyists Facing a Tough Fight with New Minority Government," *Globe and Mail*, 6 July 2004, B1; Conrad Yakabuski, "Ottawa Should Help Bombardier" *Globe and Mail*, 6 October 2004, B1; Simon Tuck and Bertrand Marotte, "Canada, Brazil to Resume Subsidy Talks," *Globe and Mail*, 30 September 2004, B3; Bertrand Marotte, "Bombardier Rival Strikes Regional Jet Deal with China, *Globe and Mail*, 13 September 2004, B3.

2. Dennis C. Kinlaw, "What Employees See Is What Organizations Get," *Management Solutions*, March 1988, 38–41.

3. Michael A. Verespej, "Balancing Act," *IndustryWeek*, 15 May 2000, 81–85.

4. John McMorrow, "Future Trends in Human Resources," *HR Focus*, September 1999, 8–9.

5. Ibid.

6. Robert B. Reich, "The Company of the Future," *Fast Company*, November 1998, 124–150.

7. Teresa Rivas, "Money Doesn't Buy Happiness for Workers," *Globe and Mail*, 13 September 2006, C10.

8. Liberal Party of Canada website [accessed 7 December 2004] www.liberal.ca/bio_e .aspx?&id=35045

9. "Western Electric Hawthorne Studies Collection," Harvard Business School website [accessed 23 April 2005] www.library.hbs.edu/hc/wes/collections/ labor/other/content/1001955886/; Barry L. Reece and Rhonda Brandt, *Effective Human Relations in Organizations*, (Boston: Houghton Mifflin, 1999), 17.

10. Douglas McGregor, *The Human Side of Enterprise* (New York: McGraw-Hill, 1960).

11. Rudy M. Yandrick, "Help Employees Reach for the Stars," *HRMagazine*, 1 January 1997 [accessed 26 April 2004] www.highbeam.com

12. Richard L. Daft, *Management*, 6th ed. (Mason, Ohio: Thomson South-Western, 2003), 554–555.

13. Eryn Brown, "How to Get Paid What You're Worth," *Business 2.0*, May 2004, 102–110.

14. Adam Horowitz, Mark Athitakis, Mark Lasswell, and Owen Thomas, "The 101 Dumbest Moments in Business," *Business 2.0* [accessed 24 April 2004] www.business2 .com; "The Best & Worst Managers of 2003," *BusinessWeek*, 12 January 2004, 55–85; Gretchen Morgenson, "It's Awards Time on Wall Street: From Epic to Comic Wall Street

Watch," *International Herald Tribune*, 30 December 2003 [accessed 24 April 2004] www.highbeam.com; Rick Moriary, "Low-Flying Airline; American Struggles to Recover from 9/11, Bankruptcy, Executive Pay Scandal," *The Post-Standard*, (Syracuse, NY), 15 December 2003 [accessed 24 April 2004] www.highbeam.com

15. Stephen P. Robbins and David A. DeCenzo, *Fundamentals of Management*, 4th ed. (Upper Saddle River, NJ: Prentice Hall, 2004), 289.

16. Bob Parks, "Where the Customer Service Rep Is King," *Business 2.0*, June 2003, 70–72.

17. Reich, "The Company of the Future."

18. Shirley Won, "Wanted: More Skilled Labour, and Quick," *Globe and Mail*, 13 September 2006, C10.

19. Kelly Barron and Ann Marsch, "The Skills Gap," *Forbes*, 23 February 1998, 44–45.

20. Andrew Wahl, "Leaders Wanted," *Canadian Business*, 1–14 March 2004, 31–35; Laura Bogomolny, "Lessons from an Ancient Land," *Canadian Business*, 1–14 March 2004, 33; John S. McClenahen, "The Next Crisis: Too Few Workers," *IndustryWeek*, May 2003, 41–45; Ken Dychtwald, Tamara Erickson, and Bob Morison, "It's Time to Retire Retirement," *Harvard Business Review*, March 2004, 48–57; Paul Kaihla, "The Coming Job Boom," *Business 2.0*, September 2003, 97–105; Stephanie Armour, "More Moms Make Kids Their Career of Choice," *USA Today*, 12 March 2002, 1B; Aaron Bernstein, "Too Many Workers? Not for Long," *BusinessWeek*, 20 May 2002, 126–130; Steven A. Nyce and Sylvester J. Schieber, "The Decade of the Employee: The Workforce in the Coming Decade," *Benefits Quarterly*, First Quarter 2002, 60–79; Paul Gores, "Economist Calls Recession Mild, Predicts Labor Shortage Will Return," *Knight Ridder Tribune Business News*, 10 February 2002; Nancy Pounds, "Nation Expert Sees Skilled Worker Need Despite Recent Layoffs," *Alaska Journal of Commerce*, 28 October 2001, 19.

21. Stephanie Armour, "Companies Hire Even as They Lay Off," *USA Today*, 15 May 2001, A1.

22. Exhibit is adapted from Jennifer Laabs, "The New Loyalty: Grasp It. Earn It. Keep It." *Workforce*, November 1998, 35–39.

23. Michelle Kessler, "Days of BMW Signing Bonuses Long Gone," *USA Today*, 14 April 2002, 3B.

24. Barbara Moses, "How to Survive the Great Unknowns," *Globe and Mail*, 15 September 2004, C3.

25. Jennifer Laabs, "The New Loyalty: Grasp It. Earn It. Keep It," *Workforce*, November 1998, 35–39.

26. Emily Thornton, "No Room at the Top," *BusinessWeek*, 9 August 1999, 50; Michael A. Lev, "Lifetime Jobs May Be at Death's Door as Japan Tradition," *Chicago Tribune*, 11 October 1998, sec. 5, 1, 18.

27. Randy Ray, "Workplace Theft Takes a Big Toll," *Globe and Mail*, 4 August 2004, C1.

28. John Greenwald, "Spinning Away," *Time*, 26 August 1996, 30–31.

29. Stephanie Armour, "Blame It on Downsizing, E-Mail, Laptops, and Dual-Career Families," *USA Today*, 13 March 1998, B1; Jennifer Laabs, "Workforce Overload," *Workforce*, January 1999, 30–37.

30. Michelle Conlin, Peter Coy, Ann Therese, and Gabrielle Saveri, "The Wild New Workforce," *BusinessWeek*, 6 December 1999, 39–44.

31. Richard L. Daft, *Management*, 4th ed. (Fort Worth, TX: Dryden Press, 1997), 771.

32. Stephanie Armour, "Workplace Demands Taking Up More Weekends," *USA Today*, 24 April 1998, B1; Laabs, "Workforce Overload."

33. Armour, "Workplace Demands Taking Up More Weekends."

34. Laabs, "Workforce Overload."

35. Michael A. Verespej, "Stressed Out," *IndustryWeek*, 21 February 2000, 30–34.

36. Verespej, "Balancing Act."

37. Wallace Immen, "Job Stress, Home Stress Linked," *Globe and Mail*, 14 July 2004, C3.

38. Joanne Cole, "De-Stressing the Workplace," *HR Focus*, October 1999, 1, 10.

39. Jennifer Bresnehan, "The Elusive Muse," *CIO Enterprise*, 15 October 1997, 52; Kerry A. Dolan, "When Money Isn't Enough," *Forbes*, 18 November 1996, 164–170.

40. Tim Larimer, "Having Fun Yet? *Time*, November 2003; Harvey Meyer, "Fun for Everyone," *Journal of Business Strategy*, March–April 1999, 13–17; Erika Rasmusson, "A Funny Thin Happened on the Way to Work," *Sales and Marketing Management*, March 1999, 97–98; Peter Baker, "Work: Have Fun. And That's an Order," *The Observer*, 3 January 1999, 11+; Melanie Payne, "Chuckle While You Work," *San Diego Union-Tribune*, 19 October 1998, E1–E2; Maggie Jackson, "Corporate America Lightens Up: Laughing Workers Are Happy Workers," *The Salt Lake Tribune*, 4 May 1997, E1; Diane E. Lewis, "Employers Find Humor Can Improve Morale, Profits," *Boston Globe*, 1 April 1997, C5; R. J. King, "Here's a Laugh: Speaker Shows How Office Humor Helps," *Detroit News*, 15 February 1996, B3; Katy Robinson, "Use Laughter to Brighten Your Office," *Idaho Statesman*, 18 October 1995, 1.

41. Linda Beamer and Iris Varner, *Intercultural Communication in the Workplace*, 2nd ed. (New York: McGraw-Hill Irwin, 2001), xiii.

42. Kamal Dib, "Diversity Works," *Canadian Business*, 29 March–11 April 2004, 53; Wallace Immen, "How Visible Minorities Can Close the Gap," *Globe and Mail*, 19 November 2005, B11.

43. Virginia Galt, "Older Workers a Drain? Not a Chance, Study Finds," *Globe and Mail*, 23 May 2007, B5.

44. Nina Munk, "Finished at Forty," *Fortune*, 1 February 1999, 50–66.

45. Ibid.

46. Amy Charmichael, "Female Executives Talk Shop and Share Know How," *Globe and Mail*, 12 July 2004, B13.

47. Virginia Galt, "Glass Ceiling Still Tough to Crack," *Globe and Mail*, 4 May 2005, C1.

48. Wallace Immen, "Despite Breakthrough, Glass Ceiling Still Perplexes Women," *Globe and Mail*, 9 March 2007, C1.

49. Daft, *Management*, 4th ed. 462–463.

50. E. Armstrong, "My Glass Ceiling Is Self-Imposed," *Globe and Mail*, 15 December 2004, B15.

51. Shirley Won, "Women Climbing the Ranks at Banks," *Globe and Mail*, 8 November 2004, B15.

52. Joseph White and Carol Hymowitz, "Broken Glass: Watershed Generation of Women Executives Is Rising to the Top," *Wall Street Journal*, 10 February 1997, A1, 6; Reed Abelson, "A Push from the Top Shatters a Glass Ceiling," *New York Times*, 22 August 1999, Y21, Y23.

53. Wallace Immen, "The Plague That Haunts Us Still," *Globe and Mail*, 8 September 2004, C1

54. Michael Barrier, "Sexual Harassment," *Nation's Business*, December 1998, 15–19.

55. Marianne Lavelle, "The New Rules of Sexual Harassment," *U.S. News & World Report*, 6 July 1998, 30–31.

56. Valerie Marchant, "The New Face of Work," *Canadian Business*, March 29–April 11 2004.

57. Sherry Noik-Bent, "By Being Visible: How to Manage Multicultural Maze," *Globe and Mail*, 24 November 2004, C1.

58. Virginia Galt, "Western Union Remakes 'Canadian' Image," *Globe and Mail*, 23 November 2004, B1.

59. Mahlon Apgar IV, "The Alternative Workplace: Changing Where and How People Work," *Harvard Business Review*, May–June 1998, 121–136.

60. "9-to-5 Not for Everyone," *USA Today*, 13 October 1999, B1.

61. Charlene Marmer Solomon, "Flexibility Comes Out of Flux," *Personnel Journal*, June 1996, 38–40.

62. Virginia Galt, "Telecommute—and Save the Environment," *Globe and Mail*, 28 April 2007, B23.

63. Susan Campbell, "More Hartford, Conn.–Area Workers Telecommute to Beat Winter Blues," *Hartford Courant*, 5 February 2004 [accessed 24 April 2004] www.highbeam.com

64. Doreen Carvajal, "It's All about the Coffepot," *International Herald Tribune*, 4 February 2004 [accessed 24 April 2004] www.highbeam.com

65. Apgar, "The Alternative Workplace."

66. Carol Leonetti Dannhauser, "Who's in the Home Office?" *American Demographics*, June 1999, 50–56.

67. Apgar, "The Alternative Workplace."

68. Melanie Warner, "Working at Home—The Right Way to Be a Star in Your Bunny Slippers," *Fortune*, 3 March 1997, 166; Lin Grensing-Pophal, "Employing the Best People—From Afar," *Workforce*, March 1997, 30–32.

69. Kemba J. Dunham, "Telecommuters' Lament," *Wall Street Journal*, 31 October 2000, B1, B8.

70. Carvajal, "It's All about the Coffepot."

71. Lisa Chadderdon, "Merrill Lynch Works—At Home," *Fast Company*, April–May 1998, 70–72.

72. Shari Caudron, "Workers' Ideas for Improving Alternative Work Situations," *Workforce*, December 1998, 42–46.

73. Rich Karlgaard, "Outsource Yourself," *Forbes*, 19 April 2004 [accessed 24 April 2004] www.highbeam.com; David Kirkpatrick, "Big-League R&D Gets Its Own eBay," *Fortune*, 3 May 2004 [accessed 24 April 2004] www.highbeam.com; Joseph N. Pelton, "The Rise of Telecities: Decentralizing the Global Society," *The Futurist*, 1 January 2004 [accessed 24 April 2004] www.highbeam.com

74. Marjo Johne, "Flextime? That's so 2005," *Globe and Mail*, 9 April 2007, B6.

75. Catherine Yang et al., "Low-Wage Lessons," *BusinessWeek*, 11 November 1996, 108–110.

76. Martha Irvine, "Organizing Twentysomethings," *Los Angeles Times*, 7 September 1997, D5

77. Konrad Yakabulski, "Wal-Mart Faces Battle of Quebec," *Globe and Mail*, 16 February 2005, F16; Bertrand Marotte, "Union Weighs Public Boycott of Wal-Mart," *Globe and Mail*, 12 February 2005, A11; Virginia Galt, "Wal-Mart Loses Labour Appeal in Saskatchewan Court," *Globe and Mail*, 24 November 2004, A1; Barrie McKenna, "Unions Starting to Make Inroads at Wal-Mart," *Globe and Mail*, 23 August 2004, B1; Tu Thanh Ha, "Wal-Mart Employees in Quebec Win Union Approval," *Globe and Mail*, 3 August 2004, A1; Patrick Brethour, "Wal-Mart Hails Saskatchewan Court Ruling on Rights in Union Drives," *Globe and Mail*, 28 July 2004, B1.

78. "UPS Workers End Two Day Strike," *Globe and Mail*, 24 November 2004, B12.

79. Nicholas Van Praet, "Alcoa Will Let Strike Roll On," *The Gazette* (Montreal), 8 October 2004, B3; Alcoa website [accessed 19 December 2004] www.alcoa.com/locations/becancour/en/home.asp

80. Susan Carey, "United Grapples with Summer of Widespread Discontent," *Wall Street Journal*, 8 August 2000, A2; Laurence Zuckerman and Matthew L. Wald, "Crisis for Air Traffic System: More Passengers, More Delays," *New York Times*, 5 September 2000, A1, C12.

81. National Union of Public Employees website [accessed 2 July 2007] www.nupge .ca/news_2007/n29my07a.htm; Norma Kozhaya, "Striking Study: Quebec's

Anti-Scab Law Increases the Number and Duration of Walkouts," *The Gazette* (Montreal), 3 September 2002, B3.

82. Bill Beacon, "World Stars Wake Up to Pay Cut," *Globe and Mail*, 11 December 2004, S5.

83. International Labour Organization, *World Labour Report*, 4 November 1997 [accessed 7 November 1997] www.ilo.org

84. Virginia Galt, "Their Backs against the Wall, Unions Are Opting for Compromise," *Globe and Mail*, 5 July 2004, B1; Lloyd G. Reynolds, Stanley H. Masters, and Colletta H. Moser, *Labor Economics and Labor Relations*, 11th ed. (Upper Saddle River, NJ: Prentice Hall, 1998), 497; Indiana University News Bureau, "Trends in U.S. Labor Movement," *Futurist*, January–February 1996, 44; Barbara Presley Noble, "Reinventing Labor: An Interview with Union President Lynn Williams," *Harvard Business Review*, July–August 1993, 115–125.

85. Virginia Galt, "More Strife in Public Sector Collective Bargaining," *Globe and Mail*, 17 December 2004, B5.

86. Greg Keenan, "Ford Canada, Union Reach Buyout Pact," *Globe and Mail*, 5 January 2007, B4.

87. Michael Arndt, "Salvation from the Shop Floor," *BusinessWeek*, 3 February 2003, 100–101; Stanley Holmes, "Boeing: Putting Out Labor Fires," *BusinessWeek*, 29 December 2003, 43; Jill Jusko, "Nature Versus Nurture," *IndustryWeek*, July 2003, 40–42; David Kiley, "Foreign Companies Cast Long Shadow on UAW Negotiations," *USA Today*, 6 August 2003, B1.

88. See Note 1 for case sources.

89. Donald P. Shuit, "Board Games," *Workforce Management*, November 2003, 37–44; "The Pros and Cons of Online Recruiting," *HR Focus*, April 2004, S2; Efraim Turban, Jae Lee, David King, and H. Michael Chung, *Electronic Commerce: A Managerial Perspective* (Upper Saddle River, NJ: Prentice Hall, 2000), 164–168; Marlene Piturro, "The Power of E-Cruiting," *Management Review*, January 2000, 33–38; "Online Recruiting: What Works, What Doesn't," *HR Focus*, March 2000, 11–15; "More Pros and Cons to Internet Recruiting," *HR Focus*, May 2000, 8; Christopher Caggiano, "The Truth about Internet Recruiting," *Inc.*, December 1999, 156; Peter Buxbaum, "Where's Dilbert?" *Chief Executive* [accessed 2 March 2000] www.chiefexecutive.net/mag/150tech/part1c .htm; James R. Borck, "Recruiting Systems Control Resumé Chaos," *InfoWorld*, 24 July 2000, 47–48; Bill Leonard, "Online and Overwhelmed," *HR Magazine*, August 2000, 36–42; Milton Zall, "Internet Recruiting," *Strategic Finance*, June 2000, 66–72; "Why Your Web Site Is More Important Than Ever to New Hires," *HR Focus*, June 2000, 9; Rachel Emma Silverman, "Recruiters' Hunt for Resumés Is Nocturnal Game," *Wall Street Journal*, 20 September 2000, B1–B4.

Chapter 11

1. Shoppers Drug Mart website [accessed 24 May 2007] www.shoppersdrugmart.ca; Marina Strauss, "Cosmetics Add Lustre to Shoppers' Results," *Globe and Mail*, 1 May 2007, B4; Marina Strauss, "Shoppers Ramps Up Premium Cosmetics Offerings," *Globe and Mail*, 21 April 2007, B6; Marina Strauss, "New CEO at Shoppers to Push Private Labels," *Globe and Mail*, 8 March 2007, B8; Zena Oliknyk, "Look Who's Eating Loblaws," *Canadian Business*, 26 February 2007, B44; Angela Barnes, "Defensive Picks the Best Offence," *Globe and Mail*, 4 April 2007, B16; Marina Strauss, "Shoppers Targets an Upscale Move," *Globe and Mail*, 19 January 2007, B4; CBC News, "Jean Coutu Selling U.S. Drugstores," [accessed 4 May 2007] www.cbc.ca/money/story/2006/08/24/ jeancout-riteaid.html; Shirley Won, "Shoppers Aims for Up to 300 Big-Box Stores," *Globe and Mail*, 20 September 2006, B3; Marina Strauss, "Shoppers Nabs Clinique to Crack Cosmetic Big Leagues," *Globe and Mail*, 15 September 2006, B10; Shirley Won, "Cosmetics Primp Up Shoppers' Bottom Line," *Globe and Mail*, 9 February 2006, B4; Marina Strauss, "Shoppers Sees Gold in Private Labels," *Globe and Mail*, 3 January 2005, B1, B2; Rasha Mourtada, "Face Lift: Shoppers CEO Glenn Murphy Has Injected New Life into an Old Brand," *Canadian Business*, 9 November, 2003, 91–95; Sheila McGovern, "We Won't Get Distracted: Coutu," *The Gazette* (Montreal), 27 October 2004, B1, B10.

2. "AMA Approves New Marketing Definition," *Marketing News*, 1 March 1985, 1.

3. Marina Strauss, "It Doesn't Pay to Be a Snob, Holt Renfrew Finds," *Globe and Mail*, 11 September 2007, B1, B6.

4. Special Olympics website [accessed 12 May 2007] www.specialolympics.ca

5. Al Ries and Jack Trout, *The Immutable Laws of Marketing* (New York: HarperCollins, 1994), 19–25.

6. Stan Choe, "Businesses Still Barter, in Simple or Complex Exchanges," *Charlotte Observer*, 30 March 2004 [accessed 5 May 2004] www.highbeam.com

7. Hudson's Bay Company website [accessed 27 May 2007] www.hbc.com/hbc/careers/ why/development

8. Terry G. Vavra, "The Database Marketing Imperative," *Marketing Management*, 2(1) (1993), 47–57.

9. Peter Fingar, Harsha Kumar, and Tarun Sharma, *Enterprise E-Commerce* (Tampa, FL.: Meghan-Kiffer Press, 2000), 24, 109.

10. Barbara Whitaker, "House Hunting with Cursor and Click," *New York Times*, 24 September 1998, D1, D5.

11. Pierre M. Loewe and Mark S. Bonchek, "The Retail Revolution," *Management Review*, April 1999, 38–44.

12. Saturn Canada website [accessed 7 June 2004] www.saturncanada.com/ssi/english/ vehicles/saturn/different/experience.html

13. John Gray, "Tailoring the Message: In a Multicultural Society All Ads Are Not Alike," *Canadian Business*, 29 March–11 April 2004, 65.

14. Stephen Power, "Porsche Aiming to Reach Broader Class of Car Buyers," *Globe and Mail*, 8 December 2006, B17.

15. *Globe and Mail* website [accessed 7 June 2004] www.theglobeandmail.com/servlet/ story/RTGAM.20040531.wrigin131/ BNStory/spec

16. Pamela Paul, "It's Mind Vending," *Time*, 15 September 2003; Hallmark website [accessed 4 May 2004] www.hallmark.com; "Every Day, 10,000 Baby Boomers Turn 50; Nobody Said Getting Old Would Be Easy," *Seattle Post-Intelligencer*, 27 March 1997 [accessed 4 May 2004] www.highbeam.com

17. James C. Anderson and James Narus, *Business Market Management: Understanding, Creating, and Delivering Value*, 2nd ed. (Upper Saddle River, NJ: Pearson Prentice Hall, 2004), 111–114; Philip Kotler and Gary Armstrong, *Principles of Marketing*, 10th ed. (Upper Saddle River, NJ: Pearson Prentice Hall, 2004), 215, 224–226.

18. Nancy Beth Jackson, "Opinions to Spare, Click Here," *New York Times*, E1, E7.

19. Marina Strauss, "Retailers Take a Flyer on Target Marketing," *Globe and Mail*, 24 May 2006, B6.

20. Canada's Personal Information and Electronic Documents Act [accessed 2 June 2004] www.privcom.gc.ca/information/ 02_05_d_08_e.asp; Linda Stern, "Is Orwell Your Banker?" *Newsweek*, 8 April 2002, 59; Mike France and Heather Green, "Privacy in an Age of Terror," *BusinessWeek*, 5 November 2001, 83–87; Amy Harmon, "F.T.C. to Propose Laws to Protect Children Online," *New York Times*, 4 June 1998, C1, C6; Andrew L. Shapiro, "Privacy for Sale," *The Nation*, 23 June 1997, 11–16; Bruce Horovitz, "Marketers Tap Data We Once Called Our Own," *USA Today*, 19 December 1995, A1–A2; Stephen Baker, "Europe's Privacy Cops," *BusinessWeek*, 2 November 1998, 49, 51.

21. Louisa Wah, "The Almighty Customer," *Management Review*, February 1999, 16–22; James Lardner, "Your Every Command," *U.S. News & World Report*, 5 July 1999, 44–46.

22. Hal Lancaster, "Managing Your Career: Giving Good Service, Never an Easy Task, Is Getting a Lot Harder," *Wall Street Journal*, 9 June 1998, B1.

23. TechEncyclopedia, TechWeb.com [accessed 4 May 2004] www.techweb.com; Ganesh Variar, "Only the Best Survive: The Combination of Integration and BI Were the Standouts of the 2003 IT Landscape," *Intelligent Enterprise*, January 2004 [accessed 4 May 2004] www.highbeam.com; Angoss website [accessed 4 May 2004] www.angoss .com

24. Janet Willen, "The Customer Is Wrong," *Business97*, October–November 1997, 40–42; William H. Davidow and Bro Uttal, *Total Customer Service: The Ultimate Weapon* (New York: Harper & Row, 1989), 8; Valarie A. Zeithaml, A. Parasuraman, and Leonard L. Berry, *Delivering Quality Service* (NewYork: Free Press, 1990), 9; George J. Castellese, "Customer Service . . . Building a Winning Team," *Supervision*, January 1995, 9–13; Erica G. Sorohan and Catherine M. Petrini, "Dumpsters, Ducks, and Customer Service," *Training and Development*, January 1995, 9.

25. Bruce Horovitz, "You Want It Your Way," *USA Today*, 5–7 March 2004, 1A–2A.

26. Lisa Taekuchi Cullen, "Have It Your Way," *Time*, 23 Novemeber 2002, 42–43.

27. Don Peppers, Martha Rogers, and Bob Dorf, "Is Your Company Ready for One-to-One Marketing?" *Harvard Business Review*, January–February 1999.

28. Malcolm H. B. McDonald, "Ten Barriers to Marketing Planning," *Journal of Product and Brand Management*, Fall 1992, 51–64.

29. Brian Grow and Gerry Kermouch, "The Low Carb Fight Ahead," *BusinessWeek*, 22 December, 2003, 48.

30. Intrawest website [accessed 3 June 2004] www.intrawest.net

31. Keith McArthur, "Coke's Healthy Water War," *Globe and Mail*, 26 May 2007, B3.

32. Gordon S. Jepson and M. Susana Diaz, "New Canadian Food Labelling Regulations," [accessed 8 June 2004] www.com/articles/new_canadian_food_labeling_regulations.pdf

33. Transport Canada website, "ecoAUTO Program Rebates," [accessed 26 May 2007] www.tc.gc.ca/programs/environment/ecotransport/ecoauto.htm

34. May Wong, " Encyclopedias Gather Dust in Internet Age," *AP Online* [accessed 5 May 2004] www.britannica.com; Leslie Kaufman, "Playing Catch-Up at the On-Line Mall," *New York Times*, 21 February 1999, sec. 3, 1, 6; Gary Samuels, "CD-ROMs First Big Victim," *Forbes*, 28 February 1994, 42–44; Richard A. Melcher, "Dusting Off the Britannica," *BusinessWeek*, 20 October 1997, 143–146.

35. Malcolm McDonald and John W. Leppard, *Marketing by Matrix* (Lincolnwood, IL: NTC, 1993), 10; H. Igor Ansoff, "Strategies for Diversification," *Harvard Business Review*, November–December 1957, 113–124; H. Igor Ansoff, *Corporate Strategy* (New York: McGraw-Hill, 1965).

36. Scott Hays, "Exceptional Customer Service Takes the 'Ritz' Touch," *Workforce*, January 1999, 99–102.

37. Marina Strauss, "U.S. Retailer Eyes 'Tween' Market," *Globe and Mail*, 30 January, 2007, B1, B2.

38. Jennifer Barron and Jill Hollingshead, "Making Segmentation Work," *MM*, January–February 2002, 24–28.

39. Kimberly E. Mock, "Good Credit Skills Are Essential for Georgia's College Students," *Athens Banner-Herald*, 23 February 2004 [accessed 4 May 2004] www.highbeam.com; Charles Haddad, "Congratulations Grads—You're Bankrupt," *BusinessWeek*, 21 May 2001, 48; Christine Duas, "Colleges Target Card Solicitors," *USA Today*, 12 March 1999, B1; Lisa Toloken, "Turning the Tables on Campus," *Credit Card Management*, May 1999, 76–79; "Credit Cards Given to College Students a Marketing Issue," *Marketing News*, 27 September 1999, 38.

40. Keith J. Tuckwell, *Canadian Marketing in Action*, 6th ed. (Toronto: Prentice Hall, 2004), 149.

41. Philip Kotler, Gary Armstrong, and Peggy Cunningham, *Principles of Marketing*, 6th ed. (Toronto: Prentice Hall, 2005), 341.

42. M. Dale Beckman and John M. Rigby, *Foundations of Marketing*, 8th ed. (Toronto: Nelson, 2003), 61.

43. Horacio D. Rozanski, Gerry Bollman, and Martin Lipman, "Seize the Occasion," *Strategy and Business*, Third Quarter 2001, 42–51.

44. David Shani and Sujana Chalasani, "Exploring Niches Using Relationship Marketing," *Journal of Business and Industrial Marketing*, 4 (1993), 58–66.

45. Courtland L. Bovée, Michael J. Houston, and John V. Thill, *Marketing*, 2nd ed. (New York: McGraw-Hill, 1994), 224.

46. Sarah Dougherty, "Bell Mobility, Virgin Target Youth Market," *The Gazette* (Montreal), 30 March 2004.

47. Marina Strauss, "Michael Gold Aims at 100 More Stores," *Globe and Mail*, 23 November 2006, B7.

48. Gary Armstrong and Philip Kotler, *Marketing: An Introduction*, 5th ed. (Upper Saddle River, NJ: Prentice Hall, 2000), 201–204; WestJet website [accessed 9 June 2004] http://c2dsp.westjet.com/internet/sky/about/index.jsp

49. Jim McElguinn, "Child's Play: Max Valiquette Makes Youth Marketing Look Easy," *Canadian Business*, 15–28 March 2004, 42.

50. Armstrong and Kotler, *Marketing: An Introduction*, 206.

51. Armstrong and Kotler, *Marketing: An Introduction*, 329.

52. Michael Solomon and Elnora Stuart, *Marketing, Real People, Real Choices*, 3rd ed. (Upper Saddle River, NJ: Prentice Hall, 2003), 263.

53. Lev Grossman, "The Quest for Cool," *Time*, 8 September 2003, 48–54.

54. Paul Funder Larsen, "Better Is . . . Better," *Wall Street Journal*, 22 September 2003, R6, R11.

55. Philip Kotler and Gary Armstrong, *Principles of Marketing*, 9th ed. (Upper Saddle River, NJ: Prentice Hall, 2001), 296.

56. Claudia H. Deutsch, "Deep in Debt Since 1988, Polaroid Files for Bankruptcy," *New York Times*, 13 October 2001, C1, C14.

57. Bruce Horovitz, "Cookie Makers Bake Up New Twists," *USA Today*, 27 March 2001, 3B.

58. Canadian Intellectual Property Office website [accessed 9 June 2004] http://strategis.ic.gc.ca/sc_mrksv/cipo/help/faq_tm-e.html#1

59. Claudia H. Deutsch, "Will That Be Paper or Pixel?" *New York Times*, 4 August 2000, C1, C4.

60. Eric N. Berkowitz, Frederick G. Crane, et al., *Marketing*, 5th Canadian ed. (Toronto: McGraw-Hill, 2003), 307.

61. General Mills Canada, provided by Denise Nelson, Communications Department, 14 June 2004.

62. Armstrong and Kotler, *Marketing: An Introduction*, 234.

63. Andy Hoffman, "More Kit Kats Is Good. Too Many Is Not," *Globe and Mail*, 9 September 2006, B3.

64. Thomas T. Nagle, "Managing Price Competition," *Marketing Management*, 2(1) (1993), 38–45; Jagdish N. Sheth and Rajendra S. Sisodia, "Feeling the Heat," *Marketing Management*, 4(2) (Fall 1995), 21.

65. Gurumurthy Kalyanaram and Ragu Gurumurthy, "Market Entry Strategies: Pioneers versus Late Arrivals," *Strategy & Business*, Third quarter 1998 [accessed 16 June 1999] www.strategy-business.com

66. See Note 1 for case sources.

Chapter 12

1. Mountain Equipment Co-op website [accessed 3 July 2007] www.mec.ca; MEC Facts, press release from Tim Southam, MEC Communications Specialist, 29 April 2004; *Computer World Canada*, 18 May 2001; *Canadian Retailer* (May/June 2001).

2. Mona Aubin, Bombardier Communications; Matthew McClearn, "Bombardier's Bank," *Canadian Business*, 29 March 2004, 20.

3. Lisa Chadderdon, "How Dell Sells on the Web," *Fast Company*, September 1998, 58, 60.

4. Gregory L. White, "GM Is Forming Unit to Buy Dealerships," *Wall Street Journal*, 24 September 1999, A3; Joann Muller, "Meet Your Local GM Dealer: GM," *BusinessWeek*, 11 October 1999, 48.

5. Philip Kotler and Gary Armstrong, *Principles of Marketing*, 9th ed. (Upper Saddle River, NJ: Prentice Hall, 2001), 435.

6. "Hallmark, a New Name in Mass Retailing," *Supermarket Business*, March 1997, 84; Daniel Roth, "Card Sharks," *Forbes*, 7 October 1996, 14; Julie Rygh, "Hallmark Cards Find Success with New Expressions Brand," *Knight-Ridder/Tribune Business News*, 31 August 1997, 831B0958.

7. Katarzyna Moreno, "UnbeComing," *Forbes*, 10 June 2002, 151–152; Avon Canada website, www.avon.ca

8. Keith McArthur, "PepsiCo Breaches the Walls of Coke's Fortress McDonald's," *Globe and Mail*, 13 March 2007, B1, B10.

9. Inditex (Zara) website [accessed 1 May 2005] www.inditex.com/en/who_we_are/stores; Richard Heller, "Galician Beauty," *Forbes*, 28 May 2001.

10. Colleen Gourley, "Retail Logistics in Cyberspace," *Distribution*, December 1996, 29; Dave Hirschman, "FedEx Starts Up Package Sorting System at Memphis Tenn. Airport," *Knight-Ridder/Tribune Business News*, 28 September 1997, 928B0953; "FedEx and Technology—Maintaining a Competitive Edge," PresWIRE, 2 December 1996.

11. Canada Post Annual Report 2006, Canada Post website [accessed 2 August 2007] www.canadapost.ca

12. Gregory Ellis, Kanetix co-founder [accessed 24 March 2004] www.kanetix.ca

13. Keith McArthur, "Teens, Moms Targeted in Oven Ready Pizza War," *Globe and Mail*, 21 February 2005, B4.

14. Mark Maremont, "How Gillette Brought Its Mach3 to Market," *Wall Street Journal*, 15 April 1998, B1, B4; Jeremy Kahn, "Gillette Loses Face," *Fortune*, 8 November 1999, 147–148.

15. Brad Dorfman, "Gillette Profits Rise on Battery, Razor Sales," *Forbes*, 4 November 2003.

16. David J. Morrow, "From Lab to Patient, by Way of Your Den," *New York Times*, 7 June 1998, sec. 3, 1, 10.

17. Amy Barrett, "Schering's Dr. Feelbetter?" *BusinessWeek*, 23 June 2003, 55+; "FDA Gives Final Approval to Loratadine, Generic Equivalent of Claritin," *Biotech Week*, 17 September 2003, 235–236; Morrow, "From Lab to Patient, by Way of Your Den."

18. Mike Drexler, "Media Midlife Crisis: The Changes are Monumental," *Adweek*, 9 February 2004 [accessed 6 May 2004] www.highbeam.com; Kevin J. Delaney and Robert A. Guth, "Beep. Foosh. Buy Me. Pow." *Wall Street Journal*, 8 April 2004, B1, B7; Stuart Elliot, "Advertising," *New York Times*, 14 April 2004, C8; Melanie Wells, "Kid Nabbing," *Forbes*, 2 February 2004, 84–88; Kimberly Palmer, "Highway Ads Take High-Tech Turn," *Wall Street Journal*, 13 September 2003, B5; Brian Hindo, "Ad Space," *BusinessWeek*, 12 January 2004, 14; Ellen Neuborne, "Dude, Where's My Ad?" *Inc.*, April 2004, 56–57; Erin White, "Look Up for New Products in Aisle 5," *Wall Street Journal*, 23 March 2004, B11; Ronald Grover, "Can Mad Ave. Make Zap-Proof Ads?" *BusinessWeek*, 2 February 2004, 36; Mathew Boyle, "Brand Killers," *Fortune*, 88–100.

19. Michelle Marchetti, "What a Sales Call Costs," *Sales and Marketing Management*, September 2000, 80–82.

20. David Prater, "The Third Time's the Charm," *Sales and Marketing Management*, September 2000, 100–104; Gary Armstrong and Philip Kotler, *Marketing: An Introduction* (Upper Saddle River, NJ: Prentice Hall, 2000), 454.

21. Salesforce.com website [accessed 2 August 2007] www.salesforce.com

22. Direct Marketing Association website [accessed 23 November 1997] www.the-dma.org/services1/libres-home1b.shtml

23. Karl Moore, "Gotta Get That Buzz," *Marketing*, 28 June–5 July 2004, 9.

24. Keith J. Tuckwell, *Canadian Advertising in Action*, 6th ed. (Toronto: Prentice Hall, 2003), 28; CRTC website, www.crtc.gc.ca; Advertising Standards Canada website, www.adstandards.com

25. Keith McArthur, "CRTC Ponders Impact of Product Placement," *Globe and Mail*, 21 November 2005, B1, B10.

26. "Nick Gillespie Discusses the Personalized Cover of Reason Magazine and the Possibilities of Database Technology" (interview), *Talk of the Nation*, National Public Radio, 4 May 2003 [accessed 6 May 2004] www.highbeam.com; Kevin J. Delaney, "Will Users Care if Gmail Invades Privacy?" *Wall Street Journal*, 6 April 2004, B1, B3; Allison Fass, "Spot On," *Forbes*, 23 June 2003, 140; "Hey You! How about Lunch?" *Wall Street Journal*, 1 April 2004, B1, B5.

27. John Heinzl, "Drug Makers Said to Skirt Canadian Restrictions on Ads," *Globe and Mail*, 12 February 2002, B1.

28. David Leeder, GlobeandMail.com, 15 October 2003.

29. "Direct Hit," *The Economist*, 9 January 1999, 55–57.

30. Sarah Lorge, "Banner Ads vs. E-Mail Marketing," *Sales and Marketing Management*, August 1999, 15.

31. Canadian Fraud Laws [accessed 25 March 2004] www.canadianlawsite.com/fraud.htm

32. Zoom Media press release, 4 December 2003; "Zoom Media Acquires Toronto Billboard Firm," Globe and Mail website [accessed 2 August 2007]; Zoom Media website [accessed 29 March 2004] www.zoom-media.com; Additional information provided by Chantal Goncalves, Communications and Marketing Manager [30 April 2004].

33. Armstrong and Kotler, *Marketing: An Introduction*, 409.

34. Paulette Thomas, "'e-Clicking' Coupons On-Line Has a Cost: Privacy," *Wall Street Journal*, 18 June 1998, B1, B8

35. William M. Bulkeley, "Rebates' Secret Appeal to Manufacturers: Few Customers Actually Redeem Them," *Wall Street Journal*, 10 February 1998, B1, B8.

36. Lisa Z. Eccles, "Point of Purchase Advertising," *Advertising Age Supplement*, 26 September 1994, 1–6.

37. Raizel Robin, "Let the Games Begin," *Canadian Business*, 5 August 2003, 17.

38. Keith McArthur, "Bell Beats Out Telus to Sponsor B.C.'s 2010 Olympics," *Globe and Mail*, 19 October 2004, B1, B22.

39. Keith McArthur, "Air Canada Near Olympics Sponsorship Deal," *Globe and Mail*, 19 January 2007, B5.

40. Betsy Morris, "The Brand's the Thing," *Fortune*, 4 March 1996, 72–86.

41. Catherine McLean, "Virgin's Sir Richard Makes Wireless Pitch," *Globe and Mail*, 2 March 2005, B4; Catherine McLean, "Virgin Mobile Set to Ring Up Canada," *Globe and Mail*, 17 February 2005, B1, B8.

42. Verne Gay, "Milk, the Magazine," *American Demographics*, February 2000, 32–33.

43. Armstrong and Kotler, *Marketing: An Introduction*, 405.

44. Keith McArthur, "Annoying But Successful. Whither the Beavers?" *Globe and Mail*, 23 April 2007, B4.

45. Janet Smith. "Integrated Marketing," *American Demographics*, November 1995, 62.

46. See Note 1 for case sources.

47. Peter Wolchack, "E-Tail Success: Watch the Pennies," *Backbone Magazine*, January/February 2005, 6; Richard Bloom, "On-Line Shoppers Click Up Sales," *Globe and Mail*, 28 December 2004, B1; Kevin Bartus, "Measuring What Works Online," 27 September 2004, 15, 16; Allison Kaplan, "Retailers Taking New Approach to Internet," *Knight Ridder Tribune News Service*, 11 June 2002, 1; Gerry Khermouch and Nanette Byrnes, "Come Back to Papa," *BusinessWeek*, 19 February 2001, 42; Rebecca Quick, "Returns to Sender," *Wall Street Journal*, 17 July 2000, R8; Greg Farrell, "Clicks-and Mortar World Values Brands," *USA Today*, 5 October 1999, B1, B2; Ranjay Gulati and Jason Garino, "Get the Right Mix of Bricks and Clicks," *Harvard Business Review*, May–June 2000, 107–114; Anne Stuart, "Clicks & Bricks," *CIO*, 15 March 2000, 76–84; Jason Anders, "Sibling Rivalry," *Wall Street Journal*, 17 July 2000, R16; William M. Bulkeley, "Clicks and Mortar," *Wall Street Journal*, 17 July 2000, R4; Allanna Sullivan, "From a Call to a Click," *Wall Street Journal*, 17 July 2000, R30; Suein L. Hwang, "Clicks and Bricks," *Wall Street Journal*, 17 April 2000, R8, R10; Jeffrey Rothfeder, "Toys 'R' Us Battles Back," *Strategy and Business*, Quarter 2, 2000; Dennis K. Berman and Heather Green, "Cliff Hanger Christmas," *BusinessWeek E.Biz*, 23 October 2000, EB30–EB38; Jerry Useem, "Dot-Coms What Have We Learned?" *Fortune*, 30 October 2000, 82–104.

Chapter 13

1. "Canada's Closely-Watched Tech Giant," CBC News website [accessed 10 August 2007] www.cbc.ca/news/background/Nortel/; Simon Tuck, "Nortel 'Back in Game', CEO Tells Shareholders," *Globe and Mail*, B9; Nortel website [accessed 10 August 2007] www.nortel.com; Mark Evans, "Nortel to Begin Results Update on Jan. 10," *National Post*, National Edition, 9 December 2004, FP4; Kevin Restivo, "Nortel CEO Says He's Red-Faced by Financial Report Delay," *National Post*, National Edition,

30 November 2004, FP3; Simon Avery, "Nortel Accounting Woes 'an Embarrassment,'" *Globe and Mail*, 30 November 2004; Mark Evans, "Nortel Wins US\$1B Order from Sprint," *National Post*, National Edition, 8 December 2004, FP4.

2. Robert Stuart, "Accountants in Management—A Globally Changing Role," *CMA Magazine*, 1 February 1997, 5.

3. Talisman 2006 Annual Report, Talisman website [accessed 17 August, 2007] www .talisman-energy.com/cr_online/2005/ econ-financial_and_operating_statistics.html

4. Jeffrey E. Garten, "Global Accounting Rules? Not So Fast," *BusinessWeek*, 5 April 1999, 26; Elizabeth Macdonald, "U.S. Accounting Board Faults Global Rules," *Wall Street Journal*, 18 October 1999, A1.

5. Matt Krantz and Gregg Farrell, "Fuzzy Accounting Raises Flags," *USA Today*, 22 June 2001, 1B.

6. Daren Fonda, "Revenge of the Bean Counters," *Time*, 29 March 2004, 38–39; Greg Farrell and Andrew Backover, "Stage Is Set for Auditors, Management to Clash," *USA Today*, 20 February 2003 [accessed 9 May 2004] www.highbeam.com; Thomas A. Fogarty, "Accounting Oversight Agency Targets Abusive Tax Shelters," *USA Today*, 21 November 2003, 3B; Janice Revell, "The Fires That Won't Go Out," *Fortune*, 13 October 2003, 139–142; Jeremy Kahn, "Do Accountants Have a Future?" *Fortune*, 3 March 2003, 115–116; David Henry and Mike McNamee, "Bloodied and Bowed," *BusinessWeek*, 20 January 2003, 56–57; Thaddeus Herrick and Alexei Barrionuevo, "Were Auditor and Client Too Close-Knit?" *Wall Street Journal*, 21 January 2002, C1, C5; Jeremy Kahn, "One Plus One Makes What?" *Fortune*, 7 January 2002, 88–90; Nanette Byrnes, "Auditing Here, Consulting over There," *BusinessWeek*, 8 April 2002, 33–34; Nanette Byrnes, "Accounting in Crisis," *BusinessWeek*, 28 January 2002; 42–48; Ken Brown, "Auditors' Methods Make It Hard to Catch Fraud by Executives," *Wall Street Journal*, 8 July 2002, C1, C16.

7. "Summary of SEC Actions and SEC Related Provisions Pursuant to the Sarbanes-Oxley Act of 2002," SEC website [accessed 9 May 2004] www.sec.gov; "Sarbanes-Oxley Act's Progress," *USA Today*, 26 December 2002 [accessed 9 May 2004] www.highbeam .com

8. David Henry and Amy Borrus, "Honesty Is a Pricey Policy," *BusinessWeek*, 27 October 2003, 100–101.

9. Iraj Pourian, "Bill C-198 Compliance," *Globe and Mail*, 27 September 2007, B1.

10. Ben Worthen, "A Funny Thing Happened on the Way to Compliance (It Got Easier for CIOs)," *CIO*, 1 December 2003 [accessed 9 May 2004] www.cio.com; "SEC Approves Listing Exchange Rules," *Internal Auditor*,

1 December 2003 [accessed 9 May 2004] www.highbeam.com; Henry and Borrus, "Honesty Is a Pricey Policy."

11. Dennis Callaghan, "Sarbanes-Oxley: Road to Compliance," *eWeek*, 16 February 2004 [accessed 8 May 2004] www.eweek. com; Ellen Florian, "Can Tech Untangle Sarbanes-Oxley?" *Fortune*, 29 September 2003, 125–128; Thomas Hoffman, "Big Companies Turn to Packaged Sarb-Ox Apps," *Computerworld*, 1 March 2004 [accessed 8 May 2004] www.computerworld .com

12. Frank Evans, "A Road Map to Your Financial Report," *Management Review*, October 1993, 39–47.

13. Reuters website [accessed 19 August 2007] http://stocks.us.reuters.com/stocks/ ratios.asp?rpc=66&symbol=RCI

14. David H. Bangs, Jr., "Financial Troubleshooting," *Soundview Executive Book Summaries* 15, No. 5 (May 1993).

15. SureShot Dispensing Systems website [accessed 17 August 2007] www .sureshotdispensing.com/aboutus.html

16. CN website [accessed 17 August 2007] www.cn.ca/about/media/news_releases/ 2006/4th_quarter/en_News20061129.shtml

17. Manual Schiffres, "All the Good News That Fits," *U.S. News and World Report*, 14 April 1998, 50–51; Janice Revell, "Annual Reports Decided," *Fortune*, 25 June 2001, 176; "The P&L: Your Score Card of Profitability," *The Edward Lowe Report*, August 2001, 1–3.

18. Adapted from Adam Horowitz, Mark Athitakis, Mark Lasswell, and Owen Thomas, "The 101 Dumbest Moments in Business," *Business 2.0* [accessed 3 August 2004] www.business2.com

19. Judy Monchuck, "Paramount Sticks to Capital Spending Plans" Report on Business.com [accessed 17 August 2007] www.reportonbusiness.com/servlet/story/ RTGAM.20070809.wparamount0809/ BNStory/robNews/home

20. See Note 1 for case sources.

Chapter 14

1. Sinclair Stewart, "Canadian Banks: World Beaters," *Globe and Mail*, 25 May 2006, B6; Canadian Bankers Association website [accessed 3 August 2007] www.cba.ca/en; Paul Waldie, "Central Bank Suggests Mergers No Threat," *Globe and Mail*, 11 June 2004, B3; Paul Viera, "Ottawa Still Cool on Bank Mergers," *Financial Post*, 5 July 2007; Susan Monroe, "Canadian Bank Mergers Decision," 14 December 1998, Canada Online [accessed 17 June 2004] http://canadaonline.about. com/library/weekly/aa121498.htm; Rob Ferguson, "Bank Mergers 'Unlikely' Before 2005; Issue Remains Hot Potato for Consumers, Analyst Says RBC Centura Plans to Open 60 More Branches in U.S.," *Toronto Star*, Ontario Edition, 10 September 2003,

C1; Ross Kerber, *Boston Globe*, 3 October 2007 [accessed 12 October 2007] www.boston. com/business/articles/2007/10/03/nj_bank_ purchase_boosts_network/

2. Canadian Bankers Association website [accessed 8 August 2007] www.cba.ca/en/ viewDocument.asp?fl=5&sl=111&tl= &docid=453&pg=1

3. "Fair Isaac Launches Strategy Science Institute; First Educational Forum Spurs Client Empowerment in Applying Advanced Analytics to Improve Critical Business Decisions," *Business Wire* [accessed 10 May 2004] www.highbeam.com; Fair Isaac website [accessed May 10 May 2004] www.fairisaac.com; "Idea Bank," *Orlando Sentinel*, 5 August 2002 [accessed 10 May 2004] www.highbeam.com

4. Mandy Andress, "Smart Is Not Enough: Cards Must Also Be Easy and Useful," *InfoWorld*, 16 October 2000, 94; Mary Shacklett, "American Express' Blue is Setting the Pace in U.S. Smart Card Market," *Credit Union Magazine*, September 2000, 16A–17A.

5. Walt Bogdanich, "Criminals Focus on ATMs, Weak Link in Banking System," *New York Times*, 3 August 2003, 1, 22; Richard Burnett, "Florida Warns of Credit Card Fraud at Gasoline Pumps," *Orlando Sentinel*, 26 January 2004 [accessed 10 May 2004] www.highbeam.com; Tom Lowry, "Thieves Swipe Credit with Card Readers," *USA Today*, 28 June 1999, 1B; Elaine Shannon," A New Credit-Card Scam," *Time*, 5 June 2000, 54–55; Linda Punch, "Card Fraud: Down but Not Out," *Credit Card Management*, June 1999, 30–42; Bill Orr, "Will E-Commerce Reverse Card Fraud Trend?" *American Bankers* Association, April 2000, 59–62.

6. Scott Woolley, "Virtual Banker," *Forbes*, 15 June 1998 [accessed 28 July 1999] www.forbes.com/forbes/98/0615/6112127a .htm; Dean Foust, "Will Online Banking Replace the ATM?" *Yahoo! Internet Life*, November 1998, 114–118.

7. Canadian Deposit Insurance Corporation website [accessed 8 August 2007] www.cdic.ca

8. Bank of Canada website [accessed 8 August 2007] www.bank-banque-canada .ca/en/index.html

9. Department of Finance website [accessed 8 August 2007] www.fin.gc.ca/toce/2005/ fact-cfsse.html, www.fin.gc.ca/toce/2001/ bank_e.html

10. Yahoo! Finance website [accessed 7 August 2007] http://ca.finance.yahoo.com

11. Peter Elkind, "The Secrets of Eddie Stern," *Fortune*, 19 April 2004, 106–127.

12. Paula Dwyer, "Breach of Trust," *BusinessWeek*, 15 December 2003, 98–108.

13. Derek DeCoet, "Flaherty's Trust Bombshell Will Open Investors' Eyes to Dividend Growth," *Globe and Mail*, 11 November 2006, B1; Department of

Finance website [accessed 9 August 2007] www.fin.gc.ca/news06/06-061e.html

14. "Stockbroker Alleges Flaherty 'Ruined' His Life," *Ottawa Citizen*, 7 August 2007; DeCoet, "Flaherty's Trust Bombshell Will Open Investors' Eyes to Dividend Growth."

15. TSX website [accessed 9 August 2007] www.tsx.com/en/investor_relations/financials/market_statistics.html

16. New York Stock Exchange website [accessed 9 August 2007] www.nyse.com

17. James K. Glassman, "Manager's Journal: Who Needs Stock Exchanges? Not Investors," *Wall Street Journal*, 8 May 2000, A42.

18. Julie Bort, "Trading Places," *Computerworld*, 27 May 1996, 1051.

19. Neil Weinberg, "The Big Board Comes Back from the Brink," *Forbes*, 13 November 2000, 274–281.

20. Lee Copeland, "After-Hours Trading," *Computerworld*, 27 March 2000, 57.

21. John R. Dorfman, "Crash Courses," *Wall Street Journal*, 28 May 1996, R12–R13.

22. Chris Isodore, "AT&T, Kodak and IP, out of Dow," CNNMoney website [accessed 9 August 2007] http://money.cnn.com; Katrina Brooker, "Could the Dow Become Extinct?" *Fortune*, 15 February 1999, 194–195; Anita Raghavan and Nancy Ann Jeffrey, "What, How, Why—So What Is the Down Jones Industrial Average, Anyway?" *Wall Street Journal*, 28 May 1996, R30; E.S. Browning, "New Economy Stocks Join Industrials," *Wall Street Journal*, 27 October 1999, C1, C15.

23. TSX website [accessed 9 August 2007] www.tsx.com

24. E.S. Browning, "Journal Goes 'Decimal' With Nasdaq Tables," *Wall Street Journal*, 2 August 2000, C1; "SEC Orders Decimal Stock Prices," *Chicago Tribune*, 29 January 2000, sec. 2, 2.

25. Scott Adams, "Stocks That Can Stand Up in a Storm," *Globe and Mail*, 8 August 2007, B13.

26. Karen Howlett, "Alberta Reverses on Single Regulator," *Globe and Mail*, 22 February 2007, B1.

27. SEC website [accessed 21 December 2000] www.sec.gov/consumer/jdatacom.htm

28. David Diamond, "The Web's Most Wanted," *Business 2.0*, August 1999, 120–128.

29. Thor Valdmanis and Tom Lowry, "Wall Street's New Breed Revives Inside Trading," *USA Today*, 4 November 1999, 1B.

30. Doug Steiner, "Pump and Dump," *Report on Business*, April 2007, P23.

31. Rebecca Buckman, "NASD Maps War on Claims on Internet," *Wall Street Journal*, 24 March 1997, B98W.

32. Peter Carbonara, "The Scam That Will Not Die," *Business Credit*, 1 July 2003

[accessed 10 May 2004] www.highbeam.com; "Profile: Recent Confidence Scams from Nigeria Have Their Roots in Depression-Era Scam That Targeted the Midwest," *All Things Considered*, National Public Radio, 29 July 2002 [accessed 10 May 2004] www.highbeam.com; Jim Stratton, "Notorious E-Mail Scam Snares Savings of Volusia, Fla., Retiree," *Orlando Sentinel*, 23 December 2003 [accessed 10 May 2004] www.highbeam.com

33. Andrew Pollack, "Some Records of Stewart's Broker Subpoenaed," *New York Times*, 9 July 2002, C11; Constance L. Hays and Andrew Pollack, "Stewart Image and Company Built upon It Take Battering," *New York Times*, 4 July 2002, C1.

34. See Note 1 for case sources.

35. Canadian Bankers Association website [accessed 8 August 2007] www.cba.ca; Mark Sievewright, "Traditional vs. Virtual Service," *Credit Union Magazine*, February 2002, 26; Eileen Colkin, "Citibank," *Information Week*, 27 August 2001, 30; Andrew Ross Sorkin, "Put Your Money Where Your Modem Is," *New York Times*, 30 May 2002, G1; Erica Garcia, "What's Left of the Online Banks," *Money*, October 2001, 167; Jathon Sapsford, "Consumers Take Notice of Online Banks," *Wall Street Journal*, 28 November 2000, C1, C19; Lauren Bielski, "Online Banking Yet to Deliver," *ABA Banking Journal*, September 2000, 6, 12+; Heather Timmons, "Online Banks Can't Go It Alone," *BusinessWeek*, 31 July 2000, 86–87; Mark Skousen, "Online Banking's Goodies," *Forbes*, 12 June 2000, P366+; Tony Stanco, "Internet Banking—Some Big Players, But Little Returns so Far," *Boardwatch*, March 2000, 86–90; Carrick Mollenkamp, "Old-Line Banks Advance in Bricks-vs.-Clicks Battle," *Wall Street Journal*, 21 January 2000, C1.

Appendix A

1. Wendy Stueck, "B.C.'s Dossier Wins Name Game Battle," *Globe and Mail*, 12 December 2006, B7.

2. Bill Shaw and Art Wolfe, *The Structure of the Legal Environment: Law, Ethics, and Business*, 2nd ed. (Boston: PWS-Kent, 1991), 635.

3. Thomas W. Dunfee, Frank F. Gibson, John D. Blackburn, Douglas Whitman, F. William McCarty, and Bartley A. Brennan, *Modern Business Law* (New York: Random House, 1989), 164.

4. Bartley A. Brennan and Nancy K. Kubasek, *The Legal Environment of Business* (New York: McGraw-Hill, 1990), 183.

5. "'03 Derby Controversy: Santos Seeks $48M in Damages for Libel," *Newsday*, 10 May 2004 [accessed 16 May 2004] www.highbeam.com

6. Brennan and Kubasek, *The Legal Environment of Business*, 184.

7. "Reasonable Product-Limit Liability Form," *Nations Business*, 1 September 1997, 88.

8. Betrand Marotte, "Hit to Mega Brands Expected," *Globe and Mail*, 17 May 2007, B19; Betrand Marotte, "Mega Brands Battles Trouble in Toyland," *Globe and Mail*, 9 April 2007, B1.

9. Dunfee et al., *Modern Business Law*, 569.

10. Dunfee et al., *Modern Business Law*, 236.

11. Dunfee et al., *Modern Business Law*, 284–297; Brennan and Kubasek, *The Legal Environment of Business*, 125–127; Douglas Whitman and John William Gergacz, *The Legal Environment of Business*, 2nd ed. (New York: Random House, 1988), 196–197; *The Lawyer's Almanac* (Upper Saddle River, NJ: Prentice Hall Law & Business, 1991), 888.

12. Brennan and Kubasek, *The Legal Environment of Business*, 128.

13. Richard Blackwell, "Jumping Ship? Ruling Tips Balance in Your Favour," *Globe and Mail*, 17 January 2007, B9.

14. Roy Furchgott, "Opposition Builds to Mandatory Arbitration at Work," *New York Times*, 20 July 1997, F11; Barry Meier, "In Fine Print, Customers Lose Ability to Sue," *New York Times*, 10 March 1997, A1, C7.

15. Richard M. Steuer, *A Guide to Marketing Law: What Every Seller Should Know* (New York: Harcourt Brace Jovanovich, 1986), 151–152.

16. Dunfee et al., *Modern Business Law*, 745, 749.

17. Brennan and Kubasek, *The Legal Environment of Business*, 160; Whitman and Gergacz, *The Legal Environment of Business*, 260.

18. Caroline Alphonso, "It's Game Over in Trivial Pursuit Legal Match," *Globe and Mail*, 26 June 2007, A3.

19. Henry R. Cheeseman, *Business Law*, 4th ed. (Upper Saddle River, NJ: Prentice Hall, 2001), 324.

20. James Connell, "Tech Brief: Apple Look-Alike Suit Settled," *International Herald Tribune*, 7 June 2001, 17; David P. Hamilton, "Apple Sues Future Power and Daewoo, Alleging They Copied Design of iMac," *Wall Street Journal*, 2 July 1999, B4; "Injunction Is Issued Against Makers of iMac Look Alikes," *Wall Street Journal*, 9 November 1999, B25.

21. Canadian Intellectual Property Office website [accessed 10 August 2007] http://strategis.gc.ca/sc_mrksv/cipo/patents/pt_main-e.html.

22. Jerry M. Rosenberg, *Dictionary of Business and Management* (New York: Wiley, 1983), 340.

Company/Brand/Organization Index

A

A&W, 453
Accel, 313
Accenture Ltd., 296
Acer, 204
Addition Elle, 15
Adobe, 353
Adtranz, 294
Advertising Age, 73
Advertising Standards Canada, 387
Agilent Technologies, 306
AgriTECH Park, 122
Agrium, 145
AIM Trimark, 338
Aim Trimark, 451
Air Canada, 14, 56, 73, 232, 238, 264, 391, 456, 483
Air New Zealand, 56
Airbus, 16
Alcan Inc., 150, 250, 282, 317
Alcatal-lucent, 202
Alcoa, 150, 317, 374
Aldo Shoes, 26
Algoma Steel, 38
Aliant, 317
Alimentation Couch-Tard, 143
Allen-Edmonds, 248
Altitude Concepts, 196, 220–221
Amazon.com, 10, 103, 114, 163, 166, 176, 231, 329, 379, 402
America Online (AOL), 149
American Airlines, 301
American Express, 183, 211, 264, 443
American Idol, 384
American Institute of Certified Public Accountants (AICPA), 412
American Marketing Association (AMA), 333
American Stock Exchange, 454
Amy's Ice Cream, 161
Anheuser-Busch, 61
AOL, 104
Apple, 166
Apple Computer, 482
Apple iPhone, 29, 168, 170, 182
Apple iPod, 166, 168
Apple iTunes, 166, 168, 188–189
The Apprentice, 272
Archer Daniels Midland, 145
Arthur Andersen, 71
Association of Tennis Professionals (ATP), 220

Astral Media, 274
AT&T, 313
ATB Financial, 261
Atkins Nutritionals, 344
Automobile Protection Association (APA), 90
Avis, 140, 145, 269
Avon, 376
AvtoVaz, 57

B

Ballard Power Systems, 168
Bang & Olufsen, 354
Bank of Canada, 18, 19, 21–22, 344, 447, 466
Bank of Montreal (BMO), 18, 211, 276–277, 310, 440
Bank of Nova Scotia, 57, 145, 440
Barnes & Noble, 402
Barrick Gold, 145
Barron's, 457
Bâton Rouge, 148
Bauer, 127
The Bay, 336, 400
BC Hydro, 18
BCE, 146, 282, 453
Beaver Lumber, 134
Bell Canada, 16, 76, 391, 393
Bell Mobility, 152, 348
Bellagio, 141
Ben & Jerry's, 89
Benetton, 91
Berkshire Hathaway, 449
Bertelsmann BMG, 328
Best Buy, 340
Big Brothers And Big Sisters, 288
Big Switcheroo, 261
Bike Friday, 239
Black & Decker, 205, 276, 373
BlackBerry, 2, 28–29, 59, 140, 232
Blackstone Group, 145
Bluenotes, 348
BMW, 228, 254, 349
BNI, 110
Boeing, 5, 16, 57, 187, 210, 236, 238, 244
Bombardier, 6, 16, 41, 57, 108, 145, 178, 237, 294, 306, 319, 320–321, 374, 411
BorgWarner Automotive (BWA), 182
Bose, 53
Boston Consulting Group, 440
Bre-X, 74
The Brick, 123

British Columbia Hockey League (BCHL), 127
British Petroleum, 200, 212
Broadlane.Com, 263
Burberry, 376
Burger King, 120, 391
Burton and Sims, 17
Business Development Bank of Canada, 20, 115, 122
Business Objects, 270
BusinessWeek, 74, 168

C

Cadillac, 85
Caisse De Dépôt, 145
Calian Technologies, 284
Calvin Klein, 338
Cameco, 145
CAMI, 56
Canada 3000, 483
Canada Post, 379
Canada Small Business Financing Program (CSFB), 125
Canadawide, 371
Canadian Association of Business Incubation, 122
Canadian Auto Workers, 319
Canadian Bankers Association, 442
Canadian Business, 277, 457
Canadian Business Online, 69
Canadian Deposit Insurance Corporation (CDIC), 447
Canadian Grand Prix, 388
Canadian Human Rights Commission, 310
Canadian Imperial Bank of Commerce, 18, 71, 95, 311, 440
Canadian Institute of Chartered Accountants (CICA), 410
Canadian Intellectual Property Office, 482
Canadian National Railway, 178, 251, 428
Canadian Radio-television and Telecommunications Commission (CRTC), 387
Canadian Red Cross, 5
Canadian Securities Administrators (CSA), 463
Canadian Standards Association, 90, 106
Canadian Tire, 84, 134, 276, 277, 357, 374
Canadian Unlisted Board (CUB), 454
Canadian Venture Exchange, 463

Canadian Youth Business Foundation (CYBF), 122
Capital One, 341
Cara Operations, 120
Carnival Cruise Lines, 237
Cascades, 88–89
Cashway Building Centres, 134
Cassis, 15
Caterpillar, 170
CBC, 348
C.D. Howe Institute, 18, 466
Centre d'Entreprises et d'Innovation De Montréal, 122
Cerberus Capital Management, 254
Certified General Accountants of Canada, 282
Cervejarias Kaiser, 36
CFL, 333
Chapters, 56
ChemConnect.Com, 263
Cherry Automobile Company, 25
Chester Dawe, 134, 153
Chevron, 263
Chez Cora, 118
China Aviation Industry Corporation (AVIC), 320–321
Chiquita, 52
Chrysler, 25, 244, 246, 254
CIBC World Markets, 248, 283, 460
Cinar, 93
Circle K, 57
Cirque du Soleil, 10, 141
Cisco Systems, 304
Claritas Corporation, 347
Claritin, 383
Clinique, 362, 376
CNN, 186
Coast Capital Savings Credit Union, 146
Coca-Cola, 10, 125, 174, 186, 345, 357, 376, 384
The College of Physicians and Surgeons of Nova Scotia, 284
Commerce Bancorp, Inc., 466
Commtouch, 464
Competition Bureau, 477
Compusearch, 347
Conference Board of Canada, 95, 276, 305, 319
The Co-operators, 146
Coors, 36, 61
Corona, 55
Corporate Knights, 69, 94
Cossette Communication Group, 272
Costco, 280
Couche-Tard, 57
Covisint.Com, 263
Credit Union Central of Saskatchewan, 146
Crescendo, 382
Curtis Lumber, 153

D
DaimlerChrysler, 187, 233, 234, 254
Dangdang.Com, 103
Danier Leather, 93
Danvin, 117
Davies Howe, 327
Dealerskins, 3

Delissio, 382
Dell, 163, 169, 186, 205, 235, 276, 374
Deloitte, 109, 413
Delta Air Lines, 274
Delta Hotels, 264
Desjardins Group, 146
Direct Marketing Association, 386
DIRECTTV, 302
Disney, 58
DoCoMo, 28, 59
Dossier, 477
Dove, 53
Dun & Bradstreet, 121, 424
Duracell, 53

E
Easton, 127
Eat, Shrink, and Be Merry, 126
eBay, 110, 166, 176
Eddie Bauer, 402
Embraer, 16, 41, 294
Enbridge Inc., 94
Encyclopedia Britannica, 345
Energy Brands, 345
Enron, 70, 179
Environics Research Group, 77
Era Integrated Marketing Communications, 338
Ernst And Young, 141
Essar, 38
Esso, 59
Estée Lauder, 362
e-Steel.Com, 263
Ethical Funds Company, 81–82, 84

F
Facebook, 110, 163
Fair Isaac Corporation, 443
Federal Trade Commission, 477
FedEx, 122, 168, 183, 250, 379
F.G. Lister, 371
Financial Accounting Standards Board (FASB), 410
Firestone, 71
FirstEnergy Capital Corporation, 181
Fisheries and Oceans Canada, 20
Foodusa.Com, 263
Forbes, 457
Ford, 71, 244, 246, 319, 348
Fort Angrignon, 208
Fortune, 457
Forzani Group, 90
Franchise Solutions, 118
Future Power, 482
Future Shop, 379, 400

G
Gap, 402
Gateway Computers, 481
Gatorade, 357
GE, 81, 174, 374
GE Capital, 252
General Mills, 344, 358–359
General Motors, 53, 56, 143, 177, 201, 246, 250, 276, 319, 348
Genius Babies, 313
George Foreman Grill, 387

Ghandi, 174
Gildan Activewear, 47, 238, 375
Gillette, 53, 382
Gl``462, 460
GlaxoSmithKline, 202
Globe And Mail, 108, 174, 269, 457
Globe Electric Company, 88
Good Earth Cooking, 208
Google, 139, 163, 387
Green Gear Cycling, 239
Greenpeace, 89
Gretzky, Wayne, 174
Grey Cup, 388

H
Habitat Conservation Trust Fund, 95
Hallmark, 339, 376
Harley-Davidson, 210, 246
Harry Rosen, 183, 184
Harvey's, 16, 118
Hawthorne Western Electric, 297
Head & Shoulders, 53
Health Canada, 387
Heineken, 36, 55
Hertz, 264
Hewitt Associates, 284, 313
Hewlett-Packard, 176, 306, 307, 308, 310
HipIce, 115
The Hockey Company, 127, 148
Hockey Equipment Certification Council, 106
Hold Renfrew, 333
Holiday Inn, 56, 186
Hollinger International, 71, 74
Holt Renfrew, 170, 376
The Home Depot, 134, 143, 146, 153, 249, 269
Home Hardware, 134, 146, 153
Honda, 26, 53, 186
Hummer, 85
Hyatt Hotels, 141
Hydro Québec, 18

I
IBM, 6, 235, 263, 276, 313
IDA, 332
IGA, 204
ImClone Systems, 464
imvescor inc., 148
Inco, 92
Indigo, 56, 402
Industry Canada, 107
IndustryWeek, 168
Infinity, 338
Intel, 213, 275, 276, 391
International Monetary Fund, 460
International Organization For Standardization, 182, 252
International University Consortium for Executive Education, 296
Internet Retailer, 394
Intrawest, 345
Intuit, 415
Investor's Business Dailyl, 457
Ipsos Reid, 207
Irving Oil, 4, 5, 197, 275
Itech, 106, 114, 127

J

Jack Victor Ltd., 238
J.D. Power and Associates, 213
Jean Coutu, 332
Jeep, 228
Jetsgo, 456
The Jim Pattison Group, 141, 142
Jockey, 55
John Hancock Financial, 185
Johnson & Johnson, 84
Justice, 346

K

Kanetix, 379
Katz Group, 332
Keebler, 356
The Kefg, 453
Kellogg, 60
Kelsey's, 120
Kentucky Derby, 479
KFC, 56, 60, 73
Kia, 238
Kingsoft, 103
Kingston Technology, 262
Knowledge Universe Education, 108
Kodak, 59, 213, 357
Korn/Ferry International, 272
KPMG Peat Marwick, 138
Kraft, 344, 382
Kruger, 141
Kumon, 120

L

La Senza Girl, 346
Labatt, 36
Labrador Inuit Association, 92
Land Rover, 209
Lands' End, 102, 308
Lansing, 134
LeapFrog, 108
Léger Marketing, 393
Lemon-Aid, 90
LevelSeas.Com, 263
Levi Strauss, 152, 286
Lexmark, 357
Limited Too, 346
LinkedIn, 110
LivePerson.com, 16
Liz Claiborne, 205
Loblaw, 332, 357
Looney Tunes, 356
Louis Vuitton, 376
Lowe's, 134
Lucent Technologies, 202, 313
Lufthansa, 56

M

M&M Meat Shops, 284, 340
Mac's Convenience Stores, 143
Mad Science, 120
Magna International, 57, 108, 202,
    228, 284
Magna Steyr, 228, 254
Mandela, Nelson, 174
Manitoba Telecom Services (MTS), 415
Manulife Financial, 185

Marineland, 351
Market Regulations Services (RS), 463
Marketing magazine, 387
Marriott International, 315
MasterCard, 442
Maybelline, 362
McCain Foods Ltd., 10, 141, 197, 382
McDonald's, 56, 376, 474
Mediagrif Interactive Technologies, 163
Mega Brands, 479
Mercedes, 228, 251, 349
Merck, 56
Merck Frosst Canada, 269, 276, 314
Meridian Golf, 232
Merrill Lynch, 274, 313, 463, 480
MGM Grand, 141
Miami Herald, 479
Michael Gold, 348
Microcell, 427
Micron, 106
Microsoft, 109, 112, 168, 172, 176,
    207, 235
Mikes, 148
Milestone's, 120
Mini Cooper, 228
Mirage, 141
Miss Sixty, 338
Mission Hockey, 127
Mission-Itech, 127, 148
Mitsubishi Motors, 430
MLS.Ca, 337
Molson, 36, 40, 55, 61, 150, 333
Monster.ca, 306
Montana's, 120
Montreal Canadiens, 150
Montreal Green Fund, 95
Moody's Investors Service, 282, 450, 457
Motion Picture Association
    of America, 53
Motorola, 109, 406
Mountain Building Supplies, 134
Mountain Equipment Co-op (MEC), 16, 84,
    370, 394
Mountain Quest, 208
MXM, 15

N

Napster, 166
NASDAQ (National Association
    of Securities Dealers Automated
    Quotations), 454
National Association of Securities
    Dealers, 454
National Bank, 440
National Post, 457
Natural Resources Canada, 210
Nestlé, 359
NetEase, 103, 104
New York New York, 141
New York Stock Exchange (NYSSE), 454
New York Times, 81
Newsweek, 429
Nexen, 145
NHL, 333
Nike, 10, 127, 205, 233, 348
No Bully for Me, 217

Nokia, 170, 182, 336
Nortel, 19, 71, 74, 103, 282, 406, 431–432

O

Oakley, 53, 127
Office Systems, 207
Olsten, 330
1-800-GOT-JUNK, 119, 120
Ontario Hydro, 18
Ontario Power Generation (OPG), 305
Ontario Securities Commission, 406, 431,
    460, 477
Ontario Teachers' Pension Plan, 145
Oprah Winfrey, 174
Oticon, 200
Outward Bound Canada, 208
Owens Corning, 386

P

Panasonic, 53
Paramount Energy Trust, 430
Parasuco Jeans, 238, 338
Parkad Media Ltd., 390
PeaceWorks, 84
Pechiney SA, 150
Peerless Clothing Inc., 238
Penningtons, 15
PepsiCo, 59, 308, 371, 376
Petro-Canada, 77
PetroCosm, 263
Pfizer Consumer Healthcare, 284
Pharma Plus, 332
Pitney Bowes, 310
Pizza Delight, 148, 353
Pizza Hut, 60, 118
Play It Again Sports, 120
Polaroid, 355
Polywheels Manufacturing, 304
Porsche, 168, 246, 338, 349, 375
The Portables, 47
Pratt & Whitney, 374
Price Chopper, 204
PricewaterhouseCoopers, 121
PRIZM, 347
Procter & Gamble (P&G), 53, 125, 311,
    356, 384
Prudential Insurance, 353
Psyte, 347
Public Company Accounting Oversight
    Board (PCAOB), 412
Publishers Clearing House, 73
Purolator, 336

Q

Quaker Oats, 357
Quebecor, 145
Queen's University, 466
QuickBooks, 415
Quo. Makeup, 363

R

Radio Shack, 287
RBC Dominions Securities, 274, 480
RealNetworks, 166
Reebok, 127, 148
Reitmans, 15

Remarkable Moments, 122
RE/MAX, 120
Réno-Dépot (Building Box), 134
Report on Business, 145, 457
Research in Motion (RIM), 2, 4, 6, 19, 27, 28–29, 59, 140, 232, 448
Retail Council of Canada, 394
Retired Worker, 110
Reuters, 38
Revlon, 362
Revy, 134
Rexall, 332
Richard Mund Pottery, 108
Rising Crust Pizza, 382
Rite Aid, 332
Ritz-Carlton Hotels, 213, 341, 346
Robert Morris Associates, 424
Rogers Communications, 204, 276, 427
Rogers Cup, 220–221
Rollerblades, 17
Rona, 134, 141, 153, 374
Roots, 371
Royal Bank (RBC), 18, 172, 269, 297, 305, 312, 379, 440, 466
Royal Group Technologies, 180
Running Room, 114
Russell Metals, 248
RW&CO, 15
Ryze Business Networking, 110

S
SABMiller PLC, 61
Sage, 415
SAS Institute, 284
Saskatchewan Junior Hockey League (SJHL), 127
Saskatchewan Labour Relations Board, 316
Saturn, 215, 338
Schering-Plough, 383
Schick, 382
Scores, 148
Sea-Doo, 178
Sears Canada, 91, 376
Second Cup, 16, 118, 120, 235
Security Home Mortgage Corporation, 447
SEI Investments, 209
Sequent Computer Systems, 251
Shoppers Drug Mart, 332, 340, 362, 376
Sico Paint, 374
Simply Accounting, 415
Sina, 103, 104
Singapore Airlines, 56
Sirens, 348
60 Minutes, 141
Skechers, 401
Ski-Doo, 178
Sleep Country Canada, 400
smart car, 233, 234
Smart Set, 15
Sobeys, 204

Sohu, 103, 104
Solectron, 233
Sony, 166
Special Olympics Canada, 334
Spiderman 3, 391
Spitz Sunflower Seeds, 59
Spoke, 110
Sport Chek, 90
Sport Mart, 90
Spring, 308
Standard & Poor's, 168, 450, 457, 459
Standard Life, 379
Staples, 371, 477
Star Alliance, 56
Starbucks, 56, 281, 315, 342
Starwood Hotels, 263
Stitches, 348
Subaru, 85
Sub-Zero, 375
Sun Life, 373
Sun Microsystems, 200
Sunbeam, 175
Super Bowl, 388
SureShot Dispensing Systems, 428
Suzuki, 56
Suzy Shier, 91, 348
Swasko Jewels, 115
Swiss Chalet, 120

T
Taco Bell, 60
Talisman Energy, 411
TBWA/Chiat/Day, 213
TD Banknorth, 466
Telus, 69, 70, 84, 95, 146, 283, 453
Tennis Canada, 220
Terpac Plastics Inc., 107
Teva Pharmaceutical Industries, 56
Texaco, 263
Texas Instruments, 211, 213
Thomson, 38
Three a.m. Advertising, 388
3Com, 276
3M, 17, 81–82, 84, 307
Thyme Maternity, 15
Tim Hortons, 56, 118
Time Warner, 149
Toronto Fashion Incubator, 122
Toronto Stock Exchange (TXS), 454
Toronto-Dominion Bank, 18, 282, 440
Totem Building Supplies, 134
Toyota, 41, 52, 170, 239, 248
Toys "R" Us, 400
Treasure Island, 141
Tremor, 384
Trident Precision Manufacturing, 251
Trivial Pursuit, 482
TSX Group, 463
Turf Builder, 374
Tween Brands Inc., 346
Tyco, 71, 74

U
Unilever, 53, 89
United Airlines, 56
United Hardware Wholesalers, 134
United Parcel Service, 10, 50, 120
United Technologies, 413
University of Alberta School of Business, 185
University of California at San Francisco Medical Center, 251
University of Western Ontario, 466
Urban Planet, 348
US Secretary of Energy, 210
US Securities and Exchange Commission, 406, 411

V
Value America, 162
Value Line, 457
Vancity Savings Credit Union, 146, 261
Viagra, 388
Virgin Group, 348
Virgin Mobile, 152, 391
Visa, 200, 442
Voisey's Bay Nickel Company, 92
Volkswagen, 145, 228, 234
Volvo, 170, 350

W
Wall Street Journal, 457, 458
Wal-Mart, 6, 143, 163, 166, 170, 203, 280, 316, 332, 400
Warner Brothers, 356
Western Union, 311
WestJet, 10, 16, 73, 230, 266, 268, 287–288, 348, 353, 456
White Spot, 118
Whittier Canada Enterprise Inc., 110
Winter Olympics, 391
World Bank, 43
World Trade Organization, 40, 42–43
World Wildlife Fund, 84
WorldCom, 71
Wyndham Worldwide, 145

X
Xerox, 109, 177, 206

Y
Yahoo!, 102, 104, 163
Yamaha, 53
YouTube, 139, 163
Yuk Yuk, 160
Yum! Brands, 60

Z
Zara, 378
Zellers, 89
Zoho.Com, 263
Zoom Media, 390
Zoomerang, 340

Subject Index

Note: **boldface** indicates key terms and the pages on which they are defined.

A

Aboriginal peoples, and diversity
    initiatives, 311
absolute advantage, **37**
accountability, 199, 412
accountant, 407–410
accounting
    accountability, 412
    accountants, 407–410
    defined, **407**
    described, 407
    fundamental concepts, 414–416
    process, 417
    rules of, 410–413
    software, 415
accounting equation, 414
accounts payable, 419
accounts receivable turnover ratio, 426
accrual basis, 416
accrued expenses, 420
acid-test ratio, 426
acquisition, 148
activity ratio, 426
administrative law, 478
administrative skills, 185
advertising
    categories, 388–390
    corporate, 389
    defined, **386**
    described, 385
    individualized, 387
    objectives, 387
after-hours trading, 462
agency, 481
aging population, 309
airlines, 13–14
alternative work arrangements, 312–314
amortization, 416
analytic system, 230
angel investors, 125
annual report, 429
arbitration, 317
Asia-Pacific Economic Cooperation
    (APEC), 43
assembly-line layout, 241
asset, 414, 418
assistive technologies, 269
Association of Southeast Asian Nations
    (ASEAN), 43

attrition, 285
auction exchange, **454**
audit, **409**
auditor's report, 429
Austin, Paul, 174
authority, 199
authorized share, 448
autocratic leaders, 175
automated teller machine (ATM), 446
automatic guided vehicles (AGVs), 246
avian influenza, 60
avoidance, 217

B

B2B exchanges, 263–264
baby-boomers
    disposable income, 6
    and market segmentation, 346
    and staffing challenges, 269, 305, 309
background checks, 273
balance of payments, 38
balance of trade, 38, 39
balance sheet, 418–420
Balsillie, Jim, 28
Bank Act, 447
bank mergers, 466
bank rate, 21
bank safety, 447
bankruptcy, 483
Bankruptcy and Insolvency Act, 483
barriers to entry, 7
batch-of-one production, 232
bear market, 457
Beaudoin, Laurent, 321
Beddoe, Clive, 73, 268
beef, 41
behaviour modification, 304
behavioural segmentation, 347
benchmarking, 183
benefits, 281–285
Bennett, Richard, 447
Bezos, Jeff, 114, 176, 380
Big Six banks, 447
Bill C-198, 70, **413**
Bingham, Gordon, 330
bird flu, 60
Black, Conrad, 70
blackout, 181
blended learning, 276

blue-chip stock, 458
board of directors, 145
Bogor Goals, 43
Bombardier, J. Armand, 294
bond, 420
bond
    Canadian government securities bonds, 450
    corporate, 450
    corporate bond ratings, 450
    defined, **449**
    income trusts, 452–453
    mutual funds, 451–452
bonus, 280
book value, 449
bookkeeping, 407
bot capabilities, 6
bottom line, 420
boycott, 317
brainstorming, 212
brand, 356
brand equity, 357
brand mark, 356
brand name, 356
Branson, Richard, 392
BRIC, 36, 47, 58
broker, 456
brokerage firm, 445, 447
Bronson, Rick, 160
budget, 429–430
Buffet, Warren, 449
bull market, 457
burnout, 307
Burns, Randy, 106
Burns, Robin, 106, 114
business, 4
business analytics, 187
business combinations, 148–152
business cycle, 19
business cycle, 21
business ethics. *see* ethics
business-format franchise, 118
business intelligence (BI), 187
business law
    agency, 481
    bankruptcy, 483
    consideration, 480
    contract performance, 480–481
    contracts, 479–481
    copyrights, 483

damages, 478
definition, 478
intellectual property, 481
intentional torts, 478
negligence, 479
negotiable instruments, 483
patents, 482
power of attorney, 481
product liability, 479
property transactions, 481
torts, 478
trademarks, 482
warranty, 481
business ownership. *see* forms of business ownership
business plan
blueprint, 116
creating, 485
defined, **114**
importance of, 114–116
software, 484
business services, 354
business-to-business (B2B) exchanges, 263–264
business travel, 13
buyer exchange, 263
buyers' decision process, 337
buyer's perspective, 14

C
caisse populaire, 444, 447
calendar year, 418
Canada
and absolute advantage, 37–38
aging population, 309
balance of trade, 39
banking environment, 447
diversity, 309
dollar, 46
economic report card, 27
economic system, 11, 12
and foreign investment, 58
greenhouse gases, 86
legal system, 477–483
restrictive import standards, 41
securities regulation, 460
Supreme Court, 478
takeover bids in 2007, 40
top 10 corporations, 142
venture capital, 126
Canada Awards for Excellence (CAE), 252, 284
Canada Labour Code, 273
Canada Pension Plan, 281
Canada Savings Bond, 450
Canadian Centre for Occupational Health and Safety (CCOHS), 20
Canadian Environmental Protection Act, 85
Canadian Food Inspection Agency (CFIA), 20
Canadian legal system
administrative law, 478
agency, 481
bankruptcy, 483
Bankruptcy and Insolvency Act, 483
business law, 478
Charter of Rights and Freedoms, 478
common law, 478

consideration, 480
contracts, 479–481
copyright, 483
damages, 478, 480
intellectual property, 481
intentional tort, 478
libel, 479
negligence, 479
patents, 482
power of attorney, 481
product liability, 479
property transactions, 481
Sale of Goods Act, 478, 480, 481
slander, 479
statutory law, 478
Supreme Court of Canada, 478
torts, 478
trademarks, 482
warranty, 481
Canadian radio-television and Telecommunications Commission (CRTC), 20
Canadian Wheat Board (CWB), 20
capacity planning, 237
capital, 9
capital budgeting, 430
capital-intensive businesses, 5
capital investment, 430
capital items, 354
capital structure, 123
capitalism, 10–11
cardio meetings, 220
Carty, Donald, 301
cash basis, 416
cash flow, 428–429
category killer, 372
Catellier, Brigitte, 274
cause-related marketing, 84, 334
cellular layout, 241
centralization, 201–203
certified general accountant (CGA), **408**
certified management accountant (CMA), **408**
chain of command
centralization vs. decentralization, 201–203
defined, **199**
described, 199–200
span of management, 200–201
change, managing, 177–178
channel, 351, 371
channel conflict, 376
Charest, Micheline, 93
Charter of Rights and Freedoms, 478
chartered accountant (CA), 408
chartered bank, 443, 447
Chen, Steven, 139, 140
cheque, 442
chief executive officer, 144
Chilton, Dave, 126
China
counterfeit economy, 54
Internet growth, 103–104
choice, consumers' right, 91
circular flow, 22
civic responsibilities, 81
Clean Air Act, 87
clicks and bricks, 402

close the books, 417
closed corporations, 141
closed-end fund, 451
closely held companies, 141
co-branding, 357
coaching, 176–177
code of ethics, 76
cognitive dissonance, **337**
Cohen, Ben, 89
cohesiveness, 216
collateral, 124
collective bargaining
defined, **315**
negotiating, 315–317
options, 317–319
process, 316
command team, 210
commissions, 280
committee, 210
common law, 478
common shares, 139
communication
ethical behaviour, 73
labelling, 90
as management skill, 185
marketing, 392–393
telemarketing scams, 75
Communications Environmental Excellence Initiative, 69
communism, 11
Community Environmental Award, 84
comparative advantage theory, 37
compensation
defined, **279**
executive, 280
compensatory damage award, 478
competition
analyzing, 169–170
defined, **15**
fair and honest, 72–73
fostering, 17–18
in free-market system, 15–17
in labour, 319
monopolistic, 16
Competition Act, 17, 90, 388
Competition Bureau, 18, 20, 90
competitive advantage, 16
compliance management software, 413
components, 354
computer activity monitoring, 278
computer-aided design (CAD), 244
computer-aided engineering (CAE), 244
computer-aided manufacturing (CAM), 244–245
computer-integrated manufacturing (CIM), 245
Comrie, William, 123
concentrated marketing, 348
conceptual skills, 185
conflict
causes, 216–217
in channels, 376
dealing with, 218
defined, **216**
resolution, 217
conflict of interest, 74, 412
confrontation, 218

consideration, 480
consumer decision process, 337
consumer demand, 360
Consumer Packaging and Labelling Act, 90
consumer perceptions, 360
consumer price index (CPI), **24**
consumer products, 354
consumer promotion, **391**
consumerism, **90**
consumers' rights, 90–92
contingency leadership, **176**
continuous improvement, 184
contract, 479–481
contract electronics manufacturers, 233
contract performance, 480–481
control
    and channel selection, 375–376
    cycle, 180–182
    as management function, 180–184
control chart, 252
controller, **408**
controlling, **180**
convenience products, 354
convenience store, 372
conversion process, 230, 231
convertible bond, **450**
convertible preferred share, 449
cookie jar accounting, 406
cooperative advertising, **389**
cooperatives, 146, 147
copyright, 483
corporate accountant, 408
corporate advertising, 388
corporate bond, 450
corporate bond ratings, 450
corporate campaigns, 317
corporate culture, **178–180**
corporations
    advantages, 141–143, 144
    characteristics, 143
    defined, **139**
    disadvantages, 143–144
    governance, 144–146
    ownership, 139–141
    parent company, 144
    private, 141
    public, 141
    subsidiary, 144
    top 10 Canadian, 142
Corruption of Foreign Public Officials Act, 55
cost accounting, **407**
cost, and channel selection, 375
cost-based pricing, 360–361
cost leadership, 170
cost of capital, 123–124
cost of good sold, **421**
cost-plus pricing, 360–361
coupon, **391**
Crazy Plates, 126
credit, blunder, 430
credit card
    defined, **442**
    to finance businesses, 126
    questionable marketing, 347
    rules, 473
    skimming, 444
credit union, 444, 447

creditors, 407
Criminal Code, 388
crisis communications plan, 392
crisis management, **171–172**
critical path, **241**
cross-functional team, **210**
cross-promotion, **391**
cultural differences
    checklist, 53
    ethical behaviour, 76
    in global environment, 50–52
    knowledge of, 59
culture
    and buyers' decision, 338
    and marketing strategy, 345
culture clash, 149
cumulative preferred share, 140, 449
currency, **441**
current asset, **418**
current liability, **419**
current ratio, **426**
customer databases, 340–341
customer divisions, **204**
customer focus, 183
customer relationship management
    (CRM), **342**
customer satisfaction, 27
customer service, **333**
customization, 58
customized production, **232**
cyberbanks, 375
cybernetworking, 110

D
D'Alessandro, Dominic, 185
damages, 478, 480
data mining, 342
database marketing, **340**
David, George, 413
day order, **456**
day trader, 456
de la Riva, Jorge, 126
dealer exchange, **454**
debenture, **450**
debit card, **442**
debt ratio, **426**
debt-to-equity ratio, **426**
debt-to-total assets ratio, **427**
debt versus equity financing, 124
decentralization, **201–203**
deceptive pricing, 360
decision making, **185–186**
decision-making meetings, 219
decision process, 338–340
decision support systems, 187
decline stage, 356
deed, 481
defined benefit plans, 281
defined contribution plans, 282
deflation, **24**
defusion, 217
delegation, **199**
Dell, Michael, 286
demand
    defined, **13**
    forecasting, 237
    in human resources, 267

demand curve, 14
demand deposit, **441**, 442
Deming Prize, 253
democratic leaders, **175**
demographic challenges
    aging population, 309
    gender equality, 310
    glass ceiling, 310
    globalization, 309
    sexual harassment, 310
    workforce diversity, 308–309
demographics, 7, **346**
Denove, Chris, 375
Department of Human Resources & Skills
    Development (HRSD), 20
department store, 372
departmentalization, **203–204**
depth, 359
deregulation, 18
Deripaska, Oleg, 254
devaluation, 48
DeZen, Victor, 180
differentiated marketing, 348
differentiation, 170
direct mail, **388**
direct marketing
    defined, **386**
    described, 385
    vehicles, 388
discharge, 480
discount broker, 456
discount pricing, **361**
discount store, 372
discretionary order, **456**
discrimination, **93**, 274
dispatching, **243**
disposable income, 6
dissatisfier, 268, 298
distribution
    exclusive, 375
    intensive, 375
    and marketing mix, 351
    physical, 376–379
    selective, 375
    strategy. *see* distribution strategy
distribution centre, **379**
distribution channel
    alternative, 374
    defined, **351**
    described, 371
    factors influencing, 375–376
    length, 374–375
    primary types of, 374–375
    selecting, 372–376
distribution mix, **372**
distribution strategy
    defined, **371**
    and the Internet, 380
    marketing channels, 372–376
    marketing intermediaries, 371–372
    physical distribution, 376–379
diversity initiative, **94**, 311
diversity, of the workforce, 308–309
dividend, **140**
divisional structure, **203–204**
Dodge, David, 8, 466
dot.com crash, 162–163

double-entry bookkeeping, 415
Dow Jones Industrial Average (DJIA), 458
Dow Jones Sustainability Index, 69
downsizing, 112, 306
Drucker, Peter, 198, 336
drug testing, 274
dual roles, 214
Duck, Michael, 428
dumping, 41
dumpster diving, 73
Dunlap, Al, 175
Dunn, Frank, 406, 431
Durfy, Sean, 268
Dutton, Robert, 153

E
e-cruiting, 329–330
e-training, 276
earnings per share, 424, 429
Ebbers, Bernie, 70
ecoAUTO Rebate Program, 345
ecology, 85
economic conditions, and marketing
    strategy, 344
economic contraction, 19
economic expansion, 19
economic indicators, 24, 25
economic payback, 339
economic shocks, in global economy, 60
economic stability, 19
economic system
    defined, 10
    described, 8–10
    free-market system. see free-market
        system
    planned system, 11–12
    types of, 10–12
economics, 8
economies of scale, 37, 148
economy, mixed, 11
efficiencies, 148
electronic banking, 446
electronic commerce (e-commerce), 7
electronic communication network
    (ECN), 455
electronic data interchange, 247
electronic economy, 8
electronic funds transfer system (EFTS), 446
electronic performance monitoring
    (EPM), 278
embargo, 41
emerging markets, 47–48
employee assistance programs (EAPs), 284
employee benefits, 281–285
    defined, 281
    employee assistance programs, 284
    employee share-ownership, 283
    family benefits, 283–284
    insurance, 281
    pension plan, 281–282
    retirement benefits, 281–283
    RRSP, 282–283
    stock options, 283
employee involvement, 182
employee retention, 268
employee share-ownership plan
    (ESOP), 283

employees
    burnout, 307
    equality, 93–94
    loyalty, 306
    safety and health, 94
    and social responsibility, 93–94
    temporary, 269
    training and development, 275–277
Employment Equity Act, 93–94, 310
enterprise resource planning (ERP), 249
entrepreneurs
    characteristics, 113
    defined, 9
    described, 110
environment, 84–90
Environment Canada, 20
Environmental Protection Compliance
    Orders (EPCOs), 85
equilibrium price, 15
equipment, 354
equity theory, 300–301
estimates, time projections, 242
ethical behaviour. see also ethics
    checklist, 79
    communication, 73
    competition, 72–73
    conflict of interest, 74
    cultural differences, 76
    decision making, 79–80
    described, 72–74
    employee survey, 78
    factors influencing, 74–78
    in global economy, 27
    insider trading, 74
    knowledge, 76
    not causing harm, 74
    organizational behaviour, 76–78
    telemarketing scams, 75
    whistle-blowing, 78
ethical dilemma, 80
ethical lapse, 80
ethics, 70–72
ethics. see also ethical behaviour
euro, 45–46
European Union (EU), 43–45
exchange process, 335
exchange rates
    Canadian dollar, 46, 48
    defined, 48
    and international trade, 48–49
    U.S. dollar, 48
excise taxes, 22
exclusive distribution, 375
executive dashboards, 187
executive information systems, 187
exercise price, 283
expectancy theory, 301–302
expense, 420
expense items, 354
expert-think, 213
Export Development Canada (EDC), 20, 55
export management companies, 55
export trading companies, 55
exporting, 55, 58
express contract, 479
extended-hours trading, 462
eXtensible Markup language, 247

external auditor, 409
extrinsic rewards, 299

F
facility
    layout, 239–241
    location, 238
factors of production, 9
factory/retail outlet, 372
fair disclosure, 463
family benefits, 283–284
federal debt-to-GDP projections, 23
female business owners, 111–112
film industry, 49
final use, 26
finance company, 445
finance department, diagram, 409
financial accounting, 407
financial analysis, 407, 423–427
financial control, 430
financial institutions and services
    automated teller machine, 446
    bank mergers, 466
    bank safety, 447
    Big Six banks, 447
    brokerage firm, 445
    caisse populaire, 444
    Canadian banking environment, 447
    chartered bank, 443
    credit union, 444
    cyberbanks, 375
    deposit financial institutions, 443–444
    electronic banking, 446
    electronic funds transfer system, 446
    finance company, 445
    insurance company, 444
    line of credit, 445
    loan, 445
    non-deposit financial institutions,
        444–445
    pension fund, 445
    security dealer, 445
    trust company, 443
financial management
    budgeting, 429–430
    cash flow monitoring, 428–429
    defined, 427
    planning, 428
financial news
    analysis of, 457–460
    the Internet, 458
    interpreting, 459–460
    market indexes, 458
    newspaper bond quotation, 460
    newspaper mutual fund quotation, 461
    newspaper stock quotation, 459
financial plan, 428
financial ratios, 424–427
financial statements
    analyzing, 423–427
    annual report, 429
    balance sheet, 418–420
    income statement, 420–422
    ratio analysis, 424–427
    statement of cash flows, 422
    trend analysis, 423
    understanding, 417–422

financing
    cost of capital, 123–124
    debt financing, 124
    equity financing, 124
    long-term, 123
    private, 125–126
    short-term, 123
    for small business, 123–126
Fiorina, Carly, 310
first-line managers, 174
fiscal policy, 22
fiscal year, 418
fixed asset, 418
fixed automation, 245
fixed-position layout, 241
Flaherty, Jim, 452
flat organization, 200–201
flexible manufacturing system, 245–246
flextime, 312
floating exchange rate system, 48
focus, 170
focus groups, 340
Ford, Henry, 168
forecasts, 168, 237, 267–268
foreign direct investment, 57–58
foreign exchange. see exchange rates
form utility, 336
formal buying process, 340
formal organization, 197
forms of business ownership
    characteristics, 136
    cooperatives, 146, 147
    corporations, 139–146
    income trusts, 146–148
    partnerships, 137–139
    sole proprietorship, 135–136
    strategic alliances and joint ventures, 152
franchise
    advantages, 119
    cost of, 120
    defined, 118
    disadvantages, 120
    evaluating, 118
    types of, 118
franchisee, 118
franchising, international, 56
franchisor, 118
fraud
    credit card, 444
    securities, 464–465
free-market system
    competition, 15–17
    defined, 10
    described, 10–11
    government role in, 17–23
    macroeconomic view, 15–26
    monitoring performance, 24–26
    supply and demand, 12–13
free-rider, 213
free trade, 36, 41
Free Trade Area of the America
    (FTAA), 43
Friedman, Milton, 80
FTSE 100 Index, 459
full-service broker, 456
fun, 308
functional layout, 240

functional structure, 203
functional team, 210

G
Gantt chart, 241, 242
Gantt, Henry T., 241
Gates, Bill, 112, 126, 168, 176
gender equality, 310
General Agreement on Tariffs and
    Trade (GATT), 42
general expense, 422
general partners, 137
general partnership, 137
generally accepted accounting
    principles (CAAP)
    defined, 409
    described, 410–411
    strictness of, 411–413
generic products, 357
geodemographics, 347
geographic divisions, 204
geographic segmentation, 347
Gilbert, Mike, 388
glass ceiling, 112, 310
global economy. see also international trade
    barriers, 51
    business environment, 49–60
    challenges of, 26–29
    cultural differences, 50–52
    economic shocks, 60
    and EU, 43
    free trade, 36
    impact on service businesses, 7–8
    international trade, 37–49
    legal differences, 52–55
global fund, 451
globalization
    defined, 26
    ethics and social responsibility, 95
    of the workforce, 309
goal, 170, 381
goal-setting theory, 303
Godsoe, Peter, 145
golden handshakes, 280
golden parachute, 152
golden parachutes, 280
Goodnight, Jim, 284
goods-producing businesses, 5–7
government
    competition, 17–18
    economic stability, 19
    environmental protection, 85–88
    fiscal policy, 22
    influencing money supply, 21
    measuring output, 26
    monetary policy, 19–20
    protectionism, 40
    regulation and deregulation, 18
    role in free-market system, 17–23
    and stakeholders, 18–19
grant, 283
green marketing, 90, 388
Greenfield, Jerry, 89
Grenier, Carl, 390
Grenier, Jean-François, 196
Groia, Joseph, 93
gross domestic product (GDP), 26

gross national product (GNP), 26
gross profit, 421
groupthink, 213
growth fund, 451
growth stage, 355
Guaranteed Income Supplement, 281
guaranteed investment certificate
    (GIC), 442

H
Hachborn, Walter, 134
Haney, Chris, 482
hard-wired, 245
Harrison, Hunter, 251
Hawthorne effect, 297
health Canada, 20
health care costs, 319
Heilbroner, Robert, 12
Herzberg's Two-Factor Theory, 268,
    298–299
high-growth ventures, 108
highly regulated industry, 18
hiring process, 271–275
Hopper, Ben, 119
horizontal structure, 203
horizontal team, 210
hostile takeovers, 150
housing starts, and economic indicators, 24
Howe, Bob, 327
human relations. see also human resources
    management (HRM)
    alternative work arrangements, 312–314
    collective bargaining, 315–319
    defined, 295
    demographic challenges, 308–312
    employee demotivation, 295–304
    job sharing, 313
    and labour unions, 315–319
    staffing challenges, 304–308
    today's workforce, keeping pace with,
        304–316
    understanding, 295
human resources, 9
human resources management (HRM).
    see also human relations
    compensation, 279–280
    defined, 267
    e-cruiting, 329–330
    employee benefits, 281–285, 281–285
    evaluating job requirements, 270
    forecasting, 267–268
    functions of, 267
    hiring, 271–275
    outsourcing, 269–270
    performance appraisal, 278–279
    planning, 267–270
    promoting and reassigning, 285
    recruiting, 270–271, 329–330
    retiring employees, 286–287
    steps of, 268
    stress, 327
    supply and demand, 267–268
    temporary employees, 269
    terminating employees, 286, 287
    training and development, 275–277
Hurley, Chad, 139, 140
hybrid structure, 206

hygiene factors, 268, **298**
hypermarket, 372

I
Iginla, Jarome, 338
Immelt, Jeffrey, 81
implied contract, 479
importing, 55
incentives, 280
income fund, 451
income statement, 420–422
income taxes, 22
income trust, 452–453
incubators, 122
index fund, 451
Industry Canada, 20
industry fund, 451
inflation, 24
informal organization, 197
information overload, 307
informational meetings, 219
initial public offering, 124
injunction, 319
The Innovation Killer, 213
Innu Nation, 92
insider trading, 74, 464
installations, 354
instant messaging, 6
institutional advertising, 388
institutional investor, 145
insurance company, 444, 447
insurance, employee benefits, 281
intangibility, 353
intangible service, 350
**integrated marketing communications
   (IMC), 393**
intellectual property, 481
intensive distribution, 375
intentional tort, 478
internal auditor, 409
international fund, 451
international law, 477
International Monetary Fund (IMF), 43
international trade
   Asia-Pacific Economic Cooperation
      (APEC), 43
   blunder avoidance, 59
   checklist, 53
   emerging markets, 47–48
   foreign direct investment, 57–58
   forms of, 55–58
   franchising, 56
   fundamentals of, 37–49
   General Agreement on Tariffs and Trade
      (GATT), 42
   importing and exporting, 55
   International Monetary Fund
      (IMF), 43
   language, 59
   licensing, 55–56
   local customs, 59
   measurement of, 38–39
   packaging, 59
   product strategies, 58–60
   promotion of, 42–43
   promotions, 59
   reasons for, 37–38

research, 59
restrictions, 40–42
strategic alliance, 56
trading blocs, 43–47
translation, 59
World Bank, 43
World Trade Organization (WTO), 42–43
Internet
   in China, 103–104
   and distribution strategy, 380
   electronic economy, 8
   financial news, 458
   opportunities, 8
   security and privacy, 8
   and small business, 110–111, 122
   speed of business, 8
interpersonal skill, 185
interviews, 272
intrapreneurs, 110
intrinsic rewards, 299
introductory stage, 355
inventory
   control, 378
   defined, **247**
   management, 91
inventory control, 248
inventory turnover ratio, 426
Ishikawa, Yasuko, 274
issued share, 448

J
Japan
   employee loyalty, 306
   labour shortage, 305
job analysis, 270
job description, 270
job enrichment, 307
job insecurity, 307
job redesign, 307
job sharing, 313
job shops, 246
job specification, 270
Jobs, Steve, 29, 166, 174, 188–189
joint venture, 56, 152
junk bond, 450
just-in-time (JIT) system, 248

K
kaizen, 252
Kennedy, John F., 90
King, William Lyon Mackenzie, 447
knowledge, 9
Koeppl, Thorsten, 466
Koffler, Murray, 330
Kozlowski, Dennis, 70
Kuhn, Don, 296
Kyoto Protocol, 86

L
labelling, 358
labour-intensive businesses, 5
labour, shortage, 304–305
labour unions
   collective bargaining, 315–319
   defined, **315**
   described, 315
   today, 319

lagging indicators, 24
laissez-fair leaders, 176
Laliberté, Guy, 141
Landes, Chuck, 412
landlord, 481
late trading, 451
law
   administrative, 478
   business. *see* business law
   Canadian legal system. *see* Canadian
      legal system
   common shares, 478
   definition, 478
   and hiring, 273–274
   international, 477
   and marketing strategy, 345
   sources of, 478
   statutory, 478
Lay, Kenneth, 70
layoffs, 286
Lazardis, Mike, 28–29
lead time, 238, 247
leadership
   characteristics, 175
   continuum, 177
   styles of, 175–176
leading, 174–180. *see also* leadership
leading indicators, 24
lean production, 248
lease, 420, 481
legal issues, in global economy, 52–55
Lemoinek Jacques, 116
length, 359
Leonides, Bob, 359
leveraged buyout (LBO), 148
liability, 414, 418–420
libel, 479
licensing, 55–56
lifestyle business, 108
light bulb ban, 88
limit order, 456
limited liability partnership, 137
limited partners, 137
limited partnership, 137
line-and-staff organization, 200
line of credit, 445
line organization, 199
liquidity, 141, 417
liquidity ratio, 424
Lizarraga, Yara, 306
load fund, 451
loan, 124, 420, 445
local advertising, 389
LoCascio, Robert, 16
lockouts, 318
logistics, 378
long-term liability, 419
Looneyspoons, 126
loyalty, 306
Lu, Cleve, 338

M
MacGee, James, 466
MacKenzie, Patricia, 69
macroeconomic view, 15–26
mad cow disease, 41, 60
Malcolm Bridge National Quality Award, 253

management
of change, 177–178
controlling function, 180–184
of corporate culture, 178–180
of crisis, 171–172
defined, 167
failure, 186–187
functions of, 167–184
leading function, 174–180
organizing function, 172–174
planning function, 167–172
production and operations. *see* production and operations management (POM)
pyramid, 173
skills, 185–186
management accounting, **407**
management by objectives (MBO), 303
management pyramid, 172
manufacturing. *see* production and operations management (POM)
manufacturing franchise, 118
manufacturing resource planning (MRP II), 249
Mao, Robert, 103
margin trading, 456
market, 10, **346,** 383–384
market coverage, 375
market indexes, 458
market maker, 455
market order, 456
market segmentation
behaviour, 347
defined, **346**
demographics, 346
described, 346–348
geodemographics, 347
geographics, 347
psychographics, 347
usage, 348
market share, 346
market timing, 451
market value, 449
marketable securities, 429
marketing
concentrated, 348
concept, 336–342
defined, **333**
described, 333–334
differentiated, 348
exchanges and transactions, 335
the four utilities, 336
needs and wants, 335
role of, 334–336
strategy. *see* marketing strategy
undifferentiated, 348
marketing channel. *see* distribution channel
marketing channels, 351
marketing communications, integrating, 392–393
marketing concept
building relationships with customers, 341–342
defined, **336**
research and databases, 340–341
understanding today's customers, 336–340
marketing intermediary, 371–372
marketing mix
defined, **350**

distribution (place), 351
price, 350
products, 350
promotion, 351
marketing objectives, 360
marketing plan, 343
marketing research, 340–341
marketing strategy. *see also* strategic marketing planning
defined, **346**
developing, 346–352
market coverage, 349
market segmentation, 346–348
marketing mix, 350–351
planning, 343–352
positioning your product, 349, 351
pricing, 360–361
product strategies. *see* product strategies
target markets, 348–349
Maslow's Hierarchy of Needs, 297–298
mass customization, 232
mass production, 232
master production schedule (MPS), 241
matching principle, 416
material requirements planning (MRP), 248
materials handling, **379**
matrix structure, 204–205
maturity stage, 356
Mayo, Elton, 297
McCallum, John, 297
McGregor's Theory X and Theory Y, 299–300
McLellan, Anne, 145
media, 389
media mix, 390
mediation, 317
meetings, 218–219
mentor, 177
Mercosur, 43
merger, 148
mergers and acquisitions, 18
advantages, 148
Canadian banks, 466
defences, 150–152
defined, 148
disadvantages, 149
failure rate, 151
recruiting independent retailers, 153
trends, 149–150
micro-segments, 348
microelectromechanical systems (MEMS), 245
middle managers, 173
middlemen, 371
Millar, Amy, 161
Milton, Robert, 73
mission statement, 168, 169
mixed capitalism, 11
mixed economy, 11
monetary policy, 19
money
characteristics and types of, 441–443
defined, **441**
supply, 21
money-market deposit account, 442
money-market fund, **451**
monopolistic competition, 16
monopoly, 16
moral personality, 82
morale, 295

mortgage bond, 450
motivation
behaviour reinforcement, 304
defined, **295–296**
goal setting, 303
key factors, 296
strategies, 302–304
theories of, 297–302
motivators, 268, **298**
Mowat, Dave, 261
Mulroney, Brian, 145
multinational corporations (MNCs), 58
multiplier effect, 22
Mund, Richard, 108
Murphy, John, 305
mutual funds, 451–452

N
NASDAQ (National Association of Securities Dealers Automated Quotations, 454
national advertising, 389
national brand, 356
National Energy Board, 20
National Fraud Information Centre, 74
natural environment, and marketing strategy, 345
natural resources, 9
near money, 442
needs, 335
negative reinforcement, 304
negligence, 479
negotiable instrument, 483
net income, 420
network structure, 205–206
Neufeld, Cameron, 119
new world order, 25
news conference, 392–393
news release, 392–393
niche marketing, 348
Nicholls, Christine, 112
Nikkei 225 Index, 459
no-load fund, 451
non-participators, 214
non-profit organizations, 5
norms, 216
North American Agreement on Environmental Cooperation (NAAEC), 85
North American Free Trade Agreement (NAFTA), 46–47, 85
Novak, John, 248

O
Oberg, Lyle, 460
objective, 170
O'Brien, Wendy, 276
occupational safety and health, 94
off-price store, 372
offshoring, 235
Old Age Security, 281
oligopoly, 16
on-line trading, 463
one-to-one marketing, 342
online retailer, 372
open-book management, 182
open-end fund, 451
operating expense, 421

operational plan, 171
operations management. *see* production and
    operations management (POM)
order processing, 378
organization chart, 197
organization structure
    centralization, 201–202
    chain of command, 199, 199–203
    decentralization, 201–202
    defined, 197
    departmentalization, 203
    divisional structures, 203–204
    flat organization, 200–201
    formal, 197
    functional structures, 203
    hybrid structures, 206
    informal, 197
    job responsibilities, 198
    matrix structures, 204–205
    network structure, 205–206
    span of management, 200
    tall organization, 201
    work specialization, 198
    workforce organization, 203–206
organizational culture, 178–180
organizational-customer decision process,
    339–340
organizational products, 354
organizing, 172–174
orientation, 275
Orlikow, Gordon, 272
Ouchi's Theory Z, 300
outplacement, 286
outsource
    advantages, 233
    blunder, 251
    defined, 112
    described, 228
    and human resources management,
        269–270
    and network structure, 205
over-the-counter (OTC) market, 454
Owens, Bill, 406
owners' equity, 414, 420

P
packaging, 357
Paille, Lisa, 261
par value, 449
parent company, 144
participative management, 182
partnership, 137–139, 420
partnership agreement, 139
passbook savings account, 442
patent, 482
Patten, Rose, 310
payroll taxes, 22
penetration pricing, 361
Pennycook, Rod, 172
pension fund, 445
pension plan, 281
pension plan, 282
performance appraisal, 278
performance, contract, 480–481
performance metrics, 187
perishability, 353
permission marketing, 388
perpetual inventory, 248

*Personal Information Protection and
    Electronic Documents Act
    (PIPEDA)*, 341
personal property, 481
personal selling, 385–386
persuasive advertising, 381
philanthropic, 84
physical distribution
    defined, 377
    inventory control, 378
    materials handling, 379
    order processing, 378
    steps in, 377
    transportation, outbound, 379
    warehousing, 379
picketing, 317
place, 351, 371
place marketing, 334
place utility, 336
planned system, 11–12
planning
    capacity, 237
    for crisis, 171–172
    defined, 167
    human resources, 267–270
    as management function, 167–172
    material requirements, 248
    strategic, 167–171
plans
    operational, 171
    strategic, 168–171
    tactical, 171
Podleski, Greta, 126
Podleski, Janet, 126
point-of-purchase (POP) display, 391
poison pill, 151
pollution
    business efforts to reduce, 88–90
    defined, 84
    government efforts to reduce, 85–86
    Kyoto Protocol, 86–87
    pervasiveness of, 84
positive reinforcement, 304
possession utility, 336
power of attorney, 481
Precious Metals Marking Act, 90
predictive analytics, 443
predictive modelling, 443
preferred share, 140
premium, 392
presence awareness, 6
price, 350
price-based pricing, 361
price changes, 24
price controls, 11
price discrimination, 360
price-earnings multiple, 460
price-earnings ratio, 460
price elasticity, 360
price fixing, 360
price skimming, 361
pricing strategies
    consumer demand, 360
    consumer perceptions, 360
    cost-based, 360–361
    developing, 360–361
    discounts, 361
    government regulations, 360

marketing objectives, 360
    penetration, 361
    price-based, 361
    skimming, 361
primary market, 454
prime interest rate, 21
principal, 449
privacy, and marketing databases, 341
private accountant, 408
private brand, 356
private corporation, 141
privatizing, 12
problem-solving team, 209
process-complete departments, 204
process divisions, 204
process layout, 240
product, 334, 350, 353–354
product advertising, 388
product continuum, 353
product divisions, 204
product franchise, 118
product identities, 356–358
product innovation, 17
product layout, 241
product liability, 479
product life cycle
    decline, 356
    defined, 355
    described, 355
    growth, 355
    introduction, 355
    maturity, 356
product line, 358
product mix, 358
product placement, 384, 387
product strategies
    branding, 356–357
    developing, 352–360
    for international markets, 58–60
    labelling, 358
    packaging, 357
    process, 352–353
    product identities, 356–358
    product life cycle, 355–356
    product line, 358–359
    product mix, 358–359
    product types, 353–354
product variables, 381–384
production
    conversion process, 230
    defined, 119
    mass production, 232
    outsourcing, 233
    service delivery, 230–231
    value chain, 230
production and operations management
    (POM), 245
    computer-aided design (CAD), 244
    computer-aided engineering (CAE), 244
    computer-aided manufacturing (CAM),
        244–245
    customization, 232
    defined, 119
    designing, 235–244
    electronic data interchange, 247
    flexible manufacturing systems, 245–246
    technology, 244–247
    understanding, 229–235

production forecasts, 237
production process
   facility location, 238
   forecasting demand, 237
   managing, 247–253
   product quality, 251–253
   scheduling work, 241–243
   supply chain, 235–237, 247–250
professional advice, 7
profit, 4
profit motive, 5
profit sharing, 280
profitability ratio, 424
**program evaluation and review technique
   (PERT), 241,** 242
promotion
   defined, **351**
   described, 381
   elements of, 385
promotional mix
   advertising and direct marketing,
      386–388
   advertising categories, 388–390
   defined, **385**
   direct-marketing vehicles, 388
   elements of, 385
   personal selling, 386
   public relations, 392
   sales promotion, 391–392
promotional strategy
   defined, **381**
   goal setting, 381
   integrated marketing communications, **393**
   market approach, 383–384
   marketing communications, 392–393
   mix selection, 385–392
   product variables, 381–384
   television commercials, 384
property, 481
property taxes, 22
property transactions, 481
prospecting, 386
protectionism, 36
protectionism, 40
proxy, 145
proxy fight, 150
psychographics, 347
psychological testing, 274
public accountant, 409
*Public Company Accounting Reform and
   Investor Protection Act,* 411
public corporation, 141
public goods and services, 22
public relations, 385, 392
publicly traded, 141
pull strategy, 383
punitive damage award, 478
purchasing, 247
pure competition, 15
push strategy, 383

Q
quality, 27, 180
quality assurance, 252
quality circle, 209
quality control, 252
quality of work life (QWL), 307
quick ratio, 426

Quinn, Jane Bryant, 429
quotas, 41

R
Rabe, Cynthia Barton, 213
Rasulo, Jay, 58
ratio analysis, 424
raw materials, 354
real property, 481
rebate, 391
recession, 19
recruiting
   defined, **270**
   e-cruiting, 329–330
   process, 270–271
reference groups, 338
refreezing behaviours, 178
Registered Retirement Savings Plan (RRSP),
   282, 451
regulating and deregulating industries, 18
Regulation Fair Disclosure (FD), 463
regulations. *see also* business law
   and marketing strategy, 345
   and pricing strategy, 360
reinforcement theory, 304
relationship managers, 198
relationship marketing, 341
reminder advertising, 381
replacement chart, 268
responsibility, 199
restrictive import standards, 41
resumé, bomb hoax, 271
retailer, 371–372
retained earnings, 420
retirement benefits, 281–283
retiring employees, 286–287
return on investment (ROI), 424
return on sales, 424
revenue, 420
Ries, Al, 335
rightsizing, 306–307
Roberts, Paul Craig, 235
robots, 244
roles, 167
round-the-clock trading, 462
routing, 241

S
S&P/TSX 60 Index, 459
S&P/TSX Composite Index, 458
safe products, 90
Saffran, David, 207
salaries, 279
Sale of Goods Act, 478, 480, 481
sales promotion, 385, 391–392
sales taxes, 22
samples, 391
Santos, Jose, 479
Sarbanes-Oxley Act, 70, 411–413
SARS, 60
Saudi Arabia
   and absolute advantage, 37
   restrictive import standards, 41
scabs, 318
scheduling, 241
Scholz, Hanz, 239
Schwartlander, Johannes, 141
Schwarz, Jeff, 122

Schwarzenegger, Arnold, 101
scientific management, 297
secondary market, 454
sector fund, 451
secured bond, 450
secured loans, 124
securities, 448
securities investments
   bonds, 449–453
   Canada Savings Bond, 450
   Canadian government securities
      bonds, 450
   common shares, 449
   convertible bond, 450
   corporate bonds, 450
   debenture, 450
   income trusts, 452–453
   mutual funds, 451, 451–452
   preferred shares, 449
   secured bond, 450
   shares, 448–449
   Treasury bill, 450
   types of, 448–453
securities markets
   auction exchange, 454
   brokers, 455–456
   buying and selling, 454–457
   day order, 456
   dealer exchange, 454
   discretionary order, 456
   filing requirements, 463
   financial news, analysis, 457–460
   fraud, 464–465
   industry challenges, 460–463
   insider trading, 464
   limit order, 456
   margin trading, 456
   market order, 456
   NASDAQ (National Association of
      Securities Dealers Automated
      Quotations, **454**
   on-line trading, 463
   orders to buy and sell, 456
   over-the-counter (OTC) market, 454
   predicting, 462
   primary market, 454
   Regulation Fair Disclosure (FD), 463
   regulation of, 463–465
   secondary market, 454
   securities exchanges, 454
   short selling, 456
   stock exchange, 454
   stock specialist, 454
   stop order, 456
security dealer, 445
selective distribution, 375
self-image, and buyers' decision, 338
self-managed team, 209
seller's perspective, 14
selling expense, 421
service businesses
   defined, **5**
   and demographics, 7
   employment breakdown, 7, 9
   growth of, 6–8
service delivery, 230–231
setup costs, 245
sexism, 310

sexual harassment, 310
shared workspaces, 140
shareholders
    defined, **139**
    described, 407
    equity, 420
shares, 448–449
shark repellent, 152
short selling, 456
short-term financing, 419
Shreiber, Jurgen, 330
sickouts, 318
Siegel, Bud, 248
SIO 9000, 252
situational factors, in buyers' decision, 339
situational leadership, 176
Skilling, Jeffrey, 70
skills inventory, 275
skimming
    credit card skimming, 444
    price skimming, 361
Skonberg, Carol, 115
slander, 479
slowdowns, 318
small and medium-sized businesses
    (SMEs), 107
small business
    assistance, 122–123
    business plans, 114
    characteristics, 108–110
    checklist, 115
    defined, **107**
    described, 107
    downsizing and outsourcing, 112
    economic role, 107–108
    failure, 121–122
    female owners, 111–112
    financing, 123–126
    franchises, 118–121
    increase in number, 110–113
    innovation, 108–110
    ownership options, 117–121
    resources, 108
    start-up companies, 117
    starting, 113–123
    time break-down, 109
smart card, 442
Smith, Adam, 10–11, 198
Smith, Fred, 122, 168
social audit, 84
social class, and buyers' decision, 338
social networking, 110
social responsibility
    civic responsibilities, 81
    defined, **70**
    diversity initiatives, 94
    environmental, 84–90
    global, 27, 95
    increasing, 84–94
    light bulb ban, 88
    perspectives, 80–84
    philanthropy, 84
    safe products, 90
    social audit, 84
    and stakeholders' rights, 83
    toward consumers, 90–92
    toward employees, 93–94
    toward investors, 92–93

social trends, 345
socialism, 12
socioemotional role, 214
sole proprietorship, 135–136, 420
Sotto, Elmer, 110
span of control, 200
span of management, 200–201
special-event sponsorship, 391
special-purpose team, 210
specialization, 198
specialty advertising, 392
specialty fund, 451
specialty products, 354
specialty store, 372
specific performance, 480
staff, 200
staffing challenges
    described, 304
    diversity initiatives, 311
    employee burnout, 307
    employee loyalty, 306
    health care costs, 319
    international competition, 319
    quality of work life, 307
    rightsizing, 306–307
    skilled labour shortage, 304–305
stakeholders, 18, 83
stale pricing, 451
Standard & Poor's 500 Stock Index
    (S&P 500), 459
standardization, 58
standards, 180
Stanton, John, 114
stare decisis, 478
start-up companies, 117
statement of cash flows, 422
statement of financial position, 417
statement savings account, 442
statistical process control (SPC), 252
statistical quality control (SQC),
    252–252
statutory law, 478
Stewart, Martha, 464
stock
    blue-chip stock, 458
    defined, **124**
stock certificate, 139
stock dividends, 140
stock exchange, 454
stock options, 283
stock specialist, 454
stock split, 448
stop order, 456
strategic alliance, 56, 152
strategic marketing planning
    competition, evaluation of, 344
    current marketing situation, 344–345
    external environment, 344
    internal strengths and weaknesses, 344
    market coverage, 349
    marketing mix, 350–351
    objectives, 346
    opportunities, 346
    performance review, 344
    positioning your product, 349, 351
    pricing, 360–361
    process, 343
    target markets, 348–349

strategic plans
    defined, **167**
    steps of, 168–171
Strauss, Paul, 153
stress, 327
strike, 317
strike-breakers, 318
Stronach, Frank, 108, 228
subsidiary corporations, 144
subsidies, 41
succession planning, 268
Sun, David, 262
Supan, Julie, 140
supermarket, 372
supervisory managers, 174
supplier exchange, 263
supplies, 354
supply, 13, 268
supply and demand, 12–13
supply chain
    coordinating, 247–250
    defined, **236**
    described, 235–237
    management, 249–250
supply-chain management (SCM),
    249–250
supply curve, 14
Supreme Court of Canada, 478
SWOT analysis, 169–170
synergies, 148
synthetic system, 230

T
T-bill, 450
tactical plan, 171
taking the company private, 152
tall organization, 201
tangible objects, 350
target for the overnight rate, 21
target markets, 348–349
targeted email, 388
tariffs, 41
task force, 210
task-specialist role, 214
tax accounting, 407
Tax Fairness Plan, 146, 452, 453
taxes, 22
Taylor, Frederick W., 297
teams
    advantages and disadvantages,
      212–213, 214
    characteristics of, 214–215
    committees, 210
    conflict, 216–218
    cross-functional, 210
    defined, **207**
    described, 207–208
    functional, 210
    meetings, 218–219
    problem-solving, 209
    roles, 214–215
    self-managing, 209
    special-purpose, 210
    stages of development, 216, 217
    task forces, 210
    team-building activities, 208
    types of, 209–212
    virtual, 211–212

technical skills, 185
technology
  accounting software, 415
  assistive technologies, 269
  business intelligence (BI), 187
  compliance management software, 413
  computer-aided design (CAD), 244
  computer-aided engineering (CAE), 244
  computer-aided manufacturing (CAM), 244–245
  computer-integrated manufacturing (CIM), 245
  credit scoring software, 443
  data mining, 342
  e-training, 276
  electronic data interchange, 247
  electronic economy, 8
  and employee burnout, 307
  in global economy, 28
  groupware, 140
  individualized advertising, 387
  instant messaging, 6
  Internet. *see* Internet
  inventory management, 91
  marketing, 91
  and marketing strategy, 345
  nanotechnology, 245
  on-line trading, 463
  and production, 244–247
  robots, 244
  security, 91
  and service businesses, 7
  and small business, 110–111
  social networking, 110
  telecommuting, 314
  telepresence, 50
  tracking devices, 91
  website creation, 111
  wireless networking, 199
telecities, 314
telecommuting, **312–313**, 314
telemarketing, 388
telemarketing scams, 75
telepresence, 50
television commercials, 384
Tellier, Paul, 178
tenant, 481
tender offer, 150
terminating employees, 286, 287
termination, 286
testing, in hiring, 274
Textile Labelling Act, 90
Theory X, 299
Theory Y, 299
Theory Z, 300
360-degree review, 278

Thurow, Lester, 12
time deposit, 441
time utility, 336
top managers, 172
tort, 478
total quality management (TQM), 182–184
trade allowance, 392
trade deficit, 38
trade dress, 482
trade promotion, 392
trade restrictions, 40–42
trade surplus, 38
trademark, 356, 482
trading bloc
  defined, 43
  European Union (EU), 44–46
  NAFTA, 46–47
transaction, 335
transaction costs, 456
transactional leaders, 176
transformational leaders, 176
Transport Canada, 20
transportation, 379
Treasury bill, 450
treasury stock, 420
trend analysis, 423
Trout, Jack, 335
Trump, Donald, 272
trust company, 443, 447
TSX Venture Exchange, 458
Tu, John, 262
turnover rate, 268
The 22 Immutable Laws of Marketing, 335

U
undifferentiated marketing, 348
unemployment, 24
unfreezing behaviours, 178
United States, and free trade, 40
units, 453
Universal Child Care Benefit, 283
Universal Product Code (UPC), 358
unlimited liability, 135
unsecured loans, 124
unsought goods, 354
usage, and market segmentation, 348
utility
  defined, **336**
  four forms, 336
  and marketing intermediaries, 371

V
value chain, 230
value chain. *see also* supply chain
value pricing, 361

Vanderbilt, William, 80
venture capital, 126
venture capitalists, 125
vertical structure, 203
video news release, 392
virtual meetings, 218
virtual organization, 205
virtual reality, 244
virtual team, 211
virtual whiteboards, 140
vision, 168
Voisey's Bay, 92

W
wages, 279
Wagoner, Rick, 177
Waksal, Samuel D., 465
wants, 335
Ward, John, 301
warehouse, 379
warehouse club, 372
warehousing, 379
warranty, 481
washroom advertising, 390
The Wealthy Barber, 126
website creation, 111
Weinberg, Ronald, 93
Weinstein, Edward, 88
Welch, Jack, 174
Welstead, Linda, 110
Welstead, Sarah, 110
whistle-blowing, 78
white knight, 152
wholesaler, 371
width, 359
Wiedeking, Wendelin, 168
Wilshire 500 Index, 459
Winn, Craig, 162
wireless networking, 199
Wismer, Janice, 276
women
  in boardrooms, 145
  as business owners, 111–112
  and glass ceiling, 310
Woods, Mike, 108
work specialization, 198
worker buyout, 287
working capital, 426, 429
working capital accounts, 428
world-class manufacturers, 253

X
XML, 247

Z
Zafirovski, Mike, 406, 431

Photo Credits

Chapter 12

Page 369, The Image Works; pages 370 and 394, Mountain Equipment Co-op and Grahame Quan Photography; page 374, The Canadian Press (Ryan Remiorz); page 375, AP/World Wide Photos; page 376, courtesy of Holt Renfrew; page 379, courtesy of Canada Post; page 382, Margot Granitsas/The Image Works; page 387, Robin Nelson; page 388, The Canadian Press/Adrian Wyld; page 390, courtesy of Chantal Goncalves Communications; page 391, ™ and © 2007 Marvel Characters, Inc. Spider-Man 3, the Movie: © 2007 Columbia Pictures Industries, Inc. All rights reserved. Used with permission. The Burger King © advertisement is used with permission from Burger King Brands, Inc.; page 392, J.P. Moczulski; page 393, courtesy of Cossette Communications Group and Bell Canada.

Chapter 13

Page 405, Landov; pages 406 and 431, The Canadian Press (Tobin Grimshaw); page 411, Superstock, Inc.; page 415, courtesy of Sage Software; page 420, Superstock/Maxximages.com; page 430, Bob Firth Photography/ImageState/International Stock Photography Ltd.

Chapter 14

Page 439, John Stuart/Mira Imaging Inc.; pages 440 and 466, The Canadian Press (François Vachon); page 446, Michael Krasowitz/Getty Images, Inc.—Taxi; page 447, Ariel Skelley/Corbis NY; pages 451 (top), Canada Saving Bond certificate images used and altered with permission of the © Bank of Canada; page 451 (bottom), courtesy of AIM Trimark; page 454, Corbis NY; page 463, Pat Sullivan/AP/World Wide Photos.

Appendix A

Page 477 (left), Rafal Gerszak; page 477 (right), John Morstad; page 478, Panos Pictures; page 479, *Chicago Tribune*/MCT/Landov; page 482 (top), © 2008 Horn Abbot Ltd. © 2008 Hasbro. All rights reserved; page 482 (bottom), Chris Hondros/Newsmakers/Getty Images, Inc.—Liaison.

Appendix C (on the website)

Page 4 (left), Mark Richards/PhotoEdit; page 4 (right), The Canadian Press (Adrian Wyld); page 9, Mark Wilson Photography.